LONDON
LOUISE NICHOLSON'S
DEFINITIVE GUIDE

LONDON

LOUISE NICHOLSON'S DEFINITIVE GUIDE

THE BODLEY HEAD

LONDON

For Nick

Jacket illustration: detail of 'The Thames and
Tower Bridge', c.1906, by André Derain.
© ADAGP, Paris and DACS, London 1987.

British Library Cataloguing in Publication Data

Nicholson, Louise, *1954 May 1*—
London, Louise Nicholson's definitive guide.
1. London (England)—Description—1981–
—Guide-books
I. Title
914.21'04858   DA679

ISBN 0-370-31032-2

Original maps by David Hart

Photoset by Rowland Phototypesetting Ltd
Bury St Edmunds, Suffolk

Printed in Great Britain for
The Bodley Head Ltd
32 Bedford Square
London WC1B 3EL
by St Edmundsbury Press Ltd,
Bury St Edmunds, Suffolk

First published in 1988

Contents

List of maps

Acknowledgements

To attempt to write a general guide book to a city as complex as London is surely madness. And I would not have got far without the overwhelming generosity of many people, both Londoners and visitors. They gave unreservedly their time, their professional expertise and their personal London knowledge and tips. Most of all, they gave encouragement. Their contribution to the following chapters has been invaluable and I am deeply grateful.

I would like to thank most warmly the staff of the London Tourist Board and the information desks of the cities of London and Westminster and the 11 Inner London boroughs. I am also grateful to the institutions, companies, hotels and restaurants who hosted me during my research.

In addition, I am especially indebted to Jane Akner, Katharine Alabaster, Reid Anderson, Clive Aslet, Caroline Audemars, Sheena Barbour, Miss Beaumont, Bill Bentley, Lucy Berge, Louis Berney, Elizabeth Black, Sonia Blech, Erica Bolton, Gordon Brearley, Stephen Brook, Anthony Brown, Peter Bufton, Charlie Burgess, Keith Butler, Richard Byron, Barbara Callahan, Alison Cathie, Sally Anne Clairecourt, Sally Clarke, Teresa and Toby Clarke, Hugo Charlton, Joyce Cohen, Frank Copplestone, Julia Cox, Gillian Craig, Shona Crawford Poole, Alan Crompton-Batt, Iain Dobson, Nina Drummond, Roger Eastaby, Margaret Eliot, Peregrine Elliott, Bill Ellis, Chris Ellmers, Sally Emerson, Anthony Everitt, Evelyn Feeney, Kevin Flude, John Freeborn, Ylva French, Paul Gambaccini, Maureen Garland, Gilly Gibbons, Giles Gordon, Piers Gough, Peter Greene, Nigel Greenwood, Mary Gunther, Julie Hacker, Andrew Hamilton, Helen Hamlyn, Nicola Hancock, Anthony Hanson, John Hardy, Belinda Harley, Teresa Harris, Peter Hartley, Dennis Hearn, Robert Hewison, Don Hewitson, Caroline and George Hill, Caroline Hobhouse, Niall Hobhouse, Avril Jones, Colin Jones, Joan Jones, Stephen Jones, Pierre Kauffman, Sir Michael Levey, Howard Lichterman, Jean Liddiard, Fiona Lindsay, Sarah Lindsay, Richard Linenthal, Magnus Linklater, Barbara Lloyd, Andrew Logan, Geoffrey Lovell, Vivien Lowenstein, Katie Lucas, Alan Marcuson, Fay Maschler, Sean Mathias, Peter Matthews, Ian McKellen, Brigadier KJ Mears, Anna Moffat, Joe Mordaunt Crook, Enid Nixon, Geoff Opie, Willie Mostyn Owen, Ian Mylles, Jon Nicolson, Penny Owens, Chrissie Painell, Dr David Parker, Michael Parkin, Jasper Partington, Indar and Aruna Pasricha, Julian Payne, Sherwin Pearson, Simon Peers, Michael Pick, Steve Pinder, Olga Polizzi, Ken Powell, Alan Powers, Jane and Stephen Quinn, Rachel Radford, Michael Ratcliffe, André Richards, Jansis Robinson, Phillis Rogers, Malcolm Rogers, Robert Rogers, Michel Roux, Rosalind Runcie, Nabil Saidi,

Andrew Saint, Emma St John-Smith, Neena and Adarsh Saran, Anthony Sargeant, Jon Savage, Deborah Scott, Christopher Sear, Maggie Sedwards, Chris Senior, Commander Charles Shears, Giles Shepard, Peyton Skipwith, Daphne Slater, Alice Smith, Christina Smith, David Smith, Juliet Simpkins, Gavin Stamp, Robert Sterling, Mark Strong, Howard Stutton, Isabella Szredzki, Carol Taylor, Ben Tindall, Martin Thompson, Mrs Tom, Trevor Turner, Lucia van der Post, Wendy Varkar, Elizabeth Villiers, Tim Wapshott, Nick Ward, Tim Waterstone, Anthony Weaver, Ben and Joan Weinreb, Paul Whitfield, Graham Wiffin, Katharine Wilkinson, Geoffrey Woolley and Adam Zamoyski.

I am particularly grateful to Hermione Hobhouse and Richard Williams who enabled me to devote my early years in London to learning about the city. My family contributed their strongly held opinions. My husband, who has shared all my London years and filled them with happiness, has given constant support and wise advice.

David Hart created the clear maps from my scatty references. Fred Pearson generously applied his extensive London knowledge to reading the manuscript. Corinne Hall and Margaret Cornell tackled the daunting tasks of editing, proof-reading and indexing.

About the author

Louise Nicholson grew up in Surrey and studied History of Art at Edinburgh University before she achieved her first ambition: to live in Central London. Arriving in 1976, she first worked for the Victorian Society campaigning for the conservation of buildings, then joined Christie's, the auctioneers, to work in the art market-place. In 1981, she achieved her second aim: she and her husband bought a dilapidated Georgian house in Islington, which they are restoring. That year she became a freelance journalist and has since written extensively on the arts – especially in London – in *The Times*, *Financial Times*, *Observer* and elsewhere. Between writing and conservation campaigning, Louise Nicholson also travels widely, particularly to India for which she has written a guide, *India in Luxury: A Practical Guide for the Discerning Traveller*.

Preface

When I was a child, the treat of the school holidays was a day out in London. It was a wonderful ritual planned by my mother and me from what it soon became clear was remote rural Surrey. On the big day, we caught an early train to Waterloo, then hopped on and off buses (sitting on top floors of double-deckers) and dipped in and out of the big stores, down the Piccadilly arcades and along the back lanes. We bought presents (there was always someone getting married or having a birthday), toys and clothes (and hideous school uniform additions) until the day's list was ticked off. Then to a museum or gallery – smooth Barbara Hepworth sculptures at the Tate one time, Hogarth prints another, exquisite Islamic manuscripts the next. Eyes dizzy and feet exhausted, we took a taxi – a wicked luxury – to Fortnum & Mason where I gobbled a waffle piled high with strawberries and cream while my mother sipped a cup of tea. Finally home, laden with parcels, giddy and elated with our day.

In June, 1976, these tastes of London became a permanent feast. University finals over, I crammed my worldly possessions into my Mini and drove south from Edinburgh to London. It was The Hot Summer. London was on show: the palaces and stucco terraces gleamed, the parks and squares were crowded with Londoners enjoying their city as never before. The pubs and restaurants overflowed onto the pavements; theatregoers sitting in the upper circle wore swimsuits to keep cool. It was an extraordinary welcome to an extraordinary city.

A decade later, the thrill of living in London has not diminished. My thirst for exploring is not quenched: there is always so much left untouched for another time – forays into the Inns of Court, traditions to catch in the City, old villages lurking behind wide public roads. My curiosity is not satisfied: there are always new layers of London to explore – the money-markets in the City, horticultural shows in Vincent Square, or climbing up Westminster Cathedral tower for a bird's-eye view. And London is always changing – perhaps now more than ever before.

There are tricks for getting the best out of London. Londoners have taught me many; I have learned others by trial and error. In this book I have tried to dispel some of the myths, explain some of the mysteries and share some of the secrets. My aim has been to make visiting London easier, more rewarding and more fun. I have tried to entice you down streets and through doors you might not notice, and to persuade you to wander the parks, eat new types of food and go to unusual theatre and music-making. Above all, I want you to share my love of London. I would not choose to live in any other city.

To a great extent, I had intended this to be the guide to London I would have found invaluable on my arrival. But that guide is impossible to write. London is too big, too dense, too complicated. It is a glimmer of that richness which I have tried to describe.

Louise Nicholson, 1988

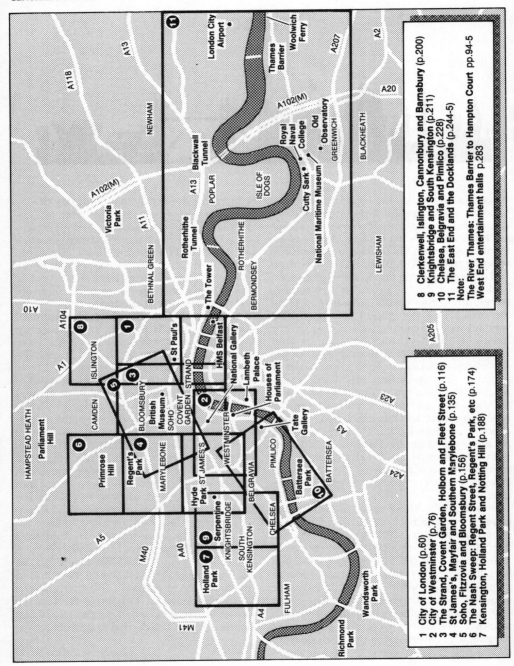

CENTRAL LONDON

1 City of London (p.60)
2 City of Westminster (p.76)
3 The Strand, Covent Garden, Holborn and Fleet Street (p.116)
4 St James's, Mayfair and Southern Marylebone (p.135)
5 Soho, Fitzrovia and Bloomsbury (p.156)
6 The Nash Sweep: Regent Street, Regent's Park, etc (p.174)
7 Kensington, Holland Park and Notting Hill (p.188)

8 Clerkenwell, Islington, Cannonbury and Barnsbury (p.200)
9 Knightsbridge and South Kensington (p.211)
10 Chelsea, Belgravia and Pimlico (p.228)
11 The East End and the Docklands (p.244–5)
Note:
The River Thames: Thames Barrier to Hampton Court pp.94–5
West End entertainment halls p.283

Arriving and Surviving

London is very big. And it overflows with people, events and action. Arriving for the first time is at once exhilarating and daunting. There is so much – almost frustratingly too much. To help you get clued up as fast as possible and to steer you through the confusion so you can enjoy all it has to offer, here are the facts, figures and tips for London survival and London happiness.

Arriving by air

(For leaving London, see end of chapter.)
In 1986 the majority of the 7,570,000 visitors to London arrived by air at Gatwick or Heathrow airports. Both are well equipped with services, so, if post-flight energy is buoyant, this is a good moment to change money, buy bargain travel passes (at Heathrow, see pp. 7–8) and pick up a tourist information pack to browse through on the way in.

GATWICK   The world's third busiest airport lies 30 miles south of Hyde Park Corner and handles more than 16 million passengers a year. There are two terminals, South and the new North (opened spring 1988), each self-contained and equipped with the full range of services and Duty Free shops. The free *Airport Information* giving latest details on all facilities is published every six months and available from the Information Desks in the arrival halls. Useful telephone numbers include:
Customs   (0293 517711) There are limits to the quantity of goods that may be brought into the UK, with different sets of rules for the EEC and the rest of the world. Passengers arriving from EEC countries may currently bring in substantially more spirits and wines if they are purchased 'duty paid' (e.g. in a supermarket) and not 'duty free'. Beyond the import limit for any items, duty is payable and passengers should go through the red channel to leave the customs hall.
Disabled passengers   For all disabilities, including the inability to walk very far, it is important to alert the airline when booking, then contact them on arrival; they will arrange the help needed at each stage through the airport. To find out more, send for the booklet *Care In The Air* from The Air Transport Users' Committee, 129 Kingsway, London WC2 (242 3882).
Information   (0293 28822) for both terminals.
Lost property   For possessions left on an aircraft or mislaid by an airline, contact the airline or handling agent immediately (see p. 22 for tel nos); for property lost in the airport, go to the office in South Terminal below the Departures Concourse (0293 503162).
Medical centre   In South Terminal, near Gatwick Village; staffed 24 hours a day; call-out fee for doctors sometimes payable; to call an ambulance, dial 2222 on any grey or white telephone or 999 on any public telephone.
Worship   The Chapel in South Terminal on the third floor of Gatwick Village is open to all faiths at all hours (0293 603857 for Anglican Chaplain; 0293 503851 for Roman Catholic Chaplain).

HEATHROW   The world's busiest airport lies 15 miles west of Hyde Park Corner. More than a thousand planes land and leave on some days; more than 70 airlines use it and up to 38 million passengers pass through every year. There are four terminals, each equipped with quantities of services, most of which function when the terminal is open; the newest, Terminal 4, is where Concorde arrives. The fine details of facilities and times are constantly changing; a free, 60-page *Airport Information* booklet published every six months has the latest information including a list of airline inquiry numbers, useful when checking your return reservation. This and other advice is available from the Airport Information Desk in each terminal, indicated with a question mark and a black and yellow sign. Each terminal also has a Travel Information Centre stocked with London Transport information and travel passes. And each has a bank, left baggage counter, nursing mothers' room, post office and, except Terminal 4, a hotel booking desk. Useful telephone numbers include:

Customs   (750 1523/5151), see Gatwick.

Disabled passengers   see Gatwick.

Information Desks   Terminal 1 – mostly British and Continental flights (745 7702/3/4), Terminal 2 – mostly Continental (745 7115/6/7), Terminal 3 – mostly intercontinental arrivals (745 7412/3/4), departures (745 7067), Terminal 4 – mostly BA, intercontinental, Concorde, Paris and Amsterdam flights (745 7139).

International Business Centre   Terminal 2 (759 2434).

London Tourist Board   Two desks. At the Underground station for Terminals 1, 2 and 3, open daily 9am–6pm, and at Terminal 2 Arrivals Concourse, open daily 8am–8pm; both supply the excellent free Travel and Tourist Information Pack.

Lost property   For possessions left on a specific plane or airline bus, contact the airline directly; for baggage lost by an airline and for claims, contact Tate Aeroservices (897 3408); for property lost in the airport, go to the office in Car Park 2, opposite Terminal 2 (745 7727).

Medical centre   Queen's Building (745 7047); staffed 24 hours a day.

Passenger assistance   The following help with such problems as being met, sorting out flight delays and transfers, advising on visas and other document problems and even flight bookings: Airport Assistance Ltd (897 6884); Tate Aeroservices (897 3408); Thomas Cook Ltd (897 8249).

Worship   St George's chapel (745 4261) is under-ground, opposite Terminal 2; an ecumenical chapel open 24 hours; services in various denominations.

LONDON CITY AIRPORT   This new airport in the Docklands, opened in November 1987, is designed for businessmen commuting to and from London for meetings – the catchline of one airline using it is 'only six miles from the Bank of England'. Check-in time is 15 minutes, the City and Docklands offices are on the doorstep, facilities include a fully-equipped business centre, and the management claim to 'knock an hour off any journey to Europe'. But the customer pays for these privileges: all seat prices are Club Class. Initially, flights are between London and Paris (10 a day), Brussels (three a day) and Plymouth (one a day); future extensions will include Amsterdam, Rotterdam, Düsseldorf, the Channel Islands and Manchester. Useful information includes:

Address   King George V Dock, Silvertown, E16.

Airlines   Brymon, in association with Air France (0752 707023); and Eurocity Express, in association with Sabena Belgian World Airlines (511 4200).

Facilities   Bank, brasserie, bureau de change, business centre open to all travellers, car hire (Hertz and Europcar), estate agent, florist, hotel reservations agency, newsagent.

Information   (474 5000) for all queries including airlines.

Airport to city centre

The fastest and easiest way is by train from Gatwick and by Underground from Heathrow, then a taxi or local bus for the last leg to your hotel. Coach from either is second best but easier if you have lots of luggage; Airliner is the cheapest door-to-door service. A taxi from Gatwick is prohibitively expensive, as is a taxi from Heathrow. For all road transport, traffic during the morning rush hour, 7–9.30am, slows almost to a standstill.

GATWICK–LONDON BY TRAIN   The station is right inside the South Terminal, with escalators down to the platforms; a shuttle train connects from North Terminal. To avoid ticket queues at the barrier, you can buy your ticket in the customs hall while waiting for your baggage to arrive off the plane. Trains leave for Victoria Station (where the largest tourist information centre is) every 15 minutes from 6.20am until 10.35pm, then hourly throughout the night. The non-stop journey takes 30 minutes.

GATWICK–LONDON BY COACH   Among the variety of coach and bus services, Flightline 777 express coaches leave for Victoria Coach Station every 30 minutes from 6am until 11pm. The non-stop journey takes just over an hour, but longer when traffic is heavy.

GATWICK–LONDON BY AIRLINER   A minibus service that delivers passengers right to their London address, daily from 7am to 7pm. To use it effectively, you need some sterling or dollars in your pocket on arrival, and some change for the telephone. While waiting for your suitcases to arrive in the baggage hall, you telephone 759 4741 to book the minibus and will be told the cost (rated according to distance) and the booking number. By the time your bags have come up and you have passed through customs and followed the yellow-and-black signs to the coach station, the Airliner representative will probably have your minibus ready; if not, the wait should be short. Of course, it is possible to use Airliner once you have been to the bank, too.

HEATHROW–LONDON BY UNDERGROUND   The airport has two Underground stations, one serving Terminal 4, one serving Terminals 1, 2 and 3. At Terminal 4 station the luggage trollies can be pushed up to the platform; at the others they must be left beside the escalator down to the platform. Trains leave Terminal 4 on Mon–Sat from 4.59am until 11.41pm, on Sun from 5.52am until 11.43pm. Trains leave roughly every three minutes during the Mon–Fri morning and evening London rush hours (7–9.30am and 4.30–7pm), every 10 minutes at other times. The journey takes about 40 minutes to South Kensington, 50 minutes to Piccadilly, 55 minutes to King's Cross. Trains follow the Piccadilly Line into London and connect with other lines to reach all 268 London stations including the British Rail train stations.

HEATHROW–LONDON BY AIRBUS   Among the variety of coach and bus services, the two Airbus routes pick up from all four terminals and deliver to several places in London. Tickets can be bought in sterling or in US, Canadian, French or German currencies. The A1 bus leaves Terminal 1, 2 and 3 station every 20 minutes daily 6am–5pm, then every 30 minutes until 10.20pm; it calls at Terminal 4 station and then delivers to Cromwell Road/Earls Court Road, Cromwell Road (Forum Hotel), Knightsbridge/Hyde Park Corner, Grosve-nor Gardens and Victoria Station; the Heathrow–Victoria journey takes about 60 minutes. The A2 bus leaves Terminal 1, 2 and 3 station every 30 minutes daily from 6.40am until 9pm; it calls at Terminal 4 and then delivers to Kensington Hilton Hotel, Notting Hill Gate, Queensway Station, Lancaster Gate Station, Bayswater Road/Albion Street, Marble Arch, Oxford Circus, Bloomsbury Bonnington Hotel, Russell Square and Euston Station; the Heathrow–Euston journey takes about an hour.

HEATHROW–LONDON BY AIRLINER   See Gatwick for how the system works. The telephone number is the same.

HEATHROW–LONDON BY TAXI   Worthwhile for the convenience of door-to-door service – and it is now acceptable to reduce costs by sharing a taxi. However, during the rush hour you merely sit in queues and watch the meter tick up, so it is better to brave the Underground or bus and then take a short taxi ride in Central London. The taxis are found at the taxi ranks, the only places they are permitted to pick up passengers; any private car driver who approaches you in the terminus is best ignored (and is certainly not licensed to ply for trade). At the taxi rank, the driver is obliged to take you, as long as the journey is under 20 miles – the distance from Heathrow to the east side of Central London; above that, he is justified in refusing your trade, but if he does take you, the meter fare system remains the same and there should not be an extra charge. See also Movement, p. 7 below.

LONDON CITY AIRPORT BY ROAD   A Green Line bus leaves for the City and the West End every 30 minutes. For personal transport, there are taxis and two car-hire firms (Hertz and Europcar).

Information

LONDON TOURIST BOARD (LTB)   Victoria Station Forecourt, SW1; open Easter–Oct daily 9am–8.30pm, Nov–Easter Mon–Sat 9am–7pm, Sun 9am–5pm. The essential first stop. This is the central LTB office, with comprehensive information on London, a hotel booking service and adjoining bookshop (tel 734 3450 ext 294, open daily) stocked with the latest books and maps. Staffed by extremely knowledgeable and helpful people and stacked high with leaflets, most of them free, a few with a nominal charge. There are maps for roads, buses and Underground, a monthly events sheet and such publications as *Weekend London* and *Holiday London*. It is also worth asking staff for a sheet of their memo-pad, on the back of which is a useful area map of Victoria – helpful for finding all the main transport booking offices and termini (bus, coach, rail, Underground, tours) and Post Office. Their Telephone Information Service is 730 3488; open Mon–Sat 9am–6pm (automatic queueing system). Their Riverboat Information Service is 730 4812; for more on Thames travel, see p. 93.

Their outposts are at:

Harrods, Fourth Floor, Knightsbridge, SW1 (730 1234); open during store hours which are usually Mon, Tues and Thurs–Sat 9am–6pm, Wed 9.30am–7pm.

Heathrow Terminal 1, 2 and 3 Underground Station Concourse, Heathrow Airport; open daily 9am–6pm.

Heathrow Terminal 2, Arrivals Concourse, Heathrow; open daily 8am–10pm.

Selfridges, Services Arcade, 400 Oxford Street, W1 (629 1234); open during store hours whose summer opening times are Mon–Sat 9am–6pm, Thurs until 7.30pm.

The Tower of London, West Gate, EC3; open daily Apr–Oct 10am–6pm.

Note: the excellent free LTB information pack is available also by post.

LOCAL TOURIST INFORMATION CENTRES Often staffed by knowledgeable locals who supply solid information plus invaluable tips.

City of London Information Centre, St Paul's Churchyard, EC4 (606 3030); open Mon–Fri 9.30am–5pm, Sat 9.30am–1pm (Nov–Mar until 12.30pm). Information includes the monthly brochure *Events in the City of London*, church opening times, lunchtime concerts, tours of livery company halls and the host of traditional City events and ceremonies.

Clerkenwell Heritage (Islington Visitor) Centre, 33–5 St John's Square, EC1 (250 1039); open Apr–Sept Mon–Fri 9am–6pm, Sat–Sun 2–5pm, Oct–Mar Mon–Fri 10am–5pm. Excellent guided walking tours (including buildings rarely open to the public) leave here Apr–Sept daily at 2.30pm, whatever the weather; for a tour during other months, telephone to arrange.

Greenwich Tourist Information Centre, Cutty Sark Gardens, SE10 (858 6376/854 8888 x2318); open Apr–May daily 11am–4pm, June–Aug daily 11am–5.30pm, Sept–Oct daily 11am–4.30pm, Nov–Mar Sun only, 11am–4pm.

Richmond Tourist Information Centre, Old Town Hall, Whittaker Avenue, Richmond, Surrey (940 9125); open Mon–Fri 10am–6pm (Wed until 8pm), Sat 10am–5pm, Sun 10.15am–4.15pm (late Oct–Dec until 3.15pm).

Tower Hamlets Tourist Information Centre, 88 Roman Road, E2 (980 3749/4831); open Mon–Fri 9am–5pm. This large central office is soon setting up satellite offices throughout the borough.

Twickenham Tourist Information Centre, District Library, Garfield Road, Twickenham, Middlesex (892 0032); open Mon–Fri 10am–6pm (Wed and Sat until 5pm, Tues until 8pm).

BRITISH TRAVEL CENTRE   12 Regent Street, Piccadilly Circus, SW1 (730 3400); open Mon–Fri 9am–6pm, Sat 10am–4pm. Packed with information on the rest of Britain, with reliable advice behind the desk; also some London information and a bookshop well stocked with London and Britain guides.

LIBRARIES   Local libraries are always worth visiting. They often have information on local events and, for the curious, local history sections and art collections. Some of the more useful are listed at the top of the Day by Day walks, see pp. 55–260; some of the national libraries are listed on pp. 210–12; for the British Library, see pp. 167–8.

LONDON MAGAZINES   For London information, the best are the weekly *Time Out* (publishes on Wed) and *City Limits* (publishes on Thurs). Both have more than 100 pages of closely typed, fact- and tip-filled, opinionated pages setting out the London scene for the next eight days; features and gossip on the latest events and crazes; listings of events from children's fun and poetry readings to theatre and late night movies. One or other is an essential first-stop buy, after which it is well worth spending an hour or so fathoming how to use it and how many events you can squeeze into one afternoon. In addition, the annual *Time Out Guides* devoted to Shopping, Eating Out and Student London (published Sept) are invaluable and the *Time Out* Filofax guides now include Shopping, Eating, Children, Sport & Fitness and Visitors' London. *The Illustrated London News* provides a glossy, more selective monthly look at the capital. Hotels stock the free *London Planner*.

OTHER MAGAZINES   A deluge of magazines fills the racks of London newsagents. Here are a handful of the more interesting: Weeklies include *The Spectator*, well written and reactionary; *The New Statesman*, not-so-well written and left wing; *The Listener*, published by the BBC, well written and of general interest; *Punch*, the essence of old-fashioned British humour; and *Country Life*, excellent architecture articles, quantities of estate agents' advertisements for those dreaming of owning a country mansion. Fortnightlies include *Private Eye*, full of gossip for journalists, lawyers and politicians; incomprehensible to most others but they still read it avidly. Monthlies include *Business*, about personalities around the London (ie, the world) business scene; *Harpers & Queen* (which advertises itself as 'the world's most intelligent glossy'), razor-edge writing on high style, high life and high snooping through the smart set's keyholes; *Cosmopolitan* for more sane, mainstream women's lives; *Blitz*, *The Face* and *ID* for the sharp side of streetwise London life; *Architectural Review* for inside views on the new facades; *Apollo* for the dramas, discoveries and personalities in the art world; and *Landscape* for vibrant comment on all aspects of British buildings and countryside.

NEWSPAPERS   The British consume almost 15 million newspapers daily and 18 million on Sundays. London offers a wider range of daily and weekly newspapers than any other city. The quality newspapers published Mon–Sat from London are *The Times*, the *Daily Telegraph*, *The Independent*, the *Guardian* and the *Financial Times* (the pink one). All carry home and foreign news, City news, sports and arts, the television and radio programmes for the day, and advertisements for most West End theatres and cinemas. *The Times*, the *Daily Telegraph* and *The Independent* publish a Court Circular setting out what the Royal Family is doing so you can go and spot them; what traditional ceremonies and processions are taking place; what important lunches and dinners with distinguished guests are being given; and, on Saturday, a handful of the most interesting Sunday church services and their music. *The Times* has a daily Information Service giving a selection of the day's exhibitions, walks, music and other events. Saturday editions usually carry arts advertisements for the following week's concerts. The better London evening paper is the *Evening Standard*, published Mon–Fri, first edition out around noon, strong on nightlife listings and consumer London. On Sunday the *Observer*, the *Sunday Telegraph* and the *Sunday Times* all publish multi-section papers with in-depth news, arts and sports reports and a colour magazine. In addition, there are all the tabloid papers, the specialist papers (the *Racing Times*, etc) and a very wide selection of foreign newspapers; see Newsagents on p. 335 for stockists.

RADIO   The four BBC national networks are Radio 1, pop; Radio 2, easy listening; Radio 3, classical music; Radio 4, talk, news and plays – this is where you might hear John Le Carré reading his latest novel or Anna Massey reading Queen Victoria's diaries. The BBC World Service broadcasts 24 hours a day, but beware: programme times are usually published GMT, so add an hour in the summer, see Time, p. 11. The three London networks are BBC Radio London, mixed programming, soul music; Capital Radio, 24-hour pop and London local affairs, very lively, runs Capital Help Line, Kidsline (see Telephone services, below) and the Fringe Theatre Box Office (see p. 290); LBC, 24-hour talk, phone-in and poor news programmes. Finally, the pirate stations: on Medium Wave find the well-established Radio Caroline 558; on FM, between BBC 2, 3 and 4, find the pirates, mostly black, sometimes Greek, who broadcast for just a few hours; the Network Radio page of *City Limits* publishes some programmes. See Television for publications.

TELEVISION   There are four networks. BBC1 and BBC2 are funded by public subscription and have no advertisements, so programmes are ad-free. BBC1 mixes current affairs with entertainment programmes; its breakfast show is non-stop news; its main news programmes are at 6pm and 9pm. BBC2 mixes entertainment with more specialist programming and culture, and screens the late-night and early-morning Open University programmes. ITV (run by Thames Mon–Fri, by London Weekend Television Sat–Sun) is the most lightweight network; its breakfast programme 'TV-am' mixes a little news with plenty of entertainment; main news programmes at 5.45pm and 10pm. Channel 4 has entertainment and deliberately minority audience programmes; its main news is at 7pm. For sports coverage, see p. 339. For programming, see the daily newspapers or, for fuller information, the two weekly magazines: *Radio Times*, which publishes programmes for BBC1, BBC2, the four BBC radio networks and Radio London, together with frequencies; and *TV Times*, which gives details of ITV and Channel 4 programmes.

TRAVEL AGENTS   Many firms will arrange your stay in London, with trips off into the countryside or further afield. Two with knowledgeable and sensitive staff and good track records are Abercrombie & Kent, Sloane Square House, Holbein Place, London SW1 (730 9600/235 9761); and Supertravel, 22 Hans Place, SW1 (589 5161). See also Tailor-made touring, p. 39.

Communications

POSTAL SERVICE   Stamps are only on sale at post offices, although hotel Head Porters sometimes keep a supply for guests. Post offices are usually open Mon–Fri 9am–5pm, Sat 9am–noon. The Trafalgar Square Post Office, 24 William IV Street, WC2 (930 9580), on the east side of Trafalgar Square, is open Mon–Sat 8am–8pm, Sun and Bank Holidays 10am–6pm; if there are special celebration stamps on sale (always at Christmas; sometimes during the year), there will be stocks of them here.

TELEPHONE   British Telecom is the private company (virtually a monopoly) which runs the British telephone system. It is a vast and complicated system of which some parts work well, some do not.
Finding a number   The London Directory comes in four volumes, listed alphabetically by subscriber's name; an additional Yellow Pages section lists companies and services under type, from taxis and tea brokers to toy makers and tropical plants. If there is no directory, the Directory Inquiries number for the London area is 142, almost perpetually engaged and when you do get through it is necessary to have the name, initial and full address otherwise they may refuse to give the number. For a number in the rest of Britain dial, 192; for one outside Britain, dial 153.
Finding a telephone   Hotel phones usually carry a hefty surcharge which is worth checking before you start dialing. Public payphones are found in the streets, in big stores and other public places. To confuse, they currently exist in seven types: coin-operated payphones which accept 2p, 10p and 50p coins; coin-operated payphones which accept all coins up to £1; phonecard phones which accept only British Telecom Phonecards (obtained from newsagents, post offices, chemists, etc and best

bought in small denominations in case they get lost); credit-call payphones which accept Visa, Mastercard (Access), Diners Club and American Express cards, as well as British Telecom Phonecards, with a minimum charge of 50p; payphones on British Rail inter-city trains, accepting phonecards (obtained from the buffet); payphones with limited facilities such as no access to the operator (often in pubs); telephones marked '999 calls only' or 'no cash calls' which give access only to emergency services and the operator. Inevitably, when you find a public phone that is free and in working order it operates a system for which you are not prepared.
Making a call   To call within London, dial the seven figures. To call outside London, it is substantially cheaper to dial direct (possible for most of the world) using the codes listed in the Code Book and at the beginning of the A–D volume of the London directory; they are divided into local, national and international codes. It is not unusual repeatedly to get a crossed line, a continuous note (unobtainable) or a short, repeated note (engaged). The telephonist of a good hotel will do the leg work and ring you when a connection is made – one American businessman who stays at Claridge's always delivers chocolates to the telephonists on his arrival and always gets his connections quickly. Useful numbers include:
Operator for UK calls: 100. This is also for alarm wake-up calls and UK transfer charge calls.
Operator for international calls: 155. This is also for transfer charge calls (calling collect).
UK Telemessage: 191.
International Telemessage: 190; International Telegrams: 193.
Call costs   Assessed according to the distance, the time of day and the length of the call. For UK calls, the local distance rate takes in all of London and there are three time rates: peak, Mon–Fri 9am–1pm; standard, Mon–Fri 8–9am and 1–6pm; and cheap, Mon–Fri 6pm–8am and Sat–Sun all day and night. For most international calls, the cheap rate is 6pm–8am; and for Australia, New Zealand, Hong Kong and Singapore an extra daily Economy Rate operates midnight–7am and 2.30–7.30pm. All charges increase if the call is connected by the operator instead of being dialled direct.
Telephone services   These are a few of the most useful:
Alarm Call: 100, for booking a wake-up call.
Artsline: 388 2227; open Mon–Fri 10am–4pm, Sat 10am–2pm; an arts and entertainment service for

disabled people, giving information on how to reach venues, where best to sit in them and what facilities are available.

Capital Helpline: 388 7575; open Mon–Fri 9.30am–5.30pm and Wed 7–9pm; run by Capital Radio, gives confidential telephone advice on any subject.

Children's London: 246 8007; a week of events on a recorded tape.

Daily Telegraph Information Service: 353 4242; open Mon–Fri 8am–8pm, will answer almost any factual query, much used by bored secretaries betting one another bottles of champagne for the answer.

Kidsline: 222 8070/4640; open Mon–Fri 9am–4pm during school holidays, Mon–Fri 4–6pm during term-time; run by Capital Radio, gives children's events.

Gay Switchboard: 837 7324, a daily 24-hour service for gay men and women; Lesbian Line: 251 6911.

Leisureline: 246 8041 English; 246 8043 French; 246 8045 German; a daily 24-hour service giving a selection of London events.

London Regional Transport and Travel: 222 1234; a daily 24-hour service with an automatic queueing system, gives routes, times and prices of London travel.

London Tourist Board: 730 7488; open Mon–Sat 9am–6pm with an automatic queueing system, for all London information.

Restaurant Switchboard: 888 8080; open daily 9am–9pm; free help to find the restaurant with the right atmosphere, cuisine and price; will also reserve a table.

Riverboat: 730 4812, for Thames travel information.

Sportsline: 222 8000; open daily 10am–6pm, for information on where to watch and play any sport, plus gives results.

Stock Exchange Information: 246 8026, for the Financial Times Share Index and Business News Summary.

Teledata: 200 0200; a daily 24-hour service giving information on anything from locksmiths (when you have lost your key) to late-night eating and minicabs.

Traveline: 246 8021; a daily 24-hour service for traffic conditions on road, rail, air and sea.

Weatherline: 246 8091; for predictions on the unpredictable British weather.

Movement

Public transport is good, but the prices are high, the distances great and the time spent getting somewhere is often longer than the time spent there. So here are some tips on London movement. To stand the prices on their head, buy a London Travelcard – even the smart Knightsbridge shoppers use them. To beat the size of London, plan your day with a map so that it has a degree of geographic logic and you do not spend most of it criss-crossing the city. To use the best transport method for each journey, it is worth remembering that the Underground slices through the city whatever the time of day, whereas buses and taxis are victims (and causes) of the Monday to Friday rush-hour jams, roughly 8–10am and 5–7pm in the centre, continuing later on late shopping nights (see p. 325). And the most important home truth is that when it rains all taxis disappear and buses only come by if they are full and not going to stop.

To make the most of over- and underground transport, consult Judy Allen, *London By Bus and Tube*, a Nicholson guide.

TRAVEL INFORMATION CENTRES The central one is at Victoria Station, open daily 8.30am–9.30pm; equipped with free maps of day and night bus routes and the Underground and all information on cheap tickets. Others are at these Underground stations: Euston, King's Cross, Piccadilly Circus, Oxford Circus and St James's Park, all open daily except Oxford Circus (closes on Sun) and St James's Park (closes Sat, Sun). London Transport Enquiries telephone service (222 1234), operates 24 hours a day and has an automatic queueing system, so just hold on.

TRAVEL PASSES Regular fares are worked out according to length of journey and the five zones, so a short journey that crosses a zone can be more expensive than a longer one that does not. A travel pass bypasses the problem, saves ticket queues and pays for itself within two or three journeys.

Travelcards Valid for unlimited travel by Underground and most buses; priced according to the number of zones included and the length of validity – one day, a week, a month, a year. (A one-day card covers all zones.) Children under 5 travel free; children aged 5–13 pay child fares; children aged 14–15 pay child fares but need proof of age plus a passport photo; adults need a passport photo. On sale at Travel Information Centres and (except for 14–15-year-olds' cards) all Underground stations.

Capitalcards Similar to Travelcards, with the addition of British Rail travel.

Visitor Travelcards Similar to Travelcards but no

7

need for a photo, are valid for one, three, four or seven days and come with free discount vouchers. The catch: must be bought before arrival in London, e.g. at a travel agent or tour operator in the UK or worldwide.

UNDERGROUND   The fastest way to cross London. The network has nine criss-crossing lines stopping at 268 stations. The lines are colour-coded both on the Underground map and in the direction lights of the older stations. First trains run around 5.30am; last trains around midnight (each station displays the time of its last departure); then each station is closed. The whole system is known as the Tube, although strictly speaking only part is the Tube; to find out more, see p. 264.

DOCKLANDS LIGHT RAILWAY   The new railway, opened by the Queen in 1987, runs from the Tower eastwards through the Isle of Dogs to end opposite Greenwich. For more, see p. 255.

BUS   The nicest way to cross London, especially sitting in the front seat of the top deck of a red double-decker when the thrill of the ride combines with sightseeing; for good sightseeing routes, see p. 261. First buses run around 5.30am; last buses around midnight, when the more skeletal Night Service takes over until about 6am. On the one-man buses the driver also sells the tickets and expects passengers to have the exact money ready.

TAXIS   Known as cabs. The drivers of the London black cabs have to pass a gruelling set of exams called The Knowledge to show they know where every London street is and the shortest route to it. It takes about three years to do the course, and each year only 700 of the 5,000 who sit the exam pass. This puts them in a class apart from the taxi drivers of any other capital city. The much loved old cabs, the FX4 design, considered by many to be part of the London character, have had a new rival since 1987, the ugly Metrocab. To find out more, visit the London Taxi Museum, 1–3 Brixton Road, SW9 (735 7777), telephoning beforehand.
Hailing a taxi   First spot one whose yellow light shines 'For Hire' – many people leap about the street at booked taxis with no light on. The driver is obliged to take you if the journey is less than six miles and within the London boundary – late at night, he is likely only to take a final fare if it is on his route home. Once inside, the meter will be set; charges increase in the evening and on Saturdays, more after midnight and on Sundays, with fixed-

price extras for people and baggage. If in doubt about the charge, the Fare Table is displayed in the passenger area. The driver is obliged to follow the shortest route unless you ask him to avoid a specific traffic jam or you agree to his suggestion of another route. To complain, make a note of the driver's number (beneath the Fare Table) and contact the Carriage Office (278 1744).
Telephoning for a taxi   Most firms charge a small fee for collection. A good one is Radio Taxis: 286 0286/272 0272/272 3030/253 5000; operates a daily, 24-hour service; uses black cabs only and has a fleet of more than 2,500; takes immediate and forward bookings which can be paid for or put on a customer's account and settled monthly; reliable for women to use alone at night.

MINICABS   Drivers are not required to take exams, usually do not have the correct insurance and often do not have meters. If you use one, it is important to agree a price in advance and to have a rough idea of the route. Abbey Car Hire (727 2637) operates 24 hours a day and is reputable.

BICYCLE   One of the best ways to explore London is by bicycle, peddling through back roads and stopping to admire buildings, relax in parks and dip into museums. You can bike through some parks, too. For details of hiring, survival tips and suggested routes, see p. 262.

MOTORCYCLE   A good way to move about independently and cover plenty of mileage without getting exhausted. Hiring is straightforward: driving demands a British or any foreign licence. Charges are around £12 per day, reductions for a weekly hire, with a £50 deposit. It is wise to buy a copy of *The Highway Code* from a newsagent before starting off. A reliable company is: Scootabout, 59 Albert Embankment, SE1 (582 0055).

CAR   Driving in London during weekdays is best avoided. Most of the time is spent in traffic jams, looking for a parking place or trying to master the one-way system to reach a car park. When you give up in desperation and leave the car illegally parked, a parking ticket arrives on the windscreen and a clamp on the wheel; freedom is won at a cost of almost £40 and several hours' wait. Driving is easier at weekends, but parking restrictions last all day on Saturday. Better by far to invest in a London travel pass (see p. 7). If you do have a car or hire a car:

The law   It is worth buying a copy of the *Highway Code* from a newsagent. Driving while under the influence of relatively little alcohol is an offence that is increasingly strictly upheld.

Hiring   Almost any car can be hired, from a simple gad-about Ford Fiesta to a chauffeur-driven Rolls Royce Silver Spirit. It is worth booking in advance for the weekends and in the summer (wedding time). Hiring from Central London is cheaper than at the airport. The driver needs to show a driving licence and to be over 18 (sometimes 21 years old); it is worth taking out the full insurance options offered by the company. Reliable firms include:

Avis, main London office at Marble Arch, 68 North Row, W1 (629 7811); British central reservations 848 8733.

Budget Rent-a-Car, 171–5 Brompton Road, SW3 (581 5363/584 6465).

Godfrey Davis Europcar, head office at Davis House, Wilton Road, SW1 (834 8484); chauffeur-driven reservations, (834 6701).

Guy Salmon, 7–23 Bryanston Street, Marble Arch, W1 (408 1255).

Hertz, head office at 1272 London Road, SW16 (679 1799).

Parking   National Car Parks are scattered throughout London and marked on the bigger maps (Nicholson, *A–Z*); their prices vary considerably and are worth checking.

Petrol   The 24-hour petrol stations include the underground car park, west side of Park Lane, W1; Chelsea Cloisters Garage, Sloane Avenue, SW3; 170 Marylebone Road, NW1; 195 Marylebone Road, NW1.

Breakdown   There are two big membership services in Britain, worth joining even if you are intending to do a small amount of driving as the annual fee is less than the cost of a single towing from a motorway breakdown to the nearest garage: The Automobile Association (AA), Fanum House, 52 London Road, Twickenham, Middlesex (891 1441), whose 24-hour breakdown service for London is 954 7373, with automatic queueing system; The Royal Automobile Club (RAC), 49 Pall Mall, SW1 (839 7050), whose 24-hour breakdown service for London is 0923 33555 for stranded cars north of the Thames, 681 3611 south of the Thames.

If membership is not worth the bother, Olympic Breakdown Service, 32a Goldney Road, W9 (286 8282/286 1869) will do both roadside repairs and tow the car away if necessary.

BRITISH RAIL   There is nothing quite as exciting as taking a day trip out of London by train, catching it early enough to have full English breakfast on board. Within London, shorter train journeys include the North London Link and the trips out to Greenwich or Hampton Court. For more on trains, see pp. 264–76. To decide where to go and to book a ticket, visit the British Travel Centre (see p. 4) stocked with leaflets promoting cheap deals for excursions, weekend breaks, awaydays, citysavers, Sunday lunch excursions, Britain Shrinkers, etc. There are nine mainline railway stations serving Britain and the Continent, each with a 24-hour telephone inquiry service:

Liverpool Street and Fenchurch Street, serving Eastern England including Cambridge (283 7171)

King's Cross, serving West Yorkshire, North East England and Scotland (278 2477)

Euston and St Pancras, serving the Midlands, North Wales, North West England and Scotland (387 7070)

Paddington, serving the West of England, West Midlands and South Wales including Oxford and Bath (262 6767)

Waterloo, Victoria and Charing Cross, serving South and South East England (928 5100)

London factsheet

MONEY   The sterling currency is decimal, 100 pence to £1. The coins are 1p, 2p, 5p, 10p, 20p, 50p and £1 (with a £2 coin coming soon); the notes are £5, £10, £20 and £50. Useful coins for telephones, entries and vending machines are 10p and 50p. The pound coin comes in four designs representing the four UK countries: an oak for England, a thistle for Scotland, a leek for Wales and a flax plant for Northern Ireland. In speech, £1 is often referred to in slang as a quid, £5 as a fiver, £10 as a tenner, especially in street markets.

Banks   These often give a better exchange rate than bureaux de change–and it is worth checking the rates to see which bank gives the best deal. No commission is charged on travellers' cheques issued in sterling or other currencies provided they are cashed at an affiliated bank (eg Chase Manhattan–Barclays); you will need to show your passport. Normal banking hours are Mon–Fri 9.30am–3.30pm; a few banks operate longer hours including some branches of Barclays and NatWest which open on Saturday mornings and some branches of the Bank of Scotland which remain open until 5.30pm. The main high street banks, many of their branches in splendid buildings, are:

Bank of Scotland, head office 38 Threadneedle Street, EC2 (628 8060); branches include 57 Haymarket, SW1 (839 6283).

Barclays, head office 54 Lombard Street, EC3 (283 2161); many branches include 119 Marylebone Road, NW1 (723 9211); 1 Pall Mall, SW1 (930 2383).

Coutts, head office 440 Strand, WC2 (379 6262); branches include 162 Brompton Road, SW1 (589 5205); 23 Hanover Square, W1 (491 4070).

Lloyds, head office 71 Lombard Street, EC3 (626 1500); many branches include 79 Brompton Road, SW3 (589 2223); 39 Piccadilly, W1 (439 8921).

Midland, head office Poultry, EC2 (606 9911); many branches include 237 Brompton Road, SW3 821 1344); 16 King Street, Covent Garden, WC2 (240 7222); 79 Piccadilly, W1 (629 4656).

National Westminster (NatWest), head office 21 Lombard Street, EC3 (280 4444); many branches include 161 Brompton Road, SW3 (589 6641); 34 Henrietta Street, Covent Garden, WC2 (836 4155); 63 Piccadilly, W1 (493 2271).

Royal Bank of Scotland, head office 67 Lombard Street, EC3 (623 4356); branches include 44 Brompton Road, SW3 (581 5914); 1 Fleet Street, EC4 (353 4080); 48 Haymarket, SW1 (930 1396).

For American Express, see under USA in the Home from Home section, p. 16.

Bureaux de change These are usually open very long hours and often at weekends (according to the season), so they are useful for changing a small amount of money to tide you over until the banks open. However, it is essential to check carefully the commission rate and other charges before entering into a transaction; there are many rip-off dealers. The LTB has a brochure of approved dealers together with the code of conduct they should abide by. The following firms, all with many branches, are reliable:

Erskine, head office 22 Leinster Terrace, W2 (402 5128); branches include 15 Shaftesbury Avenue, W1 (734 1400) and 3–5 Coventry Street, W1 (437 7167); both open daily, 24 hours.

Lenlyn Ltd, head office 84 Petty France, SW1 (222 5953); branches include four at Victoria Station and 7 Grand Buildings, Trafalgar Square, SW1 (930 4247).

Thomas Cook, head office 45 Berkeley Square, W1 (499 4000); biggest London branch at 1 Marble Arch, W1 (402 9424), usually open Mon–Fri 8am–7pm, Sat 8.30am–5.30pm, Sun 10am–1pm. Other branches, many open on Sat, include 103 Cheap-side, EC2 (606 8722); 108 Fleet Street, EC4 (353 2166); Harrods, Knightsbridge, SW1 (730 1234); 104 Kensington High Street, W8 (937 3673); 21 Old Brompton Road, SW7 (581 4577); 126 Queensway, W2 (727 1501); 100 Victoria Street, SW1 (828 0437).

Lost credit cards These are the telephone numbers to dial immediately you discover a loss:

Access, with Lloyds: 0702 352233; with Midland: 0702 352244; with National Westminster: 0702 352255; with Royal Bank of Scotland: 0702 351 381.

American Express: For cards: 222 9633; for travellers' cheques: 0273 675975.

Diners Club: 0252 516261.

Eurocheque: 588 3600.

Visa-Barclaycard: 0604 21100.

MEASUREMENTS After a half-hearted attempt to become European, the British have given up. While liquid is officially measured in litres, food cartons marked with gram weight, and weather temperatures published in Celsius, most British still think in pints, pounds and Fahrenheit. To help visitors get in tune, here are a few basic conversions:

Length 1 centimetre = 0.39 inch; 1 metre = 1.09 yards; 1 kilometre = 0.62 miles. Conversely, 1 inch = 2.54 centimetres; 1 foot = 30.48 centimetres; 1 yard = 0.91 metres; 1 mile = 1.61 kilometres.

Area 1 square metre = 1.19 square yards; 1 hectare = 2.47 acres; 1 square kilometre = 0.39 square miles. 1 square foot = 0.09 square metres; 1 square yard = 0.83 square metres; 1 acre = 4046.9 square metres.

Capacity 1 litre = 0.22 gallons. 1 pint = 0.57 litres; 1 gallon = 4.55 litres.

Weight 1 gram = 0.03 ounces; 1 kilogram = 2.2 pounds. 1 ounce = 28.35 grams; 1 pound (16 ounces) = 0.45 kilograms; 1 stone (14 pounds) = 6.35 kilograms.

Dry measures 1 US pint = 0.97 UK pints = 0.55 litres.

Liquid measures 1 US pint = 0.83 UK pints = 0.47 litres; 1 US gallon = 0.83 gallons = 3.79 litres.

Temperature Freezing point is 0 degrees Celsius and 32 degrees Fahrenheit. Thus, −18C = 0F; −10C = 16F; 0C= 32F; 10C = 50F; 20C = 68F and, optimistically, 30C = 86F.

Clothes sizes Some sizes differ between the UK and US; some also differ from the Continent – still firmly referred to as Europe in the rag trade, as if Britain did not belong. Men's suits have the same UK and US sizes but different Continental sizes; thus UK/US32 = Eur42; UK/US34 = Eur44; UK/

US36 = Eur46; UK/US38 = Eur48. Men's shirt collar sizes are measured in inches in the UK, in centimetres on the Continent; thus UK14.5 = Eur37; UK15 = Eur38; UK15.5 = Eur39.5; UK16 = 41cm. Women's UK sizes are different in the US and on the Continent; thus UK10 = US8 = Eur38; UK12 = US10 = Eur40; UK14 = US12 = Eur42; UK16 = US14 = Eur44. Shoe sizes have similar triple sizing; thus UK4 = US5.5 = Eur37; UK5 = US6.5 = Eur38; UK6 = US7.5 = Eur39; UK7 = US8.5 = Eur40.5.

TIME Greenwich Mean Time (GMT) is calculated from London (to stand over the zero degree mark, see p. 108). This is too simple for the British who now have two times, Winter Time (the GMT time) and British Summer Time. At the end of March the clocks are wound back an hour; at the end of October they are wound forward. The dates vary because the change is always on a Saturday night. The dates rarely coincide with any Continental time changes, so their time, usually one hour ahead, is occasionally the same as Britain's for a short spell.

WORLD TIME To calculate local standard time outside Britain, add or subtract the number of hours from the GMT time – but remember to take into account British Summer Time and any Continental summer times. Continental cities are usually one hour ahead. Abu Dhabi +4; Adelaide +9.5; Athens +2; Brussels +1; Chicago −6; Delhi +5.5; Hong Kong +8; Jerusalem +2; Kuala Lumpur +8; Manila +8; Melbourne +10; Moscow +3; New York −5; Oslo +1; Ottawa −5; Paris +1; Peking +8; Perth +8; Riyadh +3; San Francisco −8; Singapore +7.5; Sydney +10; Tokyo +9; Toronto −5; Vancouver −8; Washington −5.

London layout

THE MAP The first thing to realise about London is that it does not fit onto a single sheet map. It is too big. Ideally, you need two maps: a single sheet of Central London to see how one part relates to another, and a book of maps with a street directory for the whole city. The best single sheet map is the Ordnance Survey map of London Central, scale 1:10,000. There are two good books of maps, both commonly referred to as 'The A to Z', both published in several sizes: *The London A–Z Street Atlas*, Deluxe edition is best; and the much easier to use Nicholson's *London Streetfinder*, with clearer maps and more precise references, so street-plotting is faster. (The Nicholson is no relation to this author.) For map-reading in the rain, Bartholomew's *Handy Map of London* is a cleverly designed, laminated, folded sheet with map on both sides, very easy to use.

SIZE There is Inner London, 123.806 square miles. Then there is Outer London, 486.031 square miles. Together they form Greater London, 609.837 square miles. (Central London is a delightfully vague term used by everyone. It may mean anything from the small area surrounding Piccadilly and Shaftesbury Avenue to all of Inner London.)

POPULATION Reached an all-time high of around 10 million in the 1930s and 1940s, then declined until just recently when it began to stabilise. According to the Central Statistical Office, in 1986 the population of Inner London was 2,511,700 and of Outer London 4,263,500, making a total of 6,775,200. Added to that were the visitors during that year, an astonishing 7,570,000, half of whom came for a holiday, the rest for business, study or to visit friends and relations. The current population of the UK (England, Scotland, Wales and Northern Ireland) is 56,763,300.

ADMINISTRATION Since the abolition of the Greater London Council in 1986, there is no single body to run London. It has gone back to muddling through, its responsibilities shared among various bodies. Inner London is the political, commercial and entertainment hub. It is composed of the Cities of London and Westminster and of 11 boroughs who each now run many of the parks, sports and recreation services. Their information services supply quantities of brochures, maps and information, from cycling routes and how to find a babysitter to where to play tennis, where to hear a local concert or where to join in a community event. These are the main offices and the Information Desk telephone numbers:
City of London: City of London Information Centre, St Paul's Churchyard, EC4 (606 3030)
City of Westminster: Westminster City Hall, Victoria Street, SW1 (828 8070)
Camden: St Pancras Library, 100 Euston Road, NW1 (278 4444)
Greenwich: Tourist Information Centre, Cutty Sark Gardens, SE10 (854 8888)
Hackney: Town Hall, Mare Street, E8 (986 3123)

Hammersmith and Fulham: Town Hall, King Street, W6 (748 3020)

Islington: Town Hall, Upper Street, N1 (226 1234)

Kensington and Chelsea: Town Hall, Hornton Street, W8 (937 5464 for general information; 373 6099 for parks and sports)

Lambeth: Town Hall, Brixton Hill, SW2 (274 7722)

Lewisham: Town Hall, SE6 (690 4343)

Southwark: Town Hall, Peckham Road, SE5 (703 6311 for general information; 703 3499 for leisure and amenities)

Tower Hamlets: Town Hall, Patriot Square, E2 (980 4831)

Wandsworth: Town Hall, SW18 (871 6000)

POSTAL DISTRICTS   Every address has its postal district at the end, from E1 to W14. These help enormously in giving an instant idea of where a restaurant, shop or friend is located in the huge city, and for coordinating three or four visits in one area. They are arranged roughly geographically taking the City of London, the commercial centre, as their reference point. Thus E1 infers the address will be a little east of the City while SW3 infers it will be well to the south-west, SW10 even further off. To confuse, EC1–4 are inside the City of London but WC1 and WC2 stretch across Bloomsbury and Covent Garden. With the royal and political centre at Westminster (SW1), London's smart residential areas developed on that side, and today the fashionable hotels, shops and restaurants tend to be in the W and SW bracket.

Body and soul

EMERGENCIES   To report an emergency, note the address of the event and then find the nearest telephone, dial 999 (no money or card needed) and ask for police, fire brigade or ambulance. To report an accident, robbery or incident that is not an emergency, go to the nearest police station within 24 hours. At an entertainment centre or at any public event there are always representatives of St John Ambulance Service who will give first aid.

HEALTH

National Health Service   EEC nationals are entitled to free medical treatment under the National Health Service for illness arising during their stay in Britain. Citizens of some other countries are entitled to free medical treatment and subsidised dental treatment if they become ill while in the UK, including: Australia, Austria, the Channel Islands,

Finland, the German Democratic Republic, Gibraltar, Hong Kong, Hungary, Iceland, the Isle of Man, Malta, New Zealand, Norway, Poland, Sweden and the USSR. Citizens of neither the EEC nor countries with the reciprocal health arrangements with Britain must pay for everything – the emergency ambulance, the hospital treatment, the prescriptions and time spent with doctors, dentists, etc. Therefore, medical insurance is essential. To take out insurance on arrival in Britain, complete and return a Medisure form (available from a post office). For more information, contact the Department of Health and Social Security (DHSS), Alexander Fleming House, Elephant & Castle, SE1.

National Health Hospitals   Several have 24-hour casualty departments including:

The London Hospital, Whitechapel Road, E1 (247 5454)

Middlesex Hospital, Mortimer Street, W1 (636 8333)

University College Hospital, Gower Street (entrance in Grafton Way), W1 (387 9300)

Westminster Hospital, Dean Ryle Street, Horseferry Road, SW1 (828 9811)

Private hospitals   Many, particularly in northern Marylebone. They include:

The London Clinic, 20 Devonshire Place, W1 (935 4444), patients referred by a practitioner, no accident centre.

The Cromwell Hospital, Cromwell Road, SW5 (370 4233/2525), with full 24-hour out-patients department (not accident centre).

The Princess Grace, 42 Nottingham Place, W1 (486 1234), patients referred by a practitioner, no accident centre.

Medical Express, Chapel Place, W1 (499 1991) is a private walk-in casualty clinic which also offers a comprehensive health screening service.

SPECIAL HEALTH SERVICES

Alternative medicine   For information, buy a copy of the current *Yearbook for Complementary Medicine*, which gives a list of reputable sources of help in London, set out by area and subject. For more advice, contact the Institute of Complementary Medicine, 21 Portland Place, W1 (636 9543). See also Homoeopathy and Osteopaths, below.

Blind people   For all advice including which museums have facilities for the visually handicapped, contact The Royal National Institute for the Blind, 224 Great Portland Street, W1 (388 1266).

Chemists   See p. 326.

Contraception and pregnancy   Brook Advisory Centre, 233 Tottenham Court Road, W1 (323 1522), with 11 London clinics; Family Planning Association, 27–35 Mortimer Street, W1 (636 7866), with phone-in advice service; and Pregnancy Advisory Service, 13 Charlotte Street, W1 (637 8962), whose services include 'morning after' contraception.

Deaf people   For all advice, from deaf aids to public loop systems, contact:

The Royal National Institute for the Deaf, 105 Gower Street, WC1 (387 8033); or The Royal Association in Aid of the Deaf and Dumb, 27 Old Oak Road, London W3 (743 6187). The Ear, Nose and Throat Hospital, Gray's Inn Road, WC1 (837 8855) will replace batteries and repair leads for NHS patients and will, in emergency, loan NHS patients an aid. Hearing Aids, 146 Marylebone Road, NW1 (486 3638) supplies new aids.

Dentists   The Dental Emergency Service (584 1008) operates 24 hours a day, referring people in pain to their nearest open surgery, either private or National Health.

Diabetics   For help and advice, contact the British Diabetic Association, 10 Queen Anne Street, W1 (323 1531).

Heart sufferers   For a card listing the emergency pacemaker centres in the UK, contact The British Heart Foundation, 102 Gloucester Place, W1 (935 0185). London pacemaker centres include Guy's Hospital, SE1 (407 7600); The National Heart Hospital, W1 (486 4433); St Bartholomew's Hospital, EC1 (600 9000).

Helplines   These are a few of the specialist telephone services:

Alcoholics Anonymous: 352 9779.

British Pregnancy Advisory Service: 222 0985.

Gamblers Anonymous: 352 3060, a daily, 24-hour service.

Health Line: 980 4848/981 2717/980 7222, open daily 10am–10pm, for advice on any subject.

National Society for the Prevention of Cruelty to Children (NSPCC): 580 8812, a daily, 24-hour service.

Rape Crisis Centre: 278 3956; 24-hour number 837 1600.

Release: 289 1123, for counselling on drug use and referral.

Samaritans: 383 3400, a daily 24-hour service, sympathetic listeners to any problem, especially depression.

Homoeopathy   For a register of homoeopathic practitioners and chemists stocking homoeo-pathic medicines, contact the British Homoeopathic Association, 27a Devonshire Street, W1 (935 2163). The Royal London Homoeopathic Hospital is at Great Ormond Street, WC1 (837 3091); chemists include Ainsworth's Homoeopathic Pharmacy, 38 New Cavendish Street, W1 (935 5330).

Inoculations   If you are travelling on from London, the following offer the latest advice and give the jabs and prescriptions: The British Airways Immunisation Clinic, 75 Regent Street, W1 (439 9584), open Mon–Fri 8.30am–4.30pm, best to book; Trailfinder, 46–8 Earls Court Road, W8 (938 3444); and Thomas Cook, 45 Berkeley Street, W1 (499 4000). For more in-depth help, visit the Hospital for Tropical Diseases, St Pancras Hospital, 4 St Pancras Way, NW1 (387 4411).

Migraine   The Princess Margaret Migraine Clinic, Fulham Palace Road, W6, (741 7833) offers a 24-hour emergency service Mon–Fri.

Opticians   The following have a good stock of lenses, frames, contact lenses and cleaning equipment and can offer same-day service, although unusual lenses take longer. First Sight Opticians, 229–31 Regent Street, W1 (499 8777), optician and workshop on site; For Eyes, 261 Oxford Street, W1 (491 7004), workshop on site. In an emergency, go to Moorfields Eye Hospital, either at City Road, EC1 (253 3411) or High Holborn, WC1 (836 6611), both with 24-hour service.

Osteopaths   To find a trained and registered osteopath, contact The General Council and Register of Osteopaths, 1–4 Suffolk Street, SW1 (839 2060).

WORSHIP   The Queen is head of the Church of England with the Archbishop of Canterbury as spiritual leader. London's many churches are worth visiting for their architecture and monuments and to listen to fine singing and organ playing, whatever faith you follow. For worship, London is so cosmopolitan that almost every religion and denomination is represented. To find a suitable and sympathetic place of worship, it is best to contact the headquarters of that body, a few of which are listed below. For church music, see below (p. 294).

Christianity   The British Council of Churches, 2 Eaton Gate, SW1 (730 9611) welcomes visitors by appointment.

Baptist Union of Great Britain and Ireland, Baptist Church House, 4 Southampton Row, WC1 (242 7815). More than 260 churches including Bloomsbury Central Baptist Church, Shaftesbury Avenue, WC2 (836 6843).

Church of England, Church House, Great Smith Street, SW1 (222 9011). The two poles of the Church of England in London are demonstrated by All Saints, 7 Margaret Street, W1 (636 1788), high Anglican with a fine liturgical and musical tradition in a fine building, and All Souls, Langham Place, W1 (580 4357), a very popular evangelical church with overflow halls and close circuit television. There are many shades in between. St Paul's Cathedral (see p. 66) has good music; Southwark Cathedral (see p. 61) celebrates the liturgy with imagination and has good music; St Mary's Bourne Street, 30 Bourne Street, SW1 (730 2423) and St Paul's Knightsbridge, 32 Wilton Place, SW1 (235 3460) are high Anglican and social, in fine settings; St Bartholomew-the-Great (see pp. 201–2) keeps to the traditional service in one of London's oldest churches; Temple Church (see pp. 131–2) and Lincoln's Inn Chapel (see p. 126) have the barristers' collegiate atmosphere; The Chapel Royal (see p. 138) has regal splendour; St Martin-in-the-Fields (see p. 88) has a large and friendly foreign congregation; St Mary's, Marylebone Road, NW1 (935 7315) is the centre of liaison between medicine and faith, and St Peter ad Vincula (see pp. 102, 104) is in the middle of the Tower of London. To find the special services in Royal Peculiars, see p. 138.

Church of Scotland, Crown Court, Russell Street, WC2 (836 5643); churches include St Columba's Church, Pont Street, SW1 (584 2321).

Lutheran Council Great Britain, 8 Collingham Gardens, SW5 (373 5566); services at St Anne & St Agnes, Gresham Street, EC2.

Methodist Church, Conference Office, 1 Central Buildings, Matthew Parker Street, SW1 (222 8010); services with preaching at Wesley's Chapel (see p. 68) and Central Hall Westminster, Storeys Gate, SW1 (222 8010).

Moravian Church, 3 Muswell Hill, N10 (883 3409).

The Roman Catholic Church in England and Wales, Catholic Media Office, 23 Kensington Square W8 (938 2583); services in Westminster Cathedral (see p. 92); The Oratory, (see p. 215) for traditional liturgy and mass in Latin on Suns, 8am; St Etheldreda (see p. 128); Church of the Immaculate Conception (Farm Street), 114 Mount Street, W1 (493 7811); the old Portuguese Chapel, Warwick Street, W1 (437 1525); Ealing Abbey (Benedictine), Charlbury Grove, W5 (998 2158); for a list of churches, see the London telephone directory under 'Catholic'.

Salvation Army, International Headquarters, 101 Queen Victoria Street, EC4 (236 5222).

United Reformed Church, 86 Tavistock Place, WC1 (837 7661).

Islam   The Council of Mosques, 46 Goodge Street, W1 (636 7568); many of the half million Muslims in London come regularly to the Central Mosque, 146 Park Road, NW8 (724 3363) see p. 182.

Judaism   Central Enquiry Desk, Board of Deputies of British Jews, Woburn House, Upper Woburn Place, WC1 (387 4044). Over the centuries, London has acquired more than 200 synagogues. About 80% of synagogue members belong to Orthodox synagogues but there are also Liberal (similar to Reform in the US) and Reform (similar to Conservative in the US) synagogues. The London community also includes Sephardi and Oriental congregations and Chasidic synagogues. Central London synagogues include: New West End Synagogue, St Petersburgh Place, W1 (229 2631), Orthodox Ashkenasi; The Spanish and Portuguese Synagogue, Bevis Marks, EC3 (289 2573), Orthodox Sephardi; Ohel David Synagogue, Lincoln Institute, Broad Walk Lane, Golders Green Road, NW11 (455 3491), Orthodox Eastern (Oriental).

Home from home: Embassies to national clubs

Embassies and consulates are good sources of practical information. They will advise not only on visas but on where to find national cultural societies, clubs, newspapers, places of worship and the offices for national airlines and banks – Canada House even produces an information booklet. The staff of national tourist offices help with international travel and have good tips on London life. For airlines details, see Checking Out, below.

AUSTRALIA   Australian High Commission, Australia House, Strand, WC2 (438 8775). The Australian Tourist Commission, 20 Savile Row, W1 (434 4371). National Australia Bank Ltd, 6 Tokenhouse Yard, EC2 (606 8070). Australian British Chamber of Commerce, Suite 615, Linen Hall, 162–8 Regent Street, W1 (439 0086). Club: The Walkabout Club, 25–6 Craven Terrace, Lancaster Gate, W2 (402 7633).

BELGIUM   Ambassade de Belgique/Belgian Embassy, 103 Eaton Square, SW1 (235 5422). Belgian National Tourist Office, 38 Dover Street, W1

(499 5379). Banque Belge Ltd (Societé Générale de Banque), 4 Bishopsgate, EC2 (283 1080). Belgo–Luxembourg Chambers of Commerce in Great Britain, 36 Piccadilly, W1 (434 1815). Club: Anglo–Belgian Club, 60 Knightsbridge, SW1 (235 2121).

CANADA   Canadian High Commission/Haut Commissariat du Canada, Canada House, Trafalgar Square, SW1 (629 9492), publishes the fact-packed booklet *Welcome*. Canadian Government Office of Tourism is in Canada House (629 9492). National Bank of Canada, Princes House, 95 Gresham Street, EC2 (726 6581). Canada–UK Chamber of Commerce, 1–3 Lower Regent Street, SW1 (930 7711). Clubs: Canada Club, c/o Mr JT Spurgen, Wood Gundy Ltd, 30 Finsbury Square, EC2 (628 4030); Maple Leaf Luncheon Club, c/o Mrs Noble, 1 Mount Street, W1 (491 3430).

DENMARK   Kongelig Dansk Ambassade/Royal Danish Embassy, 55 Sloane Street, SW1 (235 1255). Danish Tourist Board, Sceptre House, 169–73 Regent Street, W1 (734 2637). Den Danske Bank, Danske House, 44 Bishopsgate, EC2 (628 3090). For commerce, contact the Commercial Section at the embassy. Club: Danish Club (founded 1863), 62 Knightsbridge, SW1. Church: The Danish Church, 4 St Katharine's Precinct, Regent's Park, NW1.

FINLAND   Embassy of Finland, 38 Chesham Place, SW1 (235 9531). The Finnish Tourist Board, 66–8 Haymarket, SW1 (839 4048). Union Bank of Finland, 44–6 Cannon Street, EC4 (248 3333). Commercial Section, Embassy of Finland, 46/7 Pall Mall, SW1 (839 7262). Club: Anglo–Finnish Society, c/o 42D Compayne Gardens, NW6 (624 5817). Church: Finnish Seamen's Mission, 33 Albion Street, SE16 (237 1245).

FRANCE   Ambassade de France/French Embassy, 22 Wilton Crescent, SW1 (235 8080). French Government Tourist Office, 178 Piccadilly, W1 (491 7622). Crédit Lyonnais, 84 Queen Victoria Street, EC4 (634 8000). French Chamber of Commerce, 54 Conduit Street, W1 (439 1735). Clubs and societies: Institut Francais du Royaume-Uni, 17 Queensbury Place, SW7 (589 6211) for a lively cultural programme; Centre Charles Péguy, 16 Leicester Square, WC2 (437 8339); for more, contact the French Consulate General, 24 Rutland Gate, SW7 (581 5292). Church: Notre Dame de France, 5 Leicester Place, Leicester Square, WC2 (437 9363), see also p. 159.

GERMANY   Embassy of the Federal Republic of Germany, 23 Belgrave Square, SW1 (235 5033). German National Tourist Office, 61 Conduit Street, W1 (734 2600). Deutsche Bank AG, 6 Bishopsgate, EC2 (283 4600). German Chamber of Industry and Commerce, 12 Suffolk Street, SW1 (930 7251). Society: Goethe-Institut London, 50 Princes Gate, Exhibition Road, SW7 (581 3344/7). Church: Evangelische Christus Kirche, Montpelier Place, SW7 (589 5305).

GREECE   Greek Embassy, 1a Holland Park, W11 (727 8040). Greek Tourist Agency, 320 Regent Street, W1 (580 3152). National Bank of Greece, 50 St Mary Axe, EC3 (626 3222). For commerce, contact the embassy. Society: The Greek Institute, 34 Bush Hill Road, N21 (360 7968). Church: The Greek Cathedral Church of Aghia Sophia, Moscow Road, W2 (229 7260/4643), see also p. 198.

INDIA   High Commission of India, India House, Aldwych, WC2 (836 8484). Government of India Tourist Office, 7 Cork Street, W1 (437 3677). Bank of India, 11–16 Telegraph Street, EC2 (628 3165). For commerce, contact India House. Clubs: Bharatiya Vidya Bhavan, 4a Castletown Road, W8 (381 3086), lively cultural programme plus information on London temples; Royal Asiatic Society, 56 Queen Anne Street, W1; Sanskritik Centre of Indian Arts, 17 Holdenhurst Avenue, N12 (346 5401); Tara Arts Centre, 356 Garratt Lane, SW18 (871 1458); details of many more from the Cultural Section of India House.

IRELAND   Irish Embassy, 17 Grosvenor Place, SW1 (235 2171). Irish Tourist Board, Ireland House, 150 New Bond Street, W1 (493 3201). Bank of Ireland, 36 Moorgate, EC2 (628 8811). For commerce, contact the embassy.

ITALY   Italian Embassy, 14 Three Kings Yard, W1 (629 8200). Italian State Tourist Office, 1 Princes Street, W1 (408 1254). Banco di Roma, 14 Eastcheap, EC3 (623 1681). Italian Chamber of Commerce, Walmar House, Regent Street, W1 (637 3153); Italian Trade Centre, 37 Sackville Street, W1 (734 2412). Clubs: Italian Cultural Institute, 39 Belgrave Square, SW1 (235 1461). Church: St Peter's Italian Church, 4 Back Hill, EC1 (837 1497).

JAPAN   Japanese Embassy, 46 Grosvenor Street, W1 (493 6030); Information Centre at 9 Grosvenor Square, W1 (493 6030). Japan National Tourist

Organisation, 167 Regent Street, W1 (734 9638). Bank of Japan, 27 Old Jewry, EC2 (606 2454). For commerce, contact the embassy. Clubs: Japan Association, 43 King William Street, EC4 (623 5324).

NETHERLANDS Ambassade van het Koninkrijk der Nederlanden/Royal Netherlands Embassy, 38 Hyde Park Gate, SW7 (584 5040). Netherlands Board of Tourism, 25–8 Buckingham Gate, SW1 (630 0451). AMRO (Amsterdam/Rotterdam Bank), 101 Moorgate, EC2 (638 2700); ABN (General Bank of The Netherlands), 61 Threadneedle Street, EC2 (628 4272). Netherlands-British Chamber of Commerce, The Dutch House, 307–8 High Holborn, WC1 (405 1358). Clubs: The Anglo-Netherlands Society, Unilever House, PO Box 68, EC4; Neerlandia, The Dutch Club, c/o 18 Egerton Terrace, SW3 (581 0171). Church: The Dutch Church, Austin Friars, EC2 (588 1684).

NEW ZEALAND New Zealand High Commission, New Zealand House, 80 Haymarket, SW1 (930 8422). Tourist office at New Zealand House. Bank of New Zealand, BNZ House, 91 Gresham Street, EC2 (726 4060). NZ–UK Chambers of Commerce and Industry, Suite 615, Linen Hall, 162–8 Regent Street, W1 (439 0086). Clubs: For information on the London Maori Club, London New Zealand Cricket Club, New Zealand Society and others, contact New Zealand House.

NORWAY Royal Norwegian Embassy, 25 Belgrave Square, SW1 (235 7151). Norwegian National Tourist Office, 20 Pall Mall, SW1 (839 6255). Union Bank of Norway Ltd, The Old Deanery, Deans Court, St Paul's Churchyard, EC4 (248 0462); Scandinavian Bank Group, Scandinavia House, 2/6 Cannon Street, EC4 (235 6090). Norwegian Chamber of Commerce, Norway House, 21/4 Cockspur Street, SW1 (930 0181). Clubs: Anglo–Norse Society, 25 Belgrave Square, W1; Norwegian Club at Norway House. Church: Norwegian Seamen's Church, 1 Albion Street, Rotherhithe, SE16 (237 5587).

POLAND Embassy of the Polish Peoples Republic, 47 Portland Place, W1 (580 4324); Consulate General of the Polish Peoples Republic, 73 New Cavendish Street, W1 (636 6032), for passports. Polish Tourist Office (ORBIS), 82 Mortimer Street, W1 (637 4971). Bank Hadlowy W Warszarie SA, 4 Coleman Street, EC2 (606 7181). For commerce, contact the Polish Commercial Counsellor's Office,

15 Devonshire Street, W1 (580 5481). Clubs and societies: Polish Cultural Institute, 34 Portland Place, W1 (636 6032); The Polish Institute and Sikorski Museum, 20 Princes Gate, SW7 (589 9249), see p. 218; The Polish Hearth Club, 55 Princes Gate, SW7 (589 4670). Church: St Andrew Bobola's, 1 Leysfield Road, W12 (743 8848).

PORTUGAL Portuguese Embassy, 11 Belgrave Square, SW1 (235 5331). Portuguese National Tourist Office, 1 New Bond Street, W1 (493 3873). Banco Totta & Acores, 68 Cannon Street, EC2 (236 1515). Portuguese Chamber of Commerce and Industry, 1 New Bond Street, W1 (493 9973). Club: Portuguese Community Centre, 7 Thorpe Close, W10 (969 3890). Church: Portuguese Chaplaincy, 165 Arlington Road, NW1 (267 9612).

SPAIN Spanish Embassy, 24 Belgrave Square, W1 (235 5555). Spanish National Tourist Office, 57 St James's Street, SW1 (499 0901). Banco de Bilbao, 100 Cannon Street, EC4 (623 3060). Spanish Chamber of Commerce, 5 Cavendish Square, W1 (637 9161). Clubs and societies: Spanish Club, 5 Cavendish Square, W1 (580 2750); Spanish Institute (Instituto de España), 102 Eaton Square, SW1 (235 1484). Church: Spanish Catholic Chaplaincy, 47 Palace Court, W2 (229 8815).

SWEDEN Swedish Embassy, 11 Montagu Place, W1 (724 2101). Swedish National Tourist Office, 3 Cork Street, W1 (437 5816). SwedBank, The Old Deanery, Dean's Court, EC4 (236 4060). Swedish Chamber of Commerce, 18 Bentinck Street, W1 (486 4545). Clubs: The Swedish Club, 24 Brewer Street, W1 (734 6311). Church: The Swedish Church, 6 Harcourt Street, W1 (723 5681).

SWITZERLAND Swiss Embassy, 16–18 Montagu Place, W1 (723 0701). Swiss National Tourist Office, 1 New Coventry Street, W1 (734 1921). Schweizerischer Bankverein (Swiss Bank Corporation), 99 Gresham Street, EC2 (606 4000). For commerce, The Swiss Mercantile Society, 35 Fitzroy Square, W1 (636 2892). Clubs and societies: City Swiss Club, 99 Gresham Street, EC2 (606 4000); New Helvetic Society, c/o 23 Pembroke Gardens Close, Edwardes Square, W8 (602 0149); for more, contact the embassy. Church: The Swiss Church, 79 Endell Street, WC2 (836 1418).

USA Embassy of the United States of America, Grosvenor Square, W1 (499 9000); visa enquiries

499 3443. Various state tourist boards with offices in London include: Florida Department of Commerce, 1/55 Park Lane, W1 (493 1343); New York State, 25 Bedford Square, WC1 (323 0648); State of Florida Department of Commerce, 1/55 Park Lane, W1 (493 7064). American Express: The biggest branch is 6 Haymarket, SW1 (930 4411), open Mon–Fri 9am–5pm, Sat 9am–noon; for travel, business arrangements, travellers' cheques. The bureau de change here opens June–Sept Mon–Fri 9am–5pm, Sat noon–8pm, Sun and Bank Holidays 10am–8pm; Oct–May Mon–Fri 9am–5pm, Sat noon–6pm, Sun and Bank Holidays 10am–6pm. Other branches include: 78 Brompton Road, SW1 (584 6182); 52 Cannon Street, EC4 (248 2671); 89 Mount Street, W1 (499 4436); 147 Victoria Street, W1 (828 7411). American Chamber of Commerce (UK), 75 Brook Street, W1 (493 0381); British–American Chamber of Commerce, Suite 311, 19 Stratford Place, W1 (491 3361). Clubs and societies: For a full list, see fortnightly newspaper, *The American*, which publishes a *Guide to American Organizations and Institutions in Great Britain*. It includes The British–American Arts Association, 49 Wellington Street, WC2 (379 7755).

USSR   Soviet Embassy, 18 Kensington Palace Gardens, W8 (229 6412). Soviet Consulate, 5 Kensington Palace Gardens, W8 (229 3215). For tourism, contact Aeroflot, 70 Piccadilly, W1 (493 7436). For commerce, contact the embassy; for clubs and societies, contact the consulate. Society: Great Britain–USSR Association, 14 Grosvenor Place, SW1 (235 2116). Church: The Russian Church: All Saints, Ennismore Gardens, SW7 (584 0096); The Russian Orthodox Church in Exile: Dormition Church, Emperor's Gate, SW7 (373 7924).

Hot tips

CULTURE SEEKERS   The cultural calendar runs non-stop. See the London Year Directory, p. 352, to get yourself acquainted with what's on where this month.

London has a legion of arts societies. Some have membership schemes (all welcome, no expertise needed) which bring a variety of perks: free entry into museums that charge an entrance fee; membership of others brings the opportunity to see inside buildings usually closed to the public, to enjoy guided tours and to attend events and lectures. These are a handful:

The Arts Council   105 Piccadilly, W1 (629 9495). Not a membership society but a body that receives government money to support the arts in Britain, from performances at Covent Garden to exhibitions of avant-garde art. Their art exhibition platforms are the Hayward Gallery on the South Bank for major shows and the Serpentine Gallery in Hyde Park for smaller, usually contemporary shows (see pp. 117 and 191). Recently less generous in its patronage.

English Heritage   Membership Department, PO Box 43, Ruislip, Middlesex; Fortress House, 23 Savile Row, W1 (734 6010) for general enquiries. Secures and preserves architectural and archaeological sites and runs almost 400 properties in England. London work includes running the Blue Plaque scheme (see p. 56); then recommending some buildings to be listed (see Pressure groups, below); and administering properties including the Banqueting House, Chiswick House, Hampton Court Palace, the Jewel Tower at Westminster, Kensington Palace, Kenwood, Kew Palace, Lancaster House, London Wall at Tower Hill, Marble Hill House, Ranger's House, the Tower of London, and the Chapter House and Pyx Chamber of Westminster Abbey. Membership gains free entry to all.

The National Association of Decorative and Fine Arts Societies (NADFAS)   38 Ebury Street, SW1 (730 3041). Of its London groups, Westminster runs an especially lively events programme.

National Art Collections Fund   20 John Islip Street, SW1 (821 0404). Membership helps the Fund to contribute money towards the efforts of museums and galleries to buy works of art; it also brings a number of benefits including good events. Objects recently bought by London museums with NACF help include Constable's 'The Opening of Waterloo Bridge' (Tate), the Achaemenian bronze ibex (British Museum), the Islington Cup (V&A).

National Trust   36 Queen Anne's Gate, SW1 (222 9251). Owns more than 250 historic buildings in England, Wales and Northern Ireland, as well as gardens, parks and tracts of countryside–members have free entry to all. Runs a shop at The Blewcoat School, 23 Caxton Street, SW1; publishes an annual Handbook (in March). London properties include the Blewcoat School, Carlyle's House, Fenton House, the George Inn at Southwark, Ham House, Osterley Park – both Ham and Osterley are run by the Victoria & Albert Museum. Criticised as elitist and undemocratic in its approach to property acquisition, but should improve. See also p. 90.

The pressure groups   These campaign to preserve

the better buildings and townscapes. Much of London has been destroyed by developers – an obvious example is almost every house in Park Lane; but some parts still stand because of the people that fought for them – Covent Garden, Whitehall, Knightsbridge and much more. The groups recommend to the government that it protects some buildings by listing them as Grade I (exceptional national importance), Grade II* (more than special national importance) or Grade II (special national importance) and protects areas by making them Conservation Areas. In turn, they are consulted when applications are made to alter buildings already protected. They work closely with local groups and try to stimulate public awareness of our surroundings. Membership supports their work and brings access to lectures, events, tours and outings, often to buildings otherwise closed to the public. Each group looks after a particular period of architecture, evident from its name: The Ancient Monuments Society, St Andrew by the Wardrobe, Queen Victoria Street, EC4 (236 3934); The Society for the Protection of Ancient Buildings, 37 Spital Square, E1 (377 1644); The Georgian Group, 37 Spital Square, E1 (377 1722); The Victorian Society, 1 Priory Gardens, Bedford Park, W4 (994 1019); The Thirties Society, 3 Park Square West, NW1 (286 5143/ 486 3805). The Civic Trust, 17 Carlton House Terrace, SW1 (930 0914) represents almost 1,000 local amenity societies and building preservation trusts, several of them in London.

Museum and art gallery societies The British Museum, Royal Academy, Tate Gallery, Victoria and Albert Museum and others run membership societies. Benefits vary but might include free entry to the museum and to special exhibitions within them which have a separate entrance fee; reduced prices in the museum shop; cut-price catalogues; late night and Sunday morning openings; evening talks and concerts; previews of new shows and galleries; a magazine and a catalogue for mail order shopping. At the same time, membership supports museum work. In addition, there is National Heritage, 9a North Street, SW4 (720 6789) which supports the work of all museums and galleries in Britain; membership perks include previews of new shows. The Furniture History Society, based at the Dept. of Furniture and Interior Design at the V&A (see p. 225), runs an impressive and lively events programme.

London societies As expected, many. Here are two good ones:

London Topographical Society, Membership Secretary Trevor Ford, 59 Gladesmore Road, South Tottenham, N15 (802 0595), devoted to the study and appreciation of London's history and topography and its publication; and The London Society, Room U722, The City University, Northampton Square, EC1 (251 1590), whose interests are broader and who run events, publish a journal and have a lending library. The London Library (see p. 134), open to members and really more like a club, has a very rich collection of London material.

To find out more The annual *Museums & Galleries in Great Britain and Ireland* (published November; about £3 but free to National Heritage members) lists all the vital information for 1,200 places; *Historic Houses, Castles and Gardens* (about £3.25) has details on another 1,300. For more in-depth guides: Malcolm Rogers's *The Blue Guide: Museums and Galleries of London* (1986), sensitive while being exhaustively informative; and GMS Scimone and MF Levey's *London Museums and Collections* (1986), informative and illustrated. Heather Waddell's *London Art and Artists Guide* is particularly strong on contemporary art – galleries, studios, art bookshops and artists' materials.

To learn more Christie's (see p. 140), Sotheby's (see p. 147), the V&A (see p. 225) and other institutions run art courses; the Architectural Association (see p. 166), the Royal Institute of British Architects (see p. 179) and many specialists societies and training colleges run lecture courses; and the Inner London Educational Authority (ILEA) runs an exhaustive programme of short courses on every conceivable subject (details from local borough offices, see p. 11).

ROOTING OUT YOUR ROOTS While thousands of people have arrived in Britain over the centuries, thousands have left for a new and better life. To trace your British ancestors, or to employ others to do so for you, contact the following: The College of Arms, Queen Victoria Street, EC4 (248 2762), see p. 64; The Institute of Heraldic and Genealogical Studies, Northgate, Canterbury, Kent (0227 68664), who work worldwide and produce a fascinating journal, *Family History*; The Society of Genealogists, 14 Charterhouse Buildings, Goswell Road, London EC1 (251 8799), equipped with an excellent library and professional help. Other useful bodies include: The British Records Association, The Charterhouse, Charterhouse Square, EC1 (253 0436); The Business Archives Council, 185 Tower Bridge Road, SE1

(407 6110); The National Register of Archives, Quality Court, Chancery Lane, W2 (242 1918), search room open to the public; and St Catherine's House, 10 Kingsway, WC2 (242 0262) which holds registers of all British births since 1837.

BUSINESSMAN'S LONDON   Much of what the businessman needs to know should be contained above.

At work   For business services, the LTB is expert and experienced in all details of conference arrangements and business meetings. The Institute of Directors, the largest organisation of its kind, is at 116 Pall Mall, SW1 (839 1233). The deluxe hotels have full business facilities and the Central London Yellow Pages telephone directory lists every kind of translation, typing, video, audio visual and computer service imaginable; see also Telephone services, see pp. 6–7. Useful addresses include: Central Translations Ltd, Gucci House, 27 Old Bond Street, W1 (493 5511/499 7370) for fast translations by mother-tongue translators; London International Service, 185 Brecknock Road, N19 (485 7270/671 1971), for language services and study visits; Triangle Translations, 25 Horsell Road, N5 (609 9740) for translations; Your London Office, 10 Upper Berkeley Street, Portman Square, W1 (486 2637/262 7448/262 7927), where members have secretarial, telephone, telex, word processing, mail and message services, together with conference and catering facilities. To improve your own English, avoid the rip-off sharks operating throughout London and contact the Association for Recognised English Language Teaching Establishments in Britain (242 3136) who publish a thick brochure of English language courses recognised by the British Council. For a reliable courier service, door-to-door around the world: DHL's London telephone number is 890 9000, and TNT Skypack's is 561 2345.

At play   Since many hours are inevitably spent being hosted, or hosting your hosts, it is perhaps worth glancing through the introduction to the Food and Drink chapter (see p. 301). Now for a few tips. In London it is not normal to telephone someone at home before 8am or after 11pm unless they specifically say so. If invited to someone's home, it is best to arrive slightly after the given time, say at 8.15pm if invited for 8pm; and a host or hostess is always flattered to receive a bunch of flowers (see p. 333) or box of chocolates (see p. 334). If invited to a gentleman's club, the guest may not pay for anything, should wear a tie and jacket and should not smoke in rooms where food is served. Breakfast meetings tend to be in the deluxe West End hotels, often the Savoy or Waldorf, or at the Institute of Directors, at around 8am; lunch meetings tend to be around 1pm and dinner between 8 and 9pm. If there is a theatre outing, dinner usually follows at around 11pm – so have an early evening sandwich if necessary. To thank hosts, it is easy to telephone a florist to send flowers by Interflora (see p. 333) or telephone Prezzies, 10 Sicilian Avenue, WC1 (831 8098) who will send anything you wish, from a basket of fruits to a hand-made bottle of perfume; payment for both firms by credit card.

To find out more, consult *The Economist Business Traveller's Guide to Britain* (1987).

CHILDREN'S LONDON   The British may not be known for indulging children, but London is packed with children's dream events and places. At a practical level, the big stores have rooms for nursing mothers; many restaurants serve half portions; travel is often less than half price for children. Many of the galleries and museums run weekend and holiday projects; there are three toy museums; and there are children's theatres and cinema clubs. For play supervised by playworkers, contact the Adventure Playground Association, 28 Underwood Road, E1 (377 0314) and the Inner London Pre-school Playgroup Association, 314 Vauxhall Bridge Road, SW1 (828 1401). To find out more, *Time Out* and *City Limits* have sections devoted to children's events. The following books are all good value: Susan Grossman's *Have Kids Will Travel – The Complete Holiday Handbook for Parents* (1987); M Nathenson and D Long's *London Without Tears* (1986); and Christopher Pick's *Children's Guide to London* (1985). See also Telephone services, above, and Entertainments chapter, pp. 292, 297 and 299 below.

Babysitters   Good hotels will provide a babysitter. London has few crêches, so childminding firms are in demand and need to be booked well in advance for weekends. Reliable ones include: Childminders, 67a Marylebone High Street, W1 (935 9763); Babysitters Unlimited, 271–3 King Street, W6 (741 5566); The Nanny Service, Oldbury Place, W1 (935 6976); Solve Your Problem Ltd, 25a Kensington Church Street, W8 (937 0906); Universal Aunts Ltd, 250 King's Road, SW3 (351 5767).

DISABLED PEOPLE   They are very well looked after in London. By telephoning a theatre, museum or other public place before setting off, facilities can usually be arranged. For more help, see above for Artsline in Telephone services and entries under Body and Soul. To find out more, consult the excellent Nicholson Guide, *Access in London* (1984).

FREE AND ALMOST FREE LONDON   It is a myth that London is expensive. It is as expensive or cheap as you make it.

Almost free London   Travel is made cheap by a London travel pass or by renting a bicycle – many Londoners bike. Food is made cheap by avoiding places near the tourist areas (as elsewhere in the world), by avoiding fast food in favour of ethnic (Indian, Chinese, etc.), and by making use of the street food markets such as Berwick Street and enjoying a picnic in a park. The cinema is half-price on Monday; theatre tickets are sold half-price daily; and if you want to snoop on the smart side of life, no one charges for strolling through the Art Deco Promenade of the Dorchester – although their tea is a tempting blow-out.

Free culture abounds   Unlike the rest of the world, the majority of the museums and galleries are free (as are their lectures, gallery talks and films), even if one or two have recently fallen prey to charging entrance fees. As for free entertainment, it would be hard to do the rounds to pick it all up. Here are a few ideas. Changing the Guard at Buckingham Palace and again at Horse Guard's Parade; daily entertainment in Covent Garden; visiting Lloyd's in the City; attending a BBC TV or radio show that is being recorded; lunchtime music in churches and parks; the parks themselves; the great cemeteries (Highgate, Brompton, Kensal); (almost free) Kew Gardens; wandering through Harrods to 'enter a different world' but without buying any of it; debates in the Houses of Parliament; tirades at Speakers' Corner on Sunday; watching a trial at the Old Bailey or a game of cricket at Putney or Kew; early evening music at the Barbican and National Theatre, or later jazz or folk in a pub; a constant stream of annual street traditions and processions and another stream of local festivals with street entertainment and free concerts, theatre and fairs. For more ideas, see M Peplow and D Shipley's *London For Free* (1986).

SUNDAY LONDON   While Londoners lounge in bed with the Sunday newspapers, visitors have the city to themselves for a few hours. This is their chance to hear fine music in the cathedrals, royal chapels and churches, to wander the parks in peace, to hop on a boat to Greenwich, Kew or Hampton Court, to take a picnic to Osterley or Ham House or go to Brick Lane or Petticoat Lane street markets. Hotels are the best places for the traditional roast Sunday lunch; the museums open in the afternoon, usually 2–6pm; and a walk around Hampstead stimulates the appetite for Louis Patisserie and other hilltop tea-rooms. Sunday evening is good for getting into popular films and, where open, fashionable restaurants (Londoners stay in) and good for pub music. West End theatres are closed but fringe, pub and children's theatres are not. To find out more, see J Whitaker's *London on Sunday* (1985).

HOLIDAY LONDON   While thousands of Londoners head for the countryside, the visitor is left with an eerie, empty, silent city. The big holidays are Christmas (extended right through until New Year by more people every year) and Easter. At both, the best indoor entertainment is the music in the churches; at Easter, outdoor entertainment includes carnivals, fêtes, fairs and sport and, if the weather is good, spring daffodils and crocuses in the parks. Bank Holidays are on Jan 1 (New Year's Day), Good Friday, Easter Monday, the first Mon in May (May Holiday), the last Monday in May (Spring Holiday), the last Monday in August (Late Summer Holiday), Dec 25 (Christmas Day), Dec 26 (Boxing Day). For all these, museums and galleries tend to close, so it is wise to telephone first; restaurants and entertainment centres tend to stay open; and there is usually a good choice of outdoor festivities which locals enjoy with gusto, especially in more residential areas. See also the London Year Directory, pp. 352–6.

The practical details

TIPPING

Hairdresser   The tip is usually 50p to the assistant who washes the hair, then 10–15% to the hairdresser.

In hotels and restaurants   It is vital to check carefully exactly what service charge has already been added (see p. 303 on restaurant bills). If in doubt, ask. If no tip is included, the normal amount is 10–15%, depending on the quality of service. Porters would usually expect 50p per suitcase, depending on its size and how far it is carried; cloakroom attendants should be given 20p, as should lavatory attendants.

Taxis   The tip is usually 10%, a little more if the driver has leapt out to help with baggage or waited while you go to a shop; the commissionaire who found you the taxi should receive 50p.

No tips   It is not the custom to tip at garages, in theatres, in cinemas, in concert halls, or in pubs and bars (unless there is waiter service).

LOST AND FOUND   If property is stolen, it is important to report it to the police within 24 hours.

Lost on a train or bus   Try to note the number or route of the vehicle. Then go to London Transport Lost Property Office, 200 Baker Street, NW1 (486 2496), open Mon–Fri 9am–2pm; goods arrive there up to two days after they are handed in.

Lost in a taxi   Contact the nearest police station, or the taxi office at 15 Penton Street, N1.

Lost in an airport   See Arriving, see p. 1.

Lost in a park   Telephone or visit the Park Attendant or Park Police. For Royal Parks, telephone each park's police as follows: Green Park 858 1969; Hampton Court/Bushy Park 977 0277; Hyde Park 434 5212; Kensington Gardens 723 3509; Regents Park 935 1259; Richmond Park/Osterley Park 940 0654. For borough parks, telephone the borough Information Desk, see p. 11 above.

Lost credit card and travellers' cheques   Report to the head office of the bank concerned, see Money (p. 10).

Lost passport   Report to the nearest police station, then to your embassy or consulate (see p. 14).

CLEANING AND MENDING CLOTHES   Dry cleaners outside hotels are substantially cheaper than inside, as are some laundries. Especially good cleaners who also do some mending include:

Celebrity Cleaners, 155a Wardour Street, W1 (437 5324); excellent for fancy work such as beadwork; do not clean silk or do repairs; Jaeger come here for their in-house cleaning.

Lilliman & Cox, 34 Bruton Place, W1 (492 1644/ 629 4555); a top cleaner to entrust with top outfits; collection and delivery service which must be booked by telephone the preceding Friday; basic repair service for zips, hems, pocket inner-linings, buttons, etc, takes a week.

Sketchley; several branches, some with a special Fast Cleaning Service which takes two hours if clothes are delivered before 1pm; some with a basic repair service which is fastest where there is an on-site tailor. Good Sketchleys include 49 Maddox Street, W1 (629 1292), the branch Liberty use for

their in-house cleaning; 99 Tottenham Court Road, W1 (636 3723), with on-site tailor.

COBBLERS   Some shoe shops have a good tame cobbler; most do not. Fifth Avenue Shoe Repairs, 41 Goodge Street, W1 (636 6705), open Mon–Fri 8.30am–6pm, Sat 8.30am–1pm; a proper cobbler in the old tradition. There are heelbars at most British Rail and Underground stations and in many department stores.

LOCKSMITHS   Usually charge a call-out fee and a repair/break-in fee, so can be expensive. Reliable ones include: Market Locks, 251 East India Dock, E14 (515 2121), 24-hour service; North London Locksmiths, 79 Grand Parade, Green Lanes, N4 (800 6041), 24-hour service. Heelbars (see Cobblers) cut keys.

ANOTHER PAIR OF HANDS   Several firms supply help in any form, from housekeeping and cleaning to childminding and ironing – even sewing on buttons. They include Solve Your Problems Ltd, 25a Kensington Church Street, W8 (935 9763); Universal Aunts Ltd, 250 King's Road, SW3 (351 5767).

WORDS OF WARNING   Writing as a Londoner, it would be nice to be able to say all Londoners are honest. They are not. It is madness to keep large amounts of money either with you or in your flat or hotel room; professional thieves are not stupid and choose their victims carefully. For a small fee but peace of mind, it is worth lodging documents and valuables in the safe of the bank where you change your money; and most hotels have a safe. Next, be streetwise, and not just against pickpockets. Although the big tourist attractions are magnets for millions of visitors because they are indeed stunning set pieces and historically fascinating and very beautiful, it is best to spend your money a little way off, where the Londoners do. Prices rise according to what the merchant reckons he can get away with. There are rip-off merchants at all levels – a journalist disguised as a tourist was recently charged £4.25 for an ice-cream bought from a van near Buckingham Palace (normal price 30p), was taken on a 20-minute circular drive by a taxi-driver instead of directly to the address a few hundred yards away, and was asked to pay £161 for a one-course meal for two people washed down with a bottle of sparkling wine (advertised as Champagne). Be warned.

COMPLAINING

Hotels   It is best to inspect your room on arrival, before officially checking in, and to ask for another if necessary. If you are not satisfied with the hotel, speak to or write to the manager.

Restaurants   If the food or service is not to your liking, it is best to speak to the manager, not the waiter.

Shops   The law protects the consumer very well, see p. 321 for details.

Taxis   Again, the consumer is well protected, see Movement, p. 8.

If you have any problems during your stay in London, it is best to write the details down carefully, complain to the management in writing and, if not satisfied, write to the London Tourist Board, see (p. 3).

Checking out of London

THE AIRLINES   It is wise to arm yourself with your return flight number and then check your ticket reservation with either the Central London or the airport desk of your airline. If there is a delay or cancellation, this saves waiting at the airport. Also, before you start travelling it is important to know whether you depart from South Terminal or North Terminal at Gatwick or from Terminal 1, 2, 3 or 4 at Heathrow; this affects where you arrive in the airports. The airlines' local telephone numbers should be printed on the airline ticket; otherwise, they are listed in the telephone directory. The principal ones include:

Code: R = special ticket reservation number

       G = Gatwick airport number; where no number is given, telephone 0293 31299

       H = Heathrow airport number

Aer Lingus, 223 Regent Street, W1 (Ireland and Europe: 734 1212; transatlantic: 437 8000; G:0293 502074; H:745 7017)

Aeroflot Soviet Airlines, 70 Piccadilly, SW1 (493 7436; H:759 2525)

Air Canada, 142 Regent Street, W1 (493 7941; R:795 2636; H:759 2331)

Air France, 158 New Bond Street, W1 (499 9511/8611; 24-hour information: 897 8409; H:759 2311)

Air India, 17 New Bond Street, W1 (491 7979; H:897 6311)

Alitalia, 205 Holland Park Avenue, W11 (745 8200; R:602 7111; H:759 1198); also an office at 27 Piccadilly, W1 (745 8286)

American Airlines, 6th floor, Portland House, Stag Place, Victoria Street, SW1; and 421 Oxford Street W1 (834 5151; G:0293 502078).

British Airways, 75 Regent Street, W1 (897 4000, automatic queueing system; 897 4567 for Concorde and first class passengers; 439 9584 for immunisation and health advice; G:0283 502075; H:759 2525); Concorde, Intercontinental and Paris and Amsterdam flights leave from Terminal 4, the rest from Terminal 1

British Caledonian (part of British Airways), Victoria Station, SW1 (834 9411; R:668 4222; G:0293 518888 for reservations, 0293 25555 for inquiries)

British Midland, 129 Kingsway, WC2 (831 6680; H:745 7321)

Cathay Pacific, 123 Pall Mall, SW1 (930 7878; G:0293 518033)

Dan-Air, 36 New Broad Street, EC2 (638 1747; G:0293 502068; H:759 2525)

Finnair, 14 Clifford Street, W1 (629 4349, R:408 1222; H:745 7534)

Japan Air Lines, 5 Hanover Square, W1 (629 9244; R:408 1000; H:759 9880)

KLM Royal Dutch Airlines, Time & Life Building, New Bond Street, W1 (493 1231; H:568 9144)

Lufthansa, 10 Old Bond Street, W1 (408 0442; H:759 5642); also an office at 28 Piccadilly, W1 (408 0322)

Malaysian Airline System (MAS), 25 St George Street, W1 (499 6286/7769; H:759 2695)

Pakistan International Airlines (PIA), 45 Piccadilly, W1 (741 8066; R:734 5544; H:759 2544)

Pan American World Airways (Pan Am), 193 Piccadilly, W1 (409 0688; 409 3377 for fly-drive; 735 0747 for arrival inquiries; H:759 2595)

Qantas: Qantas House, 395 King Street, W6 (748 3131; H:759 2595)

Scandinavian Airlines Services (SAS), SAS House, 52/3 Conduit Street, W1 (734 6777; G:0293 518033; H:745 7576)

Sabena, Belgian World Airlines, 36 Piccadilly, W1 (437 6960; H:745 7292)

Singapore Airlines, 143 Regent Street, W1 (439 8111; H:759 2525)

Swissair, Swiss Centre, 1 New Coventry Street, W1 (734 6737; R:439 4144; H:745 7191)

Thai Airways International, 41 Albemarle Street, W1 (499 9113; H:759 2331)

Trans World Airlines Inc (TWA), 200 Piccadilly, W1 (636 4090; H:759 5352)

Virgin Atlantic Airways, 7th floor, Sussex Street House, High Street, Crawley (0293 38222; G:0293 502105)

PACKING   If you have bought goods from shops operating the Retail Export Scheme so that you can reclaim the VAT tax, it is important to have all the VAT407 forms to hand and preferably the goods, too (see p. 321). For air travellers, most hotels will be able to weigh your luggage so that you can gauge any overweight problems and prepare for the worst; passengers are only permitted one piece of hand baggage, the rest must be checked in.

SHIPPING THE SHOPPING   If you cannot carry your booty, the following shippers are all well established, reliable and can also ship works of art, or even a vintage car. It is important to check insurance carefully; it is worth making a list of what is to be shipped and then shopping around to compare rates. Allport Freight Ltd, 42 Wigmore Street, W1 (486 6406); Astral Shipping & Packing, Cambrian House, 509/11 Cransbrook Road, Ilford, Essex (518 0327/8); Excess Baggage Company, Block 6, Avonmore Trading Estate, Avonmore Road, W14 (603 7173/4/5/6; 474 4743); The Cargoshop Ltd, 5 Maddox Street, W1 (629 0308); James Bourlet & Sons Ltd, 3 Space Waye, Feltham, Middlesex (751 1155), specialise in fine art; Vic Pearson & Co Ltd, 7 Munton Road, SE17 (703 8351), specialise in fine art.

MONEY   There are no currency restrictions. It is worth having some sterling with you in case of delays at the airport. Overweight charges and duty free shopping can be paid for with credit cards. There is no airport tax to pay.

TO THE AIRPORT   Travelling to the airport by road will take substantially longer during the Mon–Fri evening rush hour, 4–7pm, which is worst on Fri.
London–Gatwick by train   The Gatwick Express trains leave Victoria Station for the non-stop, 30 minute journey every 15 minutes from 5.30am until 11pm, then hourly throughout the night. A combined Underground-Gatwick Express ticket can be bought at any Underground station and saves a final queue.
London–Gatwick by coach   Coaches leave Victoria Coach Station every 30 minutes from 5.40am until 10.40pm. The journey takes roughly 70 minutes.

London–Gatwick by airliner   This minibus service operates 24 hours a day from door to airport. To use it, telephone 759 4741 at least 48 hours before your flight is due to leave. You give details of your flight number; you are given a price quote, a booking number and a pick-up time.
London–Heathrow by underground   Reached on the Piccadilly Line. The first train arrives at Terminal 4 station Mon–Sat at 6.29am, Sun at 7.48am; the last train arrives at Terminal 4 station Mon–Sat 1.03am, Sun at 18 minutes past midnight; trains reach the Terminals 1, 2 & 3 station five minutes later. For frequency of trains and length of journey, see p. 3.
London–Heathrow by airbus   Two bus routes pick up around London and deliver to all four terminals. The A1 bus leaves Victoria daily every 20 minutes from 6.40am until 5pm, then every 30 minutes until 9.15pm. The A2 bus leaves Euston Station daily every 30 minutes from 6.25am until 3pm, then every hour until 9.15pm. Both collect in reverse order from delivery, see Arrivals, above. Depending when you join the bus, the journey takes about an hour.
London–Heathrow by Airliner   The same as for Gatwick.
Gatwick–Heathrow link   Should there be a disaster and you find yourself at the wrong airport, or your flight is cancelled and the replacement on offer leaves from the other airport, there are connections. Services include Jetlink 747 buses every 30 minutes between Gatwick and Heathrow non-stop, with an hour's break around midnight; and Speedlink buses every 20 minutes from 6am, last bus from Gatwick at 10pm, last bus from Heathrow at 11.10pm (tel for both 668 7261).
London–London City Airport by road   see p. 3.
Airport survival tips   If you forgot to send postcards, cards and stamps are on sale but must be posted before going through customs; there are no post boxes beyond. To fill in extra hours of waiting, the rooftop spectators viewing galleries at both airports are open during the day only (small charge, buffet, shop): Gatwick's is on top of South Terminal; Heathrow's is on top of Queen's Building and has a licensed bar, book shop, amusement arcade and playground. Once through passport control, the bars in international departure lounges are usually open continually from 7am until 10.30pm.

Hotels:
A comfortable, convenient bed

To wake in a river suite of the Savoy Hotel and stroll a few paces to a magnificent drawing room bathed in shimmering light reflected off the Thames, there to sit and gaze at the view while sipping coffee delivered by the butler, would make a perfect start to anyone's day. And so handy for Covent Garden, Bloomsbury, the City and the West End, too. The Savoy is the pinnacle of the comfortable and convenient hotel bed. But it remains the stuff of dreams for most people.

More attainable – and equally special – are the increasing number of small hotels in old London houses. Some are simple, some are awash with chintz and puffed-up cushions; most are comparatively inexpensive and family run. Standards are often high, with spotlessly clean, well-serviced rooms. And most have a warm atmosphere and a staff who make time to pass on their London knowledge and tips. You feel you are living in a home, inside a corner of London, rather than observing the city from the outside.

Between these two extremes of grand showiness and intimate friendliness lie the quicksands of London hotel-land: the middle market. For while the deluxe hotels, despite their cheekily high prices, compare well with those in similar-sized capitals around the world, and the house-hotels compare well

with their Continental versions, the middle-market hotel is often deplorable: ferocious prices demanded for characterless, grubby, badly appointed rooms and minimal service. Older ones have redeeming Edwardian grandeur in the hallways; insiders nickname the newer ones 'concrete bed factories'. Exceptions are rare but, happily, on the increase.

So, contrary to the myth, you do not need to win on the horses to afford a clean, well-appointed and well-serviced room in London. But you do need to be steered through the quicksands. Your hotel may be a large part of holiday enjoyment; or it may be an efficient machine that is part of your business life; or it may be merely a bed to sleep in while most waking hours – and most savings – are spent out and about. You may want a sumptuous gourmet hotel restaurant on one visit, to be near the theatres on another; you may prefer a private flat when you come with your family, or a friendly home or a club when you come alone.

For every visitor to London, the right hotel is the key to happiness in the city. To help you find the bed you want, in an environment you like, with the services you need and at a price that does not burn a hole in your pocket, here are some warnings, tips and a few suggestions.

Tips, facts and warnings

FINDING A BED

General information The essential manual is the thick booklet *Where to Stay in London*, published annually (usually November) by the London Tourist Board and on sale at the Victoria Information Centre (see p. 3), at bookshops throughout Britain and by post by sending £1.95 (1988 price) to 26 Grosvenor Gardens, London SW1 (730 3450). A team of Londoners keep their eyes and ears open and inspect the whole range of hotels, guest houses, apartments and bed and breakfast hotels, cramming their expertise into 80 pages of up-to-date addresses, prices and facilities. In 1986, the LTB introduced their own Crown Classification System, a version of the star-rating system, awarding some of their recommendations up to five crowns. But beware; not all establishments in the booklet have been classified yet and some hotel groups (notably Trusthouse Forte, Crest and Rank) have opted out of the scheme.

Specialised information In addition to *Where to Stay in London*, the LTB stock free leaflets on staying with London families, renting apartments and other specialised accommodation. For armchair inspection of 30 Central London hotels brimful of character, consult Wendy Arnold's *The Historic Hotels of London* (1986).

Beware Standards rise and fall at alarming speed. Miserable hotel experiences are often the result of using an out-of-date guide book or a personal recommendation that is several years old. Whatever information you have, it is always best to confirm its accuracy with the hotel at the time of booking.

BOOKING A BED

The London year Surprisingly, there are still not enough hotel beds in London. The season runs March to November, then pauses for Christmas. While it is best to book well in advance, many hotels will have accepted provisional group bookings and will say they are fully booked. However, some group bookings are inevitably cancelled two to three weeks before the date of arrival. So a hotel theoretically fully booked when you asked for a room four months ahead of time may well have space the week before you arrive. It is worth trying.

Deciding what you need The principal reason for most hotel disappointments is that the guest did not work out his or her needs before choosing a hotel. If it is important to you that your window opens or that there is no traffic outside your window; that you have double glazing for peace, or air-conditioning or a view; that you have a direct-dial telephone, a trouser press, a hair-dryer, a particular newspaper delivered daily or a radio you can tune; then the only way to ensure you have it is to ask. But remember, service in London costs money. So if you do not need a telex, an en suite bathroom, 24-hour room service, an in-house swimming pool or air-conditioning, it is best not to waste your money on a hotel providing them and choose something more modest.

Advance booking direct with a hotel Even if your exploratory booking is by telephone, it is essential to confirm it in writing or by telex or Fax, and to arrive with a copy of the confirmation – over-booking happens in London, too. It is also important to confirm the following with your booking:

The arrival and departure dates, with flight details if possible; rooms are usually let noon-to-noon, so if your flight arrives early in the morning you may need to book for the previous day to ensure your room is ready – depending on their generosity, the hotel management may charge you for the whole extra day.

The room price and what is included – VAT at 15% and service charge at 10–12% usually are, continental or full English breakfast may be. (See also A Bargain Bed, below.)

The method of payment you wish to use to settle the bill – credit card, travellers' cheques, cash, etc. Smaller hotels may not take the full range of credit cards.

The type of accommodation you need, such as twin beds or a double bed, bathroom with bath or shower, an extra bed for a child, etc.

The terms of your stay, such as room only, room with all meals, etc.

Any special request you made, such as a high floor with a view.

Any special room facilities you need, such as a writing table, a reading lamp or a cot.

Any special hotel facilities you need, such as secretarial, conference, fast laundry service, bouquets of flowers, room service meals, a Fax service (increasingly available) etc.

Any disabilities, which might make climbing stairs difficult, for example; or any special needs, such as a special diet.

Deposits and cancellation fees To confirm an advance booking, many hotels ask for a deposit, the amount to depend upon the length of stay and the size of the party. At the end of your stay, this is deducted from the bill. However, if you have to cancel the reservation shortly before arrival, or fail to arrive, or leave earlier than your agreed booking-out date, you may be breaking a legally binding contract. Your deposit may be forfeited and there may well be an additional cancellation fee should the hotel be unable to re-let your room. So it is best to advise the hotel as soon as possible of any change of dates.

Advance booking through an agency   For a fast service, a good travel agency (see p. 6) will find a room but a fee is usually payable; hotel groups have central reservation offices (see below); and EXPOTEL offers a free and efficient booking service (see Bargain Bed, below). Skola Homes, 27 Delancy Street, NW1 (380 0636) will find an economical bed in a guest house, hostel or with a family. The LTB runs an Accommodation Booking Service: send details in writing six weeks in advance of your arrival to the LTB, 26 Grosvenor Gardens, SW1; they will make a provisional booking on your behalf but you must then confirm it direct to the hotel together with a deposit of the first night's payment and also send a copy of the confirmation to the LTB.

Booking on arrival   There are LTB information desks at Heathrow (see p. 2) and at the Tourist Information Centre at Victoria Station (see p. 3); at both, the current booking fee is £3, there is a communication charge, and the provisional reservation is made with the restriction that you must confirm it by checking into the hotel by a certain agreed time. At London City Airport there is a hotel booking desk.

Making your own booking on arrival   It is quite likely that you can go into a pleasant-looking hotel and find there is a room free, whatever time of the year (see The London year, above). But if you arrive late or with little luggage and without a prior reservation, you may be asked to pay in advance, so be sure to inspect your room first.

CHECKING INTO THE BED

Checking in   Before signing in, it is always worth inspecting the room selected for you. If something is not right, now is the moment to change it, not after you have unpacked and cannot be bothered and are then dissatisfied for the rest of your stay.

Hotel porters   Worth making friends with. In a good hotel, the head porter is a reliable source of information. If you need to hire a car, to book a restaurant, to buy theatre tickets or to do some complicated shopping, he is your man. He knows London well and can obtain the unobtainable for London shows and events (with a mark-up, naturally); but he should advise you when not to pay the outrageous prices demanded for fashionable events. In addition, top porters are part of an international network and have been known to secure a room in a fully booked Paris hotel, to have birthday flowers delivered to a beloved in Texas and to find country cottages to rent for a week's holiday.

In a family-run hotel, the family are the source of local knowledge and tips and usually very generous with their time.

Services   Lamentably bad in most London hotels compared to their equals in New York, Tokyo, Singapore and New Delhi. The excuse is the price of labour. Indeed, where services exist, they are expensive. So it is best to check the prices in the hotel services brochure in your room before ordering. The small house-hotels often give charming personal service at no extra cost; and at the other end of the scale, the Savoy Group and Dorchester still maintain old standards with maids and butlers in attendance on every floor.

Keeping clean and tidy   Given that most hotels work a system of noon-to-noon room-letting, it is remarkable that almost all demand that laundry be sent before 9am if it is to be returned the following day. Thus, a one-night stay precludes having any laundry done – notable exceptions are the Tower Hotel and Intercontinental (with in-house laundry). In addition, costs are high. As for ironing (pressing), a daytime or overnight service is equally rare outside the deluxe hotels; and the old tradition of putting shoes outside the door to have them cleaned overnight has disappeared in all but the smartest. So it is best to come prepared to do any instant washing, and to pack a travelling iron and shoe-cleaning equipment. Unless you ask, linen and towels are not changed daily outside deluxe hotels.

DIY room service   With the cost of labour, many middle-market hotels have installed kettles and a basket of sachets so that guests can make their own drinks. To take economy further, one food writer claims eggs cook wonderfully in kettles, but you should be careful not to let them burst by popping them in after the water boils.

Alcohol   Where a room has a mini-bar, it should be fully stocked and locked when you arrive. The porter will unlock it (and may give you a separate key for it) and ensure the price list is on show – the mark-up is usually high.

Telephone   There are hotel mark-ups. Before ringing all your friends in London and back home, it is worth checking on the hotel rates and any surcharges for assistance. Trusthouse Forte hotels have an exemplary multi-lingual printed card explaining their system. See also p. 6 on British Telecom.

Complaining   A complex network of laws protects the guest, insisting upon clear price information, good fire precautions, adherence to the Trades Description Acts of 1968 and 1972, and much more. If something goes wrong, however small, it is important to complain at the time of the incident, when all may be settled amicably. If not, and you feel it was serious, make a written complaint to the manager as soon as possible. If still dissatisfied and the hotel is part of a group, write to the head office. If all else fails, write to the London Tourist Board, 26 Grosvenor Gardens, SW1, who do not have legal powers but will do what they can on your behalf; or write to your travel agent.

CHECKING OUT OF THE BED

Transport   If you have an early start, it is best to order a taxi the previous day or to check carefully that the Underground or bus service you need will have started.

Packing   After the inevitable London shopping sprees, your baggage will be heavier than when you arrived. The hotel porter will weigh it so that you can reorganise the heavy items into hand luggage or prepare to pay extra airline charges.

Wake-up calls   Most hotels will give a wake-up call. But so many have gone wrong that it is best to set your own alarm – planes do not wait for passengers.

Settling the bill   It is usually possible to settle the previous night if you are leaving early in the morning. When checking the bill, it is important to note any extra service charges. It is usual after a long stay to give an extra tip to a regular room maid or waiter and to anyone else who has been especially helpful.

A BARGAIN BED   London hotel prices are high, but you can often lower them. Despite claims that there are too few beds in London, reduced rates abound, particularly around the slack periods of Christmas and Easter. When making an advance booking, or when checking in, it is always worth asking for a discount – it can be up to 35%, even

more. You will be amazed how often you are successful. Here are a few ideas:

Package deals   Trusthouse Forte, Thistle Hotels and other chains produce annual brochures offering a huge range of mid-week and weekend packages that may include theatre tickets, a London Travelcard, free places for children, no supplement on single rooms, free breakfast, etc. For addresses, see Hotel Groups, below.

Deluxe dreams come true   Even the grandest hotels now offer weekend deals, when their weekday high-flyers are gone. The Savoy Group, the Dorchester and the Ritz have packaged up magical weekends that may include two nights for the price of one, with champagne breakfast thrown in free; and their midweek prices often drop at Christmas and New Year, the time when their buildings are beautifully decorated and elaborate dinner-dances at bargain prices are staged in grand rooms.

Business hotels   Both mid-market and thoroughly up-market ones suffer at weekends, so it is well worth asking for a reduction; the usual deal is Friday to Sunday nights for the price of two, sometimes including breakfast (which is usually good at business hotels).

Refurbished hotels   Almost manic activity fills many London hotels now, as rooms are updated, newly fitted and given pretty wallpapers. Sometimes this follows years of neglect; sometimes it is because the local borough forbids a new hotel to be built so this is the only route to change. Once re-opened, the hotel seduces clients back with reduced rates; so you can stay in a sparkling new room (and cope with its teething problems) at a sparkling low rate.

Airline deals   Major airlines such as British Airways, Pan Am and TWA (see p. 22) often have liaisons with Central London hotel groups, including deluxe ones. Not only can you book your room in advance through the airline but you may get up to 20% off the regular rate. The airline will have a list of associated hotels.

EXPOTEL   More than 200 hotels in Britain, many of them in London, have clubbed together to offer a free booking service and reduction of 12–15%, all bookable by telephone (568 8765).

Accommodation options

HOTEL GROUPS: CENTRALISED BOOKING, GOOD DEALS   The benefit of booking with a group is that you can make several bookings in one operation – near the airport, in Central London, around the countryside, around the world. Groups often have brochures offering package deals and extra hotel events at holiday periods. While some British groups have recently undergone major upheavals to improve their looks and services, others remain disappointing. In the middle and upper market, the Thistle Hotels and Trusthouse Forte are at the top of the ladder, with Edwardian Hotels and Sarova Hotels rising. In addition, several up-market international groups have an impressive London member – Hyatt, Intercontinental, Meridien, Four Seasons, Taj – but the Holiday Inns and Hiltons here have to struggle to match their sisters in the US.

From modest to grandest, here are some of the current best. As Fax facilities are increasing, it is worth making an initial request by telex for a Fax number.

Bonnington Hotels, Southampton Row, London WC1 (tel 242 2882; telex 261591); three modest, good value Bloomsbury hotels: the Bonnington, Cora and Wansbeck.

Best Western Hotels, Vine House, 143 London Road, Kingston upon Thames, Surrey (tel 541 0033; telex 881 4912); good value, middle-market; hotels include the London Tara, winner of the 1986 Best Value for Money worldwide poll taken by *Executive Travel Magazine* and EXPOTEL.

Crest Hotels, 20–6 Cursitor Street, London EC4 (tel 430 0991; telex 83377); middle market; hotels include the Regent Crest, Bloomsbury Crest and Marlborough Crest. Airport hotel: Gatwick Crest Hotel.

Edwardian Hotels, 66–8 Cromwell Road, London SW7 (tel 581 5151; telex 919867); completely refurbished, middle market; hotels include the Grafton, Kenilworth, Mountbatten, Savoy Court, Stratford Court and Vanderbilt.

Four Seasons Hotels, Hamilton Place, Park Lane, London W1 (tel 499 0888; telex 22771/267349; fax no.: 01 493 1895 GP2/GP3); the Canadian group has the most deluxe businessman's hotel in town, Inn on the Park.

Hilton Hotels, 6 Bedford Avenue, London WC1 (tel 631 1767; telex 21373); identikit deluxe hotels worldwide; London ones include London Hilton on Park Lane and Kensington Hilton. Airport hotel: Gatwick Hilton International.

Holiday Inns International Reservation Centre, 10–12 New College Parade, Finchley Road, London NW3 (tel 722 7755; telex: 27574); just about uphold their promise to produce the same high quality conditions worldwide; hotels in Chelsea, Marble Arch, Mayfair and Swiss Cottage.

Hyatt Hotels, 2 Cadogan Place, London SW1 (tel 235 5411; telex 21944); deluxe style, quality and efficiency in their one London hotel, the Hyatt Carlton Tower.

Intercontinental Hotels, Dorland House, 14–16 Regent Street, London SW1 (tel 930 5981; telex 265834); their deluxe London hotels are Hotel Intercontinental, Mayfair Intercontinental, Britannia Intercontinental and Portman Intercontinental.

Ladbroke Hotels, PO Box 137, Watford, Hertfordshire (tel 0923 46464; telex 897618); middle market; hotels include Ladbroke Charles Dickens, Ladbroke Clive, Ladbroke on Park Lane (Curzon), Ladbroke Hotel, Ladbroke International, Ladbroke Leinster Towers, Ladbroke Park Plaza, Ladbroke Royal Kensington, Ladbroke Sherlock Holmes and Ladbroke Westmoreland.

Leading Hotels of the World, 15 New Bridge Street, London EC4 (tel 0800 181123; telex 265497; Fax no. 353 1904); the London members of this consortium of international deluxe hotels are the Savoy, Berkeley, Claridge's, Connaught, Hyde Park and Inn on the Park.

Marriott Hotels, Grosvenor Square, London W1 (tel 493 0281); the up-market international group's smart London hotel is the London Marriott.

Meridien Hotels, Piccadilly, London W1 (tel 734 8000; telex 25795); the French group have brought high deluxe style to their one London hotel, Le Meridien Piccadilly.

Mount Charlotte Hotels Ltd, 2 The Calls, Leeds (tel 0532 439111; telex 557934); quality middle market; hotels include Hospitality Inn Bayswater, Kennedy, Kingsley, London Ryan, Mount Royal, Park Court, Royal Scot and White's.

Norfolk Capital Hotels Ltd, 8 Cromwell Place, London SW7 (tel 581 0601; telex 23241); quality middle market; hotels include Royal Court and the refurbished Norfolk.

Prestige Hotels, 1–15 King Street, London W6 (tel 741 9164); a consortium of about 40 high quality, mostly British hotels whose London members include Dukes, Inn on the Park, The Ritz and The Stafford.

Rank Hotels, 4 Harrington Gardens, London SW7 (tel 373 8191; telex 915888); quality upper-middle market; hotels include the Athenaeum, The Gloucester, Royal Garden, Royal Lancaster and The White House.

Sarova Hotels, 11 Thurloe Place, London SW7 (tel 589 6000; telex 917575); middle-market Kenyan group, recently much improved; hotels include the Green Park, Londoner, Pastoria, Mostyn, Rembrandt, Regency Hotel, Rubens and Washington.

Savoy Group of Hotels, central booking through Leading Hotels of the World (see above); deluxe down to the last detail; the hotels are The Savoy, The Berkeley, The Connaught and Claridge's; the group also owns Simpson's-in-the-Strand restaurant.

Sty-al Hoteliers, 125 London Street, London W2 (tel 723 3386; telex 266059); two good value, modest hotels, the Royal Norfolk and the Warwick House.

Sheraton Hotels, central booking through Sheraton Reservations System (tel 0800 353535; telex 261534); the deluxe hotel group has one member in London, the Sheraton Park Tower. Airport hotels: Sheraton Heathrow and Sheraton Skyline.

Taj Hotel Group, central booking through Utell, Banda House, Cambridge Grove, London W6 (tel 741 1588; telex 27817); the Indian group has brought exotic style to the deluxe St James's Court Hotel.

Thistle Hotels Ltd, 5 Victoria Road, London W8 (tel 937 8033; telex 24616); exceptionally friendly staff working in prettily refurbished middle market hotels with good service; hotels include the Cadogan, Kensington Palace, Lowndes, Royal Horseguards, Royal Trafalgar, Royal Westminster, Selfridge and The Tower Hotel.

Trusthouse Forte Hotels, St Martin's House, 20 Queensmere, Slough, Berkshire (tel 0753 73266; telex 847836); after a blitz of refurbishment and internal improvement, the set of London hotels in their international chain ranges from economical Regent Palace up to deluxe Hyde Park Hotel, a member of Leading Hotels of the World; others include Brown's, Cavendish, Cumberland, Grosvenor House, Hyde Park Hotel, Kensington Close, Regent Palace, Russell, St George's, Strand Palace, Waldorf and Westbury; the group also owns the Café Royal restaurant. Airport hotels: Ariel, Excelsior, Post House and Skyway, all at Heathrow; Post House at Gatwick.

Vienna Group of Hotels, 16 Leinster Square, London W2 (tel 286 5294; telex 24923); two small, good value, modest hotels, The London House Hotel and the West Two Hotel.

A CONVENIENT BED: THE AREAS   As Central London is huge, the right place is as important as the right bed. A bed the wrong side of the centre means losing hours sitting in taxis in the traffic queues, waiting for buses or negotiating several different lines to make an Underground journey. So, while searching for a suitable hotel, it is worth perusing the street map and the Underground map to ensure it is in the best place for your needs. Some areas are better equipped with hotels than others; and hotels of one type tend to cluster together. To help you find a convenient bed, here is an area by area breakdown.

The City and the Docklands (see maps on pp. 60 and 244–5)   You are supposed to work, not sleep, here. Almost no hotels, although some will be built in the regenerating Docklands. Currently, The Tower (Thistle) is the only quality one, with New Barbican as a reserve – and a good Youth Hostel for pre-City students. Otherwise, businessmen should head for the other end of Fleet Street (a ten-minute walk from the City) to the Howard, Savoy, Strand Palace or Waldorf; or go further west to St James's and Mayfair (see below), the hot spots for classy hotels and business entertaining.

Westminster (see map on p. 76)   To be on hand to spot the royals, the prime minister, the pomp and the pageantry, nearby hotels range from the deluxe St James's Court and an excellent middle-market group (Goring, Royal Horseguards Hotel, Royal Trafalgar, Royal Westminster and Rubens) to the modest Pastoria off Trafalgar Square.

The River Thames (see map on pp. 94–5)   There are splendid river views from river-facing rooms on the fourth to ninth floors of the middle-market Royal Horseguards Hotel, on any floor of the smart Howard Hotel and, for a blow-out, from the River Suites of the Savoy (sometimes bookable as weekend deals, see Bargain Bed, above).

Strand, Covent Garden, Holborn (see map on p. 116)   Along the Strand, the linkline between the City and Westminster, the Strand Palace and Waldorf are more realistic propositions than the Savoy for most people; in Covent Garden, the grand Mountbatten on the west side contrasts with the charming and tiny Fielding house-hotel opposite the Opera House.

St James's, Mayfair and southern Marylebone (see map on p. 135)   Stuffed with up-market and deluxe hotels for shoppers, holiday-makers, honeymooners and businessmen, with some traditional clubs who open their doors to visitors. In St James's, find the pampering Dukes, Stafford, Ritz, Cavendish and the more modest Royal Overseas League. On the north side of Piccadilly, in Mayfair, find the Holiday Inn, Brown's, Chesterfield,

Claridge's, Dorchester, Grosvenor House, Le Meridien, London Marriott, Westbury and Park Lane, the more economical Flemings and Green Park hotels, the University Women's Club, and a businessmen's trio at Hyde Park Corner: the deluxe Hotel Intercontinental and Inn on the Park and the less deluxe Hilton. In south Marylebone, the middle market Cumberland, Londoner, Selfridge and Ramada (formerly Berners) and the upmarket Portman Intercontinental and Churchill are well placed for serious Oxford Street and Mayfair shopping; and Bentinck House, Kenwood House and Redlands are small house-hotels.

Soho and Bloomsbury (see map on p. 156) In Soho, the delightful and simple house-hotels Manzi's and Hazlitt's, but not much else. In Bloomsbury, the wide choice of good value accommodation includes some middle-market, exuberant Edwardian hotels, such as the Hotel Russell, Kenilworth, Kingsley and Waverley, and plenty of modest hotels and bed and breakfasts rambling through the terraces of the Bloomsbury squares – Academy, Bedford Corner, Bloomsbury Park, Bonnington, Crescent, Langland, St Athan's and Wansbeck; the central YMCA and YWCA are here, too.

The Nash sweep (see map on p. 174) To be right beside Regent's Park for morning jogging, choose between the large White House on the east side and the small, cosseting Dorset Square Hotel on the west side. To be right by Portland Place, the modest Hallam Hotel or the middle-market St George's. To be by Piccadilly Circus, the Regent Palace.

Kensington, Holland Park and Bayswater (see map on p. 188) To have Kensington Gardens on your doorstep and the South Kensington museums within walking distance, the middle-market Kensington Palace is best of the options, with good park views from the Royal Garden Hotel. The middle-market London Tara and Kensington Close are huge and well equipped; the smart Halcyon in Holland Park and the Portobello are charming house-hotels and Holland Park has the best positioned Youth Hostel in London: an old mansion surrounded by gardens. In Bayswater, the south-facing rooms of Central Park Hotel, Royal Lancaster and White's all overlook Kensington Gardens; the Royal Park Hotel is in three Victorian houses tucked behind them the Victoria Garden is nearby.

Knightsbridge and South Kensington (see map on p. 211) A good area for small, charming house-

hotels. To overlook Hyde Park, choose between Edwardian grandeur at the Hyde Park Hotel, deluxe style at the Berkeley and the north side of the circular Sheraton Park Tower; the middle market has the excellent Basil Street; the house-hotels include the small and designer-decorated Capital and L'Hotel and the simpler Beaufort, Claverley, The Knightsbridge and the Knightsbridge Green Hotel. In South Kensington, Blakes is whacky and chic, the London International, Norfolk and Rembrandt are big and good quality; but the nicest hotels here are the many small house-hotels which range from the smart Number Sixteen and Cranley Place to the simpler Alexander, Aster, Brompton, Garden House, Gore, Prince, Swiss House Hotel and Sydney Place Hotel.

Chelsea, Belgravia and Pimlico (see map on p. 228) For deluxe and stylish, the Hyatt Carlton Tower hovering between Chelsea, Belgravia and Knightsbridge, or the Berkeley overlooking Hyde Park; for up-market, the Belgravia Sheraton; for middle-market, the Cadogan, Lowndes and Royal Court; for good value, the Wilbraham. This is also a good area for small and house-hotels: in Chelsea, the chic Fenja and No. 11 Cadogan Gardens and the simpler Blair House, Eden House, Flaxman House and nearby Annandale and Willett hotels in Sloane Gardens; in Belgravia, the smart Ebury Court and the simpler Chesham House, Chester House and Diplomat; in Pimlico, the award-winning Elizabeth and Oxford House.

THE RANGE: FROM DUCK-DOWN TO DORMITORY, THE VITAL STATISTICS

Dream deluxe hotels Only a few of the great old London hotels provide a time-capsule dream; however smart the new hotels are, none manages to leave the realm of reality. The old hotel buildings are magnificent; the service sublime. You need to pinch yourself occasionally to know it is real. If you cannot afford to stay in them, reach for the sky with a package deal (see Bargain Bed, above) or at least daydream of doing so over a stylish cocktail or tea.

Claridge's (Savoy), Brook Street W1 (tel 629 8860; telex 21872); best bathrooms in London, and corner suites so big a grand piano lurks in a corner.

The Connaught (Savoy), Carlos Place, W1 (tel 499 7070; telex 296376); the epitome of discretion: the world famous who mean it when they say 'I want to be alone' stay here.

The Dorchester, Park Lane, W1 (tel 629 8888; telex 887704); the pea-green Oliver Messel Suite is less inviting than the other sumptuous suites and rooms.

The Ritz, Piccadilly, W1 (tel 493 8181; telex 267200); smaller than it looks, with white and gold rooms and the great ground floor promenade to the most beautiful dining room in town.

The Savoy (Savoy), The Strand, WC2 (tel 836 4343; telex 24234); splendid river suites and Art Deco rooms, each one different; also has apartments.

Deluxe hotels The newly built deluxe hotels are slick and stylish in every detail: the refurbished ones in Victorian and Edwardian buildings have a softer character. All provide most services – at a price – and have in-house extras such as florists, newsagents, hairdressers, health clubs, fashionable restaurants, good bars and full business facilities. Some are a complete bubble world – the Berkeley, Churchill, Hotel Intercontinental, Hyatt Carlton Tower, Inn on the Park – and are so well equipped that you need never step outside to explore London. 1987 basic single-room rates started well over £100 – and rose high. (Hotel group in brackets after hotel name.)

Belgravia Sheraton, 20 Chesham Place, SW1 (tel 235 6040; telex 919020)

The Berkeley, Wilton Place, SW1 (tel 235 6000; telex 919252); corner suites have enormous roof-top patios for party-givers.

Blakes, 33 Roland Gardens, SW7 (tel 370 6701; telex 8813500)

Brown's (THF), Albemarle Street, W1 (tel 493 6020; telex 28686)

Capital Hotel, 22–4 Basil Street, SW1 (tel 589 5171; telex 919042)

The Churchill, Portman Square, W1 (tel 486 5800; telex 264831)

Dukes, 35 St James's Place, SW1 (491 4840; telex 28283)

The Holiday Inn, Mayfair, W1 (tel 493 8282; telex 24561; fax 6292827)

Hotel Intercontinental London (Inter-Continental), 1 Hamilton Place, Hyde Park Corner, W1 (tel 409 3131; telex 25853)

Hyatt Carlton Tower, 2 Cadogan Place, SW1 (tel 235 5411; telex 21944)

Hyde Park Hotel (THF), Knightsbridge, SW1 (tel 235 2000; telex 262057)

Inn on the Park (Four Seasons), Hamilton Place, Park Lane, W1 (tel 499 0888; telex 22771)

Le Meridien (Meridien), Piccadilly, W1 (tel 734 8000; telex 25795)

London Hilton on Park Lane, 22 Park Lane, W1 (tel 493 8000; telex 24873), the higher the room, the better the view.

London Marriott (Marriott) Grosvenor Square, W1 (tel 493 1232; telex 268101)

Mountbatten (Edwardian), Seven Dials, Covent Garden, WC2 (tel 836 4300; telex 298087)

The Park Lane, Piccadilly, W1 (tel 499 6321; telex 21533)

The Portman Intercontinental (Inter-Continental), 22 Portman Square, W1 (tel 486 5844; telex 261526)

St James's Court (Taj), 41–54 Buckingham Gate, SW1 (tel 834 6655; telex 938075), also apartments.

Sheraton Park Tower, 101 Knightsbridge, SW1 (tel 235 8050; telex 917222)

Stafford, 16 St James's Place, SW1 (tel 493 0111; telex 28602)

The Westbury (THF), New Bond Street, W1 (tel 629 7755; telex 24378)

Middle-market hotels At all levels, the best are usually the refurbished old buildings, but there are a few new ones with character; most have friendly staff and good business facilities but lack the more indulgent services. 1987 basic single-room rates were between £40 and £100.

Basil Street Hotel, 8 Basil Street, SW3 (tel 581 3311; telex 28379)

Bedford Corner, Bayley Street, WC1 (tel 580 7766; telex 296464)

Bloomsbury Park, 126 Southampton Row, WC1 (tel 430 0434; telex 25757)

Bonnington, 92 Southampton Row, WC1 (tel 242 2828; telex 261591)

The Cavendish (THF), Jermyn Street, SW1 (tel 930 2111; telex 263187)

Cadogan (Thistle), Sloane Street, SW1 (tel 235 7141; telex 267893)

Central Park Hotel, 49 Queensborough Terrace, W2 (tel 229 2424; telex 27342)

The Chesterfield, 35 Charles Street, W1 (tel 491 2622; telex 269394)

The Cumberland (THF), Marble Arch, W1 (tel 262 1234; telex 22215)

Flemings, 7–12 Half Moon Street, W1 (tel 499 2964; telex 27510)

Goring, 15 Beeston Place, Grosvenor Gardens, SW1 (tel 834 8211; telex 919166)

Green Park (Sarova), Half Moon Street, W1 (tel 629 7522; telex 28856)

Hotel Russell (THF), Russell Square, WC2 (tel 837 6470; telex 24615)

Howard Hotel, Temple Place, WC2 (tel 836 3555; telex 268047)

New Barbican Hotel, Central Street, EC1 (tel 251 1565; telex 25181)

Kenilworth (Edwardian), Great Russell Street, WC1 (tel 637 3477; telex 25842)

Kensington Close (THF), Wrights Lane, W8 (tel 937 8170; telex 23914)

Kensington Palace (Thistle), De Vere Gardens, W8 (tel 937 8121; telex 262422)

Kingsley (Mount Charlotte), Bloomsbury Way, WC1 (tel 242 5881; telex 21157)

Ladbroke at Park Lane, formerly the Curzon (Ladbroke), Stanhope Row, Park Lane, W1 (tel 493 7222; telex 24665)

Londoner (Sarova), Welbeck Street, W1 (tel 935 4442; telex 894630)

London International, Cromwell Road, SW5 (tel 370 4200; telex 27260)

London Tara, Scarsdale Place, W8 (tel 937 7211; telex 918834)

Lowndes (Thistle), Lowndes Street, SW1 (tel 235 6020; telex 919065)

Norfolk (Norfolk), 2–10 Harrington Road, SW7 (tel 589 8191; telex 268852)

Pastoria, St Martin's Street, Leicester Square, WC2 (tel 930 8641; telex 25538)

Ramada, formerly New Berners, Normandie House, Berners Street, W1 (tel 636 1629; telex 25759)

Rembrandt (Sarova), Thurloe Place, SW7 (tel 589 8100; telex 295828)

Royal Court (Norfolk), Sloane Square, SW1 (tel 730 9191; telex 296818)

Royal Garden (Rank), Kensington High Street, W8 (tel 937 8000; telex 263151), best views from high floors

Royal Horseguards (Thistle), Whitehall Court, SW1 (tel 839 3400; telex 917096)

Royal Lancaster (Rank), Lancaster Terrace, W2 (tel 262 6737; telex 24822)

Royal Park Hotel, 2–5 Westbourne Terrace, W2 (tel 402 6187/8); also two apartments.

Royal Trafalgar (Thistle), Whitcomb Street, WC2 (tel 930 4477; telex 298564)

Royal Westminster (Thistle), Buckingham Palace Road, SW1 (tel 834 1821; telex 916821)

Rubens Hotel (Sarova), 39–41 Buckingham Palace Road, SW1 (tel 834 6600; telex 916577)

St George's (THF), Langham Place, W1 (tel 580 0111; telex 27274)

The Selfridge (Thistle), Orchard Street, W1 (tel 408 2080; telex 22361)

The Strand Palace (THF), Strand, WC2 (tel 836 8080; telex 24208)

The Tower Thistle (Thistle), St Katharine's Way, E1 (tel 481 2575; telex 885934)

Victoria Garden, 100 Westbourne Terrace, W2 (tel 262 1161; telex 892676)

The Waldorf (THF), Aldwych, WC2 (tel 836 2400; telex 24574)

Waverley House, 130–4 Southampton Row, WC1 (tel 833 3691; telex 296270)

The White House (Rank), Regent's Park, NW1 (tel 387 1200; telex 24111)

White's Hotel (Mount Charlotte), Lancaster Gate, W2 (tel 262 2711; telex 24711)

The Wilbraham, 1 Wilbraham Place, Sloane Street, SW1 (tel 730 8296)

House-hotels This is where the charm of staying in a London house, the caring personal service and usually reasonable prices combine to make a perfect base for a London visit. Most are family-run; rooms range from simple to over-chintzed; some rooms do not have bathrooms en suite; full breakfast is often included in the price but other meals tend not to be served; businessmen who need telex, Fax and other services should check carefully what is available. The 1987 basic single-room rate is given since it varies from the economical £16 to the pricy £150 for the one of the new cluster of fashionable, designer-decorated house-hotels. And, as size varies considerably, the number of rooms is given.

Academy, 19–21 Gower Street, WC1 (tel 631 4115; telex 24364), 23 rooms, from £23

Alexander, 9 Sumner Place, SW7 (tel 581 1591; telex 917133), 51 rooms, from £50

Annandale House, 39 Sloane Gardens, SW1 (tel 730 5051), 12 rooms, from £20

Aster House, 3 Sumner Place, SW7 (tel 581 5888; telex 8950511), 13 rooms, from £38

The Beaufort, 33 Beaufort Gardens, SW3 (tel 584 5252; telex 8951210), 29 rooms, from £75

Bentinck House, 20 Bentinck Street, W1 (tel 935 9141; telex 25247), 118 rooms, from £22.20

Blair House, 34 Draycott Place, SW3 (tel 581 2323/4/5), 17 rooms, from £27

Brompton, 30 Old Brompton Road, SW7 (tel 584 4517), 17 rooms, from £25

Chesham House, 64–6 Ebury Street, SW1 (tel 730 8513; telex 912881), 22 rooms, from £20

Chester House, 134 Ebury Street, SW1 (tel 730 3632; telex 915869), 12 rooms, from £16

The Claverley on Beaufort Gardens, 13–14 Beaufort Gardens, SW3 (tel 589 8541/4740), 36 rooms, from £35

Cranley Place, 1 Cranley Place, SW7 (tel 589 7944/7704), 14 delightful rooms, from £30

Crescent, 49–50 Cartwright Gardens, WC1 (tel 387 1515), 29 rooms, from £17

The Diplomat, 2 Chesham Street, Belgrave Square, SW1 (tel 235 1544; telex 263250), 27 rooms, from £35

Dorset Square, 39/40 Dorset Square, NW1 (tel 723 7874; telex 263964), 29 beautiful rooms, from £52

Ebury Court, 26 Ebury Street, SW1 (tel 730 8147), 39 rooms, from £37

Eden House, 111 Old Church Street, SW3 (tel 352 3403), 14 rooms, from £35

11 Cadogan Gardens, SW3 (tel 730 3426; telex 8813318), 58 pretty rooms, from £64

The Elizabeth, 37 Eccleston Square, SW1 (tel 828 6812), 25 rooms, from £22

The Fenja, 69 Cadogan Gardens, SW3 (tel 589 7333; telex 934272), 14 pretty rooms, from £60

The Fielding, 4 Broad Court, Bow Street, WC2 (tel 836 8305), 26 rooms, from £32

Flaxman House, 104–5 Oakley Street, SW3 (tel 352 7284/3610), 20 rooms, from £16

Garden House, 44–6 Egerton Gardens, SW3 (tel 584 2990), 30 rooms, from £21

Gore, 189 Queen's Gate, SW7 (tel 584 6601; telex 296244), 54 rooms, from £54

Hallam, 12 Hallam Street, Portland Place, W1 (tel 580 1166), 23 rooms, from £28

Halcyon, 18 Holland Park, W8 (tel 727 7288; telex 226721), 44 swish rooms, from £150

Hazlitt's, 6 Frith Street, Soho Square, W1 (tel 439 1524), 24 rooms, from £28

L'Hotel, 28 Basil Street, SW1 (tel 589 6286; telex 919042), 12 beautiful rooms, from £90, this is the baby sister to the deluxe Capital Hotel

Kenwood House, 114 Gloucester Place, W1 (tel 935 3473/9455), 16 rooms, from £18

The Knightsbridge, 10 Beaufort Gardens, SW3 (tel 589 9271), 20 rooms, from £24

Knightsbridge Green, 159 Knightsbridge, SW1 (tel 584 6274), 23 rooms, from £46

Langland, 29–31 Gower Street, WC1 (tel 636 5801; telex 28151), 28 rooms, from £16

Manzi's, 1 & 2 Leicester Street, Leicester Square, WC2 (tel 734 0224/5/6, 16 rooms, from £22

Number Sixteen, 16 Sumner Place, SW7 (tel 589 5232; telex 266638), 33 well-furnished and pretty rooms, from £40

Oxford House, 92–4 Cambridge Street, SW1 (tel 834 6467/9681); 17 rooms from £16.

Portobello, 22 Stanley Gardens, W11 (tel 727 2777; telex 21879); 25 rooms, from £46

Prince, 6 Sumner Place, SW7 (tel 589 6488), 20 rooms, from £24

Redland House, 52 Kendal Street, W2 (tel 723 7118/2344), 25 rooms, from £20

St Athan's, 20 Tavistock Place, Russell Square, WC1 (tel 837 9140/9627), 31 rooms, from £18

Swiss House, 171 Old Brompton Road, SW5 (tel 373 2769/9383), 16 rooms, from £22

Sydney Place, 6 Sydney Place, SW7 (tel 584 5637), 13 rooms, from £18

Wansbeck, 4–6 Bedford Place, WC1 (tel 636 6232; telex 261591), 33 rooms, from £20.50

Willett, 32 Sloane Gardens, SW1 (tel 824 8415), 17 rooms, from £23

Clubs Several of the St James's clubs have bedrooms, open to members of that club and of clubs with a reciprocal membership. And their emancipation has led to membership for men and women. So, if you are a member of a club in your own country, it is well worth finding out what the reciprocal memberships are with London clubs since these rooms are very central and good value. Other newer London clubs, such as the University Women's Club, open their doors more freely. Here is a selection:

The American Club, 95 Piccadilly, W1 (tel 499 2303), three double rooms; open to men and women with USA citizenship, or close US connections are needed.

The Caledonian Club, 9 Halkin Street, SW1 (tel 235 5162), 31 rooms; membership open to those with Scottish parents or grandparents and to those who have served in a Scottish regiment and to those with close Scottish connections.

East India Club, 16 St James's Square, SW1 (tel 930 1000; telex 938041), 48 rooms; with its full title East India, Devonshire, Sports and Public Schools Club Ltd, membership is open to most people, but ladies can only become associates.

Royal Overseas League, Over-Seas House, Park Place, St James's Street, SW1 (tel 408 0214; telex 268995), 72 rooms, many refurbished; membership open to all British and Commonwealth citizens, wherever they live.

St James's Club, 7 Park Place, SW1 (tel 629 7688; telex 298519), 44 suites and studios; founded by Peter de Savary in 1981 and quality-equipped with everything from business facilities to arrangements for helicopter hire; membership is open to all men and women.

The Sloane Club, 52 Lower Sloane Street, SW1 (tel 730 9131; telex 264010), 112 rooms; founded as a ladies' club in 1922, now revamped and luxuriously refurbished and open to all, men and women.

The United Oxford and Cambridge University Club, 71 Pall Mall, SW1 (tel 930 5151), 39 rooms; membership open to men and women (although women become lady associates only) who graduated from either of the two universities.

The University Women's Club, 2 Audley Square, South Audley Street, W1 (tel 499 6478/2268), 24 bedrooms; founded in 1886, membership open to all women graduates and similarly qualified women – men can become dining members only.

Hostels If you are prepared to share a room, the best, well-located, bargain London beds are in hostels. Some have rooms for married couples; some have sports and restaurant facilities. It is wise to book well in advance for the summer months; you may need to give references, to be over 18 years old, to take out membership or to pay a small deposit when booking.

International Students House, 229 Great Portland Street, W1 (tel 631 3223); rooms for singles and married couples, plus 11 family flats.

London Hostels Association, 54 Eccleston Square, SW1 (tel 828 3263 for reservations, 828 1545 for administration); the central reservations address for a dozen hostels, some single sex and some mixed.

Youth Hotels Association, Trevelyan House, St Albans, Hertfordshire (tel 0727 55215); their five hostels in London, all well sited, are at: 38 Bolton Gardens, SW5 (tel 373 3083), 111 beds; Carter Lane, EC4 (tel 236 2965), 282 beds; King George VI Memorial Hostel, Holland House, Holland Walk, W8 (937 0748); 84 Highgate West Hill, N6 (tel 340 1831), 62 beds; 4 Wellgarth Road, NW11 (tel 458 9054), 220 beds.

YMCA Central Club, 112 Great Russell Street, WC1 (tel 637 1334; telex 22683); one-month minimum stay but so popular (excellent location and superb facilities) that booking four months ahead is essential even in winter; rooms for singles and married couples aged 16–40.

YWCA Central Club, 16–22 Great Russell Street, WC1 (tel 636 7512); rooms for singles and married couples.

Apartments For a longer stay, especially for a family, renting an apartment or house is considerably better value than a hotel and gives greater freedom. The price range is enormous, depending not only upon decor and address but on the level of personal service available; there is usually a deposit to pay and a minimum length of stay, with rates reducing for long-term lets. The houses and flats may be furnished to be let permanently or be a family home let while the family is abroad. Furnished service flats are similar to hotel accommodation but are self-contained and have catering facilities. As with booking into a hotel (see above), it is essential to check all terms and conditions carefully; an agency will help with this.

Information: The LTB provides a useful leaflet, *Apartments and Self-catering Accommodation in London*.

Agencies: The following have a good reputation for their sensitivity and skill at finding quality apartments in up-market areas. Chestertons Residential, 40 Connaught Street, W1 (tel 262 5060); Douglas & Gordon, 5 Ellis Street, Sloane Street, SW1 (tel 730 0666; telex 929520); Fleet Estates, 1001 Park West, Kendal Street, W2 (tel 723 8488; telex 946240); and Hampton & Son, 6 Arlington Street, SW1 (tel 493 8222). Flatland, 69 Buckingham Palace Road, SW1 (tel 828 9302) cater to a wider range of pockets. Blandings, The Old Vicarage, France Lynch, Stroud, Gloucs (tel 0453 882544; telex 43214) let anything from a London town house to a Lake District cottage or a Scottish castle. For a full list, contact the Association of Residential Letting Agents, 18–21 Jermyn Street, SW1 (tel 734 0655).

Apartments: The following is a tiny selection, at all prices.

Ashburn Garden Apartments, 3–4 Ashburn Gardens, SW7 (tel 370 2663; telex 946240); Mr Aresti's one- and two-bedroom apartments are serviced by a friendly and helpful staff.

Aston's Budget Studios, 39 Rosary Gardens, SW7 (tel 352 2221); Shelagh King runs good value, pretty rooms, sought after by up-market students on art courses, so book early.

Chelsea Cloisters, Sloane Avenue, SW3 (tel 584 1002; telex 937067); smart apartments with business facilities, let for a minimum of three months to companies registered in the UK.

Clifton Lodge, 45 Egerton Gardens, SW3 (tel 584 0099; telex 936238; toll free no. 1-800-642-2747); Martin Langdon's sumptuously decorated service apartments attract diplomats and high-flyers.

Carlos Place, 1 Carlos Place, W1 (tel 491 4165); nine elegant, top-class apartments, the penthouse with private patio.

Dolphin Square Trust Ltd, Dolphin Square, SW1 (tel 834 9134 for reservations, 834 3800 for guests); Mrs King runs the most impressive block of flats in London (see p. 241) – 138 good value apartments equipped with everything from swimming pool and squash courts to a shopping arcade.

Draycott House, 10 Draycott Avenue, SW3 (tel 584 4659; telex 916266); top-class, well furnished serviced apartments with one to three bedrooms, many with two bathrooms, one with a roof garden; business facilities, cooks and valets.

47 Park Street, W1 (tel 491 7282); David Mlinaric designed most of the interiors of the sumptuous apartments which are run like a house-hotel and where guests can order up the Roux brothers' creations from La Gavroche restaurant below.

Lees Place, 10 Lees Place, W1 (491 7055); Laura Ashley style luxury in Mayfair. If full, the management liaise with a block of equally formal informality around the corner, Mayfair Apartments, 9 Charles Street, W1 (tel 493 7874).

Middleton Court, 13–15 Sloane Gardens, SW3 (tel 730 5055); Mrs Wise runs 12 good value apartments just by Sloane Square.

Ryder Street Chambers, 3 Ryder Street, Duke Street, SW1 (tel 930 2241); Valerie May runs seven one-bedroom apartments, handy for art shoppers.

St James's Court, Buckingham Gate, SW1 (tel 834 6655; telex 938075); 92 apartments and 18 suites in the up-market, refurbished hotel.

Staying with a London family To plunge right into London life, stay with a London family. Prices are cheap, the minimum stay is usually three nights, breakfast is usually included – and you may make lifelong friends. When booking, it is just as important to check what you need, what you expect from the family (to be included in their lives or not), and what the conditions are (see Booking a Bed, above). The various agencies include the reliable London Homes, PO Box 730, SW6 (tel 748 4947; telex 896559), run by Thea and Jean Druce for 10 years, more than 70 homes in and around London; and The Welcome Stranger, 11 Lower Common South, SW15 (tel 788 7047), Mrs Roger Worboys co-ordinates more than 40 homes in Britain, of which nine are in Putney, Fulham and Chiswick.

Hotels outside central London For country house comfort or fresher air, with nearby public transport to Central London, here is a handful of special hotels.

North London: Frognal Lodge, 14 Frognal Gardens, off Church Row, London NW3 (tel 435 8238; telex 8812714), 17 rooms in a Hampstead house; Grims Dyke Hotel, Old Redding, Harrow Weald, Middlesex (tel 954 4227; telex 946240), ex-home of WS Gilbert set in 20 acres of splendid gardens, 48 rooms; Hendon Hall Hotel, Ashley Lane, Hendon, London NW4 (tel 203 3341; telex 8956088), modernised Georgian mansion with 22 rooms; La Gaffe, 107–11 Heath Street, London NW3 (tel 435 4941), three rooms in a Hampstead house; Sandringham Hotel, 3 Holford Road, London NW3 (tel 435 1569), a house with a walled garden, in Hampstead village and near Hampstead Heath; Heath Swiss Cottage Hotel, 4 Adamson Road, London NW3 (tel 722 2281; telex 297232), 15 rooms in a Victorian home beautifully furnished with the owner's pictures and antique furniture.

West London: 52 Mount Park Road, Ealing, London W5 (tel 997 2243), guest house with two charming double rooms. Runnymede, Windsor Road, Egham, Surrey (tel 0784 36171; telex 934900), a modern hotel set in 10 acres of gardens and overlooking the Thames, 124 rooms; Shepperton Moat House, Felix Lane, Shepperton, Surrey (tel 0932 241404; telex 928170), modern hotel set in an 11-acre garden beside the Thames, 190 rooms.

South-west London: The Wilderness, 19 Inner Park Road, Wimbledon Common, London SW19 (tel 788 3146); guest house with three double rooms and large private sitting and dining rooms.

Airport hotels Probably most useful on your way out of London. If your flight is very early in the morning, you can struggle out of bed five minutes before check-in time; if your flight is delayed, the airline may offer to put you in a local hotel; most airport hotels run a courtesy coach to and from the airport. At other times, the transport from Central London hotels to both Heathrow and Gatwick is easy and fast at most hours (see p. 23).

At Heathrow:

Hotel Ibis, 112–14 Bath Road, Hayes, Middlesex (tel 759 4888; telex 929014); the best of the airport economy hotels, simple rooms and good restaurants.

Post House (Trusthouse Forte), Sipson Road, West Drayton, Middlesex (tel 759 2323; telex 934280); middle-market, very near the airport.

Sheraton Heathrow, Bath Road, West Drayton, Middlesex (tel 759 2424; telex 934331); up-market, efficient Sheraton style.

Sheraton Skyline, Bath Road, Hayes, Middlesex (tel 759 2535; telex 934254); up-market Sheraton style with tropical garden, swimming pool and cabaret.

At Gatwick:

Gatwick Hilton International, Gatwick Airport, Gatwick, West Sussex (tel 0293 518080; telex 877021); its advantage is the covered walkway linking it to the airport terminals, so you feel you are already in the departure lounge.

Gatwick Crest Hotel, Langley Drive, Tushmore Roundabout, Crawley, West Sussex (tel 0293 29991; telex 877311); quieter and cheaper than the Hilton.

Instant London:
Follow my leader

If London is too vast or huge to contemplete tackling alone, there is an army of guides to lead you by the hand. They offer coach tours, walking tours, general tours, in-depth tours, light-hearted tours, academic tours and thematic tours. You can rent a guide to explore churches, find your grandmother's grave or just go shopping. Here are some of the best, together with some tips of how to get the best out of the avalanche of information.

Tours

The first view of London, whether you arrive from Scotland or San Francisco, is of an overwhelming and vast muddle. London is at last before your feet, waiting to be explored; but there is no clear centre, no obvious place to begin. Evolved from two competing cities, London and Westminster, and their encircling villages, centuries of growth have gobbled it all into a single sprawling mass with no apparent order. So, more than in any other city, a day-one guided spin round the tourist highlights (well visited because they really are wonderful) helps make at least a little sense of the London map. Even for the most world-weary traveller, it pays dividends. After the overview, orientation and solo exploring is much easier. Or, for more extensive guided help, there are tours of every sort, from good value coach trips to pricey tailor-made individual tours in

chauffeur-driven cars, from in-depth specialist walks to the gloriously extravagant airship ride over the capital. Here are a few suggestions, with recommendations for some tried and tested companies with good reputations. **Be warned** Guiding is big business in London. Of the hundreds of companies producing glossy tour brochures, many use untrained guides and charge deceptively cut-price or greedily exorbitant prices. To avoid a disaster, check your guide is qualified. Intensive learning precedes the tough driver-guide examination set by the London Tourist Board (LTB). Those who pass are well prepared for solid guiding in London and on day tours out from the city; many go on to do a Blue Badge training. A Blue Badge guide has the top training and is suitable for those who want very detailed knowledge. To become one, there is a tough, six-month training and examination, again run by the LTB. Once trained, all Blue Badge guides wear their blue badge while working, and most join the Guild of Guide Lecturers (established in 1950), which issues an annual List of Registered Guides, their special interests, their permits to places usually closed, their knowledge of Britain outside London and which additional languages they speak. For more information, contact The Guild of Guide Lecturers, 2 Bridge Street, SW1 (839 7438). But to book a Blue Badge guide direct, contact Tour Guides Ltd, 2 Bridge Street, London SW1 (839 2498).

TIPS FOR TOUR-TAKERS

Choosing a tour For a coach tour, it is worth comparing rivals to find the nearest to your ideal route at the best price. Hotels and information centres have racks of brochures. Prices vary for almost identical popular trips in and out of London, so toothcomb the brochures and check if meals, entrance fees, etc. are included and whether there is enough time at a favourite spot or too much at another. A full day's immersion, possibly taking two half-day tours back to back, is the best use of time and money.

Tailor-made tours The advantages can outweigh the extra cost. The client chooses a route and timing exactly right for his tastes and London schedule, mixing museums with parks and even shopping; and the guide provides a door-to-door service; but it is up to the client to pump his personal guide's knowledge to get full value.

Walking tours Usually led by well informed enthusiasts, who dig behind the facades of familiar streets and attract loyal London supporters learning about another corner of their city. They last about two hours, are cheap and, most importantly, do not need booking, so an on-the-spot decision can be made according to mood and weather. Even so, take an umbrella.

Tour booking This is a dilemma. With the cold British winters, some tours only run in summer; and with the unpredictable British summers, many tours are best enjoyed on a sunny day. However, some good tours and specialist tours fill up and need to be booked in advance. To make a booking, contact the tour operator, your hotel Head Porter or a travel agent. Cancellation charges vary in time limit and price.

Guiding Some coach tours use a tape instead of a live guide: the advantage is usually a choice of languages; the disadvantage is an overkill on facts and no jolly anecdotes or up-to-date information to fill in traffic jam hold-ups. If the guide is to be English-speaking, it is worth checking that the mother tongue is English (even with a Blue Badge guide) – London is complicated enough without having to adjust to an unfamiliar foreign accent. As with any other country, avoid the tourist shops which coach-trip guides might suggest; the museum shops en route are best for quality and price. And a good guide deserves a good tip.

Complaints If the tour or guide was not as promised, complain to the company and, if still unsatisfied, to the LTB.

PANORAMA TOURS

London Transport Sightseeing Tour LT information centres (see p. 7) (24-hour telephone 222 1234) and LTB centres (see pp. 3–4). Four departure points for tours in English: Victoria Street (opposite Victoria Underground Station), the south-west side of Marble Arch (by Speakers' Corner on Park Lane), Piccadilly Circus (on the east side of Haymarket) and Baker Street Station (on Marylebone Road); tours leave regularly 10am–5pm, with extended summer hours. Tours in French and German leave from Baker Street only, check times. All Blue Badge guides. 1986 prices £5 for adults, £3 for children. The best of the quickies and at a bargain price, using Blue Badge guides and with no need to buy in advance (although prices reduce for those who do). Just hop onto one of LT's 50 restored classic, double-decker red buses (now out of regular use) for a good value, superbly guided, 90-minute spin that takes in Westminster, St Paul's and the Tower. Even competitors 'really recommend' this one.

Other coach panoramas Evan Evans' London Highlights and Thames Cruise tour; Frames Rickards' A Look at London tour and Panoramic London with Thames River Cruise tour; all run every morning and afternoon. Harrods London Panorama leaves at 9.15am and then regular intervals throughout the day. For all, booking is essential (see below).

Airships Industries UK Ltd Skycruise reservations Office, c/o Brevis Marketing Services Ltd, Hille House, 132 St Albans Road, Watford, Hertfordshire (0923 54606). Flights from Radlett Aerodrome, reached by train from St Pancras Station to St Albans and then by taxi or train to Radlett (about 30 minutes). Season May–October (peak season June–September), Mon–Fri with weekend flights in high season; five or six flights a day. 1987 prices £125 per person rising to £150 in high season. This is luxury. A dozen big spenders sway up through the air currents to 1,000 feet for a 75-minute, exhilarating airship ride over London, equipped with an aerial map and helped by the co-pilot to spot the dome of St Paul's, the green belts of parks and the silver, snaking Thames, fingertips almost touching the NatWest Tower, peeking behind walls into Buckingham Palace gardens and onto the unlikely confusion of Harrods' rooftop. Pure magic on a clear day.

C B Helicopters Westland Heliport, Lombard Road, SW11 (228 3232). Season Apr–Sept; several flights on every alternate Thurs; essential to book but if the weather is bad the date can be re-arranged or money refunded; 1987 prices £40 per person for 15-minute trip; maximum of four passengers per trip. More intimate than the airship, and noisier – but cheaper. The 15-minute dash takes passengers along the Thames from Battersea to the Tower and back, with commentary from the pilot. Of course, helicopters can also be hired for special trips on any day.

COMPANIES OFFERING A VARIETY PACK OF TOURS Choice reduces in winter, with fewer tours in London and some outside cancelled (e.g. Blenheim closes).

(Windsor note: the State Apartments of Windsor Castle are closed when the Queen is in residence, including June and July; St George's Chapel closes to prepare for large ceremonials; but plenty remains to be seen, see p. 275.)

Evan Evans 27 Cockspur Street, Trafalgar Square, SW1 (24-hour telephone 930 2377, telex 8950152) and 136 Wigmore Street, SW1. Six pick-up points and collection from 17 hotels; seven tours also guided in French, German, Italian and Spanish; Blue Guides throughout. Founded in 1930, a solid and experienced company with a wide range of tours under four headings: half-, full-day and evening London tours (London Highlights and Thames Cruise; City of London, Crown Jewels and Tower; Great London Nights Out, etc); half-day tours out of town (Greenwich, Windsor, etc); full-day tours out of town (from Windsor and Bath to Ascot races and Brighton, etc, all good); and two-eight day tours outside London (Scotland, Wales, Ireland and Europe, etc). Booking essential.

Frames Rickards 11 Herbrand Street, WC1 (sightseeing telephone 837 3111, telex 25493; national tours 637 4171, telex 916052). Five pick-up points (their own underground coach station is gloomy); six tours in French, German and Spanish; Blue Guides throughout. Well run company with good tours under six headings: morning tours (Panoramic London and Thames Cruise; London West End, etc); afternoon tours (Chartwell, Greenwich, Windsor, London City, etc); evening tours (Elizabethan banquet, Thames cruise, etc); whole day tours (Blenheim Palace, Cambridge, Stratford, Windsor, etc); mini-tours of three–four days; extended tours of six–seven days. The morning West End and afternoon City make a good full-day bash at London. Booking essential.

Harrods Luxury Tours Knightsbridge, SW1 (telephone 581 3603, tleex 24319). Pick-up point at Door

nine of Harrods, near the Hans Road/Brompton Road corner. All with guides except the London Panorama which has the less satisfactory headset system with taped commentary in eight languages (English, French, German, Italian, Japanese, Portuguese, Spanish, Swedish). With Harrods style, the coaches are custom built, with air-conditioning, extra large (and clean) windows and reclining seats; multi-lingual stewards serve drinks and biscuits and there are lavatories on board. Five tours: half-day Panorama, full-day London, Stratford and Blenheim (Warwick in winter), Windsor and Hampton Court, and Bath and Stonehenge (summer only). Full-day London is the only full-day tour with a double decker, thus better views; and the lunch is quality. Booking essential.

London Tour Company 162/8 Regent Street, W1 (telephone 734 3502/3, telex 912881). Five pick-up points; Blue Badge guides throughout. Solid London introductory tours (Mon, Thurs and Sat) and sunset tour; Thames cruises include Sunday lunch, Richmond to Hampton Court, and dinner; plus evening walks (Soho, Haunted London, etc) and trips out of town. Booking essential.

London Transport Guided Sightseeing LT information centres (see p. 7) (24-hour information 222 1234 and LTB information centres (see pp. 3–4). Courtesy motorcoaches cover three routes and 22 stops to collect passengers and deliver them to Wilton Road Coach Station, Victoria, SW1, where tours begin. Seven tours in Spanish; other languages for groups by arrangement; Blue Badge guides throughout. Another set of reliable, well-run tours with caring guides, these ones under three headings: London tours (London Day, Westminster and Changing of the Guard, Sunday London, A Night on the Town, etc); River and coach trips (London Views and Lunch Cruise, Greenwich and the Thames Barrier, Windsor, etc); and country tours (Windsor, Hampton Court, Stratford, Oxford, Winchester, etc). Their London Day is a good introduction. Booking essential; unsold tickets on sale at Wilton Road Coach Station.

TAILOR-MADE TOURING

Take-a-Guide 11 Uxbridge Street, W8 (24-hour telephone 221 5475, telex 918744). In the US: 63 E 79th Street, New York, NY100021 (telephone 212 628 4823, toll-free 800 223 6450, telex 620115). Frederick Pearson founded the company in 1960 and runs his own thorough course for his guides who all take the LTB driver-guide and often the Blue Badge examinations. Top quality service from well-trained guides, tailor-made trips of any length in and out of London, from in-depth sightseeing to chic shopping; choice of car, door-to-door service and the advantage of a New York office.

Tour Guides Ltd 2 Bridge Street, SW1 (24-hour telephone 839 2498, telex 946240). The booking bureau for the Guild of Guide Lecturers (Blue Badge guides, see p. 37) and the Driver Guide Association, whose driver-guides are all Blue Badge. Tiptop standards for almost any demand, be it a literary walk, a picturesque drive or visit inside a special interior; worth taking advantage of deep knowledge. Book in advance for special demands; straightforward guiding often available almost immediately.

British Tours Ltd 6 South Molton Street, W1 (telephone 629 5267, telex 27702). Founded in 1958 to offer personal guiding on wheels, their much-praised driver-guides (with the LTB qualification) tailor a variety of London tour outlines to clients' wishes and whims (the big sights, an introduction, shopping, children, etc), adding a good range of out of town trips.

Go-by-Guide 60 Clapham Common Northside, SW4 (350 2408). Barbara Weston produces a brochure with well-designed full- and half-day London suggestions, plus trips out, but her driver-guides (with the LTB qualification) 'will take people anywhere they wish', too.

Grosvenor Guide Service 30 Harwood Road, SW6 (736 9779). Judy Hoade and Katie Lucas, both extremely knowledgeable about London and Britain, show their clients the big sights with added extras not usually on public offer – a visit to the Houses of Parliament includes lunch in the Strangers' Dining Room and to the Old Bailey is guided by a barrister and includes lunch in an Inn of Court (these take time to prepare, so book early). Valued for their relaxed but informed friendliness and their practical as well as cultural help.

TOURS OF DISCOVERY FOR THE MORE CURIOUS Just a few of many, ranging from lightweight fun to seriously academic, but always run with vitality by committed enthusiasts.

Citisights of London 102a Albion Road, N16 (24-hour telephone 241 1323). Send for winter and summer programmes. No booking needed; most leave from the Museum of London at 2.30pm. Kevin Flude and his bright team of historians and archaeologists lead exemplary walks that reveal London's growth and the latest views and discoveries that contribute to its complex and exciting history. Their dozen walks, bursting with good information and vitality, range from historical themes (Roman, Medieval, Victorian) to London stars (Shakespeare, Pepys) and areas (South Kensington, City, Soho). Top quality; not a dull second. To take all of them consecutively over a season would be an ideal London introduction; and part of the ticket price goes to the London Archaeological Trust.

Cockney Walks Cockney Museum, 32 Anworth Close, Woodford Green, Essex (504 9159). No booking needed. Keen historians and off-duty teachers bring alive the Jewish East End, Cockney Whitechapel and the East End spirit in the hidden alleys.

Discovering London 11 Pennyfields, Warley, Brentwood, Essex (0277 213704). Send for the summer or winter programme, enclosing an s.a.e. No booking needed. Alex and Peggy Cobham have an astounding knowledge and a loyal London following. Their walks begin at an Underground station, roam around Sherlock Holmes's London, Historic Westminster, the Charm of Chelsea and much more. Inside tours include Kensington Palace, the National Portrait Gallery, the British Museum and Westminster Abbey; special tours by arrangement. The really keen can buy five walk tickets for the price of four.

Docklands Tours Museum of Docklands Project, Unit 39 and 41, Cannon Workshops, West India Dock, E14 (515 2612). Three tours a month, booking well ahead essential. Knowledgeable museum workers explain the sights from a coach that leaves the Museum of London to inspect the new and old of the Docklands, going south of the river, then back and through Wapping, Limehouse, round the Isle of Dogs and into the Royal Docks to the Visitors' Centre (refreshments) where the Museum of Docklands have their workshops and some of their treasures informally on show. Then, back to the museum.

Historic Docklands No fixed address (telephone 515 3000 x 3510, telex 894041 LDDCG). Coach pick-up points Embankment and Tower Hill Underground stations; booking advisable. The London Docklands Development Corporation's tour shows off their rebuilding of the docklands while pointing out the remaining walls, warehouses and administrative buildings of the great port, with cakes on a barge or a pint in an East End pub to finish.

London Arts Discovery Tours 4 Elia Street, N1 (278 0646). Groups only, no single bookings.

Howard Lichterman and Richard Barran have created the obvious London thematic holiday lasting several days, the theatre. With a skilful mixture of private events in historic houses, tours behind the scenes, meetings with directors, actors and critics, and tickets for the best shows in town, this is a theatre fan's dream trip.

London Walks 10 Greenbrook Avenue, Hadley Wood, Barnet, Herts (4118906). No booking needed. Send for the winter or summer programme, enclosing an s.a.e. within Britain, a $2 money order if overseas. Rain or shine, Mr and Mrs McCannah run a heavy programme of walks (up to four a day) that take in Dickens's London, Hampstead, the City, Thameside, Bloomsbury, pubs, Sherlock Holmes, Jack the Ripper and more, their popularity meriting their bargain walkabout tickets.

Streets of London 32 Grovelands Road, N13 (822 3414). No booking needed. Send for autumn/winter and spring/summer programmes. Michael Lermer and his guides, many with academic backgrounds, lead a dozen well-balanced, far from intense walks, from Political London and Aristocratic London to Sherlock Holmes and pubs. They have a stock of extra themes for private tours and will 'devise a completely new tour around any part of London and on any subject'. 50% come back for a second trot.

Thameside Venturers 6 Church Manor Way, Abbey Wood, SE2 (317 7722, after 6pm). Fred Sage, who has worked as a stevedore and seaman, reveals the less obvious Thames history (where George Oglethorpe sailed to found Savannah in Georgia, where Admiral Philip set sail for Australia) on his walks, and will happily seek out the haunts of somebody's docklands ancestors.

Tragical History Tours Ltd Sunnymead, 1 Bromley Lane, Chislehurst, Kent (467 3318). Send for brochures. Booking essential, except for the Murder trip. Michael Jones runs five popular coach tours; a half-day Bus Trip to Murder (with a hit list including Jack the Ripper and Sweeney Todd; London on Sunday; Lost London (from caves to Bob Hope's birthplace and Charlie Chaplin's home); Literary London (ending at Keats's house); and the day-long Ghost Bus to Chislehurst caves, Penshurst Place and England's most haunted village.

MEMBERSHIP WALKS The several conservation, architecture and arts societies run walks in and around London. The guides are excellent, the price cheap (sometimes more for non-members, but it goes to the cause), and the walks often include entry into otherwise closed buildings. To contact each society directly, see pp. 17–18; otherwise, peruse the choice listed in the London and national newspapers (especially on Fridays and Saturdays) and the weekly *Time Out* and *City Limits*.

WET DAY TOURS Walking is miserable in the rain; and coach windows fug up while traffic grinds to a halt. But there are alternatives. In addition to Discovering London's inside tours, there are tours to take around houses, theatres, institutions and museums. See Rain Rain Rain chapter, p. 277).

LEADERLESS TOURS

Culture Bus 60 St James's Street, SW1 (629 4999). No booking needed; buy tickets on board. Yellow and white buses drive an elaborate figure of eight round Central London, stopping 20 times for passengers to hop on or off. The outer limits of the route are the Albert Memorial, the Tate Gallery, the Tower and Madame Tussaud's. The idea is to visit high spots in your own time; then, clutching a Culture Bus ticket, jump on the yellow bus to the next cluster of goodies or, perhaps, stay on board for two or three stops until something takes your fancy. Thus, freedom coupled with convenience. Tickets are valid for one day, and if bought after 1pm, for the next day too; there are also three-day rover tickets.

LEADERLESS WALKS There are many printed thematic walks round London. The advantage is that you can do a little at your own pace, have a break, then return for more another day. Here are four tried and tested good ones:

The London Wall Walk published by the Museum of London (1985). A walk around the original line of the City Wall, from the Tower to the Museum of London, seeking out chunks of Roman and later wall and the explanatory blue panels at each of the 21 sites.

Londinium: A Descriptive Map and Guide to Roman London published by Ordnance Survey (1981). Despite the quantities of archaeological finds in the City's recent and current upheavals, this remains a good introduction to London's beginning. Roman London is plotted in pink over a modern map (where the Thames is so narrow now) together with 20 viewpoints of things to see (starting at Newgate) and more pink blobs of sites excavated that make you want to rush to the Museum of London or British Museum to see them on show.

The London Silver Jubilee Walkway published by Richard Stone (revised edition, 1979). Created to celebrate the Queen's Silver Jubilee in 1977 and aiming to provide a pot pourri of Central London's history, the 10-mile walk is divided into seven sections, each self-contained, the whole route usefully guided with markers set into the pavement. To do it all, the start is Leicester Square, then through Westminster and over Lambeth Bridge, along the south bank right to Tower Bridge, then back through the City, Fleet Street, Holborn and Covent Garden.

London Walks by Anton Powell, published by Robson Books (1985). Of all the books of walks. this stands out for Mr Powell's sheer enjoyment of the city. Opinionated, well observed and full of amusing anecdotes, his four walks round Adelphi and Covent Garden, the Inns of Court, St James's and Chelsea (each with a map) have such sparkle that Mr Powell seems one of the party.

Royalty and pageantry:
Who's who and where to find the shows

The British monarchy stars in one of the best shows in London and certainly the longest-running one. It began when Edward the Confessor, king of England 1042–66, made London his capital. Displays of royal pageantry have marked coronations, marriages, deaths and battle triumphs. During Queen Victoria's reign, regular royal parading was stepped up to keep her subjects happy – Londoners blew £250,000 on street decorations for her Diamond Jubilee pageant in 1897 and were delirious with 'Jubilee fever' for the whole year.

Today, the star of the royal shows boasts an astounding pedigree: the Queen can trace her blood-descent back through 62 monarchs to Egbert of Wessex who in AD829 became the first king of the English. Since the death of Llywelyn the Last in 1282, Wales and England have shared the same monarchy; and Scotland was added when James VI of Scotland became James I of England in 1603. The Queen and her family provide a continuous calendar of ceremony, formal display and glittering glamour. It may be the grand spectacle of the annual State Opening of Parliament or the high society Ascot races; the nightly Ceremony of the Keys at the Tower or a royal gala film screening in aid of charity. Or it may be the modest but impressive Changing the Guard ceremony at Buckingham Palace. The show is non-stop, the events are surprisingly accessible and most of them are free.

Meanwhile, in the City of London, the merchants maintain much of the pageantry which evolved when they were effectively the rulers of the wealthy Port of London. After Henry FitzAilwin became the first Mayor of London in 1192, the merchants' increasingly ostentatious spectacles and rituals reinforced their financial power both locally and over the sovereign upstream at Westminster: the monarch's sword is still humbly lowered when entering the City of London; the gates of the Tower of London, the monarch's fortress, are slammed shut and locked each night against the unruly London mob. Inside the City of London walls the Lord Mayor, the City livery companies (the guilds founded to train and protect craftsmen), and the city churches continue to stage an impressive, often quirky, calendar of pageantry that sometimes rivals the royal one. It ranges from the splendid day-long Mayor's Parade and the cart-marking ceremony at Guildhall to the Vintners' Company road-sweeping parade and church ceremonies such as the Blessing of the Throats or the Bubble Sermon.

Parallel to the royal and City merchants' parading, there is a string of annual ceremonies throughout Central London, mixing folklore, history, tradition and pageantry. Some celebrate London's heroes and villains – Charles I, Samuel Pepys, Guy Fawkes Night, Remembrance Sunday, Tyburn Walk. Others focus on London's communities –

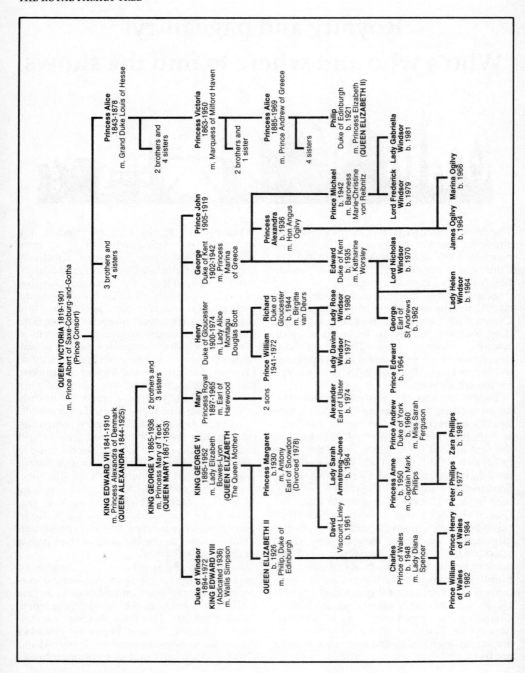

QUEEN VICTORIA 1819-1901
m. Prince Albert of Saxe-Coburg-and-Gotha
(Prince Consort)

Princess Alice
1843-1878
m. Grand Duke Louis of Hesse

2 brothers and
4 sisters

Princess Victoria
1863-1950
m. Marquess of Milford Haven

2 brothers and
1 sister

Princess Alice
1885-1969
m. Prince Andrew of Greece

4 sisters

Philip
Duke of Edinburgh
b. 1921
m. Princess Elizabeth
(**QUEEN ELIZABETH II**)

3 brothers and
4 sisters

KING EDWARD VII 1841-1910
m. Princess Alexandra of Denmark
(**QUEEN ALEXANDRA** 1844-1925)

2 brothers and
3 sisters

KING GEORGE V 1865-1936
m. Princess Mary of Teck
(**QUEEN MARY** 1867-1953)

Duke of Windsor
1894-1972
KING EDWARD VIII
(Abdicated 1936)
m. Wallis Simpson

KING GEORGE VI
1895-1952
m. Lady Elizabeth
Bowes-Lyon
(**QUEEN ELIZABETH**
The Queen Mother)

Mary
Princess Royal
1897-1965
m. Earl of Harewood

2 sons

Henry
Duke of Gloucester
1900-1974
m. Lady Alice Montagu
Douglas Scott

Prince William
1941-1972

Richard
Duke of Gloucester
b. 1944
m. Birgitte
van Deurs

Alexander
Earl of Ulster
b. 1974

**Lady Davina
Windsor**
b. 1977

**Lady Rose
Windsor**
b. 1980

George
Duke of Kent
1902-1942
m. Princess
Marina
of Greece

Prince John
1905-1919

**Princess
Alexandra**
b. 1936
m. Hon Angus
Ogilvy

Prince Michael
b. 1942
m. Baroness
Marie-Christine
von Reibnitz

**Lady Gabriella
Windsor**
b. 1981

**Lord Frederick
Windsor**
b. 1979

James Ogilvy
b. 1964

Marina Ogilvy
b. 1966

Edward
Duke of Kent
b. 1935
m. Katharine
Worsley

George
Earl of
St Andrews
b. 1962

**Lord Nicholas
Windsor**
b. 1970

**Lady Helen
Windsor**
b. 1964

QUEEN ELIZABETH II
b. 1926
m. Philip, Duke of
Edinburgh

Princess Margaret
b. 1930
m. Antony
Earl of Snowdon
(Divorced 1978)

David
Viscount Linley
b. 1961

**Lady Sarah
Armstrong-Jones**
b. 1964

Charles
Prince of Wales
b. 1948
m. Lady Diana
Spencer

**Prince William
of Wales**
b. 1982

**Prince Henry
of Wales**
b. 1984

Princess Anne
b. 1950
m. Captain Mark
Phillips

Peter Phillips
b. 1977

Zara Phillips
b. 1981

Prince Andrew
Duke of York
b. 1960
m. Miss Sarah
Ferguson

Prince Edward
b. 1964

the Pearly Harvest Festival, the Clowns Service, Horseman's Sunday and Chinese New Year, or the Church year – Christmas, Epiphany, Pancake Day and Easter. Street markets and local community fairs and arts festivals abound, keeping alive the traditional street traders' and entertainers' skills and maintaining the distinctive character of each district; see the traders' shows at Petticoat Lane on Sundays, the entertainers daily in Covent Garden.

To help you seek out the best of the royal pageantry, to know more about the star performers and to find old and new royal haunts, here is the vital information with some facts, figures and tips. To find out what is on this month, see the London Year Directory, p. 352. To find out what ceremonies are taking place in the City, visit the City of London Information centre, St. Paul's Churchyard (606 3030). To find out where the daily and weekly street markets are, see p. 325.

Getting clued up

BOOKS ABOUT ROYALS   Royal picture books abound; you merely stroll into a good bookshop (see p. 330) such as Hatchards (royal books on ground floor) or Waterstone, decide upon the size, weight and price range and then take your pick. For something more informative and small enough to carry around, these are among the best:

Hamilton, A: *The Royal Handbook* (1985); the essential manual for the inside story on each royal – details on age, homes, interests, patronage, sports, coaches, aeroplanes, servants and diagrams to help you find the best viewing point at the big events.

Hibbert, C: *A Guide to Royal London* (1987); adapted from Ben Weinreb and Christopher Hibbert's mammoth and authoritative tome, *The London Encyclopaedia*, the A–Z form runs from Albert to the Duke of York, taking in the Crown Jewels, Marble Arch and the State Opening of Parliament, with a profusion of illustrations.

For something more lighthearted:

Adamoli, V: *Utterly Trivial Knowledge: The Royalty Game* (1987); questions to fox royal fans, whose answers supply yet more useless but amusing royal facts.

Hamilton, A: *The Royal 100, A who's who of the first 100 people in line of succession to the British throne* (1986); the royal countdown, with plenty of photographs and a huge fold-out family tree with Queen Victoria the matriarch at the top and some of her 200 descendants (which include Norwegians, Roumanians and Yugoslavs) sprawled over three pages.

THE ROYAL FAMILY: WHO'S WHO   Here are the vital statistics for the nucleus of the royal family, whose family surname is Windsor; see family tree (opposite) for more members. On the birthday of a major royal, there is a gun salute, 'Happy Birthday' is played at the Changing of the Guard, and there is sometimes a carriage procession. Royal patronage, hobbies and sports are a clue to which events in and near London are likely to be graced by a royal presence.

The Queen   Elizabeth II. Title: Her Most Excellent Majesty Elizabeth the Second, by the Grace of God of the United Kingdom of Great Britain and Northern Ireland and of Her other Realms and Territories Queen, Head of the Commonwealth, Defender of the Faith. Born on April 21, 1926, at 17 Bruton Street, London W1, she was christened Elizabeth Alexandra Mary and married Philip Mountbatten (Duke of Edinburgh) on November 20, 1947 at Westminster Abbey. In 1952, she succeeded to the throne and was crowned on June 2, 1953. Official residences: Buckingham Palace; Windsor Castle, Windsor; Palace of Holyroodhouse, Edinburgh. Private residences: Sandringham House, Norfolk; Balmoral Castle, Aberdeenshire. Interests: horse-racing, bloodstock breeding and dogs – the Queen's racing colours are purple with gold braid and scarlet sleeves, black velvet cap with gold fringe; the Queen's labradors live at Sandringham while her five corgis often travel with her; and she also has three 'dorgis', the result of a romance between one of her corgis and Princess Margaret's dachshunds. Children: The Prince of Wales, The Princess Royal, The Duke of York and Prince Edward.

The Duke of Edinburgh   Title: HRH the Prince Philip, Duke of Edinburgh, Earl of Merioneth and Baron Greenwich. Born on June 10, 1921 on Corfu island, Greece, he married Princess Elizabeth (later the Queen) on November 20, 1947. Patronages include: Chancellor, universities of Edinburgh, Cambridge and Salford; Admiral of the Fleet; Marshall of the Royal Air Force; President, World Wildlife Fund; President, International Equestrian Federation. Interests: equestrianism, carriage driving, polo, sailing, cricket.

The Prince of Wales   Heir to the throne. Title: HRH The Prince of Wales. Born on November 14, 1948, he was christened Charles Philip Arthur George and married Lady Diana Spencer on July 29, 1981, at St Paul's Cathedral. Residences: Kensington Palace; Highgrove, Tetbury, Gloucestershire; Tamarisk, St Mary's, Isles of Scilly. Patronages include: Chancellor, University of Wales; President, The Prince's Trust; Patron of more than 30 organisations including the Welsh National Opera and the Royal Opera Covent Garden. Interests: polo (often to be seen playing at Smith's Lawn, Windsor, see p. 346), music, skiing, sailing, gardening, water-colour painting.

The Princess of Wales   Born on July 1, 1961, Lady Diana Frances Spencer married Prince Charles on July 29, 1981, at St Paul's Cathedral and is still affectionately referred to as 'Lady Di'. Patronages include: Welsh National Opera, Malcolm Sargent Cancer Fund for Children, the National Children's Orchestra. Interests: fashion, children, fishing, skiing and music. Children: William Arthur Philip Louis, Prince William of Wales and known by his father as Wills, born on June 21, 1982, and second in line to the throne; Henry Charles Albert David, Prince Henry of Wales and known as Prince Harry, born on September 15, 1984, and third in line to the throne.

The Duke of York   Born on February 19, 1960, and christened Andrew Albert Christian Edward, he married Sarah Ferguson on July 23, 1986, at Westminster Abbey and is fourth in line to the throne. Residence: Buckingham Palace. Interests: flying, canoeing, exploring and photography.

Prince Edward   Born on March 10, 1964, and christened Edward Antony Richard Louis, he is fifth in line to the throne. Residence: Buckingham Palace.

The Princess Royal   Born on August 15, 1950, and christened Anne Elizabeth Alice Louise, Princess Anne married Captain Mark Phillips on November 14, 1973, at Westminster Abbey and is sixth in line to the throne. In 1987, the Queen conferred the title Princess Royal upon her. Residence: Gatcombe Park, Minchinhampton, Gloucestershire. Patron-

ages include: Chancellor, London University; President, Save the Children Fund, British Academy of Film and Television Arts, British Olympic Association. Interests: equestrianism. Children: Peter Mark Andrew Phillips, born in 1977 and seventh in line to the throne; Zara Anne Elizabeth Phillips, born in 1981 and eighth in line to the throne.

The Queen Mother   Title: Her Majesty Queen Elizabeth The Queen Mother. Born on August 4, 1900 at 21 St James's Square, London SW1, Lady Elizabeth Angela Marguerite Bowes-Lyon married Bertie, the second son of George V, on April 26, 1923, in Westminster Abbey. They had two daughters, the Queen and Princess Margaret. When Edward VIII abdicated on December 11, 1936, in order to marry his beloved Mrs Simpson, his younger brother Bertie became George VI. His wife became Queen Elizabeth, his consort, until his death on February 6, 1952, since when she has been known as the Queen Mother. Residences: Clarence House, London; The Royal Lodge, Windsor; Birkhall, Balmoral, Aberdeenshire; Castle of May, Caithness. Patronages include: Lord Warden and Admiral of the Cinque Ports; Chancellor, Dundee University; President, Royal College of Music; Master of the Bench, Middle Temple. Interests: horse-racing (she has had more than 340 winners), fishing and gardening; the Queen Mother's racing colours are blue with buff stripes and blue sleeves, black cap with gold tassle.

Princess Margaret   Born on August 21, 1930, and christened Margaret Rose, the Queen's sister married Antony Armstrong-Jones (Lord Snowdon) on May 6, 1960 (dissolved 1978), at Westminster Abbey and is ninth in line to the throne. Residences: Kensington Palace; Les Jolies Eaux, Mustique. Patronages include: Chancellor, Keele University; Master of the Bench, Lincoln's Inn; Colonel-in-Chief, Queen Alexandra's Royal Army Nursing Corps; Vice-President, St John Ambulance. Interests: music and ballet. Children: Viscount Linley (a designer, see Souvenirs, below), born in 1961 and tenth in line to the throne; Lady Sarah Armstrong-Jones, born in 1964 and eleventh in line to the throne.

The Duke and Duchess of Gloucester   Born in 1944, Prince Richard, Duke of Gloucester is the second son of Henry, George VI's younger brother, and his wife Princess Alice, and is twelfth in line to the throne. In 1972 he married a Dane from Odense, Birgitte van Deurs; his nickname is Proggy (Prince Richard of Gloucester). Residences:

Kensington Palace; Barnwell, Northamptonshire. Patronages (more than 50) include: Patron, Society of Engineers, the Victorian Society and the Homeopathic Research Foundation Trust; President, Cancer Research Campaign. Interests: architecture (the Duke is a trained architect), conservation, photography, skiing. Children: Alexander Windsor, Earl of Ulster, born in 1974 and thirteenth in line to the throne; Lady Davina Windsor, born in 1977 and fourteenth in line to the throne; Lady Rose Windsor, born in 1980 and fifteenth in line to the throne.

The Duke and Duchess of Kent　Born in 1935, Edward, Duke of Kent is the son of George VI's youngest brother, and is sixteenth in line to the throne. In 1961, he married Katharine Worsley. Residences: York House, St James's Palace; Anmer Hall, King's Lynn, Norfolk. The Duke's patronages include: Chancellor, Surrey University; Grand Master, United Grand (Freemasons') Lodge of England; President, Royal Institution, All-England Lawn Tennis and Croquet Club; Vice-Chairman, British Overseas Trade Board. Interests: skiing, riding, private flying, opera, photography, tennis. The Duchess's patronages include: Chancellor, Leeds University; Patron, Age Concern, British Epilepsy Association, The Samaritans, The Spastics Society. Children: George, Earl of St Andrews, born in 1962 and seventeenth in line to the throne; Lord Nicholas Windsor, born in 1970 and eighteenth in line to the throne; and Lady Helen Windsor, born in 1964 and nineteenth in line to the throne.

Prince Michael of Kent　Born in 1942, Prince Michael is the Duke of Kent's younger brother and married Baroness Marie-Christine von Reibnitz, an Austrian and a Roman Catholic, in 1978. Her religion disqualified him from the throne. Residence: Nether Lypiatt Manor, Gloucestershire. Prince Michael's patronages include: President, Royal Automobile Club, Society of Genealogists, Institute of the Motor Industry and the Kennel Club. Interests: flying, hunting, squash and skiing. Princess Michael's patronages include: Trustee, Victoria and Albert Museum; Patron, British Ski Federation, Breast Cancer Research Trust, Society of Women Artists, Royal Shakespeare Theatre Trust. Children: Lord Frederick Windsor, born in

1979 and twentieth in line to the throne; Lady Gabriella Windsor, born in 1981 and twenty-first in line to the throne.

Princess Alexandra　Born in 1936, Princess Alexandra is the Duke of Kent's sister and is twenty-second in line to the throne. In 1963 she married the Hon Angus Ogilvy. Residences: Thatched House Lodge, Richmond; Friary Court, St James's Palace. Princess Alexandra's patronages include: Vice-President, British Red Cross Society; Chancellor, Lancaster University; Patron, Guide Dogs for the Blind Association; President, Alexandra Rose Day (founded by Edward VII's queen, Alexandra). Children: James Ogilvy, born in 1964; Marina Ogilvy, born in 1966.

THE COURT YEAR: FINDING THE QUEEN
Buckingham Palace is the Queen's principal residence; the Royal Standard flies above it when she is in town. The official palace is still St James's, to which foreign ambassadors are accredited; here is the office of the Lord Chamberlain, head of the Royal Household of some 400 people who keep the show on the road. Working around her various commitments, the Queen usually moves to her other residences at fairly regular times: Sandringham for New Year and January (private); Windsor Castle from mid-March to early May and for all of June (both times with her Court); Holyroodhouse, Edinburgh, two weeks from the end of June or early July (with her Court); Balmoral for August and September (private); Windsor Castle for family Christmas from mid-December to the end of the month (with her Court). Her foreign visits tend to be in October–November and February–March.

PAST ROYALS: WHO WAS WHO　Julius Caesar invaded Britain in 55BC, and again in 54BC. But London's history begins with the invasion of Emperor Claudius in AD43, a few years after which he built the first London Bridge. After Emperor Honorius recalled his Romans in 410, London rose again under the Saxons – Egbert (ruled 802–39) united England as one kingdom in 829, and the Saxon Edward the Confessor made London the capital of England. So, from Edward to Elizabeth II, here is a checklist of who was on the throne.

Anglo-Saxons

Edward the Confessor	born c1003	ruled 1042–66
Harold II	born c1020	ruled 1066

Normans (1066–1154)

William I, the Conqueror	born 1027	ruled 1066–87
William II	born 1060	ruled 1087–1100
Henry I	born 1068	ruled 1100–35
Stephen	born c1097	ruled 1135–54

Plantagenets (1154–1399)

Henry II	born 1133	ruled 1154–89
Richard I	born 1157	ruled 1189–99
John	born 1166	ruled 1199–1216
Henry III	born 1207	ruled 1216–72
Edward I	born 1239	ruled 1272–1307
Edward II	born 1284	ruled 1307–27
Edward III	born 1312	ruled 1327–77
Richard II	born 1367	ruled 1377–99

Lancastrians (1399–1461)

Henry IV	born 1367	ruled 1399–1413
Henry V	born 1387	ruled 1413–22
Henry VI	born 1421	ruled 1421–61

Yorkists (1461–85)

Edward IV	born 1442	ruled 1461–83
Edward V	born 1470	ruled 1483
Richard III	born 1452	ruled 1483–5

Tudors (1485–1603)

Henry VII	born 1457	ruled 1485–1509
Henry VIII	born 1491	ruled 1509–47
Edward VI	born 1537	ruled 1547–53
Mary I	born 1516	ruled 1553–8
Elizabeth I	born 1533	ruled 1558–1603

Stuarts (1603–1714)

James I (and VI of Scotland)	born 1566	ruled 1603–25
Charles I	born 1600	ruled 1625–49

(The Commonwealth 1649–53, The Protectorate 1653–9)

Charles II	born 1630	ruled 1660–85
James II	born 1633	ruled 1685–8
William III & Mary II	lived 1650–1702 & 1662–94,	ruled 1689–1702
Anne	born 1665	ruled 1702–14

Hanoverians (1714 onwards, known as the Windsors since 1917)

George I	born 1660	ruled 1714–27
George II	born 1683	ruled 1727–60
George III	born 1738	ruled 1760–1820
George IV	born 1762,	Prince Regent 1811, ruled 1820–30
William IV	born 1765	ruled 1830–7
Victoria	born 1819	ruled 1837–1901
Edward VII	born 1841	ruled 1901–10
George V	born 1865	ruled 1910–35

Edward VIII	born 1894	ruled 1936, abdicated 1936
George VI	born 1895	ruled 1936–52
Elizabeth II	born 1926	ruled since 1952

OUT AND ABOUT WITH THE ROYALS   If there is no live ceremony or show today, there is plenty of royal spirit in the museums, palaces, parks, churches and streets. Here are a few ideas.

Putting a face to the name   The best first stop is the National Portrait Gallery (see p. 88) to see all the monarchs lined up with their supporters, detractors, sycophants and lovers. The great portrait painters paid loyal and lavish attention to the gold-encrusted robes, the jewels and the crowns but they also revealed in the monarchs' faces the characters living behind the icon-like images of royal mystique. Outside the gallery, the many royal statues that add dignity to the London streets and squares include George IV and Charles I in nearby Trafalgar Square. And there is a fine view through the gates of Admiralty Arch down the Mall to the grandest of the nine statues, two medallions and two busts of Queen Victoria (see pp. 89–90). In Westminster Abbey, every monarch from Edward the Confessor to George II has a magnificent monument. To find out more, consult Arthur Byron's *London Statues: A guide to London's outdoor statues and sculpture* (1981).

Royal homes to visit   Royal homes past and present are dotted throughout London. They range from the gloriously decorated and atmospheric Kensington Palace, with royals still living in the back wing, to the recently rediscovered palace of Edward III at Rotherhithe, merely a lingering ghost of a royal presence. The most exciting royal home to visit is Buckingham Palace, where the public can visit two corners of the Queen's principal London residence: the Queen's Gallery and The Royal Mews (see p. 91). Others to seek out include: the Banqueting House, the only remaining part of Whitehall Palace (see p. 87), Clarence House (see p. 138), Greenwich, for palace memories in a still palatial setting (see p. 107); Hampton Court Palace (see p. 112); Kensington Palace (see p. 189); Kew Palace (see p. 268); Lancaster House (see p. 138); Marlborough House (see p. 136); the Tower of London (see p. 101) and the Palace of Westminster, including Westminster Hall (see p. 85) and the Jewel Tower (see p. 85). Archaeologists can seek out remains of royal palaces at Richmond (see p. 268), Southwark (see p. 62) and Rotherhithe (see p. 259). And it is well worth taking the train out to see Windsor Castle (see p. 275).

Royal art collections to visit   The Queen is guardian of one of the finest art collections in the world, held in trust for the nation. She puts much of it on public show (although rarely the great stamp and Fabergé collections). See especially the changing exhibitions at the Queen's Gallery at Buckingham Palace (see p. 91), the Crown Jewels and royal robes at the Tower of London (see p. 103), the Court Dress Collection at Kensington Palace (see p. 190), and both the Old Masters in the State Apartments and the separate Exhibition of Old Master Drawings at Windsor Castle (see p. 276). In addition, past royals have given magnificent collections to national museums, notably George II's gift in 1757 to the infant British Museum of 10,500 volumes from the Royal Library followed by George III's gift of his 120,800 books (see p. 166), now all part of the British Library; and Victoria's gift of Renaissance pictures to the National Gallery. And there are more royal treasures to see in their homes which are open to the public.

Royal parks to visit   It is thanks to our monarchs, who jealously guarded their hunting, partying and promenading playgrounds, that Central London has huge parks, magnificently landscaped and planted and often dotted with royal pavilions. Today all but the private garden of Buckingham Palace are open to the public, although they still belong to the Crown. They are: Bushy Park (see p. 114), Green Park (see p. 143), Greenwich Park (see p. 107), Hampton Court Park (see p. 112), Hyde Park (see p. 150), Kensington Gardens (see p. 190), Primrose Hill (see p. 184), Regent's Park (do not miss Queen Mary's Garden where several roses, all labelled, have been named after monarchs, see p. 180), Richmond Park (see p. 273), St James's Park (see p. 89). And the Royal Botanical Gardens at Kew were a royal foundation (see p. 267). See also p. 350 on London parks.

Royal churches and chapels to visit   Since Henry VIII broke with Rome in 1533, the monarch has been the head of the Church of England, with the Archbishop of Canterbury as the spiritual leader. However, the clergy of twelve churches and chapels owe their allegiance directly to the sovereign rather than to their local bishop. Known collectively as Royal Peculiars, five of them are Chapels Royal and open to the public (although some only on Sunday for services): Chapel Royal St James's Palace (see p. 138), Queen's Chapel (see p. 136), Chapel Royal Hampton Court (see p. 114), and two at the Tower of London: St John's (see p. 102) and St Peter and Vincula (see p. 102). Of the other Royal Peculiars, St George's Chapel Windsor (see p. 276) is well worth visiting. And, most spectacular of all, Westminster Abbey (see p. 75) was built for the royal theatre of coronation, was the royal necropolis from Edward the Confessor to George II and houses the Coronation Chair and the Scottish Stone of Scone. But the Abbey was deemed too small for the wedding of the Prince and Princess of Wales, so they were married in St Paul's Cathedral (see p. 65).

Shop where the Royals shop   Surprisingly to many, the royals are not puppets who need only to be wound up to wave and perform their tricks. They go shopping, like anyone else. Although many royal shopping baskets are filled by the royal servants, good places to spot a real royal shopping expedition are the General Trading Company, Fortnum & Mason and, of course, Harrods. Other royal shops are easy to identify: to really live like a queen or dress like a duke, spot the royal warrants over shop entrances. The warrant system started in medieval times; today, some 800 shops hold warrants to supply the Queen, Queen Mother, the Duke of Edinburgh and the Prince of Wales – and Harrods and Hatchards hold all four. One of the best concentrations of royal warrant shops is in St James's and Piccadilly (see p. 138), conveniently close to two royal homes, St James's and Buckingham Palaces. To find out more, consult Nina Grunfield's *The Royal Shopping Guide* (1984).

THE SHOWS

Finding the show   The London Tourist Board publishes Alika Georgiou and Peter Wood's booklet *Traditional London* (1987); available, with a host of other books on royals and pageantry, from the LTB bookshop in the Tourist Information Centre, Victoria Station Forecourt. LTB also stocks a free up-to-date list of traditional events, and will give more information on their Telephone Information Service, 730 3488 (see p. 3 for details).

Newspapers and magazines: *The Times* lists all royal activities and many City and traditional events on the Court Circular page and in its daily Information Service. *Time Out* and *City Limits* give exhaustive lists of the week's royal and traditional events.

Shows that need tickets   While the majority of royal and traditional events have most of their pageantry on the street for all to see, a few are best seen from the inside for which a ticket and some pre-planning is necessary. For instance, Trooping the Colour is much more interesting if you have a ticket for the stands; being in the Royal Enclosure during Ascot Week is to rub shoulders with the royal family as the Queen enjoys her favourite occupation, horse racing; you see none of the Garter Ceremony procession at Windsor unless you have a ticket to get inside the castle; and the same applies for the Ceremony of the Keys at the Tower of London (for application systems and dates, see below). That said, some events are firmly by invitation only, no applications: you can only wait and hope to be invited by the Queen to a garden party, or by the Lord Great Chamberlain to the State Opening of Parliament when even the standing room in Parliament Square is reserved for parliament staff.

Watching a show   To attend a show with a procession, especially one along the Mall, it is worth arriving early to get a good place at the front of the barrier, taking something to eat during the wait, a plastic bucket to stand on for a better view and possibly a small radio to tune in to the commentary. Major events (State Opening of Parliament, Lord Mayor's Show, Ascot, State visits by foreign dignatories, etc) are broadcast simultaneously on television and radio, and give those not present a ringside seat.

After the show   If you attended the show, there are usually highlights on every news programme that evening – get a closer view of the star players and, perhaps, spot yourself waving in the crowd. The following day's newspapers will have pictures; the following Sunday newspaper magazines may have colour pictures; and the women's monthly magazines and *The Illustrated London News* are likely to have picture stories. Glossy books of photographs recounting every moment of a major event, such as a wedding or jubilee, are in the shops just days later. Royal tours to foreign lands have whole television programmes devoted to them, usually broadcast at the weekend.

Royal souvenirs   Beware: mountains of overpriced tat and trash are sold in the shops around Buckingham Palace and Windsor Castle. To find quality royal mementoes, try the shops inside these and the other royal homes open to the public (see above). In addition, Gered Wedgwood and Spode at 173 Piccadilly, W1 (629 2614) stocks a good range of china decorated with royal designs. To buy something designed by a royal, visit David Linley Furniture, 1 New King's Road, SW6 (736 6886) to pick up a photo frame, letter rack, nest of boxes or to order some furniture. To have your picture taken by a royal, make an appointment with Patrick Lichfield, professional photographer (and cousin to the Queen), 20 Aubrey Walk, W8 (727 4468), or Lord Snowdon, ex-husband of Princess Margaret, 22 Launceston Place, W8. And to have your own party organised by a royal, employ Lady Elizabeth Anson, another of the Queen's cousins, who runs Party Planners (see p. 299). As well as books about royals, there are some by royals – the latest of eight by Prince Philip is *Men, Machines and Sacred Cows* (1984); Prince Charles wrote *The Old Man of Lochnagar* (1983); and Lichfield and Snowdon have published tomes of their photographs.

THE ROYAL SHOWS AND HOW TO SEE THEM   To make the most of a big event in or out of London, royal spotters need to do a little homework.

To obtain tickets, apply well in advance and ensure you complete any forms correctly. To obtain tickets at the last minute, apply to one of the reliable ticket agencies (see p. 284), but be prepared to pay for the privilege. Answering classified advertisements in the newspapers is a risk it is best to avoid.

Badminton Horse Trials   Initiated by the Duke of Beaufort in 1949, Londoners are among the 250,000 spectators who in early May take a trip out of town to watch four days of tough horse and rider discipline, from dressage to cross-country, with informally dressed royals keenly watching and participating and the winner receiving the Whitbread Trophy – Captain Mark Phillips has won it four times. More information from Badminton Horse Trials, Badminton, Avon (045421 272/732).

Beating Retreat   The splendid show by the marching and drilling bands of the Household Division, with plenty of drums and cymbals, has its roots in the traditional ceremony that marks dusk, the retreat of the sun. It is held on Horse Guards Parade in late May or early June (evening performances by floodlight), followed by a similar display a few days later, confusingly known as Beating or Sounding Retreat. To attend, apply for tickets from the end of February onwards from

Premier Box Office, 1b Bridge Street, SW1 (839 6815/836 4114).

Ceremony of the Keys   Each night for more than 700 years the gates of the sovereign's fortress, the Tower of London, have been solemnly locked against the London mob by the Chief Yeoman Warder of the Tower. The seven-minute-long ceremony is magical: the Tower stageset is floodlit, the Chief Warder wears a long red coat and Tudor bonnet and carries a lantern and the Queen's Keys, the huge oak doors of the Middle and Byward Towers are slammed and locked, and the bugles sound the Last Post at 10pm. To attend, apply well in advance from your home address (applications from hotels are not accepted) to The Resident Governor and Keeper of the Jewel House, Queen's House, HM Tower of London, EC3, giving your name, the date you wish to attend (and alternative dates), the number of people (up to seven), and enclosing a stamped, addressed envelope.

Changing the Guard   Since the restoration of Charles II in 1660, the Household Division has protected the sovereign. The Household Division is composed of the Household Cavalry (two regiments, the Life Guards and the Blues and Royals) and five Foot Guards regiments (Grenadier, Coldstream, Scots, Irish and Welsh). Today, guard mounting (without the Queen's presence) takes place at four palaces in London: Buckingham Palace (Queen's residence), St James's Palace (official Court palace), Horseguards Arch (opposite the previous palace, Whitehall) and the Tower of London (royal fortress); and at Windsor Castle outside London.

At Buckingham and St James's palaces (see p. 91): This is the best one to watch. At 11am, the old guard of the Foot Guards forms up in Friary Court, St James's Palace, before marching to music up the Mall to Buckingham Palace. The new guard meanwhile arrives from Wellington Barracks via Birdcage Walk (or sometimes from Chelsea Barracks via Buckingham Gate). The bands of both guards then play music for half an hour while the guards march and the palace keys are symbolically handed over by the captain. All is done by noon. To help identify the guards: Grenadiers have evenly spaced tunic buttons and a white plume on the left side of their bearskin caps; Coldstreams have their buttons grouped in twos and a red plume on the right side of their bearskins; the Scots have buttons grouped in threes and no plume; the Irish have their buttons grouped in fours and their mascot, an Irish wolfhound, leads them on parade; and the

Welsh have their buttons grouped in fives and a seven-inch plume of white and green feathers on the left side of their bearskins. The ceremony takes place daily Apr–July, on alternate days Aug–Mar but is cancelled in very bad weather.

At Whitehall: At about 10.30am (but 9.30am on Sun), the mounted new guard of the Household Cavalry leaves Hyde Park Barracks and rides down the Mall to arrive at Whitehall half an hour later. It forms up facing the old guard in Horseguards (but in Tiltyard in winter); two sentries are posted in the boxes facing Banqueting House; and the old guard returns to the barracks. The ceremony is daily, provided alternately by the Life Guards (red tunics, white helmet plumes) and the Blues and Royals (blue tunics, red helmet plumes). The dismounting ceremony is at 4pm.

At the Tower of London: A short ceremony on Tower Green at noon, only when the Court is officially at Buckingham Palace.

At Windsor: When the Queen is officially in residence, a ceremony with music at 11am in the Quadrangle; when the Queen is absent, the place is Castle Hill (summer) or outside the guard-room (winter). It takes place daily Apr–July, on alternate days Aug–Mar (alternating with the guard change at Buckingham Palace).

Cowes   Boats of every size and sophistication crewed by sailing maniacs from students to City businessmen gather on the Isle of Wight at the beginning of July for the world's oldest and most prestigious yacht regatta, affectionately known as Sacred Cowes Week and with origins in the eighteenth century. Up to 600 races a day skim up and down the Solent, the channel between the island and the mainland – tricky to sail but with good banks for grandstand views. The Admiral's Cup is run on alternate years. Smart relaxation and gossip is at the Royal Yacht Squadron. The Duke of Edinburgh used to compete; his sons still do; his daughter regularly attends; his wife occasionally does. To attend, book a hotel room early in the year, or take a day-trip; to find out more, contact the Cowes Combined Clubs Committee, 17–19 Bath Road, Cowes, Isle of Wight.

Christmas Day   The Queen and her family attend Christmas morning service at St George's Chapel, Windsor. The Queen's Christmas message is broadcast on television and radio.

The Derby   At pretty Epsom race course on the North Downs, Derby Day has drawn the crowds since 1780. More informal than Royal Ascot, coachloads of day-trippers jostle with royals and socialites on the first Wed in June. Either pay at the gate or, to get into the Paddock, apply after Jan 1 to The Secretary, Racecourse Paddock, Esher, Surrey (03727 26311).

Garter Ceremony   At St George's Chapel, Windsor, the Queen attends the thanksgiving service for the Order of the Garter. The oldest British order of Christian chivalry and the highest of the non-military honours, it dates from 1348 when, according to legend, the Countess of Salisbury's blue garter fell from her thigh while she was dancing with Edward III. The king picked it up and quipped to his joking courtiers '*Honi soit qui mal y pense*' (Shame on him who thinks evil of it), which became the motto of the order. The honour is in the Queen's gift and there are only 24 Knights Companion (with some additional royals). At the ceremony, usually on the Monday of Royal Ascot Week in June (see below), the Queen straps a blue-and-gold garter to a new knight's left leg and then joins other knights, all wearing blue sashes, in the lavish procession to the chapel. To apply for tickets to watch the procession inside the castle (the chapel is closed to the public), apply early in the year to the Lord Chamberlain's Office, St James's Palace, SW1. Without a ticket, you see nothing but it is all televised.

Gun salutes   If you like a big bang, these are the fixed dates when you can enjoy one: Feb 6 (Accession Day), Apr 21 (Queen's real birthday), June 2 (Coronation Day), June 10 (Prince Philip's birthday) and Aug 4 (Queen Mother's birthday). There are also salutes for Trooping the Colour (Queen's official birthday), the State Opening of Parliament and to honour some visiting heads of state. On these days, the King's Troop, Royal Horse Artillery assembles in Hyde Park at noon and use six gun carriages to fire a 41-gun salute (21 for the Royal Salute, 20 for the capital). Later, the Honourable Artillery Company assembles in the Tower of London at 1pm and fires a 62-gun salute (41 for the royal Tower, 21 for the City of London).

Henley Royal Regatta   One of the prettiest stretches of the Thames provides the setting for an international rowing regatta where men wear boaters and striped blazers and flirt with girls in flowing dresses and everyone drinks pint after pint of Pimm's and devours bowl after bowl of strawberries and cream. Founded in 1839, it runs during the first week of July, the finals usually clashing with the Wimbledon tennis finals; royals usually attend mid-week, families at the weekend. Best of all is to spend the day in a pleasure boat; second best is to apply for enclosure tickets to The Secretary, Regatta Headquarters, Henley-on-Thames, Oxfordshire (0491 572153); third best is to be invited to one of the many business entertainment tents or to go to the public areas.

Remembrance Sunday This is the memorial day for the members of the armed forces and the allied forces who gave their lives in the two world wars. On the Sunday nearest to November 11 (the date the armistice to end the First World War was signed), the Queen and members of the royal family assemble at the Cenotaph in Whitehall; gunfire marks the start and end of a two-minute silence at 11am; bugles sound the Last Post; the Queen, members of the royal family and representatives of British and foreign governments and of the services lay wreaths; and the Bishop of London conducts a short service. On the eve of Remembrance Sunday, the Royal British Legion present a Festival of Remembrance at the Royal Albert Hall, with another two-minute silence after which a million poppies cascade down from the dome. There are two performances: the Queen and royal family attend the evening one; the public can apply for tickets for the afternoon one from the Box Office, Royal Albert Hall, Kensington Gore, SW7 (589 8212).

Royal Ascot The poshest race week in Britain, first held in 1711 by Queen Anne, a keen horsewoman, and now held for four days (Tues–Fri) in mid-June, with Gold Cup Day (Thurs) the smartest day of all. The Queen and her family and guests stay at Windsor Castle. Each day of Ascot Week she and her guests leave the castle by car at 1.35pm, changing into carriages at the Ascot Gate of Windsor Great Park and then driving down the course to join the crowds decked out in formal morning dress, sparkling uniforms and, for the women, gloriously showy hats. As a major event in the social calendar, anyone can arrive and pay to enter the public areas but entry to the Royal Enclosure is difficult and governed by strict rules: no undischarged bankrupts, no one who has served a prison sentence, everyone to wear formal dress, women to wear hats. To apply for tickets to the Royal Enclosure, write between Jan and Mar to Her Majesty's Representative, Ascot Office, St James's Palace, SW1, giving the full name of each applicant, but only family members can apply (foreign residents apply to their embassy or high commission); then complete the form that is sent back (you will need a sponsor who has attended at least four times recently). To attend the rest of the course,

take a train from Waterloo to Ascot, pay on the turnstiles, and get a good view of the Queen's carriage drive from the public enclosure opposite the winning post. To apply for other tickets or to buy a box (costing £2,000–£6,000), apply to Grand Stand Office, Ascot, Berkshire (0990 22211). To see the royal party clambering into their carriages at the Ascot Gate, apply early in the year to the Deputy Ranger, Crown Estate Office, Windsor Great Park, Berkshire. See also p. 345.

Royal Galas When a royal attends a gala show of theatre, ballet, music or film, ticket prices shoot up and the profit usually goes to a charity favoured by the royal guest of honour. Watch the newspapers for advertisements of events. When booking seats, it is worth asking where exactly the royal box is so that you can select seats with a good view of it – in West End theatres it is usually on the right if you are facing the stage.

The Royal Maundy Originating in the twelfth century, the ceremony commemorates Christ washing the feet of the Disciples on the eve of the Crucifixion. Until 1730, on Maundy Thursday, the day before Good Friday, the sovereign would wash the feet of some of his subjects and distribute alms to the poor. Today the Queen performs only the second part. The ceremony is held in Westminster Abbey every four years, visiting other cathedrals for the three in between. The number of recipients of each sex chosen for service to Church and community) equals the age of the monarch. The Maundy Money is distributed after the first and second lessons of the service, packed in a red purse (token money representing the food and clothing given in early times) and a white purse (coins adding up to the monarch's age). The cathedral is decided upon early in the year and applications for tickets (essential) should be made direct.

Royal Garden Parties Given in July at Buckingham Palace, the three parties are by invitation only (glorious garden, less glorious tea); but the invitees, dolled up in morning dress and silks, promenade along the Mall from about 2.30pm (see also p. 91).

Royal Tournament First held in the Agricultural Hall in Islington (see p. 208), in 1880 this is now the Armed Forces' action-packed display of virtuosity given in aid of service charities for 20 days in July at Earls Court in west London, with royals taking the salute. To attend, apply from mid-March to the Royal Tournament Box Office, Earls Court Exhibition Centre, Warwick Road, SW5 (373 8141).

State Opening of Parliament Usually held in late

Oct or early Nov to mark the new parliamentary year, this is royal pageantry at its best. (If there is a general election, Parliament is dissolved and after the election the Queen opens a new parliamentary session and the autumn ceremony is by-passed.) At 11am, the Queen leaves Buckingham Palace in the Irish State Coach, processing along the Mall, across Horse Guards Parade, through the Arch and down Whitehall to the Lords entrance of the Houses of Parliament – the Imperial State Crown is taken separately. The rest is best seen on television: the Queen processes to the throne in the Lords' chamber and, after the ceremony of summoning the Commons, reads the Queen's Speech outlining the government's programme for the coming session (see p. 83).

State Visit to Scotland In the first week of July, the Queen usually takes up residence at Holyroodhouse, Edinburgh. To see the Ceremony of the Keys in the palace forecourt on her arrival, just watch through the railings. During the week, you can glimpse the procession moving up the Royal Mile from Holyroodhouse to St Giles' Cathedral if there is an investiture of a Knight of the Thistle (the Scottish equivalent of the Garter). *The Scotsman* publishes details of her other commitments.

Swan Upping The Queen and two City livery companies, the Vintners and the Dyers, own the swans on the Thames and in July there is an annual count and marking of them (see p. 100).

Trooping the Colour Although its original function was to display the regimental colour (flag) to the sovereign's army so that they would recognise it on the battlefield, the ceremony now celebrates the sovereign's official birthday and is usually held on the second Saturday in June. That day, the Queen assumes the role of both sovereign and Colonel-in-Chief of the seven regiments of the Household Division and dresses in the uniform of the Foot Guards whose colour is being trooped. At 11am, she arrives by carriage (until 1987 she attended on horseback) at Horse Guards Parade where the Birthday Parade is performed before her; returning to Buckingham Palace, she appears on the balcony for the RAF fly-past at 1pm. To attend, send a stamped addressed envelope and a letter requesting one or two tickets only to Brigade Major, Headquarters, Household Division, Horse Guards, Whitehall, SW1, to arrive between Jan 1 and Mar 1; successful applicants in the ballot are then notified and asked to pay for their tickets. As 50,000 people apply for the 4,000 public places, it is worth asking in your original letter to be included in the two other ballots held for tickets to the full dress-rehearsals on the two preceding Saturdays.

Wimbledon By the end of the All-England Lawn Tennis Championships held at Wimbledon in south London, live and television spectators have acquired an automatic lilt to their necks, like toy dogs on the back shelf of some cars. The competition begins in mid-June and usually lasts two weeks, longer if it pours with rain and disrupts the schedule. The prizes for the world's smartest tennis tournament are awarded by the Duchess of Kent; the Princess of Wales is often in the royal box in the Centre Court. See also pp. 273 and 348. To attend, apply by the end of December to enter the combined ballot for Centre Court and Number One Court to the All-England Lawn Tennis and Croquet Club, Church Road, Wimbledon, SW19, then complete the form that is sent to you. Or, apply to the same address to join the public ballot for standing-room for the last four days. Or, turn up and queue for the seat tickets kept back and sold daily or for a ticket merely to wander the grounds and outside courts (plenty of play early in the tournament), pot of strawberries in hand.

London day by day:
Exploring the centre on foot

London has been going like a fair for almost 2,000 years. The following 12 walks are merely the briefest introduction to the centre of this vast, multi-layered city. Here are just a few of the people, events and places that have shaped London's history, politics, buildings, parks and culture.

Perhaps there are two things to bear in mind that help make sense of the sprawling metropolis. First, there are two cities: the City of London (known as the City), founded by the traders and merchants who still reign in their Square Mile; and the City of Westminster (known as Westminster), which developed later and became the headquarters for the sovereign and his or her court and government. Secondly, the River Thames was until recently London's nerve centre – the source of its wealth and the motorway for most of its traffic. London buildings, London work and London pleasure were focused on the river.

The walks are arranged to fulfil different needs. This is not a museum trail; there should be something to please everyone. The most dedicated and curious might follow them in chronological order, from the City's London Bridge, built after the Romans gained their British foothold in AD43, right up to the current regeneration of the Docklands. Together they unravel a little of the story of London's growth – although there are constant deviations as the story is any-

thing but straightforward. Less ambitious explorers might just want to wander a tempting route on a sunny day and drink in the mood of the area, while others will be seduced into the first art treasure-house and emerge glazed-eyed at sunset. Still others might head for the magnificent lush parks, pause for a lunchtime concert in a Wren church, dawdle around Covent Garden watching the entertainment or window-shop their way around Mayfair. There is no strict form to the walks. They are merely a taste of the 6,000 miles of streets, the 200 or so museums and the quantities of art galleries, churches, fine houses and monuments. They are a springboard to stimulate the curious: select the bits that interest you, delve down the lanes that fascinate you and enjoy the parts that amuse you.

Introduction

Each walk is set out on similar lines. First, there are suggestions for where to plot out the area from above. When you get up high, it is quite astonishing how the landmarks never seem to relate to one another as you had imagined; and the twisting river constantly confuses. Furthermore, London has no obvious axis – every Londoner develops his own mythical idea of The Centre built around where he works, lives and plays; the rest of this huge city often remains a blur. The starting point of each walk is usually some-where near good breakfast haunts and the end is, if possible, near a good sunset gazing spot and somewhere to have tea or a drink. Then there are tips for good moments to explore the area, where to find out more about it and, finally, what festivals or events might be going on. For food and drink along the way, from breakfast to dinner, there is the page reference to that area in the Food and Drink chapter.

As you wander the streets and squares between dips into beautiful churches, splen-did houses, great institutions and museums, there are all sorts of things to notice. Here are just a few.

BENCHES   The parks and churchyards often have wooden benches inscribed with the name of the donor – Regent's Park, St George Hanover Square Gardens off Mount Street. The grand Vic-torian townscapes were equipped with elaborate, wrought-iron benches by the state – some Victoria Embankment benches have sphynxes and camels.

BLUE PLAQUES   These are put up on buildings which have been occupied by someone of historical significance. Each gives the name, dates and reason they are to be remembered. The scheme was started by the Royal Society of Arts – Lord Byron was given the first plaque in Holles Street in 1867 – and then taken over by the London County Council, who were succeeded by, first, the Greater London Council and now English Heritage. However, only one plaque per person is permitted (Mozart's is at 180 Ebury Street, although he stayed in several London houses during his visits) and the scheme operates very slowly, so local societies have begun to honour their distinguished parishioners with their own plaques, too.

BOUNDARY MARKS   The boundary bollards for many London parishes survive, for instance for St Paul's Covent Garden and St James's Clerkenwell. The grandest boundary marks are for the City of London, topped by a griffin rampant; the best known is in the middle of the road at the west end of Fleet Street. (Even the Queen must stop in her carriage here to be granted permission to enter the City of London.)

CLOCKS   The many splendid public clocks almost remove the need for a watch. The best known is on top of the tower known as Big Ben. Performing clocks are outside Fortnum & Mason (Messers F & M trot out in livery), Liberty's (St George lances the dragon), The Swiss Centre (ring-ing bells) and Neal's Yard (gardeners water the flowers), all on the hour. Ones that advertise their trade include the *News of the World* and *Evening News* clocks in Bouverie Street, Burberrys, Harvey Nichols and Sun Alliance in Cheapside; ones that do not include St James's Palace, Somerset House, Selfridges and Bracken House.

COAL-HOLE COVERS   The London terraced house was brilliantly economical in its use of space. The owners used the best floors, leaving the attics for the servants and the basements for house man-agement, extending under the pavement for cel-lars. Thus coal could be delivered directly through the coal-hole in the pavement without dirtying the house. Many ornamental coal-hole covers still exist, and some are even used for their original purpose.

DOORWAYS   The tops of doors are often deco-rated: a semi-circular, highly decorative fanlight (good ones throughout Islington, Barnsbury and Canonbury), an elaborate shell design or perhaps a carving with allusions to the building's owner or function – a man holding a palette over the Pall Mall house where Gainsborough lived, the alle-gorical figure of Justice at the Old Bailey. Victorian and Edwardian doors are often decorated with panels of coloured glass in plant designs or Art Deco ones with bold sunrays. Highly polished brass door furniture includes elaborate knockers – a lion, eagle, ram, leopard or fox. On the big step outside the door there is often an old boot-scraper on one side to remove the mud of the filthy streets (in the days of mud, horses and potholes) before going inside.

DRINKING FOUNTAINS   A Victorian contri-bution, and often very charming – see them in Birdcage Walk, Exchange Buildings and Victoria Tower Gardens. Their doubly philanthropic aim was to provide clean water to help combat disease and to lure the public away from wicked gin.

FIREMARKS   Before the London Fire Engine Establishment was founded in 1833, the individual insurance companies put a firemark on each house insured so that the fire engines could identify it. Surviving firemarks include those in Goodwins Court and Groom Place (see also p. 68).

HORSE TROUGHS   Well into the 1930s many London supplies and market goods arrived by horse-drawn cart. So the drinking troughs now filled with flowers, as on Clerkenwell Green, once provided thirsty horses with refreshment.

LIGHTING   Both lamps and lamp-posts were often designed to match their architecture, from elegant Georgian ones to the ornate Victorian ones of Victoria Embankment (with dolphins twisting round them), Wimpole Street, Finsbury Square, Lambeth Bridge and Holborn Viaduct. The most popular nineteenth-century one was the four-sided lantern, lit by gas but now mostly converted to electricity. Today, gas lighting still illuminates parts of London – Middle Temple, in front of Buckingham Palace, parts of Covent Garden. Beside the front doors of older, grand houses there are sometimes street torch extinguishers and oil lights, as around St James's Palace.

MILESTONES   Much of what is now London lay outside the city until recently. There are milestones marked with the distance to London along Kensington Gore, at Kensington Court, on Haverstock Hill, etc.

PILLARBOXES   As the British postal system is run by the Royal Mail, each pillarbox has the sovereign's monogramme on it, usually beneath the letter opening. Some of the prettiest boxes were erected under Victoria and Edward VII and a few still remain.

POSTERS   Pinned on church railings, front doors and notice boards or attached to trees or stuck up on pub windows and doors, these are the vital clues for local activities – concerts, theatre, music hall, bring-and-buy sales, home-made Sunday teas in churchyards, summer fêtes, etc. The yellow posters are often for the National Gardens Scheme and give information on local private gardens open to the public for one or two days (see p. 351).

PUBS   Victorian and Edwardian pubs may be decorated on the outside with fancy lettering proudly announcing the ales and the brewery, windows with engraved or coloured glass and a hanging pub sign with a painting illustrating the name, often inspired by a local legend or trade or by loyalty to the Crown – Jack The Ripper, Nell of Old Drury, The Printer's Devil, The Builders Arms, The Prince Albert and Queen Victoria. Inside, original fittings may include the mahogany bar and ornate engraved glass.

RAILINGS, GATES AND BALCONIES   Often extremely decorative ironwork. Railings and gates surround houses, public buildings, squares and gardens with an almost endless variety of patterns; balconies are at their most delicate and elaborate outside the first-floor salons. They are easy to date as they usually followed the fashions of the day; many have formalised plant designs, some give a clue to the owner – a crest, a mitre.

SHOP-FRONTS AND STREET SIGNS   Not all shop-fronts have succumbed to flat, plate-glass dullness. Good ones cluster in and around Jermyn Street, Artillery Row, Old Bond Street, Woburn Walk; dramatic modern ones include Joseph in Sloane Street. Shop-owners who possess Royal Warrants to supply the Queen, the Queen Mother, the Duke of Edinburgh or the Prince of Wales (see p. 138) often proudly display the appropriate royal crest above the door – Harrods has all four. The many witty street signs advertising shops include an umbrella for Smith's, a hat for Bates, an artist's palette for Windsor and Newton, a gardener for Suttons seeds; there is a splendid string along Lombard Street to advertise banks and insurance companies.

SQUARES   The square is the most distinctive characteristic of the London layout. Covent Garden Piazza (1631), built on the Bedford estate and designed by Inigo Jones, was the blueprint when it was first built: individual houses behind a uniform facade, looking across an open space. Lincoln's Inn Fields, with magnificent central garden, survives better to give an idea of an early square. As Georgian London expanded, the square was an integral part of the estates developed by the gentry. Bedford Square still sniffs of the Georgian social order when the wealthy lived in the houses with grand entrances, their first floor drawing rooms overlooking the central gardens, gates at the corners to keep out the riff-raff, mews lanes behind for stables, servants and tradesmen. Today, the squares have lost their gates, the mews houses are often bijou homes (particularly in Belgravia and Knightsbridge), but many gardens are still private and accessible only to surrounding residents who each have a key.

STATUES AND SCULPTURE   London's international heroes crowd the streets and squares in perpetuity, from kings and commerce barons to Charlie Chaplin, Winston Churchill and Abraham Lincoln; good concentrations include Parliament Square, Trafalgar Square, Waterloo Place, Embankment Gardens. Many buildings are coated with stone, stucco, terracotta and tile decoration; especially good ones are the Bibendum Building (built by Michelin) for tiles, the Natural History Museum and the London Transport headquarters.

STREET ENTERTAINMENT   Busking in the Underground and along the shopping streets varies from delightful to unbearable; the best is provided by music students (as at South Kensington), the worst by ageing hippies with electric guitars. At Christmas, bands of carol singers on street corners and at the entrances to Underground stations fill the air with 'Once in Royal David's City' and collect for charity. Regular, regulated busking fills Covent Garden.

STREET NAMES   In the City, they often reveal the street's original trade – Butcher Row, Staining Lane, Milk Street; in the West End, they often reveal the aristocratic family who owned the estate and built the houses – Bedford, Russell, Grosvenor. Unlike other cities, London rarely renames streets to honour recent heroes.

STREET VENDORS   The florists and fruitsellers beside Underground stations and in strategic spots have usually traded on that site for generations and know all the local gossip. Newsboys – their name however old they are – sell morning and evening papers; seasonal street vendors hawk summer strawberries, winter-hot roasted chestnuts, and football team colours and rosettes before big matches; charity workers give little paper brooches in exchange for contributions to Alexandra Rose Day and other causes. And rip-off merchants sell tat.

TELEPHONE BOXES   British Telecom is attempting to rip down and sell off the splendid old telephone boxes, the best of which were designed by Giles Gilbert Scott in 1924, revised by him in 1935 – see the ones (now listed) beside Bow Street magistrates court.

WARDS   The City is divided into administrative wards, often marked with oval plaques on buildings – Candlewick, Queenhithe, Cripplegate.

WEATHER VANES AND FINIALS   Often extremely delicate decorations for the tops of spires, towers and domes, many wittily revealing the function of their building – Justice tops Old Bailey, a cargo ship brings eastern goods to Liberty's store, another ship tops Trinity House. The bowl of fire on the Monument to the Great Fire of 1666 was originally planned to be a statue of Charles II, but he complained that the people of London would blame him for the disaster, so there are neutral flames instead.

The City: Merchants and money-power

Mapping it out from above: Monument; St Paul's Cathedral.
Starting point: London Bridge. Access by Underground: Monument.
Good days to explore: Weekdays to see inside the financial trading centres, the majority of churches and the pubs; weekends for a peaceful walk.
Vital equipment: 10p pieces for telescopes at St Paul's.
Information: City of London Information Centre, see p. 4.
Refreshment suggestions: see p. 309.
Local festivals: City of London Festival, two weeks in July. Non-stop quality events throughout the City, often in buildings otherwise closed to the public; information from City of London Informa-

tion Centre or the City Arts Trust, Bishopsgate Hall, 230 Bishopsgate, EC2 (377 0540). Summer in the City, first week of August, a week of family entertainment all day every day; one of a series of festivals run by the Barbican throughout the year; information from The Barbican Centre, Silk Street, EC1 (638 8891).
Local library: Guildhall Library, Aldermanbury, EC2 (606 3030), Mon–Sat, 9.30am–5pm; no reader's ticket or appointment necessary. An astounding reference library devoted to the history and development of London, well-stocked with manuscripts, books, maps and prints, and equipped with an inquiry desk with experts in history, topography, genealogy and heraldry; good shop.

Money makes the City go round. For almost two thousand years the City merchants' ruthless addiction has bought them social status and political power – sometimes more than even the monarchs of Westminster. Money seems to course through the veins of the workers who daily surge into the Square Mile. They have their own language of 'bottom lines', 'golden hellos' and 'marzipan boys' that is as fast-changing as their cars and spectacle designs. Until recently, their vital tool was the Thames. Even today, retired Londoners remember when the backdrop to the City was rows of terraced houses with a forest of soaring masts behind them belonging to exotic red and green ships from the Far East, unloading in the docks. But the market place has moved from noisy, crowded wharfs and jostling, over-loaded ships to computer-furnished concrete temples where precocious City workers make split-second,

million-dollar deals with New York and Tokyo. Now the backdrop is a forest of landbound, ever taller sky-scrapers.
Surprisingly for a tiny area which was devastated by fire in 1666 and by bombs in the Blitz, which underwent drastic rebuilding last century and during the 1960s, and where conservation has always been a firm second to financial gain, plenty of old buildings and old traditions stoically survive. Today, the merchants' power is to be contested by the hi-tech revolution of the Docklands' resurgence east of the City walls. But London began here. And recent archaeological activity is revealing more of its early history. So, rather than just visiting St Paul's and a couple of Wren churches, it is well worth exploring some of the back lanes, seeking out a chunk of Roman wall, dropping in to the Museum of London or watching the whizzkids perform on Europe's fastest financial stages.

Standing on the middle of **London Bridge** is a good place to begin. When the Romans invaded in AD43, the Thames had already served as the Bronze and pre-Roman Iron Age traders' highway since it conveniently spilt out opposite the main route onto the Continent, the Rhine. The triumphant Emperor Claudius needed a river crossing between his ports in Kent and the capital of his new Roman province, Colchester. Latest finds suggest

he waited seven or eight years to build a wooden bridge, choosing a site about 20 metres downstream of the present bridge, where the tidal waters were deep enough for a port, the marshy south bank was at its most firm, and the north bank rose to a flat platform protected behind by marsh and to the west by a stream, the Walbrook. It was a site so ideal that when Boudicca, queen of the Iceni tribe, burnt down blossoming Londinium port in

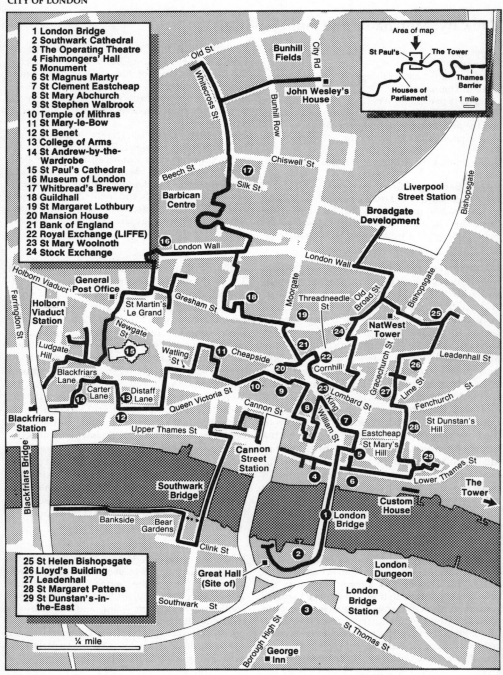

1 London Bridge
2 Southwark Cathedral
3 The Operating Theatre
4 Fishmongers' Hall
5 Monument
6 St Magnus Martyr
7 St Clement Eastcheap
8 St Mary Abchurch
9 St Stephen Walbrook
10 Temple of Mithras
11 St Mary-le-Bow
12 St Benet
13 College of Arms
14 St Andrew-by-the-Wardrobe
15 St Paul's Cathedral
16 Museum of London
17 Whitbread's Brewery
18 Guildhall
19 St Margaret Lothbury
20 Mansion House
21 Bank of England
22 Royal Exchange (LIFFE)
23 St Mary Woolnoth
24 Stock Exchange

25 St Helen Bishopsgate
26 Lloyd's Building
27 Leadenhall
28 St Margaret Pattens
29 St Dunstan's-in-the-East

Area of map
St Paul's — The Tower
Houses of Parliament
Thames Barrier
1 mile

Bunhill Fields
John Wesley's House
Old St
Whitecross St
Bunhill Row
Chiswell St
City Rd
Beech St
Silk St
Barbican Centre
London Wall
Liverpool Street Station
Broadgate Development
Bishopsgate
Moorgate
London Wall
Threadneedle St
Old Broad St
NatWest Tower
Gresham St
General Post Office
St Martin's Le Grand
Newgate St
Ludgate Hill
Blackfriars Lane
Carter Lane
Distaff Lane
Watling St
Cheapside
Cornhill
Lombard St
Gracechurch St
Leadenhall St
Lime St
Fenchurch St
St Dunstan's Hill
Queen Victoria St
Cannon St
King William St
Eastcheap
St Mary's Hill
Lower Thames St
Holborn Viaduct
Holborn Viaduct Station
Farringdon St
Blackfriars Station
Blackfriars Bridge
Upper Thames St
Cannon Street Station
Southwark Bridge
Bankside
Bear Gardens
Clink St
Great Hall (Site of)
Southwark St
George Inn
Borough High St
London Bridge
London Bridge Station
Custom House
The Tower
London Dungeon
St Thomas St

¼ mile

60

AD60, it was promptly rebuilt and became the financial and economic capital of Britain – the great queen (died AD61), 'very tall, in appearance terrifying, in the glance of her eye most fierce', cheered her horses on against the Roman foe who had not only plundered her kingdom but had flogged her and raped her two daughters; when she saw their ultimate victory, she probably took poison.

Despite two thousand years of levelling, rebuilding, flattening and reclaiming of the land – raising the level by eight metres in places – the view of the City from the bridge still betrays the shape of the land as the Romans found it: the original hill straight ahead, the Walbrook valley to the west, a second hill (surmounted now by St Paul's Cathedral), and the River Fleet marking the western boundary. They built their forum and basilica on the first hill, their fort set back on the second, and houses, baths and temples towards the riverside. Around AD200 they encased their city in a three-mile-long wall pierced by seven gates. London did not burst out of this wall for a thousand years. And when it did, it established its own areas. The boundaries of the City – meaning the City of London – only increased northwards a little and westwards along Fleet Street to confront its long-time rival, the City of Westminster.

After Emperor Honorius renounced responsibility for London in AD410, the city endured a bleak period, improving under the Kentish and Mercian traders, then under the Viking Danish conquerors who were defeated in 886 by Alfred, the Saxon and Christian king of Wessex. The Saxons quickly re-established Lundenwic, as they called it, as an international market.

Within a hundred years, London was England's wealthiest and most populous city. Its inhabitants swelled from about 18,000 in 1100 to 50,000 in the 1340s. And its trading and royal strengths made London the political centre of an increasingly unified England. As cargo was constantly heaved on and off its busy wharfs, untold wealth flowed into the city. International prestige soared. Despite a century of population decline following the Black Death (the European epidemic of bubonic plague that ravaged London's population 1348–50), fine churches and palaces were built, quality imports consumed, the export cloth trade strengthened. Bigger wharfs were built right along the city's waterfront, roughly from what is now Blackfriars Bridge (two bridges to the west) to Custom House (just before the Tower).

Then, a growing population of some 75,000 at the beginning of the sixteenth century leapt to an astonishing 200,000 by the end. London was the fastest growing European city, the size of Paris and Milan. Indeed, resources were so strained and streets so congested by the flood of immigrants that a royal proclamation of 1580 forbade any more new houses being built or old houses being sub-divided. Nevertheless, the crush went on, the wealth poured in. By 1700, with about 575,000 inhabitants, London was the wonder of Europe.

Until 1729, throughout this extraordinary expansion, London Bridge was the only span across the Thames. Successors to the Roman crossing were burnt down – even blown away – until Peter de Colechurch, encouraged by Henry II, built a 19-arched, fortified, stone one in 1176, soon cluttered up with multi-storeyed, wooden houses. It became the scene of triumphant processions: the Black Prince with his prisoner King John of France (1357), Henry V returning from Agincourt (1415), Charles II reclaiming his throne (1660). It was also the place for the ghoulish custom of par-boiling traitor's heads, dipping them in preservative tar and spiking them onto the fortifications. William Wallace, a Scot, went on show first (1305); Thomas More (1535), Thomas Cromwell (1540) and many others followed. The bridge was finally replaced by John Rennie's new one 20 metres upstream, opened in 1831 by William IV. But this elegant span went to Lake Havasu City, Arizona, USA, in 1971 when concrete cantilevers replaced it.

The Roman military supply base set up south of the bridge in AD70 makes Southwark London's earliest suburb. Because the railway lines chop up communication in London, it is easiest to visit the oldest part of it now. **Southwark Cathedral**'s heyday was as a fine thirteenth-century Augustinian priory church in the diocese of far away Winchester. It then became so down-at-heel after the Reformation that parts became a bakery, cottages and pig-sties before it was elevated and saved late last century in response to south London expansion. Today, after nineteenth-century restoration, it has a remarkable Gothic choir, chancel and east end chapels, and countless interesting monuments (tel 407 3708; open daily; good local congregation at Sunday services 9am, 11am and 3pm). The easiest way into the cathedral is by the east door on the road; or go through the archway on the road, down the steps just beyond and walk along the south wall to the west entrance in Cathedral Street.

See also the nearby lofty wall and rose window

of Winchester Palace's Great Hall (fourteenth century); the ancient brothel area of Clink Street whose prison inspired the slang phrase 'in the clink', meaning in prison; and the **Kathleen and May**, a restored coastal trading schooner berthed in St Mary Overy Dock (tel 403 3965; open daily 10am–5pm; charge) beside a converted warehouse, Old Thameside Inn (good views), all found by turning right out of the cathedral's west door.

On the other side of Borough High Street shines the sparkling new London Bridge City (see p. 260). And to the south lie two special museums: the **London Dungeon**, a scary, award-winning exhibition of medieval witchcraft, torture and horrors arranged in spine-chilling, life-like tableaux (28–34 Tooley Street, SE1, tel 403 0606; open daily Apr–Sept 10am–5.30pm, Oct–Mar 10am–4.30pm; charge; café); and **The Operating Theatre** set up in 1821 in the apothecary herb garret of the Georgian buildings which then formed the nucleus of St Thomas's Hospital, now the Chapter House of Southwark cathedral (St Thomas Street, SE1, tel 407 7600; open Mon, Wed, Fri, 12.30–4pm; closed Aug and parts of Dec–Feb; charge). Beyond it is the stately Guy's Hospital (1722–80). And down Borough High Street is a National Trust-owned pub, **The George Inn** (begun 1676), London's only remaining galleried inn, which was also a hotel and theatre. Beside it stood the Tabard Inn where Chaucer's pilgrims set out for Canterbury in his *Canterbury Tales* – Geoffrey Chaucer (c1340–1400) was both poet and civil servant; as a diplomat he visited Italy, Flanders and France; he became Controller of the Customs and Subsidy of Wools, Skins and Tanned Hides; in 1374, the king granted him the honour of a pitcher of wine, delivered by the king's butler daily.

At the north end of Peter de Colechurch's bridge stood medieval London. Its walls with seven double gateways and towers surrounded a city of flimsy wooden houses (600 might be flattened in a gale) with the spires and towers of 139 churches spiking into the sky, the narrow streets echoing with church bells and trading bustle all day. On the river, dotted with swans and teeming with fish, spices and gold arrived from the east, silk from China and arms from Scythia. On the lush pastures outside the walls lay monasteries to the north and a wreath of prosperous villages – Bethnal Green, Stepney, Islington and Marylebone – supplying London with fresh milk, fruit and vegetables. To the east rose the royal castle, the Tower; to the west, the king's palace, two miles upstream at Westminster. It was an astonishing spectacle for travellers (best imagined today from the Monument).

At the north end of today's London Bridge stands the **Fishmongers' Hall**. 96 City livery companies exist, mostly descended from the medieval craft guilds founded to maintain standards and protect the interests of their members. When London's wealth was in trading silks, gold and food, they were active members of City government. They built magnificent halls, stocked them with fine plate and pictures, embellished their local churches and bought extensive lands which royal charters have enabled them to own in perpetuity. Each company had its own uniform, or livery, later worn only by senior members who were known as Liverymen – hence livery companies. But their prestige value meant that by the fifteenth century admittance could be by inheritance rather than trade. Today few members of the Skinners, Salters and Ironmongers companies would have a clue about how to practise their trade. But members of the new Actuaries (1979), Arbitrators (1981) and Builders (1976) companies all practise their craft.

Power may be reduced, but some old companies are still wealthy landowners (the Mercers own tracts of Covent Garden) fulfilling their educational role while fiercely upholding their traditions (see p. 352). About 30 possess halls, often magnificent buildings housing some of the finest private collections in the City. This is especially true of the Twelve Great Companies who reflect their medieval stature in a strict order of precedence. Top cats are the Mercers, Grocers, Drapers, Fishmongers and Goldsmiths, of which the last two are still actively involved in their trade. A few halls have open days and host City of London Festival events in July (see p. 59); a few welcome interested visitors by written appointment.

One such is the Fishmongers' Company, whose double arms of the salt fishmongers (dolphins) and stock fishmongers (crossed dried fish) adorn their fine Greek Revival building (1831–4), the winning competition design by Henry Roberts and George Gilbert Scott. Treasures inside include a medieval embroidered funeral pall, the dagger that the fishmonger and Mayor William Walworth is believed to have used to kill Wat Tyler in 1381, and pictures by Romney, Hicks and Chambers as well as Pietro Annigoni's 1955 portrait of the Queen, familiar on stamps and bank notes. There is also a portrait of Thomas Doggett, the actor-manager of the Drury Lane Theatre and loyal Hanoverian who founded the Coat and Badge boat race on the Thames in 1715 to celebrate the accession of George I. The company still runs the race annually, in July, and welcomes the winner to a celebratory dinner at the hall with a fanfare of trumpets. The Fishmongers lost their lucrative monopoly on fish trading, but they still have two fishmeters who, since the time of James I, have inspected all fish sold in the City (Fishmongers' Hall, EC4, 626 3531; apply to the Archivist for a guided tour.) Opposite is the 1920s Adelaide House, answering Greek Revival with exotic Egyptian grandeur.

At the end of the bridge, the steep, cobbled Monument Street drops down to the right to the **Monument** commemorating the Great Fire, the most devastating of all London's fires. It broke out at a baker's in nearby Pudding Lane on the night of September 2, 1666, raged for four days and nights and destroyed four-fifths of the City including some 13,200 houses, almost all the domestic buildings. The diarist, Samuel Pepys, went to see it by boat the first day, noting 'poor people staying in their houses as long as till the very fire touched them, and then running into boats or clambering from one pair of stair by the waterside to another . . . the wind mighty high and driving it (the fire) into the city . . . after so long a drought'. There was little water to quench it. The flames eagerly ate up the tar and pitch of the closely built houses and the oil and brandy in the warehouses. 'But little was or could be done . . . it still increasing and the wind so great . . . and over the Thames with one's face in the wind you were almost burned with a shower of firedrops.' That evening, from a south bank alehouse, he watched it spread 'up the hill of the City, in a most malicious bloody flame, as one entire arch of fire . . . of above a mile long. It made me weep to see it. The churches, houses, and all on fire and flaming at once, and a horrid noise the flames made, and the cracking of houses at their ruine.' Pepys buried his wine and parmesan cheese, sent his wife and gold to Woolwich, and climbed the steeple of All Hallows by the Tower to witness 'the saddest sight of desolation that I ever saw'.

Nothing comparable struck London again until the Blitz bombings of the Second World War which laid waste a third of the City. 320 years later, in 1986, the Bakers' Company apologised, rather late in the day. The Monument went up sooner, in 1671–7. The white Portland stone Doric column 202 feet high, the distance from the careless baker's, was appropriately designed by Sir Christopher Wren, grand architect of post-Fire London. But a flaming urn tops it instead of his idea of gilded flames and a statue of the king. From the top of the dark, tightly spiralling climb of 311 steps, hardly improved since Dr Johnson found it so gloomy, there is a superb view over the gilt-topped spires of Wren's post-Fire churches still poking above most of their neighbours (except the Lego-like skyscrapers to the north). The Tower is mapped out to the east, and the river twists south up to Westminster (open Mon–Fri, Mar 31–Sept 30 9am–6pm, Oct 1–Mar 30 9am–4pm; Sat and Sun 2–6pm; charge; no left luggage facilities, maps at top out of date). For the less adventurous, the ascent up to the Stone Gallery of St Paul's is more comfortable (see p. 66).

The walk through some of the City's older streets to St Paul's gives an idea of how Wren's cathedral dominated post-Fire London, Wren's London. His massive cathedral dome hovered like a great protector above the dark and narrow lanes where new brick and stone houses, replacing the burnt wooden ones, huddled around the spires, towers and steeples of his 51 churches (of which 23 still stand). Indeed, Wren added some spires later, for effect, to improve the skyline of his new city.

At the bottom of Fish Hill Street, almost underneath the bridge, the fishmongers' church is Wren's **St Magnus Martyr** (1671–85), with a magnificent interior and one of his best towers (added 1705 – its arches spanned the footpath of Old London Bridge and the stones lying on the right were part of the bridge) (626 4481; open Tues–Fri, 9.30am–10am; Sat and Sun 9.30am–1pm). Back up Pudding Lane, left along Eastcheap and right into King William Street, Wren's **St Clement Eastcheap** (1683–7) tucked into the first lane on the right may be the church of the nursery rhyme 'Oranges and Lemons say the bells of St Clement's', referring to the medieval fruit cheape or market (226 6992; open Mon–Fri, 9am–5pm).

Further up King William Street, Curtis Green's London Life Assurance Building (1925–7) merits a peek inside before turning left down Abchurch Street to find a little square with welcome benches and Wren's wonderfully spacious **St Mary Abchurch** (1681–6) decorated with William Snow's painted dome and, for once, a definitely genuine and signed Grinling Gibbons limewood reredos. Almost all the furnishings are original: the gilded Pelican in her Piety; the higher pews, some of which had kennels for worshipper's dogs; and the sword-rests on the two front pews for the Lord Mayor's Civic Sword (242 3734; open Mon and

Wed–Fri, 11am–4pm). It is worth nipping down across Cannon Street to look at the restored nos. 1 and 2 Laurence Pountney Hill (1703). In complete contrast, Arup Associates' Bush Lane house (1976) on Cannon Street looks like an elaborately wrapped parcel – the stainless steel tubes are water-filled for fire protection.

Back up St Swithin's Lane, the Narrow Mansion House Place and St Stephen's Row lead to **St Stephen Walbrook** (1672–9, Baroque spire added in 1717). This is Wren's miniature try-out of what he hoped to do for St Paul's: a cross-in-square plan with a large central dome, the centralised plan encouraging a closer relationship between priest and worshippers. Post-war restoration is finally complete, with the addition of Henry Moore's circular, stone central altar – nicknamed 'The Camembert' by its detractors (283 4444; open for services on Mon at 1.05pm, Fri at 12.30pm (music recital) and Sun at 1–1.10pm only). This is perhaps Wren's most majestic church and interior, the beautifully coffered dome complemented by stunning, seventeenth-century furnishings given by the Grocers' Company. His fellow architect Sir John Vanbrugh was buried here in 1726. More recently, the Rector, the Revd Chad Varah, founded the Samaritans organisation here in 1953 to help the lonely and desperate.

By Bucklersbury House in nearby Queen Victoria Street, a big chunk of Roman London, discovered in 1954, has been re-assembled. It is the ground level of the **Temple of Mithras**, built in AD240 and devoted to a favourite Roman mystery cult of Mithras, the Persian god of heavenly light whose demands for honesty, purity and courage appealed to the tough Roman merchants and soldiers. Further down, Wren's St Mary Aldermary (1682, restored) sits on the right.

Watling Street runs to the right of St Mary's, probably an offshoot of the Roman road linking Dover to St Alban's. By Ye Old Watling Public House (1668), which claims Wren and his workers as regulars, Bow Lane leads up to Wren's **St Mary-le-Bow** (1670–83), so-called for the arches in the Norman crypt. Its soaring tower and spire housed the Bow Bells. They sounded the daily curfew in the fourteenth century, after which no one could carry a sword in the street 'unless some great lord or other substantial person of good reputation'. The practice continued until last century – hence the tradition that a true Cockney must be born within their sound (248 5139; open Mon–Fri, 9am–4pm). Bow Lane, the old shoe-making area,

opens into **Cheapside**, the central marketplace of medieval London off which ran each craftsman's lane – Milk, Wood, Friday (for fish) and Sopers (grocers). Returning to Watling Street, Bread Street is where the poet John Donne (1573–1631) was born. He married his 16-year-old bride, Sir Thomas More's niece (c1600), and later became Dean of St Paul's (1621) and one of the foremost preachers of his time, speaking 'like an angel from a cloud' (Izaak Walton).

The first full view of St Paul's is at the end of Watling Street. Tempting as it is to rush in, a roundabout route to the west door is much nicer. Turning left, Sir Albert Richardson's Bracken House (1956–9) is the first post-war building in England to be listed and protected from demolition. It was built as the headquarters of the *Financial Times* newspaper (founded 1888). Until the paper moved to the Docklands and sold its home to the Japanese company Ohbayashi for £143 million in 1987, you could pick a copy of the *FT* from a suitably pink stand. Down Distaff Lane, Wren's hillside St Nicholas Cole Abbey (1671–7) looks across the Thames over his solitary tower of St Mary Somerset (1686–95). However, **St Benet** (1677–83), the tiny church with garlanded windows on Paul's Wharf, is a Wren delight. It was begun by Wren's principal stone-mason, Thomas Strong, who lived in this parish (723 3104; open Sun for 10.45am and 3.30pm services and by arrangement). Beneath it is the City of London School for boys, founded in 1442, whose brand new building sits on a raft over the four-lane Blackfriars Underpass and was designed by former pupil Tom Meddings.

Crossing back over Queen Victoria Street, the elaborate iron gates of the **College of Arms** (1671–7) are a rogue addition brought from Hertfordshire in 1956 (Queen Victoria Street, EC4, tel 248 2762; open Mon–Fri, 10am–4pm; free. To trace your British family tree, make an appointment with the Officer in Waiting). Godliman Street leads up towards the south side of St Paul's. But by turning left near the top into Carter Lane there is St Paul's Deanery on the right (1670, the interior now offices), peaceful Wardrobe Place (nos 3–5 built about 1710) on the left, the Renaissance graffito decoration of FC Penrose's St Paul's Choir School (1875) further along on the right (now the fanciest Youth Hostel in London) and more domestic survivors down St Andrew's Hill. At the bottom, **St Andrew-by-the-Wardrobe** (1685–95) is on the left (tel 248 7546; open Mon–Fri,

10am–6pm). It was so-called because it was near the King's Wardrobe established by Richard III in 1361 to store the extensive royal ceremonial gowns and as a place where supplies for the royal household at Westminster were ordered. As the last and cheapest of Wren's city churches – it cost £7,000 16s and 11d – this plain building is quite the opposite of St Stephen Walbrook. Almost opposite, the **Telecom Technology Showcase** is a treat for those inquisitive about Britain's hi-tech but not always reliable telephone system (135 Queen Victoria Street, EC4, tel 248 7444; open Mon–Fri, 10am–5pm; free).

Moving west, Puddle Dock is the site of the Norman riverside Baynard's Castle which was given to the Black Friars. These Dominican monks, patronised by Edward I (1272–1307), built up a wealthy, influential and landed monastery. Parliament met here, and Emperor Charles V came to stay. Broken up during the Dissolution of the Monasteries in 1538, the refectory became a playhouse and by the seventeenth century Blackfriars was a fashionable artistic quarter where playwrights Ben Jonson and William Shakespeare and court painter Anthony Van Dyck lived – a tradition revived by the Mermaid Theatre (1959). It was also a printing centre: for the *London Gazette* (founded 1665); for the 'Wicked' Bible, the Bible edition whose copy-readers were heavily fined for failing to notice the word 'not' was missing from the seventh commandment (1631); for the *Daily Universal Register*, founded in 1785 by bankrupt Lloyd's underwriter John Walter who renamed it *The Times* three years later (the paper is now printed in Wapping); and recently for *The Observer* (founded 1791), Britain's oldest Sunday newspaper, who occupied *The Times*'s old building 1976–88 (before moving to Battersea). At the end of the street the monks are remembered by the Black Friar, a splendid Art Nouveau pub (1875 and 1904), twinkling mosaics outside, bronze monks and marble within.

Up Blackfriars Lane and past the Society of Apothecaries' fine hall (1668), there is a good view on the left of Wren's St Brides, Wren's tallest (226ft) and most famous steeple (see p. 129). It inspired the elaborate, brandy-soaked cakes of pastry cook William Rich (1755–1811), who lived at no. 3 Ludgate Hill and who set the style of wedding cakes today. Pilgrim Street opens onto Ludgate Hill, the impressive approach to Wren's cathedral. Opposite sits St Martin Ludgate (1677–87), a quiet foil to his masterpiece. Turning right, the first view of his centrepiece is sadly wrecked by Juxon House (1963–4) which blots out the left half of the cathedral. Just before this building, down Ave Maria Lane, there is a taste of pre-Fire London in Amen Court: a row of seventeenth-century canons houses with later doorside torch snuffers and a tiny garden at the far end.

Wren's **St Paul's Cathedral** is the fifth church dedicated to London's patron saint to be built on this spot. It is the first English cathedral to be built by a single architect, the only one with a dome, the only one to be built between the Reformation and the nineteenth century, and the only one in the English Baroque style. As the cathedral church for the diocese of London, an enormous area covering all of London north of the Thames, it is above all a church for Londoners in contrast to the national and royal role of Westminster Abbey.

The first St Paul's was wooden, founded by King Ethelbert of Kent for Mellitus whom St Augustine made first bishop of the East Saxons in AD604. After a fire, the bishop and saint Erkenwald rebuilt it in stone (675–85), an exercise repeated after Viking destruction (962). After another fire in 1087, Old St Paul's with its long Norman nave was finally dedicated in 1240. By 1313 a new, fashionable Gothic choir made the cathedral 596 feet long, the largest in Europe apart from Seville and Milan. And the next year, with the 489 feet high spire completed, it was the tallest of all. Legends tell of pilgrims flocking to adore the miracle-working relics of St Erkenwald, the coffers overflowing, the cathedral glowing with rich decoration.

Later legends tell of the fifteenth-century heresy and witchcraft trials where judges sent the damned to be burnt alive at nearby Smithfield. And in the sixteenth, rousing Reformation sermons at Paul's Cross, the open-air pulpit by the south wall, culminated in ripping down the grand high altar in 1549, and hacking to pieces the carvings, tapestries and tombs. Next, the soaring spire was struck by lightning, shops and houses were built up to the walls, and horses and tradesmen jostled for space in the nave. Even the combined energies of James I, Charles I, Archbishop Laud and architect Inigo Jones failed to save the decaying pile. And when the Civil War broke out in 1643, parliamentarians sold the scaffolding and the nave became a cavalry barracks.

After the Restoration of the monarchy in 1660, Charles II set up a Royal Commission and chose as surveyor **Christopher Wren** (1632–1723), a young man of brilliant intellect, energy and influence who would create the City skyline still seen today. Some

50 of his 70 buildings in and around London still stand. Son of the Dean of St George's, Windsor, he was schooled at Westminster before studying astronomy, mathematics and anatomy at Oxford. Soon he was Professor of Astronomy at Gresham College London, and at Oxford, busily inventing writing duplicators and transparent bee-hives. He was one of the founding members of the Royal Society (see p. 176) and moved in court circles of power, endearing himself to the restored ruler with a model of the moon.

Wren's work on St Paul's began quietly, with two schemes for restoration. Then, ten days after the Great Fire of 1666 began, with Old St Paul's turned to dust, his ideas transformed to a grand scale. His plan was totally to rebuild the city centre with bold wide boulevards and piazzas. The Londoners could not take it. The clergy rejected the cathedral design as too modern. However, in 1669, aged 37, Wren became the King's Surveyor-General. The next year, parliament passed a fund-raising tax on coal arriving at London port to finance a new cathedral and churches, but not a new city. Early in 1675, the clergy rejected his next idea, a domed Greek cross with curving corners whose Great Model (1673–4) is now in the Crypt. Too modern and too Italianate, they said. So Sir Christopher reverted to a long nave in the English tradition, won the clergy's blessing, and received the sensitive king's Royal Warrant later in 1675 with the rider that Wren could make 'variations, rather ornamental than essential'. He quickly chopped off three nave bays, raised the aisle walls, removed the spire from the dome and added a monumental vestibule at the west end. Wren was now Surveyor to St Paul's Cathedral, a post he held until his death 48 years later.

When the site was cleared, Wren noticed that the old stone brought to mark the centre of the new cathedral was appropriately inscribed 'resurgam', 'I shall rise again'. He had the word carved beneath the phoenix decorating the south door pediment. Meanwhile, the foundation stone was laid in 1675 and the bulk completed by 1698, using strong horses and men to haul the Portland stone up the narrow lanes from the quays. In 1708, Wren's son put the last stone on the lantern surmounting the triple-layered dome, still the second largest in the world. New St Paul's had cost £721,552. Inside, the adornments began with Grinling Gibbons's choir-stall carvings and Jean Tijou's Sanctuary gates. More recent additions include Holman Hunt's own copy of his painting 'The Light of the World' (1900, south aisle, the original is at Keble College, Oxford).

Today, 100 people including librarian, vergers, organist, choristers, plumbers, stonemasons, electricians and cleaners keep the cathedral in working shape. It is a place of public triumph, the scene of the state funerals of Nelson (1806), Wellington (1852) and Churchill (1965); of thanksgiving services for Queen Victoria's Diamond Jubilee (1897) and the Silver Jubilees of George V (1935) and the Queen (1977); and of the fairytale marriage of Prince Charles to Lady Diana Spencer (1981). It is also a vast nineteenth- and twentieth-century sculpture court. Since about 1790, the cathedral has accepted statues of benefactors of the nation: heroes (Nelson, Wellington, Kitchener, Gordon), writers (Dr Johnson, John Donne), artists (Reynolds, Constable, Sargent, Munnings), politicians, musicians and many more including a later Surveyor to St Paul's (1819–52), CR Cockerell (north transept), and the recent memorial to the dead of the Falklands and Korean wars (Crypt).

It is a massive building to visit. Magical moments are a quiet, early-morning wander, candle-lit winter evensong, the 12 pealing bells on Sundays at 10am and 2.45pm, and grand July masses with full choir and orchestra. Unmagical moments are afternoons, when the coachloads arrive – the cathedral has 2.5 million visitors a year. On entering, with screen and organ now removed, there is a clear view up the length of the cool grey-and-white building. The elegant Dean's Staircase is under the south-west tower. Right under the dome, the translation of Wren's epitaph reads 'If you seek his monument, look around you'. Down in the Crypt, the words are found again above Wren's gravestone and here you can see the Great Model, the audio-visual programme and the Treasury.

Then the climb, 530 steps to the top. The first and painless part is up to the Whispering Gallery (with a map of the dome construction half way up the staircase), rewarded by good views of James Thornhill's monochrome frescoes (1716–19) in the 64,000-ton dome. William Richmond's mosaics in the dome and Salviati's in the quarter domes and spandrels holding it up were commissioned after Queen Victoria commented in 1872 that the building was 'dirty, dark and undevotional'. Next up, the Stone Gallery is outside, its broad platform equipped with telescopes (10 pence pieces) to make the best of the magnificent **view** and with benches for weary legs. Finally, the giddy spiral up to the narrow Golden Gallery puts you on top of a toytown London. (For information, tel 248 2705; cathedral open daily 7.30am–6pm, free; Crypt, Treasury and all Galleries open Mon–Fri 10am–4.15pm, Sat 11am–4.15pm, charge. Excellent bookable guided Super Tours run Mon–Sat at 11am, 11.30am, 2pm and 2.30pm, lasting about 1½ hours, charge. Good shop.)

Trees, branches and springtime daffodils surround St Paul's. To the north, behind Wren's Chapter House, Paternoster Square, a concrete, post-war atrocity soon to be replaced by more sympathetic buildings, is relieved by Elizabeth Frink's sculpture of a ram and four sheep being driven by the Good Shepherd (1975). Behind the square, Wren's Christ Church tower (1677–87) rises in elegant isolation. In front of the **General Post Office** on King Edward Street there is a statue of Roland Hill, founder of the uniform penny postage in 1840. Underneath is the only underground Post Office Railway in the world. Opened in 1927, the six-mile-long track linking the six London sorting offices carries up to 50,000 mail bags each day (to join a fascinating tour, contact the Post Office Controller, King Edward Building, EC1, tel 239 5024). Inside, the counters stock all the latest philatelic stamps. And upstairs the National Postal Museum displays thousands of beautiful stamps (sections for India and the Commonwealth), dainty decorated stamp boxes and the proof of the first printing plate for the Penny Black, which was franked as the world's first stamp on May 6, 1840 (tel 432 3851; open Mon–Thurs 10am–4.30pm, Fri 10am–4pm; free).

Cutting through Angel Street to St Martin's le Grand, Gresham Street is straight ahead, where the Goldsmiths' Company in Foster Lane and the Pewterers' Company in Oat Lane have splendid collections in their halls, the first open during their regular exhibitions of contemporary goldsmithing (tel 606 7010), the second by appointment with the Clerk (tel 606 9363). On St Martin's le Grand stands one of four London churches dedicated to the seventh-century Saxon abbot and patron saint of travellers, St Botolph. Each is by a gateway, this one sited at Aldersgate, so that the faithful could pray before a journey.

Just beyond it lies the **Barbican Centre** (1959–81). Looking on the good side, it has three virtues. First, it was the only dream that became reality for the great post-war developers who wanted to turn London into a vast and desolate high-rise, high-walkway nightmare – similar plans to wipe out Covent Garden, Knightsbridge and Whitehall were shelved. Second, war damage here was so bad that few buildings were demolished to make way for it. Third, if you can find your way into this maze (many Londoners still come to the arts complex by taxi because they cannot find the entrance), the residential blocks are grouped around a restored St Giles Cripplegate (1545–50), a huge stretch of Roman wall and defences, and a fine arts complex providing museum, galleries, concert hall, informal entertainment, restaurants, a vast and lush greenhouse (open Sat, Sun only) and the two London theatres for the Royal Shakespeare Company (for more information, see p. 287).

The splendid **Museum of London** is the easiest part to reach, up a spiral stairway by the road junction just past St Botolph's. Powell and Moya's building (1975) is a treasure-house of London's history that beats most others. Opened in 1976, the collection is the amalgamation of the Guildhall Museum, founded in 1826 and focusing on City antiquities, and the London Museum at Kensington Palace which opened in 1912 and focused on every aspect of London's cultural history. The collection is especially strong in costumes and, with so much current building in London, recent archaeological finds. Indeed, the museum is built on top of the west gate of the Roman fort. Every item reveals something about the people, with maps, models and music to make each period come alive. Rooms are arranged chronologically, so it is easy to plunge into the grand Roman villa life of imported glass, pottery and wine, forgetting about delights to come such as the illuminated tableau of the 1666 Great Fire, the painted virginals in the panelled room of a wealthy Stuart merchant, ghoulish Georgian prison cells complete with wall graffiti, a Victorian music hall and the 1920s Selfridge's Art Deco lifts. (London Wall, EC1, tel 600 3699; open Tues–Sat 10am–6pm, Sun 2–6pm; free. Roman west gate open monthly on the first Tues, 10.30am–noon, and the third Fri, 2.30–4pm. Full programme of lectures, workshops, special exhibitions, regular 'Made in London' film seasons; Friends of Fashion society; excellent bookshop, good restaurant with garden.)

Meandering through the Barbican and out of the Barbican Centre main door into Silk Street, the keen can strike north for four things well worth a short walk. **Whitbread's Brewery** (1749) is in Chiswell Street, courtyard and buildings restored, a row of fine houses opposite. Up Whitecross Street and left into Garrett Street, the **Whitbread Stables** are where the brewery's 16 shire horses live, who deliver the beer to City pubs (Garrett Street, EC1, tel 606 4455 x 2534; open Mon–Fri, 11am–3pm and by appointment; charge; shop). **Bunhill Fields** are found back down Whitecross Street and left along Chequer Street and Dufferin Avenue: a tree-filled burial ground where the friendly gardeners will put down their rakes to show you where Defoe, Blake, Bunyan and others lie buried – they also sell the guidebook. Opposite the gateway at the far end, **John Wesley's House** and **Chapel** is across the road. This is where Wesley (1703–91), who was inspired by German Moravian brethren to found Methodism, lived (from 1779) and built the Methodist chapel (1777–8); house and chapel (with crypt museum and foundry chapel) both interesting (Wesley's House, 47 City Road, EC1, tel 253 2262; open Mon–Sat 10am–4pm, Sun after the 11am service with preacher; combined charge for house and chapel museum; free on Sun). Milton finished *Paradise Lost* round the corner; Margaret Thatcher was married in the Chapel; and Britain's newest national newspaper, the *Independent*, has offices up the road. It is a short walk back to the Barbican Centre.

Braving the windy walkways, **London Wall** is such a post-war disaster that Terry Farrell is to pull down the Lee House and Moorgate slabs and give us stone facades, huge arches and much missed trees. It leads to Aldermanbury and down into the political and financial heart of the City. On the way, at no. 20, the **Chartered Insurance Institute** has a tiny historic collection of London's pitiful fire-fighting equipment and the best set of British insurance firemarks. Firemarks were essential when flames regularly gobbled up whole streets and valuable cargo and fire fighting was understood to mean merely pulling down the burning house. Until 1833, when the London Fire Engine Establishment was founded, it was the insurance companies who sent parties out to fight fires in their clients' homes, identified by firemarks (tel 606 3835; open by appointment Mon–Fri, 9.15am–5pm; free). One or two are still visible on old London facades (see p. 57).

Further down Aldermanbury, **Guildhall** is on the left, political powerhouse of the City since the twelfth century. Its entrance is round in Gresham Street, behind St Lawrence Jewry (1670–87) whose grand Corinthian east front is in fact Wren's model design for St Paul's and whose post-war interior is suitably sumptuous for the Lord Mayor's official

worship and society brides' weddings, with receptions at daddy's company Hall.

The first known mayor, the prosperous merchant Henry FitzAilwin, was installed at Guildhall in 1192 to run a relatively simple, blossoming City. Today, the Lord Mayor is head of the City Corporation which governs a modern city of infinite complexity. He is its Chief Magistrate and Chairman of its two governing bodies: the Court of Aldermen (who with the City Livery Companies elect him annually) and the Court of Common Council (elected the first Friday in December, meet fortnightly, open to the public). Within the City, he ranks first before everybody, except the monarch. Outside the City, he ranks after the Privy Councillors and may ask for an audience with the monarch. He is Admiral of the Port of London, Head of the Lieutenancy, Chancellor of the City University and has the password to the Tower (see p. 101). The Lord Mayor's Election (September 29) and his Admission (Friday before Lord Mayor's Parade), and the election (June 24) of his two Sheriffs (the London governors before there were mayors) are conducted with sombre ceremony and plenty of pomp, culminating in the Lord Mayor's Parade on the second Saturday in November. It was the merchants who won the City Corporation its charter. As medieval London's trading increased, so did the merchants' wealth and their lust for power. So they played a winner's game with the king, who lived outside the walls at Westminster. The monarch depended upon the merchants for money. Each time he came with begging bowl, like any canny financier they gave just enough and demanded more privileges in payment. The weaker the king's authority, the more power and freedom he had to give to win the merchants' support. Thus, Henry I (1100–35) gave them the right to collect their own taxes and choose their own sheriffs, even though the sheriff theoretically represented royal authority; and Richard I (1189–99) gave them the lucrative management of the Thames (see p. 97).

Finally, in 1215, King John agreed that the elected mayor of London symbolised the City's independent status from royal Westminster's. He had effectively given London away. The merchant-financiers had their charter and promptly acted like monarchs. The democracy and equality of London's citizens, who since Saxon times had all met by St Paul's to discuss any aspect of London life, was exterminated. Weekly husting meetings at Guildhall resolved commercial disputes, a system organised into an elected Common Council during Edward I's reign (1272–1307). Each ward, or area, had its own court. And a new social class was created, citizenship, a status that could be bought, inherited or won after seven years of apprenticeship to another citizen, neatly cutting out two-thirds of Londoners including most foreigners and small traders. But even citizens played no part in government. The election of the mayor was solely by the heads of the 24 wards, the aldermen, usually wealthy merchants. In essence, government was a closed shop run by the big families in the lucrative wool, cloth and wine trades. The Common Council fixed tolls for country goods entering the City, collected royal customs on foreign goods, and made byelaws on public order, on buildings, on fire precautions, on who could trade where, on when taverns could open and even dictated when slops were to be emptied from the overhanging upper windows into the narrow, bustling streets.

The ruling merchants sought yet more money. They tightened up the trading regulations. A foreign or provincial trader could only stay in London for 40 days, could only sell to a citizen, could only deal with another foreigner through a citizen, and could not own a shop. French merchants from the Somme stayed longer by paying for the expensive upkeep of the City's water conduit (see p. 152); the Germans stayed by maintaining Bishopsgate. With little left to give, Henry III (1216–72), King John's son, had to pawn his jewels to the 'nauseously rich' Londoners in 1248 to continue building his extravagant Westminster Abbey.

Edward I began to restore some balance by giving foreign merchants the contracts for the royal household that had previously been held by the aldermen. Under Edward II, the London craftsmen formed the societies that became the City Livery Companies (see p. 62). Membership became the only necessary qualification for citizenship. Soon members became aldermen, and some became mayor, as did Fishmonger Walworth in 1381 (see p. 62). His successor, John of Northampton, made more improvements, establishing a council of citizens elected by the people of each ward to advise the king, the origin of today's Court of Common Council.

The most famous craftsman to become mayor was Richard, or Dick, Whittington. He arrived from Gloucestershire, served a mercer's apprenticeship and made a fortune, partly by supplying silk to the king. He was elected a member of the Common Council, then an alderman, then a sheriff, then three times Master of the Mercers' Company and, between 1397 and 1419, four times Mayor. Folk legends and songs were composed about him, some including his cat; and today the best-known memorial to him is a stone cat at the bottom of Highgate Hill.

It was during his lifetime that the grand new Guildhall (1411–40) was begun, and soon after that mayors upgraded themselves to Lord Mayors. Guildhall's medieval crypt is the largest in London, a vast, vaulted stone room with a painted ceiling and lit by large windows either end. Upstairs, in its newer Hall, the City's influential role is still officially acknowledged when the prime minister publicly accounts for government policy in a speech at the Lord Mayor's Banquet. It is held the Monday after the Lord Mayor's Show to the music of trumpet fanfares and Handel's mayoral *March from Scipio*. (Aldermanbury, EC2, tel 606 3030, open Mon–Sat, 10am–5pm; free.) Also here are the 700 exquisite clocks, watches and clock keys collected by the Clockmakers' Company, shown together in one room filled with the gentle and reassuring tick-tock of the longcase clocks (tel 606 3030; open Mon–Fri, 9.30 am–5pm; free), and the Guildhall Library, founded by Richard Whittington (see above).

The Lord Mayor's official residence, Mansion House, is close by, reached along Gresham Street past Old Jewry, home of the medieval Jewish financiers who prospered under William I (for Christians, to loan money and charge interest was a sin), then suffered appalling persecution (which included Henry III extorting £420,000 in over-taxing) before Edward I finally expelled them in 1290. They did not return for 400 years. At the end of Gresham Street, Wren's **St Margaret Lothbury** (1686–90) is straight ahead, on the left. Worth dipping in to see the huge carved screen with barleystick columns and soaring eagle (1689), the tester carved with frolicking cupids over the pulpit, the brass candelabra and ironwork sword-rests (606 8330, open Mon–Fri, 8am–5pm).

Turning down Prince's Street to Mansion House Square, the heavy facade of **Mansion House** (1739–52) looks up from the south side, its optimistic pediment frieze showing London defeating Envy and bringing in Plenty. Built on the site of the big Stocks Market, whose traders were moved off to Fleet Market, it was the first Lord Mayor's residence – before, they used their own homes and Guildhall. George Dance the Elder designed it, advised on the Mayor's requirements by his Swordbearer and Common Cryer. The result now includes a theatrical Egyptian Hall, chimneypieces of marble and stone to keep both guilds happy, the current mayor's favourite paintings from the stunning City Corporation collection, tapestries woven at Windsor, a gold telephone given in 1936 to mark the millionth one made in Britain, and a gold vault storing so much gold that mere silver sits in corner shadows. (Mansion House, EC4; to visit, apply in writing to the Principal Assistant for a guided tour on Tues, Wed or Thurs at 11am and 2pm; free.)

Across the road, the marble public halls of Lutyens's Midland Bank Head Office (1924–39) are well worth a look. To the west, the castle fantasy of Mappin and Webb (1870) has been acquired by developer Peter Palumbo, who has been forced to shelve both his 25-year-old dream for a Mies van der Rohe design and his follow-up design by James Stirling, now being revised.

Back in **Mansion House Square**, the world of high finance begins. The pinstriped, brolly-clutching money men – few bowlers are worn today – and power-suited money women who surge over London Bridge and disgorge out of Monument, Mansion House, Bank and Moorgate Tube stations every morning, *FT* (*Financial Times*) well-read, mostly head in this direction. All day, the tense young whizzkids making it big in the international corporations are obsessed by one thing only, the bottom line – net income after tax.

But when they disappear into their money-making temples, clues to their computer-fast working pace can be seen on the streets. Messengers constantly dart out of one sky-scraper to run through the narrow passages and courts into another. Street-walking Stock Exchange dealers call up clients on their portable radios. Standing at the traffic lights, an investor tips off a pal: 'You want to fill your boots with this one.' In a world still dominated by men, female secretaries emerge to gossip in lunchtime queues at tiny sandwich bars while their employers go off to enjoy expense-account lunches. But bottom-liners are likely to continue working, grabbing their brie roll and Perrier from the trollies wheeled to their desks. Here in Mansion House Square, friends and lovers meet to enjoy summer sunshine and blue-coated men from the Royal Exchange pop out for a breather. The different markets – the Royal Exchange, Stock Exchange, Baltic Exchange, Lloyd's and others – make this little area an international financial hothouse, even if the Big Bang of 1986 moved much of the action back into offices. Whether you are interested in money or not, the buildings are often

magnificent and the market floors (fast becoming redundant as technology takes over) are fascinating, free theatrical shows, the actors' shouted jargon and speedy dealing rivalling the medieval traders of Cheapside.

But first, the **Bank of England**. It sits fortress-like on the north side of Mansion House Square. Sir John Soane's walls (1788–1808) survive around Sir Herbert Baker's rebuilding (1921–37; for drawings and model of Soane's lost building, see p. 125). The 1694 charter granted by William and Mary required the bank to 'promote the Publick Good and Benefit of our People' (the king's statue is on the Threadneedle Street wall). In fact, they needed money to pay for war with France. It was the brainchild of a Scottish merchant, William Paterson: the public invested £1,200,000 and the Bank lent this capital to the government. Trading was in the Mercers' and Grocers' Halls before moving here, where the first Governor, Sir John Houblon, had lived. Expansion followed. But in 1797, when government financing of more French wars meant the Bank could not exchange notes for gold, James Gillray drew his political cartoon of 'Political Ravishment or the Old Lady of Treadneedle Street in Danger', a nickname that stuck. In 1928, it became the sole issuer of banknotes in England and Wales (Scottish banks issue their own), although private stockholders owned the Bank until nationalisation in 1946. Today about five million banknotes are printed and destroyed daily.

London is now the world banking centre – more than 300 banks have offices here – with the Bank of England in charge. It is not a government department but acts as banker to the government and the banking system, regulating the money flow between them. It advises the government on financial policy, supervises much of the City, funds the government and the country's foreign exchange reserves. Its 2.25 million accounts include the government and the leading high street banks, known as clearing banks. Under its Governor, a prime minister's appointment for a five-year term, its divisions range from Money Markets and Foreign Exchange to Economics and Industrial Finance. Well worth getting inside to see the Roman mosaic at the bottom of the seven-storey cantilever staircase, the reconstructed Soane Room, the Court Room equipped with a weather vane to estimate a ship's arrival after sightings in the Channel, and the museum – the gold vaults remain firmly locked. (Bank of England, Threadneedle Street,

EC2; apply in writing to the Information Division for guided tours; free.)

Now for the markets. Beside the Bank is Sir William Tite's ponderous **Royal Exchange** (1841–4). This is one of the places where a new sovereign is proclaimed, beneath Richard Westmacott's pediment sculpture of triumphant Commerce. The merchant, Mercer and financier Thomas Gresham (1519–79) founded an Exchange, or bourse, for international commerce in 1566 (proclaimed 'Royal' by Elizabeth I in 1570), aiming to transfer the financial and commercial capital of northern Europe from Antwerp to London. Trading continued until 1939, although increased pace and quantities meant specialist traders set up separate meeting places, often in local coffee houses. When the wealth was flowing into Georgian London, samples of a shipment were inspected before it was sold off at auction (there might be 60 a day) until separate sale-rooms were set up for the soft commodities, the origin of London Fox Futures and Options Exchange (see p. 73).

In 1982, it became the home of the London International Financial Futures Exchange, known as **LIFFE**. Providing a worldwide market for futures and options in a time zone between the US and Far East, it is now the largest such exchange outside the US, with more than 20,000 contracts exchanged daily. On the colour-coded floor, members have hi-tech, worldwide communications booths round the edge. Officials wear blue jackets, trainees yellow ones. Traders, often in red jackets, perform a lightning-fast show in the octagonal pits, shouting a code that is reinforced by hand signals (palm outwards for selling, palm inwards for buying, fingers whirling for the number of contracts and quoted prices) while their deals light up on a vast overhead board transmitted worldwide within seconds. Even if you do not understand, it is still fine theatre. (Royal Exchange, EC3, tel 623 0444; open Mon–Fri, 11.30am–1.45pm; free. Go late to see the action when the Chicago market wakes up.)

Leaving Mansion House Square, **Lombard Street** leads off to the left. Lombards was the English pejorative term for the Italian financiers from Genoa, Lucca, Siena, Florence and Venice who succeeded the expelled Jews as royal financiers (to satisfy the Church, their transactions were covered by Bills of Exchange, not sinful interest payments). Its decorative banking signs, a medieval tradition, show it is still a banking street. At the top is Nicholas Hawksmoor's beautifully composed **St Mary Woolnoth** (1716–27). Its rector, John Newton (1725–1807), a reformed slave-trader who wrote the hymn 'Amazing Grace', inspired his parishioner the politician and philanthropist William Wilberforce (1759–1833) to achieve the abolition of slavery (slave trading abolished 1807; slavery in the British Empire abolished 1833) (tel 626 9701; open Mon–Fri, 9am–4.30pm). Further along lived Gregory de Rokesley who outstripped Whittington by being Mayor eight times between 1274 and 1285. And Lloyd's Coffee House, origin of Lloyd's Insurance, moved here from Tower Street after Edward Lloyd's death in 1713.

Turning left into George Yard, a knot of old lanes hides some City workers' favourite haunts: the George and Vulture, the Jamaica Wine House (site of the Jamaica Coffee House where the Baltic Exchange began), Simpson's restaurant and the tranquil garden of St Michael Cornhill. Emerging into Cornhill, the little statue of a décolletée lady opposite is one of many charming fountains erected in London by the Metropolitan Drinking Fountain and Cattle Trough Association (founded 1859), a society whose dual philanthropic aim was to curb less sober gin-drinking and destroy the enemy cholera by supplying pure drinking water.

Cutting through Finch Lane, across Threadneedle Street and into Old Broad Street, the new **Stock Exchange** (1964–69) building is on the left. However, its stage is newly redundant since the 1986 Bing Bang, when office computers replaced handshake dealing. In the beginning, when the merchant venturers focused their coffee-house dealing on New Jonathan's in Threadneedle Street in 1773, they renamed it the Stock Exchange Coffee House. It was formally constituted 25 years later, in 1802, with about 550 subscribers and 100 clerks. Today, there are about 3 million direct shareholders and another 25 million indirect shareholders via pension schemes, life assurance, etc. As in any market, the number of shares is finite. So, brokers buy and sell for their clients through jobbers who play the fast and risky game of making sure that shares bought are actually available and shares sold can be disposed of.

When the action was on the trading floor, jobbers would scuttle about, shout and simultaneously talk to yellow-badged dealers, silver-badged members and into their portable telephones. Talk would be of strong, hard and firm rising prices, of dull, soft or plain flat falling ones. Off the floor, they would dip into the windowless brokers' boxes where telephones buzzed back to City offices with news of a bull (rising) or bear (falling) market. These men – and a handful of women – would deal with billions of pounds, making split-second decisions. Tension ran so high that jokes were essential relief – sometimes, a pillar on the floor was used as a wicket for a game of cricket in a slack moment. (The Stock Exchange, EC2, 588 2355; Visitors' Gallery is still open Mon–Fri, 9.30am–3.15pm; free. Regular talks and film, with reservable seats; touch-sensitive screens explaining every aspect of the Stock Market; classy souvenir shop stocks the games *Strike It Rich* and *Bulls and Bears*.)

Continuing up Old Broad Street, Philip Hardwick's City of London Club (1832–33) at no.19 was founded by a group of bankers as a local drop of St James's (to visit the interior, telephone 588 7991 for an appointment). Richard Seifert's **NatWest** Tower (1981) is one of the recent prestige bank buildings in the City. Its tower is 600 feet tall and currently the tallest building in Britain, the second tallest in Europe and the tallest cantilevered building in the world. The tower's plane is the shape of the NatWest logo, a permanent advertisement to aircraft passengers. Built on clay, it has massive concrete foundations and is designed to move to adjust to winds. Sadly, neither tower nor its top-floor gallery is open to the public. North of here, at the top of Old Broad Street and next to Liverpool Street Station, the total redevelopment of the 10-acre **Broadgate** site is currently under way, to designs by Arup Associates. Begun in July 1985, it is the largest single development in the City and, when complete, will house offices (including American Express), restaurants, shops, sculptures and two new city squares where there will be theatre, concerts and winter ice-skating. Aiming at character, not concrete rent-a-slab, this is a foretaste of the massive Docklands development east of the City (see p. 246).

Cutting east round the NatWest Tower and across Bishopsgate into Great St Helen's, **St Helen Bishopsgate** (begun in the fifteenth century) is the largest surviving medieval church in London. Dedicated to the British mother of Emperor Constantine, it has two naves, one added for a convent. As a fashionable Elizabethan and Jacobean church, there are fine memorials to the city aristocrats – Thomas Gresham, ambassador Sir William Pickering, merchants Sir John Crosby and Sir John Spencer, Alderman Richard Staper and others (tel 283 2231; open Mon–Fri, 9am–5pm).

Carrying on into St Mary Axe, the **Baltic Ex-**change is up to the left. Founded in the seventeenth century in the Jamaica Coffee House behind St Michael Cornhill, this is now the only international shipping exchange in the world, with a membership of about 750 companies who claim to handle approximately three-quarters of the world's cargo movement. Trading on the grand floor also includes two daily sessions for five other markets. They are called open out-cry, when two bells signal the start and end of frantic dealing in futures and commodities (for grain, potatoes, meat, soya bean and freight), and hundreds of contracts are exchanged within minutes. (The Baltic Exchange, St Mary Axe, EC3, tel 623 5501; apply to join guided visits on Wed, Thurs or Fri at 11.30am and 12.30pm; free.) Moving down St Mary Axe, St Andrew Undershaft (1520–32) is another medieval gem; its interior is now a Christian teaching centre.

Already you can see the towers of Richard Rogers' startling new **Lloyd's** building (1981–6). Lloyd's was founded as a marine insurance market in the 1680s in yet another coffee house, this time Edward Lloyd's in Tower Street, which later moved to Abchurch Lane off Lombard Street. Coffee-house informality persisted until rooms were leased at the Royal Exchange in 1774, after which a society of underwriters evolved, legally formalised in 1871 and then magnificently housed by Edwin Cooper (1925–8, destroyed). Today, more than three-quarters of Lloyd's annual £6,000 million premium income comes from overseas. And more than half is from non-marine sources such as aeroplanes and cars. Almost anything can be insured, from a bathtub sail across the Channel to an actress's legs. Lloyd's has even insured a space rescue operation from the US, the first insurance of its kind.

In May 1986, business moved to Rogers' building, well worth visiting. The core is the Room (the market floor), a spectacular glass-roofed atrium the height of St Paul's Cathedral. It is connected to its three surrounding galleries by illuminated, glass-sided escalators and serviced by six exterior towers where glass-bubble lifts slide up and down. Here, amid the dark-suited hubbub, an insurance broker will seek out an active underwriter – that is, one actually sat at his underwriting box rather than walking about. The deal clinched, the underwriter has accepted an insurance risk for his personal profit – or loss – and is liable to meet his commitment with all his private wealth. However, the underwriters represent about 370 syndicates who in turn have memberships of up to several thousand 'names' (members) whose collective declared resources in 1986 were £14,105 million. So the risk is spread. Just as well since although more than £25 million in premiums is accepted daily, about £8 million is paid out daily. And catastrophes demand much more, such as the $100 million paid out after the 1906 San Francisco earthquake. In the centre of the Room, Lloyd's maritime origins persist: the Lutine Bell housed in the rostrum is still rung to signal important marine news, twice for bad, once for good. And maritime disasters are recorded in the casualty book. (Lloyd's of London, Lime Street, EC3, tel 623 7100; museum (including Lloyd's Nelson Collection) and viewing gallery open Mon–Fri, 10am–2.30pm; free; souvenir shop).

South-east of here lie yet more markets. The Metal Market and Exchange Company, known as the London Metal Exchange, is in Plantation House (1934–7), whose great doors depict the tea, coffee, rubber and spices of Britain's colonial wealth. (Plantation House, Fenchurch Street, EC3; to visit, apply to Brian Reidy and Associates at Plantation House on tel 626 1828 for tours Mon–Fri at noon; free.) And at St Katharine Dock outside the city, London Fox Futures and Options Exchange (dealing in coffee, sugar and cocoa) and the International Petroleum Exchange (dealing in gas oil, heavy fuel oil, gasoline and crude oil) moved into Commodity Quay in 1987, where there is a viewing floor over their combined long exchange floor (Commodity Quay, East Smithfield E1, tel 481 2080; viewing gallery open Mon–Fri 9.15am–1pm and 2.30–5.30pm; free).

Behind Lloyd's, in Gracechurch Street, **Leadenhall** is the City's most central non-financial market. Horace Jones's curved arcades (1881) house florist, cheese shop, fishmonger, grocer, pub, restaurant, several butchers hung with braces of pheasant, and a champagne and caviar shop for the City slickers' snacks. Under here, on the hill leading up from London Bridge, stood the Roman basilica and forum, the heart of Roman London (see p. 61).

So the City's newest landmark is almost on top of its oldest. And having now glimpsed a little of London's history in between, a short walk leads down and over the river for a sunset view of its graceful spires and hi-tech towers.

Cutting down Lime Street, left into Fenchurch Street and then right into Rood Lane, Wren's **St Margaret Pattens** (1684–9) retains its tall simple spire and interior joinery (623 6630; open Mon–Fri 9am–4pm). On down St Mary at Hill, the Watermen's Hall (1792–4) is at the bottom right corner. There are still members of the Honourable Company of Watermen, remnants of the 3,000 sturdy Elizabethan oarsmen who ferried people between Westminster and the City, and whose descendants fiercely fought plans for a second bridge (see p. 98). To the left, the romantic secret garden of bombed-out **St Dunstan-in-the-East** hides behind Wren's surviving tower (1699) at the end of St Dunstan's Lane. Straight ahead, Horace Jones's proud building (1874–7) for Billingsgate fish market is topped by fish-shaped weather vanes. Since Roman times, this was the site for raucous, early-morning shouting and acrid smells. And the fishmongers kept a beady eye on their lucrative trade from the London Bridge hall, until William III finally broke their monopoly in 1698. But in 1982 the market was exiled to the Isle of Dogs and the building, converted by Richard Rogers, now houses the City's newest money market, for Citicorp (not open to visitors).

Under London Bridge Lower Thames Street turns into **Upper Thames Street**. Here other company halls kept watch over the network of lanes running down to the wharfs where lightermen loaded and unloaded ships' cargo. Beyond Cannon Street railway station, there is a good cluster of halls on the right. The Tallow Chandlers (1670–2), Skinners (1790) and Dyers (1839–40) have theirs in Dowgate Hill. The Innholders (c.1670) have theirs on College Street near Wren's last city church, St Michael Paternoster Royal (1686–94, heavily restored), and near the grand doorways (c.1680) in College Hill. Beyond Southwark Bridge, the Vintners (1671 and 1870) are on the left and Wren's St James Garlickhithe (1674–87) on the right, with original interior woodwork and another later steeple (1713) (tel 236 1719; open Mon–Fri, 9am–5pm).

Finally, over Southwark Bridge and to the right, **Bankside** stretches to Blackfriars Bridge. When theatres were banned from the City in 1574, this became the local entertainment centre with theatres, bear-baiting, brothels and taverns until the Puritans put an end to fun by closing the playhouses (1642). The Rose (1587) and Swan (1596) theatres were followed by Cuthbert and his son Richard Burbage's Globe (1599, moved from Stepney, see p. 250). Here some of Shakespeare's plays were first performed; Shakespeare arrived in London in 1593. It later burnt down during a performance of *Henry VIII* (1613). Now a small-scale, Tudor-style theatre (not a reconstruction of the Globe as no one knows exactly what it looked like) is being built as part of the International Shakespeare Globe Centre (to open 1992, tel 261 1353 for information). Meanwhile, the **Shakespeare Globe Museum** describes the London and theatre of Shakespeare's time (1 Bear Gardens, Bankside, SE1, tel 928 6342; usually open Tues–Sat 10am–6pm, Sun 2–6pm; charge, best to telephone before going).

It was here that Wren lived, on Cardinal's Wharf, watching his city and cathedral being built. Before G G Scott's Battersea Power Station (1929–55), houses at nos. 49, 50 and 52 survive from the eighteenth century; beyond are the delightful Hopton almshouses (1732) set back in Hopton Street, just before Blackfriars Bridge. Nearby, the new Founders Arms pub has wide terraces with steps down to the river shore. An evening riverside walk provides a stunning sunset **view** of London's first city.

Westminster: Power-palaces of church, crown and state

Mapping it out from above: Westminster Cathedral.

Starting point: Westminster Abbey; access by Underground: Westminster, St James's Park.

Good days to explore: Weekdays to see power in action; weekends to explore Parliament Square without being run over; Sunday to promenade down the Mall which closes to cars.

Vital equipment: To take full advantage of the extraordinary architecture and carving, a pair of binoculars.

Information: London Tourist Information Centre, Victoria Station Forecourt, SW1, see p. 3. Westminster City Hall, Victoria Street, SW1 (828 8070); open Mon–Fri, 8.30am–4.30pm; information on every aspect of the whole City of Westminster borough.

Refreshment suggestions: see p. 309.

Local Festivals: For daily and annual royal and parliamentary pageantry, see p. 51.

Local library: Westminster City borough runs 12 libraries stocked with a million books. In this area, two are especially good. Central Reference Library, St Martin's Street, WC2 (tel 798 2034/2036); open Mon–Fri 10am–7pm, Sat 10am–5pm; over 100,000 books and 800 journals include parliamentary and EEC papers, worldwide telephone directories and travel timetables, local information desk, a strong performing arts section and a separate Fine Arts Library (tel 798 2038). Victoria Library, 160 Buckingham Palace Road, London SW1 (tel 798 2187); open Mon–Fri 9.30am–7pm; Sat 9.30am–5pm; a collection amplified by the Central Music Library, the principal public music library in London (books/scores/journals) (tel 798 2192), and archives of local history dating back to the fifteenth century (documents, newspapers, playbills, maps, engravings), with well-staffed inquiry desk (tel 798 2180, closes Sat 1–2pm).

Westminster was London's second city to be born and became its second power centre. In the eighth century, an abbey was established on a marshy spot about three miles upstream and round a southward bend from the London port founded by Emperor Claudius 700 years or so before. His had been a carefully selected spot. This was more haphazard. But by the mid-eleventh century Edward the Confessor had built a bigger abbey and begun the Palace of Westminster. Soon Westminster was the seat of royal rule for governing England, then Britain, then a globe-encircling empire.

Kings were patrons of the abbey, where they began and ended their rule with coronation and burial. Their governments quarrelled and shouted nearby. And their successive palaces, corridors buzzing with gossip and intrigue, were built further and further from the muddy river bank, leaving the decision makers beside the water.

Today, Westminster is still the centre of government. The Queen was crowned at Westminster Abbey. Her government meets beneath the crown-tipped, fancy pinnacles of the Palace of Westminster, where MPs burst blood vessels in fiery debates. When the Division Bell sounds for a vote, calmer colleagues drain their pints at St Stephen's Tavern and leave the comfy sofas of their flats around Westminster Cathedral to scuttle back to the House. Whitehall is lined with minsterial corridors of the government machine. At Trafalgar Square it meets the Mall, the royal processional route. Here, between colourful banners and waving subjects, carriages bearing the Queen, her family and state visitors are pulled by horses to Buckingham Palace.

In an area so packed with royal and political history, the best place to begin is **Westminster Abbey**. It is a building at the core of British history. Every ruler has been associated with it; many are buried here. And more than 5,000 people are remembered inside, ranging from Thomas Bilson (1547–1616), who put the finishing touches to James I's Authorised Version of the Bible, to Edmond Halley (1656–1742), a Londoner who predicted the return of the comet named after him.

The Abbey's origins are cloudy. The site was unattractive Thorney Island, formed where the

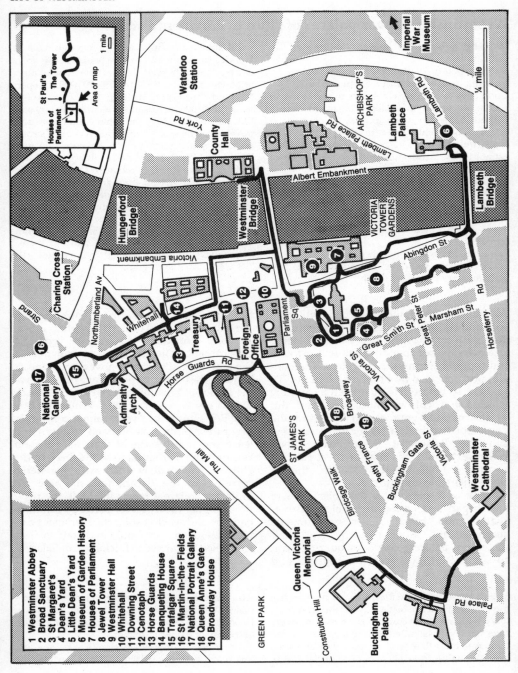

1 Westminster Abbey
2 Broad Sanctuary
3 St Margaret's
4 Dean's Yard
5 Little Dean's Yard
6 Museum of Garden History
7 Houses of Parliament
8 Jewel Tower
9 Westminster Hall
10 Whitehall
11 Downing Street
12 Cenotaph
13 Horse Guards
14 Banqueting House
15 Trafalgar Square
16 St Martin-in-the-Fields
17 National Portrait Gallery
18 Queen Anne's Gate
19 Broadway House

Tyburn river split to flow down beneath what are now Downing Street and Great College Street and into the Thames. Sebert, king of the East Saxons, possibly founded the church of St Peter here in 604, the year his uncle Ethelbert founded St Paul's. Certainly, King Edgar (957–75) gave land; kings Athelstan (924–39), Ethelred (979–1016) and Canute (1016–35) gave relics; and St Dunstan, Bishop of London, gave a dozen Benedictine monks in about 960. But it was Edward the Confessor (1042–66) who dreamt of a new palace with an extensive monastery next door and an abbey church fit for royal burial, imitating the private royal foundations in the rest of Europe. The Danes had driven him into exile in Normandy, where he vowed he would make a pilgrimage to St Peter's in Rome if he recovered his kingdom. Back on the throne, political conditions forbade him from fulfilling his vow. So Pope Leo said he could restore the monastery at Westminster instead. The pious king gave extensive lands, began his palace and replaced the Saxon church with a Norman one. It was consecrated on December 28, 1065. Eight days later Edward died, to be canonised in 1161. Harold, ambitious son of the ambitious Earl Godwin of Wessex, succeeded him, possibly initiating the tradition of coronation in the Abbey. Less than a year later, Harold had died in the Battle of Hastings and Saxons cheered as their Norman Conqueror, William I (1066–87), was crowned on Christmas Day.

Henry III (1216–72), a fervent disciple of Edward the Confessor, began the Abbey we see today, lavishing money on it at the expense of his kingdom. In 1220 he laid the foundation stone of the Lady Chapel and enjoyed a second coronation at the Abbey the next day (his first was at Gloucester in 1216). And in 1245 he began rebuilding the whole church, starting from the east. He wanted a sumptuous building in the latest European style. It was to be a shrine to Edward the Confessor, a grand coronation church and a royal necropolis. Master Henry de Reyns, now believed to have been English, was his designer.

Fourteen years later Master Henry had built the eastern end. It is a triumph of design and technique, blending English and French Gothic. The wide transepts, elaborate mouldings on the main arches, polished Purbeck marble and sculptured decoration are all English marks. But the apse with radiating chapels sliced by tall windows, the rose windows and carved angels of the transepts, the recessed doors of the north entrance, the flying buttresses and the overall sense of soaring height are French. They were inspired by recent achievements at Rheims, which the king had seen in 1243, and at Amiens and La Sainte Chapelle. Master Robert of Beverley continued Master Henry's work. By the time of the king's death the choir and five bays of the typically long English nave were complete. And the special part of the design was evident: the coronation theatre, with the choir pushed down the nave to make space for a huge, high stage, while the audience sat in the transepts, nave and two layers of galleries.

And there building stopped for a century, the elegant, 103-feet-high nave awkwardly joined to the Confessor's stumpy Norman one. It was under Abbot Litlyngton that work started again in 1376. And with money from Cardinal Langham, Richard II, Henry V and the pilgrims who flocked to the Confessor's shrine, all but the West Towers were completed by 1532 – Christopher Wren designed them and then Nicholas Hawksmoor modified them and John James finished them (1745). Henry VII (1485–1509) financed his delicate chapel (1503–12) hooked onto the east end, its cobweb-fine stone-work and elegant fan-vaulting a Tudor feat probably designed by Robert and William Vertue. (It replaced Henry II's Lady Chapel, and is dedicated to the Blessed Virgin Mary.)

The monks' happiness with their completed Abbey was short-lived. When Henry VIII (1509–47) had no male heir after twenty years of marriage, the corridors of power buzzed with 'the king's great matter', his divorce. Finally, he broke with Rome in 1533 to marry Anne Boleyn, who promptly gave him a daughter (Elizabeth I). The monarch was now head of the Church in England, signalling the end of medieval life in London and the beginning of modern British history. And the Dissolution of the Monasteries began three years later (see p. 202). Benedictine Westminster, one of the earliest and richest monasteries, became Crown property in 1534 and closed in 1540. By this time some 800 religious houses belonged to Henry, who then sold two-thirds of this massive quantity of land to his wealthier subjects to finance wars with France.

The church became a cathedral for sixteen years, when the expression 'robbing Peter to pay Paul' evolved because part of the Abbey revenues went into St Paul's coffers. The monks were restored in 1556 during Catholic Mary's brief rule (1553–8). Then Protestant Elizabeth (1558–1603) ascended the throne. She was crowned in January 1559 when 'the Queene, with great majestie, rode through

London to Westminister, against which time the Lord Mayor and citizens of London had furnished the streets with stately pageants, sumptuous showes and devices'. The next year she closed all the religious houses Mary had revived. And the church became what it is today: the Collegiate Church of St Peter at Westminster, whose Dean is answerable to the monarch directly. Thus the Abbey, as it is known, is one of twelve Royal Peculiars in Britain (see p. 138). But this did not exempt it from the reforming zeal of Cromwell's men in the next century. During the Commonwealth (1649–53) and Protectorate (1653–9) that followed Charles I's execution, they cleared the Abbey of its treasures, used the nave as a barracks, the choir as a preaching hall and put their tobacco on the High Altar. Cromwell, Henry Ireton (who had signed the king's death warrant) and others were buried in the Abbey. But after the Restoration, when Charles II was on the throne, they were disinterred, hanged at Tyburn (where Marble Arch is, see p. 151) and the heads of Cromwell and Ireton displayed on the spikes of Westminster Hall.

The Abbey is a daunting building to visit. The number of monuments makes it difficult to enjoy the beauty of the architecture; the crowds of visitors destroy the atmosphere. Magical moments are 8am Communion in St Faith's Chapel and then a wander in the silent nave and cloisters; 9.30–10am in the Royal Chapels, before the tours and when the vaulting on the east side is well lit; Wed evenings, especially in winter; and the Sung Evensongs on weekdays (except Wed) at 5pm and on Saturday at 3pm.

Inside the west door, there is a good view up Master Henry's church, over Edward Blore's gold Gothic Choir screen front (1834) to the distant chantry of Henry V – the nave chandeliers (each about 10 feet tall) were given by the Guinness family in 1965 on the Abbey's 900th anniversary. Already, you can see how the monuments are layered up the walls and piled high in corners, some with incongruous neighbours, others remembering people whose greatness needed to be qualified by long explanatory inscriptions. There are kings, politicians, scientists, poets and philanthropists. By no means all were virtuous. And some simply paid to be there. The Abbey coffers suffered after the monastery was closed in 1540, so the burial rights were opened up. From the late sixteenth century to the late nineteenth century – when it was stopped on moral grounds – the well-connected and well-to-do could buy their places in the Abbey. In the nave, several monuments are worth seeking out: the contemporary wooden panel-painting of Richard II (1377–99); the green marble slab to Sir Winston Churchill (1874–1965); the Tomb of the Unknown Warrior (1920) from the First World War, the unidentified body covered with French soil under Belgian marble and surrounded by poppies (the last full-bodied burial in the Abbey); the tomb of Poet Laureate Ben Jonson (1574–1637), whose friends minimised on space, and therefore cost, by burying him vertically; and, in the screen, William Kent's memorial (1731) to Sir Isaac Newton (1642–1727), whose friendship with the Dean removed the problems caused by his controversial theories on gravitation and the world's shape.

When the monastery was active, the screen divided lay worshippers from monks. Blore's colourful screen still encloses the ancient pulpit. Henry III's building, with its deeply cut decoration on the walls, extends one bay beyond it. Inside the pinnacled choirstalls, there is a seat for the Queen, one for her Dean, and others for the representatives of the Commonwealth countries who celebrate their Commonwealth Days with annual services here. The crossing, site of the coronation theatre, is beyond, with the High Altar as its backdrop and the Coronation Chair stored behind.

When the Queen was crowned Elizabeth II in June 1953, 250 people in nine processions escorted her here. The ceremony lasted nearly four hours, during which she was crowned according to an updated version of the service devised by St Dunstan for King Edgar's coronation at Bath in 973. Past monarchs have had problems. William I thought the cheers of acclamation were a rebellion. Richard II's shoe fell off. George IV almost fainted in the July heat, then flirted with Lady Conyngham. One lord fell down the stairs towards Queen Victoria, the Archbishop put the sapphire ring with its ruby cross on the wrong finger, and her maids made a muddle of her train. And Edward VII's crown was almost put on back to front. There were no calamities for Elizabeth II. The complicated rites went without a hitch. In all, she sat on the three chairs – State, Throne and Coronation; wore three sets of clothes – white for anointing, royal for investment and royal purple Robe at the end; was crowned with St Edward's Crown but left wearing the Imperial State Crown; was given a Bible, shown to her people and received homage from her peers; had trumpets, drums and guns sounded in her honour; and finally processed out into the pelting rain, the air ringing with the pealing bells and the National Anthem. An audience of 7,000 watched, all seated hours before she arrived. And the next day the cleaners discovered how they coped: picnic debris and empty whisky and brandy bottles were found under their seats.

From the crossing there are good **views** of two rose windows, the North one by James Thornhill, who was responsible for the dome paintings at St Paul's. George Gilbert Scott's restoration of the Abbey meant the Apostles' feet were chopped off to fit the old glass into his new tracery. And there is a fine **view** back up the narrow north aisle.

On the way to Henry VII's Chapel, the north side of the Sanctuary houses sumptuous medieval and Renaissance tombs. Inside the chapel, there are chairs to make the dizzy-high vaulting easier to enjoy. The older choirstalls have remarkable misericord carvings in the Albrecht Durer tradition (under the seats; if they are not turned up, ask an official). Originally painted and gilded throughout, the chapel is used for Holy Communion on great feast days. It is also the special chapel of the Order of the Bath, a royal honour revived by George I in 1725 as a military order consisting of the sovereign, a grand master and 36 knights. Now there are more members, so only some senior knights have stalls with their stallplates and huge banners erected above their choirstall (done at the Installation Service held every four years to fill vacancies left by deceased knights). Hugh Easton's east window (1947) remembers men of the Royal Air Force killed in the Battle of Britain (July–Oct 1940). Here, at the east end of the chapel, Oliver Cromwell spent two peaceful years after a right royal funeral when his effigy, draped in royal robes, crown, sceptre and orb, lay in state at Somerset House and was then hauled on a carriage through streets lined with soldiers and mourners.

Now the royal necropolis begins. Henry VII (1485–1509), his Queen Elizabeth of York and James I (1603–25) are in this chapel, as are Edward VI (1547–53) and the last monarch to be buried in the Abbey, George II (1727–60) – after this, Windsor became the royal burial place. The north and south aisles of the chapel contain tombs of royal women: Elizabeth I (ruled 1558–1603) with her half-sister Queen Mary (ruled 1553–8) to the north; Mary Queen of Scots (lived 1542–87) in the south, with Charles II (1660–85), William III (1689–1702) and his Queen Mary II (died 1694, and Queen Anne (1702–14) in a vault below, at the east end.

Turning back, Edward the Confessor's Chapel lies at the heart of the Abbey, behind the high altar. Roman Catholic pilgrims still visit St Edward's Shrine, where the steps are worn down by their predecessors who knelt there. Henry V (1413–22), whose royal gold helped build the church, is at its entrance. He died of dysentery in France, so the body was brought back preserved in a barrel of herbs and spices. Inside the chapel, the saint is surrounded by his devotees: Henry III (1216–72), who began this great building; Edward I (1272–1307), the first king crowned in it; Edward III (1327–77), whose shield and sword of state are also deposited there; and his grandson Richard II (1377–99), who employed Henry Yevele to continue building the Abbey and to build both his grandfather's and his own fine monuments. The chest containing the Confessor's body was carried here by Henry III, his brother and his two sons on October 13, 1269, a date still celebrated; but the shrine is Queen Mary's post-Dissolution restoration. The fifteenth-century stone screen at the west end of the chapel is carved with scenes from the Confessor's life, and in front of it sits the Coronation Chair built by Edward I around the sacred Stone of Scone he pinched from Scotland in 1296. His successor, Edward II (1307–27), was the first king to be crowned on the chair and stone, a tradition upheld ever since except at the double coronation of William and Mary, where it seems Mary was given a separate chair. Edward III's sword and shield rest beside it.

At the end of the south ambulatory, just inside the gates, the tomb in the recess on the right is perhaps King Sebert's, possibly the founder of the first St Peter's church here. And round the corner to the left is Poets' Corner, a misnomer for a forum of writers, scholars, divines, dramatists and poets who fill the south transept with beautifully carved angels high above. Geoffrey Chaucer (c.1343–1400) set the fashion. Edmund Spenser (1553–99) reinforced it. Other poets here include Ben Jonson (buried in the nave), John Dryden (1670–89) who managed to praise both Cromwell and then the restored Charles II, William Wordsworth (1770–1850), Alfred, Lord Tennyson (1809–92). Shakespeare, Milton, Kipling, Longfellow, Austen, Eliot, Shelley, Goldsmith, the Brontë sisters, Thackeray, Hardy, Handel, Purcell, Sheridan and Garrick are also remembered here. So are Nicholas de Litlyngton (Abbot 1362–86) who steamed on with building the nave and monastery, and Richard Busby (1606–95) who ran Westminster

School for 55 years and was the most celebrated schoolmaster of his day.

There are several treats left. First, the two big wall-paintings on the south wall of Poets' Corner (1280–1300). Then, through a little door in this wall, St Faith's chapel is a cell of tranquillity, decorated with a fourteenth-century painting in rich green and red. Beyond is the octagonal, light-drenched space of the Chapter House (1250–3), with original picture-tile floor and wall-paintings. The Abbot would meet his eighty or so monks here and give them their daily tasks. Later, Henry III's Great King's Council met here (1257) and soon after it became the Parliament for the Commons for three centuries, until the end of the fourteenth century. Later the Commons moved into St Stephen's Chapel in the old Palace of Westminster (see p. 82), their home for 300 years. The restored Pyx Chamber (1065–90) and the museum stocked with gruesomely realistic wax effigies painted and dressed up for funeral processions (Charles II, Elizabeth I, William III, Nelson, etc) are nearby. (For information, tel 222 5152; nave and cloisters open daily 8am–6pm, free; Royal Chapels (ie everything east of the screen) open Mon–Fri 9am–4.45pm, Sat 9am–2.45pm, charge; Chapter House, Pyx Chamber and Museum open daily 10am–4pm in winter, 10am–6pm in summer, charge; the whole Abbey open free of charge each Wed, 6–7.45pm, when amateur photography is permitted; the whole Abbey is closed before major national services. Excellent guided Super Tours (include otherwise closed Jerusalem Chamber and Jericho Parlour) run Mon–Fri, Apr–Oct 10am, 10.30am, 11am, 2pm, 2.30pm and 3pm, Nov–Mar 10am, 11am, 2pm and 3pm; Sat 10am, 11am and 12.30pm; charge; bookable at 20 Dean's Yard, SW1, tel 222 7110. Good shop; substantial official guide-book but see also *New Bells Cathedral Guide to Westminster Abbey* by Christopher Wilson and others (1986).)

Leaving the Abbey through the Cloisters to emerge into Dean's Yard, an arch straight ahead and on the right leads back to the Abbey west door. This is **Broad Sanctuary**, where the monastery gave refuge to fugitives from the civil law until it became such a mire of thieves and murderers that James I closed it. Beyond here huddled the medieval town of Westminster, with congested and often squalid alleys and, later, some of London's worst slums, filling the gap between the Abbey, palace and park. It was slowly cleared up in the eighteenth century to make way for a bridge, up-market houses and finally Parliament Square. Victoria Street, now void of character, was sliced through in 1844.

Today, Broad Sanctuary looks across to Powell Moya and Partners' sparkling new Queen Elizabeth II Conference Centre (1986), furnished with art commissioned from Paolozzi, Richard Kindersley, Jennifer Jones and other British artists. It sits between the French Baroque, domed Methodist Central Hall (1905–11) and the former Middlesex Guildhall (1906–13). To the right, just beyond the Abbey's north transept, is the restored **St Margaret's** (1480–1523, tower 1735–7). Old glass remembers Milton (married here) and Raleigh (buried here); new glass is by David Piper; the font (1641) is by Nicholas Stone. Officially Westminster's parish church, it is really the House of Commons' parish church where Members have worshipped since the Speaker of the House of Commons chose it on Palm Sunday, 1614, in Puritan preference to the ritualistic Abbey service. The front pew is still Mr Speaker's, and distinguished MPs are given memorial services here. Following the example of Pepys and Milton, Winston Churchill was married here in 1908 (222 6382, open daily 9.30am–4.30pm).

In **Dean's Yard**, MPs and Westminster School jostle for office space. In 1461, the Abbey's school was moved into no. 19, then part of the monastic guest house, and given its first lay headmaster. At the Dissolution in 1540 it went secular, thus saving some of the old monastic buildings it still occupies. In 1560 Elizabeth I endowed it. High-achieving former pupils have included Ben Jonson, Christopher Wren, Edward Gibbon and, more recently, Andrew Lloyd Webber. Relations with both Abbey and Crown are still close, and scholars have the privilege of acclaiming a newly crowned sovereign first. The main school buildings are in **Little Dean's Yard**, found through an arch in the east side of the square. Among the beautiful buildings are Henry Yevele's College Hall (1360s, part of the Abbot's house, now the dining room), Lord Burlington's College (1722–30) and Ashburnham House, which incorporates part of the twelfth–sixteenth century Prior's House (Dean's Yard, SW1, tel 222 3116; open during Easter school holidays Mon–Fri, 10am–4pm; charge). The 900-year-old Abbey Garden is at the back of the yard, a lingering atmosphere of monastic contemplation filling its peaceful walls; good view of Victoria Tower, connection through to Little Cloister (open on Thurs, Apr–Sept 10am–6pm, Oct–Mar 10am–4pm; free;

no dogs). Returning to Dean's Yard and then through an arch on the left, Great College Street leads into an eighteenth-century London backwater developed by Sir James Smith, still mostly residential, with dream houses for successful politicians. Down Barton Street and Cowley Street, across Great Peter Street and through Lord North Street, Thomas Archer's Baroque St John's Church (1714–28, now a concert hall with good crypt café) is the focus of Smith Square. Party politics fills the air: the Conservative headquarters are here; Labour were here (now flown south of the river); and the Social Democrats are in Cowley Street.

Along Dean Bradley Street and right into Horseferry Road, Lambeth Bridge leads over the Thames to **Lambeth Palace**, London home of the Archbishops of Canterbury since 1207. Here John Wycliff was questioned about his 'heretical and depraved' ideas attacking church property and powers (1378), ideas that inspired Lollardy, the biggest heresy movement of late medieval England. Here Archbishop Laud was attacked for his worldly extravagances (1640); Oliver Cromwell's men danced in the chapel; and the first Lambeth Conference (1867) was attended by 76 bishops from Britain, America and the colonies.

Here the humanist Thomas More was questioned when accused of treason (1533, executed 1535) by Thomas Cromwell (executed 1540), Henry VIII's chief minister who organised the break with Rome, which made the monarch Head of the English Church and the Archbishop of Canterbury his representative, as is true today. Henry's archbishop was Thomas Cranmer (1489–1556), who annulled his marriage and later drafted the Book of Common Prayer (first published 1549). Since 1980, Robert Runcie has been Archbishop, known for his tolerance, accessibility and diplomatic skills. The restored medieval, Tudor and Jacobean palace contains the ancient crypt, Tudor gatehouse, soaring Great Hall with library, Lollards' Tower and fashionable portraits of past archbishops. Mrs Runcie, the Archbishop's wife, is reviving the gardens. (Lambeth Palace, SE1; apply in writing to the Bursar several months in advance to join a guided tour; free. Apply to the Librarian to consult the fine library.)

Beside the Tudor gatehouse stands St Mary-at-Lambeth (1851–2, fourteenth-century tower), now the Tradescant Trust's **Museum of Garden History**, a living garden history museum where plants known in the seventeenth century fill the churchyard to honour Charles I's royal gardeners, the botanists John Tradescant and his son, also John. They collected 'all things strange and rare' (now in the Ashmolean Museum, Oxford) and are both buried here in a handsome tomb (Lambeth Palace Road, SE1, tel 261 1891/373 4030; open Mar–mid Dec, Mon–Fri 11am–3pm, Sun 10.30am–5pm; charge). The palace and church are all that survive of pre-eighteenth-century Lambeth when the surrounding marshland was just right for good duck-shoots, and transport across the Thames was a raft-like horse ferry that carried a gentleman and his coach, horses and footmen.

South of here, along Lambeth Road, an alley by some Georgian houses on the left leads to peaceful Archbishops Park, a 10-acre chunk of Lambeth Palace garden opened last century to give rosy cheeks to the local poor (nice views of Palace). The fascinating **Imperial War Museum** is 15 minutes' walk further. Founded in 1920 as the national museum of twentieth-century war, the collection squeezes into the old Bedlam asylum building (1812–15). It covers every aspect of war, civil and military, up to Vietnam. It is far more than a *Boy's Own* museum. As well as a Bristol B2F Fighter, an Anderson Shelter and Montgomery's caravan office, there are satirical carvings of Churchill and Lloyd George, the ventriloquist AL Hardon's Douglas doll who entertained troops, German straw overboots for protection against Russia's cold, early colour film of the Americans in the Pacific, and some of the 10,000 posters and paintings by Stanley Spencer, Paul Nash and other war artists. A new gallery devoted to National Service opened in 1986. (Lambeth Road, SE1, tel 735 8922; open Mon–Sat, 10am–5.50pm; Sun, 2–5.30pm; free. Guided half-hour lectures, film shows, special exhibitions, quality shop (mail order catalogue); cafe inside and lawns outside. Reference departments for art, documents, firearms, film, books and sound open by appointment. The museum also runs the Cabinet War Rooms (see p. 90), HMS *Belfast* (see p. 104) and Duxford Airfield, near Cambridge.)

Before returning to the north bank there is a good **view** of the **Palace of Westminster**, known as the **Houses of Parliament**, from Albert Embankment by Lambeth Palace. Looking at the long river facade is also a good way of seeing how the pulse of British government works. (To see inside, see p. 84.) This palace replaces the rambling old one which a fire destroyed in 1834. Only Westminster Hall, the cloisters and crypt of St Stephen's chapel, and the Jewel Tower survived. Edward the Confessor had begun the old palace, next to his abbey; but Winchester was really the capital of the peripatetic court. When William the Conqueror (1066–87) had taken London, 'overflowing' with people and 'richer in treasure than the rest of the kingdom', he needed its support. Its Saxon sophistication, its commercial prowess and its political self-reliance were in the hands of its rich and ruthless merchants. To keep watch on them, he lived and held court at nearby Westminster. And to remind them of his military strength he built the White Tower (see p. 102) in the south-east corner of the City of London. From now, Westminster Palace was the principal royal residence until Henry VIII moved into his elegant Whitehall Palace in 1512.

Meanwhile the foundations of parliament were laid in the palace's Westminster Hall, built by William II (1087–1100). Here Edward I (1272–1307) presided over the Model Parliament in 1295. Elected knights, citizens and burgesses attended, the lower clergy sitting with the lords to advise the king, and the general principles of government were agreed. The Lords met in the king's presence in the glorious Painted Chamber. But as the century progressed, the Commons began to meet separately in the Abbey Chapter House. During these years the Good Parliament (1376) acted against Edward III's corrupt court and mistress, Alice Perrers (whom they banished for corrupting judges); the Shortest Parliament (1399) met for one day to depose Richard II; and Henry VIII's Reformation Parliament (1529–36) ended Church domination of parliament and made the Commons more powerful than the Lords.

1547 was the year Henry died and the fast-moving Reformation secularised the royal chapels. Soon the Commons were meeting in the exquisite St Stephen's Chapel built by Edward I and completed by Edward III (1327–77) – tantalising pieces survive in the British Museum, see p. 167. Members sat in the choirstalls; the Speaker's chair replaced the altar – possibly the reason why Members still bow to the Speaker's chair today – and a table for the Speaker's Mace, the symbol of royal authority, replaced the lectern. To vote, the antechapel became the lobby where Members in favour (the Ayes) assembled, while Members against (the Noes) remained in the chapel.

This ex-chapel was the make-do building for the House of Commons for almost 300 years, with galleries added for Scottish and Irish members after the Acts of Union with Scotland (1707) and Ireland (1800).

Meanwhile, with king and canons gone, Members and officials sprawled over the rest of the extensive palace. In the cellars beneath the White Chamber where the Lords met, Guy Fawkes and his six Catholic conspirators were caught plotting to blow up James I and both Houses on November 5, 1605, a day still commemorated by burning effigies on bonfires (see p. 355). In the Commons, Charles I overstepped the mark in 1642 by bursting in and demanding the arrest of five Members, to which the Speaker neatly replied for all his Members that he could only speak 'as this House is pleased to direct me'. Since then, no anointed sovereign has entered the Commons Chamber. Later parliaments have included Charles II's Cavalier Parliament (1661–78), the longest to sit consecutively, and the Unreported Parliament (1768–74), which imposed reporting sanctions which Dr Samuel Johnson and others quickly broke to satisfy news-hungry Londoners – Johnson with reports thinly veiled as coming from Swift's imaginary land of Lilliput.

Then came the fire. Piles of notched elmwood tallies had been used to keep the national accounts until 1826. After this, the redundant tallies were used as firewood. On October 16, 1834, too many were put in the giant furnace. By next morning, the palace was reduced to a smouldering ruin. While carts wheeled state papers to safety, soldiers held back the huge crowds. Firemen dragged their engines inside Westminster Hall, squirted water into the roof and saved it. St Mary Undercroft, the crypt of St Stephen's, also survived (now beautifully restored and used for Members' and Peers' weddings and their children's baptisms).

For the rest, William IV's parliament, centre of his kingdom and empire, needed a new headquarters. So a competition was held for a design in the Gothic or Elizabethan style, both considered appropriately majestic and authoritative. The winner of the 97 entries was by Charles Barry (1795–1860), who provided the practical plans, and Augustus Welby Pugin (1812–52), an ardent Gothicist and Catholic convert who did all the detailed designing (and then died, mad, aged 40). The battle of the tastes was patched up into a stormy truce. The building cost over £2 million and was almost complete by 1847. The main unfinished parts were the Clock Tower (finished 1858) and the Victoria Tower (finished 1860). It was a masterpiece, symbolising a strong nation confident of its future. The young Queen Victoria (1837–1901) and her consort, Prince Albert, encouraged artists to add frescoes to Pugin's painstakingly designed Minton floor tiles, panelled ceilings, stained glass and fireplaces – even inkwells, umbrella stands, keyholes and screws. Apart from the rebuilding of the relatively dreary Commons Chamber after war damage, this recently scrubbed and restored Gothic fantasy encasing the innermost corridors of power amid ravishing sumptuousness is now as good as the day it was completed.

Looking at it from across the river, the facade is 320 yards long, decorated with statues of rulers from William the Conqueror to Victoria. Behind it, covering an eight-acre site, lie two miles of corridor, 11 courtyards, almost 1200 rooms and 100 staircases. Nevertheless, space is cramped and many MPs have to share offices scattered around Westminster. The Strangers' (non-Members) and Members' dining rooms and bars spill out onto the wide terraces, flanked by the Peers' (left) and Commons (right) libraries. As the courts will not interfere in the internal affairs of this High Court of Parliament, the bars here close on the rising of the House, often well past midnight. Inside, the machine of the constitutional monarchy operates more as an organism than an organisation.

Victoria Tower (323 feet high) at the back on the left, stores more than 3 million documents, including a master copy of every Act of Parliament since 1497. A day-time flag flying on top shows parliament is sitting. The string of main chambers runs down the centre of the building, furnished in royal red for the Lords, sombre green for the Commons.

On the left, the magnificent Royal Gallery leads to the House of Lords, perhaps the most splendid room of all. Once a year, usually November, the Queen arrives in her State Coach, comes in through Victoria Gate and sits enthroned here at the State Opening of Parliament, her lords and bishops around her as she reads the Queen's Speech, written by the government in power. This sets out the programme for the session, the parliamentary year. About a hundred laws are passed in a session, each going through various discussion stages between its beginning and becoming an Act. While the real power lies with the Commons, the Lords are an important checking body which reviews, revises and amends legislation. There are over a thousand Lords, including about 760 hereditary peers, about 340 life peers – some created each year in the Queen's New Year and Birthday Honours Lists – and 26 archbishops and bishops. About a quarter of them attend regularly. During debates, the Lord Chancellor sits on the Woolsack,

a red cushion stuffed with wool from England, Wales, Scotland, Northern Ireland and the Commonwealth Countries, while Members apparently slumped asleep are in fact listening intently to the loudspeakers installed low into the backs of the benches. It was in this splendid room that the Commons met 1941–50 while their bombed chamber was being rebuilt.

Beyond the Lords is Peers' Lobby and the Central Lobby, topped by a spire (300 feet tall). Inside, the octagonal, domed waiting hall is coated with carvings, statues and huge mosaics of four patron saints: St George (England), St Patrick (Ireland), St David (Wales) and St Andrew (Scotland). This is where Strangers (non-Members) come to listen to debates in the Strangers' Gallery or to see their MPs, who are here called by their constituency, not their name. Behind Central Lobby is St Stephen's Hall, built on the site of the chapel where the Commons developed many of its conventions (studs mark the place of the Speaker's chair and the table for his Mace). And beyond it, on the right, is William II's Westminster Hall (see p. 85).

Still looking from the river, to the right of Central Lobby, Members' Lobby leads to the House of Commons where the power struggle is played out. The players are the 650 MPs, elected at least every five years when the government calls a General Election – in 1987, only 41 women were elected MPs, one of them Margaret Thatcher for her third term as Britain's first woman prime minister. All British citizens over the age of 18 may vote. The party with the largest number of MPs is traditionally invited to form the government and the prime minister, its leader, forms a Cabinet of Ministers. About half a million civil servants – 12,000 of them beavering away in Whitehall–inform and advise the Ministers who then discuss policies and priorities at weekly cabinet meetings. The prime minister in turn informs the Queen of the government's progress and plans at an audience each Tuesday at Buckingham Palace.

Most Commonwealth countries have adopted some of the system that evolved at Westminster, especially the fundamental concepts of universal suffrage and of the ministers in power depending upon the House of Commons for their authority, making government and an elected parliament inseparable. Some say Australia has clarified the British system for their own, often robust, purposes. Certainly, India sometimes telephones Westminster to discuss a parliamentary point.

The layout of the Commons follows that of St

Stephen's Chapel. The Speaker, who chairs the debates, sits centrally, with the government in power on his right, the Opposition on his left. The prime minister and senior ministers sit on the government front bench, their 'shadows' opposite, both firmly behind red lines that were originally there to prevent sword-fights. As elsewhere in the building, there is not enough room, but the 437 seats are rarely all taken. Before business can start, the Speaker and Sarjeant at Arms arrive in procession. The Serjeant places the Mace, symbol of the royal authority delegated to the Commons, on the table, and the Chaplain says prayers before Members sit down. Now play begins and as many people as there are in the Chamber can enter the Strangers' Gallery.

As the action hots up, front bench spokesmen bash their Despatch Boxes to make a point, while backbenchers cheer or jeer. All sorts of insults are hurled in the verbal slanging matches, but never the word, 'liar'. In the galleries above the Speaker, shorthand flies across pads as the Press report the show and Hansard reporters make the official record which is then printed overnight. When it is time to vote, the Division Bells ring long and loud through every corridor of the building and in several Westminster offices, pubs, restaurants and homes. MPs not at the debate have eight minutes to down their pints or drain their claret glasses to nip along to the Aye or Noe Division Lobby parallel with the Chamber.

A debate in the Commons is one of the best free shows in town. The real cut and thrust is during prime minister's Question Time, when the main sparring partner is usually the Leader of the Opposition (Tues and Thurs, 3.15–3.30pm). The regular Question Times, Mon–Thurs at 2.30–3.30pm, are also good. For a gentler pace and easy entry, go the same days in the evening, between 6pm and 10pm – the light above Big Ben tells you if they are still sitting after that. Friday is a quiet day. The Lords, restored to glittering glory, rarely has queues and is worth visiting any time. (St Stephen's Entrance, The Houses of Parliament, SW1, 219 3000; for Commons information, 219 4272; for Lords information, 219 3107.) The parliamentary session is from mid-October to the end of July, with short breaks at Christmas and Easter. Generally, the Lords sit Mon–Wed at 2.30pm, Thurs at 3.30pm and occasionally on Fri at 11am, rising when business ends; to watch, join the right hand, shorter queue at St Stephen's Entrance at any time. Generally, the Commons sit

Mon–Thurs at 2.30–10pm or later and Fri 9.30am–3pm but rarely later; to watch, joing the long, left hand queue at St Stephen's Entrance but be warned: ticket holders only will be admitted at 2.30pm Mon–Thurs (tickets available to British residents from their MP, to non-British residents from their consulate); non-ticket holders will probably get in by 4.15pm or, much more easily, after 6pm Mon–Thurs and after 9.30am on Fri. Small bookstall stocks good guides; classy shop open only to MPs and their guests.

Finally, the Clock Tower is on the right, affectionately known as Big Ben, the name of its bell. The clock's history is an epic of disasters. When in 1844 Charles Barry planned a 316-foot-high tower with the world's biggest and best clock designed by the Queen's clockmaker Benjamin Vulliamy, the Royal Astronomer demanded extraordinary accuracy. Eventually EJ Dent (died 1853, succeeded by Frederick Dent), who made King's Cross Station clock, was chosen to make the clock. When it was made, the tower was still unfinished. When the bell was cast at Stockton-on-Tees, delivered by boat and put up, the tone was thought no good. When the clapper was doubled in weight, the bell cracked. When the new bell, cast at Whitechapel, was fitted with the old quarter bells, it too cracked, but only a little, so it was left. When the clock was put up, the mechanism was not strong enough to push round the cast-iron hands so they were remade in gunmetal. Even then, the 14-foot-long minute hand would fall several feet after it passed 12, so it was again re-made in hollow copper. As for whom the bell honours, perhaps Sir Benjamin Hall, Commissioner of Works at the palace, perhaps Benjamin Caunt, an 18-stone popular boxer who kept the Coach and Horses pub in St Martin's Lane.

On May 31, 1859, clock and bell went into operation. The dials are 23 feet in diameter; a minute space is one foot square; the hour hand is nine foot long. The chimes imitate St Mary's Church, Cambridge and are said to be based on the aria in Handel's *Messiah*, 'I know that my redeemer liveth'. When the full tune is chimed before each hour, the apt words to sing along are 'All through this hour Lord be my Guide/And by Thy Power no foot shall slide'. The BBC has broadcast the chimes at midnight on New Year's Eve since 1923; it broadcast them throughout the Second World War to signal that London was still free and today it broadcasts the midnight chimes daily. Strangely, Big Ben was not tolled for Victoria's funeral, but he was for those of subsequent monarchs. British weather has kept the disasters coming: in January 1987, freezing air changed the cheery *'boing'* sound to a thud.

Back over Lambeth Bridge, the riverside **Victoria Tower Gardens** are peopled by Auguste Rodin's bronze 'Burghers of Calais' (1915), the brave men whose lives were spared after they gave their town keys to Edward III in 1347, and a statue of Emmeline Pankhurst (1857–1928), the suffragette who, it is said, was the last inmate of the cell at the bottom of Big Ben (1902) but who in 1918 won the vote for women over thirty years old. Across the road lies the three-storeyed, moated **Jewel Tower** (1365–6, probably built by Henry Yevele), a survivor of the old palace. Built as a giant royal safe for Edward III's jewels, gold and furs, it later housed the Lords' records (1621–1864) and now displays beautiful fragments of lost Westminster buildings (Abingdon Street, SW1; open Mon–Fri, 9.30am–1pm and 2–6.30pm but until 6pm Oct 16–Mar 14; charge). Just beyond, in Old Palace Yard, you can see the back of the Abbey and how even the buttresses of Henry VII's chapel were pierced and carved to look lighter.

The Westminster facade of parliament, decorated with pre-Conquest kings, is opposite, jutting forward for the public entrance to St Stephen's Hall and Central Lobby and for William II's magnificent **Westminster Hall**. Built in 1097–9, it was 240 feet long, 68 feet wide and had six foot thick walls. Richard II rebuilt it in 1394–9, employing Henry Yevele as mason and Hugh Herland to give it a spectacular hammerbeam roof where some of Henry VIII's tennis balls were recently found.

This hall was the country's administrative centre. William II's brother, Henry I (1100–35), called his first Grand Council here and initiated its use as a law court. In the thirteenth century, the Model Parliament (1295) met here and the hall became the official Law Courts until 1882 (when they moved to the Strand, see p. 132). Sir John Oldcastle (1417, the model for Shakespeare's Falstaff), Thomas More (1535), Guy Fawkes (1605) and Charles I (1649) were tried here, as was Warren Hastings whose trial for corruption when he was governor-general of India lasted from 1788 to 1795, the longest in Westminster Hall's history. King John (1199–1216) was first of many monarchs to enjoy a lavish coronation banquet here – at Edward I's, more than 450 pigs, 400 sheep and 22,500 birds were gorged. George IV (1820–30) staged the last one, when guests were 'literally a blaze of diamonds'.

More recently, George VI lay in state here (1952), as did Sir Winston Churchill (1965).

The area from parliament up to Trafalgar Square is like a huge, outdoor sculpture park devoted to government heroes. It begins with crusader King Richard I (1157–99) and a king-like Oliver Cromwell (Lord Protector 1653–9) outside parliament. A posse of prime ministers and notable men fills Parliament Square (where plans to close the south side to traffic will make it less dangerous to reach).

The first is Sir Robert Peel (1788–1850), who founded the Metropolitan Police, was twice prime minister (PM) and died out riding on Constitution Hill. Benjamin Disraeli, Earl of Beaconsfield (1804–81) follows, a brilliant Jew who was baptised in 1817, became a flamboyant MP opposing Peel, was twice PM and pushed through the second Reform Act (1867) to double the electorate. Behind him Abraham Lincoln (1829–1906), sixteenth president of the US, and George Canning (1770–1827), who, before he became PM, fought one Commons debate as a real duel – but outside the House. Next is Edward Stanley, Earl of Derby (1799–1869), who fought for the abolition of slavery and was three times PM. Round the corner are Henry Temple, Viscount Palmerston (1784–1865), long-time Foreign Secretary and then twice PM; Field-Marshal Jan Smuts (1870–1950), President and then PM of South Africa; and the large bronze of Sir Winston Churchill (1874–1965). A soldier, journalist, historian and painter, he won his Conservative seat in 1902, switched to the Liberals in 1904, switched back in 1924 and was a brilliant war leader during his first premiership (1940–5). He was PM again 1951–5.

Along Bridge Street and past Members' Entrance, where a ringing bell and a lighted lamp on the corner means a Member wants a taxi, Westminster Bridge provides more good **views**. Proud Queen Boudicca and her rearing horses guard it, but the Roman city she devastated in AD60 lay well down river and around the corner.

County Hall (1911–22 and 1931–3), another palatial pile, sits at the south end (wide riverside terraces). It was designed by Ralph Knott for the London County Council formed out of the Metropolitan Board of Works in 1889 to run the amorphous mass of Victorian London – except, of course, the fiercely autonomous City (still independent today). Until then, London had been more successful at governing a far-flung empire than its own muddled affairs. The LCC was the first single body with substantial power to run the whole of London and be elected by Londoners. At last one administration ran everything from planning and public transport to parks and education. In 1965, it became the Greater London Council, increasing its domain from 117 square miles to 610 square miles containing 7 million people. But in 1986, Parliament abolished it. County Hall, with a 700 yard river frontage, 2,390 rooms, 10 miles of corridor, a marble-columned Chamber and a basement shooting range, went up for sale. London is back to muddling through, one of the few world capitals with no overall governing body. But many LCC and GLC achievements still stand, including the vital sewers (see p. 99), two tunnels under the Thames, six bridges rebuilt over it, quantities of housing, and the London Green Belt which in its first year, 1938–9, doubled the city's open space.

On the north side of the bridge, Victoria Embankment leads eastwards past the Norman Shaw Building (1886–90, 1906), the red and white striped Scottish castle designed by Richard Norman Shaw for the Metropolitan Police but now used as an annexe for parliament – former prime minister Harold Wilson, in retirement, had his office in one of the turrets. The cut through Richmond Terrace opens into grand **Whitehall**, part of the ancient thoroughfare linking Westminster to the City. Cardinal Thomas Wolsey (c. 1475–1530) lived here at York Place, which stretched from the river to Whitehall. Created Cardinal and Lord Chancellor in 1515, he dominated both Church and state and reigned here in royal splendour until, failing to win Henry VIII's divorce, he tumbled from favour in 1529. The king took a fancy to his home, so he moved in, renamed it **Whitehall Palace**, and added grand halls (one painted by Holbein), gardens, orchards, a bowling green and two bridges over the public thoroughfare to the royal entertainment centre: four tennis courts, a cock-pit and a tiltyard for tournaments and bear-baiting. He issued house rules: inmates were to be 'of unity and accord' and not to be 'grudging, rumbling or talking of the King's pastime'. In other words, no squabbling, no gossiping.

Whitehall became Henry's London home, within a day's ride or river journey of 13 other royal homes including nearby St James's (see p. 136), Greenwich (see p. 107), Hampton Court (see p. 112) and Windsor (see p. 275). He married two of his six wives here, Anne Boleyn and Jane Seymour, and he died here in 1547. It then remained the principal London royal residence until William and Mary (1689–1702) moved up the hill to Kensington

Palace (see p. 187) because the dank river air aggravated the king's asthma. It was here that the Stuart kings lived in astonishing splendour. James I (1603–25) dreamt of rebuilding the 2,000-room palace (only the Banqueting House was built). Charles I (1625–49) built up the outstanding royal art collection, littered with canvases by Rubens, Van Dyck and Titian. Oliver Cromwell both lived and died here. Charles II restored the monarchy (1660–85), entered London over London Bridge on May 29, 1660, his thirtieth birthday, and was crowned on April 23 the following year. Helped with money from Louis XIV, he imported French fashions to the Whitehall court and was patron to Wren's buildings, Lely's paintings and Purcell's music, while, with his queen in one apartment and his mistresses in others, he set the Palace humming with masques, gossip and intrigue. When his successor James II (1685–8) fled after three years on the throne, the Dutch Prince William of Orange and his wife Mary (James II's daughter), both Protestants, were offered the crown here. They left soon afterwards for the clean air of Kensington and Hampton Court palaces. When yet another London fire wiped out Whitehall Palace in 1698, St James's Palace nearby became the main London royal residence, where Queen Anne (1702–14) and the early Hanoverians lived and held court (see pp. 136–7).

Whitehall now slices through an estate of grandiose government houses instead of a palace. Emerging from Richmond Terrace, **Downing Street** (closed to the public) is opposite. In 1735, George II gave no. 10 to Sir Robert Walpole, Earl of Oxford (1676–1745), a skilful politician who managed to remain First Lord of the Treasury (effectively prime minister) for some years (1715–17, 1721–42) despite an earlier spell in prison for corruption. Since then, it has been the official residence of the prime minister, although some have preferred to stay in their own house, as Mary Wilson did in 1974 when Harold Wilson was re-elected as prime minister for the second time. The prime minister to live here for the longest time in recent history is Mrs Thatcher. Born in 1925, a grocer's daughter in Grantham, Lincolnshire, Margaret Hilda Roberts graduated from Oxford and worked first as a research chemist. She became the second Mrs Thatcher when she married her millionaire husband Denis whom she met at a political gathering. She then trained as a barrister and had an undistinguished political career until being unexpectedly catapulted up to become the first woman leader of the Conservative Party in 1976. Britain's first woman prime minister, she has enjoyed a record three general election victories in a row – the first since Lord Liverpool – with her uncompromising mix of market economics and domineering personal style.

No. 11, destined for the Home Secretary, has been the Chancellor of the Exchequer's home since early last century. No. 12, bought for the Judge Advocate, is now the Party Whips' office, where MPs mobilise fellow MPs and Lords of their party, whipping up support and votes on issues in Committees and in the House. All three Downing Street houses have internal connecting doors and link to the Cabinet Office building on Whitehall.

The street nestles between the Foreign Office, known as the FO, and the Treasury. Sir George Gilbert Scott designed the Foreign Office (1868–73) in fashionable Victorian Gothic, but changed it to a sensible classic Italianate palazzo to please his Conservative patron and prime minister, Lord Palmerston. It houses the Foreign and Commonwealth Offices. In front, in the middle of the road, the simple and refined **Cenotaph** (1920), designed by Sir Edwin Lutyens, was put up in 1919 as a temporary monument to the dead of the First World War. It was given Portland stone permanence the next year and is the focus of the Remembrance Sunday ritual (see p. 53). The long facade of the Treasury (1733–1844) built by William Kent, Sir John Soane and Charles Barry, leads up to Henry Holland's fine front (1787) added to earlier Dover House (1745–8), now the Scottish Office.

Beyond is **Horse Guards** (1745–55), on the site of Henry VIII's tiltyard. This long, dull building by William Kent and John Vardy provides a double-sided backdrop for the theatre of daily and annual pageantry. On the Whitehall side, the Cavalry Regiments of the Household Division (the Life Guards and the Blues and Royals) are on daily duty (guard changed hourly; see p. 51). Within the archway, the two sentries change duty every two hours. Through the arch to the Park side, the Parade Ground is the stage for two annual events: Beating Retreat (see p. 51) and, on the Saturday nearest the Queen's official birthday, Trooping the Colour, (see p. 54). In the southern corner, there is a fragment of one of Henry's tennis-court walls and a good view of Kent's part (1733–6) of the Treasury Building.

Opposite, the Ministry of Defence looms large behind Gwydyr House (1772), the Welsh Office, and one of London's finest treasures, **Banqueting**

House (1619–22). When James I dreamt of rebuilding his palace, this is as far as he got. Designed by Inigo Jones, it was possibly the first London building to be coated in Portland stone. It stood large, ordered and gleaming amid the unplanned sprawl of Henry's small-scale Tudor brick palace. It amazed everyone. Horace Walpole called it 'the model of the most pure and beautiful taste'. When Whitehall Palace burnt down, this is what survived. Inside, the crypt was for the king's small parties. The double cube room upstairs was for lavish court ceremony and entertainment. The stunning ceiling painted by Peter Paul Rubens (1634–6) for Charles I honoured the king's father, James I of England and VI of Scotland. The panels celebrate the unifications of the two countries and show the joyous benefits of wise rule – but not joyous enough to prevent Charles being beheaded on a scaffold outside one of the windows on January 30, 1649, a day remembered annually (see p. 352). Eleven years later, Charles II celebrated his restoration to the throne here. The paintings, for which Rubens was paid £3,000 and given a knighthood, are some of the finest in London (Whitehall, SW1, tel 930 4179; open Tues–Sat 10am–5pm; Sun 2–5pm; charge).

A splendid contemporary equestrian statue of Charles I, made by the Huguenot Hubert Le Sueur in 1633, looks down Whitehall from the south side of **Trafalgar Square**. When the Civil War broke out, it was hidden in the crypt of St Paul's, Covent Garden, then sold off by Cromwell's men to a brazier, who kept it intact while selling false mementoes of it to loyal Royalists and triumphant Puritans. Later, Charles II erected it here at Charing Cross in 1675, on the site where Edward I set up the largest and last of 12 crosses marking the funeral route of his wife, Eleanor of Castile, from Nottinghamshire to Westminster Abbey in 1290. Before the cross was pulled down in 1647 (there is a nineteenth-century replica in front of nearby Charing Cross Station), it was a great meeting place, where Dr Johnson saw 'the full tide of human existence'.

Trafalgar Square honours Horatio, Viscount Nelson (1758–1805), who went to sea aged 12, was an admiral at the age of 39 and after a string of sea triumphs, including the battles of St Vincent and the Nile, was created Baron Nelson of the Nile (1798) before being killed as he defeated the French and Spanish at Trafalgar in 1805. Originally the mews for royal hawks, then royal stables, the whole area was cleared in 1830 ready for John

Nash's grand plan (see p. 176). As Nash died before the site was ready, Sir Charles Barry inherited the plan. The statue of Nelson, minus an eye lost at Calvi (1794) and an arm lost at Santa Cruz (1797), went up on its 185-foot high column in 1843 (wreath laid on October 21). The hero looks down Whitehall towards Old Admiralty (1725–8) (tucked behind Robert Adam's screen (1759–61)), his headquarters and the place where his body lay in state. The gentle lions by Landseer were added in 1868. The fountains and pools (1939), some of London's most beautiful, are Lutyens' very last works in London and favourites for a cold, midnight dip to welcome the New Year. Lesser naval heroes stand at the top of the square. And the equestrian statue of the 'idle, extravagant and unpopular' George IV (see p. 177) steals no glory from the newly scrubbed sailor. (Beware of feeding the pigeons: they are liable to perch on your head.)

The square's west wall is Sir Robert Smirke's porticoed Canada House (1824–7, staircase and library worth seeing); its east is Sir Herbert Baker's South Africa House (1935), decorated with a first-floor statue of another sailor, Bartolomeu Diaz, the Portuguese navigator who rounded the Cape in 1486. And running south-east off to the right is Craven Street where Benjamin Franklin lived at no. 36 (1757–74) while he was Agent General of the Philadelphia Assembly (the house is being restored; for information, tel 828 5959). Then there are three buildings to visit on the north side: a church and two very special museums, neither overwhelmingly big.

Of James Gibbs's London churches (see also p. 120), **St Martin-in-the-Fields** (1722–4), with giant, temple-like portico topped by a tower and steeple, became the blue-print design for countless colonial churches, especially in America. Inside, beneath the delicate Italian plasterwork ceiling, painters William Hogarth and Sir Joshua Reynolds and sculptor Louis-François Roubilac were all buried in 1762, to be followed by cabinet-maker Thomas Chippendale in 1779. Dick Sheppard, vicar 1914–27, made the first radio broadcast of a church service from here (1924) and opened the crypt to homeless soldiers, now a mission for the destitute. There are regular lunchtime concerts (930 0089/1862; church open daily 8am to 9pm except Sat, 9am–5pm).

The **National Portrait Gallery**, hiding on the left up St Martin's Place, is a visual who's who of the personalities who have made British history. Founded in 1856 to display portraits of the British

great with the Victorian hope that they would inspire others to greatness, the collection has now topped 8,000 and the stipulated rule of entry by death (except for the monarch) has been bravely broken – the Victorians needed a little time to decide if someone was lastingly worthy or merely celebrated in life. Layout is chronological. So, starting at the top, you can wander through an astonishing parade of brilliant and talented faces from the icon-like Richard II to Ben Nicholson's abstract canvas of himself and Angus McBean's photograph of Vivien Leigh, each suitably labelled. Chaucer in his floppy hat, Shakespeare, Milton, Pepys and Captain Cook jostle with politicians, royals, aristocrats and lovers – Charles II's Nell Gwynn is here, so is Nelson's Lady Hamilton. More recent arrivals are Churchill, Beatrix Potter, Cardinal Hume and the Prince and Princess of Wales. As fashions changed, people sat for a jewel from Nicholas Hilliard, an arcadian dream from Sir Peter Lely or an impression by Walter Sickert. Recent additions include Beechey's romantic Horatio Nelson, Hoppe's Thomas Hardy, John Ward's Sir Harold Acton and Lucian Freud's Lord Goodman. (St Martin's Place, WC2, tel 930 1552; open Mon–Fri 10am–5pm, Sat 10am–6pm, Sun 2–6pm; free. Lectures and guided talks, special exhibitions, excellent shop. Apply also to see pictures not on view; the annexe at 15 Carlton House Terrace houses the Library of British Iconography.)

The **National Gallery** forms the north side of Trafalgar Square. It was built (1832–8) by William Wilkins on top of the royal stables (moved to Buckingham Palace, see Royal Mews, p. 92) to form the north side and focus of Trafalgar Square. In front stands a copy of JA Houdon's statue of George Washington (1732–99), first President of the US, whose English grandfather came from Northamptonshire. The **view** from the portico is especially good at sunset. Inside, Sir Michael Levey, Director 1973–86, did much to make this one of the easiest national galleries to visit in any capital. Founded in 1824 with 38 pictures, the present collection of over 2,000 paintings gives a compact and high-quality panorama of European painting from Giotto to Cézanne – the modern and most of the British paintings are at the Tate Gallery (see p. 242), leaving the National to be relatively small and manageable. All pictures are on display, some on racks in the basement. And the building is quite small, with EM Barry's interiors (1867–76) recently restored to splendour with red damask walls, stencilling and gilding. So, glancing at the plan in the entrance, it is easy (and not far to go) to find a painting to fit your mood.

Among the succession of masterpieces are Leonardo da Vinci's cartoon of the 'Virgin and Child with Saint Anne and Saint John the Baptist' (slightly damaged by gunfire in 1987), John Constable's 'The Hay Wain' and Velazquez's 'The Toilet of Venus'. Among the new arrivals are Drouais's 'Madame de Pompadour', Stubbs' 'The Milbanke' and 'Melbourne Families', Monet's 'The Gare St Lazare' and the ravishing Rubens 'Samson and Delilah'. As Sir Michael Levey says: 'Nobody should bolt a gourmet meal. My advice is always to go slowly, slowly at a few paintings, drifting rather than rushing, and wait until one of them grabs your attention' (his *250 Paintings in the National Gallery Collection* (1987) is a helpful selection). The new Sainsbury wing, designed by Robert Venturi and his wife Denise Scott-Brown and paid for by millionaire grocer brothers John, Simon and Timothy Sainsbury, should open in the early 1990s. (Trafalgar Square, WC2, tel 839 3321, recorded information 839 3526; open Mon–Sat, 10am–6pm; Sun, 2–6pm; summer evening openings with occasional evening concerts; free. Lectures, guided tours, films, audio-visual programmes, special exhibitions, artist in residence, excellent shop, exemplary café/restaurant.)

Leaving the square by Admiralty Arch (1911), the **view** through the central gates, opened for processions, stretches ahead to Buckingham Palace with the twinkling gilt 'Victory' topping the Queen Victoria Memorial in front. This surprising patch of order is quite new. At the end of last century, the world's largest capital and the hub of its huge empire had no proper processional route for its queen-empress Victoria (reigned 1837–1901). As a grandiose memorial to her, the Mall was rebuilt as a 115-foot wide road (the old road remains beside) by Sir Aston Webb, who then extended it and gave it two focuses, the triumphal arch at one end and at the other a new palace front (1913) and the great queen's memorial (1901–11), set within a huge circle to symbolise the empress at the heart of her empire.

The old Mall was part of Charles II's plan for London's first royal public park, **St James's Park**. Soon after he was on the throne in 1660, he altered the royal playground, possibly employing the creator of Versailles, André Le Nôtre. The area had been a marshy field where women lepers from St James's hospice kept their pigs. Henry VIII liked the site, made the hospice a hunting lodge and drained the marshy field, using part as a bowling alley and tiltyard. Charles extended and redesigned it for calmer pleasures. A park and ornamental canal were laid out, stocked with deer and fruit trees and enclosed by two avenues, Birdcage Walk and the Mall. Aviaries to amuse the king lined Birdcage Walk. And on the gravelled Mall he played pell mell, another courtly French import, similar to croquet. In the park, open to the public, he strolled with courtiers, mistresses and spaniels, fed the exotic ducks and even went swimming.

For the next 150 years, with the court at Whitehall and then St James's palaces, the Mall and park were the fashionable London promenades for the *beau monde*. One eighteenth-century visitor described it as 'full of people every hour of the day', ladies 'embroidered and bedaubed as much as the French'. Another wrote 'and here we see the ministers, the courtiers, the *petits maîtres* and the coquettes; here we learn the news of the day and make our parties until it is time to dress for the Court or dinner'. Still another saw 'the whole British world of gaiety, beauty and splendour'. Later, in 1814, the Regent staged an extravagant gala here to celebrate a century of Hanoverian rule. And when he became George IV, he had John Nash remodel both park and lake (1827–9), replacing French formality with romantic curves, winding paths and plenty of shrubberies, the prototype for Victorian public parks.

Today, this 93-acre royal Park is the favourite for many Londoners. Girls bask in bikinis on bank holidays; Whitehall civil servants loll in deck chairs munching sandwiches at lunchtime; and St James's gentlemen abandon their clubs to stroll at lunchtime amid the springtime daffodils and to feed the ducks. In spy fiction, this Whitehall-St James's playground is where the loitering, raincoated, clandestine meetings take place – and real life ones happen, too. Two ornithologists tend more than 1,000 birds of about 45 species that visit from all over the world and often breed here. Weeping willows, fig trees and old London planes line the banks of the lake which, at the east end, forms Duck Island, near the Cake House (ducks fed 4pm in summer, 3pm in winter). Here too are the exotic pelicans – a tradition begun when the Russian ambassador presented some in the seventeenth century (fed with whole fish on the lawn every afternoon).

From here there is a good **view** of the Parade Ground and its Whitehall backdrop and a foreground statue of Lord Kitchener of Khartoum (1850–1916), the Irish general who avenged the death of General Gordon by defeating the Khalifa in 1898. To the right stands Louis, Earl Mountbatten of Burma (1900–79), the Second World War commander and uncle of Prince Philip, who presided over India's Independence in 1947, Pakistan's creation, and was later First Sea Lord (1955–9). Behind lies the prime minister's walled garden where the Cabinet, who meet on the first floor each Tuesday morning, have their photograph taken after the first meeting of the parliamentary session – their secretaries, with offices overlooking the flowers, are known as garden girls. Clement Attlee (1883–1967), the prime minister (1945–51) who laid the foundations of the Welfare State, used to nip out of the back door to stroll through the Park to the Oxford and Cambridge Club in Pall Mall for lunch. Just beyond stands Robert, 1st Lord Clive (1725–74), the pair to Mountbatten, for Clive established British power in eastern India. The **Cabinet War Rooms** are just beyond, a fascinating underground honeycomb used by Churchill and his War Cabinet from August 1939 to September 1945 as a meeting, planning and information centre, complete with transatlantic telephone and Churchill's bedroom (Clive Steps, King Charles Street, SW1, tel 930 6961; open Tues–Sun, 10am–5.50pm; closed on State occasions; charge. Excellent acoustiguide and shop).

The **view** southwards from the park is pure eighteenth century, the back of a terrace of smart, brick houses rising high behind Birdcage Walk trees. It is worth going to have a closer look, up Cockpit Stairs in the middle of them and into **Queen Anne's Gate** (1705). Architect and painter Sir Hugh Casson considers it 'one of the best preserved sites of early eighteenth-century domestic architecture in London . . . black railings, white window bars, and elaborately carved canopies over the panelled entrance doors, huddled like houses in a cathedral close'. The discerning collectors Charles Townley and the Revd Clayton Cracherode lived here in homes filled with marbles and books now in the British Museum (see p. 166). Here Palmerston was born, and here two of Britain's most contrasting architectural institutions have their headquarters. The Architectural Press is at no.9, publishers of books and magazines that include the monthly *Architectural Review* and weekly *Architects' Journal* (publications on sale at reception); the National Trust for Places of Historic Interest or Natural Beauty is at no.36, founded in

1895 and given powers by parliament in 1907 to declare land inalienable – protected from sale unless parliament gives permission (36 Queen Anne's Gate, SW1, tel 222 9251; membership and publications available here; see also p. 17). At the end of the terrace, Charles Holden's headquarters for London Transport, Broadway House (1927–9), has sculptures by Jacob Epstein, Henry Moore and Edward Gill on the outside and mesmerising dials in the ground-floor corridor which show where the Underground trains are on each line throughout London.

Back in the Park, the path leads over the lake where the **view** from the Park bridge is a classic: the fantasy towers and turrets of Big Ben, Horse Guards and Whitehall Court and the cupolas of the old War Office rise above this green oasis where butterflies flutter, ducks dive and birdsong fills the air. Just beyond is the bandstand (performances June–Sept, 12.30–2pm and 5.30–7pm; Suns and Bank Holidays 3–4.30pm and 6–7.30pm; deckchairs for hire).

Returning to the Mall, the **Queen Victoria Memorial** is the focus of Webb's royal route. Born in 1819 the grand-daughter of George III, Queen Victoria reigned from 1837, aged 18, to her death 63 years later in 1901, overseeing the turmoil resulting from the industrial revolution at home and the rise of the largest empire in the world overseas. Of the nine statues of her in London, this is the most lavish and its creator, Thomas Brock, won a knighthood for it. The marble queen sits looking up the Mall, surrounded by female allegories of the Victorian virtues of a commercial trading nation: charity, truth and justice happily sit with progress, manufacture, war and shipbuilding, all topped by a gold-leafed 'Victory' soaring 82 feet into the air. The ornamental gates of the surrounding Memorial Gardens were gifts from her dominions: Canada, West and South Africa and Australia.

Buckingham Palace is the latest royal London home, where the Royal Standard flies when the Queen is in residence. It began as a red-brick house built in 1702–5 by William Wilde for John Sheffield, 1st Duke of Buckingham and Normandy (died 1721), on James I's mulberry tree garden (a project for producing silk that failed). One of the finest houses in London, it enjoyed superb views straight down the Mall. It caught the eye of George III (1760–1820), who bought it in 1762 for £28,000, a bargain, as a private home for his new bride, the 17-year-old Queen Charlotte, furnishing it with pictures from other palaces, Hampton Court and

Kensington. But both king and queen moved in, later adding rooms for the king's clocks and library (now in the British Museum, see p. 166) and leaving St James's Palace to be the official residence – which it still is: new foreign ambassadors are accredited to the Court of St James and then ferried in the Glass Coach to Buckingham Palace to be received by the Queen.

But when the Prince Regent, who had been living in sumptuous Carlton House overlooking St James's Park, finally became king in 1820, aged 58, he declared that neither that nor Buckingham House were grand enough. He won £200,000 out of parliament for repairs and promptly instructed John Nash to build essentially a new palace around the shell of the old one. It was to be a three-sided court of honey-coloured Bath stone, open towards the Mall and entered through a triumphant marble arch. The king died in 1830, his palace unfinished, some treasures from Carlton House installed, and bills of £700,000. His brother, William IV (1830–7), succeeded him aged 64, eccentric, modest and preferring Clarence House (near St James's Palace) to the newly built grandeur. When Victoria came to the throne, the abandoned palace had faulty drains and creaking doors. Edward Blore was brought in to tidy it up and finish it off. He also enclosed the court with a dreary east front and sent the marble arch, which was too narrow for the State Coach, off to the top of Park Lane (see p. 151). Finally, Webb re-faced the front with soulless Portland stone.

The young queen, aged 18, moved into the Palace in 1837; but apart from her jubilee celebrations (1887 and 1897) she left it under dustsheets after her beloved Albert's death in 1861. Edward VII (1901–10), George V (1910–35) and his son George VI (1936–52) were all fond of it and gradually reduced court ceremony in favour of domesticity. Edward VII's sparkling Evening Courts and the presentation parties for debutantes to 'enter Society' – the last one held in 1958 – have been replaced by the Queen with extra garden parties, informal lunches and sherry parties, whose guests have fewer titles but often more interesting careers.

Today, it is still firmly known as 'Buck House' by Londoners, and the Queen lives in a corner of the 600-room palace, about a dozen rooms on the first floor, overlooking Green Park – the royal sitting-room has the bow window. Her children have suites above. The rest of the palace is used by the Royal Household. Modern additions include lifts, swimming pool, cinema and nuclear shelter.

Sadly, the fine rooms stocked with even finer art are not open to the public. But glimpses from this treasure chest can be seen at the Queen's Gallery and Royal Mews, both on the south side of the palace (see below). The mature, 45-acre Palace garden, where the royal corgis trot amid the Queen Elizabeth roses, pink flamingoes and a mulberry tree planted in 1609, is where the Queen entertains 9,000 guests at a time for the summer garden parties. On these July afternoons, the Mall is awash with flowery dresses and top hats and for a moment becomes once more a fashionable promenade (see p. 53).

The Queen uses a side entrance facing Constitution Hill to enter and leave the Palace. Looking at the main facade, the Privy Purse Office is on the far right for official visitors, and the Queen's Royal Standard flies above the balcony where the Royal Family wave to cheering crowds, on occasions such as after the marriage of the Prince and Princess of Wales. Below, behind the newly gilded railings, the guards do their duty, changing with music, marching and magnificent solemnity. First, the Queen's colour is trooped from St James's Palace to Buckingham Palace. Then the new guard arrive with marching band from Wellington Barracks on Birdcage Walk, and touch hands with the old guard to symbolise handing over the keys. Bands play while the sentries here and at St James's Palace and Clarence House are relieved. Once complete, the old guard march off with the bands, leaving the new guard accompanied by a few drums and pipes (Apr–July daily, Aug–Mar on alternate days. Timings are roughly: trooping the colour at St James's Palace, 11.10am; new guard on parade at Wellington Barracks, 10.15am; guards change at Buckingham Palace, 11.25am–noon. Best to see new guard, then cross the park to St James's Palace by 11am, watch the ceremony and follow the Queen's colour as it marches and plays music along the Mall to Buckingham Palace, then watch from the steps of Queen Victoria's memorial. See also p. 51).

In Buckingham Palace Gate, to the left, **The Queen's Gallery** is the only part of the Palace open to the public. It was built by the Queen in 1962 on the site of her bomb-damaged chapel. Her liveried beadles watch over exhibitions selected from the extraordinarily rich Royal Collection, one of the world's finest. Sèvres, Fabergé, stamps and old master paintings and drawings reveal past, not present, royals as the great patrons and collectors (Buckingham Palace Road, SW1, tel 930 4832; open

Tues–Sat, 11am–5pm; Sun, 2–5pm; charge. Good shop for royal fans). After sampling the palace contents, the **Royal Mews**, a little further up the road, provides a taste of Nash's building. His charming stables and coach house (1826) are storerooms for the magnificent apparel of royal ceremony, including the gold-encrusted State Coach (1761, designed for George III's coronation as an exotic symbolic picture gallery) which carried the Queen to St Paul's on the Silver Jubilee, the Glass Coach which carries new ambassadors to see the Queen, the 1902 State Landau which carried the newly married Prince and Princess of Wales back from St Paul's (1980) and the newly married Duke and Duchess of York back from Westminster Abbey (1986), and a sumptuous array of harnesses – but no horses (Buckingham Palace Road, SW1, tel 930 4832; open Wed and Thurs, 2–4pm; closed Ascot Week in June and on State occasions. Good shop for horse and royal fans).

Cutting through Bressenden Place, opposite, and then turning left into Victoria Street, **Westminster Cathedral** rises on the right. Although Westminster became the chief see after the Roman Catholic hierarchy was re-established in England and Wales in 1850, some 300 years after the Reformation, it was not until 1894 that Archbishop Herbert Vaughan appointed Catholic convert John Bentley (1839–1902) architect of a new cathedral. He demanded a wide nave for big congregations, a building utterly different from nearby Westminster Abbey, and one that could be whipped up quickly and decorated later. The answer was a style mixing Byzantine and Romanesque and materials mixing brick with Portland stone. It was built by 1903. Dedicated to the Most Precious Blood of Our Lord Jesus Christ, the first public service was the Requiem Mass for Cardinal Vaughan.

Inside, the gold cross is suspended above the huge nave which is perfumed with incense and filled with smokey, blue-lit air swirling up into the mysteriously dark, still undecorated domes. Lower down, marble coats the walls. Glorious mosaics fill many of the side-chapels, shimmering in the guttering light of candles lit by the faithful. See especially the grand Lady Chapel and the peaceful Blessed Sacrament Chapel; Eric Gill's Stations of the Cross (1914–18); and Gill's reredos in the Chapel of St George and the English Martyrs, where saints Thomas More, John Fisher and John Southworth are remembered – the body of Southworth, the last secular priest to be hung, drawn and quartered (1654), lies in a crystal casket. Work continues: Elizabeth Frink is adding a bronze. Magic moments are morning peace and sung masses on Mon–Fri at 5.30pm, Sun at 10.30am.

The Campanile, dedicated to Edward the Confessor who lies in Westminster Abbey, is surmounted by a gilt cross containing a relic of the True Cross. Its balconies, 273 feet up but painlessly reached by lift, provide a stunning **view** back over the power-palaces of crown, church and state. From Buckingham Palace, you can trace a line along the Mall to Nelson's Column, then down Whitehall to Big Ben, Houses of Parliament, the Abbey and Lambeth Palace. Immediately below, the mansion blocks are home to many MPs. Further afield rise the Post Office Tower, St Paul's dome and the City sky-scrapers. (For information, 834 7452; cathedral open daily 7am–8pm except Christmas Day, 7am–4.30pm, free; Campanile open daily Good Friday–Oct 31, 10am–5pm; charge. Apply to Sister Mary, Cathedral Clergy House, 42 Francis Street, SW1 to join a guided cathedral tour at 11.15am, 12.15pm, 2pm and 4pm. Shop.)

The river: Highway for commerce, kings and commoners

Mapping it out from above: Hungerford Foot Bridge, National Theatre terraces, Waterloo Bridge, the terrace by Greenwich Observatory. Starting point: Westminster Pier; access by Underground: Westminster. Or Charing Cross Pier; access by Underground: Embankment.

Good days to explore: It is best to decide on the spot, according to the weather. Dry, preferably sunny days are a joy; cloud makes the river rather sad; drizzle and rain reduce visibility and make a river trip pointless even in a covered boat as the windows soon mist up. Take weekday or early weekend boats to avoid queues; the Crown Jewels at the Tower are closed in February; Greenwich and Hampton Court do not open until 2pm on Sun.

Vital equipment: Raincoat or jumper as protection from the river breeze; picnic lunch for long boat trips and for Hampton Court where food is low quality and scarce; change to tip the skipper's commentary; map to plot where you are.

Information

At Westminster: LTB Information Centre, Victoria, see p. 3; Westminster City Hall, Victoria Street, see p. 75.

At the Tower: LTB Information Centre, see p. 4.

At Greenwich: Greenwich Tourist Information Centre, see p. 4.

At Thames Barrier: The Thames Barrier Centre, Eastmoor Street, SE7 (854 1373).

At Richmond: Richmond Tourist Information Centre, see p. 4.

At Twickenham: Twickenham Tourist Information Centre, see p. 4.

Refreshments suggestions: See p. 310.

Local festivals: Greenwich Festival, first two weeks of June, is a burst of 250 or more concerts, fairs, theatre, fireworks and other events, many in beautiful settings. Clipper Week, 10 days in Aug, is a string of riverside festivities. The London Marathon, Apr/May, starts here (see p. 347). Information on all three from Greenwich Entertainment Service, 25 Woolwich New Road, SE18 (317 8687). In Richmond, the Richmond Festival, mid-July, is a week of street entertainment, theatre, opera and a Teddy Bear reunion in Marble Hill Park; information from Richmond Tourist Information Centre, see p. 4.

Local libraries: National Maritime Museum Library, SE3 (858 4422); open Mon–Fri 10am–6pm, Sat by appointment, Sun 2–6pm, closing 5pm all days

in winter; access by reader's ticket, best to make an appointment; research facilities broadsheets available. An unrivalled reference collection of books, manuscripts, maps, ships' draughts, journals and pamphlets etc covers every aspect of worldwide maritime history. The Museum's Print Study Room is open by appointment Wed and Thurs. Greenwich Local History Library, 90 Mycenae Road, SE3 (858 4631); open Mon 9am–8pm; Tues, Thurs and Fri 9am–5.30pm; Sat 9am–5pm. Good reference library for the whole Greenwich area, with plenty of Thames and docks material.

INFORMATION ON TRAVEL

On the water LTB River Service (tel 730 4812 for 24-hour recorded information) knows the latest on all sailings. It is worth telephoning them or the appropriate pier to check a boat is sailing as at the start and end of the season they run according to weather and demand. Allow about 15 minutes to buy a ticket and find a good seat before departure; and check return sailing times on arrival at your destination; at 2.30pm, 3pm, 3.30pm, 4pm and 5pm. The Hampton Court journey includes two locks and timing varies according to the tides. To find out how long the upstream and downstream trip will be on a certain day, Mr Wyatt (tel 930 2062) will advise; downstream is usually faster.

There are also circular, non-stop cruises at lunchtime and in the evening, mostly with bar and food:

From Westminster Pier: For lunch on Wed, Sat and Sun, boats include River Rides (regular service plus special boats to charter) (tel 839 2349/930 0970), Tidal Cruises (tel 928 9009) and Catamaran Cruisers (tel 987 1185); for dinner, book with Seekers Tours (tel 930 1827).

From Charing Cross Pier: Evening cruises (45 mins) May–Sept, 7.30pm and 8.30pm, book with Thames Cruises (tel 930 0971).

On the land If one way by river is quite enough, there is regular public transport the other way:

To and from the Tower (bus, Underground), Greenwich (regular bus; special summer bus service around Greenwich; train to Charing Cross) and the Barrier (regular bus, express summer open-top bus from Victoria, train between Charlton and Charing Cross stations). The Charing Cross train stops at Waterloo East, London Bridge,

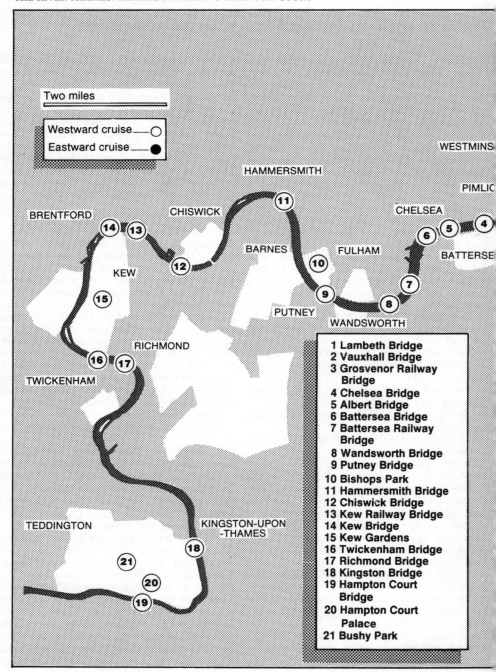

Two miles

Westward cruise —○
Eastward cruise —●

WESTMINS
PIMLIC
HAMMERSMITH
CHELSEA
BRENTFORD
CHISWICK
BATTERSE
BARNES
FULHAM
KEW
PUTNEY
WANDSWORTH
RICHMOND
TWICKENHAM
TEDDINGTON
KINGSTON-UPON-THAMES

1 Lambeth Bridge
2 Vauxhall Bridge
3 Grosvenor Railway Bridge
4 Chelsea Bridge
5 Albert Bridge
6 Battersea Bridge
7 Battersea Railway Bridge
8 Wandsworth Bridge
9 Putney Bridge
10 Bishops Park
11 Hammersmith Bridge
12 Chiswick Bridge
13 Kew Railway Bridge
14 Kew Bridge
15 Kew Gardens
16 Twickenham Bridge
17 Richmond Bridge
18 Kingston Bridge
19 Hampton Court Bridge
20 Hampton Court Palace
21 Bushy Park

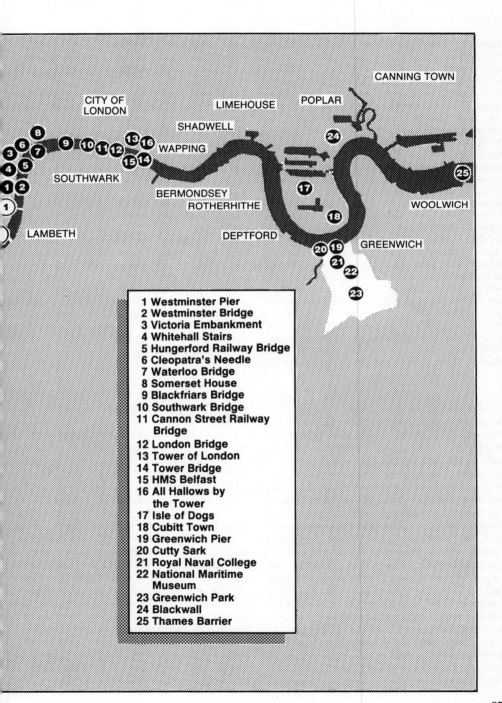

1 Westminster Pier
2 Westminster Bridge
3 Victoria Embankment
4 Whitehall Stairs
5 Hungerford Railway Bridge
6 Cleopatra's Needle
7 Waterloo Bridge
8 Somerset House
9 Blackfriars Bridge
10 Southwark Bridge
11 Cannon Street Railway
   Bridge
12 London Bridge
13 Tower of London
14 Tower Bridge
15 HMS Belfast
16 All Hallows by
   the Tower
17 Isle of Dogs
18 Cubitt Town
19 Greenwich Pier
20 Cutty Sark
21 Royal Naval College
22 National Maritime
   Museum
23 Greenwich Park
24 Blackwall
25 Thames Barrier

Deptford, Greenwich, Maze Hill, Westcombe Park, Charlton, Woolwich Dockyard and Woolwich Arsenal.

To and from Putney (bus, Underground), Kew (bus, Underground, train from Waterloo), Richmond (bus, Underground, trains from Twickenham, St Margarets and Richmond stations to and from Waterloo), Hampton Court (bus, train to Waterloo).

Boats downstream to Greenwich, etc From Westminster Pier (930 4097): Westminster Passenger Service has boats leaving for the Tower (20-min journey) and Greenwich (60-min journey) early Apr–Oct 31 every 20 mins 10.30am–4.30pm. Return sailings from Greenwich every 20 mins 11.15am–5.15pm. London Launches (tel 740 8263/930 3373) run waterbuses to the Thames Barrier (1¼hr journey) April–Oct daily 10am, 11.15am, 12.30pm, 1.30pm and 2.45pm, each returning from the Barrier 90 mins later, last sailing 4.15pm; winter months daily 11.15am and 1.30pm sailings only. Also regular circular cruises (tel 928 9009).

From Charing Cross Pier (tel 930 0971): Boats leave for the Tower (15-min journey) and Greenwich (55-min journey) Apr–Oct every 30 mins 10am–4.30pm. Return sailings from Greenwich every 30 mins 10.45am–5pm.

From Tower Pier (tel 488 0344): boats to Greenwich and, some days, to the Barrier; also boats back to Westminster.

From Greenwich Pier (tel 858 6722/3996): Campion Launches (tel 305 0333) run boats to the Barrier (20-min journey) Easter–Sept daily 11.15am, 12.30pm, 1.45pm, 3pm and 4.15pm, returning from the Barrier 30 mins later. From Barrier Gardens Pier (tel Sargent Brothers on 854 5555): Boats leave for a circular cruise (25 mins) with full commentary Easter–Sept daily every 30 mins 11am–4pm or later.

The Thames Barrier (tel 930 3373): Boats from and back to Greenwich, Westminster and, some days, the Tower.

Boats upstream to Hampton Court, etc From Westminster Pier (tel 930 2062): Boats leave for Putney (30-min journey) and Kew (90-min journey) early Apr–Oct 31, daily 10.15am, 2pm, 2.45pm and 3.30pm, returning from Kew 11.45am and then frequently 3.30–6.30pm. Boats leave for Putney, Kew, Richmond (2½hr journey) and Hampton Court (3–4hr journey) early Apr–Oct 31 daily every 30 mins 10.30am–12.30pm, returning from Hampton Court.

London exists because of the Thames. The boomtown Roman port-city founded by Emperor Claudius and renounced by Emperor Honorius rose again under the Saxons, later to be won by the Danes and then the Normans. The port was the attraction. Commerce and power blossomed, as did the number of quays and docks to load and unload rich cargo. London became the terminus for a busy water highway around the world and back. Ships set off to trade, explore, fight and govern. Some returned laden with silks, spices and jewels, others with sugar, tea and coffee. Some returned with strange plants and trees, with news of exotic lands where elephants lived, or with heroic tales of battles lost and won. Shiploads of people left to seek their fortune, serve their kind, or run away to a new life. And shiploads arrived to seek their fortune or to find refuge. From barrels of rum and bales of cotton to the Chinese, Italians, Huguenots, Jews, Greeks, Poles and Asians, the port kept London cosmopolitan in every way.

Joseph Conrad, a Polish immigrant who became a Master Seaman before devoting himself to writing, captured the greatness and romance of the Thames at the turn of the century in his novel, *Heart of Darkness*: 'The old river on its broad reach unrolled at the decline of day, after ages of good service done to the race that people its bank, spread out in the tranquil dignity of a waterway leading to the uttermost ends of the earth . . . The tidal current runs to and fro in its unceasing service, crowded with memories of men and ships it had borne to the rest of home or to the battles of the sea. It has known and served all the men of whom the nation is proud – the adventurers and the settlers . . . hunters for gold or pursuers of fame, they had all gone out on that stream, bearing the sword, and often the torch, messengers of the might within the land, bearers of the spark from sacred fire. What greatness had not floated on the ebb of that river into the mystery of an unknown earth . . . The dreams of men, the seed of commonwealth, the germs of empires.'

But the Thames was not merely the port in and out of the world's waters. It was also the local bypass. Taking a boat was a faster, cheaper and safer way to cross the City than picking through the potholes, mud, carts, pick-pockets and street-sellers in the congested alleys. It was the fast, inside route from the City merchants to the king at Whitehall and parliament at Westminster, both well upstream and around the corner. And the Thames became the heart of a network of canals that spider-webbed into Britain, providing fast cargo routes to and from the capital.

With such an overcrowded and unplanned city, the Thames became the centre of London pageantry. Robed mayors, cardinals and masters of City guilds paraded in painted boats. The king visited his string of royal palaces along the Thames. Resplendent in jewels, satins and furs, he was rowed in a gilded barge to Greenwich Palace between thousands of local rowing boats, sailing barges and the tall masts of trading and naval ships. Or he progressed gently upstream past villages, parks and forest to more palaces at Kew, Richmond and Hampton Court.

Today, Londoners have turned their backs on the Thames. It snakes silently through the capital, almost forgotten – although there has been a return of interest in the 1980s. The cargo ships, now too big to come up as far as London, use Chatham as their port. For people, Heathrow and Gatwick are the landing stages in and out of Britain. Transport within London is by land, avoiding the river with bridges and tunnels. But a boat journey through London is a great pleasure. As the river twists and turns to confuse the most compass-clear mind, London's history unfolds. Some of the buildings, statues and smugglers' pubs built facing London's busiest thoroughfare for almost two thousand years are still here, with a few up-market homes enjoying fine views and riverside gardens.

The route downstream (see p. 98) leaves one city, Westminster, for another, the City of London, then on past the Tower to Greenwich, reclining on the slopes opposite London's sparkling new third city, the revived Docklands. The route upstream (see p. 109) leaves Westminster for rural fields and parks, passing through the hearts of ancient villages that are now part of the suburban sprawl of London.

Westminster Pier is the centre of public river transport, revived in 1938 after the death of the steamboats late last century. The early Westminster monks fished near here. And today, after centuries of pollution, the Thames Water Authority has cleaned up the river so successfully that even the water-fussy salmon are back. Since the 1960s, more than a hundred species of fish have been spotted, most commonly dace, whiting, sand goby, flounder, smelt, herring, sprat and Dover sole. One fisherman caught a 64-pound conger eel in 1977, another a 33-pound pike at Twickenham in 1986; others spotted dolphin near Woolwich in 1980 and seals at Blackfriars in 1978.

It was not always so. By the last century, some 400 sewers, including parliament's, emptied their untreated contents into the Thames. Slaughterhouses, breweries, soap-works and the yards of tanners and knackers all contributed their waste. As the filthy, stinking waters sloshed up around palaces and slums, tourists refused to take boats. It was worse in summer. When the Great Stink penetrated Barry and Pugin's new waterside parliament, canvases soaked in chloride of lime were hung in the riverside committee rooms to fight it. One MP reported to the House that he and his fellow passengers on the omnibus over Westminster Bridge reached for handkerchiefs and smelling salts.

But they could do little about it. For the Thames was, predictably, run by the City Corporation. In 1197, short of cash after one of his crusades, Richard I (1189–99) handed them the river right up to Staines, together with its lucrative fishing rights. And until 1857 the City controlled it, with minimum maintenance despite parliament's complaints. After years of wrangling between sovereign and City, Queen Victoria drafted in her lawyers and the City gave back her river which by now, with the trains, bridges and pollution, was far less of a money-spinner to them. Since 1974, the Thames Water Authority has run the whole river, tidal up to Teddington (en route to Hampton Court) and tideless for 135 miles beyond to its source in the Cotswolds.

After London Bridge lost its supremacy in 1729, many road, foot and rail bridges were built and rebuilt. There are now 32 bridges between Tower Bridge and Hampton Court. **Westminster Bridge** (1738–50; rebuilt 1852–62) was London's second masonry bridge – Putney Bridge (1729) was far out of town and, anyway, made of wood. When it opened with pomp and parade in 1750, there were strict bridge rules: no dogs, and death to anyone defacing the walls. Charles Barry advised Thomas Page on the seven-arched, cast-iron replacement that blends with his parliament. In 1802, William Wordsworth crossed it in the dawn coach to Dover and wrote of the view: 'Earth has not anything to show more fair: . . . The City now doth, like a garment, wear / The beauty of the morning; silent, bare, / Ships, towers, domes, theatres, and temples lie / Open unto the fields, and to the sky; / All bright and glittering in the smokeless air' (*Upon Westminster Bridge*). Thorneycroft's bronze 'Boudicca' (1902, see p. 85) is at one end; Wordington's Coade stone lion (1837) at the other.

The watermen, who ran the boats, vigorously campaigned against Westminster Bridge, winning huge compensation: £25,000 for themselves and £21,025 for the Archbishop of Canterbury, who owned the horse ferry. Their fear was real. Back in the fourteenth century, it was the City fathers who begged the powerful watermen to limit their City–Westminster fare to twopence. By 1600, about 2,000 wherries, both small rowing boats and larger barges, ferried passengers along the Thames highway, and about 40,000 people lived off the river – bargemen, lightermen, stevedores, porters, watermen, fishermen and boat-builders. The river was lined with stairs and landing places. Humans, horses, carts, food and luggage all crossed by water. By the 1880s, with many bridges built, only 9,000 people lived off the water. The lightermen amplified their traditional work of cargo-carrying with some of the watermen's passengers. In the 1950s, several thousand lightermen still worked the Thames, some bringing newsprint from Fleet Street, rowing their hefty loads down from Purfleet with the tide. And until the 1940s, fleets of sturdy, red-sailed barges would tack across the river.

When JB Priestley opened his novel *Angel Pavement* with the words 'She came gliding along London's broadest street, and then halted, swaying gently', every reader knew that 'she' was a steamship. The empty Thames is a recent thing.

Downstream from Westminster to the Thames flood barrier

(If you are journeying upstream, turn now to p. 109)

The Thames is divided into reaches, each with a name. But this stretch, from here to Blackfriars Bridge, was un-named until it was called King's Reach to celebrate George V's Silver Jubilee (1935). County Hall (see p. 85) and then the South Bank arts complex (see p. 117) line the right bank. Sir Joseph Bazalgette's curving **Victoria Embankment** (1864–70) lines the left, an engineering feat that claimed another 37 acres for the overcrowded city from the Thames banks and simultaneously provided a wall against flooding, a riverside walk, a road, a much needed trunk sewer and an underground railway. Behind Timothy Butler's dolphin-based lamps and sphinx-ended benches rises the Norman Shaw Building (see p. 86) and the fairy-tale turrets of Whitehall Court (1884, part now a hotel) and the National Liberal Club (1887), established in the Liberal Party's heyday when William Gladstone (1809–98) was four times prime minister between 1868 and 1894.

Whitehall Stairs are in front, rebuilt by Wren for Queen Mary in 1691 as part of the riverside terrace of Whitehall Palace (see p. 86). Cardinal Wolsey, Lord Chancellor 1515–29, had lived in splendour here and would step down from his riverside York Place, robed in sable-tipped crimson satin, to be rowed in his barge to see the king at Greenwich. Evelyn watched the happy, restored Charles II come from his coronation in 1660 'Crowne Imperial on his head . . . to Westminster Stayres where he tooke Water in a Triumphal barge to White-hall where was extraordinary feasting'. But despite her terrace, Queen Mary (1702–14) claimed she could see 'nothing but water or wall' and disliked London so much she wanted to move parliament to Oxford. Hearing the rumour, a City alderman apparently remarked that as long as she was not diverting the Thames, London would do fine without out parliament. It was to Whitehall that Queen Elizabeth I's body was brought by river from Richmond (1603) and Nelson's from Greenwich (1806).

Just before Hungerford Bridge, there is a bust of

Sir Joseph Bazalgette (1819–91). His £1.55 million, three-and-a-half-mile-long embankment (built 1868–74) narrowed the river, making it run faster and, with the water flowing more freely under John Rennie's London Bridge (1831, which had fewer arches), the great Thames freeze-ups ended. Men had ridden across the river on horses (1281); people played ice football matches (1564); whole streets of shops and a printing press were erected and visited by Charles II (1683); and carriages brought crowds across the ice to watch bull-baiting and horse-racing (1684). After the last great Thames ice-fair (1813–14), the thaw came so fast that iceblocks floated away with booths, swings and people on them.

Bazalgette had another triumph. Following the cholera epidemics – an estimated 14,000 died in 1848–9 – the Metropolitan Board of Works was set up to provide a sewerage system. Bazalgette's 83-mile-long system drained a hundred square miles of buildings and his embankment trunk sewer intercepted all drains heading for the Thames and piped the muck out of London. Open in 1865, it immediately reduced the death rate. The pong endured by MPs in parliament doubtless helped push through the £4 million cost. Moored here are the *Tattershall Castle*, a paddle-steamer built in 1934 that worked in the Humber estuary and is now a floating pub, and the *Hispaniola*, once a ferry on the Firth of Clyde in Scotland, now a restaurant (see p. 310).

Hungerford Railway Bridge (1863), with foot-bridge (stunning City views), was built to carry trains right into central London, to Charing Cross Station, where the grand station hotel, still there, provided beds for Victorian visitors to the bright lights. Beyond, the South Bank's Royal Festival Hall, Queen Elizabeth Hall and Hayward Gallery are on the right (see p. 310). Charing Cross Pier is on the left, in front of Victoria Embankment Gardens where more Bazalgette reclamation has left the Duke of Buckingham's grand water-gate and steps landlocked right at the back (see p. 118). Next door are the remains of the Adam brothers' great waterside Adelphi project (1768–74, see p. 118) which sat on a plinth of tall arches where trades-men, horse-drawn carriages and carts came down to the busy broad quay. Then come the clock and smooth New York lines of Shell-Mex House (1931) and Macmurdo's bedroom wing (1903–4) of the swish Savoy Hotel (see p. 119) where the River Suites (with Terry Farrell's new ones perched on top) are taken by Danny Kaye, Meryl Streep,

Placido Domingo and other stars who can enjoy some of the most magical Thames views in London – from one balcony Claude Monet painted 18 canvases of Waterloo Bridge for his 1904 Paris exhibition. Breakfasting in the River Room beneath the suites, when the winter trees in front are leafless, is the next best thing.

With the attractions of the nineteenth-century West End, this area was the busiest for steam-boats – and the most dangerous. One exploded by Adelphi Pier in 1847, killing 30; another sank in 1878, drowning 700. Smart little paddle steamers ferried locals about; larger ones took day-trippers and holiday-makers down to the Thames estuary and the seaside; and smoke-belching steam tugs dragged strings of barges, competing with the big red sails of the fleets of sailing barges.

On the left bank, **Cleopatra's Needle** has nothing to do with the great queen. Made in 1450BC, the 86-foot-tall obelisk of pink granite weighs 186 tons, records triumphs of Rameses the Great and is the oldest monument in London. The Romans moved it from Heliopolis to Alexandria in 23BC; the Viceroy of Egypt gave it to Britain in 1819; it arrived here in 1878 when it was erected and a bundle of newspapers, coins, toys, a railway guide, some hairpins and a picture of Queen Victoria were buried underneath to give a rather crooked picture of the year to posterity. GJ Vulliamy added the bronze sphinxes in 1882; the bomb scars are from a First World War Zeppelin; and an anonymous Arab paid for it to be cleaned in 1979.

Waterloo Bridge (1811–17, rebuilt 1939–45) honours the final defeat of Napoleon in 1815 at Waterloo, near Brussels, by British and Prussian forces led by Wellington (see p. 143) and Blucher. To the fury of Londoners, John Rennie's elegant span, described by the Italian painter Canova as 'worth a visit from the remotest corners of the earth', was demolished in favour of Sir Giles Gilbert Scott's cantilevered concrete. Excellent views of its arches from the National Film Theatre's river-level restaurant, and of London eastwards to the City and south back to Westminster from on top. It was here that an early London visitor lost his hat: during the Viking raids of the ninth and tenth centuries – they stormed London with 350 ships in 851 – a ceremonial horned bronze helmet fell into the Thames (now in the Museum of London).

The best view of **Somerset House** (1776–86), London's most palatial civil servant warren, is on the left. It replaced London's first Renaissance palace (1547–50) where successive female royals lived (princess Elizabeth, Anne of Denmark, Henrietta Maria, Catherine of Braganza) until Queen Charlotte made it redundant by going to Buckingham Palace (see p. 89). Inigo Jones (1573–1652), architect of the Queen's House at Greenwich (see p. 107), the Banqueting House (see p. 87) and the Queen's Chapel (see p. 136), had apartments here. James I lay in state here in 1625 before the most extravagant London funeral ever staged, with 8,000 mourners and a total bill of £50,000.

William Chambers, architect of the new building, faced a triple challenge: to compete with what he was replacing; to outshine his rivals, the Adam brothers, who had just finished the successful Adelphi; and to produce the first major public building since Wren's Royal Naval College in 1696–1702 (see p. 107). The facade, which dropped down to the water, was later extended to left and right. From 1837 until 1973, all births, deaths and marriages in Britain were registered here, a job now done at nearby St Catherine's House, leaving the tax-collectors of the Inland Revenue to share the good views with the Courtauld Institute's magnificent collection housed in Chambers' equally fine rooms (see pp. 119–20).

Beyond, legal London stretches up from Inner Temple Garden (see p. 131). In 1858 (just before Bazalgette's clean-up), while one MP asked parliament why any foreigner would visit their new buildings when he would be welcomed by a stench which was overpowering', a lawyer wrote a tirade from the Temple to *The Times*: 'We are enveloped in the foul miasma, which spreads on either side of this repository of the filth of nigh three millions of human beings, and day and night every breath of air which we draw for the sustenance of life is tainted with its poisonous exhalations.' Moored in today's cleaner waters in front are three ships: HMS *Wellington* is the apt Company Hall for the Master Mariners, whose company was founded in 1926 and received its Livery in 1932, the first for 223 years, (see p. 62); HMS *Chrysanthemum*, a First World War sloop, and HMS *President* are both used as the London headquarters of the Royal Naval Reserve. The white steeple of St Bride's is above (see p. 129).

The silver, cast-iron griffins (1849) up on the Embankment herald the beginning of the City of London and the end of the City of Westminster. From Temple Stairs, the Queen's Swan Keeper leads the keepers of the Vintners and Dyers companies and the swanherds to a fleet of boats, banners flying, for the merry annual Swan Upping trip

to Henley-on-Thames. Their purpose is to mark the new cygnets' beaks on the way (July–Aug, see p. 354). It is said that Queen Beatrice of Cyprus gave swans to Richard I (1189–99), since when they have enjoyed royal protection. The annual count began in 1496, when stealing a swan's egg brought a year in jail. Only royals, nobles, the (almost noble) City Livery Companies and the nobles' school, Eton College, could own swans. Today, only the Queen and the Dyers and Vintners own the Thames swans, whose beaks are nicked once for Dyers, twice for Vintners and not at all for the royal birds.

On the right, past the terraces of the National Theatre (see p. 117), warehouses now jostle with office towers for television, computers and magazines. **Blackfriars Bridge** (1760–9, rebuilt 1860–9, widened 1907–10) marks the mouth of the River Fleet which had busy wharfs until it was arched over during the eighteenth century and now lies hidden beneath Farringdon Street. This was the next bridge to be built after Westminster, signalling London's expansion south of the river. When Joseph Cubitt and H Carr's bold iron arches replaced Robert Mylne's stone ones, Londoners were aghast; and when Queen Victoria, at her lowest ebb of popularity, opened it, they hissed at her carriage. **Blackfriars Railway Bridges** follow, the first (1862–4) disused (but the splendid pillars still stand), the second (1884–6) still carrying City commuters into Blackfriars Railway Station. Near here the remains of a flat-bottomed Roman sailing barge loaded with ragstone were found in 1962, a casualty during the third-century city wall building.

On the left, the stairs and wharfs lead back through narrow alleys to Wren's dome for St Paul's (see p. 65) and to the tower and spire housing Bow Bells which rang out the daily curfew for the rivermen (see p. 64). Along the front, the Mermaid Theatre is in Puddle Dock. After St Benet's church come Queenhithe Stairs, named after Matilda, wife of Henry I (1100–35), who built London's first public lavatory here. This was London's major wharf from Saxon times until the fifteenth century, when the bigger boats preferred to keep below London Bridge and Billingsgate took precedence. On the right, Bankside has radically altered since Ian Nairn wrote in only 1966 of 'the dirty water slapping around the bows of barges' (see p. 73) and the quiet, open view is dominated by Sir Giles Gilbert Scott's Bankside Power Station (1929–55).

As south London grew, **Southwark Bridge**

(1814–19, rebuilt 1912–21 to Sir Ernest George's designs) and **Cannon Street Railway Bridge** (1863–6) were added, delivering their passengers into overcrowded London. The population in the centre topped a million in 1811 and reached a peak of 4.5 million in 1901 (it is now about 2.5 million). Southwark was where haddock-smokers, bone-boilers and makers of catgut and soap worked, a place for 'all disagreeable-smelling trades'. Thousands of people were hemmed in together, living in back-to-back houses with tiny alleys ideal for thieves. On Sunday mornings, women dressed in only a shirt fought 'like wild beasts' to settle the week's grievances. It was a far cry from the palace of the Bishops of Winchester which stood on the riverfront surrounded by a 70-acre park and cathedral from 1109 to 1642 and was visited by Henry VIII. During the English Revolution of Oliver Cromwell, it became a prison for royalists and the park was leased for building soon after. The *Kathleen and May* schooner is the most recent arrival of the Thames's ships (see p. 62).

On the left bank, the Romans began their settlement around Walbrook Stream. This, their main water supply, emptied into the river just past the bridge. Their Temple to Mithras (see p. 64) and the later churches of St Stephen Walbrook (see p. 64) and St Margaret Lothbury (see p. 69) stood on its banks. But by the fifteenth century the Walbrook was covered over. St Michael Paternoster Royal looks down between the two bridges, headquarters of the Missions to Seamen since 1968 (see p. 73). The *Livery Barge Regalia*, a new floating bar and restaurant honouring the old ceremonial barges, is moored in front of deserted wharfs. Trigg Stairs Heliport does some of their job now, whisking City directors in over the traffic to deal-clinching lunches, then back to their country homes.

Under **London Bridge** (see p. 61), London's first and only crossing until 1729, the Tower looms in the distance. The deserted wharfs of Bermondsey on the right have mostly been destroyed to make way for London Bridge City (see p. 260). Goodhart-Rendel's Hay's Wharf (1931–2), incorporated into the new gleam, is a rare survivor.

Monuments to the fish trade, vital to London's diet, are on the left: the Fishmongers' Hall, church and market (pp. 62 and 73), with the gilt-topped Monument to the Great Fire of 1660 behind (see p. 63). The Romans constructed their new, 550-metre-long quay here in the third century, pushing the land forward into their river 'Thamesis' to where Lower and Upper Thames streets and St Magnus Martyr are now. Later landowners pushed it still further, encouraging citizens to dump their rubbish behind new breastworks every 30 years or so – Bazalgette was not the first land reclaimer. By the fifteenth century, Billingsgate was the main docking area, south of London Bridge whose many arches made the water fast-flowing and dangerous, like rapids. Even locals were wary of its tricky waters. When Cardinal Wolsey took his barge from Westminster to Greenwich, he prudently alighted at Old Swan Stairs (where *Regalia* is moored), paraded along Thames Street holding a vinegar-scented sponge in an orange skin to beat off the stench, and stepped back on board at Billingsgate. Just beyond, Sir Robert Smirke's long, porticoed river facade (1825) of the Custom House is the last of a succession of buildings begun in 1275.

The Honorable Company of Watermen established their hall near here (see p. 73). Watermen not only flocked to the piers, stairs and wharfs to answer cries of 'oars, oars' or 'sculls, sculls'. They also had grander jobs, rowing the gilded barges for City Livery Company parades. And, from 1422 until 1856, they took the Lord Mayor elect to Westminster to seek the king's approval, a thoroughly ritual ride given added sparkle in 1452 by an ostentatious new barge with silver oars. The Lord Mayor's pageants reached heights of extravagance in the sixteenth and seventeenth centuries. A fleet of Livery Company barges, each decorated with its arms, followed the glistening oars while the Lord Mayor elect sat in scarlet and gold splendour. For Thomas Middleton's pageant in 1613, five islands were built on the Thames and decorated with Indian fruit trees, spices and a 'faire castle especially beautified'.

With the king based away up at Westminster, such lavish displays of wealth and power by the merchants needed to be dampened with a local show of brute military strength. The **Tower of London** was the answer, built right by their source of wealth, the docks, and between them and the open sea. William I (1066–87) began it; Edward I (1272–1307) completed it. It is the most perfect medieval fortress in Britain, serving as both palace and prison. Covering 18 acres, it is now London's smallest village. 55 families live here, tending their geraniums and playing bowls on the ex-moat, their village green. The Deputy-Governor lives in sleeping quarters used by Edward I, II and III; one of the

42 Yeoman Warders, founded by Henry VII in 1485, lives where the Royal Mint was in 1590. But each night they still ceremoniously lock the gates against the dangerous London mob.

Like Westminster Abbey, the Tower is an integral part of British history since the Conquest. Memories of highest triumphs and deepest horrors fill its romantic buildings which are film-set perfection of what a tower ought to be.

The Norman conqueror quickly threw up a temporary fort between the Saxon walls and the 20-foot-high Roman ones. Later he began his Caen stone keep, the White Tower, completed by William II (1087–1100) and Henry I (1100–35). Walls were 90 feet high and 15 feet thick. The single door was on the south side, 15 feet up with a removable staircase. Inside, the four storeys watching over the double threat of London to the west and the Thames estuary to the east were well equipped with three wells, space for soldiers, servants, nobles and royalty, a banqueting hall and council chamber, the exquisitely simple St John's Chapel, lavatories on the top three floors, and an anti-clockwise spiral staircase (from top to bottom) so that defenders could fight as they went down. There was also Little Ease, a four-foot-square prison cell in the dungeons. It was an excellent defence.

Henry I added the chapel of St Peter ad Vincula (rebuilt 1520). Henry II added kitchens, bakery and gaol. Richard I (1189–99), who gave the Thames to the City, went off to the crusades leaving William of Longchamp to add wall, Bell Tower, Wardrobe Towers and ditch before he was successfully besieged by Prince John who, as king (1199–1216), strengthened it. Henry III (1216–72) began the inner wall, the moat and the royal palace, whitewashed the White Tower – hence its name – and started the menagerie. The Holy Roman Emperor gave him three leopards, Louis XIV gave an elephant and the King of Norway sent a polar bear which went fishing in the Thames on a lead. Edward I (1272–1307) completed the western inner wall with its Beauchamp Tower and most of the Outer Wall with riverside Byward Tower and Traitors' Gate. He then moved in the mint and Crown Jewels from Westminster – the jewels were all seized during Cromwell's Commonwealth. In the last 700 years, the armouries, museum and Waterloo Barracks are the main additions – the barracks built in the 1840s, when the moat was dried. Titivations include the fourteenth-century cupolas on the White Tower; Henry VIII's two large circular bastions on the north side and his half-timber houses on Tower Green including Queen's House; and some theatrical Victorian restoration.

The Tower was the stage for a succession of public shows. King Stephen (1135–54) was the first king to live there; James I (1603–25) was the last. James made the lions and bears of his menagerie give public fights which he watched from the Lion Tower. The pre-coronation festivities and processions through London to Westminster Abbey began here. At Edward I's coronation, he flung coins into tapestry-hung streets literally running with wine (1272). Before his coronation, Henry IV initiated the ceremony of the Bath when he knighted 46 nobles in the White Tower baths, after which they prayed all night in St John's chapel (1399). After his crowning, Edward IV played courtly games and picnicked on the Tower lawns (1460s). The Cheapside goldsmiths hung out cloth of gold for Henry VIII (1509). A Dutch acrobat balanced on top of St Paul's spire for Mary (1553). Elizabeth I, who as princess had arrived through Traitor's Gate, rode in a golden chariot through triumphal street arches and past loyal tableaux at her coronation (1559). Returning from exile in France, Charles II's spring festivities included a new set of Crown Jewels and was the last such pageant at the Tower (1661).

Some shows were less festive. The Barons seized the Tower, forced King John to sign the Magna Carta (1215), then imported the French Dauphin, Louis, to the Tower to be king (1216). Edward II's queen helped her lover Roger Mortimer seize the Tower, release the prisoners, give the keys to the Londoners and then rule for the prisoner boy-king, Edward III (1326). Other shows starred the London mob. While Henry III hid here, they pelted his queen with rubbish at London Bridge (1261). After Richard II made promises to Wat Tyler and his rebel peasants at Mile End, they broke into the Tower, ransacked it and dragged out their four worst enemies to behead them on Tower Hill (1381) – the king later calmed the rebels (see p. 201).

There were appalling horrors. Edward I took 600 Jews prisoner, hanged 267 of them and banished the rest (1278–9). Richard of Gloucester went off to be crowned Richard III, leaving his two prince nephews to be murdered in the Bloody Tower the next month (1483). Sir Thomas Overbury was murdered by a slow and painful three months of poison (1612). When Charles I sent six MPs here for upsetting his favourite, the Duke of Buckingham (see p.

118), one took three years to die from tuberculosis contracted in the filthy cells (1629–32). But whether king or pauper, Protestant or Catholic, many have left the Tower alive, even recently. Princess Elizabeth (later Elizabeth I) did, biding her time exercising on the ramparts between Bell and Beauchamp towers (1554); Sir Roger Casement, the Irish Nationalist and traitor, who left the Tower to be hanged at Pentonville in 1916, did not.

The pace of executions stepped up after Henry VIII's Reformation, reaching a climax of Catholic and Jesuit persecution at the end of the sixteenth century. Torture could be grisly. In 1446 when the Duke of Exeter was Constable of the Tower he had introduced the rack, known ever since as the 'Duke of Exeter's daughter'. Edmund Campion was stretched on it three times and did a spell in Little Ease, but still did not confess. The 'Scavenger's Daughter' had the opposite effect, crushing its victim with two iron hoops until blood spouted 'from nostrils, the mouth and the anus'. Father Garard, a Jesuit, was twice hung up by the hands in manacles (1597). There were also thumb screws, a spiked collar, and a dungeon below the watermark that brought up hungry rats with each tide. Execution was two-tiered: Anne Boleyn (1536) Catherine Howard (1542) and Elizabeth I's dear Earl of Essex (1601) were executed quietly on Tower Green, an exclusive privilege; but Thomas Cromwell (1540), Edmund Campion (1581) Archbishop Laud (1644), the Duke of Monmouth (1668) (whose executioner resorted to a knife when he was still alive after five chops with the axe) and many more provided entertainment and spectacle for a jeering mob up on Tower Hill. The first to be beheaded there was Sir Simon de Burley, Richard II's tutor (1386); the last, and the last in England, was a Jacobite, Lord Lovat (1747).

The best way to arrive at the Tower is by river: passing under London Bridge, you can imagine how prisoners arriving by boat saw the severed heads of previous inmates pinned on to the spikes of the old bridge, especially upsetting for Catherine Howard who saw her lover, Culpeper, there, and for Princess Elizabeth (later Elizabeth I), daughter of beheaded Anne Boleyn. Second best is to arrive by road from the west, pausing in front of All Hallows church for a first **view** of the Tower sprawling up Tower Hill, the decorative Tower Bridge beyond. Least impressive is arriving by Underground. Magical moments are early mornings, which also beat long summer queues for the Crown Jewels, and the Ceremony of the Keys at night (see p. 51); coach parties peak in the afternoon.

There is a lot to see at the Tower. The building is palace, fortress, state prison and execution site. It houses three museums and the Crown Jewels. Entering through Byward Tower, it is worth heading straight for the Crown Jewels in Waterloo Barracks, found by turning left at the Traitor's Gate and going up the stairs past the execution site on Tower Green and St Peter ad Vincula church. The rock-studded gold and silver pieces bedazzle: the ampulla and spoon for anointing the sovereign (probably first used for Henry IV in 1399, hidden from Cromwell by the Westminster monks); the luscious Imperial Mantle; the royal orbs, sceptres, rings and dozen or so crowns; the Koh-i-Nur and First Star of Africa diamonds; the Maundy Dish (see p. 53) and much more, all polished by the royal jewellers, Garrard, every February.

The White Tower houses the mystical St John's Chapel on the second floor, while the magnificent Royal Armouries museum fills the other rooms with finely fashioned French hunting spears, German jousting helmets, Italian swords and complete shining suits for kings, young princes and their horses. The collection spills over into the Waterloo Barracks where oriental armour includes a complete suite for an Indian elephant, a Turkish helmet to go over a turban and an extensive Japanese wardrobe. An executioner's mask and a Scavenger's Daughter are with the torture instruments in the Bowyer Tower behind. Modern armour of the last two centuries is housed on the east side, down past the Heralds' Museum, which traces the history of heraldry, recognising one man from another by his emblems. The art was practised by heralds who have acted as messengers, diplomats and army staff officers (to identify the enemy) since the twelfth-century crusades. Today, still appointed by the Queen and headed by the Earl Marshall (the Duke of Norfolk), they dress in gold-embroidered scarlet to play their part in the panoply of annual state pageantry, such as the State Opening of Parliament and the Order of the Garter procession (see also College of Arms, p. 64). Finally the Royal Regiment of Fusiliers has its own small historical museum here.

There are other treats to find. Up in the northeast corner, Henry III's towers and walls are now open as the Wall Walk, running from Martin Tower (good **views**) through Constable Tower (home of a Yeoman Warder) and Broad Arrow Tower (furnished to be Sir Simon Burley's chamber – knight and tutor to Richard II) down to Salt Tower (left as a classic wall tower with military basement and domestic rooms above). In the gardens towards the river there is a chunk of the third-century Roman wall by the White Tower. Here live the six Tower Ravens – if they leave, the superstition holds that the White Tower and Commonwealth will fall – tended in their wood-panelled quarters by the Raven Master who knows them by name: Larry, Hardy, George, Hugin, Mumia and Rhys.

The palace and Great Hall stood nearby, towards the river. And just here you can go out to Tower Wharf, a good refreshment spot. (Her Majesty's Tower of London, EC3, tel 709 0765; open Mar 1–Oct 31 Mon–Sat, 9.30am–5.45pm and Sun, 2–5.45pm, Nov 1–Feb 28 Mon–Sat, 9.30am–4.30pm only; charge includes Jewel House and Armouries. Yeoman Warders give entertaining tours which include St Peter ad Vincula, otherwise closed, leaving from inside the Byward Tower every 30 mins and lasting an hour. Jewel House, tel and times as for Tower but closed February, excellent catalogue; Royal Armouries, tel 480 6358, times as for Tower, excellent catalogue and on-site warders; Heralds' Museum, tel 236 9857/584 0930, open Apr 1–Sept 30, times as for Tower, charge; Fusiliers Museum, tel and times as for Tower, charge. St Peter ad Vincula open for Sunday services at 9.15am and 11am; free. To attend the nightly Ceremony of the Keys, apply well in advance in writing to The Governor, indicating the dates you prefer and leaving time for the tickets to be sent to your home address as they will not be sent to hotels, see p. 51. Extensive bookshop by West Gate; many lavatories but no refreshments; pass-out tickets available.)

There is plenty more to see on and around Tower Hill. Leaving by Wakefield Tower (collecting a re-entry ticket if you wish to return the same day), Tower Wharf stretches east and west (tel 481 1882, open Mon–Sat 7am–6.30pm or later, Sun 10am–6.30pm or later; free; refreshments). To the east lies St Katharine Dock, the first part of the old Docklands to be regenerated. The Hospice of St Katharine was founded by Queen Matilda (1146). More than a thousand houses were ripped down for Thomas Telford's docks (1824–8) which built the latest designs for the growing empire. After war bombs and the death of the docks, St Katharine closed in 1968 but was soon revived as both yacht haven and business centre (see p. 260). Now smart yachts and restored barges are moored near the old London Docks tug, *Challenge*, and a Thames estuary lightship, *Nore*. (There will be more historic ships to visit in West India Dock, see p. 257.)

Tower Bridge (1886–94) is the only bridge downstream of London Bridge. Beyond here, Londoners still depend upon ferries and tunnels (although an East London bridge beyond the Barrier is planned). Horace Jones designed it to partner the Tower in looks but to open 135 feet high for modern shipping. John Wolfe-Barry engineered it, constructing its stone-clad towers in steel to support the bascules and contain lifts up to the footbridge, now the **Tower Bridge Museum** (superb **views**) which continues underneath the south end where the steam-pumping engines of the old hydraulics are kept (Tower Bridge, SE1, tel 407 0922; open daily Apr 1–Oct 31, 10am–6.30pm, Nov 1–Mar 31, 10am–4.45pm; charge; shop). The bridge went electric in 1976 and is opened often (tel 407 0922 for times). Because the Thames is tidal, the odd height miscalculation is made and in 1986 a crane being moved by boat crashed into the gantry. Some openings are merely ceremonial, as when Sir Francis Chichester returned from sailing around the world (1967, see p. 107) and when Richard Branson finished his record-breaking Atlantic Crossing (1986).

HMS Belfast, a Second World War cruiser that is now an excellent outpost of the Imperial War Museum (see p. 81), is moored on the south bank, its sailors' rooms, machinery and weapons all on show found by climbing up and down countless ladders (Symons Wharf, Vine Lane, SE1, tel 407 6434; open daily Mar 21–Oct 31, 11am–5.30pm, Nov 1–Mar 20, 11am–4.30pm; charge; shop; café). Instead of returning over the bridge, a ferry runs across to Tower Pier (daily Feb 8–Nov 8, Sat and Sun only Nov 9–Feb 7), a survivor of the numerous ferries that criss-crossed the river, cheaper than the old bridge tolls and essential to carry dockworkers to and from work in bridgeless east London. Beneath it runs Tower Subway (1869) which carried trams and pedestrians until Tower Bridge was built.

From Tower Pier, Tower Hill leads up to **All Hallows by the Tower** (c.1000–60, 1634–5 and 1949–58, tower 1658–9), also called All Hallows Barking because the land belonged to Barking Abbey (founded 675). Well worth visiting the church and medieval crypt and vaults to trace its history from tessellated Roman pavement and Saxon arch to Tudor monuments, fine sword-rests and brasses and a tour-de-force carved font cover probably by Grinling Gibbons. The bodies of Bishop Fisher (1535) and Archbishop Laud (1645), victims of the nearby gallows, rested here temporarily. American links are strong: Admiral Sir William Penn (whose son William founded Pennsylvania state, USA, and named it after his father) was christened here (1644); John Quincy Adams (1767–1843, who became the sixth President of the US) was married here (1797) while minister resident to the court of St James's. In the crypt, the altar survives from its journey with Richard I on his crusades. (Tel 481 2928; open Mon–Fri 9am–6pm, Sat 10.30am–6pm, Sun 10am–6pm; good tours). Samuel Pepys (1633–1703), the diarist and distinguished Secretary to the Admiralty, was a friend of Penn and when the Great Fire raged in 1666 he went up 'Barkeing steeple, and there saw the saddest sight of desolation' before going round to 'eat a piece of cold meat' at the Admiral's home. Seething Lane, across the road, is where Pepys lived and where he worshipped at **St Olave's** church (fifteenth century), a rare City survivor of both Fire and bombs, with pretty churchyard and memorials inside that include one to Pepys's wife Elizabeth (by John Bushnell, 1672) and a much later one to Pepys (by Arthur Blomfield, 1884) (tel 488 4318; open Mon–Fri 8am–5pm).

From the garden of All Hallows there is a good **view** out from the City across Tower Hill which slowly changed from execution site to marine acropolis. Straight ahead lie the smooth curves of Lutyens's Mercantile Marine Memorial (1922–52). On the left, in Trinity Square, Sir Edwin Cooper's palatial Port of London Authority building (1912) is now home for an insurance company. Samuel Wyatt's Trinity House (1792–4) is behind, centre for harbour pilots and lighthouses. The gallows stood in front, now marked in the ground. Beyond rises the largest remaining chunk of Roman wall. And on the far side Sir Robert Smirke's Royal Mint (1808–9), built when money-manufacturing was moved out of the Tower, is now redundant, the mint flown to Cardiff and Smirke's royal factory to be restored and cleaned, with offices behind and a museum of Roman finds. Making a little detour left beyond the Roman wall, then left again, the Crescent (1760–70) is a tantalising remnant of George Dance the Younger's East End answer to the West End Georgian developments, his stretching north right up Vine Street.

The cityscape from Tower Pier down to the Thames Barrier has undergone two radical upheavals. The river that makes its hair-pin bends through miles of mirror-flat land used to pass thriving, ancient maritime villages, each with its own character, trades and heroes. First, the nineteenth-century docks swallowed them up to make a vast landing stage for the wealth that poured into the world's trading capital, leaving them desolate when the docks became redundant after the Second World War. Now, recently given a commercial kiss of life, they are part of the London Docklands Development Scheme, the largest urban redevelopment project in Western Europe (see p. 246).

Leaving Tower Bridge behind, Upper Pool Reach stretches to the first twist. On the right lies **Bermondsey**, where an eleventh-century abbey and some Knights Templar land (see p. 130) later became a brewing and leather centre with three and a half miles of thriving wharfs lining its riverfront from London Bridge downwards. Until recently, Courage's Brewery (1891) sweetened the air with a whiff of hops. Beyond Shad Thames Dock, the Old Justice and Angel smugglers' pubs look out from behind Cherry Garden Pier, formerly the stop for pretty pleasure gardens and a spa, now the place a ship sounds her horn if she needs Tower Bridge opened. On the left, **Wapping**'s tall warehouses, punctuated with piers and jetties leading up dark, narrow alleys, grew out of the Tudor village. In 1598 Stowe described it as 'a continual street or filthy passage with allies of small tenements and cottages'. Here Charles II's rowdy sailors lived in lodging-houses among the mastmakers and boatbuilders. It was by the Town of Ramsgate pub that wicked Judge Jeffries (see p. 131) was caught trying to escape to France disguised as a sailor. And, as the river bends, Execution Docks is where pirates were hanged and ritually washed by three tides.

This was one of the first areas to be affected by the docks. By 1800 London was the largest port in the world. At any one time, about 8,000 boats of every size and type crammed into the six-mile stretch of dockland, two miles of them above London Bridge. The greatest chaos was here at Upper Pool. 1,775 ships would be moored in space meant for 550 much smaller vessels. The muddle meant cargo unloaded by the lightermen from ships moored mid-stream was then dumped on a quay and left unguarded for weeks. It was a smugglers' and thieves' paradise. A third of port workers were on the racket; half of all cargo disappeared.

The short-term solution was the River Police, founded in 1769 at the instigation of merchants trading in the lucrative West Indies. Armed with cutlasses and blunderbusses and paid by the merchants, the police, many recruited from the watermen, used long-oared gigs to load and unload cargo. They were so effective that from 1801 the government footed the bill – London's first land policeman went on the beat 28 years later. Today's Thames Police keep most of their fleet in the next stretch of river, **Lower Pool**, near their old beat.

The long-term solution was to enclose the Docks. When the Thames was under the full force of the Industrial Revolution and the expanding Empire, the docks were built in a typically London way: large projects were discussed, none realised, and the docks were developed piecemeal by private companies. Between 1802 and 1921, docks ranging from tiny ten-acre St Katharine to the huge 245-acre Royal System cut a patchwork of mirror rectangles into the land between the Tower and Galleons Reach 10 miles downstream.

The 27-acre London Docks (1805), built on meadowland behind Wapping, were for some time the nearest to the City. Whereas wool, sugar and rum were mainly unloaded at St Katharine's, cargoes of tobacco, rice, wool, wine and brandy, as well as the exotic ivory, spices, coffee and cocoa, went into these vaulted wine cellars and magnificent, four-storey warehouses, the whole complex surrounded by a high wall. They later took over St Katharine's Dock (1828) to the west and pushed east to form Shadwell Basin. Until then, **Shadwell** was a densely populated marine hamlet where watermen, lightermen and sailors lived among the roperies, tan yards and taverns. Sir Martin Frobisher (1535–94), hero of the Armada (1588), set sail from here in search of gold and a passage to China. Captain James Cook (1728–79) stayed here between his three explorations to the Pacific which almost doubled the size of the known geographic world. Today, the pumping station behind the Prospect of Whitby pub is home to the Academy of St Martin-in-the-Fields (see p. 259).

As the river twists back to the right, the Georgian terrace of Narrow Street, including the Grapes pub (said to be the model of Dickens's Six Jolly Fellowship Porters in *Our Mutual Friend*), masks Limehouse Basin on the left. Barge-loads of coal arrived here down the Grand Union Canal that linked into the countrywide network of canal highways. **Limehouse**, named after its lime kilns, and known in Tudor times for its 'pure air', was big enough to deserve Hawksmoor's St Anne's church (1714–30) before it became a ship-building centre. In the eighteenth century, London's Chinese population first settled here, a colony of sailors who built up a Chinatown around Limehouse

Causeway and Pennyfields and who ran the exotic and legendary opium and gambling dens for their compatriots – inspiration for Sax Rohmer's fictional character, Fu Manchu. Suffering persecution from British seamen at the beginning of this century and after new rules were enforced against non-British seamen, the Chinese left. Today, their only Limehouse presence is a few street names – Ming, Canton, Pekin and Nankin – and a handful of restaurants (see Soho, p. 158, for the second wave of Chinese immigration).

On the right, Lower Pool and Limehouse Reach form the loop around Surrey Commercial Docks (1807), the only docks on the south bank. Specialising in softwood, they were built over **Rotherhithe** village, where the palace of Edward III (1327–77) has just been discovered, where his son the Black Prince had a fleet fitted out, where Henry IV came while he had leprosy and where Jonathan Swift's fictional traveller, Gulliver, was born. Before the corner, the Mayflower pub, which still sells both British and US stamps for the convenience of sailors, is near where Captain Jones set sail in the Pilgrim Fathers' boat, *The Mayflower* carrying 41 families to Plymouth, Massachusettes in America (1620) and near the church where he was later buried, St Mary's. Under the corner runs the first Thames tunnel, Marc Brunel's double Rotherhithe Tunnel (1822–43). It connects south bank Rotherhithe to north bank Wapping and was the first such footpath in the world (see also p. 259).

Round the corner, the river snakes away from Rotherhithe to make another loop, this one around the **Isle of Dogs**, a marshy peninsular drained in the thirteenth century for meadows and cornfields and barely inhabited until the West India Docks were built (1800–2), when a canal sliced across the top made it a real island. These were the enclosed and protected docks London needed: the Import and Export docks, enclosing 54 acres of water, had locks connecting them to the river. The Import Dock was three-quarters of a mile of continuous, five-storey tall warehouses. Unloading the rum and hardwood now took four days instead of four weeks. They were the first and finest of their kind.

As its population leapt, the shipyards and houses of **Millwall** arose on the west side, named after the windmills that had drained the pastureland. Here the ambitiously huge *Great Eastern* ship was built and launched (1859). At 680 feet long and six times the size of anything then afloat, it remained the largest ship built in Britain until the 1890s. Designed by Isambard Kingdom Brunel

(1806–59), whose father Marc built Rotherhithe Tunnel, the remains of the slipway it descended have just been discovered, and parts are visible at low tide. And Millwall Dock (1864–8), mostly used for grain and later swallowed up by West India Dock, championed London's first dry dock, 413 feet long. On the east side, the workers were provided with **Cubitt Town**, developed in the 1840s and '50s by William Cubitt, brother of Thomas (see p. 168) and later Lord Mayor of London. At the southern tip, where the Docklands Light Railway (1987) ends and the foot tunnel (1902) burrows across to Greenwich, Island Gardens (1895) is the spot that Wren believed gave the best **view** of his masterpiece, the Royal Naval Hospital, with Inigo Jones's Queen's House as its focus and the green Greenwich slopes framing it – as the boat stops on the Greenwich bank, it is well worth walking the tunnel to experience Wren's view.

But before the boat reaches Greenwich Pier, **Deptford** lies between Rotherhithe and Greenwich, named for its deep ford, now Deptford Creek. The Royal Dock was here, built in 1513 for Henry VIII's navy and known as the King's Yard. Here Elizabeth I visited the *Golden Hind* and knighted its captain, Francis Drake (c.1543–96), who was the first Englishman to sail round the world (1577–80) and helped defeat the Spanish Armada (1588). Here Cook's two ships, *Discovery* and *Resolution*, were equipped before his last Pacific voyage. And near here lived the diarist John Evelyn (1620–1706) who nurtured to fame a talented local carver, Grinling Gibbons, and was visited by another diarist, Pepys, who one night listened to his plays and poems and then noted rather obscurely that he 'must be allowed a little for a little conceitedness . . . being a man so much above others'.

Greenwich's heyday was under the Tudor royals – Henry VIII and his daughters Mary and Elizabeth I were all born here. The favourite of all Henry's palaces, it stood near his navy, overlooked his trading ships arriving with exotic silks and spices, and was surrounded by a magnificent park for hunting deer, hawking, jousting and frolicking with his mistresses. Much earlier, the Danes had moored their fleet off 'green reach' before Canute defeated London to become king (1016–35) and tax the wealthy Saxon city almost five tons of silver to pay off his seamen. Later, Humphrey, Duke of Gloucester and brother of Henry V, built the riverside, moated Bella Court (1427), whose fine library

became the nucleus of the Bodleian at Oxford. Around it he enclosed 200 acres to make Greenwich Park (1433), topping the hill with a watchtower.

But the setting we see today was created later. After the Tudor jollities, Anne of Denmark, James I's queen, initiated the rebuilding, employing Inigo Jones for her **Queen's House** (1616–35), his earliest surviving work and England's first Palladian villa. Completed and exquisitely decorated for Charles I's queen, Henrietta Maria, and enlarged by Jones's son-in-law, John Webb, it is ingeniously organised with bridges over the main London-Dover road that ran through the plot. Oliver Cromwell's men turned it into a biscuit factory and prison. The restored Charles II had great plans for Greenwich. Of his new palace, only a riverside wing went up (1664); but in the park, Louis XIV's Versailles creator, André Le Nôtre (see also St James's Park, (p. 89), had much earth moved, many elms and Spanish chestnuts planted and the avenues converging on the Queen's House laid out. Then, when William and Mary went west to Kensington and Hampton Court (see pp. 187 and 112), they asked Wren to build a hospital for sailors to outshine his earlier one for soldiers at Chelsea (see p. 230). Sweeping away the last of the Tudor palace, Wren cleverly built a mirror wing to Charles's, and laid grand steps up to a platform where the two U-shaped buildings of the Royal Hospital (1696–1702) face one another, leaving Queen's House between them as a distant focus, with the park beyond.

There is an enormous amount to see at Greenwich – just the park setting is mesmerising. On a day visiting the Thames, the nautical sights are the nearest and most appropriate.

Landing at Greenwich Pier, a five-minute walk through the Greenwich Foot Tunnel brings you to Island Gardens and the magnificent **view** Wren created. Back on the south bank, the handsome **Cutty Sark** tea-clipper (1869), which beat the world record in 1871 by sailing from China to England in 107 days, now displays its history and some carved figure-heads below deck and its network of rigging and masts above deck (King William Walk, SE10, tel 858 3445; open Mon–Sat, 10.30am–5pm, Sun, noon–5pm; charge). **Gipsy Moth IV** is the tiny, 54-foot ketch in which Sir Francis Chichester sailed round the world alone in 1966–7, to be knighted in Plymouth by the Queen with the sword that had knighted Francis Drake at nearby Deptford (King William Walk, SE10, tel 858 3445; open May–Sept,

Mon–Sat 10.30am–6pm; charge). Wren's baroque **Greenwich Hospital**, home to 2,710 sailors in 1815, is now the Royal Naval College (moved here from Portsmouth, 1873); but the three-part Painted Hall coated with James Thornhill's paintings and James Stuart's re-built Chapel (1718–25) are both open and well worth visiting (King William Walk, SE10, tel 858 2154; open daily except Thurs 2.30–4.45pm; free. Chapel service on Sun, 11am).

It is well worth walking downstream a few hundred yards, past the splendid Trafalgar Inn (1873) to Ballast Quay, whose view is described by poet-philosopher Peter Levi as where 'the Thames suddenly opens into a glittering sheet of water, a huge, romantic dancing floor almost empty of shipping'.

The **National Maritime Museum** fills Queen's House, the Royal Hospital School and has the hilltop Old Royal Observatory as an annex, an arrestingly beautiful museum complex. Founded in 1934, the world's largest nautical museum tells the story of Britain and the sea, that is, virtually the history of Britain: its navy, its merchants and its explorers. It is a seamans' paradise and much more. Among its boats, navigational instruments and some 2,500 ships' models, there are thousands of pictures and quantities of fine silver, porcelain and glass. Treats to seek out include the sparkling royal barges, the *Reliant* paddle steamer (West Wing), and rooms devoted to Cook and Nelson (upstairs, Queen's House), and the Great Migration to North America (East Wing). And Queen's House, with cube hall, Tulip Staircase and painted bedroom ceiling restored to seventeenth-century royal splendour (by 1989), is described by Richard Ormond, the museum's dynamic director, as 'the jewel in the Museum's many-faceted crown'. Up at the Old Observatory, Wren's Flamsteed House (1675) was built for John Flamsteed (1646–1719), first Astronomer Royal, and used by his successors until 1948, and echoes with the tick-tock of timekeepers in period rooms. Since 1833, a Time Ball on its eastern turret drops at 1pm so that passing ships can check their chronometers. The Greenwich Meridian is in the courtyard by Meridian Building, so you can stand in the eastern and western hemispheres simultaneously. (Romney Road, SE10, tel 858 4422; open Mon–Sat, 10am–5pm, Sun, 10am–5pm, closing 6pm every day during British Summer Time; charge. 30-min Gallery talks, special exhibitions in all parts, archive films, Planetarium shows, Friends soceity, quality shop for sea enthusiasts, café/restaurant. See also libraries, above.)

Just near the Observatory is the park's broad terrace – a mistake, it is said, since Le Nôtre designed the garden by correspondence and no-one told him the ground sloped. But the **view** is stunning, and on a clear day spans the Docklands and the City right back to Westminster. Finally, up the avenue, out of the gates and round to the right stands the restored, grand **Ranger's House** (eighteenth century) where the Suffolk Collection of paintings is displayed – see especially the pictures by William Larkin (died 1619) to commemorate the marriage of Elizabeth Cecil to Thomas Howard, a Suffolk antecedent (Chesterfield Walk, SE10, tel 853 0035; open daily 10am–5pm (until 4pm Nov–Jan); free; concerts).

From Greenwich Pier it is a short boatride to the Thames Flood Barrier. Down **Greenwich Reach**, Cubitt Town is on the left, in front of West India Docks where the new Canary Wharf towers will be the tallest towers in Britain, dwarfing Wren's scale (see p. 257). As the river twists back, it becomes **Blackwall Reach** where passenger ships would leave from Brunswick Wharf in **Blackwall** – in 1616 John Smith and the Virginia Settlers left to found the first permanent colony in America. Behind the wharf, Blackwall Yard was laid out in 1587 and built the great ships for the East India Company and more ships for the Royal Navy than any other yard. The wealthy and powerful East India Company, whose large ships could sail no further than Deptford, rebuilt the docks (1806), modelling them on the successful West India Docks whose design team, John Rennie and Ralph Walker, they later employed for more enlargements. Here the *Cutty Sark* clipper unloaded her valuable China tea, while other ships brought precious indigo, spices and silks from India and porcelain from China.

Opposite, Thames Ironworks and Shipbuilding Company was the last major shipyard along the Thames at London, closing in 1912 after building such ships as the iron-clad HMS *Warrior* (1860) and HMS *Thunderer* (1912).

Around the corner, in **Bugsby's Reach**, the River Lea is where King Alfred chased the Danish fleet in 896 and Izaak Walton (1593–1683, author of *The Compleat Angler*, 1653) later quietly fished. Beyond here stretched the grand finale of docklands. First came Royal Victoria (1855), then the three-quarter-mile-long Royal Albert (1880) and finally the King George V (1912–21), where the 35,655-ton *Mauritania* arrived in 1939. With electric lighting, hydraulic cranes, fridges to hold 750,000 meat carcasses, and train connections to London, they were the last word for cargo and passengers. Just fifty years later they provide passengers with an airstrip and locals with a sports centre. On the right, **Woolwich** was where Henry VIII established a Royal Dockyard in 1512 for his new navy, before his second one at Deptford. Here were built the *Great Harry* (1512) and the *Royal Sovereign* (1637).

From the boat, the huge steel fins of London's protective **Thames Flood Barrier** seem to soar higher and higher as the boat approaches them (much more spectacular than the land view). Mooted in the 1850s, it was finally begun in 1975, completed in 1982 and cost £500 million. It is the world's largest movable flood barrier, using 500,000 tonnes of concrete and endless steel to build 10 gates set between five piers housing the hydraulics to raise and lower them. It was much needed. The Thames tides are considerable, rising some 24 feet at spring tides. High tides have risen by two feet over the last century. And London, built on clay, is very slowly sinking. Furthermore, London's many floods have had lawyers rowing boats in Westminster Hall (1237), Whitehall going under water (1663) and 14 drowned in Westminster (1928). Best to visit the Barrier during its monthly raising (tel 854 1373 for dates and times). (Visitors Centre, Eastmoor Street, SE7, tel 854 1373; open daily Apr–Sept, 10.30am–6pm, Oct–Mar 10.30am–5pm; free. Disappointing displays and missable audio-visual programme, but barrier-view cafe and riverside walk.)

Upstream from Westminster to Hampton Court

The route upstream is quite different. Instead of snaking through densely packed London towards its merchant and naval centre, the boat glides out through increasingly pretty stretches, best enjoyed by sitting back and gazing at the scenery as it slowly unfolds before you.

Starting from **Westminster Bridge** (see p. 98), the sparkling-clean Houses of Parliament are on the right, where Members chat over summer drinks on the wide terraces, the Lords under red canopies, the Commons under green. **Lambeth** is on the left, where St Thomas's Hospital was named after Thomas Becket (1118–70), who as Archbishop of Canterbury resisted Henry II's efforts to bring the clergy under the jurisdiction of the secular courts, was murdered in Canterbury Cathedral, and canonised in 1173 – a story retold in TS Eliot's play, *Murder in the Cathedral* (1935). After the

Reformation, the dedication was transferred to St Thomas the Apostle. Rules demanded that patients were only fed if they struggled along to chapel, that there must be only one person to a bed and no person admitted for the same disease twice. Henry Currey's building (1868–71) is where Florence Nightingale (1820–1910) established her nursing school and revolutionised her trade, demanding for the first time that nurses be sober, honest, punctual, quiet and clean. St Thomas's nurses are still known as Nightingales see p. 177.

Beyond it rise the red bricks of Lambeth Palace (see p. 81) and then St Mary's church (see p. 81) where the harsh Captain William Bligh (1753–1817) is buried. He miraculously survived when his crew on the *Bounty* mutinied and cast him adrift in the Pacific. Later he became the equally unpopular governor of New South Wales (1805–8). It was near **Lambeth Bridge** (1861, replaced 1929–32 to Sir Reginald Blomfield's designs) that James II, fleeing the throne in 1688, took a boat across the Thames and dropped the Great Seal into the swirling waters, believing that William and Mary could not rule without it – but a fisherman caught it in his net. The large portico of the domed Tate Gallery (see p. 242), housing the Modern and British national art collections, looks down on the right, with Henry Moore's bronze, 'Locking Piece', on the riverfront. Here stood Millbank Penitentiary (1821–90), where men and women lived in three miles of cell-lined passages, many awaiting deportation which was often directly down the river steps and onto boats bound for Australia.

The first **Vauxhall Bridge** (1816, replaced 1895–1906) was the first iron bridge to span the Thames, connecting Pimlico with **Vauxhall**, a small village which gave its name to the famous and infamous Vauxhall Gardens, filled with music, dancing and merry-making and so successful that 61,000 people including the Prince of Wales came to a fancy dress ball in 1786. The wharfs of **Pimlico** lie opposite, all marshy market gardens until Thomas Cubitt's 1830s development (see p. 232). The present bridge, designed by Sir Alexander Binnie, is decorated with Alfred Drury and FW Pomeroy's eight statues of the arts and sciences, including Architecture proudly holding a model of St Paul's. Beyond, on the right, Dolphin Square (1937) has 1,250 flats served by shops, restaurant, radio station and swimming pool and was the largest block of flats in Europe when it opened. The spare heat from Giles Gilbert Scott's now redundant Battersea Power Station on the left (1929–35, now to become a fair and theme park) used to be carried under the Thames to heat the houses opposite.

Under the five-arched **Grosvenor Railway Bridge** (1850s, rebuilt 1963–7) that whisks weekenders to the Brighton seaside, riverbed finds around **Chelsea Bridge** (1851–8, rebuilt 1934) tell of a bloody battle between the Romans and British. Here on the right is the best view of Wren's Royal Hospital (see p. 229), whose gardens are the setting for the annual Chelsea Flower Show (see p. 231). On the left, the marshy land of Battersea Park (see p. 232) was firmed up and raised with the soil dug out to build the huge Victoria Dock the other side of London (see p. 110). Bathing in the Thames was once a popular pastime here – even Charles II took a dip here in 1671. RM Ordish's mixture of cantilever and suspension principles required soldiers to break step when crossing **Albert Bridge** (1871–3, later strengthened). Beyond, Mrs Gaskell, Isambard Kingdom Brunel, Hilaire Belloc and the painters James McNeill Whistler and Walter Greaves lived in the very grand houses of Cheyne Walk. And Chelsea Old Church is where Sir Thomas More (1478–1535) lies in the chapel he built (see p. 235).

Henry Holland's wooden **Battersea Bridge** (1771–2, replaced 1886–90 to Bazalgette's designs), familiar from James McNeill Whistler's painting, filled the bridgeless gap between Putney and Westminster, linking two villages on the river bend. **Battersea**, whose market gardens were famous for their carrots, melons, lavender and asparagus, centres on a cluster of grand houses and St Mary's Church (Saxon, rebuilt 1777), where JMW Turner came to watch sunsets from the tower. **Chelsea**, a 'village of palaces' in the sixteenth century (More, Henry VIII, etc), then an intellectual and artistic centre (Swift, Carlyle, the Chelsea Porcelain Works, Whistler, etc, see pp. 232–5), maintained its fishing village atmosphere down by Chelsea Creek where boats still moor on Chelsea and Cremorn wharfs.

Up Chelsea Reach and under **Battersea Railway Bridge** (1861), **Wandsworth Bridge** (1870–3, rebuilt 1936–40) connected the newly expanded Fulham to **Wandsworth** on the left. Here the Wandle tributary was used by Huguenot hatters, who made top-nots for Rome's cardinals, and Flemish iron and copper workers. This rural village was where Defoe, Thackeray and Voltaire lived but, like Battersea, all changed with the arrival of the trains. Until the last century, **Fulham** had been the fresh air attraction for manor houses and market gardens stretching from Chelsea to the Bishop of London's home, Fulham Palace, in the old heart of Fulham by Putney Bridge. Hurlingham House (1760) on the right, is a survivor, built by Dr William Cadogan, a gout expert, and soon a sports club where aristocrats played polo, skittles, croquet and tennis which is now the favourite game (see p. 340).

The wooden **Putney Bridge** (1727–9, rebuilt by Bazalgette 1882–6) was the second to span the Thames after London Bridge (see p. 61). It linked old Fulham, whose riverside All Saints parish church (medieval, mostly rebuilt 1880–1) is stuffed with fine monuments thanks to the nearby bishops, with **Putney**, a farming and fishing community that focused on St Mary's (1830s, with a sixteenth-century Chantry Chapel). Like the other Thameside villages on this stretch, its roots are Saxon, Roman and perhaps even Iron Age. Early commuters were the Tudor merchants and courtiers from their riverside mansions; Georgian growth kept the bridge busy, despite its tolls; and the arrival of both railway and Underground made it a Victorian-Edwardian suburb.

From here on the keen rowers, out in all weathers, liven up the river. The annual Easter Oxford and Cambridge University Boat Race has started from this bridge since 1845 (see p. 346). Beyond, the pier is in front of a favourite rower's pub, the Duke's Head. It is a good stop for a riverside walk up to Barn Elms Park or, on the north bank, through the 41-acre Bishops Park and Palace Grounds, home for the Bishops of London from the eleventh century until 1973. A string of keen bishop gardeners planted cedars, black walnuts, magnolias and maples, with London planes bordering the riverside walk (Bishops Avenue, SW6, tel 736 7181/7989; open daily, 7.30am–dusk). (For the keen, the riverside walk on the north bank extends right along to Hammersmith Bridge, then along Chiswick Mall (The Blue Anchor, Rutland, Dove and Old Ship pubs are all delightful), emerging at Hogarth Roundabout, near the artist William Hogarth's tiny house, see p. 270, and magnificent Chiswick House and grounds, see p. 270.)

The boat passes both parks and Harrod's Repository and Club, storage and relaxation for the great shop's employees, rounding the bend under the jazzy, castellated **Hammersmith Bridge** (1824–7, replaced by Bazalgette 1883–7). London's first suspension bridge linked **Hammersmith**, where Riverside Studios (see p. 289) front a long-time entertainment Mecca of Palais de Dance (now refurbished as Le Palais), Olympia exhibition halls, the Lyceum Hammersmith theatre and the BBC, to Barnes village and fashionable Richmond. On the right, past the rowing clubs, grand eighteenth-century houses line Lower Mall, Upper Mall and, behind Chiswick Eyot, Chiswick Mall, boats tied up to their manicured gardens shaded by willow trees. On the left, delightful **Barnes** village is tucked behind the ironwork-decorated Barnes Terrace, inspirational home to playwright Richard Brinsley Sheridan (1751–1816) and composer Gustav Holst (1874–1934).

The river loops back, past Duke's Meadows sports grounds on the right and **Mortlake** on the left, where Flemish weavers made the Mortlake Tapestries before they moved to Soho, and the local brewing trade continues at Watney's. Sir Herbert Baker and A Dryland's elegant **Chiswick Bridge** (1933), its concrete arches cased in Portland stone, links Mortlake with **Chiswick**, which fills the whole loop. The early village was back around Chiswick Mall; Strand-on-the-Green was another riverside hamlet up by Kew Bridge; and the middle was filled by Lord Burlington's magnificent villa, Chiswick House (1725–9, see p. 270), and other country estates and farms until trams, railway and finally bridge turned it from a rural retreat into a smart suburb.

Under **Kew Railway Bridge** (1864–9), the pretty, riverside Strand-on-the-Green houses have attracted painter Johann Zoffany, Arts and Crafts champion William Morris, author Nancy Mitford and others, all of whom risked finding their sitting-rooms knee-deep in water when tides were high. (The Thames Barrier, see p. 109 above, has stopped these extremes.) Beyond, the first wooden **Kew Bridge** (1758–9, rebuilt 1784–9 and 1903) carried courtiers and their entourages across from Brentford to **Kew** village, where a collection of royal retreats surrounded the green, of which Kew Palace (formerly known as the Dutch House), now inside the Royal Botanical Gardens, known as Kew Gardens) (see p. 267), still stands and was a favourite home of George II (1727–60) and George III (1760–1820). The pier is just before the gardens, whose side entrance is reached along the towpath.

On the right, after Kew Pumping Station (see p. 270), **Brentford**, well sited on the main route west out of London is where commercial traffic wiggled up the River Brent to join the Grand Union Canal. Here King Canute crushed Edmond Ironside in 1016 to become king of England, and the Royalists won a battle (1642) during the Civil War. This next stretch of river is gloriously rural, lined with the mature trees of Kew on the left and then opening for a stunning view of Syon House (see p. 269) on the right, built by Edward Seymour, Duke of Somerset, after Henry VIII dissolved Syon Monastery.

Sweeping round past **Isleworth** on the right, where orchards surrounded the village when the London Apprentice pub was built in 1741, Kew Observatory stands in the Old Deer Park on the left, built by Sir William Chambers for George III and until 1981 the Meteorological Office. Ahead lies **Richmond Lock**, **Footbridge** and **Weir**.

Now comes a good patch of pretty cottages, houses with walled gardens, waterside country pubs and grand country estates. After Maxwell Ayrton's **Twickenham Bridge** (1928–33), old **Richmond** lies on the left, known as Shene until Henry VII rebuilt and renamed his palace – its remains lie behind riverside Asgill House (1758). Here Sir Charles Asgill, wealthy banker and Lord Mayor of London, provided good entertainment to entice masters and wardens of City Livery Companies to be rowed all the way up here in their stately, gilt-covered barges, the proud merchants dressed up in velvet, jewels and decorations and entertained by musicians all the way. Beside Kenton Couse and James Paine's handsome **Richmond Bridge** (1774–7, widened 1937), the boat pauses at the pier. There are nearby riverside pubs, and Thames Skiff Hire let out beautiful old rowing boats, delightful on a summer's day.

The boat moves on, bringing good views of Richmond Hill and Park (see p. 273) as the river bends back around **Twickenham**, passing Marble Hill House (1724–9) and Park on the right, the ferry between Old Twickenham and palatial Ham House (1610) on the left and, after Eel Pie Island, Strawberry Hill on the right, where Horace Walpole built his Gothick fantasy (1748). (For more on Richmond and Twickenham, see p. 268.)

Now sails replace oars and the river is dotted with red, blue and white slashes. **Teddington Lock**, **Weir** and **Footbridge** marks the end of the tidal Thames. Between here and Edward Lapidge's elegant white arches of **Kingston Bridge** (1825–8), farms stretched from the right-hand banks inland to Bushy Park (see below, p. 114) which was enclosed by Cardinal Wolsey as part of his thoroughly royal Hampton Court estate. On the left, **Kingston-Upon-Thames** was an early fishing centre, medieval Royal Borough and major market town, whose current bridge has stone and wooden predecessors going back at least to the Conquest. Today it is affluent suburbia, where weekends take on a seaside atmosphere, with rowing and sailing clubs, riverside cottages built on stilts, jolly barbecues in boat-club gardens, plenty of gin-and-tonics in hand, and sizable yachts moored nearby.

But do not forget the right bank, where the river borders Hampton Court Park, the palace heralded by Henry VIII's gilt water-gate where the royal party would land after the royal barge and its flotilla of courtiers, maids-of-honour, servants and musicians had journeyed up the Thames – perhaps from Richmond or Kew palaces, perhaps from Whitehall, Somerset House, the Tower or even Greenwich.

The boat moors at Barge Walk beside the palace, just before **Hampton Court Bridge** (1753, latest rebuilding 1930–3), once an operatic Chinoiserie fantasy, now the clean lines of Sir Edwin Lutyens. It provides good **views** of the palace and its playful Tudor chimneys.

Hampton Court Palace blends glorious Tudor and Wren buildings with 50 acres of immaculate formal gardens, all surrounded by the extensive (some 1800 acres) and wooded Bushy and Hampton Court parks and encased in a grand loop of the Thames. Of all the royal London palaces, it is perhaps the most complete surviving testament to royal patronage at its best. For while the itinerant sovereigns moved from palace to palace, Hampton Court was a much-loved country seat from the moment Henry VIII took it over from Cardinal Wolsey in 1529 until George III came to the throne in 1760 and abandoned it to the care of 40 staff including Capability Brown who planted the Great Vine. It was the perfect setting for parties indoors, promenades along the avenues and hunting in the parks, all amid clean air and water. So it is all the more disappointing that the management has removed any spirit or sense of period inside the palace, the furnishings are dully displayed and there are few clues to the great characters who built and enjoyed it.

It was Thomas Wolsey (c.1475–1530) who in 1514 bought the country site, 15 miles south-west of London, and began to build himself an uncompromisingly royal palace with 280 rooms and a staff of 500. He was at the summit of his meteoric career. It had taken off just seven years earlier, when, aged 32, he became Chaplain to Henry VIII (1507). Dean of Lincoln and almoner to the king followed (1509); then Privy Councillor, helping Henry with his French wars (1511); then Bishop of Tournai (1513)

and Lincoln (1514) and Archbishop of York (1514) – with the bishoprics of Bath and Wells, Durham and Winchester added later. The next year he became both a Cardinal (and a Legate in 1518) and the Lord Chancellor, dominating both Church and state politics. He had the power and wealth of a king. And he enjoyed it, living ostentatiously and entertaining lavishly in palatial splendour. When England and France signed a treaty in 1527, it was here that the French ambassador and all his retinue were entertained.

Henry VIII (1509–47) watched on with increasing jealousy. Wolsey, no fool, probably tried to appease the king in 1525 by giving him Hampton Court complete with its rich stuffing of tapestries, furnishings and silver and gold plate. It did not work. In 1529, failing to win the heirless king's divorce and blackened by aristocratic plotting, Henry's richest and most powerful subject fell from favour. Henry moved in to both his London (see p. 86) and Hampton Court homes.

Henry enlarged the palace. He added courtyards, kitchens, library, tennis courts and guard room. He put Nicholas Orsain's Astronomical Clock (1540, still firmly showing the sun revolving around the earth) in Wolsey's gateway which he redecorated and named after his current (second) wife, Anne Boleyn (see Wolsey's arms on it). He put Anne's badge and initials in the carving of his new Great Hall; added a string of buildings towards his water-gate; and kept the parks well-stocked with game. Here he brought each of his wives – the palace rooms were radically altered to please each one. Jane Seymour (third) died here in 1537 giving birth to his longed-for son, Edward VI (1547–53), who became king aged 10 only to die of consumption. He married Catherine Parr (sixth) here in 1543. The Spanish Catherine of Aragon (first), gave him Edward's successor, Mary, who reigned 1553–8 and spent her honeymoon here with the unpopular Philip II of Spain. But it was Anne Boleyn (second) who provided Elizabeth, the daughter with a character to match Henry's.

Elizabeth I (1558–1603) remained unmarried. She used herself as an enticement in foreign diplomacy and an encouragement to her more eligible subjects; and using her portraits and pageantry, she created a cult image throughout her kingdom. At Hampton Court she added the Horn Room (for her collection of antlers and horns) behind the Great Hall and a triple-storeyed building near Wolsey's rooms (walls initialled and dated 1568). A keen gardener, she tended exotic delights brought from distant lands, such as tobacco and potato, presents from Raleigh, Drake and other suitors. And she made Hampton Court renowned for its masques and merriment, banquets and balls, stag-hunting and dancing. Every room buzzed with sophisticated liveliness. Plays were staged in the Great Hall, employing silk-weavers and tailors for the costumes and even creating snow for a special effect. The royal apartments were lined with gold-encrusted tapestries while ornaments and musical instruments were scattered on the inlaid tables. In 1590, the Duke of Wurttemberg declared it 'the most splendid and most magnificent royal palace of any that may be found in England, or indeed in any other Kingdom'.

James VI of Scotland succeeded her as James I of England (1603–25), initiating the Stuart line. He continued the fun, especially her traditional Christmas festivities. Over Christmas 1603, more than 30 plays were performed in the Great Hall, some including the theatre-keen queen, Anne of Denmark, some with scenery by Inigo Jones (see p. 100), and some performed by the King's Companie of Comedians, who included Shakespeare. Charles I (1625–49) amassed the unrivalled art collection (Mantegna's 'Triumphs of Julius Caesar' included), much of it removed by Oliver Cromwell's men who put Hampton Court up for sale, as they did Greenwich. When there were no buyers, Cromwell lived there for seven years until his death in 1658.

Charles II (1660–85) busily restored the royal country haven. He brought back what scattered furnishings he could find and, as at Greenwich and St James's Park, was inspired by Le Nôtre's Versailles work to built new gardens – fountains, cascades and avenues of limes where he promenaded and picnicked with his aristocratic visitors and his many mistresses. It was here he came after spending six months at Oxford during the 1665 Plague; here he received Pepys and Evelyn, both members of the Navy Board, who then dined 'with a great deal of company and much merry discourse'; here he brought his pictures to safety from Whitehall during the Great Fire of 1666; and here a string of pretty courtesans were immortalised on canvas by society portraitist Sir Peter Lely.

William and Mary (1689–1702) made sweeping changes. Driven in search of pure air, they spent most of their time at Kensington and Hampton Court. Their architect was Sir Christopher Wren, still busy with St Paul's and later to work for them at Whitehall (see p. 100), Kensington (see p. 189),

and Greenwich (see p. 107). Wren's dream was to rip down the Tudor muddle and build an English Versailles. In reality, he removed only the state apartments and built the east and south wings around the Fountain Court (1689–94). Their classic, French Renaissance lines overlook Charles's French-inspired gardens. Jean Tijou added the astounding ironwork gates; Wren the delightful riverside Banqueting House, using old bricks as a token economy. Inside, Grinling Gibbons carved yards of wood, Antonio Verrio painted acres of ceiling. The king and queen keenly watched every stone put in place. But Mary died in 1694. William moved in alone in 1699, filled it with art treasures and his wife's china collection, and spent most of his last three years there, living in modest ground floor apartments, drinking chocolate for breakfast and dying (at Kensington Palace) after he fell off a horse in the Home Park. The grand project left him in grand debt.

Queen Anne (1702–14) inherited the royal debt and the unfinished work. Wren and Grinling Gibbons completed the chapel for her (magnificent reredos); Verrio and Thornhill painted her rooms overlooking the formal gardens. And when the queen, a keen huntress, became crippled with dropsy and gout, she had the parks drained and levelled so she could chase stags from a one-horse chaise.

But the Wren rooms never saw the grand royal entertaining of Tudor and Stuart days. The Hanoverians wound down Hampton Court's life. Dull, unpopular George I hid from his subjects here, surrounded by his correct German court. George II spent quiet summers here, hunting in the parks but still dining in public in a room refitted with an ornate white chimneypiece. George III abandoned it entirely, initiating the tradition, still extant today, of providing Grace and Favour lodgings there for Crown pensioners. And in 1838, the year after she became queen, Victoria opened the State Apartments to the public. Later picture rearrangements killed the royal spirit, and in 1986 a fire devastated the royal apartments facing the Thames. Now a new team is to revitalise the palace and restore the royal atmosphere.

Throughout the centuries of jollities, state work continued. Elizabeth I debated her half-sister Mary's fate here. A stream of foreign ambassadors arrived with presents and suggestions of husbands for her. James I sat over the Conference of Divines (1604), which produced the Authorised Version of the Bible. Charles I was imprisoned by the

Parliamentarians (1647–8), but escaped along the river.

Today, magical moments for the visitor to Hampton Court are sunny days for the gardens and park, weekdays to avoid the over-crowding in the small, Tudor rooms and queues to see the Mantegna paintings and Great Vine – the cafeteria is all right on quiet days, too. It is best to explore outside first, enjoying the Gatehouse flanked by Henry's moat and protective King's Beasts (re-carved 1950), Anne Boleyn's Gateway, the Clock and Fountain courtyards and the Tudor and Wren exteriors. Then go round towards the river to explore the Privy Garden (designed for the royals' exclusive use), with high terrace walk to Tijou's 12-panel, wrought-iron screen and the water-gate (good **views**).

Back through three re-made Tudor gardens (Sunk, Pond, and Knot for aromatic herbs) to the garden buildings tucked between the river and palace. The riverside Banqueting House comes first. The Great Vine was grown from a cutting taken in 1768 from a Black Hamburg vine at Valentines Park in East London and now yields 700 pounds of fruit in a good year. The Mantegna Gallery houses his magnificent massive 'Triumphs of Julius Caesar', probably painted 1474–90, certainly bought by Charles I in 1629 for the then huge sum of £10,500. Crossing the east front, there is a tiny entrance to Henry's Tennis Courts where you may well catch the unusual game of real tennis being played. From Wren's façade, there is a good **view** up William and Mary's 700-acre formal gardens and tamed park. The clipped avenues run to the Fountain and three-quarter-mile-long Long Water, with gates either side into the Home Park for a peaceful stroll among the grazing sheep and fallow deer.

To the north of the palace lies the Wilderness, Lion Gates, Queen Anne's Maze, Laburnham Walk (dazzling golden cascade May–June), the rosebeds of Tilt Yard Gardens and the restaurant and café. The Maze, now of privet and yew but laid out in 1714 in hornbeam, merits a detour for tiny children and for eccentricity value.

Inside, it is worth seeking out Henry's huge kitchens and his Great Hall with hammer-beam roof; peeking down into the Queen's Private Chapel from the Royal Pew; pausing at the stupendous King's Staircase; and wandering the panelled Tudor rooms, the grandly decorated public Wren rooms and his more informal private rooms behind them, walls throughout hung with paintings and tapestries – and do not miss the aerial views of the gardens. (Hampton Court Palace, East Molesey, Surrey, tel 977 8441. Open Apr 1–Sept 30, Mon–Sat 9.30am–6pm, Sun, 11am–6pm; Mar, Apr and Oct Mon–Sat. 9.30am–5pm, Sun 2–5pm; Nov–Feb, Mon–Sat 9.30am–4pm, Sun, 2–4pm. Beware: winter closures include the Maze Nov–Feb; the Restaurant Oct–Mar – the café stays open throughout; and the Mantegna Gallery, tennis court, kitchens, cellars and King's Private Apartments Nov–Feb. Charges are multi-tiered: gardens, vine and Mantegna Gallery free; token charges for Banqueting Room, Maze and Courtyards; State Apartments full charge which admits to everything. Sunday services in the Queen's Private Chapel at 8.30am, 11am and 3.30pm, except Aug. Guided tours of State Apartments in summer, 11.15am and 2.15pm, unbookable; shop, café, restaurant.)

Right next door, across Hampton Court Road, the 1100-acre **Bushy Park** is totally different – wilder and seemingly further from the busy city. Although Wolsey enclosed it, the royals concentrated on the Palace's formal gardens and left Bushy mostly wild and distinctly bushy. Charles I cut a water-course from the River Cole to create the Londoford river; Wren added the mile-long double row of 274 horse chestnut trees as a royal arrival route for William and Mary (outsize chandeliers with pink and white candles in May); Queen Victoria opened it to the public (1838); and the cool and peaceful Waterhouse Woodland Park with sweetly perfumed springtime azaleas, camellias and rhododendrons was added in 1949. These and the 300 fallow deer and chirping birds (second only to Richmond Park in variety) leave London far away. From here, the easiest way back into Central London is by British Rail train from Hampton Court (the station is over the bridge) to Waterloo; but there are buses, too.

The go-betweens: The law, the letter and licence to entertain

Mapping it out from above: Hungerford Bridge; Waterloo Bridge.

Starting point: Hungerford Bridge. Access by Underground: Embankment, Waterloo.

Good days to explore: Weekdays to see the maximum of legal London (parts close at weekends and Aug–Sept); other times to wander their silent squares; weekends for Covent Garden markets. Pubs in Fleet Street and around the inns of court tend to close at weekends.

Information: There is no LTB office nearby. The nearest information centre is The British Travel Centre, see p. 4.

Refreshment suggestions: see p. 311.

Local festivals: Alternative Arts run an almost continuous festival in Covent Garden, see the programme pinned up on St Paul's Church railings; more information from 1/4 King Street, WC2 (240 5451). Other festivals include Covent Garden May Fayre, second Sun in May, puppeteers celebrate Mr Punch's birthday in St Paul's Churchyard; information from Alternative Arts or from Camden Arts and Entertainment, 100 Euston Road, NW1 (278 444); and Strawberry Fayre, third Sat in June, at St Etheldreda's Church, 14 Ely Place, EC1; information from the church (405 1061).

Local library: Nearby is the Central Reference Library, see Westminster libaries, p. 75.

The fields between the cities of London and Westminster did not stay green for long. When post-Conquest kings made Westminster a second power centre, the bridle path linking it to the merchants along the Strand and Fleet Street attracted first bishops, then Tudor noblemen and courtiers. Then came the law students, printers, journalists and writers who, from this stategic thoroughfare, served both camps with advice, intrigue and gossip. Newspapers blossomed in the eighteenth century; the courts were moved here from Westminster Hall in the nineteenth. Wigged and gowned barristers and scruffy hacks plotted scoops in Fleet Street's alley taverns, searched out stories in the Strand's coffee houses and smoking-rooms, and exchanged tips among the cauliflowers and carrots of Covent Garden market. The area became the centre for more raucous entertainment, too, with theatres, music halls, brothels and Turkish baths to amuse the City gents, literary wits and fun-loving courtiers.

Like all areas of London, it had developed piecemeal. The rich had their riverside palaces along the south side of the Strand. On the north side, the big land-owning aristocrats and smaller land-buying builders put up speculative housing. Of London's first dozen squares, half were built here.

Today, Covent Garden square has survived upheavals and mad dreams to become, with its surrounding streets, a happy marriage of rejuvenation and restoration, filling the old market halls with museums, shops, restaurants and modern markets, and adding to the area's old theatres with daily impromptu street entertainment. East of it, several squares are still the barristers' inns of court they were built to be. There is a string of calm oases stretches up from the river amid the thunderous city centre, gas-lamps lit at dusk, gates firmly closed at night. Among them are the legal theatres: the Victorian Gothic pinnacles of the Law Courts and, further east, in the shadow of St Paul's, the Central Criminal Court, where 'Justice' sparkles on top of the dome. But Fleet Street, whose printing presses have served the dramatists, the lawyers and the gossips of both City and Westminster since 1500, awaits its fate, its presses redundant, its hacks flown to clean and silent computers in the Docklands and elsewhere, leaving only their memories and pubs.

Starting on the footbridge of **Hungerford Bridge** (see p. 99), there is a stunning **view**, worth it even when trains roll noisily past in and out of Charing Cross Station. On the left, Victoria Embankment sweeps round under Waterloo Bridge (see p. 99) to Blackfriars Bridge (see p. 100). One of the wonders of Victorian London, the Embankment reclaimed land and provided road and gardens on top of the Underground steam trains and life-saving sewer (see p. 99).

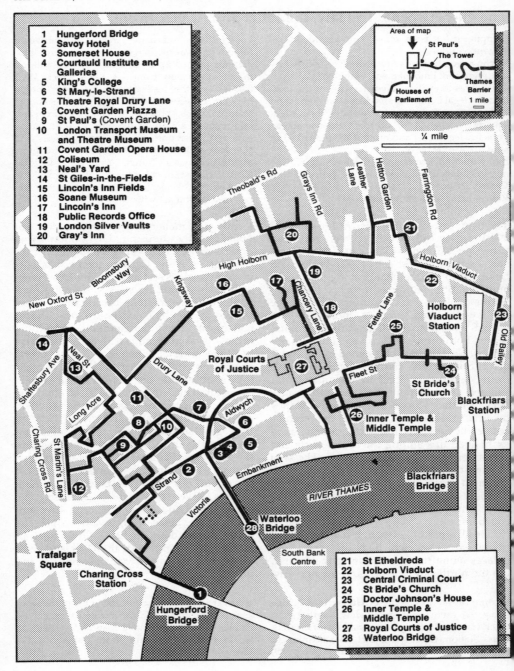

1 Hungerford Bridge
2 Savoy Hotel
3 Somerset House
4 Courtauld Institute and Galleries
5 King's College
6 St Mary-le-Strand
7 Theatre Royal Drury Lane
8 Covent Garden Piazza
9 St Paul's (Covent Garden)
10 London Transport Museum and Theatre Museum
11 Covent Garden Opera House
12 Coliseum
13 Neal's Yard
14 St Giles-in-the-Fields
15 Lincoln's Inn Fields
16 Soane Museum
17 Lincoln's Inn
18 Public Records Office
19 London Silver Vaults
20 Gray's Inn

Area of map
St Paul's
The Tower
Houses of Parliament
Thames Barrier
1 mile

¼ mile

21 St Etheldreda
22 Holborn Viaduct
23 Central Criminal Court
24 St Bride's Church
25 Doctor Johnson's House
26 Inner Temple & Middle Temple
27 Royal Courts of Justice
28 Waterloo Bridge

Well inland, you can see the line of Fleet Street (marked by St Bride's spire and the Law Courts) leading to the Strand, so-called because it ran close to the Thames. Between the road and the river ran a parade of palaces from medieval times until the eighteenth century. The bishops built their town houses, known as inns. After the Dissolution, favoured nobles redecorated them and welcomed courtly guests arriving in gilded barges at their grand watergates. Just this side of Blackfriars Bridge, Henry VIII's Bridewell Palace (1515–20) is where he entertained the Holy Roman Emperor Charles V with feasting and merriment (1522), and where the French ambassador and his friend the Bishop of Lavaur posed as 'The Ambassadors' for Holbein the Younger (1533, now in the National Gallery, see p. 88). Next door, the Spanish envoy, Corier, was put up at the Bishop of Salisbury's fine inn while he fixed up Philip II of Spain's marriage to Mary (1554). Further down, after Temple gardens, Lord Protector Somerset built Somerset House, the first English Renaissance palace (1547–50), later replaced by William Chambers' grand house for civil servants (see p. 119).

This side of Waterloo Bridge, Henry, 1st Duke of Lancaster, lavished £35,000 on rebuilding Savoy House to outshine all others (1343–70). Later, the canny 12th Earl of Arundel paid just £40 for Arundel House (1549) where Wenceslas Hollar was later to draw his famous view of London from the roof (1647). Elizabeth I lodged her favourites in some: Exeter House went to Lord Burghley, the Durham bishops' medieval house to Sir Walter Raleigh whose servant, seeing him smoking the newly imported tobacco leaf, thought he was on fire and poured a tankard of ale over him to put him out. Northumberland House, with added Robert Adam interiors, stood at No. 1 The Strand, one of the first London houses to be numbered but now gone for the sake of Northumberland Avenue – the family lion went to Syon, the Northumberland country house (see p. 269). Of these and many more, one tantalising reminder survives: the Watergate (1626) added by the Duke of Buckingham to the Bishops of Norwich's medieval house known as York House, after he evicted the eminent scientist, philosopher, lawyer and politician Francis Bacon (1561–1626).

On the right, the modern view is of the **South Bank Centre**. It was inspired by the 1951 Festival of Britain held to cheer up the British after post-war austerity and to celebrate the centenary of the 1851 Great Exhibition (see p. 212). The temporary fairs and buildings that sprawled over derelict land gave birth to a long-term scheme, now the largest arts centre in Western Europe and still growing (see p. 288), many buildings known by their initials. By this bridge, Robert Matthew and JL Martin's Royal Festival Hall (RFH 1951, 1962) started the complex: a concert hall which was the Festival's only permanent building and one of London's first post-war public buildings (original interior; later facade). South Bank Craft Centre is behind, in the Hungerford Bridge Arches. Next come the Queen Elizabeth Hall (QEH) and the Purcell Room, both small concert halls, and the Hayward Gallery behind (all 1964–7), topped by Philip Vaughan and Roger Dainton's cheerily playful neon sculpture, especially mad in high winds. The National Film Theatre (NFT, 1956–8) and the latest addition, the Museum of the Moving Image (MOMI, opens summer 1988), crouch underneath Waterloo Bridge (wonderful under-arch views). Sir Denys Lasdun's National Theatre (NT, 1967–77), lies beyond, its three theatres and surrounding survival kit the realisation of a dream first seriously mooted in 1848 (Garrick had suggested a national theatre in the eighteenth century), then championed by H Granville-Barker, GB Shaw, Laurence Olivier and others. It finally opened in 1976 under the direction of Peter Hall.

Do not be put off by forbidding concrete and breezy corners, to be resolved by Terry Farrell, architect to the administrators – Farrell's grander dreams leap back over the Thames, right up to Trafalgar Square. The whole complex is well worth exploring: outside terraces for sculpture, views and summer entertainment; inside for breakfast, bookshops, lunchtime music, art exhibitions, informal foyer entertainment, bars, supper and full evening and weekend programmes. In addition to its temporary shows, the theatrical paintings and drawings of the Maugham Collection lodged here sometimes cheer up the theatre foyer walls.

The Hayward Gallery is the Arts Council's stage for big shows, usually of nineteenth- and twentieth-century art; MOMI tells the very visual story of film and television, with presenters replacing guards, changing displays, touchable items, and moving images on inside and outside walls. (South Bank Centre, SE1; central information from Royal Festival Hall, inside the ground level, riverside entrance, tel 928 3002; most buildings and their contents open 10am–last event; excellent, bookable tours of RFH (tel 928 3002) and NT (928 0880). During exhibitions, Hayward Gallery usually open Mon–Wed 10am–8pm, Thur–Sat 10am–6pm, Sun 2–6pm; charge. For information on MOMI openings contact the NFT, tel 928 3232/ 437 4355. For more information, see p. 288.)

Returning over Hungerford Bridge and through Embankment Station, **Villiers Street** skirts Charing Cross Station (see p. 99) and still sniffs of Victorian London. Charles Dickens worked near here in a shoe-blacking factory 'a crazy tumble-down old house . . . overrun with rats'. Turning right into **Victoria Embankment Gardens** (summer evening music) by Gordon's, a tiny basement wine-bar known for its casks of sherry, **York Watergate** (1626) marks the riverbank before extra land was reclaimed by Bazalgette's engineering works. It also testifies to the crescent of palaces and is a memorial to its vainest inhabitant. Visitors passed through this rusticated gate topped by lions, family arms and pious motto – 'The cross is the touchstone of faith' – and across gardens to York House, home of James I and Charles I's favourite, George Villiers, Duke of Buckingham (1592–1628). With his looks as his passport, he shot from commoner to duke in seven years, but his tactless monopoly of Court power led to Spanish and French insults abroad and loathing from parliament and the City, ending in his murder. After the Restoration, the 2nd Duke sold York House in the 1670s to big-time property speculator Dr Nicholas Barbon on condition that the Watergate was kept and the new streets named after him – George, Villiers, Duke and Buckingham still stand, and Of Alley is now York Place.

The gate leads to **Buckingham Street** – if it is closed, go back and along Watergate Walk. Barbon's work here and, earlier, on the site of Essex House beyond Somerset House (see p. 119) began the break-up of the palaces. This street, built 1675 with later replacements, embodies the post-Great Fire regulations – the use of brick with minimal timber, the front wall running up above the roof line to make a parapet, timber windows set back from the wall, iron fire-cones to extinguish torches, etc. And its inhabitants over the years are a typical mix for the area: diarist and top naval man Samuel Pepys (1679–88 at no. 12, 1688–1701 at no. 14), writer and barrister Henry Fielding (1735 at no. 15), actress Peggy Woffington (1755–7 at no. 9), philosophers David Hume and Jean-Jacques Rousseau (1766 at no. 10), poet Samuel Taylor Coleridge (1799 at no. 21), painter William Etty (1824–48 at no. 14), the young Dickens (1834 at nos 15–16) and, significantly, the first building conservation society, William Morris's Society for the Protection of Ancient Buildings (at no. 9, see also p. 18).

Turning right, the view up **John Adam Street** gives an idea of what the radically new **Adelphi** (1768–74) was like. It was the inspiration of Robert Adam (1728–92), described by John Fleming as 'a typically hard-headed Scot, canny and remorselessly ambitious, yet with a tender, romantic side . . .'. A brilliant architect, decorator and furniture designer, his light-hearted neo-classicism perfectly suited the quiet opulence of the Georgian aristocracy. His output was enormous (later work is in Edinburgh); his influence still felt today. Having trained under his architect father in Edinburgh, he did the Grand Tour and then hit London in 1758, producing the Admiralty Screen (see p. 118) and transforming the interiors of Syon (see p. 269), Osterley (see p. 267) and Kenwood (see p. 271) houses. Then came Adelphi, a bold and imaginative scheme that ended in a mixture of tears and triumph. Robert and his brothers John, James and William, bought up the lease on Durham House and drained the muddy bay in front. Here they built an elegant quay with a network of tunnels and storage vaults leading up to the Strand and supporting a riverside Royal Terrace of smart brick houses with surrounding streets. And they named it Adelphi, Greek for brothers, after themselves. But, as no one wanted this chic address, bankruptcy followed and the houses were disposed of by lottery at £50 a ticket. However, as architecture it was the bravest and most successful speculation in town, its cool neo-classicism enlivened with rich, light ornament.

Although its centrepiece was destroyed in 1936, there are good bits left to to seek out. Turning right down York Buildings and left into Lower Robert Street, the road plunges down under one of the old arches, turns sharp right, and emerges where the quay was. Steps nearby lead up to where Royal Terrace overlooked the Thames, now Collcut and Hamp's building (1936–8) with murals of British counties and massive corner figures. Looking down into Robert Street to the right, no. 3 survives complete, showing how the riverside facade was decorated with the new flat Adam pilasters with honeysuckle strands – Robert Adam lived in no. 9. Back in John Adam Street, the Royal Society of Arts (founded 1754) is opposite, built 1772–4 for a society whose purpose was 'the Encouragement of Arts, Manufactures and Commerce' and duly decorated with exterior frieze and remarkable interior murals (1777–83) by James Barry in the lecture room.

Possessors of some of the best minds have been members: Dr Johnson was so intimidated by his fellows – Walpole, Chippendale, Gibbons, Adam – that he admitted after addressing them that 'all his flowers of oratory forsook him'. Later, it was here that Graham Bell first described his experiments with the telephone (1877). The Society played a major part in the 1851 Great Exhibition (see p. 216) and subsequent jamborees including the 1951 Festival of Britain; awarded their honours to Pasteur, Madame Curie and Fleming; and in 1867 put up a plaque to Byron in Holles Street (off Oxford Street), the beginning of the Blue Plaque tradition that now marks about 500 London houses of historical interest (see p. 56) (8 John Adam Street, WC2, tel 930 5115; apply by telephone or in writing to visit the lecture room or attend lectures; publications available from the hall in office hours). At the top of the street, no. 7 Adam Street closes the vista and is the only surviving Adelphi house to have its complete original decoration.

The **Strand** was written off in 1532 as 'full of pits and sloughs, very perilous and noisome'. Its rise was gradual. Pre-Barbon and pre-Adam, the Earl of Salisbury did his own speculation spree on part of his run-down Durham House. This New Exchange (1608), rivalled the City's Royal Exchange (see p. 71) and operated as a trading centre surrounded by galleries of shops, an early shopping precinct. By the early eighteenth century, the whole area was a fashionable shopping centre: Thomas Twining supplied tea to Queen Anne from here (1706); Ackerman made big enough profits from his prints to be one of the first to light his premises by gas (1810). After Nash's West Strand improvements in 1830–2 Disraeli declared it 'perhaps the finest street in Europe'. Worth exploring to the left now to see John Nash's pepper-pot corner (part of his huge Trafalgar Square Scheme, see p. 176) and stucco facades and, returning, to enjoy what little remains of the Jacob Epstein statues (1908) on Charles Holden's Zimbabwe House (1907) on the corner of Strand and Agar Street, disfigured after a Philistine campaign against their lewdness by Lord Beaverbrook's *Evening Standard*. Avoiding being run over, there is a good **view** down the length of the Strand to St Mary-le-Strand (see below).

By the turn of the century, the Strand was an entertainment arcade, with pickpockets and prostitutes lurking around the theatres, coffee houses and chop houses. Moving along it, the Adelphi (founded 1806, latest building 1930) and

Vaudeville (1870, where Henry Irving found fame in *Two Roses*) theatres on the left remain from the 1890s when this street had more theatres than any other. Stamp-selling Stanley Gibbons moved here in 1874; and across on the south side Simpson's Divan and Tavern (1848) was where chess fanatics lolled back on divans and between games feasted on roast beef – no chess today, but plenty of beef. To serve the fun-seekers, there were hotels: the Charing Cross back at the station; the demolished 900-room Cecil (1886), built as the largest in Europe (now Shell-Mex House, 1931); then FJ Wills' 786-room Strand Palace (1925–30) on the left, whose glorious entrance is now in the V&A (see p. 222).

But the Savoy (1884–9), which stands back on the right, is still one of the world's grandest hotels (see p. 24). Built by Richard D'Oyly Carte next to his Savoy Theatre, it was designed by TE Collcutt. Guests were managed by Cesar Ritz, fed by Auguste Escoffier, rose to their rooms by electric lift and had their diamonds lit up by the new electric lighting. When Art Deco hit London, many rooms received dramatic revamping by Basil Ionides and the entrance court was remodelled with stylish stainless steel (see it best from the Upstairs Brasserie). In the entrance court, on the right, D'Oyly Carte's Savoy Theatre (1881, rebuilt by Tugwell and Ionides 1929) was the first with electric light and staged Gilbert and Sullivan operas, opening with *Patience* (hotel and theatre well worth a peek).

Crossing Lancaster Place, **Somerset House** (1776–86) was William Chambers's ponderous answer to Robert Adam's Adelphi. Chambers (1723–96), a Scot like Adam, trained in Paris and Italy and arrived in London in 1755. He was instantly popular, starting his rise to royal officialdom the next year when he became architectural tutor to the Prince of Wales, later George II. His key to success was English Palladianism smoothed by French neo-classicism, always correct, often dull. He and Adam dominated the Golden Age of Georgian London architecture, the 1760s–90s. But they were open rivals, their differences described by Sir John Summerson as Chambers's 'sensitive eclectic conservatism' against Adam's revolution in taste. For their Strand projects, both put their best face towards their audience on the river – from where you still see most clearly how Chambers used Adam's idea of setting a big block on riverside arches (see p. 99 and nip along Waterloo Bridge).

From the Strand, a majestic, triple-arched gateway leads into the *cour d'honneur*. And above here,

Chambers's finest string of rooms, with Louis XV-inspired ceilings and fireplaces, will house the exceptional **Courtauld Institute's Galleries.** It is a stunning assembly of six private collections. Samuel Courtauld (1865–1947) gave Manet's 'Bar at the Folies-Bergère', Renoir's 'La Lodge' and dozens of other French Impressionist and Post-Impressionist canvases; Lord Lee of Fareham (1868–1947) followed with Old Masters and British, including Beechey's 'Queen Charlotte' (she who left the old Somerset House for Buckingham Palace, see p. 90); art critic Roger Fry (1866–1934) gave his collection; Sir Robert Witt (1872–1952) gave his drawings; the Mark Gambier-Parry Bequest (1966) includes Lorenzo Monacos; and Count Antoine Seilern's Princes Gate Collection (1978) has many canvases by Rubens, Tiepolo, Van Dyck and more. All this forms part of the Courtauld Institute of Art. Founded by the industrialist and art patron Samuel Courtauld in 1931 and housed in his Adam mansion, Home House, 20 Portman Square (see p. 153), with public galleries, his idea was for students at London University to study art history in the setting of fine architecture and pictures. In its new surroundings, the Institute's various departments, previously separated for lack of space, are once more united. (Somerset House, WC2; for information, contact The Trust Office, 20 Portman Square, W1, tel 935 9292; charge. Guided tours; lectures, workshops, special exhibitions, Friends society, photographic library, conservation departments, bookshop, café.)

Turning right out of Somerset House, its eastern extension is Sir Robert Smirke's **King's College** (1829–35), founded by a collection of bishops and the Duke of Wellington in God-fearing riposte to godless University College (see p. 164), both now part of London University.

Mid-road, the casket-like **St Mary-le-Strand** (1714–17) is the first of many London churches by another Scottish architect working in Georgian London, James Gibbs (1682–1754), who returned from training under Carlo Fontana in Rome to develop a style mixing the Baroque of Rome and Wren. This is also the first church built under Queen Anne's optimistic Fifty Churches Act (1711). It catered for London's growing population who had recovered from the setbacks of both the Plague and the Great Fire and was not only rapidly expanding east and west but was also being energetically lured into the dangerous camps of non-conformity and atheism. Quality won over quantity and only twelve churches were built, each

of stone, with portico and steeple. (Others include St Mary Woolnoth, p. 71, and Hawksmoor's St George's Bloomsbury (see p. 168) and his three East End churches, see pp. 249 and 258.) St Mary-le-Strand was designed to be enjoyed from all sides, so it is worth dodging the traffic to go around it (see especially the garlanded apse window). A maypole stood in front of the old church, where children danced on May Day (May 1) and near where Pepys, in 1667, noticed 'many milkmaids with their garlands upon their pails, dancing with a fiddler before them'.

North of here lies **Covent Garden**, where actors and writers have lived among the market and theatres since the seventeenth century.

Cutting through Montreal Place and up Catherine Street, Ewen Barr's Duchess Theatre (1934) is currently home for the Players' Theatre, a company in the Victorian music-hall tradition who have been ousted from their more informal home under the arches of Charing Cross Station until rebuilding is complete; under the guidance and hammer of the Master of Ceremonies, audiences sing and sway along to 'Cherries so red, strawberries ripe' and other favourites (see p. 293).

But the **Theatre Royal Drury Lane** (1811–12, interior 1931), on the right, is the place to begin looking at London's theatres. The father of West End theatres, it was first built in 1663 for Thomas Killigrew and The King's Servants as one of only two patent theatres set up after Charles II was restored to the throne – the other was at Lincoln's Inn Fields. Charles II, restored to the throne in 1660, had issued the two patents; and until the 1840s and the great Victorian expansion of the theatre, these were the only two legitimate theatres and companies – all others were illegal and could be closed at a moment's notice.

The Theatre Royal's subsequent history was illustrious in every way: buildings by Wren, the Adams, Henry Holland, Benjamin Wyatt and pillars from Nash's Regent Street for the colonnade; management by Garrick (Shakespeare seasons), Sheridan (*School for Scandal*), Charles Macready and Augustus Harris (amazing effects and annual pantomimes); acting by Nell Gwynn (1665), David Garrick (1742), Mrs Siddons as Portia (1775), Henry Kemble as Hamlet (1788), Edmund Kean (1814), Grimaldi the clown (his farewell, 1818), Charles Kean (1826) and Henry Irving (his last season, 1905); and royal mistresses – Mary Robinson for the Prince of Wales, later George III, and Mrs Jordan for the Duke of Clarence, later William IV.

More recent triumphs include Noel Coward's *Cavalcade* (1931), four of Ivor Novello's musicals (1935–9), *My Fair Lady* – about a girl from nearby Covent Garden market (1958, for 2,281 performances), and the current revival of *42nd Street* (1984).

Turning left into Russell Street, **Covent Garden Piazza** lies ahead. Here is the first of the many residential squares that shaped and characterised London's haphazard development over the next 250 years as each great estate fell prey to the glittering financial prizes of development. Its origins are ecclesiastical: a convent garden (hence its name today) belonging to Westminster Abbey. After its dissolution (1552), the 1st Earl of Bedford was given the land, an area bounded by the Strand, Drury Lane, Long Acre and St Martin's Lane. Francis Russell, the 4th Earl, saw the rent potential of the land behind his Strand-facing house. But Charles I was against London expanding. So the earl paid £2,000 for a building licence and promised his speculation would be a magnificent addition to London's beauty rather than some mere extension of streets. He then tactfully employed the favourite royal architect, Inigo Jones (1573–1652), in 1631 to build a residential square – the patron dreaming of Place des Vosges in Paris, the architect dreaming of piazzas he had seen while studying Palladio's work in Italy. The result was an innovative, ordered and airy lung in London's tight-knit alleys and streets. It was an immediate success. The houses, set behind their unified classical and stuccoed facades and arcaded ground floors, looked across the open square to the portico east end of St Paul's church. And until the lure westwards to St James's Square (see p. 139), these were high society houses – Killigrew of the Theatre Royal took one house; court painter Sir Peter Lely another.

Society's exit was accelerated after the 5th Earl exploited the central space and won a licence for a market for flowers, fruits, roots and herbs in 1671. The tone of the area plummeted. As the market expanded, so did the amusements. While literary debate by Boswell, Sheridan and Walpole filled the coffee houses, there were duels in the taverns, more than 20 gambling dens, many night cellars and pickpockets and prostitutes in the piazzas (as the arcades were now called). It was in the Piazza that Boswell, his wife neatly out of town, made his rendezvous with pretty Louisa, waiting for her 'in a sort of trembling suspense' and then taking her off in a carriage to enjoy 'a most luscious feast of a night'.

The houses behind the elegant facades were divided up into cheap lodgings, Turkish baths and brothels, earning Covent Garden the nickname 'the great square of Venus'. Meanwhile, the closure of the big Stocks Market to build Mansion House (1737) brought more traders from the City and the closure of Fleet Market (1820s) brought an onslaught. All goods were on sale here: among the apples, lavender and exotic pineapples you could find pretty birdcages, painted plates and even hedgehogs, kept as pets to curb the beetle population.

Order came when Charles Fowler's Central Market building went up in 1831, complete with Bedford arms and motto, *Che sera sera*, above the cross-axis entrances – a motto to be invoked when the Bedfords finally sold out in 1918 and put most of the profit into Russian bonds. But space was still short. Floral Hall (1860), the Flower Market (1870–2) and the Jubilee Market (1904) followed. And until the 1970s, fur-wrapped ladies and hatted gentlemen picked their way through pungent smells and moonlit cabbages and carts on their way home from the chandeliers and red plush of Covent Garden Opera House. As dawn broke, more than a thousand porters came to hump the fresh goods on and off lorries, carts and stalls, stacking up to four or five baskets on their heads. Bernard Miles, who later painted scenery at the Opera House and built the Mermaid Theatre just inside the City, remembers his first visit to London aged five, with his father, a flower salesman, 'in the back of a horse-drawn van full of geraniums', and, on arrival at 5.30am, 'all that hurly-burly of horses and carts and shouting tradesmen'. But in 1974 the market moved south of the river to Nine Elms. The black cloud of redevelopment hung over Covent Garden, the fights for its survival began, but in the end the area was saved. Now the market buildings, the deep arcades and an increasing number of streets and alleys leading off in every direction are restored and spruced up.

As Christina Smith, long-term resident and champion of the area's rejuvenation, advocates, the nicest way to enjoy Covent Garden is to mix wandering, exploring and shopping with simply sitting and watching. A good place to begin is the restored **Central Market**, its elegant central arcade flanked by two large market halls and surrounded by an arcade. Ground and basement floors are stuffed with shops and restaurants, but traders take regular stalls in the central arcade, called the Apple Market (antiques on Mon, crafts Tues–Sat) and buskers entertain daily (10am–9pm). As well as the Bedford arms above the side entrances, a memento of the past lingers on the wall of the south-west pavilion where JA Butler advertises himself as 'Herbalist & Seedsman, Lavender Water etc'.

Under **St Paul's Portico**, the only surviving part of Jones's church, Alternative Arts runs a daily programme of theatre and entertainment (10am–dusk, programme pinned up on the church railings, further information from 1/4 King Street, WC2, tel 240 5451). It follows an old tradition. Pepys watched the London debut of Pietro Gimonde's marionette show (May 1662), the birth of Pulchinella, now known as Mr Punch, whose birthday is celebrated annually here (see Festivals, p. 115). Charles James Fox (1749–1806) did his theatrical electioneering and was voted MP here. And in the opening of GB Shaw's play, *Pygmalion* (later the basis for the musical *My Fair Lady*), the Cockney Eliza Doolittle is selling violets to theatregoers here.

Beyond, in the north-west corner of the square, the ghost of Jones's dignified design breathes in Henry Clutton's Bedford Chambers (1877–9). Turning left into **King Street** (flattering Charles I), the Baroque mansion at no. 43 housed Evans Music-and-Supper Rooms, the first and most famous London music-hall, which from the 1840s to '80s reverberated with song throughout the night until morning, much patronised by the future Edward VII and his fashionable set. In this street David Garrick lived (1743–5) and the club named after him was founded (1845). Down Bedford Street on the left, iron gates topped by the Bedford arms lead to the peaceful churchyard (benches for the weary) of **St Paul's** (1631–33), Jones's 'handsomest barn in Europe' built for Francis Russell, rebuilt after a fire in 1795 and still the favourite church for the artists and actors – memorials begin with Peter Lely (1680) and Grinling Gibbons (1721, with a wreath carved by him for St Paul's Cathedral) and continue up to Sybil Thorndike, Ivor Novello, Edith Evans, Ellen Terry, Noel Coward, Charlie Chaplin, Vivien Leigh and many more. Pleasant in the afternoon, when the nave resounds to choir practice or theatrical friends greeting one another with 'darling' before a christening; pretty gas lamps at dusk, before evening concerts (tel 836 5221; open Mon–Fri 9.30am–4.30pm and for the Sun 11am service).

Turning left out of St Paul's churchyard and again into **Henrietta Street** (flattering Charles I's queen, Henrietta Maria), the explicitly titled St Peter's Hospital for Stone and Other Urinary Diseases (founded 1860) is next to where Jane Austen stayed at her brother Henry's house (1813–14). On the south side of the piazza, the restored **Jubilee Hall** (1903, conceived in 1897, Queen Victoria's Diamond Jubilee year), where foreign flowers were sold, is now a splendid, large, covered market (Mon antiques, Tues–Fri general, Sat and Sun crafts), with a sports centre above, offices and flats adjoining, and restaurants in the basement and overlooking the market area.

The **London Transport Museum** is straight ahead, in the old Flower Market. Founded in the 1920s as a collection of buses, this is now an exciting place that tells the story of the world's largest urban passenger transport system, which carries more than six million passengers a day in buses and trains that cover about half a million miles. When passengers forsook Thames river transport for the land, they progressed from the French-imported cabs and omnibuses to electric tram and trolleybuses on roads. And they hitched up their long skirts to use the Underground, which later promoted top 1920s and '30s design, including an avalanche of seductive posters – 'Soonest reached at any time, Golders Green'. The big hall contains survivors from each era, runs videos inside some buses, has plenty to climb in and to touch, and shows a selection of its poster collection (some reproduced as limited edition postcards). (39 Wellington Street, WC2, tel 379 6344; open daily 10am–6pm; charge. Special exhibitions, film shows, excellent shop stocks posters and postcards, café.)

Leaving the piazza by **Russell Street**, Russell Chambers is where Hummums stood, a Turkish bath whose new owners tried to improve its image in 1701 by forbidding 'stinking savours' and inviting clients to 'sweat and bathe in the cleanliest and be cupped after the newest manner'. Past Boswell's Coffee House, once bookseller Thomas Davies's home, where Boswell and Johnson first met in 1763, the **Theatre Museum** is a new outpost of the Victoria and Albert Museum (see p. 222), housed in more of the Flower Market. Opened in 1987, one of the richest collections in the world is on show, appropriately right among the long-time hub of theatres, the links strengthened by having a theatre ticket office in the museum hall. The giant gilt statue the 'Spirit of Gaiety' welcomes; tickets are sold from Cecil Beaton's box office formerly at the Duke of York's theatre (1950). Then, using playbills, programmes, prompt books, drawings, photographs, models, costumes and props, the basement rooms trace the history of the English stage since the seventeenth century, looking at the theatre (Noel Coward's red, monogrammed dressing-gown and slippers), opera (Boris Christoff's costume for *Faust*), ballet and music as well as puppetry, music hall, circus and rock (Mick Jagger's Jumpsuit). (Tavistock Street, WC2, tel 836 7891; galleries and theatre open Tues–Sun, 11am–7pm; shop, café and theatre ticket office open Tues–Sat, 11am–8pm, Sun, 11am–7pm; closed Mon; charge. Guided tours, lectures, workshops, theatre, special exhibitions, Friends society, shop, stage-set café.) For enthusiastic theatre fans, the main reference library is here, but the bulk of the archive material is at the National Archive of Art and Design (23 Blythe Rd, W14, tel 603 1514; open by appointment Tues–Fri 10am–1pm and 2–4.30pm; best to check first if an item is here or in the Theatre Museum).

Bow Street, where carver Grinling Gibbons (1678–1721), dramatist William Wycherley (1715) and writer and barrister Henry Fielding (1749–53) lived, leads up to the left past Floral Hall (in fact used by fruiterers not florists) to Bow Street Police Station. Although the street was named for its bow shape, its fame came with the Bow Street Runners, originally a group of thief-catchers employed by Henry Fielding to improve on the ineffective watchmen and constables in this crime-ridden area. They were paid reward money, wore no uniform, and even when Home Secretary Robert Peel founded his uniformed Metropolitan Police in 1829, continued to work for the Bow Street Magistrates' Court for another decade. Indeed, this area was so notorious for crime that in 1730 the shopkeepers complained that 'Russell Street, Drury Lane, Crown Court [are] infested with these vile people . . . fighting, robberies and all sorts of debaucheries committed by them all night long'. (To find out more, join a tour at the Metropolitan Police Historical Museum, Bow Street Police Station, 28 Bow Street, WC2, tel 434 5427; tours by appointment on Mon–Fri, 10.30am and 2.30pm; free; no children.)

Opposite stands **Covent Garden Opera House** (first built 1732, rebuilt 1809 and 1858), London home of international opera since its rival, Her Majesty's Theatre in the Haymarket (see p. 140), burnt down in 1867. Lavish from the start, the pantomimist and harlequin John Rich (who had held the other royal patent, see p. 120) moved here

from Lincoln's Inn fields. He built the first opera house on this site, for which Handel wrote a string of oratorios including *Samson and Belshazzar* (1734–7), where Mlle Salle performed perhaps the first *ballet d'action* on stage (1734) and where Goldsmith's *She Stoops to Conquer* (1771) and Sheridan's *The Rivals* (1775) were first performed. After the first fire, which also destroyed Handel's manuscripts and organ, Robert Smirke's theatre, decorated with Flaxman's freize, was the setting for first performances in English of Mozart's *Don Giovanni* (1817) and Rossini's *Barber of Seville* (1818). Then, when Her Majesty's refused to stage one of Giuseppe Persiani's operas in 1847, he left with the top singers, bought this theatre and renamed it the Royal Italian Opera House. Before the next fire, Verdi's *Rigoletto* (1853) and *Il Trovatore* (1855) had their English premieres.

The third building still stands. Designed by EM Barry, decorated with Flaxman's unburnt reliefs, the debuts include Adelina Patti's (1861). The English premieres include *Don Carlos* (1867), *Lohengrin* (1875), *Aida* (1876), *The Ring* with Mahler conducting (1892) and Puccini's *Madam Butterfly* (1905), and London premieres include Bliss's *The Olympians* (1949), Britten's *Billy Budd* (1951) and *A Midsummer Night's Dream* (1961) and Tippet's *The Midsummer Marriage* (1955). Its most recent triumph was a live relay of Placido Domingo in *La Boheme* to 5,000 opera lovers sitting and standing in the Piazza, using a huge screen and powerful loud speakers (1987). Currently the home of the Royal Opera and Royal Ballet, Bernard Haitink is Musical Director, television's Channel 4 creator Jeremy Isaacs is Director, and grocer knight Sir John Sainsbury is Chairman. Optimistic and controversial plans are afoot to spend £55 million extending right back into the piazza and creating a pastiche of Inigo Jones's arcading.

Back down Bow Street into **Wellington Street** (originally called Charles Street to flatter the king again), the Lyceum (1771, latest rebuilding 1904) is where Madame Tussaud first exhibited her waxworks in London (1802) and where the unknown Henry Irving made his name, performed his famous *Hamlet* (1874), became manager and produced a series of triumphs with Ellen Terry as his leading lady (1878–1902); it now awaits its fate as dance theatre or dance hall. Penhaligon's, housed in an old florist's shop at no. 41 and worth a peek inside, started in Jermyn Street where WH Penhaligon brewed his perfumes and pomades using bluebells, lavender and other English essences and became Court Barber to Queen Victoria. Descendants now take care of the Duke of Edinburgh.

Turning right along **Tavistock Street**, across the site of Bedford House, Charles H Fox at no. 32 has stocked every colour, cream and wig for actors' disguises since 1878. Across Southampton Street, where actor and Poet Laureate Colley Cibber lived (1714–20), as did Garrick (1750–72), lies **Maiden Lane**. Here Turner was born above his father's barber shop, Voltaire stayed when exiled from Paris (1727–8), and Rules Restaurant opposite (established 1798) was soon famous for its oysters and porter (a beer brewed from charred malt). Edward VII would sneak in by a special door to dine with Lillie Langtry; and today publishers and authors continue the habits of Dickens, HG Wells and Graham Greene and devour their boiled beef in plush pews surrounded by layers of Spy, Deighton and Wylie cartoons – worth a look inside. Dipping down into the narrow alleys that run down to the Strand, you get an idea of what a tangle of dark and dangerous lanes surrounded the open piazza: Lumley Court, Bull Inn Court and Exchange Court (its hidden grand house a real surprise).

When Covent Garden sank to its lowest, in the eighteenth and nineteenth centuries, the labyrinth of such courts spreading from the end of Maiden Lane to St Martin's Lane formed one of the city's worst rookeries – the horrifically vivid name for ghettos of cheap housing where the poor lived in squalor and misery. This one, described in the 1870s as 'a devious, slimy little reptile of a place', was where the boy Dickens worked in Chandos Place (1824–5) and where many market workers lived. Typically for London, **Bedford Street**, running up right beside it, was always 'a handsome street'. It housed first an aristocrats' finishing school, then a posse of publishers (Heinemann, Macmillan etc), and now *The Lady* magazine at one end (with weekly advertisements for nannies and nanny-hunters) and Moss Bros the dress hire shop at the other. Founded by Moses Moses in 1860, named Moss Bros by his sons, it still hires out tails and toppers for weddings, balls and Ascot races. Turning left into New Row, left into Bedfordbury and right through an archway into **Goodwins Court**, here is a saved and smartened drop of the eighteenth century, complete with gas lamps and a fire mark (see p. 68) above the arch.

The court opens into **St Martin's Lane**, where Chippendale lived and had his workshop. Here Hogarth (1697–1764) studied at the Artists'

Academy (established 1720), refounded it in 1735, attracted Gainsborough and Reynolds to work there and made it London's main art school until it became part of the Royal Academy (1768, see p. 142). Straight across are two more courts: Cecil, briefly Mozart's home (1764), now lined with second-hand bookshops; and St Martin's, where Sheeky's has served oysters since 1896. As the west boundary to Covent Garden, there are three more theatres here: the Duke of York's (1892) arrived first; then the Albery (1903), where Noel Coward's first play, *I'll Leave It To You*, was staged (1920) and where Lionel Bart's musical *Oliver* played for 2,618 performances (1960–6); and the **Coliseum** (1904), with revolving globe outside and revolving stage, electric lifts and Edwardian grandeur inside, a fine setting for Ellen Terry, Edith Evans, Lillie Langtry and Diaghilev's Russian ballet. It is now the home of the Sadler's Wells Opera Company, renamed the English National Opera, who sing in English to a full house of 2,558, London's largest theatre audience.

Moving up the hill, the northern border of Covent Garden is **Long Acre**, first a centre for coach-making, then for cabinet-making; Chippendale worked here, too. On the right, Edward Stanford (established 1852) at nos 12–14 is the world's largest map shop, its sheets describing every corner of the world stored and displayed in Herbert Read and Macdonald's handsome Edwardian shop (1901). Through Conduit Court on the right and then right again down to **Garrick Street**, the great palazzo opposite is the Garrick Club, a drop of Pall Mall appropriately strayed eastwards. For, founded in 1831 to honour the actor David Garrick (1717–79), its past members include Irving, Beerbohm Tree, Dickens, Thackeray, Trollope, Leighton and Rossetti. Portraits of actor-members line the fine rooms and stairwell where present members, still drawn from the arts or the law, dine and gossip.

Turning left into Garrick Street, then again into Rose Street, a pre-Covent Garden 1620s alley, the lane beside the Lamb and Flag pub (unmodernised, so worth a peek) leads into Floral Street; and Langley Court on the left cuts back to Long Acre. Neal Street runs off left, lined with tantalising specialist shops. Contemporary Applied Arts is at the Earlham Street junction, a large showcase for the forefront of British craftsmanship (43 Earlham Street, WC2; tel 836 6993; open Tues–Fri 10am–5.30pm, Sat 10am–4pm; free; Friends society, shop). Turning left into Shorts Gardens, a giant wall water-clock fills the wall outside Neal's Yard warehouse, a vegetarian gourmet's delight with a special line in unusual British cheeses.

Through Neal's Yard, right up Monmouth Street and into St Giles High Street, **St Giles-in-the-Fields** (1731–3) is an isolated treat. Standing first among fields, then among a large parish of squalid rookeries where the 1664–5 Great Plague started and the number of burials (1,361 in one month) destabilised the church, it was rebuilt under the Fifty New Churches Act (like St Mary-le-Strand, see p. 120). In the design competition, Henry Flitcroft beat Gibbs with a thoroughly Gibbsian design and signed his name above the door (church model in vestibule). Garrick was married here (1749), architect John Soane buried here (1837) (tel 240 2532; open Mon–Fri 9am–3.30pm and for Sun Services at 11am and 6pm). Returning down Endell Street, past George Vulliamy's Swiss Protestant Church (1853), St Martin's Hall stood at the Long Acre corner, where in 1859 Dickens gave the first of the public readings that eventually exhausted and killed him; and at nos 132–5 Long Acre on September 30, 1929 John Logie Baird broadcast the first television programme in Britain.

Turning left, Long Acre crosses Drury Lane out of Covent Garden. It was just here that rats carrying the plague arrived in 1664, in goods sent from Holland to Flemish weavers. Ahead lies **Great Queen Street** leading to Lincoln's Inn Fields, an ambitious speculation by William Newton, following hot on the heels of Covent Garden in 1635–40 and similarly under the controlling scrutiny of Charles I. With its disciplined Italian character arriving amid the gabled irregularity of all streets until then, it was known as 'the first regular street in London', a blueprint for perfect, red-brick, rectangular facades decorated with pilasters rising from the first floor to the cornice. The street's order has now gone, due in part to Ashley & Newman's tower-topped Freemason's Hall of 1927–33.

But across Kingsway (sliced through the slums in 1905, good view down to Bush House) and through Remnant Street into **Lincoln's Inn Fields**, Lindsey House down on the right at nos 59–60 reveals just how sweepingly different and handsome the whole scheme was. Possibly by Inigo Jones, its Ionic pilasters were imitated a century later by the architect of nos 57–8 next door. Lower down is Barry's Royal College of Surgeons (1835–6), where students are directly involved in major medical research and have access to the rich collection of the eighteenth century surgeon-scientist,

John Hunter, including work related to his theories of transplant surgery.

The treasure-house here is the **Soane Museum** on the north side where, from 1813 until his death, architect Sir John Soane (1753–1837) lived (moving in from no. 12 next door which he had designed for himself in 1792). He rebuilt no. 13 and filled his cunningly proportioned and decorated rooms to bursting point with his own models (Bank of England); Hogarth's paintings for 'The Rake's Progress' and 'The Election' series (unmissable, unfold them from the walls in layers); antiquities (Soane gave a three-day arrival party for the sarcophagus of Seti I which had been found in the Valley of the Kings); sculpture (Flaxman, Banks); and drawings and paintings (Turner, Watteau, Lawrence, Reynolds), all maintained with such sensitivity that it seems the old man might be found sitting reading beneath his sons' portraits in the drawing-room upstairs, daffodil yellow curtains closed against the winter chill. The house was Soane's working museum for ready reference. Current curator Peter Thornton (who succeeded Sir John Summerson, author of numerous books on London) is reviving Soane's decoration and has already re-established Soane's Model Room. (13 Lincoln's Inn Fields, WC2, tel 405 2107; open Tues–Sat, 10am–5pm; free. To enter, ring the bell; guided tours Sats at 2.30pm; ask to see the Model Room, bookstall; apply in writing to consult the architectural library and drawings and to see no. 12 where they are housed.)

Lincoln's Inn Fields and the Bloomsbury squares (see p. 168) were the seventeenth-century blueprints for the London square: private houses surrounding tree-filled gardens. Lincoln's Inn Fields is the largest in Central London, where tennis courts and a café for lunchtime lawyers are shaded by full-blown plane trees. Hovering on the edge of legal London proper, its residents have included half a dozen Lords Chancellor; Lord Mansfield (1705–93), who improved mercantile law and in 1772 declared slavery illegal in England; Sir William Blackstone (1723–80), whose *Commentaries on the Laws of England* (1765–9) were a comprehensive account of English law and the constitution; and Ramsay MacDonald (1866–1937) who lived in Lindsey House (1896–1911), the first Labour prime minister (1924, 1929–31) whose wife is remembered by a bronze in the garden near no. 3.

East of here lie the four **Inns of Court** – Lincoln's (records since 1422), Middle Temple (records since 1501), Inner Temple (records since 1505) and

Gray's (records since 1569). Originally great mansions where students and barristers lived, each is a proudly independent Honourable Society governed by Benchers who call their students to the Bar.

The Inns were probably established in the fourteenth century after Edward I's Ordinance (1292) put the equivalents of today's barristers and solicitors under the judges' control, ending the clergy's position as lawyers. At the Inns, senior barristers taught students English Common Law, not then a university subject, and a smattering of society skills such as music and dancing, vital accomplishments for ambitious barristers. The revival of interest in legal education last century, after a 200-year decline, encouraged legal London to put itself in order and centralise its activities around the Inns. The Inns became more places of work, in chambers, than places of residence. The Law Society (founded as the Law Institute, 1825) provided a united voice for public debate and also checked its more dubious members. Furthermore, the Council for Legal Education (1852) controlled training; the many small Inns were rationalised to just four; the various courts scattered around Westminster Hall and the Inns were centralised in the new and convenient Law Courts; and institutions with close legal links flocked to the area – insurance companies, banks and the Public Record Office.

But an interest in law is not a required ingredient for a delightful wander through the peaceful Inns and past a few of their satellite buildings in the surrounding streets. Lincoln's Inn Fields begins the series of quiet, restful squares where papers tied in legal red tape fill the window sills and precise minds debate finer legal points on sunny street corners and in nearby pubs.

Lincoln's Inn is across the Fields, through an entrance in the south-east corner. First housed on the Earl of Lincoln's land, it moved into the Bishop of Chichester's mansion (1412–22), bought the freehold (1580), gradually added buildings and, spared from war bombs, is the only Inn where the collegiate character of the lawyers' buildings survives intact. Inside the gate, Philip Hardwick's New Hall and Library (1843, housing one of London's oldest libraries, founded 1497) is on the left, where students clock up the required numbers of 'dinners' beneath Watts's huge fresco of 'The Lawgivers' (1859). GG Scott's fantasy mini-castle beyond is the gardeners' potting shed for the roses and lawns beyond. Ahead lies the core of the older buildings. Above the open undercroft, the foundation stone of the Chapel (1619–23) was laid by member, preacher and poet John Donne (1572–1631, nice box pews and stained glass). To the south, Old Buildings is where early lawyers lived in Old Hall (1490–2, linenfold panelling, Hogarth's painting of 'St Paul Before Felix'); it was later used as a court until the Law Courts were completed. To the north, Old Square (much by GG Scott, 1873–6) leads to Stone Buildings (1774–80); and to the east, the Gatehouse (1518, mostly rebuilt), complete with original heavy oak doors, is topped with Lincoln's Inn arms (lion rampant).

Back and around the pretty gardens on the left, New Square (1685–97) was Henry Serle's private speculation of lawyers' lodgings, later swallowed up by the Inn and changed to offices. Illustrious members of the Inn have included prime ministers Walpole, Pitt the Younger, Melbourne, Asquith, Disraeli and Gladstone; recent Law Lords include both Lords Hailsham and Lord Denning; students have included Oliver Cromwell and William Penn. (Lincoln's Inn, WC2, tel 405 1393; courtyards open Mon–Fri; gardens and chapel open Mon–Fri noon–2.30pm; these and Old Hall also open on application to the Porter's Lodge by Lincoln's Inn Fields gate; Chapel services in law terms, usually on Sun, 11.30am; apply in writing to the Under-Treasurer to visit the Watts fresco.)

Through the archway at the bottom and past Wildy the law bookseller, **Carey Street**'s bankruptcy courts (now part of the Law Courts straight ahead) are why a bankrupt person is described as being 'in Carey Street'. To the right is a favourite lawyers' pub, the Seven Stars, and a corner memorial to Sir Thomas More (1478–535), member of Lincoln's Inn who was Lord Chancellor to Henry VIII (1529–32) but executed for treason after he opposed the king's divorce. To the left, past grand no. 60 (1731–2), craftsmen work at the back of Ede and Ravenscroft in Star Yard making the various legal wigs for Bench and Bar, each made-to-measure in horsehair in about 7 weeks for around £180, their seventeenth-century styles the ultimate in the legal profession's proud conservatism – even bishops stopped wearing wigs soon after Queen Victoria's coronation.

Into **Chancery Lane**, the backbone of legal London that runs from opposite the Temple in Fleet Street, up past the Law Courts and Lincoln's Inn to Gray's Inn. Here wigged and gowned lawyers scuttle along their thoroughfare from Inn to Inn, pausing at legal buildings and shops. To the right lies Lewis Vulliamy's Law Society (1831, additions by Charles Holden, 1902). Across the road, James Pennethorne's **Public Record Office** (1851–6, John Taylor's additions 1891–6) is where 84 miles of England's government and law records since the Conquest of 1066 were at last gathered together, ordered and filed to form one of the most complete archives of any nation. The star exhibit of its museum in the old Rolls Chapel (old glass and monuments) is the Domesday Book (a minutely detailed survey of William the Conqueror's England, made 1086), while co-star documents include: Pope Clement VII confirming Henry VIII as Defender of the Faith, Cardinal Wolsey asking Henry VIII's pardon (1529), Drake reporting on the Spanish Armada (1588), Wellington's account of the Battle of Waterloo (1815), Guy Fawkes's confessions, the wills of Shakespeare and Jane Austen, Washington's letter to George III, and much more (Chancery Lane, WC2, tel 405 0741; open Mon–Fri, 1–4pm; free). Back up Chancery Lane, past legal outfitters, wig-makers and booksellers, the **London Silver Vaults** are nos 53–64, a warren of silver shops housed in the disused Chancery Lane Safe Deposit.

At the top, a little diversion across Holborn and up Brownlow Court brings you first to speculator Dr Barbon's wide and elegant **Bedford Row** (1680, most of the west side original, see especially nos 12, 13, 36 and 42–43). If it is a weekday, between May and September and between noon and 2.30pm, you can return down Bedford Row, turn left by an old hand pump, and enter **Gray's Inn** by the side gate – otherwise it is a trot back along Holborn, past Chancery Lane and in at the main gate, near the Cittie of Yorke pub where members sip their Burgundy around an iron stove (1815) saved from their Hall and decorated with their crest, the griffin.

Sir Reginald le Grey, Chief Justice of Chester (died 1308), lived in a manor house set amid lakes and windmills in open country. By 1370 it was the law students' hostel, and buildings were gradually added during its Tudor heyday. Today, after much bombing, the Gatehouse leads into South Square (1685, rebuilt), with rebuilt Library on the right. The Chapel and Hall (surviving interior includes the magnificent Tudor screen) divide it from Gray's Inn Square (1678–88) which leads on to Verulam Buildings (1803–11). These honour the member lawyer and scientist Francis Bacon (1561–1626), who advocated scientific knowledge, was a favourite of Elizabeth I, became Lord Chancellor (1618–21), was created Lord Verulam and Viscount

St Albans but was finally caught taking bribes, put in the Tower and died in debt – Pomeroy's statue (1912) of him is in South Square.

A passageway in the south-west corner of Gray's Inn Square leads to Field Court and through the elegant iron gate (1723) into Gray's Inn Gardens (1606). Laid out by Bacon, they were later known as the Walks, became a favourite promenade for seventeenth-century society – Pepys espied 'fine ladies' there – and are now a haven of green lawns and mature trees. Alec Forshaw, connoisseur of London parks and squares, revels in their 'sloping terraces of velvet lawns' where 'wisps of gardeners' bonfire smoke drift through soft afternoon sunshine'. Eminent members and students have included William Cecil (1520–98), Secretary of State and Lord Treasurer to Elizabeth I; the Earl of Southampton, Shakespeare's patron who had the *Comedy of Errors* first performed in the Hall (1594); and more recently Lord Shawcross, who was Attorney-General 1945–51 and chief prosecutor at the Nuremberg War Crimes Tribunal. (Gray's Inn, WC1, tel 405 8164; gates open Mon–Sat, Holborn gate only on Sun; The Walks open May 1–Sept 30, noon–2.30pm, extended in the Long Vacation; to visit the Library, Chapel and Hall, apply to Mrs Thom, Librarian, tel 242 8592; during law terms, after-dinner concerts on some Fris, 8pm, and Chapel services on most Suns, 11.15am.)

Turning left out of Holborn gate along **Holborn**, the restored half-timbered houses on the right (1586), with strip windows, gables and overhangs, are London's only surviving Tudor domestic architecture. Imagined as part of a narrow street full of similar houses on both sides, then Jones's Covent Garden, Barbon's Bedford Row and Serle's New Square must have seemed a startling innovation to Londoners. An arched opening among them leads to the Inner Court of Staple Inn (east side 1729–34, Hall 1581), rare surviving buildings of the small Inns, all now absorbed by the big four. Further down Holborn, a narrow passage by nos 20–3 leads to another survivor, the tiny Hall of Barnard's Inn. On the north side of Holborn, Alfred Waterhouse's red terracotta, Gothic palace for Prudential Assurance (1879 and 1899–1906), affectionately known as the Pru, testifies to their pioneering success at industrial life assurance in wealthy Victorian Britain – Dickens lived on this site while he wrote *Pickwick Papers*, remembered by a bust in the hall. Running north from here is Leather Lane market (best enjoyed during a weekday lunchtime), connected via Greville Street on the right to Hatton Garden (named after Elizabeth I's Chancellor), glittering with the diamond and silver traders' shop windows.

Turning right into it from Greville Street, then left by no. 8 down very narrow Ely Court alley and past the tiny-roomed Ye Mitre pub (1546), you emerge into **Ely Place**. Here lived the Bishops of Ely from 1290 to 1772, when they left their Temple lodgings and then went west to Dover Street. All but their private chapel was destroyed and the tranquil close was built around it. A private road owned by the Crown, its peace is guarded by a lodge, a top-hatted commissionaire and wrought iron gates closed nightly. The church, **St Ethel-dreda** (c.1300), is tucked in on the left, with a spacious nave illumined by light filtering through the stained glass windows at the east and west ends, especially magical on sunny mornings and evenings (tel 405 1061; open daily, 7.30am–7pm).

At Holborn Circus, Charles Bacon's jolly equestrian statue of Prince Albert doffing his plumed hat to the City (1874) marks the beginning of **Holborn Viaduct** (1863–9), an extravagant project that cost £2.5 million, took six years to build and was opened by Queen Victoria. It sweeps off left to connect Holborn with Newgate Street across the River Fleet valley, now Farringdon Street, the bridge section (good **views**) decorated with statues of Victorian virtues – Commerce, Agriculture, Science and Fine Arts – and four past City heroes at the corners – Henry FitzAilwin (first Lord Mayor), Sir Thomas Gresham (found of the Royal FitzAilwyn Exchange), Sir William Walworth (the mayor who stabbed the peasant rebellion leader Wat Tyler) and Sir Thomas Myddelton (who brought fresh water to London).

Across the viaduct, Holy Sepulchre Without Newgate (1666–70) is a post-Fire rebuild around the surviving soaring fifteenth-century west tower. And on the right sits EW Mountford's Wren-inspired, heavily fortified **Central Criminal Court** (1900–7), known as Old Bailey and topped by a dome inspired by Wren's at Greenwich and by Pomeroy's bronze statue of Justice, who has been a minor star of countless British crime movies. This was the site of various Newgate Prison buildings, where lack of water and ventilation promoted gaol fever, a fierce version of typhoid. Here the murderer Major Strangeways was pressed to death (1658); the Gordon Rioters pulled down one building and their enemy, Lord George Gordon, was installed in the next and died of gaol fever (1793); and crowds paid highly to watch multiple public

hangings until 1868 after which they were carried out behind the walls.

The Central Criminal Court superseded the nearby Sessions Courts in 1834. With 18 courts tightly packed on the first floor, and prisoners' cells below, the judges still carry fragrant posies on the first two days of each session in memory of Newgate stenches.

More serious parades have been to the trials of Oscar Wilde (1895), 'Brides-in-the-Bath' murderer George Joseph Smith (1915), William 'Lord Haw-Haw' Joyce (1945), JR Christie (1953) and 'Yorkshire Ripper' Peter Sutcliffe (1981). Entering by the street that gave it its nickname, Old Bailey, it is well worth exploring the interior and asking which court will be the most interesting to attend – the free show of lawyers' sharpened wits can match anything on offer in Covent Garden. When the court adjourns, barristers, journalists and relatives of those in dock adjourn too, to the pubs opposite and at the top of the hill (Central Criminal Court, EC4, tel 248 3277; courts sit Mon–Fri, 10.30am–1pm and 2–4pm; list of the day's programme by the main door).

Continuing down Old Bailey, then right down Ludgate Hill – where Old Bailey jurists stayed at the London Coffee House when they debated their verdicts overnight – and across the path of the River Fleet (now New Bridge Street), **Fleet Street** lies ahead. This main thoroughfare and royal route westwards out of the City is still pleasantly informal with a mixture of buildings accumulated over the centuries and impressive focuses both ends – St Paul's eastwards, St Dunstan's westwards.

Printing began here. William Caxton (c.1422–91) published the first book printed in England in 1477, *Dictes and Sayings of the Philosophers*, following it with almost eighty volumes hot off his press at Westminster. After his death, Wynkyn de Worde, his more commercially minded pupil, moved the press to be close to his customers, the clergy around St Paul's who almost monopolised literacy. He set up England's first press with movable type near St Bride's church, amid the bishops' mansions. Between 1500 and his death in 1535, he printed about 800 books, ending with 'Complaint of the too soon maryed', and also ran a bookshop in St Paul's Churchyard. This was where, in the 1660s, Pepys treated himself to 'two or three hours' at his bookshop, 'calling for twenty books to lay this money out upon'. From here to Aldwych, printers, bookbinders, booksellers and their essential tools, writers and their coffee-house or pub meeting-places, lined the road.

It became one of the sights of London. And when the German scientist, philosopher and wit, Georg Christoph Lichtenberg, came in 1775 he was amazed and wrote home: ' . . . on both sides tall houses . . . the lower floors consist of shops and seem to be made entirely of glass; many thousand candles light up silverware, engravings, books, clocks, glass, pewter, paintings, women's finery, gold, precious stones, . . . and endless coffee-rooms and lottery offices . . . the street illuminated as if for some festivity . . . the confectioners dazzle your eyes with their candelabra and tickle your nose with their wares . . . festoons of Spanish grapes, pineapples, and pyramids of apples and oranges, among which hover attendant white-armed nymphs with silk caps and little silk trains.' And all about the noise was tremendous: 'the hum and clatter of thousands of tongues . . . the chimes from Church towers, the bells of the postmen, the organs, fiddles, hurdy-gurdies, and tambourines . . . the cries of those who sell hot and cold viands at street corners . . . merrily shouting beggar-boys, sailors and rogues.'

Ludgate Circus, named after King Lud, built by the Romans, then rebuilt several times before being demolished with the other City gates in the 1760 traffic improvements, marks the start of Fleet Street. It replaced Fleet Bridge, near which the *Daily Courant* was published in 1702, England's first daily newspaper. On the first Fleet Street house on the right, a bronze medallion remembers Edgar Wallace (1875–1932), who rose from poor newspaper boy through journalist to Hollywood author of 170 novels. On the left, Punch Tavern is where Punch magazine was conceived in 1841, now decorated with cartoons and drawings from it. Beyond, tucked down a lane, stands Wren's **St Bride's** church (1671–8, spire 1701–3), where his tallest spire (226 ft) is a landmark soaring up from the bombed and rebuilt nave (pews given in memory of press barons, hacks and cartoonists). Underneath, the remarkable crypt (Roman ditch and pavement, medieval tiles) houses a fascinating mini-museum of Fleet Street's printing history (tel 353 1301; open daily, 8.30am–5.30pm, until 8.30pm on Sun). The churchyard behind has welcome benches, overlooks twisting Bride Lane and Bride Court, and was where William Rustell printed books by his uncle, Sir Thomas More, in the 1530s.

Back on The Street, as it was known until the newspapers left, Wynkyn de Worde set up his office at the Sign of the Sun, conveniently opposite Shoe Lane where the bookbinders worked. Around the corner, Salisbury Court leads down to Salisbury Square, where the Press Council is at no. 1, the only domestic survivor. In this square, Pepys downed 'a morning draught and had a pickled herring' for breakfast (1660); William Woodfall edited one newspaper, *The Morning Chronicle*, and founded another, *The Diary* (1789); and the painter Hogarth first met Dr Johnson, whose shaking head he thought idiotic until, according to Boswell, 'he displayed such a power of eloquence that Hogarth looked at him in astonishment'.

It was on The Street that the newspaper revolution took place last century. Alfred Harmsworth (1865–1922), the pioneer of popular journalism in Britain, bought the *Daily Mail* in 1896 and drove its circulation up to a million, the first daily newspaper to hit that figure, then joined his brother Harold to found a women's picture paper, the *Daily Mirror*, in 1903. True press barons, Alfred was created Baron, then Viscount Northcliffe, while Harold became Viscount Rothermere. The present Viscount Rothermere's group of *Daily Mail*, *Mail on Sunday* and *London Standard* were in Carmelite Street, the extension of Whitefriars Street to the south, but fled Fleet Street westwards to Kensington in 1988, taking with them the boardroom built for Lord Northcliffe.

On the left is Lutyens's headquarters (1935) for Reuter's and the Press Association, organisations set up in 1851 as co-operatives by British newspapers to provide a pool of foreign (Reuter's) and domestic (Press Association) news. Opposite, Ellis & Clarke and Sir Owen Williams' slick, glossy building (1931) was the first curtain wall building in London, put up for the *Daily Express* (founded 1900) which another press baron, Lord Beaverbrook, bought in 1915 and used brilliantly as a propaganda tool to support the Empire, further his own career – he was a member of the wartime Cabinet and a good friend of Churchill – and later to fight Britain's entry into the EEC. Further up, Elcock and Sutcliffe's building (1928–30) for the *Daily Telegraph* (founded 1855, run by the Berry family until sold to Canadian businessman Conrad Black in 1985) stands next to Peterborough Court, the name of the paper's diary column.

Beyond here, down Bouverie Street to the left, world press baron Rupert Murdoch ran the *Sun* and the *News of the World*. And until recently, other papers were not far away, either. The *Guardian* was up Farringdon Road, Murdoch's *The Times* and the *Sunday Times* beyond, the *Observer* off Ludgate Hill and the *Financial Times* behind St Paul's. Then, in 1985, Eddy Shah started *Today*, based in Pimlico and using merely journalists and computers. Technology had replaced the printers. Murdoch moved his empire eastwards to the Docklands and direct-input technology. Other papers followed. Where Fleet Street thundered with century-old presses, lorries delivering vast rolls of newsprint and nippy vans racing off to put tomorrow's papers on overnight trains, and where post-theatre passers-by could pick up tomorrow's papers today, all fell silent just a decade before the 500th anniversary of de Worde's arrival.

The alleys give an idea of what the area was like. Diving off north, Wine Office Court is where Ogilby and Morgan lived while they compiled and printed the 1676 map of London, where Oliver Goldsmith began *The Vicar of Wakefield* (1760–2), and where Ye Olde Cheshire Cheese, known as The House, is still famed for its steak and kidney puddings and retains the character of the many eighteenth-century rambling chophouses, this one patronised by succeeding generations of the local literary set – Gibbon, Boswell, Dickens, Thackeray, Mark Twain et al.

Plunging right again, through Hind Court into Gough Square, **Dr Johnson's House** (built c.1700) is at the far end. Here Dr Samuel Johnson (1709–84) lived from 1749 to 1759 while compiling his dictionary, helped by six amanuenses (of whom five were Scots) who worked in the garret at the top. Saved from demolition in 1911 by Lord Harmsworth, now tended by Johnsonian Miss Margaret Eliot, it is furnished with Boswell's coffee cup, Mrs Thrale's tea-set, a dictionary and portraits of Johnson (whose short sight makes him look very cross) and his friends (Chesterfield, who was patron of the dictionary; Boswell; the Doctor with actress Mrs Siddons; Wesley preaching). And the Doctor's character pervades all (17 Gough Square, EC4, tel 353 3745; ring bell to enter; open Mon–Sat, May–Sept 11am–5.30pm, Oct–Apr 11am–5pm; charge). Cutting down Bolt Court, St Dunstan's Court or Johnson's Court back to Fleet Street, Crane Court is next but one, where *Punch* and *The Illustrated London News* were first published and where nos 5 and 6 are the earliest surviving post-Fire houses and early works by speculator Dr Barbon. Beyond, Robert Maxwell's Mirror Group of newspapers is still at the top of New Fetter Lane. And opposite is El Vino's, a favourite haunt of male

barristers and journalists, notoriously unfriendly towards women despite the 1982 Court of Appeal ruling that they must not refuse to serve women standing at the bar.

As Fleet Street bends round, St Dunstan-in-the-West (medieval, latest building 1829–33) closes the view, its exterior adorned with a clock (1671) put up by grateful parishioners after the Great Fire halted nearby; a statue of Elizabeth I (above the vestry) from the Tudor Ludgate (1586, King Lud and his sons are inside); and Lutyens's memorial to Lord Northcliffe (1930). John Donne was rector here (1624–31); Izaak Walton was a sidesman (1629–44), whose *The Compleat Angler* (1653) was printed in the churchyard by Richard Marriott. In this bit of Fleet Street, Richard Pynson, an early printer to the king (1500–30), rolled his presses in time with de Worde's down at St Bride's; his successor, Thomas Berthelet, imported Italian binders to make the first gilt-tooled bindings in England; Richard Tottell won a patent in 1553 to print all the official books on Common Law; Jacob Tonson bought the copyright of Milton's *Paradise Lost* which he published together with works by Dryden, Congreve and Vanbrugh; and John Murray published from no. 32 (1762–1812) before moving to Albemarle Street.

Just beyond Chancery Lane, Horace Jones's mid-road memorial topped by a griffin rampant (1880) is a feeble replacement for Wren's majestic Temple Bar archway, where traders hired out telescopes for the curious to gloat at executed heads tied on firmly out of reach of grieving friends. It marks the boundary of the City of London and the City of Westminster, and it is here that on state occasions the sovereign still pauses to ask the Lord Mayor's permission to enter his city and to surrender the Sword of State, symbolising the old tension between the monarchy and its money source, the City merchants (see pp. 68–9). Catching a distant glimpse of Gibbs's tower (1719–66) soaring above Wren's tree-hidden St Clement Danes (1680), the archway opposite Chancery Lane leads into Inner Temple Lane and the law presides once more – last century, the newly centralised legal honey-pot attracted Hoare's (no. 37), Barclay's (no. 19) and Child's (no. 1) banks.

Inner Temple and **Middle Temple** derive their name from the Knights Templar, so-called because the brotherhood of knights (founded in France, 1118) who protected pilgrims journeying to Jerusalem had their base next to the Mosque of El Aska, known as the Temple of Solomon. In 1185, the

London Knights Templar moved from Holborn to the riverside and built a circular temple-church and adjoining monastery. Grateful pilgrims and monarchs fuelled their power and wealth; royal jealousy followed and they were discredited and suppressed (1312). The property was given to the Order of St John (1324) and part leased to law students for a hostel. At the Dissolution, it became Crown property, which the Benchers (senior Inn members) later leased in perpetuity (1608) and then divided (1732); but the Master of the Temple Church is still a Crown appointment.

These are the best positioned of all Inns: right on the merchant-to-royals route, with land sloping down to the river which was much increased by Bazalgette's embankment. Middle Temple Walk divides the two Inns which appear to be a single labyrinth of courts. Even if the post-bomb rebuilding (much 1950s work by Sir Edward Maufe) is often out of scale, the whole retains its peaceful, collegiate atmosphere, a delight to wander as the sun softens until at dusk the lamplighters light the gas lamps. Inner Temple gateway (1610–11) is one of the best half-timber buildings in London, and a surviving panelled and plastered room of the first floor is well worth visiting – now housing the Samuel Pepys Club and Pepysian memorabilia (Prince Henry's Room, 17 Fleet Street, EC4, no tel; open Mon–Fri 1.45–5pm, Sat 1.45–4.30pm; charge). Down the lane, where Doctor Johnson lived at no. 1, Dr Johnson's Buildings (1857) named after him are on the right, where John Mortimer, senior defence-only barrister and author of the Rumpole stories, has chambers. On the wall is a clue to identifying which Inn is which: this building is marked with the winged-horse Pegasus crest of Inner Temple. But Goldsmith Building (1861) on the left has the Paschal lamb and flag crest of Middle Temple above the main doorway. In front, the grand grave belongs to the lawyer John Hiccocks (died 1726), the plain one to the writer Oliver Goldsmith (1728–74).

Further down the lane, Farrer's Buildings (rebuilt 1876) is on the right, where Boswell took chambers to be near his friend Johnson, leading into Hare Court. Here Lord George Jeffries (1648–89), the infamous and ruthless Lord Chief Justice, had his chambers. After the Monmouth Rebellion (1685), when Charles II's illegitimate son, the Duke of Monmouth (1649–85), attempted to claim the throne from James II but was defeated at the Battle of Sedgemoor and then executed, Judge Jeffries presided over the 'bloody assizes' that followed, condemning some 300 supporters to be hanged and several hundred more to be transported to the colonies. But after James II fled in 1688, the judge died an inmate of the Tower.

Temple Church (c.1160–85, c.1220–40, later restoration) sits across the lane. One of the oldest buildings in London, its circular plan was inspired by the Dome of the Rock in Jerusalem, its chancel added later to make it 'pure Norman and pure Gothic side by side' (Pevsner). See especially the decorated porch outside and, entering by the south door, the Purbeck marble effigies of thirteenth-century Knights Templar (that of Robert de Ros, 1227, the only unrestored original). Leaving the church, Church Court is surrounded by the Knights' cloisters on the right (rebuilt 1949–50), and on the left the deceptively new Master's House (copy of the 1667 original) stands at the end of an incongrous city-centre English country garden.

But past it and through the arch, much of Wren's splendid King's Bench Walk (1677–8) straight ahead still stands, nos 1–6 with their interiors, too – Harold Nicolson and his wife Vita Sackville-West lived at no. 4 (1930–45), H Rider Haggard lodged at no. 13. The houses run down to the river opposite S Smirke's Paper Buildings (1838, where Galsworthy had chambers), behind which are Inner Temple Gardens, a **view** of them best enjoyed by peeking through the splendid gates (1730) decorated with the Gray's Inn griffin and Inner Temple Pegasus to symbolise their long friendship. Forbidden to build on their bonus land from Bazalgette's reclamation, the Benchers hosted the Royal Horticultural Society's annual flower show in their enlarged gardens (1888–1913) until it moved to Chelsea Hospital to become the Chelsea Flower Show (see p. 231). Overlooking the gardens, Crown Office Row (1953–5) juts forward, beside the neo-Georgian Inner Temple Hall (1955), Treasury and Library. Left of the Hall, a passage leads to Elm Court where two of the monastery's fourteenth-century rooms survive on the east side (now part of the Hall). Middle Temple Lane is through the archway of Lamb Building (1954) at the far corner. A few yards up, another archway leads into the narrow, paved Pump Court (c.1686, except the south side, 1951–3), where Henry Fielding (of the Bow Street Runners, see p. 123) had chambers at no. 4.

At the top of Middle Temple Lane, the official dividing line between the Inns, the gateway (1684) to Fleet Street was designed by Roger North, a bencher and amateur architect, and nos 1–3 were built soon after (1693). Returning down the lane, through Brick Court (Oliver Goldsmith's home from 1765 until his death) and Essex Court on the right, an archway (1677) leads to New Court (1676), now a misnomer for one of the oldest survivors, a seven-bay building put up by that ubiquitous speculator Dr Barbon. To the north lies Devereux Court, with the barristers' local pub tucked in the lane; to the south, steps lead down to Fountain Court where, ahead and down more steps, there is a good view over Middle Temple Gardens.

Back in Fountain Court, the magnificent Middle Temple Hall (1562–70, restored) has a double hammer-beam roof, remarkable Elizabethan screen, carved doorways, Tudor Bench Table, portraits of Elizabeth I and the Stuart monarchs (Charles I by Van Dyck), the Cupboard Table where Readers gave their lectures before becoming Benchers, and walls lined with former Readers' coats-of-arms (from 1597). This is where the great revels and masques were staged between All Saints (November 1) and Candlemas (February 2), concluded in 1601 with a performance of Shakespeare's *Twelfth Night*. It was then that Tudor sailors Drake, Raleigh and Hawkins were associated with the Inn. Dramatists Wycherley and Congreve followed, as did John Evelyn (diarist and close friend of Charles II), the ill-fated Duke of Monmouth (see above), Sir William Blackstone (resident of Lincoln's Inn Fields, see p. 125), Edmund Burke (1727–97), the influential political theorist who advocated the constitutional rights of parliament, and William Wilberforce (1759–1833), the philanthropist who achieved the abolition of slavery throughout the British Empire (1833). Today, the horn summons students to dine at 6.30pm, when they clock up their required 'dinners' in the 12 legal terms each year.

Down Middle Temple Lane, passing on the right Plowden Building (1831) and the Inn's Treasury and Library (1956–8), EM Barry's Temple Gardens (1878–9) spans the lane and is the river gate of the Temple, beyond which are nice views back up both Inns' gardens from the Embankment. (Inner Temple, EC4, tel 353 8462 for Treasurer's Office. Middle Temple, EC4, tel 353 4355 for Treasurer's Office, Plowden Buildings; Hall during legal terms, Mon-Fri 10–11.30am and 3–4pm (subject to availability); gates of both Inns usually close at 8pm but the one to Middle Temple Lane (river end) remains open. Temple Church, tel 353 1736, open daily 10am–4pm (some closures), services on Sun at 8.30am and 11.15am (except Aug and Sept).

Turning right and right again, **Essex Street** (c.1680) is a Dr Barbon development on the Essex House site, where publishers later congregated (Macmillan are still in Little Essex Street). Emerging into Fleet Street, there is a good **view** across to the turrets and towers of the **Royal Courts of Justice** (1874–82), known as the Law Courts. As usual in London, their history was protracted. By the 1830s, judges and lawyers were flitting between Westminster Courts and their overflow at Lincoln's Inn. So, helped by the new Law Society, the solicitor and law reformer EW Field launched his campaign for a single new building in 1841. Parliamentary Bills were passed in 1865; the design competition announced in 1866, won by George Edmund Street in 1868; the first brick was laid in 1874; Street died of a stroke fed by exhaustion and worry in 1881, having prepared some 3,000 drawings; and Queen Victoria opened it in 1884.

EV Lucas called it 'the most astounding assemblage of spires and turrets, and gable and cloisters, that ever sprang from one Englishman's brain'. Scrubbed clean in 1970, this last great Gothic public building in London has a cathedral-huge hall where Armstead's monument to Street is on the right, Alfred Gilbert's Victoria at the far end, and the Trial List in the centre. The porter will recommend the most intriguing or scandalous free show to watch in the surrounding court-rooms, but leave time for a cup of tea in the basement café where Court reporters tap typewriters on their knees and off-duty barristers plonk their wigs down beside the chocolate biscuits (Royal Courts of Justice, Strand, WC2, tel 936 6000; courts sit Oct–July, with Christmas and Easter breaks, Mon–Fri from 9.30am).

Opposite, Lloyds Bank (1882–3) at 222 Strand was built as the Royal Courts of Justice Chambers and crammed 400 spectators on the scaffolding when Victoria was opening the Law Courts. It is worth a dash into the banking hall (formerly restaurant) to see the glorious Doulton tilework made at Lambeth Potteries, an early scheme of tile decoration that happily mixes classical and Islamic styles and Ben Jonson characters with chrysanthemums.

If the Law Courts wiped out a disreputable Victorian slum, the crescent-shaped **Aldwych** (1900–5), an area that Alfred once gave his defeated Danes back in the tenth century, soon cleared up another patch. The island gained Marshall Mackenzie's Australia House (1912–18);

Helmle & Corbett's Bush House (1923–35), with symbolic figures of England and America and marble corridors to be manufacturers' showrooms, but since 1940 home of the BBC World Service (worth exploring the ground floor, public arcade); and Herbert Baker's India House (1928–30), India-inspired friezes outside and murals by Indians inside. The outside ring, in keeping with Covent Garden behind, has WGR Sprague's Aldwych Theatre (1905) on one corner, where Ben Travers's Aldwych farces were staged and the Royal Shakespeare Company had its London home until it moved to the Barbican (see p. 287); his twin Strand theatre (1905) at the other corner; and A Marshall Mackenzie's Waldorf Hotel (1907–8) in between.

The much loved Gaiety Theatre (1868, rebuilt 1903) was at the south-west corner, its reputation made by a string of burlesques (1868–86) followed by *The Gaiety Girl* (1893) which set the mood for musical comedy, Gaiety Girls and stage-door Johnnies. From the rebuilt theatre (demolished only in 1957), the Gaiety Girls would skip across to tea in the Waldorf's Palm Court (see p. 290), munching their cucumber sandwiches while their prospective escorts, some from nearby legal chambers, sized them up from the glass-walled bar overlooking it. The tea is still good, and a short wander away is **Waterloo Bridge** (see p. 99), the perfect spot to watch the sun set over Westminster in the west, turning to catch the last rays tickling the City spires in the east.

The Court of St James's: Society moves west

Mapping it out from above: Two good places, but both require buying a meal or a drink: Roof Restaurant, 27th floor, the Hilton Hotel (Mon–Sat buffet lunch 12.30–3pm, Sun brunch 10.30am–2.30pm, Mon–Sat 7.30–11.30pm [last orders] dinner); Hamilton's, 7th floor, the Inter-Continental hotel (Tues–Sat, evenings only; bar and restaurant). However, the view from the bridge over the Serpentine is free and remarkable, even if it is not high up.

Starting point: The Mall, by St James's Palace, access by Underground: Green Park, St James's Park.

Good days to explore: Weekdays for the art dealers, auction houses, shops and smart society (who spend weekends in the country); weekends for quiet streets and lively parks including Speakers' Corner in Hyde Park.

Vital equipment: To enter the spirit and breakfast, tea or cocktail in the grand hotels, it is best to look tidy (not necessarily smart). Contrary to popular myth, you do not have to dress up, pay or buy a catalogue to visit the auction houses.

Information: LTB Information Centre, Victoria, SW1, see p. 3; there is also an LTB outpost at Selfridges, see p. 4. For special information on Jermyn Street, the Jermyn Street Association, 15 Jermyn Street, SW1; and on Bond Street, the Bond Street Association, 180 New Bond Street, W1 (629 1682).

Refreshment suggestions: see p. 311.

Local festivals: Jermyn Street Festival, held most years, often for a week in Sept and focused on St James's Church; the whole street is like a village fete; information from the Jermyn Street Association, see above. Bond and Jermyn streets are decorated at Christmas time, mid-Nov–Jan 6.

Local libraries: See Westminster walk, p. 75. Westminster Borough libraries also include Mayfair Library, 25 South Audley Street, W1 (798 1037); Mon–Fri 9.30am–7pm, Sat 9.30am–1pm.

If you are here for any length of time, the London Library, 14 St James' Square, SW1 (930 7705); Mon–Sat 9.30am–5.30pm, Thurs until 7pm; founded in 1841 by Thomas Carlyle who was fed up with the slow service at the British Library; more than a million old and new books housed in a warren from the deepest bowels to the roof of a once-elegant St James's residence, particularly good on London, subscribes to countless specialist magazines; splendid Reading Room where gentlemen snooze in leather chairs after lunch at their club; excellent librarians and book service; membership by application to the Secretary, costs £10 monthly (a reference ticket only), £75 annually (reference and borrowing ticket) plus £18.50 for a spouse – a bargain.

Around St James's Palace, the spirit of the eighteenth-century courtiers still lingers. After the fire at Whitehall Palace in 1698, this became the official royal London palace. The whole area was built by the privileged for the privileged. The first courtiers moved west from the Strand and Covent Garden soon after the Restoration of Charles II in 1660, further encouraged by the Great Fire of 1666. They colonised the fields nearest their familiar territory, neatly filling the space between the Strand and the new court. St James's Square went up first, inspired by the Duke of Bedford's building in Covent Garden, with its elegant piazza by Inigo Jones. Development swiftly spread northwards, where half-a-dozen of the landed gentry built up their acres to form Mayfair. Pressing on further, above Oxford Street, the Marylebone and Portman estates came next and then, sneak-ing along the north side of Hyde Park, the beginnings of Bayswater.

Building followed a regular pattern: squares and broad streets of stylish mansions, with mews lanes for carriages and horses behind and nearby streets lined with select shops. For, hot on the heels of the developers came the suppliers – of a lady's perfumes and jewels, of a gentleman's hats, suits and shirts, and of two essentials for cultivated high society: art dealers to help connoisseurs and not-so-connoisseurs furnish their mansions; and clubs to help gentlemen escape from their wives.

It was these developments, perfect rich men's playgrounds bordered by three big parks for taking the air, that made this the most socially desirable residential area of London throughout the nineteenth century and until social patterns changed after the

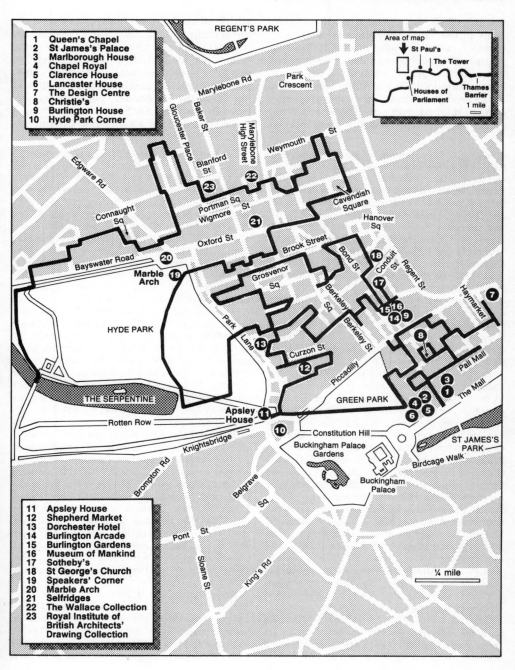

1 Queen's Chapel
2 St James's Palace
3 Marlborough House
4 Chapel Royal
5 Clarence House
6 Lancaster House
7 The Design Centre
8 Christie's
9 Burlington House
10 Hyde Park Corner

11 Apsley House
12 Shepherd Market
13 Dorchester Hotel
14 Burlington Arcade
15 Burlington Gardens
16 Museum of Mankind
17 Sotheby's
18 St George's Church
19 Speakers' Corner
20 Marble Arch
21 Selfridges
22 The Wallace Collection
23 Royal Institute of
   British Architects'
   Drawing Collection

REGENT'S PARK

Area of map

St Paul's

The Tower

Houses of
Parliament

Thames
Barrier

1 mile

Marylebone Rd

Park
Crescent

Gloucester Place

Baker St

Marylebone High Street

Blanford St

Weymouth St

Portman Sq

Wigmore St

Cavendish Square

Hanover Sq

Connaught Sq

Oxford St

Brook Street

Bond St

Conduit St

Regent St

Bayswater Road

Marble Arch

Grosvenor Sq

Berkeley Sq

Berkeley St

Haymarket

HYDE PARK

Park Lane

Curzon St

Piccadilly

Pall Mall

THE SERPENTINE

The Mall

Apsley House

Rotten Row

Constitution Hill

GREEN PARK

Knightsbridge

Buckingham Palace Gardens

Birdcage Walk

ST JAMES'S PARK

Brompton Rd

Belgrave Sq

Buckingham Palace

Pont St

Sloane St

King's Rd

¼ mile

135

Second World War. And even if the mansions of the royals and the aristocrats now mostly house diplomats and commerce, suppliers to the wealthy and discerning are still here. In the British version of the board game, Monopoly, royal blue Mayfair and Park Lane are the most expensive properties and, developed with a red hotel and some green houses, will bankrupt most players who land on them. Next along the board are the viridian green triumvirate of Bond Street, Regent Street and Oxford Street. The game echoes real life. And to enjoy this area fully, you need to enter into the spirit of the game, perhaps exploring inside Asprey's shop, taking tea at the Dorchester, perusing the pictures in the Fine Art Society or watching a few lots go under the hammer at Christie's.

Standing on the south side of the Mall, with your back to St James's Park, there is a good **view** of a clutch of palace-mansions. Ahead lies St James's Palace, the sooted brick of its garden wall a foil for the pink almond blossom of springtime. To the left are Clarence House, home of the Queen Mother, and Lancaster House; to the right, Marlborough House and then the dignified backs of Nash's Carlton House Terrace which used to culminate in Carlton House. The medallion of Queen Mary (1867–1953) in the garden wall of Marlborough House is well placed: in her widowhood, she sat at a first floor window to watch the funeral procession of her husband, George V (1935). It was here she learnt of her son Edward's love for Mrs Simpson and from here, until her death in 1953, that she watched royal processions respectfully slow down as they passed by.

The tribute to her mother-in-law, Queen Alexandra, who also lived here, is on the wall of Marlborough Road, straight ahead, the Art Nouveau bronze by Alfred Gilbert (of Eros fame, see p. 177) one of the most loving and gentle memorials in London. Just beyond is the restored **Queen's Chapel**, whose history of international worship began when Inigo Jones built the first classical church in England (1623) for Charles I's proposed Catholic bride, the Spanish Infanta, its first floor royal pew connected by an overhead passage to the Palace. The marriage fell through. Subsequent denominational services have included William and Mary's Dutch Reformed, the Hanoverians' German Lutheran (George III married Charlotte of Mecklenburg-Strelitz here, 1761), and Queen Alexandra's Danish (to visit, attend a Sunday service held Easter–end July, Holy Communion 8.30am, Sung Eucharist 11.15am, details published on Court pages of quality Saturday newspapers).

Opposite is Friary Court in **St James's Palace**. As its name suggests, the Palace started life as an Augustinian hospital. It was later a women's leper hospital dedicated to St James the Less before being bought by Henry VIII who built a hunting manor (1532) and enclosed 300 acres to the south, the present St James's Park (see p. 89). Of Henry's building, the four-storeyed Gatehouse on the right remains, with octagonal towers and linenfold-panelled doors, as does the Chapel Royal. Behind these doors lies Colour Court, one of four courts with surrounding rooms where Tudor events both happy and sad began 300 years of court activity: Mary I died here (1558), Elizabeth I (1558–1603) held merry court here. The Stuarts mixed tragedy and comedy, too: James I (1603–25) and his court laughed over Ben Jonson's masques and Charles II (1660–85) flirted and played pell-mell nearby while encouraging his friend Henry Jermyn to develop St James's fields; but Charles I (1625–49) spent his last night here before walking across the Park to his execution outside Whitehall Palace (see p. 87).

However, it was after the Whitehall Palace fire in 1698 that St James's became the monarch's principal London home until the move to Buckingham Palace in 1762. Queen Anne (1702–14), James II's second daughter, had been born here. Succeeding William and Mary (her sister), she spent her life in pain (now thought to be gout), gave birth to most of her seventeen children here (of which the longest survivor lived just 11 years), spent many hours drinking tea and playing cards, and had a long and stormy close friendship with Sarah Churchill, later Duchess of Marlborough, who lived first here and then in greater and independent grandeur at Marlborough House next door. But, despite being untrained to rule, she was a conscientious queen who oversaw, amongst other things, the Union between England and Scotland (1707).

Anne was the last of the Stuarts. By the Act of Settlement (1701), James I's great grandson George Lewis (born 1660), already Elector of Hanover, arrived peacefully to become George I (1714–27), ushering in Hanoverian rule. The court became strange indeed: its language was German, its royal servants Turkish, its climate uncultivated, its courtiers mostly Germans who did not frolick or dance, and its royal German mistresses an ugly, thin-and-fat duo nicknamed the Maypole and the Elephant and Castle. Its home-sick king, unloved by his subjects, was saved by his deep passion for music which led him to import his Kappelmeister, George Frederick Handel, who was soon giving concerts here and making his impact on English music.

George II (1727–60), thrown out of the palace after a quarrel with his father, created a rival and rather jolly court at Leicester House (where Leicester Square is) but returned here to rule over another dull court, his blinkered German obsession for court etiquette and punctuality saved by Queen Caroline of Anspach's intelligence and Robert Walpole's advice. He in turn threw his son out describing him as 'the greatest ass, the greatest liar, the greatest canaille and the greatest beast in the whole world and we heartily wish he was out of it'. The son retaliated. He was reportedly 'an obstinate self-indulgent miserly martinet with an insatiable sexual appetite', a description historians consider cruelly accurate.

However, father outlived son, and the 22-year-old grandson became George III (1760–1820). He spoke English without a German accent, worked incredibly hard, weathered the loss of America, backed the Tory William Pitt the Younger against the wild Whig Charles James Fox to become prime minister (for 23 years: 1783–1801, 1804–6) and endeared himself to the xenophobic British. Britain prospered. But in 1788 the king was suddenly afflicted by mad convulsions. He recovered the next year and survived numerous assassination attempts during the French Revolution (including one at Drury Lane Theatre), only to suffer permanent insanity from 1810, when he went to live at Windsor Castle, 'a blind old man with a long white beard, wearing a violet dressing gown and shambling around an isolated set of rooms'.

The Royal Apartments of St James's had already been deserted by George III in favour of Buckingham Palace. George IV (Prince Regent from 1811, king 1820–30) stayed put in Carlton House (see p. 175) along the road while Buckingham Palace was being aggrandised. Emerging from the Hanoverian habit of bad father and son relations, he effectively reigned for 19 years. On the good side were his high spirits, intellectual gifts, good taste and stylishness. On the bad side were the dissipation of his abilities through over-indulgence; his weak and lazy political behaviour, first opposing his father to support Charles James Fox then switching to become an ultra Tory ruler; and his legendary extravagance which jollied up court life and gave London Buckingham Palace and the great Nash sweep from St James's to Regent's parks but meant he had to marry the 'fat, coarse, vulgar and unwashed' Caroline of Brunswick in 1796 in payment for parliament writing off his debts. It was at St James's that they married, the groom drunk throughout – in stark contrast to the marriage here in 1840 of the 20-year-old Queen Victoria to her Albert.

These, then, were the royal residents of St James's Palace while the British landowners were busily building up St James's and Mayfair. But even if the Palace was not the riot of revels and pageantry of Tudor and Stuart days and much was rebuilt after a fire (1809), its romantic and fairytale exterior survives. And St James's is still the official London royal palace. Foreign ambassadors are appointed 'to The Court of St James's'. They are accredited here before riding in the Glass Coach to call on Buckingham Palace. The Queen was proclaimed here – and at Royal Exchange in the City – and she made her first speech as Queen here.

Friary Court provides the perfect stage backdrop when the Queen's colour is trooped at the beginning of the Changing of the Guard (see p. 51 for all details). Inside, Crown offices include the Ascot Office where social grandees decide who will, and who will not, be admitted to the inner sanctum of the Ascot Races, the Royal Enclosure (see p. 53). And lesser royals continue to live in the palace precincts.

To the right, Wren's **Marlborough House** (1709–11, two top storeys added 1861–3) was built for Sarah Churchill, Queen Anne's intimate friend and wife of the Duke of Marlborough (1650–1722). He was a star soldier who was made a peer for crushing the Monmouth Rebellion (1685), an earl for supporting William of Orange and Mary's succession to the empty throne left by James II (1689), and a duke for supporting Anne's succession (1702) after which he led a series of victories including Blenheim (1704), the name he gave to his palace near Oxford. The duke was laid in state here, amid the stairwell murals of his great battles and the magnificent salon with Laguerre's 'Battle of Blenheim' on the walls and Gentileschi's 'Arts and Sciences' (1636) on the ceiling – pinched by Sarah from Queen's House at Greenwich, with the queen's approval. In 1817, the lease reverted to the

Crown and real, not self-appointed, royals arrived: Prince Leopold (who left to become the first Belgian king, 1831); Dowager Queen Adelaide (1837–49), who gave Victoria her wedding banquet here; Victoria's eldest son, Edward, Prince of Wales (1861–1901), who with his wife, Alexandra, made it the centre of fashionable society and the 'best kept house in London' peopled by an army of uniformed maids and footmen; and then their son (later George V) and the widowed queens Alexandra and Mary. Since 1962 it has been the government's Commonwealth Centre (Marlborough House, Pall Mall, SW1, tel 930 2100; after current restoration, apply by telephone for guided tours on weekdays, 11am–3pm, when there are no meetings).

Round past Henry's Gatehouse – a stunning end to St James's Street – and left again into Stable Yard, Ambassadors Court has York House on its north side, a grace-and-favour residence currently used by the Duke of Kent. Ahead lies the **Chapel Royal**, much rebuilt but with the original painted ceiling commemorating Henry's short, political marriage to Anne of Cleves (1540). At Sung Eucharist on Sundays the chapel resounds with the fine church music for which it has been famous since it was built – Thomas Tallis, William Byrd and Henry Purcell have been organists (Chapel Royal, Ambassadors Court, St James's Palace, SW1; to visit, attend a Sunday service held Oct-Easter; see Queen's Chapel, above). This is one of five Chapels Royal in London; the other four are the nearby Queen's Chapel, at the Tower (St John's and St Peter ad Vincula, see p. 102) and at Hampton Court (Chapel Royal, see p. 114). The Chapels Royal are all Royal Peculiars, that is, they are not subject to a bishop but own their allegiance directly to the sovereign. In all, there are twelve Royal Peculiars, the other seven being Westminster Abbey, the Queen's Chapel of the Savoy, the Royal Foundation of St Katharine, St George's Chapel Windsor, All Saints Windsor Great Park and chapels in Buckingham Palace and Windsor Castle.

On the south side, Nash's Clarence House (1828) overlooking the Mall was built for George IV's bookish and quiet brother, the Duke of Clarence, who became William IV (1830–7) aged 64 and stayed where he was, deeming Buckingham Palace too grand and St James's Palace two small for both books and levees. Later residents included Queen Victoria's second son, Alfred, Duke of Edinburgh (1866–1900), who added another storey; Victoria's third son, the Duke of Connaught (1900–42);

Princess Elizabeth (1947–52), later Queen Elizabeth II, who lived here before her accession and gave birth to Princess Anne here; and now the Queen Mother (since George VI died in 1952), who lives in a first floor suite and comes to greet well-wishers at the gates on her birthday, August 4.

Benjamin Wyatt's grand **Lancaster House** (1825–9, formerly known as York and then Stafford House) is across Stable Yard Road, built for another of George IV's brothers, Frederick, Duke of York. When he died in heavy debt, one of his creditors, the Marquess of Stafford, who was later created the Duke of Sutherland, snapped it up (and the proceeds paid for Victoria Park, see p. 253). The 2nd Duke hired the talents of Wyatt, Robert Smirke and Charles Barry to extend the Bath stone pile and lavish its interior with French Louis-style extravagance. A spectacular staircase sweeps up to the first floor State Rooms where Victoria would visit the Duchess, her friend and Mistress of the Robes (1837–61), coming once with Albert and the Duke of Wellington to listen to Chopin play (1848). In 1913 Sir William Lever, the next owner, gave it to the nation and in 1953 the chandeliers glittered for the Queen's Coronation Banquet. Formerly open to the public, it is currently firmly closed.

Between the two houses, there is a pretty view down to St James's Park, with another to Green Park on the right. Leaving this royal corner of pristine houses with polished brass and crown-topped gas lamps, Little James Street leads round to **St James's Street** and the courtiers' outside world. Here clubs and coffee houses, already famous in Charles II's day, multiplied when the court moved in and were soon interspersed with fashionable shops and residents.

Opposite, Lock & Co at no. 6 have been making top hats, cokes (a sort of bowler), bowlers and polo caps for the best heads since Robert Davis followed his clients here from the City in 1676. Hatters to the Duke of Edinburgh, they hold a Royal Warrant. Such warrants are given to those who supply the Queen, the Queen Mother, the Duke of Edinburgh or the Prince of Wales 'By Appointment', a much sought-after honour with additional commercial advantages, for the holder may advertise his privilege by displaying the appropriate royal coat of arms on his premises, products and stationery and generally use it as a promotional draw. The idea began in the Middle Ages and touched every corner of royal life, as it does today – Henry VIII had a proud 'King's Laundresse', Elizabeth I an 'Operator for the Teeth'. William IV granted the use of the royal coat of arms; Victoria began issuing formal Royal Warrants; and today the 800 or so Royal Warrant holders, mainly in Britain, lose and gain 20–30 members a year. Like an up-market child's 'I Spy' game, the four royal coats of arms can be spotted regularly in St James's and Mayfair, still the hotbed of royal suppliers.

Both Lock and Berry Brothers and Rudd at no. 3 have beautiful panelled interiors, worth a peek. Berry Brothers are successors to the grocer William Pickering who arrived in 1703, did very well, and built the houses in Pickering Place (1730), found through the arch beside the shop – the Texan legation was here in 1842–5. As for their closest customers, the street's residents have included Sir Christopher Wren (who died here 1723), Charles James Fox (who died here 1781 in heavy gambler's debt), and the political cartoonist James Gillray (who committed suicide out of the window of no. 24 in 1815).

Down and round the corner, the wide **Pall Mall** stretches ahead. It is named after the alley for the courtiers' popular French import, *palle maile* (soon anglicised to pell mell), a game similar to croquet played here by Charles I before Charles II moved it into his new St James's Park (see p. 89). The old course became the carriage highway linking his St James's Palace with Whitehall Palace and the Strand. It was immediately fashionable and the king's mistress, Nell Gwynn, moved in among the counts and dukes (no. 79). In the next century it attracted the society portraitist Gainsborough (no. 82) and George IV's estranged wife, Mrs Fitzherbert, to whom he returned in later life (no. 105). And in 1807, part of this street of mansions, by now leading to fashionable Carlton House, was lit by FA Winsor's new-fangled gas lighting to celebrate George III's birthday on June 4.

Then, with the demolition of Carlton House in 1826 (see p. 176) and the redevelopment of its garden and stables, Pall Mall became the heart of clubland. The coffee houses here and on St James's Street and the gambling clubs of the aristocrats developed into something more substantial, more like a gentleman's home-from-home – or mansion-from-mansion, since they often took over a private mansion as clubhouse. Soon, a dozen clubs lined Pall Mall. Today, they are still exclusive havens for their members – still mostly male – and their atmosphere, language and character are consciously preserved. Behind their portals, men meet, debate and play snooker (and swim and play squash in more modern minded clubs). They eat in Coffee Rooms and take coffee in Libraries where they doze in the squishy red leather chairs surrounded by thousands of volumes tended by full-time librarians. As expected, they are unvisitable; you need to be a member of an associated club, or invited by a member. But several clubhouses look good from the outside, too.

First on the right is Robert and Sydney Smirke's mansion (1836–9) at no. 71, now home for the United Oxford and Cambridge University Club who spread next door where Queen Victoria's daughter, Princess Christian, and granddaughters lived until 1947. The Royal Automobile Club, founded in 1897 'for the Protection, Encouragement and Development of Automobilism', are in Mewes and Davis's clubhouse at no. 89, complete with post office, Turkish bath and huge pool – the spies Burgess and Maclean lunched here before fleeing to Russia. The Reform follows at nos 104–5, perhaps Charles Barry's masterpiece. The Italianate palazzo (1837–41, inspired by the Palazzo Farnese in Rome), is a purpose-built and magnificent clubhouse where the nineteenth-century Whigs congregated (Gladstone, Palmerston, Asquith) and where women now have full membership. The Travellers' is in an earlier Barry clubhouse (1828–31) at no. 106, possibly the prototype Victorian Italianate building. It was founded in 1819 when travelling was more dangerous and traveller's tales more gripping. The Athenaeum's character is quite different: in Decimus Burton's clubhouse (1827–30) closing the terrace at no. 107, the air is heavy with the high-powered conversation of government ministers, bishops and academics. Founded in 1824 by John Wilson Croker, who coined the political term 'Conservative', Athene, goddess of wisdom, stands over the entrance to this correctly classical building housing an intellectually elite club named after Emperor Hadrian's university in Rome. When HG Wells fled from new membership here back to his beloved Savile Club (see below), he apparently said 'Thank God I'm back. This is the Athenaeum of the living.'

A few yards back along Pall Mall, the road on the right leads up to **St James's Square** (begun 1665), the centrepiece of a successful development by Henry Jermyn, Earl of St Albans. Rumoured to be the secret husband of Henrietta Maria, Charles II's mother, he made a substantial fortune through influence and friendship with both royals and by 1665 had persuaded the king to part with the freehold of half St James's Fields. His plan was a central piazza with wide converging streets, the whole enclosed by Jermyn, Haymarket, Pall Mall and St James's streets. In the piazza, plots were leased to speculative builders who put up palatial mansions aimed at aristocrats who needed to be near St James's Palace – the ubiquitous Dr Barbon put up no. 4 (see p. 118). It was an astounding success, instantly the most fashionable address in London and by the 1720s housed seven dukes and seven earls – a ghost of its grandeur survives in the early rebuildings of Edward Shepherd's heavy no. 4 (1726–8), no. 5 (1748–9, refaced 1854), Henry Flitcroft's elegant Palladian row of nos. 9, 10 and 11, and James Stuart's classical no. 15 (1764–6). Flanking this are the London Library at no. 14 since 1845 (rebuilt 1896), and the East India Club, a meeting place for the empire's servants on leave in London, who built their new clubhouse over nos. 16 and 17 in 1865. Pitt the Elder, the Earl of Chatham, lived at no. 10 – now the home of the Royal Institute of International Affairs (Chatham House). The leafy central garden conceals William III on horseback.

To the east, the tactfully named **Charles II Street** (completed 1689) led straight to **Haymarket** (Nash's Regent Street sliced through later) named for its market supplying the royal mews on what is now Trafalgar Square (see p. 87). In 1662 Lord St Albans won a licence from the king to hold twice-weekly markets for cattle and sheep. But the filth was so appalling that the next Lord St Albans made a compromise with James II in 1686: he moved his cattle market off north of Green Park, but he could hold an annual 15-day fair there starting on May 1. Hugely successful, the developed area that spread out from there became known as Mayfair.

Approaching Haymarket, the vista is closed by Nash's **Theatre Royal, Haymarket** (1820–1, but first built 1720), where Henry Fielding's crude satires caused the old theatre to be closed and the Lord Chamberlain's powers of censorship to be introduced in 1737 (and only lifted in 1968). And this is where JG Phipps built the first 'picture-frame' stage and converted the pit into the stalls in the 1880s, and where manager Herbert Beerbohm Tree staged Oscar Wilde's *An Ideal Husband* (1895) before leaving to build and run **Her Majesty's Theatre** (1705, rebuilt 1789, 1869 and 1897), opposite. (Do dip into Suffolk Place and Street on the way down, a surviving snippet of Nash's improvement plan for side streets.) By then, Her Majesty's had a glowing history. It opened under the joint

management of Congreve and Vanbrugh; it staged Handel's oratorios and operas for 40 years, beginning with *Rinaldo* (1711); and in its operatic heyday Beethoven's *Fidelio* was given its English premiere here (1851), followed much later by Bizet's *Carmen* (1878). CJ Phipps's new building (1897) later had a drama school attached (1904), the nucleus of the Royal Academy of Dramatic Art, known as RADA, both run by Beerbohm Tree until 1915. When Tree played Professor Higgins in *Pygmalion*, he was so nervous that he had copies of his lines pinned to stage furniture, and prompters behind the doors, windows and sofa. Towards the top of the street, **the Design Centre** is on the right, the Design Council's wide-ranging showroom-shop for their selected British designers – well worth a look (28 Haymarket, SW1, tel 839 8000; open Mon–Sat 9.30am–5.30pm, Wed and Thurs until 8pm; Council's Design Index, good book-shop, café).

Back through the square, **King Street** leads out to the west, where an enclave of art dealers sprang up during the last century to help locals furnish – and strip – their extensive homes. Today, this is the southern tip of the St James's–Mayfair art market which stretches unbroken up to Oxford Street, one huge, sprawling and dangerously tempting mass of galleries. Dotted among them are the auction houses where dealers bet thousands, the international spenders show off buying diamonds and Impressionists, and young couples nervously bid £50 for their first furniture.

King Street (completed in 1682) is a good place to start exploring. Art dealers Spink & Son, whose specialists still include two Spink family members, moved to nos. 5–7 in 1920, but John Spink was already trading as a goldsmith in Lombard Street in 1666 – worth a look to feast on their silver, water-colours and Far Eastern art. **Christie's**, the auctioneers, are next door at no. 8. Leaving the navy to learn a more lucrative trade as a Covent Garden auctioneer, James Christie set up in 1766, putting anything that was moveable under the hammer. He soon transferred the business to no. 125 Pall Mall, and lived nearby at no. 81, next to Gainsborough's home. Clients accumulated, helped by useful friendships with Gainsborough, Reynolds and Garrick, and the flood of art from Paris during the French Revolution. His son moved to King Street in 1823, since when buyers have glided up the red-carpeted staircase to the Great Rooms to watch the heirlooms be bid up and knocked down one by one for as much as fashion, the market and the mood that day will stand. One of Christie's early local house clearances was no. 22–3 St James's Place, after its owner Samuel Rogers died in 1855, a sale that lasted 22 days and made £45,000. More recently, a single canvas by Van Gogh, 'Sun Flowers', sold for £24.75 million. Well worth a visit to see a sale on view (explanatory catalogue hung up near by), or to watch an auction where seasoned auctioneers tease and goad their bidders, pace their sale up to its climaxes and reckon they put on the best free shows in town, especially at the peak season sales in late November–early December and late June–early July – there is little activity in January and August. (Christie, Manson & Woods, 8 King Street, SW1, tel 839 9060; open Mon–Fri, 9am–4.45pm).

Just past Christie's, turning right to make a circle back to King Street, more galleries fill Bury Street (Hazlitt, Godden and Fox at no. 38), Ryder Street (Peter Nahum at no. 5) and Duke Street St James's (Harari & Jones at no. 12, by Mason's Yard, built as the Fortnum & Mason depot; Whitford and Hughes at no. 6).

Returning through St James's Square, Duke of York Street leads up past a time-warp Victorian pub, the Red Lion (c. 1880), complete with mahogany and mirrored glass, to **Jermyn Street**, which Lord St Albans gave his family name. Ahead rises Wren's much imitated **St James's, Piccadilly** (1682–84, restored 1947–54), the new estate's parish church, designed to envelop 2,000 smart souls who could all hear their preacher loud and clear. Lord St Albans, always in favour with the right people, was both friend and patron of Wren and could therefore tempt him away from his busy building of the post-Fire City. The simple brick belies a sumptuously elegant interior with Grinling Gibbons reredos and marble font, and organ from the Whitehall Chapel Royal topped by Gibbons's music-making cherubs. Locals James Christie (died 1803) and the caricaturist Gillray (died 1815) were buried here and William Blake baptised (1757); the Blake Society is based here (tel 734 4511; open daily, 8.30am–late, depending on events; lunchtime and evening recitals and lectures, courtyard market on Fri, café, garden).

Although no original house stands on Jermyn Street, the atmosphere is still as select as its specialised and long-established shops. They range from Astleys the tobacconists at no. 109 (est. 1862) and Bates the hatters at no. 21a (est. 1900) to a gaggle of shirtmakers, each quietly confident of producing a better cuff and collar than its neighbour, including

Turnbull & Asser at nos. 70–2 (est. 1885 and hold the Prince of Wales's Royal Warrant), Hilditch and Key at no. 73 (est. 1899) and New and Lingwood at no. 53 (est. 1865). Two special shops should not be missed: Paxton and Whitfield the provisioners at no. 93, started by a Suffolk cheesemonger who came to London in 1740; and Floris the perfumers at no. 89, where a Spaniard from Minorca, Juan Famenias Floris, started making the courtesans smell sweeter in 1730.

Piccadilly is found through Princes Arcade. This and Oxford Street were the ancient routes westwards out of London. But its name came when Robert Baker, a successful Strand tailor, built himself a mansion in the fields north of what is now Piccadilly Circus (see p. 177) in around 1612. Having made his fortune selling fashion-conscious courtiers the latest stiff collars, known as 'picadils', he could not escape his trading origins and his new home was nicknamed Piccadilly Hall. The street was soon developed with a dozen seventeenth-century noblemen's mansions at the east end, the string of palaces extended right up to Apsley House at Hyde Park Corner the following century where the views over Green Park made this one of the most desirable addresses in Victorian and Edwardian London. Tragically little remains, mainly due to post-war developers, not war-bombs. But it is a busy street with plenty of interest.

In this section, **Albany** is straight ahead, still a sought-after gentlemen's address. Here the garden of Viscount Melbourne's mansion (1770–4) was built over (1803–4) with two blocks of bachelors' chambers connected by a covered walkway, the rope walk, a lastingly successful conversion where Henry Holland (the owner), Gladstone and Macaulay lived and, more recently, Sir Thomas Beecham, Dame Edith Evans (when it opened to ladies), Graham Greene, Aldous Huxley and Edward Heath. To preserve its peace there are strict rules of entry, fiercely upheld: no estate agents, journalists, tradesmen, small children, animals, running, whistling or photography in the corridors.

To the right, Richard Norman Shaw's baroque Piccadilly Hotel (1905–8) is now sumptuously revamped as Le Meridien (good *views* from the restaurant behind the Ionic columns). Opposite Lutyens's heavily decorated Midland Bank (1922) is next to St James's church. Hatchards, the booksellers at no. 187, was opened by John Hatchard in 1797 and soon became a clubby place where customers such as Gladstone and Macaulay would stroll across from Albany to peruse newspapers and new books beside the fire while their servants waited outside sitting on benches. Next is Fortnum & Mason at no. 181, founded by William Fortnum in 1707 (building 1935), a footman in Queen Anne's vast Household who saw what the courtiers lacked and left to set up a grocery shop nearby to provide it all. His friend and partner soon built Mason's Yard, behind, to cope with deliveries. Still the royal grocer, although now owned by the Canadian Garry Weston, Mr Fortnum and Mr Mason appropriately present a footman's show on the outside clock every hour.

Burlington House (1715–17), on the north side behind the great stone gateway, is the survivor of the early mansions. It was built by Colen Campbell for Richard Boyle, 3rd Earl of Burlington (1694–1753), the influential connoisseur whose circle included painter William Kent and sculptor Rysbrack. Burlington pioneered the change from Wren's baroque to the more correct Italian baroque of Palladio which he thought right for the new Hanoverian king; and he built his own idea of perfection at his Chiswick country house (see p. 270). Pevsner praised Burlington House as 'the model town-house for Palladians'.

Today it is the appropriate (but much remodelled, including another storey) home of a bevy of scholarly societies – Antiquaries, Chemical, Geological, Linnean (botanical) and Royal Astronomical – surrounding the **Royal Academy of Arts** in the main house. Founded in 1768 with George III as patron, Sir Joshua Reynolds as President (statue in the courtyard) and architect William Chambers as Treasurer, it had Gainsborough as a founder member and Lawrence, Constable and Turner as early students. In 1837, it moved here from Somerset House (see p. 119) where it had already begun the traditions of holding annual Summer Exhibitions and of newly elected Academicians presenting one work to the society – Sir John Millais's 'Bubbles' (1886), long-time advertiser for Pears Soap, is here. Currently, the President is Roger de Grey. Royal Academicians (who may add RA to their name) include artists Alan Jones, Peter Blake, David Hockney, Victor Pasmore, Elizabeth Frink and Sir Hugh Casson (a past President) who loves the building's 'columns and cornices, painted ceilings, rich plasterwork, mahogany doors built like battleships'. Architect members include Richard Rogers, Norman Foster and James Stirling. And Leonard Rosoman's mural de-

corates the café. (Burlington House, Piccadilly, W1, tel 734 9052; open during exhibitions daily 10am–6pm; charge. Lectures, major exhibitions, Friends society, library, concerts, excellent shop, good café.)

Beside it runs Burlington Arcade (see below); and opposite runs its extension, **Piccadilly Arcade** (1909–10), with pretty bow-windows for yet more smart shopping. At the bottom of it, at no. 73 Jermyn Street, Lord St Albans's special friendship with Charles II is commemorated in a relief on no. 73 showing him receiving the deeds for his land.

Clubs for some of St James's most elite habitués nestle discreetly in the top half of **St James's Street**. Here Whites and Boodles were the old-established, aristocrats' clubs. James Wyatt's White's (1787–8, facade 1852) is at no. 37–8. Founded in White's Chocolate House in the 1690s and with a non-stop membership of the richest, most aristocratic and most influential men, this is the grandest of all. Known for its mad gambling, its gaming room was called Hell and in the special betting books Lord Arlington once put £3,000 on a race of raindrops down a window pane. J Crunden's beautiful Boodles (1765) is at no. 28, founded 1762 and famed for its good gambling, good food and good sociability. Henry Holland's Brooks's (1777–8) at no. 60, founded 1764, had both Charles James Fox and William Pitt as members but became a Whig stronghold. Then came Sydney Smirke's The Carlton, now at no. 69, founded 1832 in opposition to Brooks's; the inner sanctum of Tory gentlemen, where Gladstone was told by a fellow member he should be 'pitched out of the window in the direction of the Reform Club'. In T. Hopper's building (1826–7), members recently closed their eyes to Mrs Thatcher's gender as Conservative prime ministers are traditionally made members – women were only admitted on General Election night.

As you seek out these male citadels, it is worth dipping down the alleys on the right. For the block between St James's and Green Park still sniffs of this world of wealth, privilege and style. At the top, Bennett Street leads round into Arlington Street where Mewes and Davis's Ritz Hotel (1906) is London's first steel-framed building but disguised in the fancy dress of a Beaux-Arts chateau on Paris's Rue de Rivoli – see front arcade. Costing £1,000,000, it was named after César Ritz, the Swiss hotelier who founded the Savoy (see p. 119). Edwardian London loved it. Rooms cost a guinea a night, the most expensive in town and double Claridge's and the Savoy; unchaperoned ladies took tea in the Winter Garden (now called the Palm Court), the first hotel they visited alone; couples danced in the basement ballroom (now a casino) before having late supper of quail and ice-cream; and arbiters of artistic taste – Pavlova, Diaghilev and Caruso – ate in the most elegant restaurant in London – well worth walking the Long Gallery past the bar and Palm Court to see the French Louis-style restaurant overlooking Green Park.

Back in St James's Street, **Park Place** houses a club oddity at no. 14, Pratt's, where an ex-croupier turned steward would be visited regularly by his master, the 7th Duke of Beaufort, who drank and gambled with friends in the basement kitchen. Today's aristocratic members still eat round a single, basement kitchen table with room for just 14 and call all the servants George. Cobbled Blue Ball Yard comes next, and then St James's Place. Here John Vardy's Spencer House (1752–4) at no. 27, London home of the Princess of Wales's family (now leased to Jacob Rothschild's J Rothschild Holdings who are restoring it to lavish former glory), reveals the street's grand and sophisticated past; Sir Denys Lasdun's neighbouring flats at no. 26 maintain its exclusive present; and the cosy Stafford Hotel at no. 17 keeps its wines in a warren of cellars which backed onto those of Madame Prunier's renowned fish restaurant (now no more) in St James's Street.

Beyond, through an alley tunnel on the left, the lush expanse of **Green Park** extends up to Hyde Park Corner. Speckled with daffodils in springtime and carpeted with crunchy auburn leaves in autumn, this quiet, 53-acre wedge of grass and trees – including the more unusual black poplar, silver maple and silver lime – was enclosed by Henry VIII and made a royal park by Charles II. He called it Upper St James's Park, planted it, and built the snow-house in the middle to keep his wines cool for summer sipping (a mound marks the spot). Set on the western outskirts of London it was a great place for duelling, highwaymen, ballooning – one man went up on a horse, one lady dropped out monkeys once she was up – and the London favourite, fireworks. Handel's music accompanied the sparkles celebrating the end of the War of the Austrian Succession (1748) where George II was the last English king to lead his troops into battle. After splendid fireworks for Queen Victoria's coronation (1838), she later survived three assassination attempts here. Turning left down Queen's Walk, named after George II's wife, Caroline, there are good **views** of the elegant garden fronts of the St James's mansions. Through the gates by St James's Palace, it is a pleasant walk up to Hyde Park Corner, Buckingham Palace on the left and the now commercial Piccadilly on the right.

To reach Apsley House, you either risk death above ground or negotiate the warren of tunnels underneath. Today this survivor, the last of a continuous string of Piccadilly mansions, stands in isolated glory. Overlooking **Hyde Park Corner**. Constitutional Arch (1827–8) used to be the northern gate to Buckingham Palace grounds and faced the Screen (1825) in front of Hyde Park, beside Apsley House. The young Decimus Burton (1800–81) designed both and, with William Wilkins's St George's Hospital (1827), now being restored to Regency glory as a hotel, and Apsley House, they formed the impressive, neo-classical western gateway from fields into London before Belgravia was developed. In 1883 the arch was moved; in 1912 the Quadriga (Victory riding the four-horse chariot) replaced the Duke of Wellington's statue; and since the 1950s its Corinthian columns are merely outlets for the fumes of the underpass traffic of this busy road junction.

Apsley House (1771–8, then 1818 and 1828–9) is the most splendid surviving London private palace of its period. It was built by Adam for Henry Bathurst, Baron Apsley. The red brick house was then enveloped and vastly aggrandised by the brothers Benjamin and Philip Wyatt for Arthur Wellesley, Duke of Wellington (1769–1852), the nation's hero. He led a packed double life, starting as a soldier aged 18 and an MP aged 21. He was both soldier and administrator in India (1797–1804), was created duke for his various victories 1813–14, led the victory against Napoleon at Waterloo (1815), then became a Tory Cabinet minister (1818–27) before twice becoming prime minister (1828–30, 1834) and then Cabinet minister once more (1841–6). It was in 1832, when Reform rioters broke his windows and he installed iron shutters, that he acquired the nickname 'Iron Duke', not during his military escapades.

In addition to the bridge, barracks, square railway station and street named after him and his victories in London, the Duke celebrated his Waterloo triumph himself, giving an annual banquet which from 1830 until his death in 1852 was held in the great picture gallery; today the Queen hosts a royal banquet at Windsor Castle most years and the present Duke attends – England and France have been at peace with each other since

1815. And he is the only hero, royal or common, to have two equestrian statues in London, one here, one in front of the Royal Exchange (see p. 71). This house where he lived – and from where he rode on horseback to buy his books and chat with Gladstone at Hatchards – is now the Wellington Museum, with the present Duke's London home on top. It opened in 1952 and is devoted to Wellington's triumphs. All is immaculately restored, down to the railings painted pale green as he had them. Inside, see especially the Spanish royals' pictures (Goya, Velasquez, Murillo, Rubens) captured during the battle of Vitoria (1813) and later formally presented to the Duke by Ferdinand VII of Spain; the Duke's own choice of seventeenth-century Dutch pictures; Frederick William III of Prussia's gift of Berlin porcelain painted with scenes of the Duke's life; the Wellington Shield; and Canova's 11-foot-high statue of Napoleon and Lawrence's flattering portrait of the handsome Duke. And do not miss Wyatt's Waterloo Gallery (1828–30), marking the arrival of the French Louis-style in London which rampaged through high society salons, and the splendid Wyatt-amended but still very Adam rooms – ceilings, chimney-pieces, doorcases (Wellington Museum, Apsley House, 149 Piccadilly, SW1, tel 499 5676; open Tues–Thurs and Sat, 10am–6pm, Sun 2.30–6pm; charge. Lectures, bookshop).

Apsley House marks the south-west corner of **Mayfair**, a playground for the titled and glamorous from its inception with the building boom of the 1720s until society was changed by the post-war politics and economics after 1945. But physical changes began after the First World War, encouraged by an adoration of America and idolisation of the motor car. The destruction of Georgian London began. And after the Second World War, the gardens that had stretched continuously from Berkeley Square to Piccadilly in the 1920s began to disappear. However, the houses not bombed or sold to developers are now often embassies or offices. Today the world's wealthy stay in sumptuous apartments or luxurious hotels, taking to the streets dolled up in yesterday's spending spree and off to spend, spend, spend again in the boutiques, restaurants, art galleries and casinos. The great English hostesses and their private palaces have been replaced by a different, equally elite and glamorous society. There is plenty to see on a quick trot.

Park Lane, now a thundering motorway, was indeed once a narrow lane. Negotiating it and then moving northwards, the virtue of Lewis Solomon Kaye's ugly, skyline-wrecking London Hilton tower (1963) is the spectacular view from the high rooms and the rooftop restaurant (see beginning of walk) – Charles Clore's 28-storey development was the tallest building in London when it went up. Below it, a clutch of deluxe hotels followed: the Marquess of Londonderry sold out to developer Isaac Klug in the 1960s, hence the Londonderry; and bomb-damaged mansions were cleared for Sir Frederick Gibberd's Inter-Continental (opened 1975) and the confusingly named Inn on the Park (opened 1970) (only a few of whose hyper-smart guests can glimpse the greenery). Beyond the Hilton, Bauhaus hero Walter Gropius and a British team built the handy Playboy Club (1953–5), but the doors are now closed and the bunnies have hopped away. To imagine the original Park Lane, look right, to no. 5 Hamilton Place (1879–81), lavishly built for Leopold de Rothschild (now Les Ambassadeurs Club), and no. 4, Wellington's pre-Apsley House home.

Early Mayfair is found down **Hertford Street**, where the interior of Adam's no. 10 (1769–71) survives and was home to Richard Brinsley Sheridan (1751–1816), a friend of the Prince Regent, who wrote *The Rivals* (1775) and *School for Scandal* (1777) before becoming an MP (1780) and performing his own theatre as one of parliament's great orators. At the end of the street is **Shepherd Market**. This is where Lord St Albans moved his market from Haymarket (see p. 140) in 1686 and began holding his annual May Fairs, which became renowned for their bawdiness and were eventually suppressed. In 1735, Edward Shepherd, who made a tidy fortune developing much of Mayfair, laid out the charming knot of lanes and alleys which still retain their eighteenth-century scale and village atmosphere, complete with the prostitutes inherited from market days. With its cafés and grocers, this is still Mayfair village.

At the north-east corner of the market, a covered passage leads up into **Curzon Street**, which Sir Nathaniel Curzon began developing around 1720. It is full of eighteenth-century style. Opposite, royal barber Geoffrey Trumper is at no. 9 (est. 1875), where gentlemen collect their sweet-smelling violet shaving cream, browse amongst pots and potions in the mahogany-fitted rooms and perhaps have a shave. To the left, Edward Shepherd's Crewe House (1730) is a rare survivor of Mayfair's large, detached mansions set back amid lush gardens. Originally Shepherd's own house, it was given its grand, stuccoed facade in 1813, was owned by the marquess of Crewe at the turn of the century, and is now headquarters of the Thomas Tilling Group. Beside it stood Chesterfield House, replaced at the end of the eighteenth century by a since untouched gem, Chesterfield Street, with its elegant but simple three-storeyed brick fronts typical of all the Mayfair estate building. But next door, in Chesterfield Gardens, huge Ancaster House kept large-scale living alive. 35-year-old banker Adrian Hope built it in 1873 for his family of four daughters and 18 servants. In 1987 its 50-foot ballroom (the biggest private one in London), ten bedrooms, five reception rooms, gym, sauna, lift, lodge, garden and extensive staff quarters went on the market for £10 million.

On the south side of Curzon Street, a remarkable set of survivors includes Adam's no. 30 (1770–1), whose glorious first-floor ballroom and other salons are now the restaurant and gaming halls for the smart members of Crockford's Club. For the Regency addiction to gambling stretched up here from the St James's clubs. Crockford's began in Bolton Street, off Curzon Street, in 1824, just near Watier's where Byron and Beau Brummell both lost thousands at the high-stake favourites, macao and whist.

Park Lane is found by turning up South Audley Street and left along Tilney Street. Here Curtis Green's deliciously Art Deco Dorchester Hotel (1928–31), definitely worth a dip inside, was built by developers Sir Robert MacAlpine and Gordon Hotels. But those who remember say it cannot compare with what they demolished: Lewis Vulliamy's monumental private palace modelled on Rome's Villa Farnese built for millionaire RS Holford in the 1850s (a mantlepiece went to the V&A Museum). It overlooked the newly improved Hyde Park where railings replaced the wall and Decimus Burton's smart east side gates and Hyde Park Corner work made Park Lane a tip-top address. It was then that Wellington, the nation's hero, improved his Apsley House, Robert Grosvenor added his grand entrance screen to Grosvenor House (now the hotel, rebuilt 1926), the Earl of Dudley built Dudley House (1824–7) beyond at no. 100, miraculously still standing, and the terraces were tarted up with the latest Regency facades of boldly curving bays (nos 93–9 survive) – Disraeli lived in no. 93 from 1839 to 1872, and the smart Victorian heroes of Thackeray, Galsworthy and Trollope novels had houses here, including the father of Galsworthy's Soames Forsyte. (Dudley

House and the terrace are best seen returning from Hyde Park, see below.) More recently, Lord and Lady Mountbatten inherited the vast, six-storey Brook House in 1925 and lived there in a 36-room apartment eating their meals off silver plate and served by liveried footmen.

Cutting through Deanery Street to the right of the Dorchester Hotel, left up South Audley Street and then right into South Street, the industrialist Henry McLaren, 2nd Baron Aberconway, built Mayfair's last grand private home at no. 38. Ahead lies the Berkeley estate. The Royalist commander, Lord Berkeley of Stratton, was rewarded after the Restoration with a large chunk of open land. He built his mansion (1665) on the south side, the newly fashionable Piccadilly, soon bordered by Stratton and Berkeley streets. Canny descendants switched political allegiance, and the palatial house was home for Princess Anne for three years (1692–5) before William Cavendish (1641–1707) bought it in 1696. A committed Protestant who was created Duke of Devonshire in 1694 by a grateful William and Mary, his descendants made the renamed Devonshire House the focus of Mayfair society. The 3rd Duke had William Kent rebuild the house (1734–7, demolished 1924) in new magnificence; the 5th Duke's wife, Georgiana, was acknowledged First Lady of Mayfair. She hit London aged just 18 in 1774 and made the glittering house the centre for Whig opposition to George III and his Tories and aglow with a succession of balls, card parties, masquerades and routes, whose visitors were the most brilliant, sophisticated, clever and talented society that England has ever known – ranging from Sheridan, Gibbon and Dr Johnson to Charles James Fox and the Prince of Wales. Meanwhile the Duke went gambling at Brooks's, then ate boiled mackerel for his 4am breakfast.

The streets built in the estate in the 1740s over Hay Hill Farm and surrounding this vibrant court – surely a preferable alternative to George II's St James's – still match that elegance. Farm Street was for the aristocrats' coach-houses – if the later Church of the Immaculate Conception (1844–9) is open, see the Gothic interior. Turning right and right again into Hill Street, then down Chesterfield Hill to Charles Street, some houses here even retain their iron lampholders and stone obelisks. The Duke of Clarence lived at no. 22 before moving into his new Clarence House (see above). Hay's Mews runs along the back of Berkeley Square, housing the nobles' fleets of coaches and horses.

Around in **Berkeley Square**, the lofty, 200-year-old plane trees shade the surviving west side and are the site of the annual Berkeley Square ball, where modern Mayfair prancers down enough champagne to make it worthwhile for the huge car showroom to remain open for impulse Rolls Royce buys at 3am. Pevsner declared William Kent's no. 44 (1742–4) 'the finest terrace house of London', now home for two clubs for the smart jetset. The Clermont, with dramatic staircase leading up to 'the grandest drawing room of any 18th century private house in London' (so any invitation should be accepted, whatever the hour), is where poker-player Lord Lucan passed his nights in the early 1970s. Annabel's is the basement, started by Mark Birley, named after his wife and deemed by the most energetic and globe-trotting socialites to be the best nightclub in the world – 'the best service, the best people, in the best city' quipped one member. At the bottom of the same side, no. 50 is both open to all and open during the day, its walls lined from bottom to top with old and new volumes of Maggs Bros, the booksellers. When the American aristocrats conquered London, Waldorf Astor rented no. 54 in 1894, followed by Gordon Selfridge while he built his suitably palatial department store bang in the middle of the northern border of Mayfair, lucrative source of his big-spending clients.

Along the south side of Berkeley Square, then right and left up Hay Hill, the Albemarle estate was slowly developed by a consortium of businessmen and bankers who bought out the 2nd Duke of Albemarle in 1683 and demolished the nearly-new Clarendon House. This had stood in Piccadilly, a vast pile built for Edward Hyde, Charles II's Lord Chancellor, whose daughter married the future James II and was mother to two queens, Mary and Anne. Pepys nosed around it on Valentine's Day, 1666, while it was being built, and noted that from the top it had 'the noblest prospect that ever I saw in my life, Greenwich being nothing to it. And in everything is a beautiful house . . .' However, the consortium came unstuck: John Hinde, its head, went bankrupt in 1687; and Sir Thomas Bond, the financier and courtier who took building leases with fellow courtier Henry Jermyn (by then created Baron Dover) and Margaret Stafford, died in 1685. But their names last in the streets that were finally completed in the mid-eighteenth century and were already turning to commerce, especially the art trade, in the nineteenth century.

Albemarle Street is the backbone of the estate, found by going round Grafton Street, finally built

by the Duke of Grafton in the 1770s. The street's early residents included the Prince of Wales (later George II); Robert Harley, the 1st Earl of Oxford, whose heir bought land to the north and gave Oxford Street its name; and society painter Johann Zoffany and architect Robert Adam, both handily near their patrons. Now it houses the Royal Institution (founded 1799), devoted to mechanics and science, where Faraday did his electricity experiments inside while Lewis Vulliamy added his Roman temple facade to the outside (1838). At the same time, Brown's Hotel, slightly further down, was opened at no. 23 in 1837 by ex-manservant James Brown and his wife Sarah, ex-maid to Lady Byron. Here Alexander Graham Bell stayed in 1876 and made the first telephone call in England; Franklin and Eleanor Roosevelt spent their honeymoon; and Rudyard Kipling made long stays (his desk remains). Further down, it is worth nipping right along Stratton Street and into Dover Street to explore the galleries and to see Elizabeth Frink's bronze Horse and Rider (1975) on the Piccadilly corner, returning to a good gallery trio at the bottom of Albemarle Street: Marlborough Fine Art at no. 6, Thomas Agnew in the beautiful no. 3, and Connaught Brown at no. 2. Opposite, John Murray, the publishers of Jane Austen and Byron, arrived from Fleet Street (see p. 130) at no. 50 in 1812 and swiftly formed Regency London's most stimulating literary salon. Literary magnates and 'wits and bards' were the 'four o'clock visitors'. Here Byron first met Sir Walter Scott; and, despite John Murray's loyal patronage, here Byron's memoires were condemned for their naughtiness and burnt.

Back up Albemarle Street, **Royal Arcade** (1879) is the pristine, High Victorian arcade made 'Royal' because Queen Victoria bought her riding skirts from Brettel's. Chic shopping persists, ending with the chocolatiers, Charbonnel et Walker, where Madamoiselle C arrived from Paris in 1875 and the *boîtes-blanches* of plain chocolates delight the Queen today. At the end, **Old** and **New Bond Streets** formed the pre-eminent Georgian shopping street, where the *beau monde* would promenade, window-shop, spend, take lodgings above the shops and, inevitably, gamble with each other as they strolled along – Charles James Fox wagered the Prince of Wales how many cats each would see on his side of the street, chose the cats' favourite side, the sun-drenched one, and won. Gossip columnists even coined the name 'Bond Street Loungers' for these eighteenth-century Sloane Rangers. Today the street is a dazzling thoroughfare of shops world-famous for their *haute-couture*, *haute*-jewellery, *haute*-art and *haute* everything, a big-spender's or window-shopper's delight that stretches the length of Mayfair, from Piccadilly up to Oxford Street, quality all the way. And this is how it was for the Georgians, too.

Turning right down **Old Bond Street**, the tone is set in the art world of Colnaghi at no. 14, Leger Galleries at no. 13 and Arthur Ackermann at no. 3, with more Marlborough and Agnew opposite. But the Embassy Club at no. 6, the favourite inter-war haunt of the glamour set – the Mountbattens, the Prince of Wales, Lady Diana Cooper, Cecil Beaton *et al* – is a pale shadow of that cocktail-sipping, fun-loving set.

Turning left into Piccadilly, **Burlington Arcade** is a few yards along, the beginning of the great estate that surrounded Burlington House (see p. 142). As with the house, it was the enlightened 3rd Earl who laid out the streets (1718–39) and employed the great Palladian architects of the day. Although their work has mostly gone, the streets are still synonymous with culture and taste. Samuel Ware's Burlington Arcade (1815–19, second storey 1911, new entrance 1931), a continental import that became the blueprint for London arcades, was built for George Cavendish, who had inherited the estate and was fed up with locals chucking their rubbish and oyster shells (the nineteenth-century version fish and chips newspaper) into his garden. To guarantee his peace, beadles guarded the row of tiny shops and enforced the rules of no singing, no running, no carrying of big parcels, no open umbrellas and, to cope with a later invention, no bicycles, rules firmly enforced by beadles today.

Turning right into **Burlington Gardens**, no. 7 on the north side hints at the past character of the rest, although the 1720s mansion was given a new handsome facade later. Opposite it stands the **Museum of Mankind**, built by James Pennethorne in 1866–7 on Burlington House garden as the headquarters of London University, which fled to Bloomsbury in 1900 (see p. 165). Behind the thoroughly unwelcoming facade, this is the British Museum outpost for its fascinating Ethnographic Department. The world's biggest and best collection includes Eskimo snow spectacles and polar-bear trousers, an Arapaho Indian chief's feather head-dress, an Amazonian's human head mascot, a Mexican's painted skull for their Day of the Dead, the Asante West African's gold jewellery, a Zulu warrior's shield, a Bedouin's goat-hair tent and a New Guinea magical mask, all displayed to show how the peoples live, with plenty of maps and helpful booklets (6 Burlington Gardens, W1, tel 437 2224; open Mon–Sat 10am–5pm, Sun 2.30–6pm; free. Guided tours, lectures, workshops, films, six-monthly exhibitions, bookshop).

Northwards lies the estate proper. **Old Burlington Street** (1715–25) was the artery, where Colen Campbell's houses at the southern end (nos 31–2) still stand as archetypes for the simple Georgian London terrace. To the east lies **Savile Row**, named after the 3rd Duke's wife, where surviving houses include William Kent's no. 1 where Dr Livingstone was laid in state before his Westminster Abbey burial, and homes for some of the renowned tailors who started coming to the street in the last century, including Hardy Amies at no. 14, 'By appointment' Henry Poole at no. 15 and many more. It was here that the Beatles last appeared together in public, when they gave an impromptu roof-top concert on top of the Apple building in 1969. To the west lies **Cork Street**, where the latest Hockneys, Frinks and pictures by tomorrow's great artists lurk in more than a dozen galleries – try dipping in to Bernard Jacobson, Brownse & Derby, Knoedler (for Hockney), the Piccadilly, the Redfern and Waddington.

At the end of Burlington Gardens is Bond Street, with Boucheron the jeweller opposite. Turning right into **New Bond Street**, Asprey's has yards and yards of proud Victorian window, almost as good as its older Aladdin's Cave interior. Founded by a Huguenot, William Asprey, whose grandson moved here in 1847, it has served big spenders from American industrialists and Indian maharajas to the oil-rich Arabs and is one of the world's great luxury shops. Naturally, it has three of the four Royal Warrants, but just dreaming through the window and collecting the free catalogue satisfies most people. Looking up to the left at the junction with Bruton Street, Henry Moore's bronze (1953) is on the terrace of Rosenauer's Time-Life building (1952–3). This is also the junction with Conduit Street, named after Conduit Mead, a small estate owned by the City of London merchants since the fifteenth century to ensure the conduits bringing them their fresh water were safe.

Ahead, art dealers abound in the next block, with the Fine Art Society at no. 148, loved by Sickert who called it 'the best shop in London' and always worth a look. Wildenstein is at no. 147, before **Sotheby's**, the world's largest auctioneers, on the right at nos. 34–5. Founded in 1744 by

Samuel Baker who sold and auctioned books, a Sotheby nephew joined him in 1776. In 1917 the firm moved here. Then scope was widened and Christie's pre-eminence as art auctioneers challenged. Although their rooms are not as impressive as Christie's Great Rooms, it is well worth going in to inspect a sale on view and see how the international bigtime bidders discreetly nod or raise their hand to up the price another thousand for a rare piece of Sèvres porcelain (Sotheby's, 34–5 New Bond St, W1, tel 493 8080; open Mon–Fri, 9am–4.30pm; basic procedure the same as Christie's, see p. 140).

To the right of New Bond Street, the large Millfield estate covered the north-east corner of Mayfair, stretching from Conduit Street up to Oxford Street. Sir Benjamin Maddox starting laying out his elegant plan around 1715. This was the first organised Mayfair development, with square and parish church, and its immediate success with fashionable society ensured the building boom that followed. It had two other familiar ingredients: an aristocrat as principal developer, the 1st Earl of Scarsborough; and some loyal street-naming, this time to mark the Elector of Hanover arriving to become George I in 1814.

Turning right into Maddox Street, the first junction reveals the plan. Straight ahead, John James's **St George Hanover Square** church (1721–4) was built as part of the Fifty Churches Act (see p. 120) and adorned with the first portico on a London church, useful for keeping society hats and furs dry and a favourite backdrop for society weddings. Looking left, **St George Street** (simply George Street until 1938) widens as it opens into **Hanover Square** (1717), a spacious and formal design in tune with the German Court. But to get a flavour of the estate continue along Maddox Street, seeing Masons Arms Mews, then cut left along Pollen Street (Benjamin Pollen was Maddox's heir) and then left again into the square.

This is where the quality moved in, as survivors nos 16, 24, 19 and 20 show, the last two by the Huguenot architect Nicholas Dubois (who also did flashy no. 15 in St George Street). With a powerful Whig developer, early residents included the Whig general Lord Cadogan and George I's mistresses duo, 'The Maypole' and 'The Elephant and Castle'. Later, Chantry's statue of Whig politician William Pitt the Younger (1759–1806) was stood on the south side. But there was soon entertainment to tempt the Tory Bond Street Loungers when Sir John Gallini, a Swiss-Italian, opened no. 4 as the

Hanover Square Rooms (1773), packing in smart audiences for subscription concerts by Johann Christoph Bach and other box-office sell-outs. Later again, Lucile Sutherland was single-handedly revolutionising Edwardian fashion; carriages queued up daily at no. 23 where she daringly showed off her latest feminine fashions on live models who wore the dresses next to their flesh – a dramatic change from the obligatory high-necked black satin undergarment used until then.

One annual success (1785–1848) at the Hanover Square Rooms was performance of the *Messiah*, which Handel wrote during the 30 years he lived at no. 25 **Brook Street**, the street leading westwards out of the square and across New Bond Street. Passing the pretty Haunch of Venison Yard, **South Molton Street**, is on the right, its high fashion and highly priced boutiques contrasting sharply with its old name, Poverty Lane. It marks the course of the Tyburn river, which gives Brook Street its name and marks the boundary of the greatest of all Mayfair estates, the Grosvenor.

In 1677, the 21-year-old Sir Thomas Grosvenor from Eaton in Cheshire made an excellent marriage at St Clement Danes in the Strand. His bride was Mary Davies, the 12-year-old daughter of Alexander Davies who had inherited 100 acres of marshy fields here and another 400 equally open acres south of Hyde Park from his immensely rich uncle, Hugh Audley, a self-made money-lender. Their descendants developed the land, the Mayfair acres first in 1720–70, the rest from the 1820s on to form Belgravia and Pimlico. As Grosvenor coffers overspilt with the high rents from the bulk of London's prestigious addresses, the family accumulated aristocratic honours to match, reaching the top in 1874 when the 1st Dukedom of Westminster was conferred upon the head of one of the richest families in all Europe. Today, the 6th Duke oversees a 300-acre estate, his family having clung on to it through good management, good maintenance, short leases (resold at good prices), foreign property investments and selling off the Pimlico acres.

The Mayfair estate was laid out on a grand scale by Thomas's son, Richard. The centrepiece was a large square surrounded by street upon elegant street of fashionable Georgian brick houses. From the start it was the last word in smart addresses, and by the 1750s more than half the houses in Grosvenor Square and along the two grand east-west streets leading off it had titled owners. And its allure for the very rich has been continuous, so that over the years many of the simple three-storey facades have been rebuilt or dollied up with bows, porticos and stucco, according to the whims of their fashion-conscious owners.

A quick canter around front and back streets of this big estate, still remarkably intact and atmospheric in places, begins by plunging left down **Avery Row**, again following the Tyburn's course and catching tiny Lancashire Court on the left before the developers do. Across Grosvenor Street, an alley leads to Bloomfield Place. To the right, in the tangle of Grosvenor Hill, Bourdon Place and Bourdon Street, chic residences with Mercedes in the garages have replaced the mews artisans' houses and stabling. These served the houses of **Davies Street**, worth popping in here to see its untypically grand survivor, Bourdon House (1723–5), possibly built by the estate surveyor Thomas Barlow, then extended piecemeal until the 2nd Duke of Westminster left Grosvenor House on Park Lane to live in it (1916–53) – now Malletts the antique dealers, so visitable.

Back into Grosvenor Hill and left, Broadbent Street opens into **Grosvenor Street** (1720–34). One of the estate's principal and grandest streets, this and Brook Street were high society's main routes from the fairly smart Millfield and Burlington estates to the citadel of smartness, Grosvenor Square. Amid the office blocks, the remaining houses with their Edwardian fronts give a taste of the grandeur lived in by countless nobles as well as architects Robert and James Adam (1768–52), brewer and politician Samuel Whitbread (1792–8), biscuit-maker George Palmer (1881–7). One piece of full-blown Edwardian rebuilding was at no. 46 (now the Japanese Embassy's Chancellery). Here the American financier Sir Edgar Speyer, close friend of Edward VII and financier of much of London's Underground system, bought no. 44 (in fact two houses) and spent some £250,000 in 1910–11 to employ Detmar Blow (estate architect) and Frenchman Fernand Billery to give him a magnificent double mansion, with silver bath, special cellars for fruit and wine, grand salons where Debussy played, and two full staircases (one modelled on the Scale dei Giganti in the Doge's Palace) because the Duke of Westminster insisted it must be possible to part the houses again if necessary.

Brook Street (1725–31), further up Davies Street, has a similar story. Edward Shepherd, who built Shepherd Market, built nos 66 and 68 (1725), then lived in no. 72. J Pierpont Morgan's brother-in-law,

Walter Hayes Burns, arrived in the 1890s and made another double mansion at no. 69 and 71, with lift, marble pillars, maple ballroom floor, and lavish Louis XV interior, all now enjoyed by the Savile Club, whose members eat Friday night candle-lit dinners in the ballroom. But the building that is both lavish beyond belief and open to all to enjoy is Claridge's Hotel, founded by William Claridge (1855), bought by the Savoy Company (1895), rebuilt by CW Stephens (1895–9) who also designed Harrods, and stylishly extended by Oswald Milne (1931). It has been home to an almanack of the world's royals past and present, whose every wish is the morning-coated staff's desire. It is here that the Queen's royal guests on State Visits come after their few days at Buckingham Palace. Well worth a peek, even just the hall. Just beyond, the Grosvenor Estate Office is at no. 53 Davies Street, its 1820s facade hiding a splendidly panelled and plastered 1730s interior (tel 408 0988 to arrange a visit).

Moving west, **Grosvenor Square** (1725–31), grandest of all London addresses for two centuries, has been wrecked. The oval garden of this, the largest square in London after Lincoln's Inn Fields (although Belgrave competes for the prize, too), was surrounded by terraces of individual, not uniform, houses. Many of their interiors were made newly elegant by the Adam brothers in the 1770s, public settings where Britain's and then the world's nobles and politicians met to take tea, play at cards, dine, dance, or simply converse. In 1802, JP Malcolm described it as 'the very focus of feudal grandeur, fashion, taste and hospitality'. Throughout its history, half the residents were always nobles, and many were MPs if not prime ministers. To help the imagination, see no. 9 (rebuilt 1909–10) at the north-east corner and no. 4 (rebuilt 1865–6) on the east side (now the Italian ambassador's residence), and no. 38 (1865–8, facade, but the 1770s house survives behind) on the south side.

Not even the most loyal American visitor can find much to praise in Eero Saarinen's outsized, grandiose and bombastic US Embassy (1956–9) for which the west side was demolished. As the 2nd Duke retained the freehold, it is probably the only US embassy not to own the land on which it stands. Crossing the square through the garden, William Reid Dick's bronze is of Franklin Delano Roosevelt (1882–1945), who honeymooned at Brown's Hotel, became 32nd President of the US in 1932, was elected three times, repealed Prohibition, initiated the New Deal and was a close friend of Churchill.

Leaving the square at its north-west corner, **Upper Brook Street** returns to the grandeur and proportion of Brook Street, and, turning left into Blackburne's Mews and right into Culross Street, the atmosphere of old Mayfair returns. At the end, the Park Lane survivors are to left and right, nos 93–9 with jolly, bow-fronted Regency facades and no. 100 the palatial Dudley House (see Park Lane, above).

For a pleasant wander down through southern Mayfair to Hyde Park, turn back along **Upper Grosvenor Street** beside Grosvenor House Hotel, where the magnificent Grosvenor family mansion was replaced by AO Edwards, encased by Lutyens (1928) and equipped with swimming pool and skating rink which was later the US Mess for Eisenhower, Patton and other US officers during World War II and then made into the biggest ballroom in London. Turning right into South Audley Street, then left along Ernest George's lavishly ornate, pink terracotta tiled **Mount Street** (1884–9), the Connaught Hotel (1894–6) is at the end, sensitively renamed from the Coburg Hotel at the beginning of the First World War, De Gaulle's headquarters in the Second World War and now the most exclusive and discreet of all London hotels. Stars who are not crying wolf with 'I want to be alone' stay here. The entrance to the tree-filled oasis of St George Hanover Square Gardens is opposite. Through its dark, leafy shade furnished with benches given by grateful locals, a gate leads back into **South Audley Street** between the local library and the Grosvenor family chapel (1730), an outpost for the parish church in St George Street since 1831. Turning left, Thomas Goode operate in splendour from Ernest George and Peto's purpose-built, 13-roomed and sumptuously decorated shop (1875–91), luring customers in with two seven-foot-high Minton elephants at the doorway. Since they arrived on this site in 1845, their fine china and glass has been irresistible for the world's noblesse. In 1863, the Prince of Wales, newly married to his Alexandra, twice spent £1,000 in one day here when he was setting up home at Marlborough House.

To reach Hyde Park, turn right along South Street, right again into Rex Place, then left into Aldford Street, leaving a charming spot of Mayfair to dip through the subway under Park Lane.

The king's **Hyde Park** halted the eighteenth-century developers and marked the western boundary of London. Beyond was all fields and villages. Today, its 344 acres stretch across to the Serpentine lake, with Kensington Gardens beyond (see p. 190). The two parks form a 619-acre green expanse – the largest in London, an extraordinary expanse of open views and mature trees encased in another two centuries of developers' bricks.

Royal ownership has preserved Hyde Park. At the Dissolution, Henry VIII relieved the Westminster monks of it, adding a fence to keep his game in good supply for hunting and hawking (1536), which continued until 1768. Charles I (1625–49) opened it to the public, when the fashionable May Day promenades began; Cromwell sold it off in three lots for £17,000; and Charles II took it back, put up a brick wall, and made the ring road the fashionable place for 'sparkling eyes or a splendid equipage' – even Pepys went there in 1663 to be seen wearing his 'painted gloves . . . all the mode'. William and Mary, preferring to live at Kensington Palace, had 300 lamps hung along Rotten Row (an anglicisation of *Route du Roi*) which led to it from Hyde Park Corner and was plagued by highwaymen. George II's Queen Caroline added the Serpentine lake (where Londoners have splashed and swum ever since, even on chilly Christmas Day) but chopped off 200 acres beyond it for Kensington Palace. George IV had Decimus Burton build lodges along the east side and John Rennie the bridge (1826) over the Serpentine. William Nesfield and other royal gardeners have planted such treats as the mature manna ash (by Hyde Park Corner), the Caucasian wingnut (by Rotten Row) and the Chinese evergreen magnolia (by the nursery); students of Chelsea Art College sculpted some trunks of the elms killed by Dutch elm disease.

The park has been the scene of countless demonstrations, celebrations and shows, most notably the Hanoverian centenary and Napoleon's exile into Elba (both 1814, even a mock battle on the Serpentine), George IV's coronation (1821, elephant towed along the lake on rafts) and the Great Exhibition (1851, see p. 212). More recently, there were fireworks for the Queen's Silver Jubilee (1977) and the worldwide Sport Aid London route began and ended here (1986). The Big Storm of 1987 sadly uprooted some of the older trees.

For a gentle stroll to see a little of it, go straight ahead from the subway and turn left onto Broad Walk, then cut across right down past the bandstand to Rotten Row (beware of city horse-riders). The Great Exhibition (1851) was held at the far end (see p. 216), but turn right just before southern tip of the Serpentine to go through the Dell, a garden of azaleas, emerging at the restaurant beyond which are the rowing boats, canoes and pedal craft for hire (bandstand music end May–end Aug; boats for hire end Feb–early Oct, daily 10am–just before dusk).

Moving north from here, through trees and then open grass (**views** of London skyline in every direction), **Speakers' Corner** is at the north-east corner of the park. It was here that in 1855 one political Grosvenor upset Londoners so much with his proposed Sunday Trading Bill that orators stirred up a mob of 150,000 gathered here even though there was no legal right of assembly. That came in 1872, since when anyone (including you) may harangue their audience on any topic, so long as they do not blaspheme, are not obscene and do not breach the peace.

Nash's **Marble Arch** (1827) stands behind, marooned mid-roundabout. Banned from Buckingham Palace entrance because it was too narrow, this northern version of Rome's Arch of Constantine is also separated from the statue of its patron, George IV, which should sit on top but is in Trafalgar Square instead. Cars whizz round the redundant archway; only the Royal Family and the King's Troop Royal Horse Artillery may go through it. But this spot's real fame was the Tyburn Gallows, London's main public execution site from the fourteenth century until it was moved to Newgate in 1783, conveniently right outside the prison. Until then, condemned victims, often 'shaved and handsomely dressed', were processed in a cart through the city, tied to the rope under the gallows and the horse whipped so that, according to one observer, 'away goes the cart, and there swings my gentleman, kicking in the air'. Hanging days were public holidays, the authorities reasoning that such sights would deter wickedness. Crowds lined the way and jostled for space at Tyburn. The rich sat in expensive grandstand seats to watch up to 21 victims dangle to death, the frail pushing forwards to touch the dead body which was believed to possess medicinal properties.

Here St John Southworth was martyred (1654, see Westminster Cathedral, p. 92), as was Oliver Plunkett (1681), the last English martyr; and the trio of Cromwell, Ireton and Bradshaw were disinterred from Westminster Abbey, hanged here for a day and then beheaded, their heads spiked onto Westminster Hall and their bodies buried in a deep pit here. And to this day, in the nearby Tyburn Convent, the Benedictine Adorers of the Sacred Heart (affiliated to the Sacré Coeur in Paris) keep perpetual exposition of the Blessed Sacrament in memory of the 40 Catholic martyrs hanged at Tyburn, together with a museum of relics in the crypt (8 Hyde Park Place, W1, tel 723 7262; chapel open at all times, Mass at 7.30am and Vespers at 4.30pm; crypt open daily 3.30–4.15pm and 5.30–6.15pm).

Explorers may now wish to wander through the park, making their way down to the Serpentine Bridge to enjoy one of the great London views. But if St James's and Mayfair have merely whetted your appetite, an hour's trot around southern **Marylebone** just north of Oxford Street, dropping in on an astounding palace-mansion now housing a glorious art collection, gives a more complete picture of eighteenth-century high society's move west.

The subway by Speakers' Corner plunges back under Park Lane to the Grosvenor estate. It was only after the gallows went that builders moved in to develop this last corner. Cutting along Green Street, then right down Park Street and left to wiggle through pretty Lees Place (with Shepherds Place and Shepherd Close), **North Audley Street** was part of the early building. Edward Shepherd built nos 11–12 (c.1730) to which the Huguenot refugee Jean Louis Ligonier added an exquisite garden gallery (one of London's finest surviving early Georgian rooms) and later resident Samuel Courtauld (founder of the Courtauld Institute, see p. 120) invited Rex Whistler to decorate a bedroom. Beyond it, Providence Court and George Yard lead to **Duke Street**, the other principal street leading north from Grosvenor Square. Turning left and past Alfred Waterhouse's Ukrainian Catholic Cathedral (1889–91, built as the King's Weigh House Chapel) and the electricity sub-station (1903–5), incongruously practical amid so much sumptuous grandeur, the **view** stretches up across Oxford Street to tree-filled Manchester Square with Hertford House beyond (well-lit at night).

Oxford Street began as the Roman route which by-passed London and ran from Hampshire to the Suffolk coast. After a succession of names, including 'King's Highway' to flatter Charles II and 'The Tyburn Way' to mark the river it crossed at the top of South Molton Street and to honour the condemned prisoners' processional route to the gallows, it was called Oxford Street not because it led out to Oxford but because the land on the north side was bought by Edward Harley, 2nd Earl of Oxford, in 1713. A 'lurking place of cut-throats' around then, it soon smartened up to answer the newly arrived locals' needs. Built up first with theatres and entertainment halls, it became a shopping street in the nineteenth century and some of today's fruit and flower street traders are the great-grandchildren of traders who kept their barrows here.

Its most famous arrival was RF Atkinson and Daniel Burnham's Selfridges department store (1907–28), built by American retail magnate Gordon Selfridge, who strolled up from his Grosvenor Square home to watch the steel frame being coated in Ionic columns to make it London's grandest temple to Edwardian spending, still true today even if Harrods is more famous. To see how it contrasted with its surroundings, turn right and cross the north side, pass Bird and James streets and turn left through a tiny archway into Gees Court and St Christopher's Place where tiny shops have recently been given new life. Further along Oxford Street, more little shops line South Molton Street on the right (see above), while on the left Stratford Place sets the tone for Marylebone: an elegant cul-de-sac closed by gates (see the lion-topped pier) leading to R Edwin's Adamesque Stratford House (1773). Now the home of the Oriental Club, founded in 1824 for administrative bastions of the British empire who could not join the military Pall Mall clubs, it was built by the 2nd Earl of Stratford on land bought from the City merchants when water pipes replaced conduits. Since medieval times they would ceremoniously process here ostensibly to inspect the head of their valuable water conduit, in fact spending most of the day feasting in their grand banqueting hall between hunting for hare and fox.

It was on these well stocked fields that London pushed northwards. Vere Street is three streets further along, where James Gibbs's **St Peter** (1721–4, pretty interior) is the chapel-at-ease for Cavendish Square, found round to the right at the end of Henrietta Place (whose stylish drawing room of no. 11 is in the V&A museum, see p. 222). This is where the Marylebone estate began, satisfying the growing numbers of prosperous Georgian high society by expanding their hub of airy smart squares and terraces in the only direction left, north of Oxford Street. The land was owned by politician and aristocrat Robert Harley, 2nd Earl of Oxford (1661–1724), whose Tory career enabled him to rise to win Queen Anne's confidence, temporarily eclipsing the Whig Duke of Marlborough's influence (and that of his wife) so that his expensive victories during the War of the Spanish Succession (1702–13) were finally concluded in the

Treaty of Utrecht (1713). Before falling from favour the next year, Oxford acquired this chunk of land. He married Lady Henrietta Cavendish-Holles, an heiress who came with her own tract of land to the west, later developed as the Portman estate by their only child, Margaret, who married William Bentinck, 2nd Duke of Portland and a keen horse racer.

The Marylebone estate kicked off with John Prince's Cavendish Square (1717), with advice from James Gibbs. Well placed directly north of fashionable Hanover Square, it received the ultimate stamp of society approval when George II's daughter, Amelia, came to live at no. 16 (1761–80). Two stone-faced houses (1770s) survive in the middle of the north side and a statue of George Bentinck, 4th Duke of Portland (1802–48) and Tory ally of Disraeli, stands in the garden, all best seen from the restaurant of the John Lewis department store (1939) which covers both the south side and the house in Holles Street where Byron was born.

The streets around the square make a pleasant stroll. Leaving by Chandos Street in the northeast corner, one of Robert Adam's best houses, Chandos House (1769–71), built for the 2nd Duke of Chandos, closes the vista at the end. Turning left along Queen Anne Street, then right along Mansfield Street (dipping right to catch the sphinx-decorated mews houses off Duchess Street), a left turn into New Cavendish Street leads to Harley Street, a smart residential street that attracted painters Turner (no. 64, 1804–8) and Allan Ramsay (no. 67, 1770–80) before the medical profession took it over in the 1840s. Back in Queen Anne Street, Turner made nos 22–3 his gallery from 1808 until his death in 1851. Moving along to the right, then turning left down Wimpole Street, right along Welbeck Way and left down Welbeck Street, Wigmore Street is where Clark and Russell's splendid shop (1907–8) for Debenham and Freebody is ahead, opposite the Wigmore Hall (1901) on the left, a concert hall which Friedrich Bechstein built adjoining his spacious piano showrooms.

Turning right, then right again, the heart of old Marylebone village survives along the narrow winding Marylebone Lane where the medieval church of St Mary-by-the-Bourne (that is, the Tyburn river) gave the area its name. Then, cutting out of it left through Hinde Street, eighteenth-century order resumes in Manchester Square (1776–80), still almost complete, with gracious houses on three sides and Hertford House, home of **the Wallace Collection**, along the fourth. Built for the Duke of Manchester so that he could enjoy the nearby duck-shooting, it was soon bought by the 2nd Marquess of Hertford in 1797. The Hertfords were great and discerning collectors. The 1st Marquess patronised Ramsay and bought Canalettos; the 2nd was given Gainsborough's 'Mrs Robinson' by a grateful Prince Regent who enjoyed the company of Hertford's wife (his portrait hangs next to it in the ballroom); the 3rd, a society legend and close friend of the Prince Regent, bought Sèvres and Dutch seventeenth-century pictures; and the 4th, an eccentric living in the Bois de Boulogne in Paris, took full advantage of the chaos during the Revolution and snapped up first-class canvases (Fragonard, Watteau, Boucher, etc), furniture, sculpture and objets d'art to make one of the finest private collections of French art. All was left to his illegitimate son, Sir Richard Wallace, who shipped it home, renovated the house (staircase from Louis XV's Palais Mazarin) and his own Italian majolica and Renaissance armour, bronzes and gold. And his widow gave the lot to the nation, provided that it remained always in Central London.

An astounding collection set out in the palatial and immaculate house of its owners, this is one of the most magical of all London museums, revealing the lifestyle and taste of its string of discerning owners. Wandering the rooms, with pauses for fresh air on the benches of the courtyard, do not miss the Fragonards on the staircase, the two great marquetry bureaux in Wallace's dining room, and his dressing room and bathroom on the first floor. According to Malcolm Rogers, Deputy Director of the National Portrait Gallery, this is 'arguably the finest collection of French 18th century paintings and furniture to be seen in a single room anywhere' (The Wallace Collection, Hertford House, Manchester Square, W1, tel 935 0687; open Mon–Sat 10am–5pm, Sun 2–5pm; free. Lectures, bookstall).

West of Manchester Square, Fitzhardinge Street opens into Baker Street, where Sherlock Holmes still receives mail at his fictional home, no. 221B. **Portman Square** (1764–84) is across the road. Here the second survivor of Robert Adam's Central London mansions is Home House at no. 20 (1773–7), containing perhaps his best interior. Built by the widowed Countess of Home, it became the focus of an anti-court society in the 1780s, when the Duke and Duchess of Cumberland would sweep up the dramatic circular staircase to Adam's richly encrusted rooms. It was later home to the industrialist Samuel Courtauld who filled it with his collec-

tion and bequeathed both to his newly formed Courtauld Institute, to go to Somerset House in 1989 (see p. 120). Home House may open to the public under the auspices of the National Trust; but no. 21 (its entrance around the corner in Gloucester Place) is already open and, although less grand, well worth a quick look. Built in 1772 by Robert's brother, James, it now houses the **Royal Institute of British Architects' Drawings Collection**, an enormous and exceptional collection of more than 200,000 drawings, ranging from all of Palladio's studio drawings up to Lutyens and Le Corbusier, tempting morsels put on show in the modern gallery, the rest open to researchers by appointment (Heinz Gallery, 21 Portman Square, W1, tel 580 5533; open during exhibitions Mon–Fri 10am–5pm but Thurs 11am–8pm, Sat 10am–1pm; closed Aug; usually free; to see more of the house, just ask. See also p. 179).

Gloucester Place leads north from here, a remarkably intact street a mile long and lined with grand Georgian terraces. It was just this sort of simplicity that the Victorians called boring and therefore jazzed up with bright red brick and articulated fronts. Turning left off it along George Street, the little circle right through **Montagu Square**, on and left along Crawford Street (Smirke's St Mary, 1823, on the right) and back down **Bryanston Square** is well worth the detour. This last and western edge of the Portman estate was designed by Joseph Parkinson (1811) and built by a chimney sweep made good, David Porter. He named Montagu Square after the glittering and intelligent society hostess Elizabeth Montagu. She lived in nearby Portman Square where he had eaten at her annual May Day chimney sweeps' dinner – her equally famous literary gatherings included Mr Benjamin Stillingfleet whose eccentric blue instead of black stockings gave the parties the nickname Blue Stocking Society, soon to become a disparaging term for women intellectuals.

Moving down the length of Great Cumberland Place (1789), there is a good **view** of Marble Arch before turning right along Bryanston Street and then crossing Edgware Road into tiny Connaught Place which leads through to **Connaught Square** (1807–15). Small-scale, elegant and peaceful, this marked the start of a new move west and the development of **Bayswater**, the area north of Hyde Park. Known as Tyburnia, this little corner quickly prepared for society with a network of increasingly spacious squares and terraces inspired by their Marylebone and Mayfair neighbours but more and more influenced by Nash's grand, stuccoed work up at Regent's Park (see p. 180) and finally bordered along the north-west by the impressively wide and grand Sussex Gardens, now slightly down at heel. To see a little, follow **Connaught Street** left out of the square, catch the view down Albion Street on the left, but continue along **Hyde Park Street** and around Hyde Park Square, leaving it down **Clarendon Place** to see the still pristine mix of Hyde Park Garden Mews and parallel **Hyde Park**

Gardens (1830s, by John Crake). At the bottom, Victoria Gate leads into Hyde Park for the best views of their built-to-impress facades. Fountains and dog cemetery are to the right of the gate (see Kensington Gardens, p. 191). The path alongside Queen Caroline's Long Water leads down to the Serpentine Bridge with expansive sunset **views** over the royal St James's and Buckingham palaces, which drew the aristocrats here, to the suncatching spires of Westminster.

Soho and Bloomsbury: Cosmopolitan living and learning

Mapping it out from above: Nothing good, but for a classic Bloomsbury square, the view from the Architectural Association's first floor room down over Bedford Square.

Starting point: Leicester Square, access by Underground: Leicester Square, Piccadilly Circus.

Good days to explore: Soho goes non-stop Monday to Saturday, with a strange post-party quietness on Sunday; museum-stuffed Bloomsbury is best Monday to Saturday for space and calm to contemplate its treasures; but opening times vary so it is best to plan ahead – Sundays are crowded family days.

Information: The nearest is the British Travel Centre, see p. 4.

Refreshments: see p. 313.

Local festivals:

In Soho: Chinese New Year, usually celebrated in February; a terrific street carnival with lion dance in Chinese Soho.

In Bloomsbury: Several lively neighbourhood festivals through the year including Calthorpe Summer Celebrations, Gray's Inn Road, second Sat in June; Queen Square Fair, WC1, first Sat in July; Fitzrovia Fair, Fitzroy Square, W1, first Sun in July; Bloomsbury Fair, Museum Street, WC1, second Sat in July; information on all from Camden Arts and Entertainment, 100 Euston Road, NW1 (278 4000 x2452).

Local libraries:

For Soho, Westminster City's Central Reference Library, off Leicester Square, see p. 75.

For Bloomsbury: Two of Camden borough's libraries are in the area: Holborn, 32–8 Theobald's Road, WC1 (405 2705); and St Pancras, 100 Euston Road, NW1 (278 4444), both open Mon–Sat. See also the British Library (pp. 67–8).

In the quiet of early-morning Gerrard Street, Chinese locals discuss the news gleaned from *Sing Tao*, their newspaper published in Britain; a few streets north, jean-clad Italians murmur a bleary-eyed ciao over an expresso. As the sun lifts, media men meet for a croissant at Patisserie Valerie, barrow boys arrange their juicy oranges and lemons in Berwick Street and salami and pasta addicts slip into Camisa delicatessen. Gaston polishes up the glasses in the French pub. Chefs from India, Hungary, France, Malaysia, Korea, Italy and China chop, grate, blanche, fry, stir, blend and taste. Then the daily Soho party begins.

Restaurants overflow as gossip columnists spot who's lunching with whom at L'Escargot, Groucho's or Alastair Little. More modest parties compete with the Chinese for seats in their favourite dim sum parlour or flirt with Italian waiters who twist yard-long pepper mills to spice up the spaghetti. In the post-lunch lull, alley doors surrounded by flashing lights seduce the well-wined into their dark caverns for afternoon amusements. Then pubs, restaurants, bars and clubs of every conceivable type – and many inconceivable – open up, light up and switch on for the night-long party where song and chatter in every language spills out along the streets until the dawn milkman comes on his rounds.

Bloomsbury, to the north, is just as international, but the tiny Soho warren which no bus has dared to tackle is exchanged for extravagantly spacious garden squares and streets. Here scholars stroll amid the roses in pensive mood, sharp brains debate timeless philosophies over a lunchtime pint in the Museum Tavern, and students scuttle to lectures on medicine, mandarins and military campaigns. Seasoned academics normally cocooned in libraries discuss the finer points of a PhD thesis while sitting in public vulnerability in the Pizza Express. Scholars of the Indian subcontinent disappear into the bowels of Mr Vijayathi's Books from India, while professors from far-flung lands lose hours in their favourite haunts browsing and drooling over longed-for obscure volumes.

Bloomsbury is London's literary stronghold whose king is the British Museum, whose nobility are the small specialised museums and whose people are professors, lecturers and students of the University of London, the largest university in Britain. Back-pack travellers, chic New Yorkers and sari-swathed Indians stream into the British Museum, then hours later stream out again, brains giddy and feet fragile from treasure-

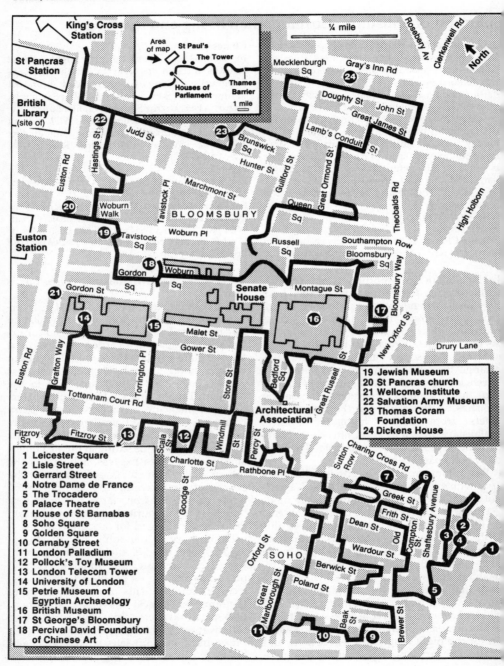

Area of map St Paul's
The Tower
Houses of Parliament
Thames Barrier
1 mile

¼ mile

North

King's Cross Station

St Pancras Station

British Library (site of)

Euston Station

Fitzroy Sq

Euston Rd

Hastings St

Judd St

Woburn Walk

Tavistock Pl

Marchmont St

BLOOMSBURY

Woburn Pl

Tavistock Sq

Gordon Sq

Woburn Sq

Gordon St

Grafton Way

Torrington Pl

Tottenham Court Rd

Fitzroy St

Scala St

Charlotte St

Windmill St

Percy St

Rathbone Pl

Goodge St

Oxford St

Great Marlborough St

Poland St

SOHO

Berwick St

Beak St

Brewer St

Wardour St

Dean St

Old Compton St

Frith St

Greek St

Shaftesbury Avenue

Charing Cross Rd

Sutton Row

Great Russell St

Store St

Malet St

Gower St

Bedford Sq

Senate House

Montague St

Russell Sq

Queen Sq

Guilford St

Great Ormond St

Lamb's Conduit St

Southampton Row

Bloomsbury Sq

New Oxford St

Bloomsbury Way

Theobalds Rd

High Holborn

Drury Lane

Brunswick Sq

Hunter St

Mecklenburgh Sq

Doughty St

John St

Great James St

Gray's Inn Rd

Rosebery Av

Clerkenwell Rd

Architectural Association

19 Jewish Museum
20 St Pancras church
21 Wellcome Institute
22 Salvation Army Museum
23 Thomas Coram Foundation
24 Dickens House

1 Leicester Square
2 Lisle Street
3 Gerrard Street
4 Notre Dame de France
5 The Trocadero
6 Palace Theatre
7 House of St Barnabas
8 Soho Square
9 Golden Square
10 Carnaby Street
11 London Palladium
12 Pollock's Toy Museum
13 London Telecom Tower
14 University of London
15 Petrie Museum of Egyptian Archaeology
16 British Museum
17 St George's Bloomsbury
18 Percival David Foundation of Chinese Art

gloating, to sit on the museum benches licking ice-creams in the summer sunshine.

So, while Soho feeds, drinks and amuses the flesh, Bloomsbury feeds the mind. To glimpse the past and present of this cosmo-politan area of London, explore beyond the streets, poking down the Soho alleys and perhaps dipping into a Chinese chemist, a French church, the Jewish Museum or Dickens's home.

In southern **Soho**, the scene is set in **Leicester Square**. At the Dissolution of the Monasteries, while the bishops' palaces in the Strand went to favoured courtiers, Henry VIII (1509–47) relieved the Abingdon monks and the custodian of St Giles-in-the-Fields leper hospital of their farmland just north of Whitehall Palace and used it to extend his hunting. At the same time the Charterhouse monks (see p. 202), who had been given Blemon-disberi (meaning Blemond's manor, later reduced to Bloomsbury) with its vineyards and swine-stocked woods by the pious Edward III, were relieved of their land, too, which went to Thomas Wriothesey, Henry's Lord Chancellor (1545), whom he made Earl of Southampton (1547). While the Southampton heirs developed their Bloomsbury acres Mayfair-style, Henry's hunting ground, known as Soho from the old hunting cry 'so-ho', was parcelled off to royal favourites who built country mansions and streets for fellow aristocrats before moving off to more fashionable areas.

The French Huguenots, early Soho immigrants, lived side by side with the aristocracy in the eighteenth century. They were joined by artists and then by a flood of nineteenth-century population overflow who lived in a seedy state surrounded by their often bawdy entertainment halls and prostitutes. This influx and the nineteenth-century cholera outbreaks sent the wealthy away. But they returned for nighttime pleasures and merriment once the late Victorians had raised the Soho tone by slicing through Shaftesbury Avenue, lining it with grand theatres. At the same time they began to eat in restaurants instead of entertaining at home, making Soho a paradise for international gourmands.

Leicester Square (1670s) is a microcosm of Soho's history. Its acres belonged to Westminster Abbey. Henry VIII took them; Charles I gave them to Robert Sidney, 2nd Earl of Leicester. He built one of London's largest Stuart houses on the north side (1631–5), entertained lavishly (John Evelyn was bewitched by a fire-eater one night), and added the handsome square after Charles II's restoration and the Great Fire both encouraged the gentry to move west (1670s). It was in a plum position. Aristocrats moved in, and the main house was rented to the rebellious Prince of Wales who held rival court here after his father, George I, threw him out of St James's Palace (1717–27, see p. 137). Among the artists who arrived were William Hogarth at no. 30 (1733–64) where he worked on his great social series including *The Rake's Progress* (now in the Soane Museum, p. 125), and Joshua Reynolds at no. 46 (1760–92), where he made his fortune painting high society in his elegant salon while entertaining Burke, Johnson and Goldsmith and acting as first President of the Royal Academy in Picca-dilly. John Hunter also lived here, at no. 28 (1783–93), amid his forest of physiological specimens now pored over by students at the Royal College of Surgeons (see p. 125).

When the gentry moved off, their empty homes became foreign hotels, Turkish baths or made made way for four great Victorian entertainment halls that characterised the square's heyday and made it synonymous with West End entertain-ment: the Alhambra (1858), a fabulous Moorish building with minarets where Queen Victoria came to see the circus; the Empire (1884), where Katti Lanner staged her mesmerising ballets; Daly's (1893), where Humperdinck's *Hansel and Gretel* had its London début in 1895; and the Hippodrome (1900) at the end of the square's north-east arm, Cranbourn Street.

Then the picture palaces arrived, bringing the exotic American culture, and glamorous Holly-wood in particular, to the West End – hours of escapist dreaming at a fraction of the cost of a theatre ticket. Mass entertainment began: the Empire changed from stage to screen (1928), the Warner West End replaced Daly's (1938), and the Alhambra became the Odeon (1937), its dra-matic geometry and black granite as stylishly mod-ern as its films. Meanwhile, Mayfair high society led by the Prince of Wales (later Edward VIII) squeezed into the basement Café de Paris on the north side to bring a touch of Hollywood glamour to Leicester Square. In its interior based on the SS *Lusitania*'s Palm Court, the glittering, champagne-drinking fun set included kings (Greece, Norway, Portugal, Spain) and stars (Noël Coward, Gloria

Swanson). They danced 'and fast, there was no shuffling around', watched the cabaret shows (Marlene Dietrich, Maurice Chevalier) and could even hire a dance-hostess – Merle Oberon and Nora Turner started here.

Today, all three cinemas are still here and the revived Café de Paris is currently the best and most star-studded (and most difficult to enter) disco club in town. In the square, John Doubleday's bronze (1981) of London's own comic hero of the silver screen, Charlie Chaplin (1889–1977), who hit Hollywood in 1914, is complete with bowler hat, stick and baggy trousers. As for the garden, locals dried their laundry in it until the geographer James Wyld bought it and, in 1851, to coincide with the Great Exhibition (see p. 212), opened his 60-foot high globe. Visitors so loved clambering up the four storeys of the gas-lit interior, walls painted with the earth's mountains and rivers, that it was a favourite London outing for a decade. Current plans are to rip up James Knowles's garden (1870s), including his Shakespeare-topped fountain surrounded by busts of its illustrious residents, and start again.

Leaving the square by the north-west corner, up past the Swiss Centre whose outside chiming clock adds to the noise of the square's street entertainers, Leicester Street leads up to **Lisle Street** (the Leicesters were also the Viscount Lisles). This, the parallel Gerrard Street and the surrounding alleys are London's Chinatown. Although early Chinese immigrants were eighteenth-century seamen employed by the East India Company and formed their Chinatown in the Docklands' Limehouse (see p. 106), a second and much larger wave arrived from Hong Kong and China in the 1950s and '60s, fleeing poverty in the New Territories, then part of British-owned Hong Kong, while the rest of communist China was closed to the world. Their dream was to run a restaurant in London, where British soldiers had returned from Second World War service in the Far East with a taste for chop suey. Today, about 100,000 Chinese live in Britain, half of them in London and concentrated here. They call their district Tong Yan Kai (Chinese Street); they read their British-published daily newspaper, the *Sing Tao*; they stoically, and rarely for immigrants to London, speak broken English; they rent out Kung-Fu videos; and they celebrate New Year with the full lion dance to scare away evil spirits and bring good luck, red envelopes of 'lucky money' and choruses of '*Gung Hei Faat Choi*' (wishing you prosperity). The shops are a revelation: paper

kites, flowers and parasols; sets of *ma-jong* and *hsiang-ch'i* (Chinese chess); statues of Buddha and Taoist deities; and grocers selling sweet and sour and stocked with mysterious-looking roots, dried fish, bottled fruits and vegetables. But all these lurk among the main trade – restaurants.

Much more than New York's SoHo district, this tiny spot *feels* Chinese. You are quite likely to be the only non-Chinese clicking your chopsticks in a restaurant or nosing about the grocer's. To see a little of it, turn left along Lisle Street to Wardour Street, where dim sum devotee Fay Maschler haunts Chuen Cheng Ku, the 'seething cathedral of Cantonese cooking' opposite – appropriately, the name of the tempting little parcels means 'touch the heart'. Right and right again is **Gerrard Street** where, either side of the Chinese red-and-gold gateways, telephone boxes and benches (courtesy of Westminster City council), you can find opera masks at no. 14, acupuncture equipment at no. 20 and kites at no. 46. After Gerrard Place on the left, with a Chinese cinema, Newport Place leads right, past odd-shaped monsters laid out at the wet fishmonger's on the corner of Newport Court. (While you are here, it is worth popping through and across Charing Cross Road to see what's on at the excellent Photographers' Gallery in Great Newport Street.) In the parallel Little Newport Street, Chinese martial arts are found at no. 10. Returning along Lisle Street, the herbal chemist at no. 24a sells dried seahorse for coughs and snakeskin for strength and the Diamond restaurant next door is a favourite late night haunt for top London chefs Anton Mosimann and Nico Ladenis.

In contrast to the recent Chinese arrivals in Soho, the French were some of the first. French Protestants fled here and were given asylum by Edward VI, together with a right to hold services in 1550, although they did not get their own church until 1893 (see Soho Square, below). The Huguenots, also French Protestants, arrived next, this time fleeing France to find religious sanctuary after Louis XIV revoked the Edict of Nantes in 1685. An estimated 13,000 came to London where James II was soon to topple to Protestant William and Mary (1689–1702). Some settled in Wandsworth (hatters and dyers, see p. 110), some in Spitalfields (silk dyers, weavers and merchants, see p. 248) and some here in Soho where they quickly gained respect as honest merchants. Indeed, by the 1730s they were so established that the area was known as Petty France, church services and baptisms were in French and there were about 800 French-speaking homes. As William Maitland wrote in 1739: 'It is easy Matter for a Stranger to imagine himself in France.' The French Revolution brought a new wave of refugees, this time mostly Catholics including many priests and nobles, among them the future Louis XVIII, Charles X and Louis-Philippe, all of whom benefitted from more than £2 million handed out by the British government (1794–1802). Naturally, many settled near here, close to their fellow countrymen.

By the 1860s, most of the 50,000 French people in England lived in London, working as merchants, artists, musicians, chefs, wine merchants, couturiers, governesses and servants, with an annual influx of another 30,000 French tourists who stayed in the 40 French hotels around Leicester Square. The area became, as one Frenchman noted, *'le quartier français du plus mauvais renom . . . une population sordide'*. The spirit of charity was aroused. Half-way along Lisle Street, turning left down Leicester Place, the Marist priest Charles Fauré employed a pioneer of the Art Nouveau movement, Auguste Boileau, to convert a Victorian panorama theatre into the church of **Notre Dame de France** with school and charity house (1865), worth going inside to see Jean Cocteau's frescoes (1960) in the north chapel (tel 437 9363/ 5571; open Mon–Sat, 9am–1pm and 2.30–6.30pm, Sun, 9am–1pm; Mass on Sat 6pm, Sun 10am and 11.30am (Gregorian Chant), all in French). Further along Lisle Street, Manzi's on the corner of Leicester Street is still a tiny, family-run French hotel with gingham cloths in the painted, ground-floor, mostly fish restaurant – easier than going over to Paris for the weekend. And turning right up Wardour Street, Chez Victor feels very *chez* Left Bank.

In 1877, with Nash's smart new Regent Street complete, parliament decided to clear up the disreputable area to the east of it and improve communications. So they destroyed some of the worst slums to widen Soho's main thoroughfare up to Bloomsbury, renaming it **Shaftesbury Avenue** after the philanthropic 7th Earl of Shaftesbury, whose Eros memorial is at the bottom in Piccadilly Circus (see p. 177). Opened in 1886, it immediately attracted a string of theatres up the west side, some still here. To the left, CJ Phipps's Lyric (1888, Rosenauer's interior 1933) built with proceeds from the hit comic opera *Dorothy*, which was then transferred from the Prince of Wales (of Leicester Square) to be the opening show. More recently, Alan Bennett's *Habeas Corpus* had an unusual cast change when, after a year's run, the author took over the part of Mrs Swabb (1974). Moving up the street, Lewen Sharp's French renaissance Apollo (1901) opened with a musical farce; WGA Sprague's Globe (1906) also opened with a musical but later staged Christopher Fry's *The Lady's Not For Burning* (1949) and Robert Bolt's *A Man for All Seasons* (1960); and Sprague's Queen's (1907, rebuilt 1959) ran the last word in matinee frolicks in 1913 with their Tango Teas of dancing, dress parade and tea – until recently, matinee theatre-goers in the West End could have a tea-tray brought to their seat.

Turning left down Shaftesbury Avenue, **the Trocadero** (1895), originally a dance hall opened by a French wine merchant, became Joe Lyons' smart, plush-seated restaurant where older Londoners remember being brought for holiday treats in the 1930s. Today, gutted and rebuilt by Fitzroy Robinson and Ove Arup (1980s), the old facade houses shops, pricey restaurants and, on the upper floors, two easily missed quality London shows – and one missable one (Trocadero, W1, all shops, restaurants and shows open daily 10am–10pm).

Guinness World of Records, inspired by the annual Guinness Book of Records, is everything Madame Tussaud's is not: well built models complemented by hands-on items, period film, tapes, moving diagrams and music, all designed to be exciting and fun. In the six worlds – earth, sport, human, animal, machine and entertainment – the most spectacular feats, facts and oddities come alive. You can watch the longest domino tumble go down, stand in the tallest man's footprint, listen to the man with the worst hiccups ever, see Pele scoring his soccer goals, inspect the fast-moving digits recording the world population as it increases by 161 a minute, watch each tallest building be eclipsed by the next (currently topped by the Warszawa Tower in Poland) and listen to the highest-paid concert pianist (Paderewski), the most-recorded song (McCartney's 'Yesterday') and the highest-selling record – Bing Crosby's recording of Irving Berlin's 'White Christmas', whose sale is 25 million to date. Justifiably popular; quietest early morning or in the evening (tel 439 7331; charge. Bookshop sells the current *Guinness Book of Records*).

The other good show is **Light Fantastic**, the largest permanent holography exhibition in the world and the showroom for holographic technology and its practical application. Wandering the large, dark room, more than a hundred apparently black screens light up as each is passed, teasing with all kinds of tricks – Heineken lager reviving a withered flower, Alice in Wonderland's Cheshire cat disappearing to leave its smile, Dizzy Gillespie puffing his trumpet and, very dramatic, the presentation model for the new science museum in Paris. Inspired by these, visitors can order their own hologram, prices starting at £1,500 for one on a credit card (tel 734 4516; charge. Shop). Finally, The London Experience, a dash through London's history using photographs, voice and music, could be so much better although the accompanying catalogue and map are good (tel 439 4938).

A larger tract of Soho lies north of Shaftesbury Avenue, a honeycomb best explored by strolling along the streets and poking down the narrow alleys and courts. **Windmill Street** leads up through the long-time haunt of prostitutes, peep shows, striptease clubs, clip joints, encounter parlours and dirty bookshops, collectively known as the Vice. But, suddenly, it has become an area of licensed (the girls can move) and unlicensed (the girls strike immobile poses) striptease clubs, fast-declining as each expired lease is refused renewal. Soho's council, Westminster, began their crackdown in June 1986. A year later, 65 sex establishments had reduced to 36, the Vice dens were opening as chic restaurants and clothes shops, the prostitutes had taken their trade to King's Cross and Bayswater, and the council had licensed just five sex establishments and three striptease shows – Sunset Strip in Dean Street, Carnival in Old Compton Street and the well known Raymond's Revuebar in Walker's Court. The red lights had dimmed.

In Soho's heyday, the Windmill was the most famous club. Inspired by the French craze for revuedeville (non-stop afternoon and evening variety shows using almost-nude girls) it launched a similar show in 1932, had a huge success and was the only London theatre to remain open throughout the Second World War – hence the epithet 'we never close', except that it finally did in 1964. To see the nearest equivalent today, turn right into Brewer Street, then left into Walker's Court to find Raymond's Revuebar, whose happy clients have included schoolboys up on the train from Eton ostensibly to have tea with an ageing aunt in Kensington. Sex tycoon Paul Raymond typifies Soho's newly scrubbed image: as the licenses are refused, he buys up property and converts it into up-market restaurants, offices and flats.

Leaving this knot of courts, best enjoyed at the full tide of evening partying, **Rupert Street** on the right leads left through Tisbury Court to glimpse the tower remains of Wren's parish church, St Anne's Soho (1680–6, tower 1717) before crossing into **Old Compton Street**. Laid out in the 1670s, it soon had more French than English residents and became Soho's main shopping street, its pubs a meeting-place for French exiles – Rimbaud and Verlaine drank here. But today, although Patisserie Valerie at no. 44 keeps the mood alive, Italians set the character of this and neighbouring streets. The nineteenth-century Little Italy of London was up in Clerkenwell (see p. 204), but some Italians came to Soho along with other Continental immigrants in the seventeenth century, especially political refugees. And whereas Clerkenwell has lost its Italians, in Soho they have consolidated their presence with a host of bars, restaurants and some of the best food shops in London. On this street alone there are the cheerful bars Pollo (no. 20) and Presto (no. 4–6), the wine shop Vinorio (no. 8), the delicatessen Camisa (no. 61 – its equal, Lina Stores, is at 18 Brewer Street), a tiny cave scented with almonds, parmesan and fresh pasta, and the wonderful Moroni's (no. 63) stocked with Italian chocolates and cigarettes, six same-day Italian newspapers and the British-printed *London Sera* and *La Voce degli Italiani* – a complete package for the homesick Florentine.

Turning left up **Dean Street** (1690), peopled by the usual Soho succession of aristocrats, French immigrants and then artists, the Venetian ambassador had his chapel here at no. 21, later converted into Caldwell's Assembly Rooms where the seven-year-old Mozart was made to perform on the harpsichord, accompanied by his four-year-old sister (1763). Nearby, at no. 28, on top of PG Leoni's Quo Vadis, an early restaurant arrival (1926), Karl Marx lived with wife, maid and five children (three of them died while here) in two rooms of squalor, 'thick dust . . . the greatest disorder . . . dirty spoons . . . Dutch clay pipes . . . tobacco ash' (1851–6, apply to Quo Vadis on 437 9585 to arrange a visit). From here, he walked to study at the British Museum Reading Room daily, though it was at up at no. 64 that he and Engels pored over the final *Neue Rheinishe Zeitung* numbers (1850).

An Italian waiter, Luigi Gamba, left the Savoy in 1903 to start a boot-making business at no. 46 to supply his fellows with more comfy shoes and was soon crafting ballet slippers for Pavlova and Nijinsky. Also in Dean Street, the French House at no. 49 was bought by Monsieur Berlemont in 1914, became a haven for the Free French during the Second World War, a favourite watering hole of De Gaulle and a clique of writers that began with Brendan Behan and Dylan Thomas and continues today under the management of Berlemont's son, Gaston. While here, do not miss narrow Meard Street on the left, built by carpenter John Meard in 1732, for an echo of the eighteenth-century residential atmosphere.

Turning right along Bateman Street, where the first Huguenots settled, then right into **Frith Street**, this is where Mozart's father took rooms at no. 20 on his return trip with his child prodigies (1764–5) and advertised tickets inviting Londoners to try his son's 'surprising Musical Capacity, by giving him any thing to play at Sight, or any Music without Bass, which he will write upon the Spot'. On January 26, 1926, there was an equally remarkable demonstration at no. 22: John Logie Baird gave his first public show of television (see his equipment in the Science Museum, p. 220). Today, Ronnie Scott introduces the world's jazz stars at no. 47. Further down, **Romilly Street** leads off left, named after law reformer Samuel Romilly, son of a third generation Huguenot watch-maker. Hiding among the Italian trattorias hung with chianti bottles is Kettner's at no. 29. Founded by Napoleon III's chef, Auguste Kettner, in the 1860s, it was one of the first Soho restaurants, became Oscar Wilde's favourite and its plush interior is now the setting for pizzas and jazz piano, Italian links strengthened by 10p of every Pizza Veneziana ordered going to the Venice in Peril Fund.

To see the grandest Shaftesbury Avenue theatre, find the **Palace Theatre** at Cambridge Circus, the mythical M16 Circus of John le Carré's spy thrillers. Designed by Collcutt and Holloway (1888–91) for D'Oyly Carte as the home for the Royal English Opera, it had green marble columns, gilded capitals, alabaster balusters, Morris & Co carpets, Doulton terracotta decoration, the latest scene-changing machinery including a three-level cellar, its own generator for 2,000 electric lamps and opened in 1891 with Arthur Sullivan and Julian Sturgess's romantic opera *Ivanhoe*. D'Oyly Carte's great dream failed. By the next year it was a variety theatre. Sarah Bernhardt played Cleopatra, Pavlova made her London début (1910), theatre manager Beerbohm Tree acted in Kipling's *The Man Who Was* (1912) and the film *The Sound of Music* played for 2,385 performances (1961–7). More recently, Andrew Lloyd Webber and Tim Rice's *Jesus*

Christ Superstar became London's longest running musical. Lloyd Webber bought the theatre when it came up for sale and is restoring it to glory (open daily 11am–3pm for lunch, entertainment and a glance round). Rice works in a peppermint-green office (including the piano) nearby. (Up at the top of the second half of Shaftesbury Avenue, London began in 1987 to answer Hollywood's pavement of stars: brass prints and signatures of Nigel Havers, Peggy Mount and others start outside the Shaftesbury Theatre and are to have additions stretching down to Piccadilly Circus.)

To right and left, **Charing Cross Road** (1880s) was cut through at the same time as Shaftesbury Avenue, with the same aims and engineer, the great Victorian Joseph Bazalgette (see p. 99). The street's supply of theatres was interspersed with bookshops, now a bibliophile's delight, especially down to the right where Zwemmer's stands at nos. 76 and 80 and round the corner at nos. 24 and 26 Litchfield Street. But Marks and Co at no. 84, to whom Helene Hanff addressed her letters, and later her book (*84 Charing Cross Road*), has gone.

Back into Soho, Moor Street leads up to **Greek Street**, named after the Greek church which stood nearby. The Greeks were an established part of the community. Galsworthy has an upper-class *Forsyte Saga* character denigrate Soho at the end of the last century as 'full of Greeks, Ishmaelites, cats, Italians, tomatoes, restaurants, organs, coloured stuffs, queer names, people looking out of upper windows . . . ' Little sign of those Greeks remains, and the Turkish Cypriots who live up in Harringay and Stoke Newington (north London), nicknamed by them 'The Capital', mostly came to London in the 1930s and then the 1950s from Cyprus, fleeing civil war and bringing their leather, catering and rag-trade skills. It was these and the Greek Cypriots (who settled in Camden Town) who saw their chance when Italians were imprisoned during the Second World War. They took over Charlotte Street's Italian restaurants (see below) and dived into pockets of Soho – basement Jimmy's round at 23 Frith Street, known for its surly-looking waiters, has now fed two generations of students with cheap *sheftalia* washed down with *Domestica*.

Moving up Greek Street, Josiah Wedgwood's London showrooms were at no. 12 (1774–97). At no. 48 (1741–2) Georges Gaudin set up L'Escargot Bienvenu restaurant around 1900 and painted his motto 'slow but sure' outside it. Restored and refurbished, it was in at the start of Soho's change from sex shops to smart socialising and is now a favourite haunt for government, media and glamour stars who trot up to the dining rooms on snail-carpeted stairs, attended by Elena Salvoni, doyenne of Soho *maitresse d*'s. Near the top of the street, past Manette Street, the **House of St Barnabas** (1746) provides the only glimpse of what grandeur Soho possessed. Behind its plain exterior, the magnificent interior (1755) fitted out for Richard Beckford (whose brother lived at 22 Soho Square and became Lord Mayor) includes splendid stucco staircase, elaborate plaster ceilings with dancing *putti*, and carved woodwork. Now a charity house for homeless women, it is well worth timing a visit (1 Greek Street, W1, tel 437 5508; open Wed 2.30–4.15pm, Thurs 11am–12.30pm; donations welcome).

Soho Square (begun 1677) was one of the first dozen squares built in London. Laid out over fields, it was equipped with grand mansions and a statue of Charles II in the garden and was a very fashionable address for a century – no. 15 survives to give an idea of the scale. In the garden, suited executives eat their sandwiches seated on benches next to down-and-outs. It was here, in the northwest corner, that Edward VI's licence, awarded to the first French Protestants in 1550, finally came to fruition with Aston Webb's Franco–Flemish brick and terracotta church (1891–3), its stone tympanum commemorating 400 years of Huguenot association with Soho. On the east side, the Irish Catholic immigrants were luckier. The trickle of Irish turned into a flood in the seventeenth century and St Giles, just east of here, became virtually a settlement of poor Irish. Father Arthur O'Leary ensured they got their St Patrick's Chapel in 1792, later replaced by John Kelly's Italianate building (1891). It was much-needed consolation for the next, bigger wave of arrivals who left the famines of 1847–8 in search of food and work and created some of the worst slums of London here: 'The misery, filth and crowded condition of the Irish cabin is realised in St Giles . . . squalid children, haggard men with long uncombed hair, in rags . . . women without shoes or stockings – a babe perhaps at the breast . . . decayed vegetables stewing in the pavement, linen hanging across the street to dry.'

Looking east down Sutton Row, a London landmark soars hideously into the sky: Richard Seifert's Centre Point (1963–7), a 398-foot high tower whose 35 floors remained empty for a decade (and are still barely occupied) while its owner merely watched its value accrue.

Turning south down Bateman's Buildings, a stroll through more Soho streets leads back westwards to its second square and then back here. Right into Bateman Street, right again into Frith Street and then left down Carlisle Street and left again into Dean Street, the Irish actress and sometime mistress of David Garrick, Peg Woffington, lived at no. 78 (1740s). Jazz fans not at Ronnie Scott's are tapping their fingers at Pizza Express. Opposite, St Anne's Court leads to **Wardour Street**, citadel of film distributors where film buffs watch reel after reel in darkened rooms. But its former fame was for its fine craftsmen (Sheraton lived at nos 103 and 147) and then, in the last century, for disreputable antique dealers who made Wardour Street the byword for fake antiques.

Crossing into Broadwick Street, **Berwick Street** is on the left, its lively street market and many of the houses dating from the eighteenth century. When the newly arrived Jews (see below, p. 170) took to the barrows at the end of last century, the market expanded to its present sprawl from here down to Peter Street. Battling through the cabbages, and perhaps joining the noisy lunchtime bargaining for reputedly the best fruit and veg in town, turn right into Peter Street, right into Hopkins Street, and then thread left through Ingestre Place to Silver Place and into **Beak Street** (1689), built by Queen Mary's Messenger, Thomas Beak. On the right, the Left-handed Shop is devoted to equipping lefties with everything from tin-openers to scissors.

Great Pulteney Street on the left was built on Sir William Pulteney's estate and the scale of its simple, eighteenth-century survivors (nos. 8–13 and 35–40) are worth keeping in mind when looking at **Golden Square** (begun 1670), found by turning right into Brewer Street and right again after Bridle Street. Here the early eighteenth-century noblesse lived in a 'very handsome place railed around and gravelled'. Later residents were embassies (the Portuguese at nos. 23–4 which survives, altered, with a charming Roman Catholic church behind), the Swiss painter Angela Kauffmann who helped the Adam brothers keep the Mayfair palace interiors up to date (1767–81 at no. 16), and now the rag trade and film companies who venture palefaced onto the garden benches at lunchtime.

Leaving it by Upper John Street in the northwest corner, Kingly Court is opposite, with **Carnaby Street** to the right of it. When London was 'swinging', this was the inner sanctum of trendiness. The Beatles were on top of the world, Mary Quant wore black and white, the Mini was the car to drive, and optimism abounded. It was the moment to be young and British. The world's long-haired hippies made their pilgrimage here to buy lime-green trousers, flower-power shirts, felt hats and necklaces. Today, the joyful 1960s spirit of enterprise, cameraderie and happiness has been soured; and the fancy-dressed young aggressively demand payment for tourist photographs. But the parallel Newburgh Street to the right, and its connecting alleys, retain their old Soho character.

Great Marlborough Street, honouring the Duke of Marlborough's Blenheim triumph (1704), is at the top of Carnaby Street. The Tudor revival black-and-white of Liberty's side building (1924) is on the left, using oak from two nineteenth-century battleships and continuing the dream inside with a galleried well and lift with linenfold panelling (see p. 178). Ahead, American Raymond Hood's Palladium House (1928), a black granite cube with Egyptian cornice by the pioneers of the New York sky-scraper, has been judged 'a notable exception to the lamentably unimaginative architecture which . . . is all too common in England'. Next to it stands the **London Palladium**. Built when variety and music-hall entertainment were at their peak with about 60 halls in London, Walter Gibbons outstripped his rivals at the Coliseum, Hippodrome and even the Palace with Frank Matcham's lavish Edwardian theatre (1910). It set him back £250,000 but received rapturous praise as 'the last word in luxury and appointment . . . not a dull note anywhere'. It had a Palm Court to seat a thousand for tea, a silver vestibule, Rose du Barri hangings and, most exciting of all, box-to-box telephones. The 2,325 seats, all of them cheap, made it second only to the Coliseum in size. From the moment it opened, the London Palladium was the home of tip-top popular variety, mixing farce, opera and melodrama. It gave its first Royal Command Performance in 1911; George Black countered the threatening talkie films with *The Crazy Gang Shows* (1930s); the annual *Peter Pan* Christmas pantomime included Elsa Lanchester and Anna Neagle as Peter (1930–8); and with the arrival of television the spectacular reviews were beamed across Britain as 'Sunday Night at the London Palladium'.

Moving eastwards along Great Marlborough Street, Poland Street (begun 1680s) is on the right, named after the King of Poland, although the Poles who arrived this century tend to live in west Lon-don (see p. 219). Here Blake worked on his *Songs of Innocence* (1785–91 at no. 28) and Shelley stayed after he was sent down from Oxford for publishing *The Necessity of Atheism* (1811, at no. 15). D'Arblay Street on the left leads through to Sheraton Street. A left into Chapel Street and then right down Fareham and Dean streets leads left into Carlisle Street and back into Soho Square.

Leaving Soho Square by Soho Street, the area north of Oxford Street (see p. 151) became known as **Fitzrovia** in the 1930s, when the streets south of Fitzroy Square and bounded by Great Portland and Gower streets became a favourite haunt of artists and writers. By constantly threading left and right to catch the best bits, it is a pleasant stroll up through them to their centrepiece.

Straight ahead lies Rathbone Place. But to the right, through Evelyn Yard, lies Gresse Street, with its several mewses, which returns back to Rathbone Place in time to dip into Ferns at no. 27, where the back wall is lined with large, old tea caddies and the air perfumed with freshly roasted coffee beans.

Next come the streets William and Francis Goodge began developing in the 1740s on fields inherited by their carpenter uncle. To the right is **Percy Street**, where Frederick Gibberd's architectural practice works at no. 8, conveniently close to the king of the area's Greek Cypriot restaurants, the White Tower at no. 1, run by the Stais family since 1938, before which it was the Tour Eiffel where Wyndham Lewis and Ezra Pound celebrated the launch of the Vorticist magazine, *Blast*. The Elysée at no. 13 is more thoroughly Greek, where 'plate-smashing is £6 per dozen'. Left and left again, Fitzroy Tavern in the Goodge boys' **Windmill Street** was where Augustus John would meet fellow artists in the 1930s and where Dylan Thomas, Cyril Connolly and George Orwell downed pints between paragraphs in the 1940s. Turning right into **Charlotte Street**, the grand route leading up to Fitzroy Square and loyally named after George III's queen, this bottom end is almost an extension of Soho: a cluster of Greek restaurants whose cheap food and outside tables bring a touch of southern European *mañana* to London summer lunchtimes.

Moving northwards and dipping right through **Colville Place** (1766), a surviving Georgian alley complete with shop fronts, two left turns lead into **Goodge Street**, whose provisions shops and pubs form the village heart of Fitzrovia. Then right up Charlotte Street and into **Scala Street** to escape into nostalgic **Pollock's Toy Museum** and see inside one of the Goodge estate houses. So wonderful were the toy theatres of Benjamin Pollock (1856–1937) – 'a penny plain and twopence coloured' – that his shop became a museum (1956), overspilt and moved here (1969) into two 1760s houses. To explore them now, clamber up the narrow staircases and in and out of tiny rooms stuffed with eighteenth-, nineteenth- and twentieth-century childhood treasures – zoetropes, humming tops, trains, model 1910 toyshop, big Punch and Judy puppets, an Italianate villa dolls' house, a 1790s Noah's Ark, the model of Pollock's print workshop and, of course, plenty of his theatres. It was one of these that the actor Ian McKellen was given by Santa Claus in 1947, 'so I did my first Shakespeare in our lounge, with scenery and cardboard cut-outs from Olivier's film of *Hamlet*, sliding Sir Laurence onto his wire and waggling him at a petite Jean Simmons – me doing both voices'. Toyshop to equal the museum (1 Scala Street, W1, tel 636 3452; open Mon–Sat, 10am–5pm; charge. Toy theatre performances, Punch and Judy and conjurer during school holidays, magic lantern shows at Christmas, telephone for times; annexe with library, tin toys, English dolls and rocking horses, open by appointment; excellent toyshop supplemented by a further shop at 44 The Market, Covent Garden, tel 379 7866).

Turning left, **Whitfield Street** runs behind the American Church which replaces George Whitfield's Methodist Tabernacle (1756) where his impressive preaching (much enjoyed by Hugh Walpole) earned it the nickname 'Whitfield's soul trap'. Left into Chitty Street and right into Charlotte Street once more, the **London Telecom Tower** (1963–6) looks like a Lego effort by a child fresh from Pollock's Toy Museum but was in fact designed by the Ministry of Works to transmit microwave messages. The tallest London tower when it went up (580 ft, surpassed by the NatWest Tower in 1981, see p. 72), the revolving roof-top restaurant was a terrific top-of-the-world outing with diagrams of the view as placements, until a terrorist bomb explosion forced its closure to the public. Charlotte Street now becomes Fitzroy Street, where Whistler and Sickert had studios, and leads into **Fitzroy Square**. Planned and begun in 1793–8, it comes a good century after Soho and Golden squares, at the end of the eighteenth-century Mayfair and south Marylebone squares and at the moment when the Bedford estate was poised to extend a chessboard of squares over Bloomsbury (see below). The Fitzroy family had

owned the land for some time, and their history riddles the area and its street names. Henry Fitzroy was Charles II's son by the Duchess of Cleveland and was matched aged nine with a five-year-old bride, Isabella Bennet, who later inherited the Arlington estates of Euston in Suffolk and Tottenham Court manor in the fields north of London. He was awarded the titles Earl of Euston and Duke of Grafton. His son, Charles, laid out Euston Road.

His great-grandson, elevated to Baron Southampton, employed the Adam brothers to lay out Fitzroy Square. The east side was built behind a unified palazzo facade of Portland stone, the south side followed (1794, rebuilt) and the west and north sides came later (1827–35), faced with the then fashionable stucco fronts. Now pedestrianised and equipped with benches and a dinner service of blue plaques, you can sit and enjoy it in peace, imagining the lives of past artistic residents. They were a magnet for the area's later artists, especially Ford Madox Brown who entertained pre-Raphaelites Rossetti and Holman Hunt (at no. 37, 1867–82) – his two guests had lived in nearby Cleveland Street; George Bernard Shaw while he was furiously writing on everything from music to politics and a being lively member of the newly formed Fabian Society (at no. 29, 1887–98); and Roger Fry who, with finance from Shaw and others, set up the Omega Workshop (at no. 33, 1913–9) to promote good design by employing young artists on a regular wage – a failure, since the best efforts were quickly copied and mass-produced by commercial firms.

In eastern Fitzrovia, moving towards the Bedford estate, the Fitzroy family names go public. Grafton Way leads off, with Grafton Mews and Fitzroy Court on the left and the YMCA for Indian Students accounting for the number of Indian restaurants (best is Lal Qila on Tottenham Court Road). On across Tottenham Court Road, the vast campus of the **University of London** begins with Alfred Waterhouse's chirpy Gothic pinnacles and turrets for University College Hospital (1897–1906) on the left (the bulk of it paid for by Sir John Maple of the Tottenham Court Road furniture shop) and William Wilkins' cool Greek Revival for University College (1827–9) straight ahead in Gower Street. This was the founder member of the university, established in 1826 by enlightened private sponsors who had three principal aims: to take non-Church of England students (Oxford and Cambridge excluded them); to remove the Church of England's influence over education; and to extend the subjects on offer, looking to Germany for models for both constitution and curriculum. Rivals sneered at the 'godless college in Gower Street' and promptly founded the strictly Church of England King's College by Somerset House (see p. 120).

But its handsome main building by the National Gallery's architect soon went up, and its medical research led to many firsts at the neighbouring hospital – first major operation in Europe using ether (1846); first antiseptic surgery by Joseph Lister, a Quaker refused by Oxbridge (1867); and first cerebral and spinal tumour removals (1884, 1887). Here too the **Slade School of Fine Art** (1871) was founded by Felix Slade to provide a less conservative and dreary approach than the Royal Academy, where Henry Tonks, William Coldstream, Lawrence Gowring, Roger Fry, Rudolf Wittkower and Ernst Gombrich have taught, and where Walter Sickert, William Rothenstein, Augustus John, Wyndham Lewis and Stanley Spencer have learnt. Well worth exploring to seek the **Flaxman Gallery** where more than a hundred spirited models by the neo-classical sculptor John Flaxman (1755–1826) stand in the octagonal room beneath the dome (tel 387 7050 to arrange a visit; free); one of London's oddities, the embalmed and clothed body of the philosopher Jeremy Bentham (1748–1832) (telephone to visit in termtime only); the Archaic lions from Koptos in the South Cloister; the **Strang Print Room**, where there are termtime exhibitions ranging from sixteenth-century German drawings to works by past Slade pupils (tel 387 7050 to visit Mon–Fri, 1–2.15pm).

Down Gower Street and round to the southern entrance in Malet Place, the **Petrie Museum of Egyptian Archaeology** is named after Sir Flinders Petrie (1853–1942), Britain's first professor of Archaeology. The pottery, beads and slant-eyed cats of the Petrie and Langton collections are so unceremoniously exhibited that visitors happily feel they are making their own discoveries (tel 387 7050; open Mon–Fri 10am–noon and 1.15–5pm, closed part of each holidays; free). Here too is Dillon's, the University Bookshop, at no. 1, always full of students calculating just how far their grant will stretch.

Leaving the temples of education, the chunk of **Tottenham Court Road** at the end of Torrington Place is the most interesting. Turning left, Smith and Brewer's distinctive Heal's (1916), with craftsmen's tools decorating the spandrels, was put up by the shop's founder, Ambrose Heal, who pro-

moted quality vernacular furniture in general and the Arts and Crafts Movement in particular. It is now owned by Sir Terence Conran, who has added a designer restaurant. Further down, in the bazaar of electrical, hi-fi and computer shops run by bright young computer brains, bargains as good as those in Hong Kong and Singapore are to be found by bartering one shop's price against another's, taking time off to plan the next move at Bernigra at no. 69, by Goodge Street Underground station, where the signor from Messina makes fresh Italian ice-cream for shoppers.

Turning left down Store Street, there is a good **view** straight along to Charles Holden's dramatic **Senate House** (begun 1932), built after his other landmark, London Transport headquarters (see p. 190). It was for the newly organised University of London whose history is yet another London saga of muddle. Founded by Lord Melbourne in 1836 essentially as an examining body, it was shuffled from Somerset House to Burlington House to Burlington Gardens (now the Museum of Mankind) before even permitting women to sit for degrees (1878). At last it was reorganised (1898–1900), with a Senate as a supreme governing body who took under its wing the various London colleges. Finally, it was given a wedge of Bloomsbury for permanent buildings (1911). Senate House went up first, Holden's stripped-classical, Portland stone facade leading to grand ceremonial rooms (stylish panelling and light-fittings). War interrupted the rest of the grand plan. Today, with 50 colleges (even ones in Scotland and Paris) and 40,000 internal and 24,000 external students, it is Britain's largest university – some colleges are larger than provincial universities – and its Chancellor is Princess Anne. It has wormed its way into hundreds of Bloomsbury buildings – spot the brass department plates on the doors – and, tragically, has been responsible for destroying many, too.

Approaching it from Store Street, the Bloomsbury loss is more apparent by seeing what remains. For beyond, Bloomsbury still survives, mostly untouched by developers' claws. Already you can see some of Gower Street's older houses standing to the right, where the actress Sarah Siddons lived and found 'the back of it is most effectually in the country and delightfully pleasant' (1784–9).

To imagine what she meant, glance down Gower Mews (built for stables and tradesmen) on the right, then go down Keppel Street and right along Malet Street past the Gower Street back gardens, returning along Montague Place to **Bedford**

Square (c.1775), Bloomsbury's only complete surviving Georgian square. This was the Bedford estate's second square, built a century after Bloomsbury Square (see p. 168) and probably designed by Thomas Leverton, who lived at no. 1. Its simple, four-storey brick houses enlivened with Coade stone decoration are relieved of repetition by making the central part of each side look like the centre of a palazzo, with pilasters, pediment and stucco. To give residents privacy, the square was gated and mewses (like Gower Mews) built behind. To give them private greenery in town, the oval garden was laid out and each resident given a key (still the case here and for many other squares). Inside, smart life was on the first floor, where Angela Kauffman, living in Golden Square, was employed to decorate some houses. When Sarah Siddons was in Gower Street, residents here included Henry Cavendish, grandson of the Duke of Cavendish (no. 11) and Lord Loughborough, the Lord Chancellor (no. 6).

Today, publishers and architects occupy the fine houses, including the **Architectural Association** at nos 34–6. Founded in 1842 by a group of students, some early members rebelled against the RIBA (see p. 179) as 'a gang of tradesmen' and against their pupillage system as 'fraud'. They set up their own school (1846) and finally moved here (1917). Now, as lively as ever, recent star students include Richard Rogers, Piers Gough and Alan Forsyth; and the club welcomes the public (36 Bedford Sq, WC1, tel 636 0974; very good bookshop open Mon–Fri; restaurant open Mon–Fri; lectures and seminars – do go up to the first floor salon for **view** over the square).

Equipped with this near-perfect experience, the later Bloomsbury squares should make more sense. As Sir Hugh Casson observes, 'dignified, formal, discreet . . . it would be no surprise, even today, to meet here a sedan chair.' But first, the British Museum, best approached by going right down Bloomsbury Street, left along Streatham Street, across into Little Russell Street, then left up Museum Street where the huge bulk looms ahead.

The **British Museum** fondly known as the BM, is the treasure-house of the national collections of archaeology and ethnography. But its four million or so objects, excluding the vast prints and drawings collection, ranges from prehistoric to quite modern – even an Art Deco bronze. The cream of it is on show, apart from the Ethnographical Department in the Museum of Mankind (see p. 147). Thousands of the less important pieces are out,

too. And it grows weekly, with finds (most major British archaeological discoveries come here), bequests (the recent Godman Bequest of Islamic Pottery will need its own gallery) and careful acquisitions (recently the Mostyn Tompion clock, the Duchess of Marlborough's solid gold ice-pails and a fantastical watercolour by Richard Dadd). So the idea of quickly 'doing' the BM is a non-starter.

Its history has been one of continual and astounding growth. Three collections stimulated parliament into action: the library and antiquities of Sir Robert Cotton (1570–1631), the manuscripts of Robert Harley, Earl of Oxford (1661–1724) and, most importantly, the extensive collection of Sir Hans Sloane (1660–1753), a physician who filled his house at no. 4 Bloomsbury Place with a vast collection of 'plants, fossils, minerals, coins, books and manuscripts', some 79,575 pieces in all which he later moved to his country house in Chelsea (see p. 229) and then suggested in his will that the government buy. They did. And in 1753 parliament passed the British Museum Act for the first public museum in London. £300,000 was raised by public lottery (which after bills and expenses were settled, left £40,000 to build the museum), Montagu House was bought and the museum opened on January 15, 1759. Rules were strict: entry by written application, only ten tickets per hour, only three hours of opening per day, and 'No Money to be given to the Servants'.

The foundation collection grew fast. George II gave the Royal Library of 10,500 volumes (1757); Sir William Hamilton gave his antique vases (1772); the Charles Townley classical sculptures came (1805); then the Lansdowne manuscripts (1807), marbles from the Parthenon and Erechtheum brought from Greece by Lord Elgin (1816), George III's library of 120,800 books (1823) and much more, including David Garrick's plays, Captain Cook's finds, Sir Stamford Raffles' Javanese collection, Felix Slade's glass and drawings, and the Bank of England's coins.

Space was tight. So Robert Smirke designed the present, appropriately neo-classical building (1823–38) around Montagu House which was then demolished to put the Ionic colonnade and portico across the front (1842), decorated with Westmacott's pediment sculpture recounting the progress of civilisation (1847–51) – an advertisement for the fuller story told inside. The courtyard was later transformed into the magnificent, blue-domed Reading Room (1854–7) by Robert's brother, Sydney Smirke (in which Karl Marx wrote

Das Kapital) and various galleries added including Sir John Burnett's Edward VII galleries at the back (1914), where there is a second entrance. Again and again, space has got tight, with short-term relief when the natural history department went off to South Kensington (1881, see p. 221), the newspapers went to Colindale (1904), the Ethnographic Department to Piccadilly (1970, see p. 147) and the Printed Books and Manuscripts departments, although still exhibiting here, became part of the **British Library** (1973), with many of the 10 million volumes of its Reference Division plus manuscripts, scores, maps, periodicals, etc, stored elsewhere. Since the 1911 Copyright Act dictates that one copy of every book, periodical or newspaper published in Great Britain must come to the British Library, more than two miles of bookshelf are added annually. To ease the strain, Colin St John Wilson's much-needed but highly controversial new British Library, a mile north of here, should open in 1991.

The BM now covers 13.5 acres, is the largest museum in Britain, employs 1200 staff and has four million visitors each year, more than most museums in the world. In the year 1987–8, the grant to run the museum was almost £14 million; in addition, gifts include the royalties from the play *Pygmalion*, bequeathed to the BM by its author, George Bernard Shaw.

To enjoy this overwhelming store of goodies, the way to start a first visit to the BM is to explore the main entrance hall, picking up a free map, an events leaflet and brochures (for BM and BL), and checking out the VDU screens for the latest information on lectures, closed galleries and exhibitions. If confused by choice, the Information Desk will explain how to find what you fancy – it is all too easy to get lost in Egyptology when paradise would be Indian sculpture. The entrance hall also has a statue of Sloane, the Reading Room straight ahead (hourly visits 11am–4pm), the BM shop and, to the left, the BM bookshop through which lies the restaurant. One temporary exhibition gallery is that way too, Room 76, with the other, Room 49, upstairs on the east side and the prints and drawings exhibitions away at the far side, upstairs (easy access via the back entrance, but 1988–9 closures probable).

Then, to explore the treasures. Every object – gold, glass, silk or marble – belongs to one of eight tightly arranged departments but, with the Reading Room in the middle, setting off for one in the wrong direction means walking three times too far.

The big stars are really quite easy to find. Basically, the British Library is on the right (east side), with the Magna Carta, Lindisfarne Gospels, Shakespeare's First Folio and the Gutenberg Bible all nearby and then Smirke's 295-foot-long King's Library, his best room, beyond, and maps beyond that (– if you get this far).

The BM departments proper fill the west and north sides and the basement and first floor. To the left (west side), also easy to reach and arranged in sequence, are the Greek and Roman Antiquities (Room 8 built for the Parthenon sculptures, the Elgin Marbles; Room 16 has stairs down to the basement where the Townley collection is out in old museum style, like a crowded Roman forum of rearing horses, fierce senators and fallen columns); then, moving back towards the entrance hall, Western Asiatic (with the Assyrian story-telling reliefs of lion hunts and palace life from Nineveh and stairs down for more from Room 18) and Egyptian Antiquities (the finest in the world outside Egypt).

Then comes the travelling. Upstairs, turn right for more Greek and Roman (west side, newly refurbished), straight ahead for Prehistoric and Roman–British (Room 35 for latest finds such as the 2,000-year-old Lindow Man) and further on to Medieval and Later Antiquities (Rooms 40 for Mildenhall and 41 for Sutton Hoo treasures; Room 44 for a concert of chiming mechanical clocks on the hour) (all south side), Room 42 houses the exquisite fragments of Edward III's St Stephen's Chapel, Westminster (see p. 82). Room 41 is the key for moving north to Room 49 for special exhibitions; then round to the north side for more Western Asiatic and Egyptian (here are the mummies of humans, cats, crocodiles and even baboons) and finally, the exhibitions (usually about three a year) from the huge Prints and Drawings collection where the English drawings alone top 20,000. Here too, on the ground floor, are the newly organised Oriental Antiquities, each gallery a peaceful cul-de-sac (therefore free of corridor visitors) housing Islamic inlaid metalwork, Indian sculptures, Turkish Isnik pottery, Chinese porcelain and soon a new rooftop gallery built for the Japanese prints.

Everyone finds their own favourites and, as with the V&A (see p. 222), each return visit reveals new delights. And glazed eyes or exhausted feet can always relax on the courtyard benches. The aims of the current Director, Sir David Wilson, seem to work: to preserve 'a universal museum' for everyone's benefit, keeping the objects as available as possible, open every day, and free. (Great Russell Street, WC1, tel 636 1555, recorded information on 580 1788; open Mon–Sat 10am–5pm, Sun 2.30–6pm; free. Guided tours, lectures, films, special exhibitions, Friends society, excellent bookshop stocks guide with map, gift shop, restaurant; apply to the relevant department to see reserve collection and use its Student Room. British Library information is as follows: For printed books, maps, music, publications, Reading Room and manuscripts, here at the BM but tel 636 1544; for oriental and philately, 14 Store Street, WC1, tel 636 1544; for newspapers, Colindale Avenue, NW9, tel 323 7535; for the India Office Library and Records, 197 Blackfriars Road, SE1, tel 928 9531; and for science, Southampton Buildings, Chancery Lane, WC2, tel 405 8721, and Aldwych Reading Room, 9 Kean Street, WC2, tel 636 1544.)

Leaving the BM, the cafés, pubs and bookshops in the little network of streets in front never fell under Nash's plan to clear them for a better view of Smirke's facade. Down Museum Street and left, Nicholas Hawksmoor's **St George's** (1716–31) is one of six churches he built under the 1711 Fifty New Churches Act (see p. 120), so smarter residents of the northern part of St Giles's parish could avoid soiling their sensibilities by picking their way through the rookeries to St Giles-in-the-Fields. To the left of its grand Corinthian portico, an alley leads round the tower (topped with George I in Roman toga) to the north facade in Little Russell Street, decorated with a two-storey Roman arcade. Turning right, then left up Bury Place and right along Great Russell Street, no. 4 Bloomsbury Place is where Sloane lived (1695–1742) while he was physician to Pepys and Queen Anne and obsessively amassing his cabinet of curiosities, spilling over into the house next door.

He overlooked **Bloomsbury Square** (c.1660), the first patch in the huge Bedford estate quilt. When the Carthusians surrendered their open acres to Henry VIII, his favoured courtier Thomas Wriothesley was rewarded with them and created Earl of Southampton (1547). A century later, the 4th Earl moved into the old manor house and, after the Restoration, demolished it to build his 'little Towne' (c.1660) 'at the bottom of a Long Field'. His new mansion overlooked a 'noble square or Piazza', a market, stables and streets for servants, cabinet-makers and bookshops. Plots of land were sold off for house-building. And the Duke of Montagu, married to his daughter-in-law, built Montagu House next door. It was a model estate

and a fashionable address, with such widespread fame that even though it was well out of London it was a top tourist attraction for princely foreigners.

Meanwhile, the Russell family, Earls of Bedford, moved in. In 1550, John Russell, owner of the Woburn, Tavistock and Taviton estates, was created Earl of Bedford. In 1694, the 5th Earl was made Duke of Bedford and Marquess of Tavistock in thanks for Protestant loyalty to William and Mary (1689–1702). His son, William, had married Rachel, heiress to the Earl of Southampton, but was executed for his Protestant conspiracies (1683). So, when both fathers died, Rachel and her son inherited the good combination of the Russell fortune, the Bloomsbury estate and a bunch of titles.

Building began; healthy Bloomsbury became fashionable. Great Russell Street was built to connect the Bedford mansion with Tottenham Court Road; the 4th Duke's widow, Gertrude Leveson Gower, built Bedford Square while her son was still a minor. But it was the 5th Duke of Bedford who saw the development potential of his estate. Around the year 1800, he started work on Bloomsbury Square. He demolished the great house and employed James Burton to put up the terrace on the north side and top landscape gardener Humphrey Repton to lay out the gardens (much altered) – Westmacott's statue of the Whig politician and *bon viveur* Charles James Fox arrived in 1816 complete with bags under his eyes and dimpled chin.

The 5th and 6th dukes controlled the overall plan, James Burton (died 1837) and Thomas Cubitt (1788–1855) developing most of the leases. Burton, an ambitious Scot and father of architect Decimus (see p. 177), became the most important London builder since Dr Barbon. He cemented his bricks from here right across north London to Regent Street and St John's Wood, ending with an estimated total house value of £2 million and a home in the middle of Regent's Park (The Holme, see p. 181). Cubitt was known for his nearby Gray's Inn Road workshops where he rationalised building methods in 1815. Instead of contracting each building trade separately for the job required on a building, he employed them all on a permanent wage – the first modern building firm in London. He succeeded Barbon and filled the gaps with better-built and more refined houses before going on to mastermind the whole of Belgravia and Pimlico (see pp. 238–40).

Gradually, an ordered, spatial sequence of elegant squares and roads was established over the

Bloomsbury estate, whose gates, mewses and gardens, like Bedford Square, reflected the clearly defined eighteenth- and nineteenth-century social order. Gating squares was abolished in 1893, and the University's arrival destroyed west Bloomsbury's character. But wandering through the best remains today, it is still easy to see their attraction for lawyers working at the nearby Inns of Court as well as generations of writers, painters and musicians.

Moving off from Bloomsbury Square, James Burton's Bedford Place (1801–5), built over Bedford House, leads to his **Russell Square** (1800–14), one of the biggest squares in London. Westmacott's statue of curly-haired Francis Russell (1765–1805), the 5th Duke and a keen agriculturist (hence the sheep and plough), looks out from the shady gardens now entirely altered since Repton laid them out but with good lawns, rosebeds and an Italian café for a post-BM breather (open daily 10am–7.30pm, opening around 8.30am in summer). Around them, houses on the west survive, where the Sedleys and Osbornes of Thackeray's *Vanity Fair* lived in fashionable style. Later, red terracotta was added to enliven dull brick for the Victorians and Charles Fitzroy Doll's Russell Hotel arrived, opening its marble doors to fancy-hatted guests on Derby Day, 1900 (grandeur worth a glimpse).

In the north-west corner, Thornhaugh Street leads into James Sim's **Woburn Square** (1825) where the Courtauld Institute Galleries hover at the top of the west side until they move to Somerset House in 1989 (see p. 120). This and Torrington Square, found round to the left, have been devastated by the University. But beyond, Raphael Brandon's steepleless University Church of Christ the King (1853), built for a Catholic sect who broke away after the announcement of the Pope's infallibility (1870), is worth a look for the Victorian carvings, stencilling and tiles, especially in the Lady Chapel.

Cubitt's **Gordon Square** (1820–60), named after the 6th Duke's wife, retains more of the Bloomsbury atmosphere. The houses are mostly inhabited by university departments whose students leave their books to hold summer tea-parties for the Egypt Exploration Society or to swot up their Jung for finals in a garden of beech trees, acacias, tall blossoming roses and twittering birds, more like Sussex than Central London. This was the heart of the Bloomsbury Group – a misnomer since their origins were at Cambridge at the end of last century, where a clique of artists and writers propounded GE Moore's philosophy that the most important things were 'the pleasures of human intercourse and the enjoyment of beautiful objects'. However, some members lived here: Virginia Stephen (1905–7, later Woolf), her sister Vanessa and Clive Bell (1911) and John Maynard Keynes (1916–46), all at no. 46; and Lytton Strachey at no. 51 (1921). Others – Roger Fry, Duncan Grant, EM Forster – were frequent visitors. The nicest way to feel the atmosphere of the square is to wander up through its garden.

But a dip into no. 53 in the south-east corner first is irresistible. This is the **Percival David Foundation of Chinese Art**, some 1500 Chinese ceramics given by scholar and collector Sir Percival (1892–1964) to the University in 1951, a serene feast of exquisitely fine craftsmanship whose perfect dishes, pots and vases in rich blue, blood red, smoky greens and buttercup yellow range from miracle survivors from the fourteenth century (the two David Vases) up to the eighteenth century. Do not miss the emperors' Ru ware on the ground floor (53 Gordon Square, WC1, tel 387 3909; open Mon, 2–5pm, Tues–Fri, 10.30am–5pm, Sat, 10.30am–1pm; free; library; erudite publications).

Through Gordon Square garden and right along Cubitt's Endsleigh Place (1825–9), his **Tavistock Square** (1806–26) survives on the west side, his houses more individual after the plain purity of the Georgian terraces. It replaced all of Burton's earlier square (1803) except Tavistock House on the east side (now gone too) where Dickens lived (1851–60) while writing *Bleak House, Little Dorritt, Hard Times, A Tale of Two Cities* and parts of *Great Expectations* and amused himself by building a little theatre in the garden where he and the London literary set staged plays for one another. Bloomsbury Group literary life followed, with Virginia and Leonard Woolf living on the south side (1924–39), where early Hogarth Press volumes were hand printed.

Today, with Bloomsbury a more international learning centre, Fredda Brilliant's bronze (1966) of the cross-legged Mahatma Gandhi (1869–1948), later visited by Jawaharlal Nehru, sits in the garden, and the **Jewish Museum** is on the north side. Wilfrid Samuel established it in 1932 to show Anglo-Jews their rich cultural heritage, and the one-room museum is stuffed with testaments of their centuries of London life. Jews have been here at least since the Conquest, making them some of the first immigrants. Although at first they suffered appalling persecution and prejudice – and were expelled wholesale by Edward I in 1290 – the British tolerance record improved after 1656, when Cromwell officially allowed them to settle here once more.

The modern Anglo-Jewish population began with refugees from another expulsion, from Spain where in the 1492 persecutions many Jews were baptised while secretly continuing to practise Judaism. Known in Spain as Marranos, a few came to London and kept up their act – Elizabeth I's physician, Rodrigo Lopez, was one. Then Rabbi Menasseh Ben Israel, a Portuguese Jew living in Holland, pushed for Cromwell's official welcome and Resettlement began. Sephardi Jews of Spanish and Portuguese origin arrived from Holland first, continuing to speak Spanish and Portuguese and working mostly as prosperous merchants. Then followers of the Ashkenazi tradition came from throughout Europe, spoke Yiddish and struggled up through the more modest trades of jewellery, clothing, groceries and hardware. The next wave came with the anti-semitic pogroms in Russia and Poland following the assassination of Tsar Alexander II in 1881, when many settled in the East End, still an area for the Jewish rag trade and leather trade. And the final wave came in the 1930s, fleeing fascist persecution in Europe. Today, about half of the 450,000 British Jews live in London, the focus now moved from Whitechapel in the East End (see p. 251) up to north and north-west London, especially Golders Green, Edgware and Stamford Hill.

In the museum, see the thirteenth-century bankers' tallies; the Portuguese Jews' silver Salver (1702) for presenting annual sweetmeats to the Lord Mayor; Staffordshire figures of Jewish pedlars; silk Torah mantles, containers and shields for the synagogues; Ketubahs for marriage contracts; a child's peep-show of a Succah scene; a table painted with a synagogue scene; Passover plates and much more, as fascinating for non-Jews as for Jews (Woburn House, Tavistock Square, WC1, tel 387 3081; open Tues–Thurs (and Fri Apr–Sept), 10am–4pm, Sun (and Fri Oct–Mar), 10am–12.45pm; free. Audio-visual, guidebook). To find out more, visit the Museum of the Jewish East End, founded in 1983 to preserve the heritage and social history of the Jewish community there. Treasures include a walk-in reconstruction of a tailoring workshop, tools of the trades (baker, tailor, cabinet-maker) and memorabilia of Yiddish theatre and Friendly societies (The Steinberg Centre, The Manor House, 80 East End Road, N3, tel 346 2288/

349 1143; open Sun–Thurs and some Fris, 10am–4pm; free; plenty of events).

Leaving this last Bloomsbury square by the north-east corner and crossing **Woburn Place** (again Cubitt, as was Endsleigh Place and Street and Gordon Street, all adjoining these last two squares), the grand memorial gates on the right belong to Lutyens' building for Annie Besant's Theosophical Society (1911–13, 1922–9), now the British Medical Association. Further up, HW and W Inwood's Greek Revival **St Pancras** church (1819–22) has an Ionic portico at the west end and reproduction Erechtheum caryatids at the east. Beyond is **Euston Road**, rebuilt (1756) by the 2nd Duke of Grafton as a by-pass for cattle being driven across London to Smithfield meat market, diverting them from the fast-smartening Oxford Street. And when the railways were built, this was the boundary line for the three great termini leading to Birmingham, Liverpool, Sheffield, Glasgow and other Victorian industrial boomtowns in the north. Competition between rival railway companies was fierce, and their magnificent showpiece termini at the nation's capital lived up to contemporary ideals: 'Railway termini and hotels are to the nineteenth century what monasteries and cathedrals were to the thirteenth century.'

Ahead, before destruction which included the Euston Arch and 'which ranks high even among the architectural crimes of the 1960s' according to architectural historian Donald Olsen, London and Birmingham Railway cut through nursery gardens to bring mighty steam trains loaded with wide-eyed passengers into London's first mainline terminus, **Euston Station**. Robert Stephenson (engineer of *The Rocket* engine) built it (1837); Philip Hardwick added his screen (1838), two hotels (1839, for rich and poor) and Great Hall (1849). The management proudly claimed that the screen's huge stone arch and the biggest Doric columns in London made it the entrance to 'the Grand Avenue for travelling between the Midland and Northern parts of the Kingdom'. British Rail tore it all down in 1963, leaving the solitary statue of George Stephenson (Robert's father and joint-engineer of the London–Birmingham line). The **Wellcome Institute for the History of Medicine** is here, with library and museum of Sir Henry Wellcome (1853–1936), founder of the pharmaceutical firm and the Wellcome Foundation (183 Euston Road, NW1, tel 387 4477; Library open to the public Mon–Sat, 10am–5pm, museum open only to medics Mon–Fri, 9am–5pm).

To see the two surviving cathedrals of the steam age at the eastern end of Euston Road, a good route is to cut through more of the Bedford estate, in the area known as **St Pancras**. Back along Upper Woburn Place and then left down Cubitt's **Woburn Walk** (1822), the local shopping precinct and now a unique Regency survivor, Burton Street is on the right. Burton Place on the left leads to Cartwright Gardens (1801), originally called Burton Crescent and built by James Burton. Sweeping round to the left and then straight along Hastings Street, the **Salvation Army Museum** is on the second floor of the corner building with Judd Street. It is an extraordinary cave brimful of memorabilia of the Sally Army's triumphs since its founding as a Christian mission by the Revd William Booth in 1865, with headquarters in Whitechapel Road to help East Enders. Here are Booth's top hat, Booth's recordings booming out, early money-tins, the bands' instruments and the bonnets 'strong enough to protect the wearers from cold as well as from brickbats and other missiles', all tended with enthusiasm by Major Robert Reeve (Salvationist Publishing & Supplies, 117–21 Judd Street, WC1, tel 387 1656; open Mon–Fri, 9.30am–3.30pm, Sats by appointment).

Turning left up to the top of **Judd Street**, the sparkling new British Library is straight ahead (see above). To the right, the Midland Railway's **St Pancras Station** amazed Victorians. Barlow and Ordish's train shed (1863–7), with 55-ton ribs spanning 240 feet and reaching 100 ft high, was an engineering feat; the whole station was built on a 20-foot-high platform to reduce the drag up out of town; and George Gilbert Scott's Grand Midland Hotel (1868–72), a true Gothic cathedral of towers and spires – although he failed to win through his Gothic plan for Whitehall (see p. 87) – was hailed by globe-trotters as the best in the empire. Since 1935 only lucky office-workers could glide up its imperial staircase; but now it is being scrubbed and restored to serve its original purpose.

To the right, the comparatively tame and simple Great Northern Railway's **King's Cross** Station was designed by Lewis Cubitt. It opened in 1850 (in time for the hoards of visitors to the Great Exhibition of 1851, see p. 212), the biggest in England, with his Great Northern Hotel (1854) built to match next door. This was London's fifth terminus, praised by some for its 'massive boldness . . . - noble span . . . it is expressive, if not beautiful', but given a cooler reception by *Building News* in

1866: 'The most careless observer . . . cannot fail to be struck with the great changes of outline which the prospect has everywhere undergone within the last three or four years . . . mainly due to the new railway termini and the gigantic hotels connected with them . . . whose roofs and turrets rise sharply above the skyline of [their] humbler neighbours.'

A stroll back through some of these older and 'humbler' neighbours in eighteenth-century Holborn makes their point. Returning well down Judd Street, St George's Garden on the left down Handel Street is a hidden patch of trees, shrubs and scented garden. The next turning leads to the **Thomas Coram Foundation for Children**. Captain Coram (1668–1751) went to sea aged 11, rose to become an expert on the American Colonies and returned home in 1732 to be horrified by the abandoned children in London, some 'left to die on dung-hills'. So he founded a hospital (an orphanage) just near here, helped and encouraged by Hogarth who donated pictures and persuaded other artists to do the same (Gainsborough, Reynolds, Copley, Rysbrack) and by Handel who gave an organ, scores (*Messiah*) and played fundraising concerts, all now on show in the rebuilt house (40 Brunswick Square, WC1, tel 278 2424; open Mon–Fri, 9.30am–3.30pm when there are no meetings, so telephone first).

Cutting through Brunswick Square gardens, then along Landsdowne Terrace and left, Coram's Fields keep the sailor's spirit alive: seven acres of the hospital's former lawns and trees, with its original entrance gates and loggias (1742–52) where adults may enter only if accompanied by a child. Prince Charles's sons, princes William and Harry, have played among their commoner peers here. Either side of the hospital, the foundation later employed SP Cockerell and Joseph Kay to build two squares, Brunswick (now virtually gone) and Mecklenburgh, whose remaining, immensely grand east side is a surprising find round to the left beyond the Fields.

Even better is the **view** south from this terrace into old **Holborn**, which marked the north-eastern edge of eighteenth-century London and is remarkably well preserved and atmospheric. It stretched from Gray's Inn Road back to Russell Square and from just here down the wide, handsome avenue of **Doughty Street** (1792–1810) to the Walks of Gray's Inn Gardens. As with the Bloomsbury squares, Doughty Street had gates either end, where porters wearing mulberry livery with the

Doughty family buttons and gilt-edged hats attended to visiting gentry. The elegant late Georgian terrace was built on Henry Doughty's estate inherited from the Brownlows who had already started building to take advantage of their prime position just north of the Inns of Court.

This is where Charles Dickens (1812–70), on the threshold of fame, came to live at no. 48, now the **Dickens House**. The only survivor of the writer's many London addresses, he lived here for under three years (1837–9) in new middle-class wealth while he completed *Pickwick Papers*, wrote *Oliver Twist* and *Nicholas Nickleby*, began *Barnaby Rudge* and emerged from his pseudonym of Boz into the literary limelight. Bought, restored (1922–5) and run by the Dickens Fellowship, who have their headquarters here, it is packed with goodies to satisfy the most ardent Dickens fan: Dickens's hideous colour scheme and carpet for his living room; his desk and chair; *Oliver Twist* in Chinese, Victorian relief scraps, Fagin Toby-jugs and Lionel Bart's musical score; Paul and Florence Dombey in stained glass; marked-up prompt copies for his readings; a copy of *The Chimes* inscribed by him and given to admirer Hans Christian Anderson, and much, much more (48 Doughty Street, WC1, tel 405 2127; open Mon–Sat, 10am–5pm; charge. Quality shop; comprehensive library; the Dickens Fellowship).

Half way along, after Roger Street (leading to Brownlow Mews on the left), the earlier end of Doughty Street is called **John Street** (1754–60, with its North and Kings mewses to the left) after Doughty's carpenter, John Blagrave. Its **view** down the popular, tree-lined Gray's Inn Walks made it instantly fashionable with City merchants and lawyers. Round to the right along Theobald's Road, **Great James Street** (1720–30), built for George Brownlow Doughty, had a similar impact by continuing the line of Dr Barbon's grand Bed-

ford Row (see p. 127). This, the centre of Holborn, is one of the most complete eighteenth-century London streets surviving.

At the bottom of it, Rugby Street leads left to **Lamb's Conduit Street** where the Victorian Lamb pub (worth a half-pint), wall-papered with music-hall photographs, was a favourite Bloomsbury Group haunt. Street and pub honour William Lamb, a wealthy clothworker and chorister at the Chapel Royal (see p. 138) who in 1577 restored the water conduit here (see the statue at the north end, past the pub). Moving west, **Great Ormond Street** (nos 55–7 probably by the ubiquitous Dr Barbon) is synonymous with the Hospital for Sick Children. Charles West was behind its foundation in 1851. A century after Coram's good work, he was equally appalled at London children's plight, this time that some 21,000 children under the age of 10 died annually, most without the option of hospital care. Immediately successful, James Barrie later gave the hospital the full copyright of his fairytale, *Peter Pan*, in 1929 to help raise funds. (Keen architecture buffs should seek out the unbombed Victorian chapel in the old building, with glorious mosaics but sad plaques to children who did not recover).

Queen Square (1708–20), named after Queen Anne, won its fame when George III, beginning to suffer from his illness, stayed here privately with Dr Wills – hence the disagreement over which ugly queen the lead statue of a pretty crowned lady represents: Anne, Caroline or (top choice) Charlotte. To the left, Boswell and Old Gloucester streets survive either side of the Italian Hospital (1899), founded to tend sick Italians.

Ahead, Cosmo Place leads out of Queen Square to Southampton Row back into Bloomsbury. Turning right, you can join Chinese students, Tibetan scholars and British Museum keepers for a drink and sundown relaxation on the shady lawns of the Bedfords' Russell Square gardens.

The Nash sweep: A great plan for London

Mapping it out from above: Primrose Hill; rooftop restaurant of St George's Hotel, Langham Place, W1 (730 0111), snacks, tea and cocktails served at sofas in front of the plate-glassed view, restaurant tables set back.

Starting point: Carlton House Terrace, at the bottom of Regent Street, access by Underground: Piccadilly Circus.

Good days to explore: If it is dry and, with luck, sunny, this is a glorious outside day; if not, there are few fascinating interiors or museums to explore and it is better to do something else. The Canal operates daily but summer weekends bring queues for boats; the Zoo is open daily but brings holiday and weekend crowds.

Information: British Travel Centre, see p. 4. The Regent Street Association, 180 New Bond Street, W1 (629 1682) is the shop-keepers association; it puts on the Regent Street lights at Christmas. Refreshment suggestions: see p. 314.

Local festivals: Regent Street has spectacular Christmas lights, mid-Nov–Jan 6. The Camden Festival, three weeks in April; especially good for jazz, opera and ethnic music and dance; information from the Camden Festival, 100 Euston Road, NW1 (278 4444 x2526). Smaller, neighbourhood festivals in Camden to catch on this walk include Midsummer at St Mary's, Primrose Hill, starting with the Primrose Hill Festival in Chalcot Square and continuing for the last week of June; Albert Street Carnival, second Sat in July, a local beano with lots to see and do; information for both from Camden Arts and Entertainment, 100 Euston Road, NW1 (278 444 x2452).

Local libraries: Westminster City Central Reference Library, off Leicester Square, see p. 75. Westminster City's Marylebone Library is on Marylebone Road, NW1 (798 1037); open Mon–Fri 9.30am–7pm, Sat 9.30am–5pm; in addition to its regular stock, it is especially rich in medical books and pamphlets (some 35,000) and in archives and local history. In Camden borough, two good main libraries are Holborn and St Pancras (see Soho and Bloomsbury walk, p. 155). The Royal Institute of British Architects (RIBA), 66 Portland Place (580 5533) houses the British Architectural Library, open to all for reference only; open Mon 10am–5pm, Tues–Thurs 10am–8pm, Fri 10am–7pm, Sat 10am–1.30pm. Books on every conceivable aspect of London's physical history, from door-knockers to drains, with excellent librarians.

It took a remarkable coincidence of royal enlightenment, architectural panache, peaceful times and a large tract of available land. Then it happened. A great plan for Central London was conceived and completed. John Nash's conception of an elegant Regency backbone for London was built. It started from St James's Park, embraced Trafalgar Square and swept up Regent Street beside the new Mayfair and Marylebone squares to a park dotted with villas and surrounded by handsome terraces and a canal to the north. Until now, London had grown bit by bit out of the needs of two city centres, one political, one commercial. Kings had built palaces for their courts; Wren had given post-Fire London its spires but had his grander plans ignored; and medieval streets remained while aristocrats began to develop their open fields. There was no unifying plan, no order. Then came Nash, who changed the whole character of the capital and influenced its subsequent growth. Nothing like it has happened since.

Londoners were amazed, especially by the park. First, the works: 'A most extraordinary scene of digging, excavating, burning, and building, . . . more like a work of general destruction than anything else.' Then, the progress, noted by Mr Hughson the builder in 1817 as: 'Not likely to receive a speedy completion' but already 'one of the greatest Sunday promenades about town'. Then, the result, when the *Times Telescope* for March, 1825, eulogised: 'Among the magnificent ornaments of our metropolis commenced under the auspices of his present Majesty, while Regent, the Regent's Park ranks high in point of utility as well as beauty, and is an invaluable addition to the comforts and pleasures of those who reside in the north-west quarter of London.' And it went on: 'A park, like a city, is not made in a day; and to posterity it must be left fully to appreciate the merits of those who designed and superintended this delightful metropolitan improvement.'

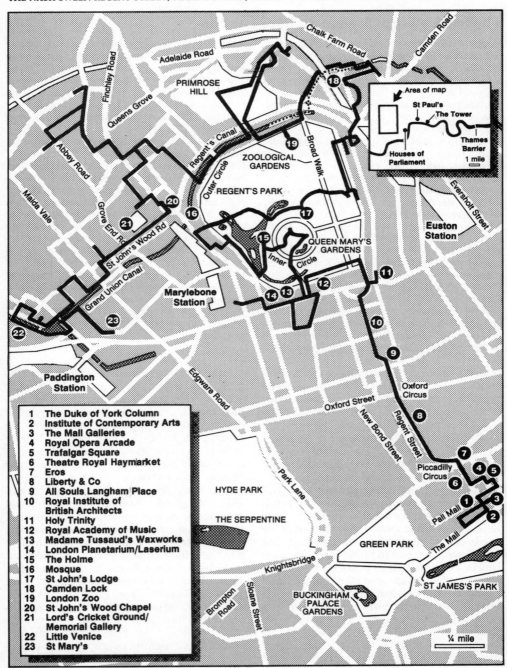

1   The Duke of York Column
2   Institute of Contemporary Arts
3   The Mall Galleries
4   Royal Opera Arcade
5   Trafalgar Square
6   Theatre Royal Haymarket
7   Eros
8   Liberty & Co
9   All Souls Langham Place
10 Royal Institute of
    British Architects
11 Holy Trinity
12 Royal Academy of Music
13 Madame Tussaud's Waxworks
14 London Planetarium/Laserium
15 The Holme
16 Mosque
17 St John's Lodge
18 Camden Lock
19 London Zoo
20 St John's Wood Chapel
21 Lord's Cricket Ground/
    Memorial Gallery
22 Little Venice
23 St Mary's

That year, with Carlton House still standing at the bottom of Regent Street, Nash's dream was a near-reality. The next year, Carlton House was demolished. The focus went. But the rest of the scheme in principle remains.

Today, choice stores line Regent Street, choice institutions line Portland Place and Regent's Park is for many people the best possible London address. Those whose bank balances forbid the immaculate, stage-set, terraces go to the hearts of the villages nearby – north Marylebone, Camden, Primrose Hill, Maida Vale and St John's Wood. But for all Londoners, part of Christmas is to visit the Regent Street lights, window-shop in Liberty's and Hamley's and peel sweet-smelling hot chestnuts bought on street corners; part of summer is to loll around the Park's lake, wander Queen Mary's perfumed rose garden at sunset and drop in on the elephants at the zoo.

Standing in the middle of **Carlton House Terrace**, beside the Duke of York Column, the **view** up Regent Street to Piccadilly Circus is wide, regal and impressive. Turning round, looking over royal St James's Park to the spires of parliament is almost as good. This is where Carlton House stood, the focus of Nash's design and home of his patron, the Prince Regent. This is where the story begins.

In 1783 George III's son, the Prince of Wales, came of age (see p. 137). He immediately moved into the modest but well placed Carlton House (eighteenth century, enlargements by Holland from 1783 on, demolished 1826) and set about transforming it into a palace. His architect was Henry Holland, a favourite of the bright Whig circle the Prince pointedly associated with to annoy his father. The result was an austerely classical facade with a Corinthian portico in the centre and – a Parisian idea – a colonnade screen set well in front. Here the handsome, curly-haired Prince lived, infusing it with his good taste, style and spirit, entertaining lavishly and repeatedly overindulging until his looks and figure crumbled. And here he squandered a fortune over the next 30 years – he was a jobless son until he became Regent in 1811 when his father became permanently insane. He demolished neighbouring houses to add new wings; he sent agents to China to buy furniture for his first-floor drawing room (they spent £441 on lanterns alone); and he gave spectacular parties including a fête (1814) to celebrate both Wellington and the Hanoverian centenary when 2,000 guests wandered in the gardens that stretched right along to Marlborough House, pausing at Nash's specially erected little buildings.

John Nash (1752–1835) is the other principal player. The son of a Lambeth millwright, he trained under Robert Taylor (architect of Stone Buildings in Lincoln's Inn Fields, see p. 125), struck out on his own to build stucco-fronted houses, went bankrupt and retired to Wales. Then he made his comeback. He met the landscape gardener Humphrey Repton, worked with him on country houses and through him returned to London and met the Prince of Wales. Then, in 1798, aged 46 and in the Prince's favour, he suddenly married a young, ambitious courtesan who acquired several children and was surrounded in scandal. Her relationship with the Prince remains a tantalising mystery. But from that day, Nash was rich, landed, influential and one of the Prince's Carlton House set.

Together, the Prince and Nash began the 'metropolitan improvements' to put provincial-looking London on a par with other European capitals. First came the land. The lease on about 500 acres of Crown property known as Marylebone Park was due to expire in 1811. Scattered with a few farms and small factories, it was just north of the aristocrats' successful speculative developments in Mayfair and Marylebone. So when John Fordyce, a bright Scot, was made Surveyor-General to His Majesty's Department of Woods and Forests in 1793, he naturally had visions of a lucrative Crown estate development. He made a survey, invited schemes from architects and, doubtless with Nash's conniving, produced a final report in 1809 suggesting a garden city for nobles linked to the Prince's home by a new street – essential for the carriages to parade their masters from these new northern limits of London down to the court, parliament and the St James's clubs. The same year, Nash, aged 57, was appointed Architect to the Department of Woods and Forests.

The year 1811 brought another set of coincidences: Marylebone Park reverted to the Crown, the Prince became Prince Regent and the tide began to turn in the Napoleonic War (1803–15), boosted by the failure of Napoleon's invasion of Russia (1812) and then Wellington's victories at

Vitoria (1813) and Waterloo (1815). The building boom began. While soldiers triumphed on the field, the Prince Regent spoke of 'quite eclipsing Napoleon' in London.

Nash, by now fully in tune with the Prince of Wales's taste, made detailed plans, highly picturesque with plenty of theatrical Parisian panoramas. There was to be a royal mile to outdo Rue de Rivoli leading from Carlton House to a huge circus (the biggest in Europe). This would open into a park dotted with villas, woody groves, a royal pleasure palace, a vast lake and a diverted canal, all surrounded by palatial terraces. The whole project carried its royal patron's name. Regent Street was built (the street remains; most buildings have been reconstructed); half the circus was built; and Regent's Park was laid out and received some of its theatrical props – but there were fewer villas, no palace, no Valhalla and a canal diversion around instead of through. And when the Prince Regent left the spotlight of his Carlton House stage in search of greater grandeur in Buckingham Palace, he demolished the house he once lived in to develop Carlton House Terrace and prettied up St James's Park as a replacement focus. At the same time, Nash sorted out the Whitehall muddle to the east. He cut Pall Mall East to link the Regent Street sweep to a new and spacious Trafalgar Square and he tidied up the beginning of the Strand, although his idea of a road north from it to fast-expanding Bloomsbury stayed on the drawing-board.

In all this, Nash's strength was for creating scenic grandeur rather than detail. His impressive exteriors and panoramas took little account of the houses behind the facades, which were often, in Summerson's words, 'identical in their narrowness, their thin pretentiousness, their poverty of design . . . the sham is flagrant and absurd'. But on the outside they were indeed magnificent metropolitan improvements, even if James Elmes's patriotic praise in 1827 is a slight exaggeration: 'Augustus made it one of his proudest boasts, that he found Rome of brick, and left it of marble. The reign and regency of George the Fourth have scarcely done less, for the vast and increasing Metropolis of the British empire . . . the Rome of modern history.'

The best way to explore it today is to wander and look, enjoying the variety, surprises and many grand vistas created by this master of the Picturesque movement – extraordinary to think that it took a public outcry to prevent the government ripping it all down for 'improvements' in the 1920s.

Carlton House Terrace (1827–32) stretches west and east, its grand cream cliffs inspired by Paris's Place de la Concorde. Front doors opened onto the gardens of the Pall Mall clubs (see p. 139); first-floor salons overlooked St James's Park. To the east, the National Portrait Gallery extension is at no. 15 (see p. 88); Gladstone's home was no. 11 (1857–75, except while he was prime minister, 1868–74), and, astonishingly, the palatial end house is still privately owned as one family's London home. To the west, the German Embassy was at nos 7–9 – German ambassador Herr von Ribbentrop's dog, Giro, was buried just west of the Duke's column; and the erudite Royal Society (begun 1640s, formalised 1660) has had Wren, Pepys, Newton and Sloane as presidents (no. 6). Beyond, the road becomes **Carlton Gardens** (1830–3), with strong French memories: de Gaulle and the Free French forces at no. 4, complete with his message broadcast after France's fall in 1940 on a wall plaque; and, round the corner, the exiled Louis Napoleon (Napoleon III) at no. 1. From the steps, Nash's Picturesque remodelling of St James's Park is clear: out went Charles II's French formality and in came a serpentine lake, winding paths and romantic shrubberies. Turning left into the Park, there is a good **view** of the terrace.

In the centre, the **Duke of York Steps** rise to the **Duke of York Column** (1833), a memorial to Frederick, the second son of George III whose campaigns were neatly expressed in the children's nursery rhyme: 'The grand old Duke of York, He had ten thousand men; He marched them up to the top of the hill, And he marched them down again.' As he died with a debt of some £2 million, Londoners remarked that the height of his column kept him out of his creditors' clutches. At the bottom of the steps lurks the **Institute of Contemporary Arts**, showing a lively programme of the latest in art, film, theatre and opinion (Nash House, The Mall, SW1, tel 930 6393; open Tues–Sun, noon–9pm; day and full membership instantly available. Good bookshop, restaurant). Further east, less avant-garde art fills more Nash basements at the **Mall Galleries**, where London art societies for illustrators, portrait painters, animal painters, etc, take turns to hang their annual shows (The Mall, SW1, tel 930 6844; open during exhibitions, usually Mon–Fri 10am–5pm, Sat 10am–1pm; usually charge).

At the top of the steps (with a good **view** back over the Park) **Waterloo Place** (1816) commemorated Wellington's triumph over the French (1815) and opened up the view from Carlton House ready for the Prince Regent and Nash's grand plan. And after the demolition of Carlton House, it retained its grandeur with two clubs: Nash's United Service on the right (1827–8), now home for the Institute of Directors (since 1978); and Decimus Burton's Athenaeum on the left (1827–30, see p. 139). Burton (1800–81) is a major character in the Nash story. Son of James Burton, one of London's most successful builders (see p. 168), he was only 18 years old when he designed The Holme in Regent's Park (see below) and swiftly followed this triumph with other Park work – Cornwall Terrace, Nuffield Lodge, Clarence Terrace and the wondrous Colosseum (gone) – before the Athenaeum, nos 1–2 Carlton House Terrace and then titivations to the United Service Club to make it a pair to his Athenaeum. The United Service was Wellington's favourite club, and the horse block built for him is still outside it.

This space, which feels like a handsome square when the cars are gone at night, has a good crowd of statues: the Duke up on his column, Edward VII in the middle, and national soldier and explorer heroes looking on. India hero Lord Lawrence (1811–79), Colin Campbell, Lord Clyde (1792–1863), who was a Glasgow-born rags-to-riches soldier, and Captain Scott (1868–1912), who took *Discovery* to the Antarctic and reached the South Pole (1912) before dying there, are on the right; Sir John Fox Burgoyne (1782–1871), one of Wellington's soldiers, and Sir John Franklin (1788–1847), who died after discovering the North-West Passage, are on the left. And beyond, pioneer nurse Florence Nightingale is one of the figures on the Guards Crimean War (1854–5) Memorial.

This is the moment to enjoy the first part of Nash's **Regent Street** (1817–23), the Prince Regent's triumphal way to his new park. It sweeps up to Piccadilly Circus, the fine **view** originally closed at the circus by Robert Abraham's replica (1819) of Inigo Jones's demolished Somerset House (see p. 119), a wonderful scenic device for Nash paid for by an extravagant insurance company manager and architecture buff. Blomfield's replacement, the County Fire Office (1913–30), has some of the same effect. Sir John Summerson, historian of London's Georgian architecture, gave the whole street high praise: 'Its amazingly successful blend of formality and picturesque opportunism could have happened nowhere and at no time but in England of the period of the Picturesque.'

Just here, the **Crafts Council**'s Waterloo Place Gallery on the left is a showcase for British craftsmen, holds exhibitions and also advises on where to seek out specific skills to commission work (12 Waterloo Place, SW1, tel 930 4811; open Tues–Sat, 10am–5pm, Thurs until 7pm, Sun, 2–5pm; charge for exhibitions). Then, before exploring further, a short detour right along **Pall Mall East** leads to Nash's other improvements in this area. Nash and GS Repton both created the very French Royal Opera Arcade (1816–8) on the left, just before the landmark tower of ugly New Zealand House (1960), where stunning views are enjoyed by guests at the almost daily roof-top cocktail parties. Straight ahead, Matthew Cotes Wyatt's George III (1836) trots out from Trafalgar Square (begun 1820), where Francis Chantrey's equestrian statue of the Prince Regent as George IV is on the far side, originally destined to top Marble Arch in front of Nash's Buckingham Palace (see p. 91). Turning left up Suffolk Street and left again into Suffolk Place (1820), these are the sole survivors of Nash's elegant side-street plans. And in Haymarket on the right, Nash's **Theatre Royal Haymarket** (1820–1, see p. 140) beautifully closes the vistas from smart St James's Square down Charles II Street.

Piccadilly Circus (1819) was Nash's triple solution to close the vista from the Prince's Royal Apartments, meet Piccadilly and start the next part of the royal route. But the circle was soon broken up when Shaftesbury Avenue was opened in 1886 (see p. 159). Theatres followed, and Piccadilly became the central meeting place it is today – and not just for Londoners. Students starting out on world explorations from Vancouver or Singapore agree to meet here. Snow or hail, there are backpacks on the steps beneath **Eros** (1893) which has become a much-loved symbol of London. In fact it portrays not Eros but the Angel of Christian Charity and was made of aluminium by Alfred Gilbert to commemorate the philanthropist and statesman Antony Ashley Cooper, 7th Earl of Shaftesbury (1801–85), champion fighter for better conditions for the insane, factory workers, chimney sweeps and colliery workers and for better housing for the poor. Surrounding it are the Criterion Brasserie and the magical Criterion Theatre (1871–4) (south side, dip inside both to see Thomas Verity's twinkling mosaics and sumptuous tiles); the London Pavilion (east) newly restored as a shopping emporium with a restaurant above (views) and a Madame Tussaud's outpost for rock star waxworks on top; Blomfield's Swan and Edgar's department store (west, 1925–7, now Tower Records); and

Blomfield's County Fire Office (west, 1927); all surrounded by walls of jolly neon lights whose arrival with the Bovril and Schweppes advertisements at the turn of the century scandalised purists.

From here, **Regent Street** swings dramatically left to its second part and the full effect of Nash's design takes off. Nash had problems, but, fortunately, as Summerson points out, 'the financier was an artist and the artist a financier'. Plots sold slowly and the idea of a unified facade was abandoned to entice moneyed men to take sites. Decimus Burton's father, James, took the lead with some but here on the corner, where individuality would not work, Nash sank his own money into the project to build the Quadrant and its curving colonnade to protect chic shoppers from the inevitable London drizzle. But within 25 years the dusky colonnades had become a 'haunt of vice and immorality' and were pulled down (1848).

Round the corner, the street swept up to Oxford Circus between the rich and poor, the land bought cheaply from the right-hand (Soho) side, then built with its main openings to attract up-market trade from the left-hand (Mayfair) side. Nash planned it as the smart shopping centre it still is. And his success was his loss, for after 80 years as a high society fashion street, where 'between three and six o'clock every afternoon . . . celebrities of wealth, nobility and the mode' came in their carriages, its shopkeepers felt cramped. Again, architects were drafted in and the whole section was redeveloped from 1916. It is this part which has been illuminated by the Regent Street Association of shops (founded 1925) since 1949. At first, only Christmas trees were lit. Then, since 1954, a whole avenue of bright lights, each year a different design, has been switched on in mid-November, often by a member of the royal family.

Walking up Regent Street today, there are several buildings worth dipping into; Austin Reed at no. 103 for the Art Deco basement barber's; the Café Royal at No. 68 for its sumptuous Grill Room, echoing the Bohemian lifestyle of its Domino Room where Wilde, Beerbohm and Whistler met; Mappin and Webb at no. 106 for its cases of silver and gold; Garrard at no. 112, jewellers to the sovereign since Queen Victoria patronised them in 1843, for the elegant interior and even more elegant jewels, with craftsmen working behind; Hamley's at nos 200–2, which opened in London in 1760, for its sheer size as probably the largest toyshop in the world; and ET and ES Hall's Liberty and Co. (1926)

at nos 210–20. Its exterior frieze of the wealth of far-off countries, and its clock give a clue to its interior full to bursting with Eastern exotic delights and top Western design. The contrasting Tudor revival back end of the store was built later (1924) from two ex-ships, HMS *Hindustan* and HMS *Impregnable*, further enriched with stained glass and Italian carving. It fitted the image of the store's founder, Arthur Lasenby Liberty, an enthusiast of all things Japanese, whose success at selling oriental fabrics and shawls led him to commission furniture to go with them, then fashion using them. He introduced the romantic, flowing Pre-Raphaelite fashion and had Ruskin, Rossetti and Whistler as customers. So stylish was he that the French spoke of 'Liberty' with bated breath and Norman Shaw said to him: 'You found things – most of them beastly, and you left them glorious in colour and full of interest!'

Oxford Circus (1912–23), where Regent Street cuts across Oxford Street (see p. 151), was rebuilt by Henry Tanner (1913–28). Beyond here, Nash went residential again to pass through the elegant Marylebone streets (see p. 152), a northern outpost of the smart set. Ahead, the splendid **view** of his All Souls (1822–4), at Langham Place, with circular portico and conical spire, neatly closes the vista before the Via Triumphalis wiggles round to the park approach. From the colonnade, a bust of Nash looks down his street. Inside, BBC lunchtime and evening concerts are often recorded (see p. 293 for how to attend). To the right, the roof-top restaurant of St George's Hotel, good for all meals and snacks, has stunning **views** right out to the distant Heathrow aeroplanes on a clear day. The hotel replaces the spectacular Langham Hotel (1864), built as a Florentine palace, opened with a 2,000-guest ball attended by the Prince of Wales, and instantly the swishest of all London's hotels, patronised by Toscanini, Dvorak, the exiled Napoleon III and the later exile, Haile Selassie.

The hotel covered part of Foley House (1767), Lord Foley's mansion for which he fought long to obtain a guarantee from the Duke of Portland, who owned the land, that his view of Hampstead and Highgate would never be interrupted by another building. However, later Foleys curtailed their privilege when, fortune gone, they sold out to Nash. The canny financier then sold on half to Sir James Langan, for whom he built Langan House (later replaced by the hotel), and half to the Crown, for his pet project. This is how Nash came to wiggle his Regent Street round to tag it on to the earlier, handsome **Portland Place** (1776–80), Robert Adam's 125-foot-wide speculative street that led from Foley House up to Marylebone Road. Adam, careful not to block Lord Foley's view, had created one of the grandest eighteenth-century London streets.

Not much of Adam survives at the bottom (but nip left to Chandos Street to catch his fine mansion on the right (see p. 152). Val Myers and Watson-Hart's Portland stone **Broadcasting House** (1931), home of the British Broadcasting Corporation (BBC), is on the right. Sculptures by Eric Gill decorate the outside with, over the main door, Prospero sending Ariel, symbol of broadcasting, out into the world. Above, on the third floor, the Director-General and Governors meet in the Board Room to decide Britain's public service broadcasting policy. Despite scores of other BBC buildings, Broadcasting House (known by BBC staff simply as 'BH') has the romance: when a bomb exploded inside in 1940, the radio continued; today there is always a flurry of star-spotters on hand to recognise singers, actors and politicians arriving (BBC publications are sold at the bookstall in the hall; to attend BBC recording sessions, see p. 293).

Broadcasting House answered a pressing need; for, just five years after the first daily programmes began to go out over the air from Savoy Hill on November 14, 1922, the new medium of wireless was a huge and fast-expanding success. Lord Reith, the Corporation's first director-general, and the government were anxious to prevent the free-for-all of commercial radio gaining a foothold in Britain as it had in the US. So the non-commerical BBC was established in 1927, after one or two sponsored broadcasts, including the enterprising (American-owned) Selfridge's fashion talk from the Eiffel Tower in Paris (1925). By 1939 about 9 million licences were held. Almost everyone in Britain listened to the BBC, whose policy was guided by 'high culture' and 'Christian morality'. But J Walter Thompson (also American) was soon sending 40 sponsored programmes a week from its studios in Bush House (see p. 133) to Radio Luxembourg.

The block between New Cavendish and Weymouth streets has more Adam buildings, with the brick fronts and honeysuckle-decorated stucco pilasters he used at the Adelphi (see p. 118). A clutch of embassies live in splendour here: the Swedish, Malaysian, Polish and Turkish (the Americans were at no. 98). But the office of the Chinese Chargé d'Affaires at no. 49, a glorious Adam survivor, was scandalously gutted against British wishes in 1981.

Beyond, just after Weymouth Street, the **Royal Institute of British Architects** is housed in Grey Wornum's Swedish-inspired building (1932–4) at no. 66. Founded in 1824, membership is by examination (since 1887). The coveted Gold Medal has recently been awarded to Sir John Summerson (1976), Sir Denys Lasdun (1977), James Stirling (1980), Berthold Lubetkin (1982), Norman Foster (1983), Indian Charles Correa (1984), Richard Rogers (1985), Japanese Arata Isozaki (1986) and Ralph Erskin (1987), many of whom have buildings in London. And Presidents have also included many architects who have contributed to London – CR Cockerell, George Gilbert Scott, Charles Barry, Alfred Waterhouse, Reginald Blomfield, Edwin Lutyens, Basil Spence and Rod Hackney. But not all the British praise the RIBA. Last century, the Architectural Association was set up in opposition (see p. 166); and recently writer and arbiter of good taste Kingsley Amis wanted to 'blow up the RIBA as thoroughly and noisily as possible in protest not at its design but at its occupants'. (66 Portland Place, tel 580 5533; open Mon–Fri, 9am–9.30pm, Sat, 10am–1.30pm. Lectures and events, information service, library (see beginning of walk, above), magnificent drawings collection currently housed at 21 Portman Square (see p. 153); good bookshop.)

At the top of this monumental approach, Nash planned the biggest circus in Europe, **Park Crescent** (1812, much rebuilt), as the formal entry into the Prince Regent's playground park, enticing society north of the London boundary of Marylebone Road. Only half was built, and that with difficulty as the first builder went bankrupt. But its sweeping and graceful curves, accentuated by simple windows and a colonnade with pairs of Ionic columns, had the desired theatrical impact. Summerson finds it one of the best parts of the whole scheme: ' . . . very lovely, unpretentious, neatly detailed . . . the simple appropriateness of Park Crescent with its Ionic colonnades is beyond criticism.'

Turning right, the thundering highway at the top was called New Road until its rebuilding in 1857, when the western part was renamed Marylebone Road, the eastern Euston Road. To the right, the tower of Sir John Soane's **Holy Trinity** (1824–8) rises in front of R Atkinson's The White House (1936, now a hotel), conceived as a northern version of Pimlico's fully serviced Dolphin Square (see p. 241), built star-shaped for maximum light and coated with cream faience tiles to keep it clean and shiny. Straight ahead, **Park Square East** and **West** (1823–5) completed the entry into the Park. Behind no. 18 Park Square East, Nash built the latest entertainment gimmick, an octagonal Diorama (1823, still there, just), where crowds flocked to sit in the rotating auditorium and be whirled past Jacques Mande Daguerre's changing tableaux recounting a story. Known to Victorians as the Palace of Light, his Mount Etna for the 1851 Exhibition staged the full eruption to live organ music accompaniment.

Beyond lies **Regent's Park**, where Nash's disciplined tract of green, punctuated with elegant amusements of garden, lake and zoo, is the epitome of a nobleman's Picturesque estate. Free from most of the houses planned for it, including the Prince Regent's, it still feels as though it belongs to a country mansion, a Syon or a Kenwood. In fact it is a perfect people's park in the middle of London, serving not one family but thousands of Londoners living in the surrounding flats and houses. It covers 472 acres, including its Primrose Hill annexe to the north. Originally part of the Abbess of Barking's grounds, Henry VIII appropriated it after the Dissolution and made it into his Marylebone hunting park, with ditch and fence to discourage poachers. Edward VI entertained the French ambassador here; Elizabeth I hunted with the Duke of Anjou (1582); and Charles I used it as security when he needed to buy gunpowder but lacked cash during the Civil War. When Cromwell sold it off, some 16,000 trees were felled and the land ploughed up. After royal reclamation under Charles II, several farms took leases and marketed their milk and hay to the capital. These, with some buildings and small factories, ended in 1811, keenly anticipated by John Fordyce, Nash and the Prince Regent.

Ignoring the tried and tested nobles' developments of squares and terraces, Nash used his country house experience to design an urban Picturesque plan of a garden city: 56 villas, each with its own garden and tree-shaded privacy to give the impression of countryside, all surrounded by romantic, cardboard cut-out panoramas of grand, stucco palaces. This utopia would have the canal and lake inside and the market for supplies outside at the north-east corner. It was a radically new approach to urban planning, the forerunner of Victorian suburbia. Building began with Park Crescent. And the best way to unfold the rest of the story is to wander the Park, dipping out to catch nearby sights and villages. For many, it is a favourite but moody London Park. American-born writer Frederick Raphael responds to it as his 'sacred and profane grove'; architectural historian Joe Maudant Crook loves 'the Rose Garden in winter, rows of benches like the British seaside' and for Ian Nairn, so difficult to please most of the time, it was 'unique: for once neither leafy nor urban, but all the elements acting together to create consciously the kind of living tissue that we sigh for.'

Going into the park, Sir Denys Lasdun's Royal College of Physicians (1960–4) is a new addition, with a newer courtyard garden. Then, cutting westwards, there are good **views** up the Broad Walk to the right, a tree-lined promenade that runs the length of the Park, right up to the Zoo in the north-east corner (park information and maps at the bottom of it). Beyond, the palace-facade terraces begin on the left. First is Nash's **Ulster Terrace** (1824–5), with bold bays at either end. Next is Nash's **York Terrace** (1824–6), divided in the middle by **York Gate** (1824–6) to keep the good **view** of Thomas Hardwick's earlier **St Mary's** (1813), with sun-catching, gilded caryatids supporting the dome. It was planned back in the 1770s to serve the fast-expanding and smartening **Marylebone**, whose northern part is best explored now. (For the southern part, see pp. 152–3.)

Down through York Gate, the tall, striped chimneys of Ernest George's **Royal Academy of Music** (1910–11) are on the left. Founded in 1774 and modelled on Italian conservatories, it was the first music academy in England. **Marylebone High Street**, across the road, passes the graveyard where painter George Stubbs was buried (1806), as were Charles Wesley and his nephew Samuel. It was up at this end of Marylebone that John Holles bought the manor house in 1708 which was inherited by his daughter Henrietta, wife of the Earl of Oxford, who then developed southern Marylebone. The high street it overlooked, fondly called 'my village green' by journalist Bernard Levin, who lives nearby, still has a strong local character and is equipped with The Prince Regent pub at no. 71, Radio London's studios at no. 35a, Maison Sange the café and patisserie at no. 105, almost unchanged since it opened in the 1920s (their cakes are a favourite with Harley Street dentists), the Casson Gallery at no. 73 selling British craftsmanship, and Quinto the secondhand bookshop at no. 83, with their purpose-built shop of c.1910 (open Mon–Sat 9am–6pm, Sun noon–6pm).

Turning right into Nottingham Street and again up Uxborough Street, **Madame Tussaud's Wax-works** museum is opposite. In 1986, 2.4 million visitors made it the top UK tourist attraction for which there is an entry change. Its fame is sadly at odds with its quality. Visitors on short stays queue for hours in rain, wind and dust, juggernauts thundering past, while there are many more wonderful things to enjoy in London, the majority them for free and without queueing. The idea was good. Madame Tussaud (1761–1850, real name Marie Grosholtz), who learnt her art from her uncle, made wax figures at Louis XVI's court and then wax heads of nobles awaiting the guillotine during the French Revolution. Next, she fled to England with her uncle's waxworks and toured the country with her show before settling near here. She increased crowds by keeping right up to date – she paid £18,000 for George IV's coronation robes and the Duke of Wellington returned every time the Chamber of Horrors altered. Madame Tussaud's sons moved the 400 waxes to this site (1884) and continue up-dating.

So, following the chronological sequence from Pepys to Picasso and Mrs Thatcher, one good star to see is Sleeping Beauty, with her breathing chest, in fact modelled on Louis XVI's mistress, Madame du Barry, by Madame Tussaud's uncle. Newer, good waxworks are the Beatles, modelled as the Fab Four, smiling in their collarless suits (these waxworks appear on their *Sgt Pepper* cover; Barbara Cartland, with her fluffy dog Twi-Twi; Joan Collins, lounging in lurex; and the tableau of Lord Lichfield snapping the Royal Family – not forgetting the Chamber of Horrors (an idea done so much better by the London Dungeon, see p. 62) and the Battle of Trafalgar. For once, photography is encouraged: 'Picture yourself with the famous', but the whole show feels slightly shabby and temporary, and the waxes vary considerably in quality (Marylebone Road, NW1, tel 935 6861; open daily, 10am–5.30pm, but earlier at weekends and in summer; charge. Good shop, with Madamae Tussaud's letter box and postmark; big café. Tussaud outposts include the London Pavilion, see p. 177 and Windsor, see p. 276).

Both events next door are good. The **London Planetarium**, opened in 1958, uses a Zeiss projector with more than 29,000 parts to take visitors on a remarkable journey among the stars, time and space – the night sky will never look the same again (same address, tel 486 1121; charge, but combined ticket with Madame Tussaud's is cheaper; 30-minute shows from 11am in school holidays, 12.15pm in termtime; last show 4.30pm; John Ebdon's catalogue is good). In the same hall, the **Laserium** show, currently the world's most elaborate, uses all the latest laser tricks to produce prancing sheep, guitars and people who dance and gyrate across the Planetarium dome, all to the beat of pop music (same address, tel 486 2242; charge; shows on Tues–Sun 6pm, Tues–Sat 7.45pm, Fri and Sat 9.15pm). Cricket fans should nip further west along Marylebone Road, then right up Gloucester Place to Dorset Square, the MCC's ground 1787–1811 (see Lord's, p. 185).

Back in the park through York Gate, the road straight ahead is York Bridge. And from its bridge there is a good **view** back down to St Mary's church. Beyond, the road winds up between Regent's College (1913) and the tennis courts (with Tea pavilion) to Nash's **Inner Circle**, a road surrounding the raised land where he envisaged a 'National Valhalla'. It was not built; instead, the Royal Botanical Society filled the 18 acres with gardens (1839–1932) until **Queen Mary's Rose Garden** was planted by the British Rose Growers' Association and named after George V's queen. It is one of the best rose gardens in Britain and one of the most romantic. Wandering through its pergolas and among its beds of flame-red 'Lover's meeting', creamy yellow 'Peaudouce' and peach-pink 'Silver Jubilee', a pot-pourri of heady perfumes fills the summer air (plenty of benches, best blooms Jun–Sept). Two of the Park's many unusually mature and fine trees are nearby, a manna ash and pillar apple. Here, too, are the small lake, with water-fowl and arched bridge to a tiny, rockery garden island; the Open-Air Theatre, founded 1932, stage for Vivien Leigh and Gladys Cooper on to Michael Crawford and Jeremy Irons (season June–Aug, matinée and evening shows, barbeque suppers, for more information tel 486 2431); and the Rose Garden Restaurant.

Leaving the garden beside the restaurant, Decimus Burton's **The Holme** (1818) is on the right. It was 18-year-old Burton's first house and the first Regent's Park villa to be completed, built for his father, James, the successful London builder who loyally supported Nash by overspending to take chunks of Regent Street. Today it is one of only three surviving villas of the eight that were built.

Beyond lies Nash's 22-acre **Boating Lake**, its arms curving picturesquely around Inner Circle, its island a successful heronry with plenty of young to spot in springtime. Here summer weekends are like seaside holidays in an old Renoir film, with kids paddling, families boating, couples flirting, locals devouring their Sunday newspapers and old dears dozing on deckchairs under lace parasols, with music drifting through the giggles and shouts from the nearby bandstand (deckchairs for hire; boats – skiffs, canoes, kayaks and ferry boats – hired from the north-west corner daily 10am–dusk; band performances scattered from end May–end Aug, Mon–Sat 12.30–4pm and 5.30–7.30pm, Sun and Bank Holidays 3pm–4.30pm and 6–7.30pm).

Following the bank down towards the left, past weeping willows and clumps of yellow irises, the next batch of terraces come in sight. From the bridge, there is a good **view**. Left is **Cornwall Terrace** (1821–3), designed by Nash and Decimus Burton, built by James Burton. Over the bridge and right, the same trio produced **Clarence Terrace** (1823). But Nash alone designed **Sussex Place** (1822), whose octagonal domes, polygonal bay windows and curved end wings made it the most eccentric of the Park's terraces, infused with some of the mood of Brighton Pavilion which he was designing for the king at the time. Next is Nash's simpler **Hanover Terrace** (1822–3). All of this scenery provides glorious, romantic panoramas from the park.

Dipping down Kent Passage to the left of Hanover Terrace, Nash's **Kent Terrace** (1827) was one of the last to be built and the only one to face outwards, so it lacks its theatrical setting. Turning right back into the Park past Burton's Hanover Lodge (1822–3), Sir Frederick Gibberd's **Mosque** (1978) is a new arrival, its gilded minaret an appropriate fantasy addition to the Park. The principal mosque in Britain, it is built on land given to the Egyptian government in exchange for land in Cairo. Although the imams have all studied at Al-Azhar University, the local faithful who flock to prayer, especially on Fridays, come from all Islamic countries of the world (146 Park Road, W1, tel 724 3363; visitors are asked to dress modestly and behave appropriately; headscarves are available). It is just here that the Crown Commissioners have taken up Nash's incomplete dream and commissioned Quinlan Terry to design six villas, each in a different style but all with Nash's free form of classicism – a Doric one, a Gothic, a Regency, an Ionic, a Corinthian and a Venetian. To inspect their progress, turn left along Outer Circle.

Straight ahead is the north-west arm of the lake where boats are hired. Beyond, Winfield House and its vast garden on the left is the American ambassador's residence, given by Barbara Hutton, the heir of FW Woolworth's stores, and now one of the few remaining private tracts of the park. Branching towards the right and over the bridge of the north-west arm of the lake (with an identification chart beside the duck and geese breeding area), **St John's Lodge** is the second of the original villas, built by J Raffield (1818), enlarged by Charles Barry (1947). Later, the 3rd Marquess of Bute leased it and had R Weir Schultz make further alterations. In 1888 he described his new home as 'terra incognita to a great many Londoners; and there is perhaps a certain piquancy about a place which almost simulates to be a country house and yet is only a shilling cab-fare from Piccadilly Circus.' More recently, it was the subject of furious controversy when the American, Frederick Koch, planned to buy it, refurbish it and put his art collection on show – a project that failed. Its magic garden, found on the east side behind a shepherd girl statue, has both perfumed roses and scented shrubs, a favourite spot for London park connoisseurs. North of here, the tiny, Tudor-style tea pavilion fits neatly into Nash's Picturesque ideals (and even stocks dog biscuits).

Striking out eastwards, beyond the Broad Walk (**views** of surreal, bare, zoo mountains on the left), there is a moment when the horizon is all green, not a building in sight. Then the Park's east side comes into focus, a long backdrop of terraces. From the south, Nash's **Cambridge Terrace** (1825) is followed by his **Chester Terrace** (1825) with projecting wings, worth exploring by popping out through Cumberland Gate to find the black and gold George IV lamp-posts and road posts and, behind the facade, a triumphal arch with the terrace's name on top. Nash's huge **Cumberland Terrace** (1827) is best seen from the park, its porticoes, courtyards and arches described by Summerson as 'the back-cloth as it were to Act III, and easily the most breathtaking architectural panorama in London'. North of it, Ambrose Pynter's St Katharine's Hospital (1826), ousted from its medieval site so that St Katharine Dock could be built (see p. 104), adds a spark of Gothic Revival to the scenery before Nash's **Gloucester Gate** (1827), with double-sized mouldings on the capitals because the builders reckoned it would look better that way, completes the terraces. But the most startling of Nash's innovations lies outside

Gloucester Gate and round to the right in Albany Street. Here, in Park Village East and West (1829), he created the model for the Victorian surburban villa, a village-like cluster of houses, each very different and set in its own garden.

Nash's idea of a canal through the Park was amended and the eight-and-a-half-mile-long **Regent's Canal** (1812–20) finally bordered the north side, running through a deep, verdant cutting. It came from the Paddington Branch of the Grand Union Canal at Little Venice to the west (see below), and passed through the Park to Camden and on to Limehouse Basin (see p. 106) and the new East London Docks off the Thames. And when it was opened in 1820, Nash and his assistant, James Morgan, went down it in the splendid City State Barge, bands playing and guns firing salutes. Until the railways came, this was the busiest stretch of canal in Britain. And afterwards, it continued to carry many of the building materials for London's expansion.

A good way to see the canal, and the best way to arrive at the Zoo, is to glimpse a little of **Camden** and then catch a boat from Camden Lock. Moving back up Albany Street, then right into Parkway and left into Oval Road, the Italianate villas of **Gloucester Crescent** (1840–60) sweep round to the right. They sit on the field of Chalk Farm, a large area given to Eton College by Henry VI, and were built soon after the completion of Regent's Park opened possibilities for a whole new tract of fashionable London development. At the end, the splendid Circular Factory (1852) was Collard and Collard's five-storey piano factory, each instrument assembled floor by floor as it was hoisted up and down a central well.

Jamestown Road round to the right leads to Camden High Street, the hub of Camden Town, and round to the left a narrow gateway leads down to the canal where there is a bridge across to **Camden Lock**. Camden's manor with its surrounding cattle pastures was inherited (1749) by the wife of John Pratt, who became 1st Earl Camden and toyed with a small amount of building. But development only took off with the arrival of an extra stretch of the Regent's Canal. Timber and coal wharfs followed – hence Serge Chermayeff's warehouses (1930) by Oval Road's bridge to the west.

Today, Camden has been gentrified, the rows of cottage-sized houses now filled with books, cleverly bought antiques, and word-processors. Camden Lock has been spruced up, its cobbles polished and its Victorian warehouses and stables converted into restaurants, craftsmen's studios (well worth exploring), Dingwalls (for jazz and rock) and Terry Farrel's TV-am studios (1983) topped with outsize breakfast eggcups. The very lively market (Sat and Sun) has stalls piled high with weaving, knitting, light-hearted antiques and second-hand books, all in a post-hippy, friendly atmosphere. Its outpost, The Old Stables, is also well worth seeking out up Chalk Farm Road (open Sat, Sun and Thurs), as are two more nearby markets back down Camden High Street, one for second-hand clothes, the other for fruit and vegetables.

To return down to the Park and Zoo, there are two options, both using the canal: walking the towpath (with various steps up to the road, mostly open Mon–Fri at 7.30am, Sat 8am, Sun 9am, closing 30 minutes before dusk), or gliding along the canal on a boat, which is more fun.

The London Waterbus Company run a scheduled service on two ex-commercial narrowboats, *Gardenia* (1947) and *Perseus* (1935), from here to Little Venice (see below), stopping at the Zoo (39 Camden Lock Place, NW1, tel 482 2550; Easter-Sept, daily service runs hourly 10am–5pm; Oct–Easter weekend only; ticket price can include the cheap deal of Zoo entrance, too). They also run fascinating but less picturesque day-trips eastwards down to Limehouse Basin (see pp. 106, 258), passing through 12 locks, the 960-yard-long Islington tunnel and rural Victoria Park, with excellent commentary along the way (summer period only, usually Sat, 9.30am–6pm, booking essential). There is also the traditionally painted narrowboat, *Jenny Wren*, which goes directly to Little Venice, without the Zoo stop (book at 250 Camden High Street, NW1, tel 485 4433/6210; Apr–Oct, daily 11.30am, 2pm and 3.30pm). Finally, before hopping onto a boat, the Regent's Canal Information Centre, housed in the old lock house on the quay, stocks a good canal brochure, the leaflet *Wildlife on the Regent's Canal* and plenty of other information (official address 289 Camden High Street, NW1, tel 482 0523; open daily 10am–1pm, 2–5pm). For the really keen, the Inland Waterways Association publish the *Canal Walks in London* booklet and have run excellent guided canal walks for over a decade (meet: Camden Underground station, 1st Sun of each month, 2.30pm, no booking necessary; more information from 114 Regent's Park Road, NW1, tel 586 2556/2510 or Melbury House, Melbury Terrace, NW1, tel 262 6711).

The trip to the Zoo leaves the double lock of Camden to pass the pretty gardens of St Mark's Crescent and perhaps a local fisherman catching a pike or roach or an old man feeding the ducks. Turning sharp right at Cumberland Basin, there is an instant scene-change to rural, leafy greenness and the Zoo, heralded by Lord Snowdon's Aviary (1963) housing the Indian and African birds. (Walkers need to come up the steps by the aviary, then cross into the Park and enter the main Zoo entrance.)

London Zoo, officially the Zoological Gardens, was part of Nash's playground park scheme and houses an extraordinary collection of animals and birds which snort, yelp, bray, screech, flap and slither their hours away in some architecturally important buildings. The well-travelled Sir Stamford Raffles (1781–1826), who established the Singapore colony to help British trade with China, stimulated the founding of the Zoological Society of London (1826, see his collections, in the BM, p. 166). Four years later, Decimus Burton's zoo opened stocked with the Society's live collection of exotic attractions – zebras, monkeys, kangaroos, bears and llamas. Despite women poking their parasols through the bars, huge popularity brought fast expansion with the arrival of the royal menagerie from Windsor (1830) and the royal zoo from the Tower (1832–4, see p. 102) with its Indian elephant and a hundred rattlesnakes. Star arrivals included the giraffes (1836) who encouraged a fashion for giraffe-patterned fabric, a giant ant-eater who gobbled 50 eggs a day (1853) and, top favourites, Jumbo and Alice the African elephants (1867). Since the giant panda arrived in 1938, cuddly toy versions have sold non-stop, encouraged by the arrival of a second panda, Chi-Chi, in 1958 (the Zoo even has a shop selling soft toy animals). As a major world centre for research, the Zoo has a string of world firsts in its history – reptile house (1843), aquarium (1853), insect house (1881).

There have been disasters, too. When the lioness died after a fall, her lion died of sorrow (1840); when the reptile keeper tried to charm a cobra, it bit him and he died (1843); when the holiday crowds left one day, Alice the elephant's trunk was a foot shorter as one visitor had chopped off a memento (1867); and when the Second World War broke out, some dangerous animals went to Ireland, but the unlucky snakes were decapitated and the edible fish cooked and eaten for dinner.

As for the buildings this century, Belcher and Joass designed the surreal mountains of the Mappin Terraces for the agile bears and goats (1913); Joass rebuilt the aquarium (1924) and Lubetkin and Tecton designed the spiral-ramped Penguin Pool (1936) – as one architectural historian observed, 'the first Modern Movement buildings experimented on animals'. Today, more than 8,000 animals squeeze into 36 acres, with a country outpost at Whipsnade Park in the Chiltern Hills near Luton (information from the Zoo). And current projects include a new coral reef aquarium for the fish and a Canadian tundra arctic wilderness for the bears and goats.

To get the best out of the Zoo, it is worth going to the main entrance first to check on feeding times and collect a map. Then, treats to seek out include the gymnast gibbons, the Asian and African elephants, the Sumatran tiger, the disguised chameleon, the rare green turtle coming up for air, carp being fed their lunch of maggots, the dazzling scarlet ibis and the Moonlight World where day and night are reversed so that nocturnal animals can be spotted by day visitors. And you may bump into the elephant wandering around before his daily summer workout of being weighed and enjoying a bath in the paddock at 3pm. (Regent's Park, NW1, tel 722 3333; open daily 10am–dusk, 6pm in summer; charge. Friends society, animal sponsor/adoption schemes – the Zoo receives no public money, good shop, Teddy Bear soft toy shop, restaurant and café. Regular feeding times include: pelicans and penguins, afternoons; cows being milked in the Children's Zoo, 3pm; sea-lions, Sat–Thurs afternoons; snakes, Fri afternoons.)

Leaving the Zoo by the main entrance, a stroll through the areas north-west of the Park can bring you back to follow the prettiest length of the canal to Little Venice. (Alternatively, boats leave Zoo Pier for Camden at 35 minutes past the hour and Little Venice at 15 minutes past the hour, see London Waterbus Company, p. 183 above.)

Walking westwards along the north side of the Park, the next footbridge over the canal on the right leads across Prince Albert Road and up onto **Primrose Hill**. This 62-acre, grassy and primrose-less mound, a favourite spot for summer kite-flying and winter tobogganing, was owned by Eton College until 1841 when they gave it to the Crown in exchange for some royal land near the school in Windsor. From the summit (209 ft), the **view** is magnificent, right over Nash's great work across the whole of Central London from St Paul's dome round to the Houses of Parliament spires – worth the climb. Behind here is Primrose Hill village, new home of the literary set (Jonathan Miller, Alan Bennett, VS Pritchett, etc) who have abandoned Bloomsbury for pretty Regency and Victorian homes with gaily painted facades and rose-filled gardens. On a sunny morning, the noise of their tapping typewriters through open windows competes with the lions' roars wafting up the hill. One local media woman recalls she has 'met friends, brought up children and changed husbands and pursued careers on Primrose Hill'.

To glimpse the village centre, leave by the north-east corner and go straight ahead along Regent's Park Road, dropping right down Chalcot Crescent to find Chalcot Square, returning up Sharpleshall Street to turn left along the local high street section of Regent's Park Road.

Back down Primrose Hill and into the Park, the next dip out is two bridges along, where Nash's Macclesfield Bridge (1815) provides a good **view** of the third surviving villa, Decimus Burton's **Grove House** (1822–4). Built for George Bellas Greenough, a cultivated bachelor who gave weekly soirées, the ground floor circular hall was surrounded by rooms, each with views over the four-acre garden to the Park, for billiards, conversation, reading and cases of his fossils and minerals. Burton's cousin later extended it; Sigismunde Goetze added murals illustrating Ovid 1909–39) – and gave the splendid wrought-iron gates to Queen Mary's Rose Garden in Inner Circle; and the Nuffield Foundation worked in it until 1986. It then went on the market for £8 million with the proviso that it must return to residential use, attracted more than 30 serious buyers and was snapped up by the Australian tycoon Robert Holmes à Court.

Over the bridge, **Prince Albert Road** is lined with apartment blocks taking greater or lesser advantage of the Park's views. Dating from 1910 onwards, they are a quick skip through twentieth-century fashions, from the Edwardian, inward-facing Northgate (1910, east end), through Robert Atkinson's balconied Oslo Court (1936), Marshall and Tweedy's round-ended Viceroy Court (1937), the huge balconies of Imperial Court (1965) and Atkinson's Stockleigh Hall (1937) to the new, speculative and characterless King's and Prince Albert courts.

North-west of here lies **St John's Wood**. Here, fields that had belonged to the Knights Templar (see p. 130), then the Knights of St John of Jerusalem (see p. 203, hence its name), were brought by City merchant Henry Samuel Eyre (1732) to become the Eyre estate. With the arrival of the Park and canal, development began in the 1840s and '50s with handsome Italianate and Gothic villas set in leafy gardens, on the model of Nash's Park Village houses but with the added innovation of semi-detached villas, too. For romantic Victorians, it was an airy and rural drop of paradise conveniently close to the city centre. Aristocrats kept their mistresses here – Napoleon III's Elizabeth Anne Howard lived here. Writers, artists and intellectuals flocked to live in 'the Wood' – George Eliot, Edwin Landseer, James Tissot, Lawrence Alma-Tadema. And by the end of the century the fashionable St John's Wood clique of painters were meeting every Saturday to draw together, selling their dramatic, often sentimental, canvases at hugely inflated prices. Many villas still stand, enveloped in that idyllic spirit.

To catch a little of the mood, go straight ahead up Charlbert Street, turning left into St John's Wood Terrace, then right up Ordnance Road, left along Acacia Road, left again down charming St Ann's Terrace and then right along Circus Road to handsome, tree-lined Cavendish Avenue, with secluded Cavendish Close at the bottom. Back out along Wellington Place and into the gardens of Philip Hardwick's **St John's Wood Chapel** (1812). (Those keen to see more villa-filled streets need to forge further along Acacia Road, across into Grove End Road and then right up Abbey Road, past the Beatles's Abbey Road Studios on the left. Left into Hill Road, around Alma Square, up through Nugent Terrace and right back to Abbey Road. Then moving further up it to explore Blenheim Road, Carlton Hill and Clifton Hill, all on the left, ending up at Boundary Road to see the Saatchi Collection of modern art in Max Gordon's building at 98a Boundary Road, NW8 (tel 624 8299, open during exhibition, Fri and Sat, noon–6pm).

Turning right out of the church and crossing the roundabout, Gilbert Bayes's stone relief on the wall, 'Play up, Play up, Play the Game' (1934), announces the veridian lawns of **Lord's Cricket Ground**. It was moved up here by Thomas Lord (died 1832) in 1811 when he sold the grounds further south (opened in 1787) for development into Dorset Square. Further along St John's Wood Road, the WG Grace Memorial Gates lead into this hallowed home of the Marylebone Cricket Club (MCC, founded 1787), cricket pilgrims can visit the **Cricket Memorial Gallery** to see the tiny maroon urn containing the Ashes, the Wisden Trophy, the

185

sparrow killed by Jehangir Khan's ball in 1936, Donald Bradman's sturdy white boots, Patrick Eager's photographs and a host of fascinating memorabilia. Winter tours are excellent for seeing parts closed to the public in the season. (St John's Wood Road, NW8, tel 289 1611; gallery open end Apr–early Sept, Mon–Sat, 10.30am–5pm, donations welcome, good shop; tours including gallery Oct 1–Mar 31, Mon–Fri, 10.30am and 2.30pm by appointment). Finally, Hamilton Terrace, on the right further along St John's Wood Road, was laid out in 1830 as a long, wide terrace of large villas and keeps the spirit of 'the Wood' alive.

Just beyond, Northwick Terrace on the left joins Aberdeen Place where a turn right leads across Edgware Road to pick up the western end of the **Regent's Canal** for a pleasant surprise at the furthest tip of Nash's great plan. For here the water, narrowboats, trees and white stucco villas of Blomfield Road and Maida Avenue (both 1840s) make this the prettiest stretch of the canal. If you arrive by boat, this view comes as a glorious surprise after the 272–yard-long Maida Tunnel. Nicknamed **Little Venice**, the best way to enjoy it is to go for an exploratory stroll punctuated with stops at the local pubs. Blomfield Road leads to the Pool where boats dock and the canal joins the Grand Union Canal. Further along, past Warwick Place (good pub and restaurant) and Clifton Villas (biggest nursery in Central London), a little bridge crosses the canal to GE Street's landmark, **St Mary Magdalene** (1868–78), one of London's best Gothic Revival churches (worth a look). Keen canal towpath walkers can press on westwards, along past the mid-air motorway, then past tall warehouses, then hedgerow flowers to find a good **view** down

into Kensal Green Cemetery (see p. 266) with its obelisks and columns and then a grassy hill on the left whose summit provides spectacular **views** over south London – and a bench to rest on.

Returning along Delamere Terrace, a path leads down onto the wide quay of the Pool, with steps at the end and then a bridge leading round to spick-and-span Rembrandt Gardens on the right. Keen architecture buffs can press on along Maida Avenue and then right down Park Place Villas to seek out J Plaw's beautifully restored **St Mary's** (1788–91) isolated on Paddington Green, with Quinlan Terry's new church hall (1981) beside (tel 262 3787 to see inside both, or apply to the vicarage) and a statue of the actress Sarah Siddons (1755–1831).

To take boats to Camden Lock from here, transport includes the London Waterbus Company; the 1906 narrowboat *Jason* (60 Blomfield Terrace, W9, tel 286 3428, service Easter–Sept, Fri–Mon at 12.30pm and 2.30pm with some trips at 10.30am and 4.30pm, picnic lunches to order).

Nash's design may not have been realised to the letter. He may have encouraged his royal patron to spend at least four times the original estimate; and the buildings may have yielded only a third of their estimated income. But the great Nash sweep from St James's Park up to Regent's Park and its canal was a hugely successful contribution to London. Crabb Robinson wrote of the Park in 1872: 'This enclosure, with the New Street leading to it from Carlton House, will give a sort of glory to the Regent's government, which will be more felt by remote posterity than the victories of Trafalgar and Waterloo.'

Kensington: Royal blessing for a rural suburb

Mapping it out from above: Two good places, both require buying a meal or drink: Royal Roof Restaurant, 10th floor, Royal Garden Hotel, W8 (937 8000; open Mon–Fri for breakfast [7.30–9.30am] and lunch, Mon–Sat for cocktails and dinner); The Roof Garden, 6th floor, 99 Kensington High Street (entrance in Derry Street), W8 (937 7994; open Sun for brunch, Mon–Fri for lunch). However, expansive and free, if flattish, views from the centre of Kensington Gardens.

Starting point: Kensington Palace, access by Underground: Queensway and High Street Kensington.

Good days to explore: Mon–Sat for antique shops in Kensington Church Street and Portobello Road area; Sat for Portobello Road antique market. Kensington Gardens imitates the British seaside on summer weekends. With few museums or interiors, a dry day is essential.

Information: Reference Library, Central Library, Royal Borough of Kensington and Chelsea, Hornton Street, W8 (see below): equipped with good guides, maps and all information on the borough.

Refreshments: see p. 315.

Festivals: Notting Hill Carnival, three days over August Bank Holiday weekend (last weekend in Aug), when the Caribbean community turn Notting Hill into a Caribbean carnival with non-stop steelbands, floats, grand processions, foodstalls and dancing, dancing everywhere; information from Carnival and Arts Committee, 7 Thorpe Close, W10 (960 5266). Contemporary Art Fair, two-day fair held in late June in the 'Peacock House' (see p. 195, below), proceeds to the Richmond Fellowship; information from The Richmond Fellowship; 8 Addison Road, W14.

Local libraries: Central Library, Royal Borough of Kensington and Chelsea, Hornton Street, W8, (937 2542); open Mon, Tues, Thur and Fri, 10am–8pm, Wed 10am–1pm, Sat 10am–5pm; this large borough's main library holds especially good collections on biography, folklore and language, art, history and topography, with a strong local studies collection for Kensington that includes books, photographs, illustrations and pamphlets (for Chelsea history, see p. 227).

Kensington is London's royal suburb. It won its superior status in 1689, the year asthmatic William III became king. He immediately forsook the dank Thameside air of Whitehall Palace and bought Nottingham House which stood with other country mansions up in the clear air near Kensington, a small village one-and-a-half miles west of Hyde Park Corner. Nottingham House was soon Kensington Palace, the queen nabbed a chunk of Hyde Park for the royal roses and the local village was smothered by courtiers' homes.

Three centuries later, the royal suburb thrives. Kensington Palace, known in court circles as 'KP', is home for the Prince of Wales, heir to the throne; Princess Margaret, the Queen's sister; the Duke and Duchess of Gloucester; and Prince and Princess Michael of Kent. In the now public palace gardens, uniformed, no-nonsense nannies push newly born aristocrats in big black prams, pausing in front of the Peter Pan statue for early induction with JM Barrie's fairytale of the boy who never grew up. And in the surrounding streets clusters of spacious, immaculate, white-stuccoed houses are decked out with designer curtains, inherited oil paintings and crested silver. These are the London homes for British families who still follow the royal year – in May the daughters dolly up in fluffy gowns for Cambridge balls; in June every Hon, Lady, Duchess and Viscountess pins on a pricey hat for Ascot races; in July sporty socialites watch tennis at Wimbledon, rowing at Henley and sailing at Cowes, peering through a haze of Pimm's cocktails and gobbling punnets of strawberries and cream. For these families, weekends are spent in The Country, a vaguely defined place that may well mean a landed home in somewhere like Gloucestershire, where the royals also have their country estates.

From its early beginnings just south of the palace, this leafy estate for the privileged spread west until all the land of the great mansions was covered, except part of Holland House grounds. As much as Chelsea, Kensington's bird-filled trees attracted artists and writers – unlike Chelsea, two artists' remarkable homes are open to the public,

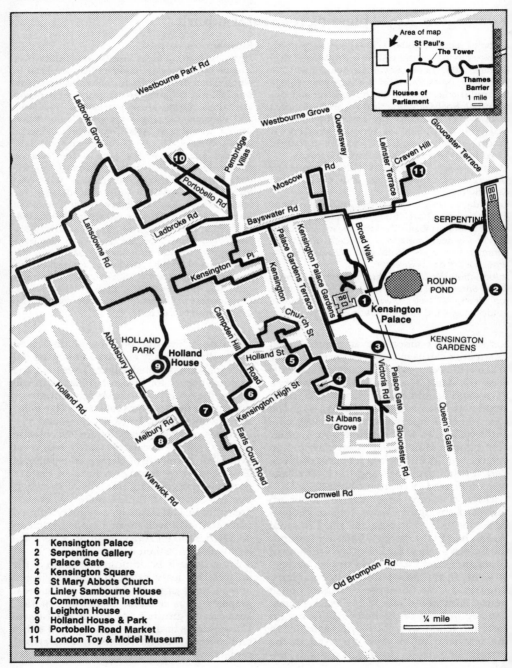

1 Kensington Palace
2 Serpentine Gallery
3 Palace Gate
4 Kensington Square
5 St Mary Abbots Church
6 Linley Sambourne House
7 Commonwealth Institute
8 Leighton House
9 Holland House & Park
10 Portobello Road Market
11 London Toy & Model Museum

¼ mile

Leighton House and Linley Sambourne House. Houses spread up behind the palace to cover Campden Hill, Holland Park and finally the hippodrome on Notting Hill. It is only here, around Portobello Road with its antique markets, writers, left-over hippie drop-outs and lively Caribbean immigrants, that the spick-and-span idyll cracks a little, quickly restored by the western part of Bayswater overlooking the royal gardens.

Free from the formality of St James's and Mayfair, and with space that enabled gener-ous street layouts, the Kensington atmosphere is almost rural, city bricks disguised with sparkling white stucco and enveloped by clouds of mauve wisteria, pink clematis and sweet-smelling honeysuckle. Indeed, much to the fury of the inhabitants – who, like all other Londoners, believe they live at the capital's epicentre – Lady 'Bubbles' Rothermere, arbiter of upper-crust taste, neatly remarked in 1980 that Regine's new up-market nightclub would fail in Kensington because it was 'too far out of London'. It duly failed.

Starting at **Kensington Palace**, this is the spot where Sir George Coppin built his Jacobean mansion (1605). It was perfectly positioned for clean air, country living and London socialising: Holland House, Campden House and other noble homes lay to the west, nursery gardens to the south-west, farms sprawling over the hill to the north-west and the king's Hyde Park to the east with, beyond it, the coffee houses, town mansions and formal Courts of Whitehall (until burnt down in 1698) and St James's Palace. The next owner was Sir Heneage Finch, later Earl of Nottingham, who rebuilt the house (1661) and became one of William III's ministers. When King William and Queen Mary bought it from Finch, they put the royal stamp of approval on an already aristocratic area. Until 1760, this joined the other palaces as one of the official residences of the ruling sovereign, after which a string of royal relatives moved in and out.

The king paid 18,000 guineas for the house but instantly brought in Sir Christopher Wren and Nicholas Hawksmoor to reconstruct and enlarge it (1689–96). King and queen, both keen landscape gardeners, laid out a 26-acre formal Dutch garden. Chivvied by the queen, some hurriedly built walls fell down, were rebuilt and the royal family moved in for Christmas 1689. Building continued, using warm red stone to create an unostentatious, informal and almost cosy home of smallish rooms with big windows, leaving Hampton Court to be the showy palace. When John Evelyn came in 1696, he reported that 'The House is very noble, tho not greate; the Gallerys furnished with all the best Pictures of all the Houses, of Titian, Raphel, Corregio, Holben . . . and others, with a world of Porcelain; a pretty private Library; the Gardens about it very delicious.'

When Queen Anne (1702–14) moved in, she added the Orangery and turned the gardens English. But the Court got little sparkle – Swift reported that the queen would sit at her levées with fan in mouth, muttering a word or two now and then and leaving immediately dinner was announced. Then came the Hanoverians. George I (1714–27) imported an army of German servants to spruce it up and got the Scottish architect Colen Campbell to add the great staircase and state rooms (1718–21) and the English William Kent to decorate them (1722–7). Queen Caroline of Anspach, wife of George II (1727–60), ignored the king's antics with his mistresses and concentrated on the gardens. When it was finally complete, George III (1760–1820) promptly went off to Buckingham Palace (see p. 89) while keeping St James's Palace for official business (see p. 137). The state apartments were abandoned, then opened to the public on Queen Victoria's 70th birthday (1889) and were the temporary home for the London Museum (1950–75, see p. 189).

The palace was the scene of several strange royal deaths. It was here that Queen Mary died of smallpox (1694); her widower William III died after his hunting accident at Hampton Court (1702, see p. 113), and still wearing bracelets of his beloved queen's hair; Queen Anne had a fatal attack of apoplexy after over-eating; and George II died in his water closet, the Hanoverian version of a lavatory.

The palace was also the scene of the most important royal birth and childhood of the next century. When George III's son, the Duke of Kent, moved in, his extravagant alterations by James Wyatt fuelled his debts so much he had to leave the country rather than enjoy the result. But he married and returned here in 1819. And on May 24 his daughter, Victoria, was born here. After her father died, Princess Victoria was brought up by her strict mother and her governess Louise Lehzen. Then, when William IV died on June 20, 1837, the Archbishop of Canterbury and the Lord Chamberlain hurried up to the palace, thumped long on the doors to rouse a porter and were then left waiting in the 5am morning chill while the king's niece was roused from 'such a sweet sleep'. When the 18-year-old princess arrived in white nightgown, shawl and loose-flowing dark hair, they told her she was queen. The next day she held her accession council here; the next night she slept in a separate room from her mother for the first time. Three weeks later she moved to Buckingham Palace on the threshold of a 64-year-old reign during which Britain's political and commercial power reached its zenith. But she did not forget her childhood home. It was Victoria who fully opened the gardens to the public (1841), opened the State Apartments (1889) and whose son fulfilled her wish and made Kensington a Royal Borough (1901).

Today's royal residents fill what is really an up-market apartment block on the west side – the Gloucesters have 35 rooms for their quarters. The royal apartments are grouped around Clock Court and well screened for privacy, so royal spotters may only see their targets as they come and go through their entrance off Kensington Palace Gardens. The public State Apartments are on the east side, overlooking the gardens, their entrance found in the north corner and marked with William and Mary's monogram. Even though all royals are long gone, the furnishings and the smallness of the rooms help retain an atmosphere of royal domesticity absent from all the other London palaces open to the public.

The plain oak staircase leads up to Queen Mary's small bedchamber with an ornate writing-cabinet, followed by William Kent's painted ceiling in Colen Campbell's Privy Chamber (1718–20, sneak a look at Wren's Clock Court through the window) and Kent's Pompeiian ceiling in the Presence Chamber, the first of its kind, later taken up by the Adam brothers. Then comes the King's Grand Staircase, designed by Wren, railings by Tijou, the walls and ceilings by Kent showing a grand Venetian-style view of a crowded gallery, inspired by Versailles and Blenheim (home of Queen Anne's close friend, the Duchess of Marlborough). Courtiers and ambassadors would have glided up

it and into Hawksmoor's King's Gallery (1695–6), the only palatial part of in this unpalatial palace. Here Kent painted the ceiling with scenes from the *Odyssey* (1725–6); William III had a wind-dial built over the fireplace connected to a roof-top weathervane; and the cream of the royal pictures hung on the walls (Rubens, Van Dyck, Ribera and Snijders are there today). Kent's finest ceiling is two rooms on, where his Jupiter and Semele crown the King's Drawing Room.

Finally, the newly restored rooms overlooking the gardens. These were altered (1834–6) for the Duchess of Kent and her daughter Princess Victoria and are now filled with Victoria memorabilia: the bedroom where she was sleeping the night she became queen has the cot used for her children; the magnificent Cupola Room (1722 on, found off the King's Drawing Room) is where she was baptised amid Kent's giant pilasters, proud Roman emperors, gilded gods and goddesses, Greek poets and philosophers and a ceiling painted to resemble coffering surrounding the badge of the Order of the Garter, the highest order of chivalry; and the Council Chamber is where the memorial to her dear Albert's triumphant Great Exhibition (1851, see p. 216) includes such ridiculous extravagances as Garrard's silver centrepiece incorporating the queen's four dogs. Before leaving, to get an idea of the strict and strange formalities of Court dress, the series of tableaux on the ground floor ends with a 1930s scene of ladies and gentlemen dressed up for an evening court reception, for it was only with the Second World War that such formal ceremony was broken and never reinstated (Kensington Palace, Kensington Gardens, W8, tel 937 9561; open Mon–Sat 9am–5pm, Sun 1–5pm; charge. Good shop for royal fans).

Kensington Gardens begins right outside the door. Its character is quite different from Hyde Park's, although the two spaces are adjacent to one another. There are no roads, plenty of planting, some statues and a general air of privacy, mystery and childhood adventure. Perhaps this intimacy comes from the palace it surrounds and its royal owners. George II would take a solitary walk in the gardens each morning and, when he and his Court were off at Richmond, first opened them 'to respectably dressed people' on Saturdays – no soldiers, sailors or servants. Queen Victoria opened them fully (1841). As for its growth, the house William III bought came with 26 acres. Queen Anne anglicised Mary's Dutch gardens, built the Orangery, laid out the Sunken Garden, took a chunk from royal Hyde Park (see p. 150) and built Rotten Row to connect to Hyde Park Corner. Queen Caroline took another, bigger tract of Hyde Park that included Buck Hill on the north side, created the Round Pond and diverted the Westbourne stream to make the Long Water (and the Serpentine in Hyde Park) – she lightened the royal coffers by £20,000 on this and other pet projects. This now makes up the 275-acre park whose official boundary with Hyde Park is not the water but the line that runs from Alexandra Gate over the Rennie brothers' bridge (1826) and straight ahead up Buck Hill Walk to Victoria Gate. Among some of the older trees is a sweet chestnut supposedly planted in 1700 and some of Britain's best hawthorns, Montpelier maples, single-leaved ashes, red oaks and swamp white oaks. (In the 1970s, an epidemic of Dutch Elm disease killed about 500 elms in Kensington and other London parks; and the Big Storm of 1987 uprooted many of the older trees.)

Taking a trip round the Park from the Palace, the Sunken Garden in front of the state apartments on the right is like a secret garden, a tunnel of pleached limes enclosing flowerbeds, pond and benches (all laid out in 1909). Ahead, Hawksmoor's restored Orangery (1704–5), decorated with Grinling Gibbons' carving and classical statuary, is where Queen Anne took tea and held summer supper parties among orange, lemon and myrtle trees (open Apr–Sept, daily 9am–4.30 if no staff shortage). Further ahead, towards the Tea Kiosk, the **view** to the left stretches to the mansions of Kensington Palace Gardens (see below). Turning back, the Broad Walk leads the length of the Park. In the eighteenth century its sustained popularity rivalled that of the Mall in St James's Park (see p. 89), later imagined by Leigh Hunt 'as if the whole recorded polite world were in flower at one and the same period, all the fashion of the gayest times of those sovereigns, blooming with chintzes, full-blown with hoop-petticoats, towering with topknots and toupees' – today, jean-clad skate-boarders and roller-skaters fly down it when park-keepers are not looking. Just by the palace, Queen Victoria's sixth child, Louise (who lived here 1880–1939), sculpted the demure statue of her mother (1893).

Branching off left, the Round Pond is where boys navigate toy sailing boats across the mini-ocean and fly hi-tech kites in summer, and skate and slide across the ice in winter. The obelisk on the left as you cross Lancaster Walk commemorates John Hanning Speke's discovery of the source of the

Nile (1864) and George Frederick Watts's powerful Physical Energy (1904) on the right is a bronze of champing horse and nude. Continuing eastwards, the garden just before the Long Water and coated with springtime crocuses is where the fairytale Peter Pan used to land for his nightly visits. For George Frampton's statue (1912) the children's hero stands playing his pipe on top of a rock where rabbits, squirrels and mice clamber and scuttle about and ethereal fairies float up towards him. The model was perhaps Nina Boucicault, the first actress to play Peter Pan in JM Barrie's play, *Peter Pan: or The Boy Who Would Not Grow Up* (1904); with royal blessing, the whole statue was set up and paid for by the playwright.

Beyond, willows weep over the quiet Long Water, where the shy herons, tawny owls, crested grebes and little grebes have been enticed back into the Park now that the boaters have been banned (identikit water-fowl information by lake). To the left, at the top of the Long Water, Prince Albert contributed to James Pennethorne's design and William Nesfield's planting for the pretty complex of loggia, terracing, fountains and sculpture (especially delightful roundels of the seasons) that make up the Italian Water Gardens (1861). There is a deep well and pump underneath to improve on the Westbourne River's 'little squirts'. Beyond the gardens, more than 200 London pets have memorials in the Dogs' Cemetery by Victoria Gate – dogs, cats and even a monkey – where the first dog was buried in 1880, the last in 1915.

Back down the waterside path and then branching right, Kent's restored Queen Caroline's Temple is on the way to Henry Tanner's tea-room (1908), now the Serpentine Gallery housing the Arts Council's twentieth-century art shows whose sculptures often spill into the surrounding parkland (Kensington Gardens, W2, tel 402 6075; open during exhibitions Apr–Oct, Mon–Fri, 10am–6pm, Sat and Sun, 10am–7pm, Nov–Mar daily, 10am–dusk; free). From here, a path to the southwest joins the richly planted Flower Walk which leads behind the Albert Memorial (see p. 216) to the Broad Walk (for more on the southern part of the gardens, see p. 216). Turning right and then left across the south front of the palace, the statue of William III (1907) honours the man who instigated the whole project (no more bandstand concerts, but children's puppet shows in the north-west playground, twice daily in Aug; for further information, tel 937 4848).

By the 1760s, when George III left the palace for

good and the gardens were a fashionable rendezvous, **Kensington** village, hugging the southwest corner of the palace, was beginning to expand. And by the middle of the nineteenth century the area was ripe for a magnificent piece of development.

Turning left, a gate in the wall leads out into **Palace Avenue**, where the Archbishop and the Lord Chamberlain arrived with Victoria's great news in 1837. Ahead, **Kensington Palace Green** has the palace's old seventeenth-century barracks on the left and provides a good view back to the west side of the palace and Wren's Clock Court. Across it lies **Kensington Palace Gardens** (1843), a wide, tree-lined avenue one-and-a-half-miles long with gatehouse either end. It was laid out over palace kitchen gardens by James Pennethorne and soon lined with such opulent mansions (mostly built 1844–70) that it was nicknamed Millionaire's Row – since the 1930s the millionaires have mostly been replaced by embassies ranging from Nepal, India and Japan to the five mansions occupied by the USSR. (But newer millionaires can snap up a flat in the converted Victorian barracks, now vacated for Sir Basil Spence's towering eye-sore on Kensington Gore (see p. 213).)

Designed as an exclusive development to attract 'the best sort of occupant', Pennethorne's plan was slow to catch on as prospective customers did not fancy opening the curtains every morning to see the soldiers scrubbing themselves in the open air. But by 1860 the rich were moving in and the *Illustrated London News* predicted that its 'imposing aspect and correct taste throughout' boded well for it 'to become a most aristocratic neighbourhood'.

It is perhaps London's grandest nineteenth-century residential street. To catch some highlights, turn right up past the seven Edwardian houses (nos 4–10 Palace Green, 1903–12) built to fund Edward VII's Windsor gardens. Then seek out no. 15 (1854–5) built for James Knowles, a self-made lace manufacturer whose meteoric career began in a Soho Square draper's shop; CJ Richardson's no. 13 (1851–4), built for the Earl of Harrington in his favourite Gothic style which he later used on his South Kensington land; and James Murray's no. 12a (1863–5) next door.

Grisell and Peto built four houses here in 1845–6: no. 12 which still has its 1860s addition of a glittering Moorish billiards room; no. 20 opposite, which changed hands for £5 million in 1986; and nos 18 and 19 next door. Back down past Palace Green,

two huge houses stand at **Palace Gate**: Frederick Hering's no. 2 Palace Green (1860–2) designed for William Makepeace Thackeray (1811–63) who incorporated his London life from days at Charterhouse school (see p. 202) to years living in Kensington into his many novels that include *Vanity Fair* (1847–8), *Henry Esmond* (1852) and *The Newcomes* (1853–5), some written in nearby Young Street (see below); and Philip Webb's no. 1 (1867–70) for George Howard who filled the interior with work by Webb, Burne-Jones, Walter Crane and other Arts and Crafts artists.

Turning left into Kensington High Street, Richard Seifert's Royal Garden Hotel (opened 1965) chops into the skyline atrociously, but provides good **views** from the Royal Roof Restaurant (see Refreshment information, above). On the right, JJ Stevenson's Flemish **Kensington Court** (1883) smothered in cake-decoration terracotta belied the novelties contained inside: hydraulic lifts in the houses, man-sized subways beneath the roads for servicing gas and water and, totally new, the whole seven-acre estate was lit by electricity supplied by a local generating station in the back garden of no. 48, home of scientist and electrical pioneer REB Crompton. It was built over the extravagant house of fraudulent financier Alfred Grant, who demolished two fine mansions and evicted 1200 poor tenants to Notting Hill in order to squander £300,000 on a house with marble staircase, cupid-painted ceilings and central heating, surrounded by gardens with orangery, bowling green and a lake for canoeing. Built in 1872, it was up for sale five years later when he went bankrupt.

Further along the high street, John Inderwick laid out Kensington New Town (1837–55), a network of charming streets built over the fields south of the park in the late Regency style but whose names honour the young queen and her husband. A walk round it begins by turning right down **Victoria Road**, originally the rural Love Lane footpath, then right along Cambridge Place and left along the footpath to find Albert Place. Crossing Victoria Road, Canning Passage leads down to Canning Place (1846), well worth a glimpse before going on to the local village centre and looking left down equally pretty Victoria Grove. On the right, Launceston Place leads down to the two arches of Kynance Mews. Half-way along the right hand section, steps on the right lead up through the garden of Christ Church and back into Victoria Road where the third turning on the left, St Alban's Grove, leads along to South End and then right up

Ansell Street and left along Thackeray Street into Kensington Square and old Kensington.

Thomas Young's **Kensington Square** (1681), set in the fields south of the village, took off the moment William III moved himself and the Court to Kensington Palace. The handsome houses – each one quite different – surround the leafy square and were mostly built in the eighteenth century. They have since attracted a steady flow of eminent occupiers, first courtiers and nobles, then artists and writers when the Court departed. Sir Richard Blackmore, the king's physician, moved into the south-west corner; Richard Steele, essayist and founding editor of *The Spectator*, was already here in 1708. Moving round it, the Jacobean nos 11–12 are the oldest unaltered houses (built 1693–1702); Hubert Parry, who composed *Jerusalem*, gave music lessons to Vaughan Williams while he lived at no. 17 (1886–1918); while Thomas Carlyle was guest of philosopher John Stuart Mill at no. 18, his manuscript of *The French Revolution* was used by a maid to light the fire and he had to write his history again; and Pre-Raphaelite painter Edward Burne-Jones lived at no. 41 (1865–7) where his Persian carpet was a present from 'Topsy', the unlikely nickname for Arts and Crafts pioneer William Morris. Leaving by Young Street (1729), also built by Thomas Young, who was an apprentice to Wren and became the foreman carpenter to William III, no. 16 (1816) is where Thackeray lived (1846–53) while he wrote *Vanity Fair*, *Pendennis* and *Henry Esmond*, whose terrific successes provided the funds for his mansion over the road in Palace Gate.

Turning left, **Kensington High Street** rose to shopping prominence as the fields gave way to bricks and then the Underground station arrived (1868). In 1870, young John Barker opened his drapery shop and did for Kensington what Mr Harrod did for Knightsbridge, ending with a huge department store that was selling three million yards of linen in the first six months of 1920 and 100,000 dresses in the first three. Next door, Charles Derry and brother-in-law Joseph Toms built up their 'Toy and Fancy Repository' (opened 1854) into a similar success, supplying fashionable furs from Siberia and providing an open lift up to the top-floor restaurant where once a week an Indian chef in full eastern dress concocted curries. In 1921, Derry and Toms sold out to Barkers. And in the 1930s, Bernard George, who lived in Thackeray's Young Street house, was employed to give both stores a facelift, a jolly Art Deco facade for

Barkers (1937–8), now the headquarters of Lord Rothermere's Daily Mail Group of newspapers (see p. 129), and a total rebuild for Derry and Toms (1933). Soon the roof gardens were laid out (1938), equipped with fountains, palm trees and high-living pink flamingoes and are still a magical oasis above London on a sunny day (see Refreshments, p. 315).

Across the road, old Kensington village clustered around **St Mary Abbots** church (1869–72), founded by the Abbots of Abingdon in the twelfth century, rebuilt (1696) to be suitable for William and Mary's worship (the palace had no chapel), then rebuilt by George Gilbert Scott, supposedly to match 'the opulence and importance of this great Metropolitan parish' but dismissed by the discerning Jones and Woodwood as 'dull'. Kensington Church Street rises to its right, originally the country lane from this village to Notting Hill with a tollgate half way up, today lined with more than 40 antique shops spilling down the hill from Portobello Road market at the top.

To seek out the early Kensington expansion, find the tiny, peaceful garden hiding behind the church and then go up Kensington Church Walk and into Holland Street where Queen Anne houses still have their panelling and powder closets. To the left, Gordon Place, home for the royal coachmen, runs as a picturesque cul-de-sac southwards and rises northwards to Pitt Street where, turning right and round the corner, the cottages of Duke's Lane are a surprising survival. Left into Kensington Church Street and then left again, Campden Grove is just below where Campden House (1612) stood, one of the country mansions that attracted the king to the area. Built by Sir Baptist Hicks, later Viscount Campden, and surrounded by a good-sized estate, this is where Charles II spent a merry fortnight celebrating his restoration to the throne (1660), where the future Queen Anne lived (1691–6) and where the 3rd Earl of Burlington spent his childhood before going on to build Burlington House (see p. 142). Turning left down more of Gordon Place and right along Pitt Street, named after Stephen Pitt who inherited the Campden estate (1751, still partly owned by his descendants), Sir Basil Spence's Central Library (opened 1977) is down Hornton Street.

Cutting right along the top of it, **Campden Hill Road** (1860s) sweeps up to the right where, on the bend, South Lodge at no. 80 is the survivor of a dozen country villas built for gentlemen to enjoy the wholesome hillside air – this one belonged to

Sir James South before it became the literary salon of novelists Ford Madox Ford and Violet Hunt at the turn of the century, meeting place for HG Wells, Arnold Bennett, Joseph Conrad and Henry James. WJ Loftie also came up here and in 1888 joined other Londoners with his ecstatic praise for Victorian bricks and Kensington growth: 'To me there does not exist in the world any scenery more impressive than the view from the summit of Campden Hill. The sea of houses surging up over all the hills round about, the innumberable chimneys, the endless streets . . . Such a scene is a marvel of earth . . . there is no city now in existence worthy to be even compared with London.'

South, a founder member of the Royal Astronomical Society, also lived nearby in New Campden House where he erected what was believed to be the largest telescope in the world in his garden (1831), commemorated by the name of Observatory Gardens. The house (1762) was built for Robert Phillimore, owner of the slopes down to Kensington High Street. His son William was early on the building scene, starting with Phillimore Place (1780s) and helped by the family agent Charles Chesterton, grandfather of the writer GK Chesterton and founder of the estate agents thriving in Kensington today, Chesterton & Co. The compact estate, built up gradually and appealing to retired officers, barristers and tradesmen rather than the nobility, contains something special in this area of private homes: public access to an interior.

Returning down Campden Hill Road, then right along Upper Phillimore Gardens, Argyll Road on the left runs down past Phillimore Place and Essex Villas to the last street to be built, **Stafford Terrace** (1868–74). Here, **Linley Sambourne House** is where the young artist (1844–1910) moved into his newly built house and, while creating cartoons for *Punch* magazine, filled it to bursting with heavy High Victorian draperies, chiming clocks, a fountain, pictures layered up dark-patterned William Morris wallpapers, shelves of china kissing the ceiling and windows brightened with coloured and engraved glass, all lovingly tended and virtually unchanged for three generations. This extraordinary survival of a complete late Victorian town house is now run by the conservation group The Victorian Society which was founded here in 1958 (18 Stafford Terrace, W8; charge; open Mar–Oct and Wed 10am–4pm and Sun 2–5pm or, for groups, by arrangement with The Victorian Society, 1 Priory Gardens, W4, tel 994 1019).

Along Stafford Terrace and down Phillimore Gardens to the high street, Matthew and Johnson-Marshall's **Commonwealth Institute** (1962) is on the right, after the grand gates of Holland Park (see below). Founded in 1887 to celebrate Victoria's Golden Jubilee and promote knowledge of her empire, multi-coloured flags of the member countries of the old British Empire, re-formed into the Commonwealth, fly outside. Using materials from Commonwealth countries for the building – eg Zambian copper for the hyperboloid roof – it is a pool of lively international activities related to the Commonwealth countries and focused around 50 permanent exhibitions (Kensington High Street, W8, tel 603 4535; open Mon–Sat, 10am–5.30pm, Sun, 2–5pm, plus some evenings; free. Temporary exhibitions, theatre/cinema, workshops, festivals, library, bookshop, restaurant).

Across the road, there is another glimpse of early Kensington: the Edwardes estate. When the 4th Earl of Holland died (1721), the young William Edwardes inherited a large tract of west Kensington (see below). He later sold off the northern part to Henry Fox (1768) and was created Baron Kensington (1776). Next, the 2nd Baron Kensington, inspired by William Phillimore's instant success with Phillimore Place, began laying out a terrace, square and surrounding streets over the hedges and fields beside the tollgate into Kensington from the west, naming them after places on his wife's estates in Pembrokeshire.

To reach the heart of it, cut down Earl's Court Road, glancing into Pembroke Place and Pembroke Mews. Then, turning right through Pembroke Square and left down Pembroke Villas (with pretty Pembroke Mews running down left), a right turn along Pembroke Road and another right leads into Pembroke Gardens. At the bottom, it turns left where pretty Pembroke Studios is on the right. A few yards back, then left, is **Edwardes Square** (1811–9). Contrary to popular myth, it was not built for officers of Napoleon's army – a rumour put about by the pro-Napoleon habitués of nearby Holland House. Rather, Louis Leon Changeur, a Frenchman living in Hammersmith, leased land from 2nd Baron Kensington, built tall, grand Earls Terrace facing the high street and then this modest, small-scale square behind. Its peacefulness and propriety, especially with the later addition of garden and Tuscan garden-house (1820), attracted lawyers, wine merchants and a steady flow of writers including Leigh Hunt (1840–51) and GK Chesterton (1901). The whole square was governed by a strict set of rules: the Trustees had to provide lamp-posts, lodges and watchmen and throw out offensive residents; while each resident had to clean the path in front of his house by 9am, never beat carpets outside the house, never exercise a horse in the garden and never let pigs roam free, all on pain of a hefty fine or hard labour for up to three months.

Leaving the square and turning right to pass Earls Terrace, **Holland Park** is the leafy residential area stretching northwards and surrounding Holland House and its spacious park. Crossing the street into **Melbury Road**, this little corner, south of Holland House, became an enclave for successful artists at the end of last century, a place where the rich indulged their most exotic dreams.

Again, there is one extraordinary interior to see: **Leighton House**, found on the left in Holland Park Road. This was the home of Frederick Lord Leighton (1830–96), who was born in Scarborough, roamed Europe, and had his painting 'Cimabue's Madonna' exhibited at the Royal Academy and bought by Queen Victoria when he was 25 years old (1855). His reputation made, he became a fashionable painter and was later President of the Royal Academy (1878–96). His friend George Aitchison designed the sizable Italianate house (1864–6) with just one bedroom – the owner did not want guests. The outside is plain; the inside deliciously rich. Leighton had the rooms decorated red with ebonised wood and gilding to show off his paintings (Burne-Jones, Millais, etc.), porcelain and furniture, a fine setting for Charles Halle and Pauline Viardot's performances at his musical soirées. The centrepiece is one of the most exotic rooms in London: the Arab Hall, created by Aitchison as an architectural showcase for Leighton's flower-patterned, lagoon blue and green tiles collected during his eastern travels (1852–77), with tinkling fountain and Walter Crane's gilt mosaic frieze to enhance the Arabian Nights mood – best seen from above as well as ground level. Leighton's studio and art palace was the first full expression of the Aesthetic Movement in England and still sustains the atmosphere of a private man passionately devoted to art (12 Holland Park Road, W14, tel 602 3316; Mon–Fri 11am–5pm but 6pm during exhibitions, Sat 11am–5pm; free. Temporary exhibitions, lectures, concerts, Friends Society, large garden).

Leighton's artistic and art-loving neighbours began next door, where painter Val Princep had a Gothic studio designed by Philip Webb (architect

of George Howard's dream in Palace Gate, see above). Back on Melbury Road, Tower House (1876–81) at no. 29 on the right at the corner was as personal as Leighton House, a Gothic dream realised by William Burges (1827–81) for himself, with thematically decorated rooms that culminated in his bedroom where the artist could lie in bed under the sea, the ceiling's twinkling night sky above, the chimney-piece topped with mermaids and walls busy with swimming fish. Next door, painter Luke Fildes lived in a Norman Shaw house, no. 31. Round the corner and on the left, Marcus Stone, illustrator of Dickens, lived at another Shaw house, no. 8 (1875–6).

More locals included sculptor Sir William Thorneycroft at no. 2, George Frederick Watts at no. 6 where he sculpted Physical Energy (in Kensington Gardens), and Pre-Raphaelite painter William Holman Hunt at no. 18. For the keen, there is one more remarkable house, found by going to the end of this road and then right to Halsey Ricardo's Arts and Crafts house for shop-owner Sir Ernest Debenham, so glittering with William de Morgan tiles inside and outside that it is known as the Peacock House (8 Addison Road, W14, now home of the Richmond Fellowship, tel 603 6373; visits by appointment, donations welcome; see also Festivals, above).

Opposite Marcus Stone's house in Melbury Road, Abbotsbury Road leads to **Holland House** and **Park** on the right. Its rich history began when Aubry de Vere was rewarded for his loyalty to William I during the Conquest with a large manor. De Vere descendants became Earls of Oxford. The manor was sold off to Walter Cope, soon to become Sir Walter, Chancellor of the Exchequer to James I. He built Cope Castle (1606–7), later known as Holland House. Its remains constitute the only E-plan Jacobean manor left in Central London. Sir Henry Rich, Cope's son-in-law, inherited and was later created 1st Earl of Holland. When the 4th Earl died, William Edwardes inherited (1721) and let off the great house and some land to Henry Fox (1746). Fox did well. In 1763, he was created 1st Baron Holland and in 1768 he bought Holland House with the fortune he had made by sneakily speculating with public funds while he was Paymaster General. But six years later his one-year-old grandson inherited as the 3rd Baron.

Much influenced by the political thoughts of his uncle Charles James Fox as he grew up, the 3rd Baron and his witty wife made Holland House the glittering, social centre of Whig politics and literature, a more influential court than the Hanoverian one. Here Sheridan, Melbourne, Palmerston and Macaulay mixed with Byron, Wordsworth, Scott and Dickens. As for their keen support of Napoleon, they even sent him jars of plum jam in Elba. The 4th Baron inherited in 1840, converted the stables into a garden ballroom and connected the nearby orangery to the house with terraces and arcades. His widow maintained her lavish entertaining by selling two chunks of park, one to the north (1886, developed as Holland Park estate) and one to the west (1873). And the show went on when Lord Ilchester inherited (1886) and made the house and gardens hum with dancing and gallivanting.

The house was bombed during the war. Afterwards, the dreamlike private garden went public (1950). This is what you see today: Holland House is the best sited and best designed student hostel in town; its facade is the backdrop for the annual outdoor Court Theatre (July–Aug); the Orangery has art exhibitions; the nearby Ice House holds smaller exhibitions (all information from the Central Library, tel 937 2542). The Garden Ballroom is the chic Belvedere Restaurant (tel 602 1238). Surrounding them are the three formal gardens: Rose, Dutch (springtime tulips and Eric Gill's statue) and Iris (with fountain), with nearby café beneath two magnificent horse chestnut trees (open daily, 10am–dusk or later during theatre season).

Then the 54-acre park, with summer cricket to the south and wooded walks to the north (May-blossoming horse chestnuts above mature rhododendrons and perfumed azaleas) enlivened by screeching peacocks, ornamental birds, a mini-zoo (despite bloodthirsty local dogs) and the Rose Walk which ends with a statue of Henry Fox with spats and stick, sitting beneath a copper beech. Intensely romantic and much less manicured than the royal parks, these richly wooded, rural slopes give an idea of what first attracted the nobility to Kensington. But writer and local Rachel Billington feels it is almost too loved and has lost its 1960s 'air of surprise . . . Now if you are a late-delivering writer you will meet your publisher or an out of work actor his bank manager, or a lover his wife' (tel 602 2226; open daily 8am–dusk. For park progress, see the Friends of Holland Park notices – 'wisteria out at last; 8 new ducklings on the pond today').

Moving up through the woods and out of North Gate, **Holland Park** (1866) is the confusing name for the estate of 87 immensely grand houses with elaborate ironwork and suitably wide steps for aristocratic arrivals. It was built by William and Francis Redford as two parallel streets with a mews running between. To see it, turn left down part one, then right past the mews and part two.

Across Holland Park Avenue lies north Kensington. Whereas neatly tended nursery gardens were kept in southern Kensington, this was an area of farms until the early nineteenth century when the combination of the post-Waterloo peace, an expanding middle class and the attraction of healthy air (the local gravel pits were supposed to give off beneficial fumes) led to the London-wide building boom taking force here, too. Two remarkable schemes went up: the Norland estate in Notting Dale and the Ladbroke estate sprawling up the hill, divided from each other by less savoury potteries and piggeries. Inspired by Nash's Regent's Park work (see p. 180) and Cubitt's Belgravia (see p. 238) and unconstrained by space, their generous layout around tree-filled gardens makes an introductory trot well worth the effort.

Over the road and slightly left, royal clockmaker Benjamin Lewis Vulliamy sold his 50-acre Norlands Farm and House to Charles Richardson (1839) who employed Robert Cantwell to lay out a small-scale Belgravia-style estate dotted with spacious, semi-detached villas (1843–68). The centre is **Norland Square** (1848), with the sort of ground floor bow windows usually reserved for the English sea-side. Through it and left, Queensdale Road leads into the wide, tree-lined Addison Avenue (1845–8), then right and right again into grand Royal Crescent (1843–8) with bold cylindrical corner turrets. In the middle, the less severe, red-brick St Ann's Villas leads to St James's Gardens (1847–68) on the right where the houses surround St James's Church (1845), the focus for Addison Avenue. It was designed by Lewis Vulliamy, the son of Benjamin who seems to have had a hand in the whole estate's layout, too.

Up Penzance Street and left into **Princedale Road**, this was the area for potteries, piggeries and brickworks. From the 1820s to '60s, potteries for tiles, flower pots and drainpipes stood beside a colony of pig-keepers, while bricks had been manufactured where St James's Gardens stands. One kiln survives in the wall of a Princedale Road furniture depository. Turning left and along Penzance Place past Pottery Lane (where John Bentley decorated the St Francis of Assisi Church, 1859–63, built for the poor Irish Catholics here – colourful, worth a look), **Clarendon Cross** has a cluster of surviving 1850s shops that served the estate, including the stucco jars advertising an oil man's shop on the corner of Portland Road. Down Hippodrome Mews to Walmer Road, the remains of another kiln are on the right.

Back and up Clarendon Cross, the hill rising ahead is where James Weller Ladbroke bought his large **Notting Hill** farm. His ambitious plan (1823) included a mile-long circular road. He kicked off with drainage and a few houses down here. Work was slow, so he let off 200 acres to Mr John Whyte (1837) who built the Hippodrome racecourse but managed to include a public footpath so the riff-raff could mingle with the gentry, and clay soil that was hopeless for the horses. It closed in 1842. Ladbroke then employed James Thomson and later Thomas Allom to embark upon a modified plan but still one for a utopian 'Garden City' with villas set in their own gardens and opening onto large communal gardens. The eastern part was laid out by WK Jenkings who came from Hereford – hence the Denbigh, Pembridge and Chepstow street names. Work began in 1844, changed to more conventional (and more lucrative) tightly built terraces after Ladbroke's death (1850), and was complete by 1870. Nevertheless, as architect and resident Ian Grant observes: 'The remarkable sense of breadth in this whole quarter, complemented by the general high standard of architectural design, singles it out from any comparable contemporary development.'

To get an idea of its grandeur, follow Lansdowne Rise left into James Thomson's Lansdowne Road which sweeps round to **Ladbroke Grove** and good downhill **views**. Turning right and then left along Ladbroke Gardens, Allom's hilltop Stanley Crescent (with his grand Stanley Gardens and Kensington Park Gardens off it) returns to Ladbroke Grove opposite St John's church (1845) with its landmark spire. To the right, Walter Gropius and Maxwell Fry's brick, steel and tile flats (c.1933). To the left, **views** down the other side of the hill look towards Holland Park – there is a story that Ladbroke built nos. 42–4 for himself, topping them with a central tower. Turning left through **Ladbroke Square** (past remarkable gardens) and left again into Kensington Park Road, the Ladbroke coat of arms adorns the square's garden gates on the left.

Down the hill and right into Chepstow Villas, **Portobello Road** leads off left and right, originally a farm track leading downhill to Porto Bello Farm, which honoured Admiral Vernon's capture of the Caribbean city of Puerto Bello (1739). Gypsies were trading horses and herbs here by the 1870s; stalls

had moved in by the 1890s for Saturday night markets lit by flaming naphtha lamps, and the antique dealers arrived in force when the large Caledonian Market at King's Cross closed in 1948 (later to reopen south of the river as Bermondsey Market). Today it is one of the longest British street markets, selling almost everything imaginable. There are records, a Portuguese patisserie and contemporary art galleries around Golborne Road and Oxford Gardens way down at the bottom of the hill and under the motorway; then the oriental carpets, haberdashery and food from there up to Westbourne Park Road; and finally the jolly bric-à-brac and serious antiques sold up at the southern end. Moving uphill between the double rows of Saturday stalls and shops, keen eyes really can pick up a bargain model car, coin or piece of Coalport (Mon–Sat but liveliest on Sat; the bottom end is the centre of the Notting Hill Carnival, see Festivals above).

Back into the quieter Ladbroke streets at the top of the market, pretty Pembridge Crescent and Pembridge Square are a few yards along to the left down Pembridge Road. Back up Pembridge Road and then right along Ladbroke Road past the Ladbroke Square mewses, Ladbroke Terrace on the left leads back to Holland Park Avenue. Here, at no. 21, lived Robert Cantwell, who designed the Norland estate.

Across from here, the scale changes radically, back to the older, tight-knit lanes and streets at the top of Campden Hill. Past Campden Hill Place, **Campden Hill Square** (1826–50) was laid out by JF Hanson who modelled it on his Regency Square in Brighton and moved into no. 2 while the rest was developed piecemeal over the next 20 years. At Christmas, the windows of its large, rambling family houses, homes for newspaper editors, playwrights and pop stars, are lit with rows of candles. At the top, **Aubrey Road** on the right has good **views** down over the Ladbroke estate and, turning left, Aubrey House (1698, remodelled 1745–66), originally built over a medicinal spring and now the only surviving Kensington country mansion. Along past the converted coach-houses in Aubrey Walk and right up Campden Hill Road, the Windsor Castle pub (1835) at no. 114 retains its local village character and was named because, it was optimistically claimed, on a clear day the view west stretched to Windsor Castle. Peel Street (1824) runs down to the left, more a lane than a street, with a cut through Peel Yard to go on down Campden Street. Then, left up Kensington Church Street past another dose of antique dealers, a left turn leads through the old Notting Hill lanes of Edge Street, across Kensington Place into Hillgate Street, right down Hillgate Place and left along Farmer Street.

Finally, a touch of palace-hugging grandeur. Turning right along Notting Hill Gate and past Palace Gardens Terrace (1860), dressed up as an avenue of pink almond blossom in springtime, the top of Kensington Palace Gardens (see above) is worth a look before glimpsing the west part of **Bayswater** crossing the road for the Edward Orme story. Orme, a Bond Street print-seller, is said to have sold two ship-loads of Notting Hill gravel to Tsar Alexander I in 1814 and bought a chunk of land with the proceeds. Certainly, a thoroughly royal and Russian-looking eagle fronts his estate. **Orme Square** (1818), overlooking the park, was where Roland Hill lived at no. 1 (1839–42) while setting up the penny post (see p. 67) and where Lord Leighton lived at no. 2 (1859–66) before building Leighton House (see above), both found at the far end. Beyond, Orme Court leads round into Orme Lane and then down gratefully named St Petersburgh Mews to **Moscow Road** where, on the left, the Byzantine revival Greek Orthodox **Cathedral of St Sophia** (1877–82) designed by John Oldrid Scott (Sir George's second son) is hung with staring-eyed, golden icons and tended by church fathers who trot across the road in full regalia to take their post-Mass coffee in Maison Bouqillon (Moscow Road, W2, tel 229 7260/4643).

Back on **Bayswater Road** which skirts the Park, an alternative Royal Academy exhibition is staged every Sunday: from early morning, the railings are hung from top to bottom with an extraordinary assortment of amateur and professional efforts, from gaudy to dull, sentimental to slick, animal portraits to endless London views – with the occasional surprise. Overlooking it all, Park-view grandeur is maintained at the top of Porchester Terrace, where JC Loudon's double villa is at nos. 3–5 (1823–6), its see-and-be-seen conservatory in front disguising the fact that the villa is divided in two. Just beyond, nos 23–4 **Leinster Terrace** (1858) appear to be just two more terraced houses; but they are merely facades hiding the unsightly railway tracks of the Underground (this stretch opened 1863).

Finally, at the bottom of the terrace and right into **Craven Hill**, the **London Toy and Model Museum** fills two Victorian houses and their gardens. Two passionate toy collectors, the Levys, founded it. He collects trains while she, a member of the Thai royal family, inherited a fine collection of dolls and made one of her own of teddy bears. These and much more fill the house, including the spectacular Bay West City (too exciting to reveal the surprise here), the miniature French town centre and a late Victorian nursery, while bigger trains puff-puff their way round the garden, thoroughly grown-up men tinker with engines in the back shed and family Thai cooks bake cakes in the living room-turned-café (23 Craven Hill, W2, tel 262 7905/9450; open Tues–Sat 10am–5.30pm, Sun 11am–5pm. Train rides, good shop, café). From here it is a short stroll down to Kensington Gardens for sunset by the Long Water, enjoying the fresh air and lush landscape that enticed William and Mary to move in and give their royal blessing to this still semi-rural idyll.

Clerkenwell to Canonbury: Uphill to fresh air, water and fun

Mapping it out from above: The hilltop fields that once gave splendid views down on the City have all been built up, sadly leaving no great vantage point.

Starting point: Smithfield Market, access by Underground: Barbican.

Good days to explore: To see Smithfield meat market in full swing, Mon–Fri (best 5–8am, but continues until midday); for Camden Passage antique market, Wed and Sat; to visit Charterhouse, Weds in Apr–July.

Information: Clerkenwell Heritage Centre, see p. 4.

Refreshment suggestions: see p. 316.

Local festivals: Clerkenwell Festival, 10 days in mid-July: concerts, exhibitions and events in the many old buildings, plus street entertainment; information from Festival Organiser, The Festival Centre, Old Sessions House, Clerkenwell Green, EC1, 354 7127. The Procession of Our Lady of Mount Carmel (Sun after July 16); Italian Catholic celebration with religious tableaux, triumphal arches, flower garlands and flags, then a street fete; information from St Peter's Church, 4 Back Hill, EC1, (837 1528).

Local Library: For the southern part of Islington borough (Clerkenwell, etc), Finsbury Library, 245 St John Street, EC1, (609 3051); open Mon, Tues and Thurs, 9am–8pm, Wed and Fri, 9am–1pm, Sat, 9am–5pm. For central Islington, Central Library, Fieldway Corner, off Holloway Road, N5 (609 3051); open Mon–Fri, 9am–8pm, Sat, 9am–5pm; the good local history collection usually open 10am–noon and 2–4pm but phone first.

Outside the walls of the tightly packed medieval City, open fields sprawled over the hills to the north. Here was fresh air after the dank Thameside atmosphere, hillside springs with clean – even medicinal – waters and open countryside with fine views down over the metropolis.

The monks took to this land first, moving onto the lower slopes of Clerkenwell and around the Smithfield execution site and livestock market of Smithfield, hard by the City walls. But it was when the royal favourites moved in after the Dissolution of the Monasteries that the area became socially acceptable. The hero of North London's transformation was Hugh Myddelton, a Welsh-born goldsmith who sank his fortune into a project to bring fresh water to the City from Hertfordshire along a man-made channel, opened with a flourish of trumpets in 1613.

By the end of the century, Londoners were flocking out to the hills' fashionable spas to drink and wallow in the health-giving waters and to while away the hours flirting, playing skittles, listening to concerts and taking tea in honeysuckle bowers. The Great Fire (1666) and then London's rapid growth pushed more people outside the walls. Development followed. Overloaded narrow boats glided through Islington on Nash's Regent's Canal on their way from the Grand Union Canal to the Thames docks. The Clerkenwell distilleries began transforming the sweet waters into wicked gin, mother's ruin. The live cattle market was ousted from crowded Smithfield to spacious Islington. And a patchwork of elegant squares and terraces covered the fields from Finsbury up through Islington and Barnsbury to Canonbury.

These houses were much too far away from the courtiers' Mayfair playground to become high society's smart addresses. But, hovering above the City, the Inns of court and Bloomsbury, they attracted merchants, lawyers and writers. Then, after a century as a forgotten and down-at-heel London backwater, regentrification began with a vengeance in the 1970s and much the same mix of people have moved back in – even craftsmen to Clerkenwell. A stroll through the streets around Smithfield meat market, medieval Clerkenwell and up through the merchants' hillside homes built over the spas and fields tells a story of northern expansion from the City that was quieter and less grand than westward growth, and still preserves much of that spirit.

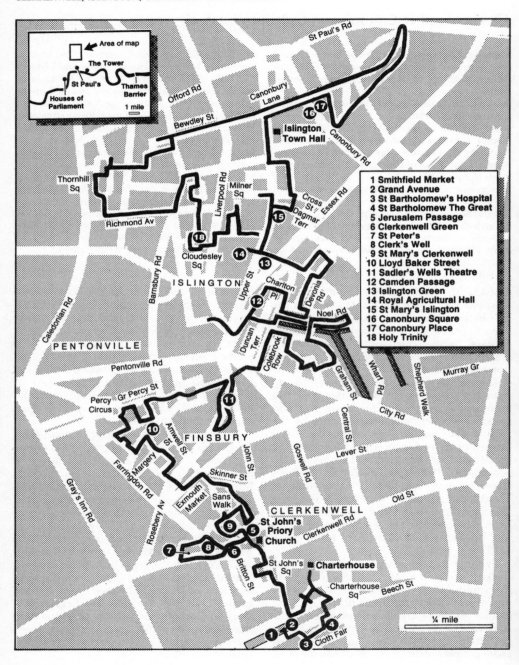

1 Smithfield Market
2 Grand Avenue
3 St Bartholomew's Hospital
4 St Bartholomew The Great
5 Jerusalem Passage
6 Clerkenwell Green
7 St Peter's
8 Clerk's Well
9 St Mary's Clerkenwell
10 Lloyd Baker Street
11 Sadler's Wells Theatre
12 Camden Passage
13 Islington Green
14 Royal Agricultural Hall
15 St Mary's Islington
16 Canonbury Square
17 Canonbury Place
18 Holy Trinity

Starting out as early as bearable, **Smithfield Meat Market** (1851–66) is the only large fresh food market left in Central London – Covent Garden vegetable market has flown to the South Bank and Billingsgate fish market has gone east to Docklands. Smithfield began as a Friday horse market (twelfth century) on the smooth field – hence Smithfield – outside the north-west walls of the City. Sheep, cattle and oxen were added before it became the official cattle market (1638). As London expanded, cows and humans competed for space. The drunken herdsmen brawled, the cows mooed and the young drovers raced their cattle through the muddy, blood-soaked streets with shrieks and thundering hooves while pious congregations attended Sunday service. Dickens describes it in *Oliver Twist*: 'The ground was covered, nearly ankle-deep, with filth and mire; and thick steam perpetually rising from the reeking bodies of the cattle . . . the unwashed, unshaven, squalid and dirty figures constantly running to and fro.'

Cleaning up the area began in 1855, when live cows were sold in the Islington suburbs (see below) and only carcasses were for sale at Smithfield, known as the 'Dead Meat Market'. Horace Jones, the City Architect of Billingsgate and Leadenhall (see p. 73 for both) markets, designed the new market: a grand avenue with four huge trading halls topped by a roof with domed corner turrets. Underground railway linked it to the newly built mainline stations for speedy transport of the meat throughout Britain, and in 1876 the refrigeration revolution began when the first frozen meat shipment arrived from America. Today, the massive container lorries arrive throughout the night. Thousands of bloody carcasses are unloaded and hung up on iron hooks the long length of the blue-painted iron arcades. Under the harsh electric light, it makes an eerie scene. Trading is liveliest from 5 to 8am, when the bummarees (as the porters are known) discard their blood-stained white coats, stamp the sawdust from their feet and adjourn to the Fox and Anchor pub for sausages, a steak and a pint of bitter. Best views from Grand Avenue; well worth a visit, if your stomach can take it, especially as it is threatened with closure.

Between the market and the City, there is a drop of old Smithfield to seek out. Facing south out of Grand Avenue, this was the 'grassy space' where Edward III held a sumptuous royal tournament for the king of France (1357) and another lasting a week to honour his mistress. A few years later, it is also where the Peasants' Revolt (1381), led from Kent by Wat Tyler, confronted Richard II and Mayor William Walworth after they had ransacked the City. While terms were being negotiated, Walworth stabbed and killed Tyler (The Fishmongers' Hall claims to hold the dagger, see p. 62), leaving the 14-year-old king to calm the rebels. Smithfield was also an alternative to Tower Hill for executions until the gallows were moved to Tyburn (see p. 151). Even then, countless witches and heretics continued to be burned, roasted or boiled alive, with the usual religious U-turns – Catholics set alight in cages under Henry VIII, Protestant martyrs burned under Mary.

The backdrop to these happenings was **St Bartholomew's Hospital** straight ahead and **St Bartholomew's Priory** to the left, one of four monastic foundations near here. Both were founded by Henry I's court jester-turned-Augustinian canon, Rahere, in 1123. Having caught malaria while on a pilgrimage to Rome, he was cured, had a vision of the saint and vowed to build a hospital in thanks when he returned home. The king gave the land, and London got its first hospital. When Wat Tyler was stabbed, the gentle Augustinian nuns tended his wound until the king's men dragged him out and chopped off his head. After the Dissolution, the hospital went secular and was later run by Elizabeth I's physician, Dr Rodrigo Lopez (1568), who was then hanged at Tyburn for trying to poison her (1594). Today, after much rebuilding by James Gibbs (1730–59) and Philip Hardwick (1834), it is worth visiting to seek out the statue (1702) of Henry VIII over the gatehouse; the Gibbs court with trees and fountain; the hospital church of St Bartholomew-the-Less (fifteenth-century tower, 1823 octagonal nave) where Inigo Jones was baptised; and the grand Baroque Great Hall and the staircase up to it, decorated with two huge murals by William Hogarth, a hospital governor (West Smithfield, EC1, tel 600 9000; to join a tour, meet at the main hospital gate at 2pm on Sun; contributions welcome).

Rahere's priory church of **St Bartholomew-the-Great** (1123, restored 1880–90) is found to the right on leaving the hospital, through a great stone arch (thirteenth century) topped by a restored, half-timbered Tudor gatehouse (1559). This arch led into the church's original west end, so the path to the present west door runs the length of the destroyed ten-bay nave (the cloisters were on the right) and into Rahere's part: the choir, ambulatory and (rebuilt) Lady Chapel. These now constitute London's oldest church, its only surviving twelfth-century monastic church and the best piece of surviving, large-scale Norman building. It is a glimpse of just how magnificent the dozen or so London monastic churches were. Inside, the powerful, circular piers and blank, honey-grey stone walls set off the minimal decoration. Rahere's tomb (1405, he was buried here in 1143) is to the left of the high altar. William Bolton's window (1515) is to the right, good for peeking at the progress of Rahere's tomb offerings and carved with a visual pun on his name, a crossbow and cask (bolt and tun); and the restored Lady Chapel is where Sir Richard Rich, who bought the dissolved monastery off Henry VIII and tore down the nave, lived before it later became a printer's office where Benjamin Franklin worked (1725) (tel 606 5171/ 1575; open daily 8am–4.30pm; bells rung Thurs 6.30–7.30pm (practice) and Sun 5.30–6.30pm; to hear the excellent choir, attend Sun Sung Eucharist 11am or Evensong 6.30pm).

This was not all Rahere did. In 1133, Henry I granted him a charter to hold an annual **Bartholomew Fair**, whose lucrative tolls went to the priory and hospital. Lasting three days, it was soon the biggest cloth fair in England, attracting the big European merchants, too. Over the centuries, fire-eaters, minstrels and theatre booths overtook more serious business until the puritanical City fathers suppressed the fair in 1855. But it is remembered in **Cloth Fair**, the narrow street found by turning right out of the church and then right again. Here nos. 41–2 give a glimpse of pre-Fire, seventeenth-century London, as do the tiny alleys of Cloth Court and Rising Sun Court leading off it. It was here that Inigo Jones was born to his draper father and, more recently, the conservation campaigner and Poet Laureate Sir John Betjeman lived.

Cutting through one of the alleys to emerge in Long Lane, turn right left down Hayne Street. Cobbled **Charterhouse Square** (1700–75) is opposite, complete with its gates to keep out the riff-raff and with two early houses at nos. 4 and 5 (c.1700).

Behind it lies **Charterhouse**, London's only medieval ecclesiastical foundation to preserve its cloister atmosphere. When Henry VIII (1509–47) broke with Rome in 1533 in order to take a second wife, Anne Boleyn, whom he hoped would give him a male heir (she gave him a daughter), he became head of the Church of England. Three years later, he consolidated his new position by embarking on a ruthlessly thorough attack on all religious houses, the Dissolution of the Monasteries. By 1540 some 800 had been closed, their

buildings and lands sold off to the highest bidder or given as cheap rewards to Court favourites. It was a tremendous upheaval that marked the end of medieval London. A whole way of life was wiped out forever. The loss was physical, social and spiritual. The buildings were torn down to be replaced by showy manors, often made in the same stone. Gone were the refuges for the sick, poor and old, the hotels for travellers and the hives of activity for the flourishing social, learned and professional societies whose members' homes were hovels compared to these spacious halls and cloisters. Gone too were the oases of spiritual seclusion and contemplation.

Of the thirteen large monastic houses in and around the City, four were in Smithfield and Clerkenwell: St Bartholomew's Priory (founded 1123), Charterhouse Monastery (founded 1370), St John of Jerusalem's Priory (founded about 1140) and Clerkenwell Nunnery (founded about 1140). Historian Arthur Bryant notes that towards the end of the twelfth century Londoners came out to Smithfield meadow, where 'high-stepping palfreys with gleaming coats were put through their paces and country folk brought their goods and livestock for sale'. People stayed on for 'summer evening walks among the suburban wells – St Clement's, Holywell, Clerkenwell – and the sparkling streams whose mill-wheels made so cheerful a sound'.

Charterhouse was the inspiration of Edward III's brave knight Sir Walter de Manny who first bought the land as a burial ground for victims of the Black Death (1347–50), the epidemic of bubonic plague that ravaged England and killed more than half of London's population. He then established the Carthusian monastery, to pray for the plague victims' souls – their origin was St Bruno's contemplative Order founded near Grenoble at Chartreuse (1084), the word then anglicised to Charterhouse. Sir Walter employed royal master mason Henry Yevele (see p. 79) to build the cells for the solitary monks and brought the water supply down wooden pipes from the hill now covered by Barnsbury (see below).

After the Dissolution, when nine monks were chained upright until they died of starvation, Sir Edward North was the first of several noble Tudor owners, none of whom tore down the cloisters. Royal links were maintained by Elizabeth's stay on the way to her coronation (1558) and James I's on his arrival in London (1603). It was Thomas Sutton, rumoured to be the richest man in England, who paid £13,000 for the buildings in 1611 to establish a school for 44 poor boys and home for 80 poor gentlemen. Past pupils of the school (which moved to Surrey in 1872) include John Wesley, Joseph Addison, Robert Baden-Powell and William Thackeray who writes about it in *The Newcomes*. The Charterhouse pensioners still live around the peaceful cloisters (much restored after war bombs) found through the stone arch beneath the Master's residence (1716). (To visit inside and outside, join the weekly guided tours Apr–July on Wed at 2.30pm, meeting inside the main archway. Otherwise, apply in writing to The Master, Charterhouse, Charterhouse Square, EC1.)

Returning out of the arch and turning right, a lane on the right leads out of the square and past tiny Charterhouse Mews. At the end, Charterhouse Street skirts the meat market and a turn right leads into **St John Street**, the old highway northwards, once lined with butchers, cowkeepers and more than 20 taverns. St John's Lane on the left rises to **Clerkenwell**. Straight ahead is Prior Docwra's **St John's Gate** (1504, restored 1903) which, with the chancel and crypt of the Priory Church, are the surviving scraps of the **Priory of St John of Jerusalem**. It is best seen from the other side. So, turning left along Briset Street, named after the Norman knight Jordan de Briset who founded the priory, and right up Britton Street (1719), built for wealthy City merchants, St John's Passage hiding on the right leads to **St John's Square**.

Now you are right inside the former priory. To the left, across Clerkenwell Road, lies the priory church; to the right the gate. This was the English headquarters of the Knights Hospitaller, a Military Order which set up hospices (houses of refuge) to give food and shelter to pilgrims going to Jerusalem and who later ruled Rhodes and then Malta, from 1522. When Wat Tyler and the peasants destroyed the whole priory (1381), Prior Docwra's palatial new buildings (1501–27) had a church that was 'the glory of North West London', gardens, orchard, fish pond, houses, courtyards and, of course, a counting house. After the Dissolution, the gate housed Edward Cave's *Gentleman's Magazine* (1731–81) on which Samuel Johnson worked so regularly that he had his own room here. It was also a parish watch house and the Old Jerusalem Tavern before the Order was refounded in a Church of England form (1831). The Order then founded St John Ambulance (1877) who teach first aid, run an eye hospital in Jerusalem and, most

obvious to Londoners, have uniformed volunteers who attend all major London events from every theatre show to football matches and royal parades, on hand to provide first aid. The Queen is head of the Order; the Duke of Gloucester the Chief Prior.

To explore the hall (1903, housing huge Maltese medicine jars) and West Tower (1504) and see the library, medals, manuscripts and silver, visit the Museum of the Order of St John found through the arch and on the left (St John's Gate, St John's Lane, EC1, tel 253 6644; open Tues and Fri 10am–6pm, Sat 10am–4pm; donation box). Across Clerkenwell Road, the circular nave of the original priory church is marked on the paving outside. Inside, the cool dark crypt (1140) has later delicate stained glass, a charming wall memorial to Sir Herbert Perrott, an alabaster effigy of Don Juan Ruiz de Vergara (died 1575), Proctor of Castile, and the tomb sculpture of thin William Weston, the last English prior before the Dissolution (to visit, join a tour from the museum on Tues, Fri and Sat, 11am and 2.30pm; or take the Clerkenwell tour from the Heritage Centre in St John's Square, daily at 2.30pm).

As well as a spiritual refuge, Clerkenwell's closeness to the City made it a practical refuge for craftsmen fleeing the fierce City guild restrictions. Printers, clock and watch-makers, jewellers and goldsmiths settled here – Smith & Co, next to the church, was founded in 1780. Today the craftsmen are returning. Here in St John Square, artists' studios fill the Victorian model dwellings of Penny Bank Chambers (1879), with more in Cornwall House on Clerkenwell Green. Part of a charitable foundation, about 80 craftsmen, ranging from jewellers and polishers to ceramics restorers, bookbinders and clock repairers, work in the two buildings (directory of craftsmen available from Penny Bank Chambers, Clerkenwell Road, EC1, tel 251 0276).

Leaving the square on the north side through **Jerusalam Passage**, Thomas Britton (1664–1714) lived in the corner house at the top, a self-taught coal-dealer who became a chemist and an antiquarian book collector (Sir John Soane bought volumes off him) and held musical evenings attended by Handel. Turning left, **Aylesbury Street** is named after the Tudor family who acquired part of the dissolved priory, built a fine mansion, used the choir as their private chapel and the crypt for storing their wine.

It leads down into **Clerkenwell Green**, the old

village centre with not a blade of grass but with Thomas Rogers's restored Sessions House (1779–82) still the focus at the bottom (worth a look) – as Clerkenwell absorbed some of the less glamorous City overspill: outposts for Newgate and Bridewell prisons were built here. Last century, the green was a rallying point for political radicals, the ancestor of Hyde Park (see p. 150). Their meeting house was no. 37 on the right. The Chartists and the Home Rulers met here; John Stuart Mill's London Patriotic Club was founded here (1872), whose Socialist demonstration from here to Trafalgar Square (1887) led to two deaths and the nickname Bloody Sunday; William Morris set up Britain's first socialist press here (1890s); and Lenin studied here and edited *Iskra* (*The Spark*), the original Bolshevik newspaper which he then smuggled into Russia (1902–3). It is now the Marx Memorial Library housing both books and the banner designed by William Morris. As a first stop for all Communists visiting London, Mikhail Gorbachov came directly from the airport on his arrival in Britain in 1984 (tel 253 1485; open Mon and Fri 2–6pm, Tues–Thurs 2–8.45pm, some Sats 11am–12.45pm). Across the Green, on the corner of Britten Street, Piers Gough has designed the multi-coloured private house with the blue-tiled roof, a rare new building for Clerkenwell.

Those keen to catch a vestige of the old Italian quarter should now nip down right past Café St Pierre, across Farringdon Road, up Ray Street and left down Back Hill to find **St Peter's** church (1863, to visit tel 837 1528). This was the centre of nineteenth-century Little Italy when a surge of street entertainers, food vendors (mostly ice-cream and chestnuts) and craftsmen increased the London Italian population to around 10,000. Here women in headscarves sat knitting in the alleys and ice-cream vendors sang Italian folk songs. Politician Giuseppe Mazzini and patron of British clown Joseph Grimaldi lived nearby (Grimaldi's first stage appearance was at Sadler's Wells); Garibaldi visited; Caruso and Gigli sang at Mass. Today, the church draws the dispersed Italians for marriages, funerals and Sunday Mass (with post-church visits to Gazzano's and Terroni's delicatessens) and the annual Procession of Our Lady of Mount Carmel (see festivals, above).

Coming down Clerkenwell Road, there is a good **view** of the City and, in the foreground across Farringdon Road, of Booth's gin distillery. This was one of several set up in the mid-eighteenth century to take advantage of the good water sup-

ply, with the Government's full blessing as it provided an outlet for the over-production of cereals (Gordon's and Nicholson's distilled here, too). It was these that helped lead to 'an orgy of spirit-drinking' in London, especially among the poor, when fiery, raw spirit or cheaper, potent cordials flavoured with aniseed or juniper berries were sold in almost every shop, children were given daily doses and adults sat tippling in the corner grocery.

Back across Farringdon Road, where keen-eyed collectors seek out lost treasures in the Wednesday and Saturday morning stalls of old books and newspapers, the **Clerks' Well** is over the railway bridge and on the left (door to it between nos 14 and 16 Farringdon Road; window exhibition about it next door; Clerkenwell walk includes a visit; otherwise apply to Finsbury Reference Library, tel 609 3051). One of many 'excellent suburban springs, with sweet, wholesome and clear water that flows rippling over the bright stones' (Fitzstephen, 1174), this was where the City's Parish Clerks staged annual mystery plays – the Skinners' Company did the same thing at Skinners' Well nearby. The well marked the western border of wealthy **St Mary's Nunnery** whose church, found back up the Green and to the left, was saved at the Dissolution by being rededicated to St James to serve the growing parish. Rebuilt (1788–92) by local architect James Carr (1742–1821), there is a good **view** of its Gibbs-inspired tower and spire from the Green; and inside the vestibule has grand benefaction boards, George England's organ is one of London's finest and ladies' modesty boards up the staircase keep their ankles hidden from prying parishioners (tel 253 1568; usually locked; to visit, join Clerkenwell walk or attend a service or concert). Like St John's Priory, the nunnery was founded by Jordan de Briset, and remains of the cloisters are traceable in the churchyard.

From the church, **Clerkenwell Close** leads round to the right, once lined with Tudor nobles' mansions set in lush gardens. Passing the Horseshoe pub, whose large garret windows suggest it was built as a watchmaker's or jeweller's home, more of today's Clerkenwell craftsmen work in the 160 units of the old school Supplies Depot, their skills ranging from millinery to precision metalwork (to find out more about a specific craft or to commission a piece, apply in writing to the Workshop Manager, 31 Clerkenwell Close, EC1, tel 251 4821). Ahead, the alley leads past St James's parish boundary bollards and along Sans

Walk to the charming, newly restored Sekforde Estate. Thomas Sekforde, an Elizabethan lawyer, retired here to his Clerkenwell mansion in 1581, bequeathing the estate revenues to the almshouses he founded in Woodbridge, Suffolk. The almshouse governors later improved the income by building over the estate (1767) and then in the 1820s laying out a triangle of modest residential streets with especially attractive doorcases and other details. To the right, **Sekforde Street** turns left past Hayward's Place cottages (1834) and left again up **Woodbridge Street**.

Skinner Street leads ahead past a pocket of modern London to a welcome patch of green on the left which marks the site of Clerkenwell's most famous resort, the London Spa. Opened around 1730 when a medieval well was rediscovered, it was soon a favourite excursion. Londoners flocked to cure every conceivable ailment with the waters while rope-dancers, singers and fireworks entertained them and local ale quenched their thirst. Just beyond, **Exmouth Market** is where Grimaldi lived at no. 8 (1822–9), where John Sedding designed the appropriately Italianate Church of the Holy Redeemer (1887) and where shoppers, exhausted by the chirpy, cheeky stallholders of the daily street market, can buy a pint of cockles or mussels from the long-established seafood stall at the bottom end.

Turning right here and crossing Rosebery Avenue, a hike through the half-dozen **Finsbury** squares that sprawled over the steep hill during the last century leads back round to Sadler's Wells at the top of Rosebery Avenue. First is **Wilmington Square**, whose northern exit runs up to Margery Street, the site of Merlin's Cave, one of several spas that dotted the open land.

Across the road, Fernsbury Street cuts through to **Lloyd Baker Street** which runs the length of the Lloyd Baker estate, from Amwell Street down to King's Cross Road. Originally owned by the Knights Hospitallers, it was inherited by the great-granddaughter of Bishop Lloyd who then married the Reverend William Baker. The clergyman and his son Thomas developed the fields from 1819, employing John and William Joseph Booth, also a father-and-son team, to design the houses. It is a modest development of great individual character, with none of the pretensions of Bloomsbury at the bottom of the hill. However, the professionals and businessmen who moved in were soon distressed by the arrival of trains and new roads and moved away to more leafy suburbs, leaving good-sized houses to be let as lodgings until the 1970s and '80s gentrification began.

Turning left down Lloyd Baker Street, then right through **Granville Square**, Wharton Street leads up the hill and right along Prideaux Place to the remains of **Percy Circus** – just below here, Bagnigge Wells was a favourite spa, opened in 1758 and highly fashionable for the rest of the century, boasting organ, distorting mirror, water temple, honeysuckle arbours for taking tea, a grotto, a bowling green and elaborate gardens with fountains and flower walks. The smart set, rumoured to include Nell Gwynn and her lover Charles II, met to sip water in the morning and stir china cups of tea with gilt spoons in the afternoon, the air filled with the soft tinkles of an orchestra. Up **Great Percy Street** and detouring right along Cumberland Gardens, then left through **Lloyd Square** and left again down Lloyd Street, Great Percy Street leads on up to Amwell Street.

Across the road lies the New River Company estate, whose centrepiece is Chadwell Mylne's handsome **Myddelton Square** (1827) built around his **St Mark's** church (1827) and a large, well-kept public garden. It honours Sir Hugh Myddelton (born 1560), hero of the New River. A wealthy Welsh goldsmith, Myddelton became MP for Denbigh and jeweller to James I. Then, when Edmund Colthurst's scheme to bring clean water to thirsty London from Hertfordshire springs floundered for lack of money, he came to the rescue, keeping Colthurst as a partner. The channel – not a river at all – was cut from the River Lea by the springs of Amwell and Chadwell and run 40 miles on a very gentle gradient that dropped just 18 feet in all, ending by running through Islington village to New River Head – a pond just behind Myddelton Square and well-placed directly above the City of London. This natural duck-pond was enlarged to make a circular basin with a 200-foot diameter. From here, the water was moved into smaller and smaller cisterns and finally sent down around the City in elm tree-trunks hollowed out as pipes.

It was an engineering feat. But with more than 600 men employed, compensation for landowners, time extensions and soaring costs, Myddelton was forced to sell his own property to raise extra cash. Finally, when the City would lend no more, the king provided funds. In 1613, the Hertfordshire sluices were opened and the New River Head filled, watched by Myddelton, the Lord Mayor and Myddelton's brother (the next Lord Mayor), with cannons firing and processions of labourers marching to drums and trumpets as the water flowed in. Myddelton received a knighthood and later a baronetcy for his work. Chadwell Mylne, son of the river's brilliant Scottish surveyor Robert Mylne, answered the demand for houses by covering the rest of the estate with handsome terraces named after the project – Myddelton, Amwell and Chadwell. And, most telling of all, fresh Hertfordshire water flows along the same path into London today.

The site of New River Head is on **Rosebery Avenue**, found by leaving Myddelton Square along Chadwell Street and turning right along Arlington Way and right again. This was the road built 1889–95 to link growing Islington with Bloomsbury and central London, spanning the old River Fleet valley on two tall viaducts. Down beyond Howard Robertson's building for the Metropolitan Water Board (1938), Austen Hall's building (1920) incorporated the fine Oak Room (Grinling Gibbons carved panelling and elaborate plasterwork) of the old Water House and left some of the pond behind (to visit, apply in writing to the Divisional Manager, Thames Water Central Division, New River Head, 173 Rosebery Avenue, EC1).

Back up the Avenue, Lubetkin and Tecton's Le Corbusier-inspired Spa Green Estate (1950) is on the right. It covers the Islington Spa which had won instant credibility and popularity in 1684 when its water was declared to be similar to that at Tunbridge Wells, the great curative Kent spa. For more than a century, a thousand fashionable Londoners hied up here every day to take the waters. In 1732, George II's daughters joined them to wander the lime-walks, to attend the weekly public breakfasts (11am–3pm), and to dance and gamble while the waters supposedly worked miracles on 'Hysterics, Vapours, Dropsies, Swellings of the Legs'. Opposite is **Sadler's Wells**. Here Thomas Sadler built a music-room (1683) beside another medicinal well. The well's waters were forsaken for other spas, but the jugglers and other entertainers worked on. Later, a company was formed (1753), the theatre rebuilt (1765) and Grimaldi and Edmund Kean performed under Tom King's management. Then, having been a skating rink, pickle factory, boxing arena, melodrama hall, scene of aquatic spectacles and music hall, it was again rebuilt with money raised by Lilian Bayliss (1927–31, designed by FGM Chancellor), since when it has lost two ballet companies to Covent Garden

(see p. 123) and an opera company to the Coliseum (see p. 124) – but continues as a theatre, has generated a new opera company and the well is still here, under a trap door at the back of the stalls. Rosebury Avenue, EC1, tel 278 6563; to join a theatre tour, write to the Backstage Tours Manager; charge).

Rosebery Avenue joins St John Street which leads up to the Angel at **Islington**. When Myddelton was cutting his River, this was the first posthouse out of London. Beyond Islington village lay handsome Tudor mansions with orchards and gardens. It was a royal favourite. Here Henry VIII hunted the woods and supposedly stopped off to dally with his mistresses in his several houses; Elizabeth I visited Sir John Spencer at Canonbury House and (perhaps) Sir Walter Raleigh in Upper Street; and James I stopped on his way down from Scotland to claim the English throne.

Before the Tudors, the Anglo-Saxons called this forested hill Gislandune (Gisla's Hill) – hence Islington. It then became part of Middlesex Forest and was owned by the canons of St Paul's who sold off Barnsbury and Canonbury manors to Ralph de Berners and the more northern manors of Highbury and Tolentone to the Knights of St John. After the Tudors, 'merry Islington' became famous for its dairy farms and its pure spring waters, so much so that it rivalled Clerkenwell as an eighteenth-century fun resort of taverns and tea-houses – already in 1667, Pepys was nipping up here after Sunday church: 'So church done, we to coach and away to Kingsland and Islington and there eat and drink.' Well out of the City, it served as a refuge from the recurrent plagues, the Great Fire and religious persecution – but several Protestants were discovered when Catholic Mary was reigning and became the Islington Martyrs, burnt at the stake in Smithfield. Well up amid fresh air and fertile soil, it became a place for educating young aristocrats and growing the City's vegetables, as well as providing pasture for cattle.

But the nineteenth-century building boom and the arrival of the Regent's Canal and the live cattle market redesigned the landscape. The village tentacles spread out as fields were coated with attractive brick terraces only to lose their appeal totally at the turn of the century, returning to favour since the 1970s. Indeed, many self-appointed know-all Londoners have no clue how to reach this lively hilltop community who live in a network of unspoilt Georgian and Victorian terraces surrounding the inner hub of antique market, fringe theatres and the newly restored Agricultural

Hall, still known as the Aggie. A wander through the Islington terraces around the New River and Canal, the old village centre, Canonbury's leafy lanes and lastly Barnsbury's spacious squares provides an introduction.

To avoid the thunderous Angel traffic intersection, cut right along Owen Street, following the New River path, and then cross Goswell and City roads where the green-painted clock advertises Smith's clock component makers seen back in Clerkenwell (see p. 203). **Duncan Terrace** lies ahead on the left with, confusingly, **Colebrooke Row** on the right, both built gradually between 1768 and 1841 – nos 1–6 this end went up in 1799–1803. Here the City stockbrokers' and merchants' handsome homes bordered the New River, now replaced by public gardens after the water pipes were put underground. Half way along, on the right, Nash's Regent's Canal (see p. 183) emerges from the 970-yard-long Islington Tunnel (1812–20), on its way to the Thames docks. Its arrival stimulated a pretty little estate of low-built houses, best explored by threading down it through Vincent Terrace, right into Quick Street, left down Elia Street past Sudeley Street and Nelson Terrace and on down Nelson Place, Remington Street and Coombs Street to Graham Street where the whacky Fallen Angel café-pub and café-restaurant is on the corner.

Turning left, Graham Street leads up and over the canal to **Noel Road** whose delightful houses with pointed Gothic windows have gardens overlooking the canal. Down on the right, steps to the canal tow-path are by Wharf Road Bridge or there is direct access out from the Narrow Boat pub. Beyond the lock, City Road Basin is across the canal, home of Islington Boat Club, with Wenlock Basin beyond. For the old river traffic, this was one of three horse-changes between Paddington and Limehouse, so stables surrounded the lock.

Moving back along the tow-path to the tunnel, there are steps back up to Colebrooke Row and ahead through Duncan Street lies bustling **Islington High Street**, the centre of Islington village. From this bottom end the Angel road crossing is to the left and Chapel Market for fruit, vegetables, flowers, fish and general bargains (an arcade of fun costume jewellery) straight ahead, a few yards up Liverpool Road (best Fri–Sun). To the right the narrow high street leads into pedestrianised **Camden Passage**, the whole strip saved from developers' hungry feelers by the residents 25 years ago. Since then, the handsome houses and charming cottages, including tiny Pierrepont Row on the right, have almost all become antique shops for furniture, prints, old games, grandfather clocks, 1920s clothes and brass door furniture, joined on Wednesday and Saturdays by numerous stallholders selling everything from silver teapots to Art Deco earrings and 78rpm records – a tantalising avenue for window-shopping and browsing, pausing for a pint at the Camden Head pub where on quiet days the dealers chat over their latest discoveries, leaving notes in their shop windows for customers wishing to find them (market Wed and Sat; other days the dealers' shops are either open or pin up a note of how to be contacted).

Half way along the Passage, **Charlton Place** (1790) on the right leads down to cut through the grandest part of Duncan Terrace (nos 50–8 were built 1791, nos 46–9 in 1794). Turning left, nos 60–5 were known as Bird's Buildings – Charles Lamb was thrilled to move into no. 64 in 1823, feeling 'like a great lord, never having had a house before'. On the other side, the oldest part of Colebrooke Row (1768, fine door-cases) had the Revd John Rule's Academy for Young Gentlemen at no. 57, his pupils benefiting from the fresh, hilltop air. Moving back past Gerrard Road, nos 20–3 and 24–8 are part of the last addition, Montague Terrace (1841), completing what is still the finest part of residential Islington. But their extension, the small-scale streets laid out over the nursery gardens and dairy north of the Regent's Canal, are worth exploring too.

Turning left down the top part of Noel Road this time (where playwright Joe Orton lived and was murdered at no. 25) then first left and left again up Gerrard Road, Devonia Road on the right runs across pretty St Peter's Street and into Raleigh Street and past **Chantry Street**. Then, turning left up Queen's Head Street and left along **Cruden Street**, a right up St Peter's Street leads to Essex Road and across to the triangular **Islington Green** with shady trees, benches and a fine statue (1862) of our hero, ruffled and bearded Sir Hugh Myddelton, looking down towards London. Collins' Museum Hall faced onto the Green, where owner Sam Collins sang comic songs while men and women swayed and sang along. Audiences – who came to let their hair down after a day at the Aggie Hall (see below) – were later entertained by Charlie Chaplin and Gracie Fields.

The Green marks the meeting of two great highways into London, Upper Street and Essex Road (first called Lower Street). When the City was at last forced to clear out the cattle causing the Smithfield squalor, this was the chosen spot. Frederick Peck's **Royal Agricultural Hall** (1861–2), fondly known as the Aggie, was built on the north side of Upper Street, using 1,000 tons of cast iron to create a vast, 130-foot-span glass-roofed central hall with smaller sidehalls for music and other entertainment. It was an instant and long-lasting success. Far from being restricted to regular cattle shows, the magnificent building was the stage for a splendid Grand Ball for 5,000 guests to honour visiting Belgian Volunteers (1869) and later the site for the World's Fair (1883–1939), started to imitate the suppressed Bartholomew Fair (at Smithfield, see p. 202 above), as well as marathon bicycle races, circuses, the predecessor of the Royal Tournament (1880–1906), Cruft's dog show (1891–1939) and even bull-fighting with Spanish matadors (1870). Its heyday over, it was closed in 1939, almost demolished and opened again in 1987. Restored, painted and sparkling bright, this is the Business Design Centre, the brainchild of Sam Morris who started work as a Billingsgate fish porter. It is the first integrated trade exhibition and permanent market for design in Britain, aimed at both buyers and sellers. The way to see inside the building is to visit the upstairs restaurant, the Designers Club, which overlooks the great hall (all three restaurants and pub are open to the public).

Moving northwards along **Upper Street**, the King's Head on the left is one of London's best-known theatre pubs. For drink, the management have stoically refused to accept decimalised currency and sell pints of bitter for pounds, shillings and pence. For theatre, the audience is fed lunch or supper in the back room where the show is then staged, often with bonus music in the bar afterwards. Just beyond it, in Almeida Street on the left, the Almeida is the newest local theatre-café, avant garde performances in the converted Literary Institute (1937) and wine and food across the courtyard. Back in Upper Street, Launcelot Dowbiggin's **St Mary's** church (1751–4) has kept its pretty old steeple, a landmark which can be seen from the Angel. A path to the left of it leads through the churchyard to **Dagmar Terrace** and another theatre, the Little Angel Marionette Theatre, where the resident company's huge puppets entertain crowds of children (and plenty of rogue adults) on Saturdays (11am and 3pm) and Sundays (3pm). To the left, the Dagmar Passage cottages open into **Cross Street** (begun c.1760) where, down on the right, the terrace up on the high pavement tumbling down the hill was described by Islington connoisseur Mary Cosh as 'among the most handsome single streets' in Islington – at nos 33 and 35, the fashion-conscious merchant owners were quick to imitate the Adam brothers' Adelphi, adding grand new door cases in the 1770s.

Back up Cross Street, then right along Florence Street and on up past the Town Hall in Upper Street, the lanes of **Canonbury** are on the right, a leafy oasis of family houses, walled gardens and general peacefulness far removed from the steamy city.

Slipping down Canonbury Lane to Jacob Leroux's **Canonbury Square** (1800), the handsome houses surrounding the public gardens are where Evelyn Waugh lived in 1928 (no. 17a) and George Orwell in 1945 (no. 27) – even when Islington was at its lowest ebb this century, Canonbury retained a seedy gentility that attracted writers and artists. Straight through the square and into **Canonbury Place**, Canonbury House (c.1780) proudly faces out from the bend, with Canonbury Tower behind, the centre of Canonbury. When Ralph de Berners granted one of his estates to the Canons of St Bartholomew's in Smithfield (1253) – hence Canonbury – Prior Bolton built the tower and mansion (much survives), again marking his efforts with the visual pun on his name: a bolt piercing a cast (tun). After the Dissolution, Henry VIII gave it to his right-hand man, Thomas Cromwell. After he fell from favour a string of nobles lived here including John Spencer (Lord Mayor in 1594) who did more building and whose daughter was lowered in a basket from the Canonbury Tower to elope with the penniless Lord Compton. The family leased it to Sir Francis Bacon (1616–25) while he was Lord Chancellor (see p. 127). But in the next century it went rather down-at-heel, when tenants included Samuel Humphreys (died 1736) who wrote words for Handel's oratorios, Ephraim Chambers (died 1740) who compiled Chambers' Encyclopedia, and Oliver Goldsmith (who lived here 1762–4). The present house was built by John Dawes, a stockbroker who leased both manor and grounds; the Tower is yet another theatre, the Tavistock Repertory Company, where two upper rooms retain their Elizabethan panelling, plaster ceilings and chimneypieces (to visit them, join the tour after the Sat evening show or apply to the manager, Tower Theatre, Canonbury Place, N1, tel 225 5111).

John Dawes also built the handsome, early stucco houses in the cul-de-sac to the right of Canonbury House (good **views** of the house and

Tower from here) – no. 6 has Prior Bolton's visual pun. Behind here, a spacious estate spread around New River (1835–50). A circular trip begins down Alwyne Villas, left along Alwyne Road, left again up Alwyne Place and then right along either sweep of Canonbury Park North or South. At the top, a gate on the right a few yards down St Paul's Road leads into the long narrow New River Park (opened 1954) which runs for half a mile along the course of Myddelton's New River. The river itself was stopped north of here in 1946 and the present waters have quacking ducks, overhanging weeping willows and plenty of waterside benches, bordered by Douglas Road and then Canonbury Grove at the bottom.

Turning right up Canonbury Road, then left back through Canonbury Square to Upper Street, Leroux's grand Compton Terrace (1806) on the right, with garden in front, contrasts sharply with the informal squares of **Barnsbury** lying across the road. Named after Ralph de Berners, who held onto the manor until 1532, these hilltop fields of rich pastures were where White Conduit springhead rose to supply the solitary Carthusian monks down the hill. Beside it, aristocrats formed the White Conduit Club (1752) to play cricket at Thomas Albion Oldfield's tea-house and dairy (now the Albion pub) until they moved to the private lawns of Dorset Square, formed the Marylebone Cricket Club and later to Lord's Cricket Ground (see p. 185). Barnsbury was also a great place for botanical gardens, holiday excursions and dairy farms. But when the trustees of William Tufnell, a minor who inherited the estate, spotted the lucrative building boom in 1822, they quickly parcelled up the land and leased it off. Thirty years later, a network of idiosyncratic squares linked by long terraces and villas covered the fields and London had another suburb.

The young Thomas Cubitt laid out much of it, before going on to make his mark in Bloomsbury (see p. 168) and then triumph in his grand speculations of Belgravia and Pimlico (see pp. 238 and 240). Its bad period under absentee landlords – Arnold Bennett's exploration in a taxi in 1925 provided an exotic sight for the poor residents – preserved it from modernisation; and the recent middle class influx, thick with writers, publishers, lawyers and journalists, has restored whole terraces to their former grandeur.

Straight ahead Islington Park leads to Liverpool Road where, turning left and then right, Barnsbury Park (1830s) is a two-storey terrace pretending to be up-market semi-detached villas. Left into Thornhill Road, **Barnsbury Square** is on the right where a hotch-potch of houses surrounds a pretty, tree-filled square. In its north-west corner hides Mountford Crescent (1837–47), where remarkably grand, stuccoed and bow-fronted villas stand in large gardens; while in the south-west corner Italianate Mountford Terrace is a rogue design more like houses in the then smarter south-west London. Down past it, into Barnsbury Terrace, then left and right, Lofting Road leads down into oval **Thornhill Square** and **Crescent** (1840–52). This is a hippodrome of a square with huge central garden, church and playground. This was the centrepiece of the Thornhill family's 85-acre development. Leaving it at the south end, turn left up grand Richmond Avenue, where William Dennis's Graeco-Egyptian terrace at nos 46–72 (1841–4) with their great doorstep sphinxes and obelisks were thought 'too marvellous' by Arnold Bennett. Turning left at the top along narrow Thornhill Road, the local pub and pretty cottages at the top of Ripplevale Grove create an intimate village atmosphere. But ahead and right down Barnsbury Street and right again into **Lonsdale Square** (1835–43), RC Carpenter's tall, ecclesiastical Gothic houses restore the estate's formality.

Straight through it and along Stonefield Street, two more little developments end the walk. First is the Stonefield Estate (1825), laid out around **Cloudesley Square**, with roads radiating out from it and the young Charles Barry's **Holy Trinity** church (1826–7) in the middle – long before his work at Westminster (see p. 82). Leaving the square to the left and crossing Liverpool Road, Theberton Street leads to **Gibson Square** (1836–9), centrepiece of the Milner-Gibson estate (1829–41) with Raymond Erith and Quinlan Terry's new Victoria Line Ventilation Shaft (1970) heavily disguised in the gardens. To end, the most idiosyncratic of all Islington squares, built on the same estate at the back of Gibson Square. This is **Milner Square** (1841), designed by Gough and Roumieu, whose attempts to jolly-up the plain Georgian house-front format with unbroken skyline frieze and close-set piers left Summerson aghast as if from 'an unhappy dream' and Pevsner citing it as proof positive of the 'disintegration of the classical proportions'. Certainly, it takes everyone by surprise. Returning through Gibson Square, then left to meet Upper Street, there is a good choice of pubs, restaurants and perhaps even a theatre to end the day up on north London's hills.

Knightsbridge and South Kensington: 1851 and all that

Mapping it out from above: Queen's Tower of Imperial College, open July–Oct (see p. 219, below), for the best viewpoint in West London; Level 6 of the Henry Cole Wing of the V&A Museum provides only a glimpse.

Starting point: Albert Gate, just east of the Hyde Park Hotel. Access by Underground: Knightsbridge.

Good days to explore: Rainy ones, when the South Kensington museum village gives shelter and educative entertainment (mostly free) – there are even underground tunnels connecting them and running to South Kensington Underground station; weekdays, when museum-keen Londoners are away at their desks, but BEWARE: the V&A is closed on Friday. Visiting the IBA's Broadcasting Gallery must be booked by letter or telephone. Harrods, with museum status, is marginally less crowded early in the morning and in obscure departments.

Vital equipment: To peer more closely at the smaller, more exquisite museum pieces, a simple magnifying glass.

Information: LTB Information Centre in Harrods, see p. 4. For the four big museums, tel 938 9000.

Refreshment suggestions: see p. 316.

Local festivals: Not much on the streets, but plenty of quiet national and international ones in the museums and always a show, demonstration or star appearance in Harrods (watch the posters at entrances and in stairwells). The Henry Wood Promenade Concerts are held in the Royal Albert Hall (see p. 293).

Local Library; Brompton Library, 210 Old Brompton Road, SW5, tel 373 3111/2; open Mon, Tues and Thurs 10am–8pm, Wed 10am–1pm, Fri and Sat 10am–5pm.

National libraries: The South Kensington museums and colleges each have extensive, richly endowed and specialist libraries which may operate slightly differently from their host bodies; some exhibit their rarer possessions; some have their own publications. Here are a selection (see also text, below):

British Geological Survey (London Base), Geological Museum, Exhibition Road, SW7, tel 938 8765; open Mon–Fri 10am–5pm, no appointment required, ask doormen for a free pass; more than 60,000 volumes, maps, reports, photographs and surveys.

Imperial College of Science and Technology, Impe-

rial College Road, SW7, tel 589 5111; open Mon–Fri 9.30am–9pm, Sat 9.30am–5.30pm; visitors should sign in but need not make appointments; one of the principal science libraries in London, the central catalogue for its 15 department libraries spread over the building is in the Central Library.

National Art Library, V&A, SW7 tel 938 8500; open Tues–Fri 10am–5pm, Sat 10am–1pm and 2–5pm; no appointment required for regular books but a Reader's Ticket is necessary for older or rarer ones, obtained by submitting a letter of recommendation and then completing a form (a temporary Ticket can often be issued on the spot); the museum's department libraries are for scholars' use by appointment.

National Library for the History of Science and Technology, Science Museum, Imperial College Road, SW7 tel 938 8000; open Mon–Sat 10am–5.30pm, no appointment required; sited outside the museum and next to Imperial College's Central Library, and focusing on history rather than current developments.

National Sound Archive Library, 29 Exhibition Road, SW7, tel 589 6603; open Mon–Fri 9.30am–4.30pm, Thurs until 9pm; the reference library of books and catalogues is open daily without appointment for browsing, then tapes can be ordered and an appointment made to return to listen to them.

Natural History Museum, Cromwell Road, SW7, tel 938 9123; open Mon–Fri 10am–4.30pm but skeleton service noon–2pm, no appointment required but best to phone first; the central catalogue for all five libraries is in the General Library (biology), the other four are for zoology, botany, entomology and palaeontology/mineralogy.

Royal College of Music, Prince Consort Road, SW7, tel 589 3643); open Mon–Fri 10am–5.30pm, no appointment required; reference reading for books and manuscripts, and listening room for records and tapes.

Royal Entomological Society, 41 Queen's Gate, SW7, tel 584 8361; (Mon–Fri, 9.30am–5.30pm, telephone appointment preferred); reference library of books and manuscripts.

Royal Geographical Society Map Room, 1 Kensington Gore, SW7, library tel 589 5466; open Mon–Fri 10am–5pm, no appointment necessary but best to phone first.

Victoria & Albert Museum Slide Library, South Kensington, SW7, tel 938 8500; open Mon–Fri

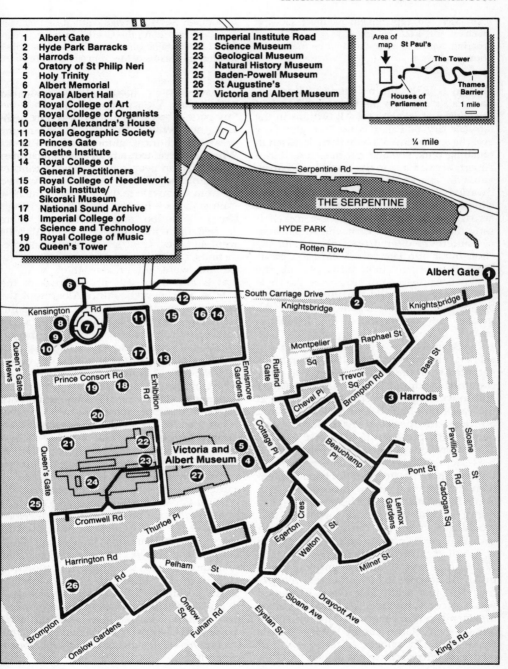

1 Albert Gate
2 Hyde Park Barracks
3 Harrods
4 Oratory of St Philip Neri
5 Holy Trinity
6 Albert Memorial
7 Royal Albert Hall
8 Royal College of Art
9 Royal College of Organists
10 Queen Alexandra's House
11 Royal Geographic Society
12 Princes Gate
13 Goethe Institute
14 Royal College of
   General Practitioners
15 Royal College of Needlework
16 Polish Institute/
   Sikorski Museum
17 National Sound Archive
18 Imperial College of
   Science and Technology
19 Royal College of Music
20 Queen's Tower

21 Imperial Institute Road
22 Science Museum
23 Geological Museum
24 Natural History Museum
25 Baden-Powell Museum
26 St Augustine's
27 Victoria and Albert Museum

Area of map
St Paul's
The Tower
Houses of Parliament
Thames Barrier
1 mile

¼ mile

Serpentine Rd

THE SERPENTINE

HYDE PARK

Rotten Row

Albert Gate

South Carriage Drive
Knightsbridge
Knightsbridge

Kensington Rd

Montpelier Sq
Raphael St
Basil St

Trevor Sq
Cheval Pl
Brompton Rd

Harrods

Prince Consort Rd

Exhibition Rd

Ennismore Gardens

Rutland Gate

Queen's Gate Mews

Beauchamp Pl

Cottage Pl

Sloane Pavilion Rd

Victoria and Albert Museum

Pont St

Cromwell Rd

Queen's Gate

Lennox Gardens

Cadogan Sq

Thurloe Pl

Egerton Cres

Milner St

Harrington Rd

Pelham St

Walton St

Draycott Ave

Sloane Ave

Brompton Rd

Onlow Gardens

Onslow Sq

Fulham Rd

Elystan St

Sloane Ave

King's Rd

10am–5pm, no appointment required; slides of much of the V&A collection to consult before ordering copies or new slides to be made; also photographs.

In addition, several foreign cultural centres blossom here, including the Goethe Institute (see p. 218), L'Institut Français (see p. 222) and the Polish Institute and Sikorsky Museum (see p. 218).

On May 1, 1851, Queen Victoria left Buckingham Palace to open the Great Exhibition of the Works of Industry of All Nations in the fairytale Crystal Palace between Rotten Row and the south side of Hyde Park. Dressed in blushing pink, she and her husband, Prince Albert, arrived inside the enormous, barrel-vaulted, sparkling-glass cathedral which dwarfed the great Hyde Park trees it enclosed. Trumpets sounded, cannon was fired across the Serpentine, a 1,000-voice choir sang the National Anthem, the Archbishop of Canterbury offered up a prayer and the choir burst into Handel's *Hallelujah Chorus*. Then four organs took turns playing the National Anthem continuously as the royal party processed round the 19-acre building before 'Her Majesty again ascended the throne, and pronounced the Exhibition open'.

25,000 spectators whooped with joy and set off to explore the 100,000 exhibits gathered from the British Isles and 40 other countries including Russia, America, China and India. There were squeaks of delight at the vast Koh-i-Nur diamond displayed in a birdcage and the jewel casket loyally decorated with portraits of the Royal Family. There were coos of wonder at the mechanical harvester pulled by a steam engine, the Philadelphian floating Gothic chapel for seamen and the exotic ivory throne given by a South Indian maharajah. There were gasps of horror at the alarm-clock bedstead that would turf its sleeper out into a cold bath instead of gently purring on a bell. And there was excited gabbling as friends met up by the 27-foot-high crystal fountain gurgling in the middle to describe to each other the wonders they had just seen. This Great Exhibition was a success, a grand celebration of mid-nineteenth-century ingenuity and ornamentation – even if the young William Morris wrote off the 'heaviness, tastelessness, and rococo banality of the whole display'.

It was Prince Albert's brain-child. The night before, Victoria noted in her diary that 'my poor Albert is terribly fagged'; the night after, she wrote: 'This day is one of the greatest and most glorious of our lives.' When the Great Exhibition closed on October 15, six million people had visited, a third of the whole population. One woman walked up from Cornwall; many arrived at the new train stations – Euston, Paddington, King's Cross, Waterloo and others; still more crossed from the Continent. And Victoria went 40 times. Contrary to pessimistic predictions, London had not run out of food, the exhibits were not broken, there were no brawls and there was no outbreak of the plague. The energetic Prince Albert took the handsome profits of some £200,000 and immediately sank them into a more permanent showcase 'in which', he hoped, 'by the application of Science and Art to industrial pursuits the Industry of all nations may be raised in the scale of human Employment, and where by the constant interchange of Ideas, Experience and its results each nation may gain and contribute something'.

The idea for the South Kensington culture campus for public learning was born. Until then, Knightsbridge was an undistinguished place to pass by before crossing Brompton and southern Kensington's famous market gardens on the way to courtly Kensington. With the Great Exhibition, all changed. South Kensington went on the map. The developers moved in, the Underground arrived to speed smart residents to St James's and Westminster, and within 25 years the silence and solitude of genteel, semi-rural Brompton was exchanged for fashionable, often showy South Kensington. Meanwhile, the modest Knightsbridge lanes began to be upgraded from working-class cottages into *bijou* residences and Charles Digby Harrod bought out his father's village grocery shop and started expanding.

It was an extraordinary transformation. In a way thoroughly uncharacteristic of London, a museum village was conceived, designed and realised, and the area around it dutifully took off and then became fashionable. From the silk-wrapped, chauffeur-driven hostess who drops into Harrods for her daily frivolity to children gawping at the dinosaurs in Waterhouse's blue-striped

Natural History Museum and crowds singing and swaying at the Last Night of the Proms in the circular Albert Hall, this is no land of dull, puritanical learning. Rather, it is a giant playground for endless discovery and astonishment, punctuated with outdoor strolls around Knightsbridge lanes and South Kensington squares.

Starting at **Albert Gate** (1846), this is where the Westbourne River ran down through the fields of west London known for their highwaymen and their aristocratic duels. There is a legend that two knights once fought on the river bridge, hence Knightsbridge. Certainly, a charter of Edward the Confessor mentions Kynesbrig in the eleventh century. It was still a hamlet when Pepys came picnicking in 1666. Later, the river was dammed to fill the Serpentine and Long Water in the royal parks (1730). And in 1826 the overflow – by now 'a great sewer' – was diverted and the area tidied up for the Belgravia aristocracy and given a gate and Thomas Cubitt's two palaces instead of gatehouses. The one on the left was built for millionaire George Hudson, 'the Napoleon of the railways', who suddenly went bankrupt before he moved in, since when it has been the French embassy.

Moving westwards along **Knightsbridge**, Archer and Green's turrets and balconies were built as a gentlemen's apartments (1888), then transformed into Hyde Park Hotel (1908), strategically placed with public rooms overlooking Hyde Park (good for watching the Household Brigade pass each morning) and an entrance overlooking newly built Belgravia and the junction of the Kensington and South Kensington roads into the West End. Queen Mary visited; Winston Churchill, Valentino and Mahatma Gandhi stayed – a goat was milked for the Mahatma's breakfast; and Princess Elizabeth, later Queen, came for her dancing lessons. Opposite, Richard Seifert's cylindrical Sheraton Park Tower Hotel (1973) rises beside Harvey Nichols, where Benjamin Harvey's local drapery (1813) did so well from passing trade during the Great Exhibition that his daughter merged with the silk buyer Colonel Nichols to form the still thriving department store, now with a roof-terrace restaurant for over-heated spenders. Other well-placed traders were the Gardiner brothers who arrived from Glasgow with their tweeds and tar-

tans (1830) and whose descendants now stock more than 300 tartans at the Scotch House.

To the right of it lies the road to Kensington with, on the right, Sir Basil Spence's **Hyde Park Barracks** (designed 1960, built 1967–70) whose red brick and concrete suddenly shoots up to a 320-foot tall tower, wrecking the Knightsbridge skyline from every corner of Hyde Park and Kensington Gardens – as the Hilton Hotel wrecks the eastern view. Here live the Household Cavalry Brigade of some 500 soldiers and almost 300 horses. Early risers can spot the green-hatted Watering Order exercising the horses in the Park around 7.30am; late risers can watch the red-uniformed Life Guards or the blue-uniformed Blues and Royals trotting along the Park's Rotten Row at 10.30am to Buckingham Palace and on to take up their duty at Horseguards (see p. 52). Nipping into the Park to see the front, the large pediment of the parkside gateway incorporates the carved horses' heads and foliage from TH Wyatt's harmless barracks (1878–9) it replaces.

Opposite, **Knightsbridge Green** is the alley leading down to the few remaining blades of the village green that once filled the angle of the two main roads and until early last century was the scene for the weekly cattle market, the local sinners' stocks and Maytime dancing. West of here, a cluster of small-scale Regency lanes lurks quietly behind the bustle, all hint of past modesty now disguised by pristine paintwork and designer interiors.

Turning right and right again, Lancelot Place leads up and left into **Trevor Square** (1818), built with its surrounding streets by Arthur Trevor Hill, soon fashionable enough to have an attic storey added and conveniently close to the barracks to house officers' mistresses. When the southern part slumped to slum level, Harrods bought it (1913) for their warehouse and garage, building tunnels under Brompton Road to the shop. Up through the square and left across Trevor Place, **Montpelier**

Square and its neighbouring lanes (1825–50) were supplied with plenty of pubs for the modest inhabitants – the King George IV, Nelson, Tea Clipper and Prince of Wales. Turning left through the square into **Montpelier Street**, Bonham's the auctioneers are on the right, founded in 1793 and still a friendly family firm with a sixth-generation Bonham on the staff (Montpelier Street, SW1, tel 584 9161; open Tues–Fri 8.45am–6pm, Mon 8.45am–8pm, Sat 2.30–5pm). Cutting along narrow Montpelier Place and left down Montpelier Walk, Rutland Mews East is on the right. It served Rutland Gate (1838–56), a larger-scale Victorian square found on the right, up a few steps and through an archway. While here, Ennismore Street and Rutland Mews South round to the left, once the stables and coachmen's quarters (spot the grooming posts), are now the Disney-perfect dolls'-house homes of City successes.

Back through the arch, down Rutland Street and left along Cheval Place, there is a splendid **view** westwards to the Oratory's dome hovering over Brompton. Busy **Brompton Road**, at the bottom of Montpelier Street, follows the old country track from Knightsbridge to the medieval Broom Farm hamlet (hence Brompton). By the seventeenth century, the fields were famous for their market gardens, especially Brompton Park Nursery run by royal gardener Henry Wise and others. Wise lived in Brompton Park House from 1698 until his death in 1738, and the 100-acre nursery sprawling in front supplied the great London gardens with flowering trees and scented shrubs, now partly covered by the V&A. Brompton remained firmly rural: in 1820 almost 600 acres were still tilled, and in the 1870s the area was still known for its healthy air, although bricks had by then triumphed over blossoms.

Harrods stands across the road, probably the world's most famous shop. For visitors, it is an established part of the London milk run, with Westminster Abbey and the Tower. For Londoners, there is a love-hate relationship: most claim they hate it but then assure you it is the best place for silk socks, toys, flowers, cheese, pedicures, tea or whatever. Certainly, its 230 departments on five floors spread over 20 acres where 4,000 staff serve 50,000 customers and the daily take is around £700,000 make it the best bazaar this side of Bombay. It is quite possible to live daylight hours entirely in Harrods's mini-city, except on lonely Sundays when it closes. There are six restaurants, five bars, legendary food halls, a lending library,

bank, pet shop, dry cleaners, dog kennels, a huge beauty parlour, antiques and jewels to gawp at, exhibitions, demonstrations, visiting stars signing their books or playing their records, everything from Indian bidi cigarettes to domestic satellite equipment to buy, a ticket agency and departments for christenings, weddings and funerals – everything except somewhere to sleep the night. Power comes from its own electricity generator; water from its three wells. Not content with selling everyone else's goods, Harrods own-make goods fill an in-house shop and Harrods green coaches do London tours. In all, a brave attempt to live up to its motto: *Omnia, omnibus, ubique* – everything, for everyone, everywhere.

Henry Charles Harrod, a tea merchant, founded the institution with a small grocery shop nearby (1849) and was pleased if his weekly takings were £20. After the Great Exhibition made the area pick up, his son Charles Digby Harrod took over (1861), expanded, was soon taking £1000 a week (1867) and then lost the lot in a fire (1883), when he wrote to his customers 'I greatly regret to inform you, that in consequence of the above premises being burnt down, your order will be delayed in the execution a day or two'. Such service drew yet more buyers, and Lillie Langtry, Ellen Terry and Oscar Wilde were early account holders (1885). Richard Burbidge took over and initiated the slogan 'Harrods serves the world' (1894), London's first escalator arrived (1898) and, with more land, Stevens and Munt designed the splendidly proud and domed Edwardian store (1901–5), with WJ Neatby's mosaic friezes and tiles in the Food Halls. Royal patronage followed: Burbidge was made a baron (1916), Princess Anne opened the new Food Halls (1983) and the store holds all four Royal Warrants (see p. 138). Its figures are mind-boggling: £6 million taken on the first sale day in January 1986, and 320 pantechnicon loads of furniture sold on the first two days; 163 brands of whisky stocked in the wine department; and Christmas sales of 18 tons of Stilton, 120 tons of Christmas puddings and 45,000 mince pies. And 40% of everything bought goes abroad, neatly packed into Harrods moss-green bags.

For some, just gazing at the 80 window displays outside or seeing the store illuminated for Christmas by 11,000 bulbs is enough. For those who venture inside, here are a few tips: best times are early morning, when the bazaar crush is less; worst times are pre-Christmas and sales. At all times there are so many people 'entering a different world' and wandering about that it is difficult to get anywhere. Information desks inside most entrances know of the day's activities and should have *The Store Guide* plan of what's where. The new escalators on the Hans Crescent side, complete with waterfall, are the fastest way to move vertically. Harrods Shop, tourist information, ticket agencies and the Georgian Restaurant are on the fourth floor. Worth a visit are the Art Deco men's hairdressing rooms (ground floor, Basil Street entrance), Neatby's tiles in the fish, meat and poultry Food Halls (centre of ground floor), the charcoal granite Perfume Hall and red velvet and white marble Cosmetics Halls (east of the Food Halls, ground floor), the Christmas decorations (third floor) and the Toy Kingdom (fourth floor) (Knightsbridge, SW1, tel 730 1234; open Mon, Tues and Thurs–Sat 9am–6pm, Wed 9.30am–7pm).

The poshest shops that swarm round this honeypot line the road back up to Knightsbridge, down Brompton Arcade to the right and into Sloane Street (see p. 237). Westwards, a short walk round the modest, rural houses of the pre-1851 fashion boom, now the choicest of addresses, ends at the site of the great Crystal Palace. But before setting off, do not miss two Art Nouveau treats in Hans Road: no. 12 by Arthur Mackmurdo (1894) and nos 14–16 by CEA Voysey (1891–2).

Moving down Brompton Road, **Beauchamp Place** serves the locals with chic shops and restaurants for large bank balances. South-west of it, the 70-acre Smith's Charity Estate was founded by Henry Smith (died 1628), a salter who rose from childhood beggary to Alderman of the City and bequeathed his estate as a charity for Christian prisoners of North African pirates. Perhaps the pirates reformed, for a century later no prisoner had claimed funds for years and the trustees put the estate's profits to use in the local parishes, increasing the finances with gradual building 1785–1880s.

Turning left, **Walton Street** (1847) turns into Walton Place (1836 on) beside George Basevi's St Saviour's Church (1839–40), with pretty Pont Street Mews behind – Basevi (1794–1845), cousin of Benjamin Disraeli and brilliant pupil of Sir John Soane (see p. 125), was one of the Charity's main architects (see also his Belgrave Square work, p. 239). Back down Walton Street, tree-filled Ovington Square (1840s) off Charity land is on the right, while the Charity's late addition of oval, redbrick **Lennox Gardens** (1885) is on the left. It was built

over Prince's Club which had been local society's sporting centre and whose lease had expired. By 1872 it had reputedly the finest cricket lawn in England and a smart, 700-long membership list with Lord Cadogan as Chairman – the rumour was that no lady entered its precincts who had not been presented at Court. That year, the Marylebone Cricket Club (MCC) moved in, returning to Lord's in 1876 (see p. 185) although England played Australia here in 1878. On the tennis courts, the club helped establish formal lawn tennis rules (size of court, height of net, method of scoring, overhead serving) and vied with Wimbledon for its prestige championships.

At the bottom of Lennox Gardens, broad Milner Street (1850s) has a row of stuccoed terraces leading off it up to Walton Street. Passing Lennox Garden Mews and going up the third terrace, First Street, a left into Walton Street leads round to Brompton Road (but to catch pretty Donne Place, turn twice left at the Walton Street bend). To the left and still on Charity land, Basevi's Pelham Crescent and Place (1827–30) across the road is an oasis of lush gardens around sparkling white-stuccoed houses – society photographer Cecil Beaton lived at no. 8 Pelham Place. To the right, Basevi's slightly grander Egerton Crescent (1840s) on the right sweeps round to Egerton Terrace (1785, much rebuilt), whose low-built Georgian houses to the right were some of the earliest Charity work. Back up the terrace and right through Egerton Gardens Mews, Yeoman's Row was built as a row of tiny cottages (1670s) bounding the Charity.

Across Brompton Road, **Brompton Square** (1822–30), now one of the smartest and most secluded addresses in Knightsbridge, was at first two terraces leading to fields until the semi-circle of grand houses sealed it into a square. With Ennismore Gardens to the north, this marked the pre-1851 boundary of developed Knightsbridge from Brompton, now known as **South Kensington**.

West of it stands the **Oratory of St Philip Neri** (1878–84, dome 1895–6), known as the London Oratory (and incorrectly as Brompton Oratory). It quickly became the focus of Roman Catholic worship in London and, despite Westminster Cathedral being built (1903, see p. 92), retains its importance. St Philip (1515–95) founded the Institute of the Oratory in Rome (1575) as a congregation of secular priests. Father Faber started the London Oratory (1849) and bought this rural site (1853) despite fellows' cries of 'too far out . . . a suburb . . . a neighbourhood of second-rate gentry and second-rate shops'. Later, 29-year-old Herbert Gribble designed the flamboyantly Baroque church in imitation of the mother church in Rome, the Chiesa Nuova. The interior is a Baroque time-warp. Around the 51-foot wide nave (only Westminster Cathedral and York Minster are wider, the Twelve Apostles by Giuseppe Mazzuoli, a pupil of Bernini, are from Siena Cathedral (thrown out when the Cathedral authorities were tidying up); the Lady Altar (1693) is from Brescia; and in St Wilfred's Chapel (south of the High Altar) the Flemish altar is from St Servatious Maestricht (early eighteenth century) – Rex Whistler painted the triptych of St Thomas More and St John Fisher and their Tyburn execution (1938). Still the smart place for Catholic christenings and weddings, Sunday choral Mass mixes solemnity with socialising (tel 589 4611/581 8701; open daily 6.30am–8pm; Mass Mon–Sat at 7am, 7.30am, 8am in Latin, 10am, 12.30pm except Sat, 6pm; Choral Mass on Sun, 11am).

Outside the eastern wall, a path leads up parallel with Cottage Place to TL Donaldson's **Holy Trinity** (1829), now in the shadow of the Oratory's great dome. Beyond, the church path leads up to the mews cottages and then left along the churchyard, emerging into **Princes Gardens**, whose informal sunken lawn with lofty trees are a public treat after the manicured and firmly locked private squares. Wandering through them and then right, past Ennismore Gardens Mews, **Ennismore Gardens** is an interesting mix of before and after the Great Exhibition: HL Elmes's attractive houses (1843–6) on the east side looked westwards across gardens to Kensington village until three huge mansions (1870s) were built with post-1851 pomposity on the west side. Turning left and up past Lewis Vulliamy's **All Saints** church (1869) with CH Townsend's facade (1892), now the home of the Russian Orthodox Church in Exile, the Prince of Wales Gate (1848) into Hyde Park lies ahead.

Here, where local children learn to ride, couples flirt over a game of tennis and old gentlemen play bowls, was the main entrance of the **Crystal Palace**, the Great Exhibition's hall. In January 1850, Prince Albert established a Royal Commission to help the Society of Arts, of which he was President, to organise the biggest exhibition yet seen in London the following year. Against cries of horror, especially from *The Times* newspaper, this was the chosen site. The hall was designed by Joseph Paxton, head of the Duke of Devonshire's Chatsworth

garden. It was an enormous greenhouse stretching back towards Knightsbridge, and given an exotic, fairytale quality by its cathedral size, the elms it covered and the extraordinary, hotch-potch collection of ingenious, extravagant and ornamented exhibits. Less exotically, until some sparrow-hawks were brought in, the Hyde Park sparrows' droppings added to the Persian carpets' patterns.

Built by 2,000 men in four months using prefabricated girders and columns as a frame for the glass walls and ceilings, it was 1,848 feet long (three times the length of St Paul's), 108 feet tall under the barrel-vault, used 900,000 square feet of glass and provided one-and-three-quarter miles of galleries. To test its strength, soldiers marched round the galleries in close formation. Contrary to prediction, it did not blow away, catch fire with the sun's rays or fall down like a pack of cards. After the show closed in October 1851, it was re-erected at Sydenham where it was the focus of an amusement park until it caught fire in 1936. Now all that remains of this 'Wonder of the World' are the concrete foundations beneath the Hyde Park grass – and possibly a cast-iron walkway recently discovered in the Agricultural Hall in Islington (see pp. 208, 274).

Moving to the left, the great Coalbrookdale Gates lead to the **Albert Memorial** (1864–76). Sir George Gilbert Scott's appropriately complex, educational, romantic and flamboyantly Gothic tribute to Queen Victoria's beloved Albert (1819–61) has the prince sitting round-backed, holding a catalogue of his Great Exhibition and overlooking his lasting legacy, the South Kensington culture centre. This was the national memorial. From the competition entries, the mourning queen chose Scott's design (1862), the money was raised from the public and parliament (£120,000), a bevy of sculptors went to work, the queen was pleased and knighted Scott (1872) and John Foley's 14-foot-high statue of the prince finally went into place (1876). In essence, it is an outsize reliquary casket. Albert sits within a Gothic canopy inlaid with enamels, precious stones and Salviati's mosaics of Poetry, Painting, Architecture and Sculpture, all mounted on a high base coated with layers of instructive statuary. Asia (a busty eastern beauty astride an elephant), America, Europe and Africa form the outer corners; a intriguing parade of 169 portraits of mid-nineteenth-century's idea of civilisation's greatest creators comes next (a certain Orcagna is rated with Giotto and Cimabue; Scott put himself between Pugin and Cockerell); Albert's deepest interests are bove – Commerce, Manufacture, Engineering nd Agriculture; and yet more allegorical figures un up to the 175-foot-high pinnacle with Faith, lope, Charity and Humility the nearest to the ross on top.

It was a fitting memorial for an extraordinary nan. When the coronation festivities were over in une 1838, Victoria's advisers turned their noughts to marriage. The queen's cousin, handome Prince Albert of Saxe-Coburg-Gotha, visited ondon the next year, the queen fell in love with im and the 20-year-old couple were married in the hapel Royal of St James's Palace in 1840. While eir marriage blossomed and bore nine children, ne queen and her husband promoted the great noral revival, starting with the Court (whose deprative and seductive ladies Albert stoically gnored) progressing to their own children (Albert vas horrified by the future King Edward's amorus antics) and setting an example for all the ueen's subjects. In formal life, Albert was more nan an invaluable support. He was adviser and rganising secretary for his wife. Disraeli noted nat 'nothing small or great was done but by his dvice' and at meetings he would quietly prompt er in German to ask her advisers pertinent quesons. Moreover, his energy had a vocational, lmost missionary quality. He threw himself into ne wholesale domestic, health, cultural, agriculural and industrial improvement of all British eople. The triumphant Great Exhibition of 1851, ith model dwellings for the poor designed by imself as one exhibit, was followed by three thers at Dublin (1853), Manchester (1857) and ondon (1862). With his foresight its profits went nto the founding of South Kensington, which was on appropriately nicknamed Albertopolis.

At last, in 1857, parliament acknowledged lbert's contribution and, to the queen's joy, gave im the title Prince Consort. But in 1861, aged just 2, Albert died of typhoid. The queen lost her ractical and psychological support, withdrew into omplete seclusion and never wholly recovered. 'israeli spoke for the stunned public who 22 years arlier had viewed with suspicion the foreigner's rrival as husband for their great queen: 'This erman Prince has governed England for twentyne years with a wisdom and energy such as none f our Kings have ever shown.'

Albertopolis stretches south from the memorial. Vhile the Royal Commission was busying itself aying up the Brompton fields and nurseries to ake the plot, Albert produced his dream plan.

Imagined from his memorial, colleges for art and science would stand either side of an avenue leading to a huge National Gallery. Beyond, museums for industrial art, trade and inventions would flank large gardens, with learned societies off to the left (the V&A site) and a concert hall to the south. And all in 'an Italian or Palladian style or architecture'. But it was not to be. Most importantly, the National Gallery would not budge from Trafalgar Square. However, the Royal Horticultural Gardens were built and Albert opened them on June 5, 1861, his last public function.

The dream that was realised, spilling down the hill from his memorial, is this: the landmark Royal Albert Hall surrounded by colleges and societies; beyond, the Royal College of Music and Imperial College of Science and Technology with its surviving Queen's Tower; the Science, Geological and Natural History museums covering the gardens (the 1862 Exhibition was held at the bottom end); the V&A off to the left; and, recently completed, the Ismaili Centre on the concert hall site across Cromwell Road.

It is a people's education park. Four museums, five teaching colleges and seven other bodies now make up the Kensington Estate, still run by the Royal Commission. The main buildings are monuments to Victorian confidence, power and panache. Dipping inside them, the sciences and arts are practised and conserved in warrens where all the technical miracles, shimmering gems and dinosaur skeletons would take a lifetime to explore. On a first visit it is best to wander and dip into the one that appeals. And do struggle up the Queen's Tower if it is open.

At the top of the hillside and on the central axis stands the **Royal Albert Hall** (1867–71). Oval, not circular, it was designed as a Hall of Arts and Sciences by two engineers, not architects, Captain Francis Fowke and Major-General HY Darracott Scott, who took Roman amphitheatres as their models. Funds were raised by selling 1,300 of the seats for £100 each on a 999-year lease, buyers to have free entry for all shows – a system only marginally modified today; and the peppercorn rent of one shilling (5 new pence) set up by the Great Exhibition commissioners still applies, paid annually on March 25. On the outside, the high frieze of cavorting figures illustrates the Triumph of Arts and Letters and was made, with help from Mintons, by the Ladies' Mosaic Class of the V&A – it was Victoria who unexpectedly announced that Royal Albert would be added to its name when she

217

laid the foundation stone. Inside, the shallow, iron and glass dome spans a huge space 185 by 219 feet and 135 feet high, another Victorian engineering triumph. But the disastrous design fault was only discovered when the Bishop of London's 'Amen' reverberated round and round and up into the 135-foot-high dome at the opening ceremony, a fault that led to the quip that a composer whose work was premiered here could be sure of a second performance (the remedy was huge saucers, hung in the dome in 1968).

During a century of non-stop action ranging from charity bazaars to boxing, highlights have included Bruckner playing Willis's 9,000-pipe, steam-engine-driven organ at the inaugural concert (biggest of all organs at that time); a 9,000 audience listening to the first gramophone concert (1906); balls celebrating 100 years of peace between Britain and the USA (1914) and the coronations of George V (1935) and the Queen (1953); and the arrival (1941) and home ever since of the highly traditional Henry Wood Promenade Concerts when for seven weeks of top class concerts the chairs are removed from the pit and impoverished music-lovers stand or sit on the floor to join the seated audience (Kensington Gore, SW7, box office tel 589 8212; tours, either a guided 90 minutes including the Queen's Box or an unguided 30 minutes, usually run June–Oct, daily from 10.30am–5.30pm, bookable by telephoning 589 3203; charge; shop).

A cluster of cultural satellites hovers nearby. Moving round Albert Hall westwards, the **Royal College of Art** was founded in 1837 as the Government Schools of Design with a brief to turn out good designers for British industry. The oldest element of the V&A (see below), it now has a separate life in HT Cadbury-Brown and Sir Hugh Casson's new building (1962–73). Further round, engineer HH Cole designed the National Training School of Music (1875), where the **Royal College of Organists** (founded 1864) now lives strangely organless behind FW Moody's maroon, blue and cream Germanic graffito facade. Just off to the right, **Queen Alexandra's House** (1884) was built as a residential home for female students attending the local institutes, its tile-coated hall leading to Henry Doulton's magnificent tile-panels in the dining room which incorporate Mozart, Handel, Della Robbia and others and established his reputation (Bremner Road, SW7, tel 589 4053; to visit become a Society member and attend a concert, or write). On round the hall, Joseph Durham's bronze Albert

on a chirpy, merry-go-round horse (1858) at the top of the steps commemorates the Great Exhibition. Then come two monumental mansion blocks of flats: striped, turreted and smart Albert Court (1890), whose entrance corridor has fireplaces, clocks and minstrel galleries; and Norman Shaw's comparatively sleek and curving Albert Hall Mansions (1879–86).

Turning right along the main road, Kensington Gore turns into Kensington Road. On the right, Norman Shaw's tall chimneys and big gables announce Lowther Lodge (1873–5), the 'country house come to town' of ex-diplomat and Member of Parliament William Lowther and, since 1911, home for the **Royal Geographical Society** (founded 1830) who sponsor explorations into the unknown and who have adorned their buildings with sculptures of Africa explorer David Livingstone (1813–73) and, round the corner, Arctic explorer Ernest Shackleton (1874–1922) (see Libraries, above).

Across the road, **Princes Gate** (1848–55) is the smart, stuccoed terrace of Park-facing houses which confusingly continues down the top of Exhibition Road. Here, at no. 49, lived Pre-Raphaelite patron Frederick Leyland, for whom Whistler, unasked, painted the Peacock Room over valuable old leather wall-coverings while the master was away, charged 2,000 guineas, was paid half, and vented his fury by adding a pile of gold coins beneath one peacock (1876, the whole room is now in the Freer Gallery, Washington). After Leyland died (1892), Burne-Jones designed his tomb which stands next to that of his son-in-law, painter Val Prinsep (died 1904) in the glorious flower-filled Brompton Cemetery found much further down Old Brompton Road (the keen should take a bus there). Next door is the **Goethe Institute** which runs a vibrant German cultural programme (50 Princes Gate, SW7, tel 581 3344). Facing the park, J Pierpont Morgan once owned no. 14, later stayed in by the boy JF Kennedy while his father was US Ambassador (1937–40) and now home for the **Royal College of General Practitioners** (founded 1952). Here too is the **Royal College of Needlework** (founded 1872), whose studio brought William Morris' crewel-work designs to life and contributed to the Queen's Coronation Robes (25 Princes Gate, SW7, tel 589 0077; courses, shop, repair service and temporary exhibitions).

But it is the **Polish Institute** and **Sikorski Museum** which provide the best glimpse inside a house as well as an extraordinary collection that orms the major Polish museum outside Poland and includes some 10,000 items ranging from the sumptuous and huge red-and-white striped tent booty from a Turkish victory, 1621) and the red-and-white Polish flag flown over Monte Cassino monastery (1944) to delicate, eighteenth-century watercolours and the Enigma machine which decoded the Germans' secret messages. The principal archives for Polish twentieth-century historians are also here. London's closely knit Polish community began to arrive in the 1790s, with larger numbers coming late last century, including Joseph Conrad. After the German invasion of Poland (1939), the Polish government-in-exile arrived with 33,000 personnel and set up in Mayfair, Belgravia and South Kensington. 150,000 Poles settled here after the war, many of them middle-class professionals. Today, the daily *Dzinnik Polski* newspaper, the Roman Catholic church and the clubs (Polish Hearth Club is round the corner) keep Polish culture, language and gossip alive. In the museum, labelling is firmly in Polish, so ask if you want to know more (20 Princes Gate, SW7, tel 589 9249; open Mon–Fri 2–4pm and the first Sat of each month 10am–5pm; free).

Exhibition Road was mostly developed by coal merchant-turned-builder CJ Freake with large mansions built in the grandiose Italianate style that was to characterise the post-1851 South Kensington homes of the wealthy. Nos. 69–72 (1860s) make the point. But William Lowther built some on his west side land, of which the one to see inside is no. 29 (1873), designed by JJ Stevenson in the quieter Queen Anne style that Norman Shaw had used for Lowther's home – red brick, tall narrow windows, decorative panels of brickwork, tall chimneys and Dutch gables. It now houses the **National Sound Archive**, an outpost of the British Museum (see p. 66) which holds around half a million recordings of some 35,000 hours of sound from early wax cylinders to modern compact discs, covering subjects from Baden-Powell, Shackleton and Mahatma Gandhi to Olivier's *Othello* performance, an owl's screech, Peking Opera and Paderewski playing the piano (29 Exhibition Road, SW7, tel 589 6603; Public Listening Service open by appointment Mon–Fri 10.30am–5.30pm, Thurs until 9pm; free. See also Libraries, above).

Turning right along **Prince Consort Road** (1887), three colleges have been incorporated into the **Imperial College of Science and Technology** (1907), now part of the University of London (see p. 164). One is on the left, the Royal School of Mines (founded 1851, another early member of the V&A Museum), which was given its monumental Edwardian building (1909–13) by Aston Webb, architect of the front part of the V&A. Statues of Otto Beit and Sir Julius Wernher decorate the entrance, its two German benefactors who came to London, made gold and diamond fortunes in South Africa and returned to endow the school. The two other colleges were the Royal College of Science, founded 1845 with Albert as President, and the City and Guilds College (founded 1884).

The **Royal College of Music** is beyond, opposite the great steps down from Albert Hall. Founded in 1882 with George Grove as first Director, who compiled *The Dictionary of Music*, it soon moved into Sir Arthur Blomfield's 'ugly and undistinguished premises' (Hobhouse) in 1904, where Vaughan Williams and Benjamin Britten were later students – its most recent addition is Sir Hugh Casson's Britten Opera Theatre (1986). The college's collection of over 500 musical instruments is stunning, based on 300 European ones given by Sir George Donaldson and some Indian ones given by a relative of Rabindranath Tagore who rushed around Europe promoting Indian music and giving collections to major cities. Treats include Haydn's clavichord, Handel's spinet, a Venetian harpsichord with seductive paintings by Transuntino (1531), a carved German recorder by Oberlender and a guitar decorated with sunflowers by Joachim Tielke (Prince Consort Road, SW7, tel 589 3643; museum open during termtime, Mon and Wed, 11am–4pm, charge; full programme of termtime concerts; Friends society; see also Libraries, above).

At the end of the road, the palatially wide **Queen's Gate** fulfilled the hopes of the Commissioners and became a fashionable street of huge Italianate private mansions. Even now, chopped up into flats or demoted to hotels, they retain their air of late Victorian and Edwardian sumptuousness and comfortable wealth, when an army of servants was running up and down back stairs while well-bustled ladies met in high-ceilinged, first-floor drawing rooms, wallpapered with overblown roses and cosily furnished with palm trees, Chinese screens, leopard skin rugs, ivory photograph frames, carved Indian tables and plenty of buttoned sofas. Indeed, no. 167, built for sugar merchant Mr Davidson in 1890 and now the Estonian Legation, is frozen in time and retains its high marble chimneypieces, lavish plasterwork, Mrs Davidson's piano and basement servants' bells marked up with the Davidson family names. Inevitably, an institution has sneaked in, this one the **Royal Entomological Society** at no. 41, founded in 1833 and boasting the world's finest library on insects (see Libraries, above). Moving down Queen's Gate, Queen's Terrace and Elvaston Place run off it on a similar scale, with pretty mewses behind.

Turning left into **Imperial College Road**, this and Prince Consort Road both slashed through the Royal Horticultural Society's gardens where, following Albert's wish 'to reunite the science and art of gardening to the sister arts of Architecture, Sculpture and Painting', Sydney Smirke and Captain Fowke had surrounded Nesfield's beautifully landscaped gardens with romantic Italian arcades (1861). They would be a glorious lung for scholars and visitors to Albertopolis today. But 21 years later the Society could not afford their upkeep, they were dismantled and a string of exhibitions used the site ending with the Colonial and Indian (1886).

It was following this that the **Imperial Institute** was founded (1887, now the Commonwealth Institute, see p. 194) and housed in TE Collcutt's grand building (1887–93) until, despite public outcry, all but the central tower was destroyed for Imperial College's new buildings – again, the University of London 'having destroyed so much more of Bloomsbury, was unmoved' (Hobhouse). Now Imperial College students have opened **Queen's Tower** (1986) and give visitors conducted tours from Boehm's statue of Victoria up the 342 stairs to the top, past the 10 bells (rung for Royal Family birthdays and when the college orchestra given their annual outdoor performance) and on up giddy-making spiral stairs to the outstanding **view** down over Albertopolis and out across the whole of west London (Imperial College Road, SW7, tel 589 5111 x3017; open July 1–end Oct, daily 10am–5.30pm; charge).

The four big museums fill the southern third of the Commission's Kensington Estate, each with its own strong character. Turning right, Exhibition Road's inner lining of ice-cream vans to supplement the inadequate museum cafés offers hot-dogs in winter and stoically remains throughout London drizzle and chill.

First on the right is the **Science Museum**, more fully the National Museum of Science and Industry. It is a thrilling five floors (with two extra topnots) where George Adams's beautiful and finely tuned microscope, a complete off-shore drill-ing rig floor with full sound effects and the inside story of what happens when you dial the emergency number 999 overturn any ideas that science might be boring for the unscientific. When the science and educational collections of the V&A were ousted to make room for more art in 1864 they came here but remained under V&A management until 1909. With Richard Allison's department store format for their home (1913), the spaces are big and natural light floods through the large windows.

Today, helped by gifts and enlightened curators, the 70 galleries covering eight acres of floorspace recount discoveries and inventions from the small-time eccentric to the bigtime that changed our lifestyles (the exciting arrival of plastic bags from America; the invention of the telephone), each ingeniously explained and demonstrated. Here are answers to all sorts of questions you never thought of asking but are suddenly keen to know about – how we move (with 1813 Puffing Billy engine and a 1909 Silver Ghost Rolls-Royce), how a plane flies (Amy Johnson's *Jason* in which she flew to Australia), how a photograph is made, or how a needle projects sounds from a record groove. With subjects arranged so that they demand more knowledge each floor up you go, budding scientists can go up and play with computers or explore the Wellcome galleries of medicine while others stay down to find three special features: the new Exploration of Space gallery on the ground floor and the basement Children's Gallery and ground floor Launch Pad, both playgrounds with plenty of audience participation, shouting and laughter. Director Neil Cossons has rightly worked out that museums 'must put as much effort into looking after their customers as they do into looking after their collections. We are', he says, 'in the leisure industry.' The museum also has two out-of-town outposts: the National Railway Museum at York and the National Museum of Photography, Film and Television at Bradford (Exhibition Road, SW7, tel 938 8000, information on 938 8111; open Mon–Sat 10am–6pm; Sun 2.30–6pm; free. Daily public demonstrations, lectures, films, good shop, basic café on fourth floor. See also Libraries, above).

The **Geological Museum** is next door, telling the story of the Earth with a startling combination of a delicate 330 million-year-old fossil of a fern blowing in the wind from Scotland, glittering canary yellow sulphur crystals from Sicily and the full re-enactment of an earthquake in Caracas. The smallest of this museum family and the latest arrival, it began in a house in Whitehall where the rocks, minerals and glass finds were supposed to illustrate how geology could help 'the useful purposes of life' (1835). It soon amalgamated with the Geological Survey (1845, set up to make geological maps of Britain), and could be inspected by 'suitably qualified persons'. Progressing to become the Museum of Practical Geology (1851), it finally outgrew its later Jermyn Street home, moved here (1924) and is part of the Institute of Geological Studies.

While the regional story of Britain is upstairs, the ground floor is devoted to the Earth's geology and minerology. Here, some 3,000 items of one of the world's best collections of minerals, natural crystals and gemstones are on show, sparkling with flaw-free fiery diamonds from Africa and Siberia, slabs of luminous deep-blue lapis lazuli from Afghanistan and tough, pale green jade from New Zealand. Exploring further, past a piece of the moon collected by the *Apollo* astronauts (1972), the best of the audience participation enticements (rocks to touch, buttons to push) is a full-sized cut-away model of a house where pushing the colour-coded buttons reveals just how many different and exotic minerals went into the car, fridge, TV, chairs and carpets. (Exhibition Road, SW7, tel 938 8765; open Mon–Sat 10am–6pm; Sun, 2.30–6pm; charge (double ticket available to include Natural History Museum). Lectures, demonstrations, films, workshops, geological walks in London; British Geological Survey information office; good shop stocking books, maps and British and worldwide stones; basic café. See also Libraries, above.) Now that the mineral and economic collections are part of the Natural History Museum (1985), an internal link to it opens in 1988.

Down and round to the right, the **Natural History Museum**, an outpost of the British Museum (see p. 167), has a stone zoo of animals and plants on the outside and their fossils and remains inside. Its foundation was the well travelled Sir Hans Sloane's collection (see p. 166) which inspired the creation of the British Museum (1753). A century later, when the natural history departments were overflowing, the 1862 International Exhibition site was given over to them and Alfred Waterhouse designed their home (1873–80). His great honey-and-blue striped Romanesque cathedral for the wonders of creation is as good as its contents. While the southern towers contained offices and fire-fighting equipment and northern ones were disguised chimneys for the heating system, the elaborate terracotta decoration scheme was planned by Sir Richard Owen, the museum's first Superintendent, to reflect the gallery plan – extant animals crawl over the zoology side on the west, extinct ones over the geology and palaeontology on the east side.

Inside, the cathedral nave is still the most impressive part. Robed Sir Richard Owen (1804–92), the energy behind the museum's creation, looks down on the huge skeleton of the 150-million-year-old Diplodocus dinosaur from Wyoming in the US, its tiny head and 26-metre-long body perpetually surrounded by small, screeching children amazed that this is not a sci-fi film set. To help explore the rest, where a tiny part of the museum's 50 million treasures are on show, there are plans, newsboard and information at the entrance. To the right, London treats include Mr Jarzembowski's find (1986) of a fossil dragonfly which was flying above the muddy swamp of London 125 million years ago, and evidence of polar bears at Kew and hippopotami, elephants and lions (real, not Landseer's) at Trafalgar Square. To the left, old mahogany cases of birds, insects, spiders and corals and shells lead to the new human biology gallery, first into a dark, womb-like room with things thudding around, then into a blast of light and a baby's-eye-view of the outsize world, with plenty of films to watch and buttons to press. In the mammal room beyond, the massive Blue whale is suspended beside an elephant one-twentieth of its size. Do go upstairs, too, to catch the **view** down over the hall on the way to the excellent Darwin Room and, up again, past the 1300-year-old Sequoia tree slice from California to the British natural history room. Fortunately, the weird shapes, dazzling colours and exotic histories of the objects and Waterhouse's building make up for the often dreary presentation. (Cromwell Road, SW7, tel 938 9123, information on 938 9378, open Mon–Sat, 10am–6pm; Sun 2.30–6pm; charge (double ticket includes Geological Museum). Lectures, films, workshops, special exhibitions, two shops, basic café, good lawns. See also Libraries, above. Internal link to its associate, the Geological Museum, see above.)

Running along the front of the museum lawns is **Cromwell Road**, the third great road the Commissioners prepared for private mansions. Named after Oliver Cromwell, who supposedly lived in a mansion at the junction with Queen's Gate, CJ Freake was again quick to start developing, kicking off in 1855 and then moving into no. 21 himself in 1860 (now the Royal College of Art's school of fashion design). The earls and lords hurried to live in healthy and open 'Brompton, or, as residents prefer to call it, South Kensington', extending smart Kensington credentials in the same way Chelsea's are today. But *The Building News*, arbiter of architectural taste, got thoroughly heated about the chosen style for the latest 'favoured locality' and attacked it for its 'meretricious unentertaining character . . . that would only suit the humdrum or the wearied follower of fashion, and would be almost agony to poets and painters'. It blasted on: 'We might almost imagine we were within the precincts of some convict establishment or military barrack', such were the oppressive 'miles of stereotype perspective of Cromwell-road or Queen's-gate'.

Softened by time and by subsequent eye-sores, South Ken, as its residents now fondly call their home, no longer seems to merit such fierce deprecation. However, the pre-Exhibition streets certainly have more charm, as a whirl round the South Ken core reveals.

Turning right, Queensbury Place is where diplomats and globe-trotters send their children to the French Lycée while they live in London. The **Institut Français** next door runs a good cultural programme (15 Queensbury Place, SW7, tel 589 6211). Further along, the small **Baden-Powell** museum devoted to Robert, 1st Lord Baden-Powell (1857–1941) and the scout movement he founded is inside a new scouts' hostel where boys doubtless 'smile and whistle simultaneously in accordance with rule 8' as PG Wodehouse's Clarence tried to (Queen's Gate, SW7, tel 584 7030; open daily 9am–5pm; free). Down the remainder of Queen's Gate, with luck popping into Butterfield's **St Augustine's** (1870–6) to feast on the patterned and coloured stones, the coloured glass and Martin Travers's glittering baroque reredos of 1928 (tel 581 1877; open daily 6–6.15pm, plus Wed, 11–11.30am, Sun for 11am service; if closed, apply to vicar's house at the end of the drive). Turning left into **Old Brompton Road**, this is the local high street with neighbourhood restaurants and shops for books, food and Arabic sweetmeats – for homesick diplomats of the many Arab embassies nearby. In Christie's South Kensington, more modest than its parent auction house in St James's (see p. 140), the hammer sometimes falls for a piece that goes straight into one of the local museums (85 Old Brompton Road, SW7, tel 581 7611; open Mon and Wed 9am–7pm, Tues, Thurs and Fri 9am–5pm; regular sales). Down the mews beyond,

future connoisseurs and arty aristocrats due to inherit well-stocked homes follow the Christie's Fine Art Course – the V&A runs a similar course for the more career-minded art historians.

Local food shops good for Hyde Park picnic-buying continue along Bute Street, and there are good **views** of the Natural History Museum towers down Glendower Place. But to see some of the prettier residential streets, turn right down **Sumner Place** (1851), then left along CJ Freake's **Onslow Square** (1846), where fashionable Thackeray lived at no. 36 (1854–62) and where Lutyens was born at no. 16 (1896). Left again and up to **South Kensington Underground Station**, the arcade leads through to **Thurloe Street** and the charming Thurloe Estate, developed in the 1820s by John Alexander who employed George Basevi as architect, who did so much on the neighbouring Smith's Charity Estate. Turning right, Thurloe Street leads into Thurloe Square where a right and left round the garden reaches South Terrace with **Alexander Square** at the end, not a square at all, more a terrace. Half way up it, **Alexander Place** leads back to Thurloe Square where a right turn leads up to South Ken's newest arrival, Sir Hugh Casson's building for the **Ismaili Centre** (on the site originally planned for the National Gallery), where the Zamana Gallery brings cultural aspects of Islam to the West (1 Cromwell Gardens, SW7, tel 584 6612/3; open during exhibitions Tues–Sat 10am–5.30pm, Sun noon–5.30pm). The great facade of the V&A is opposite.

The **Victoria and Albert Museum**, known to all as the V&A, is the national museum of art and design and the largest decorative arts museum in the world. And not only that, it includes the national collections of sculpture (best Italian set outside Italy), watercolours, portrait miniatures, art photography, wallpaper and posters, and the largest collection of Indian art outside India. Just 130 years after its opening in South Kensington, it is an encyclopaedic and truly international collection that still grows daily.

With the Horticultural Gardens, this was the only part of Albert's grand plan to see light during his lifetime. Fully aware that Britain was losing her industrial supremacy in Europe, Albert promoted the idea of a museum whose contents would be of practical instruction for students preparing to work in commerce and industry. Its hero is Sir Henry Cole (1808–82), the first director. One of the Prince's closest colleagues throughout the Great Exhibition and its aftermath, this rotund figure with wild, white hair, his little dog always scuttling along after him, was universally disliked. But his lion-sized character, energy and dynamism made him the driving force behind the Great Exhibition, the creation of South Kensington culture centre (he thought up the name) and the establishment of this museum.

Ambitiously conceived by Cole as 'a splendid collection of objects representing the application of Fine Art to manufactures', with the accent on design and craft in commerce rather than craft for craft's sake, its beginnings were more humble. A hotch-potch mixture of plaster-casts, engravings and examples of manufacture used by students of the Government Schools of Design in Somerset House (1837) were taken over by Cole, students and all, moved into Marlborough House (see p. 137), amplified with goodies from the 1851 Exhibition and renamed the Department of Science and Art (1852). Cole then moved it to South Kensington, where the students lived in wooden sheds and the museum was housed in engineer William Cubitt's corrugated iron and glass building known as the Brompton Boilers (1855–6). Just as the roses were painted for the queen in *Alice in Wonderland*, it was quickly daubed with green and white stripes before Victoria came to the opening of the South Kensington Museum (1857). It grew quickly. To the museum and art school (later the Royal College of Art) were added a science school, refreshment rooms, lecture theatre and a Museum of Construction full of marbles, cements and all the colourful ornamental enamels and tiles so popular with Victorian builders.

With no great building planned for them, Cole's keeper, JC Robinson, busily amassed objects of huge diversity and highest technical quality to educate his students and provide them with examples to emulate. The museum had soon acquired its first big collection, Sheepshanks's British paintings, quickly followed by the Bandinel Collection of pottery and porcelain, part of the Bernal Collection of glass, objects from the 1856 Paris Exhibition and the Gherardini Collection of models for sculpture, as well as old enamels, jewellery, furniture, metalwork and needlework from Europe and the Far East. And the best of contemporary work arrived – a tradition the museum was to maintain: the bulk of the 2,000 works bought annually by the design, print and drawings department are contemporary; in 1983–6, 111 of the 176 items acquired by the furniture department were twentieth-century pieces; and the museum commissions

silver, tapestry and other pieces. Furthermore, practising designer Jean Muir and design tycoon Sir Terence Conran currently sit on the V&A Board of Trustees.

As the objects accumulated, Cole's masters and keepers were fast forgetting the original practical purpose of the museum. Beautiful, interesting, odd and new things poured in, from the exquisite Canning Jewel and Shah Jahan's Jade Cup to the sizable Raphael Cartoons and the Great Bed of Ware, to huge chunks of architecture saved as tantalising reminders of the destruction of London as it expanded – a whole seventeenth-century carved-oak house facade from Bishopsgate, the Duke of Norfolk's Music Room in St James's Square, a panelled room from Clifford's Inn and James Gibbs's elegant room from Henrietta Place. Much is on show – most of the ceramics can be seen; much more is stored in the bowels or off-site; and much of the Indian department's treasures are still to be catalogued – just 2% of the 44,000 or so objects are on view (the collection was moved to the V&A temporarily when the Imperial Institute was demolished). Sir Roy Strong, Director 1974–87 and the vitality behind many recent innovations, echoed his forebears when he remarked: 'For over a century the Museum has proved an extremely capacious handbag.' Now Elizabeth Esteve-Coll, the first woman director of a major British arts institution, runs this colossal carpet-bag.

A very big building was needed to contain this fast-expanding collection. First, a picture gallery was pinned onto the Boilers, then another and still others – although the Boilers later went eastwards to be re-erected as the Bethnal Green Museum of Childhood (see p. 253). Cole's patronage of contemporary craftsmen – Godfrey Sykes, James Gamble, Frank Moody and Reuben Townroe – make some of the rooms museum pieces in their own right and the odd mosaic lunette or tiled staircase a sudden treat on the way round. A mighty slab of grand rooms was later slapped on the front to solve space problems forever but recently the V&A tentacles have tickled their way into an old neighbour for yet more room (the Henry Cole Wing) and the whole theatre department has gone to Covent Garden (see p. 122). The muddled way in which it evolved perhaps explains why it is a confusing warren to explore.

The early additions form the quadrangle and north-eastern block of the museum, a happy mix of practical structures designed by two engineer-scientists (Cole disliked his lack of control over architects) and decorated by craftsmen. The first was Captain F Fowke's Sheepshanks Gallery (1857–8) along the east side of the quadrangle. Next came the Vernon and Turner Galleries (1858–9) to the north of it, and then three smaller courts running down the east side. The spaces between were filled in to become North and South Courts (1861–2) and, to the south of them, East Court (1868–73). The south side of the pretty quadrangle (now the Pirelli Garden) was built for the National Art Library (1879) and, like the other three sides (built piecemeal 1862–1901) mixed terracotta, red brick and mosaic in what became known as the South Kensington style. The original entrance was in the north side, between an arcaded loggia and columns, leading to three splendid rooms straight ahead: the tiled Restaurant (1866, now the Gamble Room, with added chimney piece from Dorchester House, see p. 145), the tiled Grill Room to the right (1865–73, now the Poynter Room), and William Morris's Green Dining Room to the left, an early secular commission to which Edward Burne-Jones added the window (1866–9, now the Morris Room). And, at the end of the corridor to the left, Moody's splendid ceramic staircase has survived later clean-ups.

But there was still not enough room. So, in a one-off attempt to ease the crush, a competition was held, Aston Webb won and a row of huge galleries with a great entrance hall and quarter-mile-long facade were plonked in front of the existing buildings (1899–1909). As at the Albert Hall, when Victoria laid the foundation stone (her last major public engagement in London), she announced the name would be changed to honour the original spirit behind the museum. By the time Edward VII opened it, the corona-topped entrance was embellished with Alfred Drury's statues of Victoria and Albert and W Goscombe John's of Edward and Queen Alexandra, with other sculptures of British artists added by students of the Royal College of Art (George Frampton did the spandrels over the front entrance). Sir Hugh Casson, who gazed at it from his architectural practice in Thurloe Place for 30 years, thinks it 'clumsy, over-cooked' but loves the Minton-tiled tea rooms of the old part.

Finally, recent expansion to the north-west is into the handsome building (1863–73) overlooking Exhibition Road and decorated with more terracotta and Minton majolica. Ironically designed for Cole's Department of Science and Art, Gavin Stamp reckons this is 'the finest example of the South Kensington style'. First used by the School of Naval Architecture (now at Greenwich) and later by Imperial College, it is now the Henry Cole Wing, honouring the first and greatest Director. And in the Cole tradition, Douglas Coyne and Christopher Hay of the Royal College of Art designed the new iron gates to it.

Over the century, pantechnicon-loads of the museum contents have come and gone. Arrivals include the whole of the India Museum (founded 1802) and the National Art Library. Departures included part of the Royal College of Art (see above), and all of the Science Museum (see above). Still overspilling, today's V&A outposts are the Theatre Museum (see p. 122), Bethnal Green Museum of Childhood (see p. 253) and three historic houses: Apsley House (see p. 143), Ham House (see p. 269) and Osterley Park (see p. 267).

With 145 galleries totalling seven miles of gallery space arranged on six levels around four courts over the 13-acre site, plus the Henry Cole Wing, it is easy to head off for Constable paintings, Islamic metalwork or Japanese armour and get thoroughly lost in (and happily seduced by) British ballgowns or medieval ivory. More than in any other London museum, it is far more rewarding to get stuck in to one or two rooms here rather than wandering aimlessly, attempting to 'do the V&A'. It is an un-do-able museum. So it is worth working out where your favourites are before plunging in.

Inside the main entrance are an information desk, big plans, news of activities (special exhibitions, lectures, films, gallery talks, gallery closures), and the free plan – as crucial for finding as for leaving when, eyes and mind brimful and feet aching, exit signs seem to disappear. Here, too, are the current Object in Focus (from the V&A) and Object of the Month (belonging to a regional museum but bought with V&A help). Other practicalities: the excellent new shop is here, entered through Gilbert Scott's iron gates for Salisbury Cathedral chancel, 1869–72 (100 Things to See or Julius Bryant's guides are both good buys); the Friends of the V&A desk is here (privileges include 10% off in the shop); but the restaurant (best of all London museums) is away in the Henry Cole Wing. Finally, lifts down the steps either side of the main door whizz you between the four layers; and the lift in the Henry Cole Wing takes you to Level 6 and good rooftop **views**.

Then to the galleries, each glowing with masterpieces. For administration, they are grouped into ten departments: Sculpture, Ceramics, Furniture and Interior Design, Indian, Library, Metalwork, Far Eastern, Prints Drawings Photographs and Paintings, Textiles and Dress, and Theatre (at Covent Garden) – Conservation is also a department. Their galleries aimed at the non-specialists are mostly on the ground floor and the first three layers of the south-west corner; the study collections, more specialised and often less glamorously displayed, fill the rest. However, in practice it is not so clear. So here is the layout made as simple as possible.

First, the **view**: standing in Webb's domed hall, the central axis is straight ahead, a magnificent vista recently opened up. It runs through the Medieval Treasury (one of the world's best, newly restored with Trusthouse Forte money) and Gothic Art into the Pirelli Garden (coniferous incense cedars and Italian alders, pink stone and seats, open according to the weather) in the old quadrangle, where the Renaissance galleries surround the remaining three sides and the old entrance straight ahead leads to the deliciously decorated Morris, Gamble and Poynter rooms. To the right of the quadrangle are the carpets and medieval tapestries.

Still standing in the hall, the ground floor of Webb's building is laid out in three rows. Running behind his facade to the left, down a flight of steps, are the seventeenth- and eighteenth-century Continental galleries (including the Jones collection); to the right are the new Art and Design in Europe and America 1800–1900 galleries (easy-to-reach highlight; high Empire style to Frank Lloyd Wright). For the next row, rooms right of the hall lead through sculpture and then left to the two magnificent restored Victorian Cast Courts (again, one of the best; weird mixture of Spanish altarpieces, Trajan's Column and Michelangelo's David; early casts came from Marlborough House in 1852) with the fascinating Fakes Gallery in between them. Rooms to the left of the main hall contain the shop (carved London house fronts surrounding) and then the Raphael Cartoons (1515–16, designs for tapestries woven in Brussels for Pope Leo X for the Sistine Chapel, bought by Charles I, now lent by the Queen), leading right into the Dress Collection (up-to-the-minute with nine new Versace outfits; secret stairs up to musical instruments). For the third row, the magical Medieval Treasury (the best introduction to the history of European decorative arts) is flanked by magnificent collections from exotic eastern worlds: China and Japan on the right

(with the stunning new Toshiba Gallery as highlight), and Islam and India on the left.

Down the steps at the far ends of these (and the costume) rooms, a left turn and steps up lead to the new Henry Cole Wing, its entrance decorated with Rodin's sculptures (given by the artist), its arched basement the large restaurant and extra shop, its floors above devoted to prints, drawings, photographs and paintings topped by the Constable collection on Level 6, with real Constable clouds and London rooftops to see through the windows. The ground floor entrance also leads to the Twentieth Century Exhibition Gallery.

Staircases surround the sides of the ground floor, leading to the quieter upper rooms whose exquisite treasures have less star status. The front and west side of Webb's building is made of four layers: lower ground (Continental), upper ground (English Renaissance, British Art 1650–1750 including several ex-London rooms; European carvings), upper first (Georgian and Victorian British Art; Scott's plaster model for the Albert Memorial, booty from the Great Exhibition, and plenty of Arts and Crafts; Glass and French ceramics), and second floor (worldwide pottery, earthenware and ceramics). The first floor proper is in four bits. Part runs across the middle of Webb's section (musical instruments above the costumes; German stained glass; European ironwork; more glass); a fragment is reached from the Henry Cole entrance (British Art and Design 1900–60); and the bulk is in smaller rooms over the old buildings: The National Art Library, silver and church plate overlook the quadrangle; jewellery (usually with a contemporary showcase), European textiles and embroidery surround the old South Court; and the museum's north-east corner, well worth exploring, harbours pewter, plate, enamels, armour, Islamic metalwork and armour, tapestries, textiles, lace, carpets and oriental textiles, all surrounding the exciting twentieth-century study collection.

Whatever amuses or interests you, some of the most unusual or best or exotic examples are here. There is never enough time to explore; another room is always beckoning. It was Sir Roy Strong who started the slogan 'Spend a day at the V&A'. With the Great Bed of Ware already there, it would be easy to move in. (South Kensington SW7, tel 938 8500, information on 938 8365, recorded information on 518 4894; main entrance Cromwell Road, Henry Cole Wing entrance Exhibition Road; open Mon–Sat 10am–5.50pm, Sun 2.30–5.50pm, admission by voluntary donation (unnecessary for shop, restaurant and Library); late opening to 9pm of Henry Cole Wing and restaurant on some Weds, telephone to check. Guided tours, lectures, seminars, courses, special exhibitions, music and drama in the Pirelli Garden, Friends society (museum address, tel 580 4040). Department staff give opinions on objects Tues and Thurs, 2.30–4.30pm, except Furniture and Sculpture staff who give opinions on Tues only, at 10.30am–1pm and 2.30–4.30pm; no appointment necessary. In addition, Textiles and Dress and Prints and Drawings staff give opinions on Sat

10am–12.30pm by appointment. The special study rooms for Prints, Textiles and Indian art have shorter open hours than the museum. Excellent shop with a section run by the Crafts Council and with mail order service, plus smaller one in Henry Cole Wing; excellent restaurant.)

Orderly Albert would surely be horrified at the muddled growth of this mansion and its overwhelming collection that not even its curators can fully control. But his spirit still pervades the range, quality and vitality of his South Kensington centrepiece, legacy of his 1851 triumph.

Chelsea, Belgravia and Pimlico: Village lanes to stucco estates

Mapping it out from above: Nothing very high in this flat, residential area. Best to go up nearby Westminster Cathedral tower (see p. 92). Starting point: Sloane Square. Access by Underground: Sloane Square.
Good days to explore: Saturday for King's Road young fashion parades; Mon–Sat mornings to see Royal Hospital's Council Chamber; Wed and Sun for Chelsea Physic Garden; Apr–Oct to see Carlyle's House; Londoners crowd out the Tate and Clore (Turner) Galleries on weekend afternoons.
Information: The two nearest are the LTB Information Centre at Victoria. See p. 3, or its outpost in Harrods, see p. 4.

Refreshments: see p. 317.
Local festivals: Chelsea Flower Show, third week of May; annual splash by the Royal Horticultural Society; enjoyed by the Queen on Mon, RHS members Tues–Wed, public Thur–Fri with decreasing entry fee as blooms blow down; information from The Secretary, RHS, Vincent Square, SW1, 834 4333. Entry by pre-arranged ticket only.
Local Libraries: Chelsea Library, King's Road, SW3, tel 352 6056/2004; open Mon–Sat 10am–5pm but Wed only until 1pm. Especially good for local history, costume and fashion, botany and bookplates.

The red-uniformed Chelsea Pensioners totter along the King's Road, a foil to parades of teenagers swathed in the fancy dress of the latest and wildest British fashions. In Sloane Square mothers and daughters meet at Peter Jones for lunch, dressed identically with matching headscarves and handbags in unwitting imitation of Osbert Lancaster cartoons. North of here, the international set swan out of their London homes in gleaming Belgravia terraces to shop in Kenzo, Valentino or Joseph in Sloane Street or to walk huge hounds homesick for their weekend country acres. Southwards, over the railway lines, the friendly Pimlico people barter for their cabbages and Coxes in the daily street market. And in the furthest Pimlico corner, the canvases Turner and Whistler painted in Chelsea hang in the riverside Tate Gallery.

This triangle of smart residential London, whose points are Battersea Bridge, Hyde Park Corner and the Tate and whose epicentre is Sloane Square, sits snugly in the river bend, bordered by Knightsbridge and South Kensington to the west and Westminster and St James's to the east. Contrary to appearances, it was one of the last pieces to be added to the Central London puzzle.

The King's Road, public catwalk for the avant garde since the 'swinging' 1960s, was until the 1830s the private royal route from Whitehall palace to Hampton Court and other western royal retreats. From the time of Charles II to George IV, the king, queen, mistresses, courtiers and all their trunks, servants, entertainers, advisers and sycophants crammed into a coach cavalcade which then ambled out past the royal St James's Park, across the open scrubland and past Chelsea hamlet, the first of a succession of riverside fishing villages whose inland pastures were dotted with aristocratic manors set in large gardens and orchards.

Scrubland, fishing villages and manors have gone. Chelsea, the nearest of the courtly country retreats, spread up from the river bank and over the Tudor mansions as it gained eighteenth-century country opulence, helped by the frivolous Ranelagh Gardens and Wren's Royal Hospital, a western counterpart to Greenwich. Relaxed, bohemian days followed last century when Carlyle, Rossetti, George Eliot, Ellen Terry, Whistler and Oscar Wilde were among the rich literary and artistic talent living in the old village. Then, in the 1950s, the Chelsea wealthy began the still popular London fashion: buying humble houses built for workmen and artisans and dollying them up as *bijou* delights to compare with Marie Antoinette's fake farm cottages at Versailles.

Belgravia covers the scrubland that lay between Chelsea and London. By the 1830s, the new royal home was Buckingham Palace, right behind it. So the mightily grand Grosvenors, creators of Mayfair, made a well-

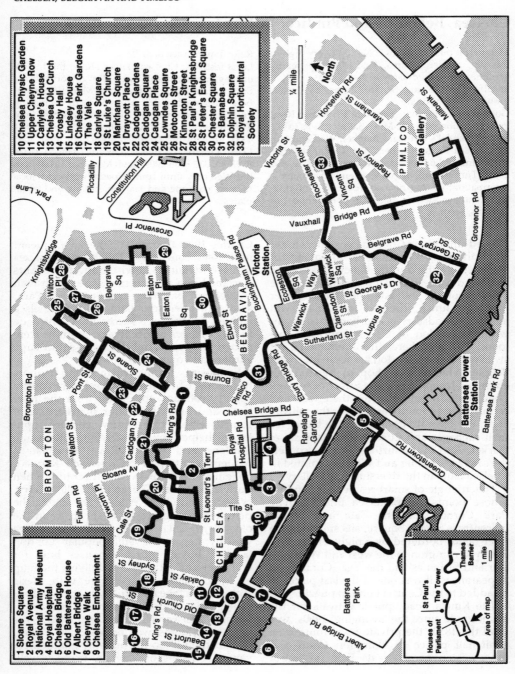

1 Sloane Square
2 Royal Avenue
3 National Army Museum
4 Royal Hospital
5 Chelsea Bridge
6 Old Battersea House
7 Albert Bridge
8 Cheyne Walk
9 Chelsea Embankment
10 Chelsea Physic Garden
11 Upper Cheyne Row
12 Carlyle's House
13 Chelsea Old Curch
14 Crosby Hall
15 Lindsey House
16 Chelsea Park Gardens
17 The Vale
18 Carlyle Square
19 St Luke's Church
20 Markham Square
21 Draycott Place
22 Cadogan Gardens
23 Cadogan Square
24 Cadogan Place
25 Lowndes Square
26 Motcomb Street
27 Kinnerton Street
28 St Paul's Knightsbridge
29 St Peter's Eaton Square
30 Chester Square
31 St Barnabas
32 Dolphin Square
33 Royal Horticultural Society

timed move to develop this remaining inner London space for their fellow aristocrats. With its grand squares and sparkling stucco terraces, it was the last London estate to be built by the rich for the rich. And no more Grosvenor acres in the neighbouring marshy bend of the Thames, Pimlico was born: more sparkling stucco for the not-quite-Belgravians and Belgravia's service industry, and even known as Lower Belgravia in early days.

A century on, modest Pimlico flourishes whereas Belgravia's grand houses have been sold up – the British nobility have always kept their country acres and disposed of town mansions when money got tight. But in estate agents' jargon Belgravia is the most 'des. res.' (desirable residence) address in town. The viscounts and lords whose grandfathers owned the Belgravia ballrooms now have mews cottages round the back as their

London pied-à-terres. More than 20 great houses have become embassies; the rest are divided up. Here a 25-year lease on the topmost flat of a once-grand townhouse sells to the seriously rich, and that usually means non-British, for the price of a whole house anywhere else in town.

An exploration of the southern Chelsea lanes needs some careful timing if you want to dip behind the facades to glimpse the Royal Hospital chapel, sniff the perfumed air of the walled botanical gardens and sense Carlyle's ghost in his time-warp house. Continuing through north Chelsea, then ordered and sparklingly posh Belgravia and the equally bleached Pimlico streets, there are a group of sumptuous late Victorian churches to see (if they are open) before the final feast of British and twentieth-century art in the Tate Gallery.

Starting in **Sloane Square**, the flower sellers and Venus fountain wrapped in the dappled light of plane trees give this glorified roundabout a Parisian air, enhanced with twinkling night-time lights in the trees – despite valiant attempts, the missing ingredient of a pavement café is forbidden by the authorities. The square honours Sir Hans Sloane (1660–1753), the well travelled and well heeled physician who became an obsessive collector while he lived in Bloomsbury (see p. 168), bought Chelsea Manor (1712), came to live here (1741), bequeathed his collection to the nation (the foundation of the British Museum, see p. 166) and left his estate to his two daughters. Clearly, there was paternal favouritism: the younger daughter, Elizabeth, wife of Charles Cadogan, 2nd Baron Cadogan of Oakley, got the lion's share and became Lady of Chelsea Manor; Sarah, wife of George Stanley of Paultons in Hampshire, got the rest.

More recently, the square gave its name to the middle-class, genteel Sloane Rangers, the set who ardently abide by a string of rigid, life-moulding rules to avoid any decision-making, from what to wear, what to cook for dinner, how to decorate their drawing rooms and where to go skiing, with helpful columns of monthly up-dating from the glossy magazines. The hub of Sloane London homes is Fulham, west of Chelsea; but the hub of

daily life is here, where quick-thinking commerce feeds Sloanes and would-be Sloanes from all over Britain with Ann Barr and Peter York's *Sloane Ranger Handbook* and puts the Sloane stamp of approval on anything bought from Peter Jones or the General Trading Company.

Cobbled and enclosed in 1771, Sloane Square is now a jolly hotch-potch focus for local life, as a spin around it reveals. With no obvious core to the area and no perches to map it out from above, this is also a good moment for orientation.

On the west side stands the local emporium: Crabtree, Slater and Moberley's once avant-garde Peter Jones store (1936) whose curved curtain wall snaking round its plot still generates praise as 'one of the finest buildings of the decade in London' (Jones and Woodward). Moving clockwise, Sloane Avenue shoots northwards to Hyde Park between Chelsea and Belgravia; to the north-east, King's Road swings off through Belgravia to the royal palaces. Walter Emden and WR Crewe's Royal Court Theatre (1887–8, bombed and rebuilt) comes next. Here Harley Granville-Barker and his team dazzled the London stage when they put on 32 plays by 17 authors in 1904–7, including the first performances of GB Shaw's *Candida* (1904), *Major Barbara* (1905) and *The Philanderer* (1907). George Devine's English Stage Company, which arrived in 1956, have added more landmark firsts including

John Osborne's *Look Back in Anger* (1956) and Arnold Wesker's *Roots* (1959). Next door, the Underground station has an iron pipe carrying the River Westbourne over the tracks on its journey from Hyde Park to the Thames, and until recently a platform pub for thirsty travellers. Southwards, Lower Sloane Street heads for the Thames between Pimlico and Chelsea and is the climax of the annual pilgrimage route to the Chelsea Flower Show, where gardeners up from the country stock up with catalogues and newly created plants before heading back home with their booty. Westwards, King's Road slices through Chelsea.

King's Road was indeed just that. Charles II (1660–85) adopted the twisting path as his private road to Hampton Court (see p. 112), open to others on production of a copper pass. Before this, the fishing village of Chelsea, probably named after its chalk wharfs and usually reached by boat, attracted enough Tudor courtiers and statesmen to be nicknamed Village of Palaces. Sir Thomas More was an early arrival (1520); the Earl of Shrewsbury, Duke of Norfolk and Henry VIII followed; Tudor Princess Elizabeth spent some of her childhood here with Catherine Parr, Henry's surviving wife. Then the kings came trotting through. George III (1760–1820) was especially fond of this route to one of his favourite palaces, Kew. Post royals, the newly public road of 1830 soon had a string of squares opening onto it, like no other road in London.

Today, these leafy openings bring relief to the otherwise solid lining of shops, pubs and restaurants that made the King's Road as synonymous with the Swinging Sixties as Carnaby Street (see p. 162). But unlike the degeneration of Carnaby Street into tat, the King's Road has kept up, revived its fashionability among the young at the time of Punk, and even spruced itself up to serve its locals. As you criss-cross it to explore, the top section has branches of the national stores, a group of antique markets follow, and the mile-long catwalk for the weird and wonderfully painted human artworks peaks at the first corner where Vivien Westwood and other leading British designers have their shops.

King's Road is the backbone of **Chelsea**, a small town with a surprisingly heterogeneous character, whose final knot joining it to London was only tied in the 1880s when Cadogan Square was built. Moving down it, a bunch of little 1830s lanes sets the tone for early Chelsea growth, charmingly small-scale and modest. Find them by turning right

up Blacklands Terrace, (dipping into John Sandoe's excellent bookshop), left along Bray Place and again down Lincoln's Street, where a right along Coulson Street and a left down Anderson Street returns to King's Road.

Across the road and a few yards further along, the **view** (best in winter) down **Royal Avenue** (1692–4, houses nineteenth century) stretches across the green lawns to the centre of Wren's Royal Hospital facade. It is a great unfinished plan. This is all that was built of William III's project to lay out an elegant link over the Chelsea and Brompton fields to Kensington Palace (see p. 187) where he had moved in 1689, the year he became king. The shady avenue, where Ian Fleming gave his suave hero James Bond his London home, opens onto Burton's Court, a green where the Pensioners play bowls and the local Brigade of Guards play cricket. The handsome eighteenth-century houses of St Leonard's Terrace run along the back, where Bram Stoker, creator of Dracula, lived at no. 18 (1896–1906) and where architect Richard Rogers (of Lloyd's, see p. 72) now lives. Ahead the **view** of the Royal Hospital is even better.

But before visiting it, the **National Army Museum** lies through Burton's Court (or around it to the left if the gates are closed) and right along Royal Hospital Road. Here, the stories of the British Army from the Yeomen of the Guard (founded 1485) to the Falklands campaign (1982) and the story of the Indian and colonial forces are told in five galleries: art, uniform, arms and two for the story of the Army. For the less soldierly, there are Spode egg stands for the King's Royal Irish Hussars, General Gordon's mother-of-pearl magnifying glass, scent bottles from Bahadur Shah's Delhi palace and the skeleton of Napoleon's horse, Marengo. For militarists, there are uniforms coated in gold braid and silk rosettes and plenty of maps, models, old films and audio-visuals in the more strictly story-telling galleries upstairs. In all, fascinating objects housed in a hideous building and displayed with cold formality (Royal Hospital Road, SW3, tel 730 0717; open Mon–Sat 10am–5.30pm, Sun 2–5.30pm; free. Lectures, workshops, special exhibitions, Friends society, good shop for boy soldiers; to use the excellent library, apply to the Director for a reader's ticket).

Back along Royal Hospital Road, a gateway on the right just before Burton's Court leads into **Royal Hospital** (1681–6, plus additions), known by many as Chelsea Hospital. Inspired by Louis XIV's

Hotel des Invalides (1670) in Paris, Charles II founded a hospice for retired soldiers (1681) and employed Sir Christopher Wren as architect. Although his work on St Paul's would continue for decades, most of the post-Fire City churches were designed and Wren now approached his first large-scale secular work. This new type of institution needed a new style of building. Wren produced the blueprint for institutional and educational buildings in Europe and America: using informal brick, the main range contains the Central Hall and Chapel behind a colonnade facing southwards to the Thames – the garden used to end at the water's edge; and the two side courts with the dormitories open to the west and east. In 1689, 476 pensioners moved in, to be given board, lodging, clothing, nursing and a weekly allowance. Wren added outbuildings (1691); Sir John Soane added more (1809–17); and today about 420 pensioners have their home here, their winter blue and summer scarlet uniforms dating from the eighteenth century cutting quite a dash when they go for a stroll up to King's Road.

To explore Chelsea's showpiece in its glorious setting, start with Soane's stables (1814) to the right of the entrance. A few yards inside, turn left along the north side of College Court to reach the central Figure Court where there are long, built-in benches for enjoying the magnificent **view** down to the Thames past Grinling Gibbons's bronze of Charles II dressed as a Roman soldier (1676, brought here 1692). On Oak Apple Day (May 29), the pensioners parade in three-cornered hats, receive double rations and decorate their founder with oak leaves to celebrate his birthday and his escape from the Roundheads after defeat at Worcester (1651) by hiding in the trunk of a hollow oak tree. On the left, the elderly gentlemen dine beneath Verrio's large canvas of Charles II in the grandeur of the panelled Great Hall – it was here that the Duke of Wellington lay in state for a week (1852) and two people were crushed to death in the crowds who came to pay their respects. Next door, the gentlemen pray in the box pews of the sumptuously decorated chapel – black and white floor, carved font, more Gibbons carving, Sebastiano Ricci's Resurrection over the altar. Beyond, the Council Chamber in the Governor's House is the most splendid part of all: Van Dyck and Lely's portraits of Charles II, Kneller's of William III and much more. Near here, another Soane building (1816) is the Secretary's Office which houses the little museum (Royal Hospital Chelsea, SW3, tel 730 0161; Great Hall and Chapel open Mon–Sat 10am–noon and 2–4pm, Sun 2–4pm; Council Chamber usually open Mon–Sat, 10am–noon but telephone to check; Museum open April–Sept, hours as for Great Hall; free. Sun services in Chapel at 8.30am, 11am (Parade Service) and noon).

Turning right, the 66-acre gardens are in two parts. On the left, the informal, undulating and tree-filled Ranelagh Gardens were set up over the house (1690) and gardens of Lord Ranelagh, Paymaster General to the Forces. From 1742 to 1803 they rivalled Vauxhall Gardens (see p. 109) as a fashionable pleasure resort. Here the *beau monde* listened to Mozart play in the orchestra, ate in the gilded and painted rococo rotunda lit with chandeliers, were painted by Rolandson and Canaletto and flirted in the Chinese pavilion beside the ornamental lake. Walpole approved it as having 'totally beat Vauxhall'; Gibbon as 'the most convenient place for courtships of every kind'; Goldsmith as full of 'fetes, frolics, fire-works and fashionable frivolity'; and Lord Chesterfield came so often he had his mail delivered here.

Today, Chelsea ladies take portable garden chairs to read library books in the shade of a chestnut tree; men sit on the benches to peruse the *Daily Telegraph*. On the right, Wren's formal gardens with 80-foot-long raised causeway flanked by canals and avenues have gone. Instead, locals walk their red setters, clipped poodles and royal corgis by the formal parterres while local children take tennis lessons (good **views** of the Hospital from the centre). It is here that, since 1913, the Royal Horticultural Society holds its annual Chelsea Flower Show in late May, a bedazzling array of prize blossoms filling vast marquees with blasts of rich colours and a heady, sweet perfume. Every serious amateur gardener in Britain comes, from the Queen and high society (who then instruct their gardeners) to window-box and allotment amateurs. The last to leave on the Friday night carry off tree-sized flowering trophies at bargain prices – the rest of the year, regular shows are in the Society's halls in Vincent Square, Pimlico (see p. 241 below) (all grounds open Mon–Sat 10am–sunset; Sun 2pm–sunset; free. Ranelagh Gardens close 1–2pm).

Leaving by the river gates and turning left, the footpaths over **Chelsea Bridge** (1934) are walled off from the road down the middle, so you have to choose your **view** eastwards (Pimlico and Battersea Power Station) or westwards (Royal Hospital and Battersea Park) before you start.

Battersea Park is London's second big park to be specifically created for Londoners rather than for royalty – the first was Victoria Park in the East End (see p. 253). It is also Chelsea's local park, so much so that the surrounding residents upgrade themselves and call the area Lower Chelsea. It fills the south bank between Chelsea and Albert bridges. The marshy fields, which disappeared under water at high tide, were given a rough embankment in the 1560s and became a place for pigeon-shooting, gypsies, duels and taverns for bawdy summer Sunday parties with donkey races, gambling, conjurers and 'shameless dancers'. On the advice of Thomas Cubitt the government stepped in (1843), the taverns were closed and 320 acres bought – 200 for a park, the rest leased for building to pay for it. In 1846, parliament authorised the creation of a park. The embankment was rebuilt; the land level raised with earth from Victoria Docks then being built east of the City (see p. 110); and Sir James Pennethorne laid it out with carriage drives encircling an ornamental lake and Old English Garden. When Queen Victoria opened it (1853), its fashion was assured. The park became the centre for the Victorian cycling craze (forbidden in Hyde Park) and a favourite place for ladies to take a morning promenade ending with breakfast by the lake. This century, artists John Piper and Osbert Lancaster laid out the Festival Pleasure Gardens to coincide with the Festival of Britain along the riverbank at Waterloo (see p. 119) (1951) and enticed eight million visitors who loved the formal flower gardens but dismissed Henry Moore's 'Three Standing Figures' as 'a piece of grotesque modern sculpture' (William Kent, 1951). The Japanese Buddhist order, Nipponzan Myohoji, and the Most Venerable Nichidatsu Fujii donated the latest addition: London's first monument dedicated entirely to peace, the London Peace Pagoda (1985).

As well as walking along the riverside path to enjoy good **views** across to the Royal Hospital and Chelsea and see the Peace Pagoda, there are special things worth seeking out. Mist's Pitch, two acres of nature reserve closed to the public but bubbling over with butterflies, is at the north-eastern corner. Pennethorne's amoeba-shaped lake (boats and café at north-eastern end) is on the south side, near the deer park. The Festival Pleasure Gardens are behind the riverside Terrace Walk, with roller-skating, break-dancing and the latest acrobatic feats performed on the athletic grounds to the west (especially at weekends), beyond the little zoo (pony rides). Pennethorne's Old English garden is near the large herb garden in the north-west corner. And mature and exotic trees, the park's most valuable possession, are dotted throughout, from the tallest known black walnut and the largest hybrid buckeye to the Chinese thuja, Kentucky coffee and the foxglove tree (for information, tel 871 7534. Café open daily Apr–Sept 10am–6pm, Oct–Mar 11.30am–5pm; boats for hire daily Apr–Sept 2.30–7pm; zoo open Apr–Sept Mon–Fri 1.30–4.30pm and Sat, Sun 11am–4.30pm, Oct–Mar weekends only).

Out of the south-east gate, the *Observer* newspaper avoided the lure of the Docklands and deserted the Fleet Street area for Queenstown Road. Beyond, Sir Giles Gilbert Scott's Battersea Power Station (1929–35) is five minutes' walk away, saved from destruction when it became redundant and now to open as a £135 million entertainment complex in 1990. Out of the western gate to the left of the lodge, old **Battersea** village is another five minutes' walk away, hidden in an industrial maze and found along Parkgate Road, right along Battersea Bridge Road and left along Battersea Church Road. It is worth the effort to see **St Mary's** church (1777), where Turner painted sunsets from the tower; the **views** across to Old Chelsea; and a cluster of fine houses – the Dutch-gabled Raven pub, the Vicarage, Devonshire House and **Old Battersea House** (1699). Possibly designed by Wren, certainly the best domestic house in the area, it has been restored to glory by the American Forbes family (of Forbes Magazine) with part of it the home for the de Morgan Collection of paintings and pottery (Vicarage Corner, SW11; for a guided tour of the de Morgan Collection, apply in writing to Mrs JP Lanchester, 21 St Margaret's Crescent, London SW15).

Leaving the park by the west end riverside gate, RM Ordish's **Albert Bridge** (1871–3), complete with toll houses (disused since 1878) provides good westwards views of Bazalgette's Battersea Bridge (1886–90), replacing Henry Holland's wooden bridge familiar from Whistler and Walter Greaves paintings. Moxley, Jenner and Partners' Chelsea Harbour village built around a yacht harbour rises beyond the houseboats and Chelsea Creek on the north bank. Northwards, **views** are of old Chelsea village. When Bazalgette's **Chelsea Embankment** (1871–4), typically dual purpose with road above and main sewer below, was slapped down from here to Chelsea Bridge, it destroyed the relationship between Chelsea and its water. And while it enticed some interesting domestic architecture at the end of last century, the imagination needs to wipe it away to enjoy the older riverside street, Cheyne Walk, which runs from east of Albert Bridge to well west of Battersea Bridge. Both parts, old and new, attracted a plethora of creative spirits last century. As Gavin Stamp observes: 'In Victorian London, the best artists tended to live in Georgian houses in either Chelsea or Hampstead. Would-be Academicians put on an architectural display in the Melbury Road ghetto and the second-rate with pretensions gravitated to Artistic Bedford Park.'

Cheyne Walk honours the Cheyne family, Lords of Chelsea Manor (1660–1712) before Sloane bought it. Its most handsome houses stand to the right behind the trees, on the site of the manor. Henry VIII had built it (1536); he gave it to his wife Catherine Parr as a wedding present (1543); his daughter Elizabeth stocked the grounds with mulberry trees while she lived here (1536–47); Lord Howard of Effingham (hero of the defeat of the Spanish Armada) and Lord Cheyne followed; and Sir Hans Sloane died here, hoping his collection would be exhibited in the house. But the collection went to Bloomsbury and Sloane's son-in-law, Baron Cadogan of Oakley, demolished the house and put up nos 19–26 (1753). Down Cheyne Mews under the archway of no. 24, ancient mulberry trees grow on an acre of the old manor grounds.

The next group, nos 15–18, are earlier (1712–19), built hard by the manor house in the Queen Anne style and equipped with splendid gates and railings. No. 18 was Don Saltero's Coffee House and Museum of Curiosities, run by a former Sloane servant who was given Sloane's cast-offs (1717–99). When in 1862 Dante Gabriel Rossetti, Algernon Swinburne, George Meredith and Rossetti's zoo with screeching peacocks all moved into no. 16, Queen's House, (1717, designed by John Witt), Chelsea's artistic tone was set. No. 16 became a centre of Bohemian, Pre-Raphaelite life in London. The peacocks fought loudly until they died behind the studio sofa; the armadillo burrowed into the kitchen next door and gave the cook hysterics; the Thames tide flushed in and out of the cellar.

Next, the later nos 7–12 (1880s) where the gallivanting politician David Lloyd George lived at no. 10. Nos 2–6 are again Queen Anne. At no. 6, Dr Dominicetti from Venice administered medicinal baths in wooden contraptions built in the garden until he went bankrupt. At no. 5, the miser John Camden Neild lived before leaving £500,000 to Queen Victoria who promptly squandered it on

her latest building project, Balmoral Castle in Scotland. At no. 4 (especially good ironwork and doorway) lived Daniel Maclise (who contributed murals to Barry and Pugin's new Westminster Palace), fellow artist William Dyce, and later the elderly George Eliot after she finally married John W Cross when she was 61 years old.

It was houses like these, Old Battersea House and the Royal Hospital that inspired the Queen Anne Movement in architecture. At last architects broke away from the rigid London formula of uniform stucco Italianate and looked at the late seventeenth-century and early eighteenth-century architecture known as the Queen Anne style, with its red bricks, bold white windows, pitched roofs and Dutch gables. Adding a few decorative features and balconies they created a newly informal, picturesque architecture. Andrew Saint, biographer of the style's leading London light Richard Norman Shaw (1831–1912), described it as 'the brick architecture of Webb and Scott pupils, adapted to London street and climate, and tricked out with archaeological trappings'. Known as Queen Anne style, the affluent and artistic middle class gave it the stamp of approval in Chelsea in the 1870s; it then rampaged through the capital. The most distinctive cluster is just here, with more in north Chelsea.

Cutting forward to the riverfront from Cheyne Walk, the newly reclaimed **Chelsea Embankment** was soon busy with builders, many of them piling up bricks to designs by Shaw, whose London work ranges from the Royal Geographical Society (1872, see p. 218) to Bedford Park (see p. 267) in west London, the first garden suburb. Here, he was responsible for Cheyne House on the corner (1875–7), then Old Swan House (no. 17, 1875–7) and Farnley House (no. 15, 1887–9). Beyond the Physic Garden, now also chopped off from its water, Shaw also designed nos 11, 10, 9 and the Clock House (no. 8, 1878–80). Then a change: Edward Godwin, who had taken the painter George Frederick Watts's actress wife Ellen Terry as mistress and became the favourite 1870s architect for the avant garde, displayed Queen Anne convention for nos 6, 5 and 4 (1876–8); and Bodley and Garner designed River House (no. 3, 1876–9), inspired by the seventeenth century Kew Palace (see p. 268).

The bottom of **Tite Street**, also part of the Bazalgette reclamation, has more Queen Anne, often with artists' large-windowed studios. John Singer Sargent lived at no. 31, Augustus John at no. 33; and Godwin designed the controversial no. 34 (now gone) for James McNeill Whistler – the American painter arrived in Chelsea in 1862, declared it 'The Wonderful Village', and lived at ten different Chelsea addresses over the next 41 years until his death in 1903. Godwin again designed the Tower House (no. 46, c.1884), a house for Oscar Wilde's rich friend Frank Miles (no. 44, 1878–9) and the interior of no. 34 for Oscar Wilde who wrote *The Importance of Being Earnest* and *Lady Windermere's Fan* during the 11 years he lived there.

Returning down Tite Street to turn right along Dilke Street and again up Swan Walk, a handful of handsome houses set behind large front gardens on the right (where the Sitwells hosted William Walton's premiere of *Façade*) overlook **Chelsea Physic Garden** on the left. Founded by the Society of Apothecaries in 1673 to grow plants for medical study, it followed others at Pisa (1543) and Oxford (1621). Visitors, plants and even trees arrived by barge to the pre-Bazalgette riverside steps. And when funds ran low, Sir Hans Sloane came to the financial rescue (1722) – Sloane studied here himself and was by then Lord of Chelsea Manor, a successful physician and a big collector of medicinal and scientific objects. Gardener Philip Miller (1691–1771, curator 1722–70) trained William Aiton (Kew's first gardener), cultivated countless plants for the first time in England, sent cotton seeds to found the staple crop of the new colony of Georgia, and wrote *The Gardener's Dictionary*, the first modern encyclopaedia of horticulture.

Today, the four-acre garden squeezes in herbs, greenhouses, England's earliest rock garden (with basaltic lava brought from Iceland, 1772) and pond with water plants. In the peaceful shade of a magnificent Willow Pattern Tree, a fruit-bearing olive and other exotic trees, the sweet-smelling grid of medicinal plants and herbs (hardy ferns, South American, Californian, Australasian, etc) is decorated with a replica of Rysbrack's statue of Sloane (original in the British Museum entrance). In the Big Storm of 1987, the garden suffered extensive damage. (66 Royal Hospital Road, SW3, tel 352 5646; open mid-April–mid-Oct Wed and Sun 2–5pm, daily during Chelsea Flower Show 2–5pm; charge. Entrance in Swan Walk, plants for sale, bookstall, courses run by the English Gardening School, teas on Sun; library open by appointment).

From here, a short cut leads back to Chelsea's old core and a house to explore inside. Crossing Royal Hospital Road, Christchurch Street leads up to a left turn into Robinson Street, then across Flood Street into St Loo Avenue. Then, with a right and left, Oakley Gardens leads through the pedestrianised part into Phene Street to pass Margaretta Terrace on the right and emerge into Oakley Street, all laid out by Baron Cadogan of Oakley in 1850, trees planted by Dr Phene.

Upper Cheyne Row (mostly 1718) across the road, is the first of a delightful maze of lanes that evoke the old riverside village. Leigh Hunt lived at no. 22 (1833–40); doll's house cottages fill the passage at the far end. Lawrence Street on the left was home for Tobias Smollett at no. 16, near where the Chelsea China Works flourished (1745–79), seeking Physic Garden models for their botanical designs. Further down, an elaborate double hood over two front doors is opposite pretty Justice Walk.

Down again and left through Lordship Place, **Carlyle's House** in handsome **Cheyne Row** (1703) is the chance to slip behind a Chelsea facade. Thomas Carlyle (1795–1881), the Scottish historian, philosopher and author of *The French Revolution* (1837), lived here from 1834 until his death, becoming an object of local curiosity and of long-distance pilgrimages to hear his fluent discourses. On arrival, he reported that 'Chelsea is unfashionable; it was once the resort of the Court and great, however; hence numerous old houses in it, at once cheap and excellent'. And of the house he wrote: 'The street is flag-pathed, sunk-storied, iron-railed, all old-fashioned . . . the House itself is eminent, antique . . . a most massive, roomy, sufficient old house . . . Rent £35! I confess I am strongly tempted.' Today, immaculately maintained by the National Trust and stocked with the great man's dressing-gown, hat, pipe, pen and all, the ghost of Carlyle welcomes Leigh Hunt in the rose wallpapered parlour, sips coffee in the back dining-room, writes in his sound-proof top room and learns from John Stuart Mill in the drawing-room of the accidental burning of volume one of *The French Revolution* (see p. 193 for where the tragedy happened). Here, too, the witty Mrs Carlyle received her admirers: Dickens, Tennyson, Browning, Thackeray, Darwin and even Mazzini. In the back garden, with cherry, vine and walnut, Carlyle would 'wander about in dressing-gown and straw hat . . . and take my pipe in peace' (24 Cheyne Row, SW3, tel 352 7087; open Apr–Oct Wed–Sun 11am–5pm; charge).

Chelsea in the nineteenth century was for Carlyle 'a singular heterogeneous kind of spot, very dirty and confused in some places, quite beautiful in others, abounding in antiquities and the traces of great men'. All this is still true, as the old heart of Chelsea shows. But first, Arts and Crafts artist William de Morgan lived at no. 30 Lawrence Street, with his pottery warehouse and showroom (1876–82) at the top end where the Church of the Holy Redeemer stands (1895). At the bottom of the street sits Boehm's statue of Carlyle (1883), complete with books. To left and right, another block of Cheyne Walk includes on the right CR Ashbee's nos 38–9 (1890s) contrasting with nos 46–8 (1711) and, after the pub, Carlyle Mansions where Henry James lived (around 1900), and a hospital on the site of Holman Hunt's house.

Then comes the focus of old Chelsea life, **Chelsea Old Church** (1157, much rebuilt). Well worth going inside to see the medieval chancel; private north chapel (1325) for the Lord of Chelsea Manor (Henry VIII married Jane Seymour here before their state wedding in 1536); private south chapel (1528) for Sir Thomas More (capitals carved by his friend Holbein); sanctuary with the tomb of More's first wife; six chained books given by Sloane; and one of the best series of monuments in a London parish church, from Lady Jane Cheyne to Henry James and, of course, Sloane (monument in the churchyard). And do not miss the new kneeler tapestries, in the churchyard, (tel 352 5627; open Mon 10am–1pm, Wed–Sun 10am–1pm and 1.30–5pm, Sun 7.30am–1pm and 1.30–7pm). More (1478–1535), who lived in Chelsea and rose to become Lord Chancellor and a close friend of Henry VIII, could not accept the king's position as head of the Church of England instead of the Pope. He was executed for treason, buried at Canterbury, canonised by the Roman Catholic Church in 1935 and given the bronze outside this church in 1969.

The village high street ran up beside the church, now Old Church Street. Half way up, Paultons Street on the left leads into Paultons Square (1830s), built by descendants of the less lucky of Sloane's daughters. The polished stucco terraces around large, shady trees are the last of the King's Road squares. Turning southwards out of it, Danvers Street was laid out over the Chelsea palace of Sir John Danvers who turned from being Charles I's minister to being a signatory to his death warrant, and whose 'prettiest contrived' (Pepys) home was the first in England to be given a formal, Italian garden. More recently, Alexander Fleming, inventor of penicillin, lived here (1929–55).

Turning right at the bottom, **Crosby Hall** is an incongruity. Built in Bishopsgate in the City as a large mansion for the fifteenth-century wool merchant, Sir John Crosby, it was later occupied by Richard of Gloucester (later Richard III), Sir Thomas More, Sir Walter Raleigh, the East India Company and a restaurant. In 1908, its Great Hall was dismantled, moved here and erected, ironically, on part of More's Chelsea garden. (In between these two houses, Jonathan Swift lived in a more modest house built on this site while he wrote *Journal to Stella* (1710–13), the diary of his political life in London.) Crosby Hall is well worth a visit to see the hammerbeam roof, oriel windows and one of three versions of More and his family painted by Holbein for More's three daughters (Cheyne Walk, SW3, tel 352 9663; open Mon–Sat 10am–noon and 2.30–5pm, Sun 2.30–5pm; free; often closed for private events on Sat).

Further along, **Beaufort Street** cuts across from Battersea Bridge and covers the site of Beaufort House, formerly More House. This was where Sir Thomas More pioneered courtly Chelsea living. He built his country house (1521) with separate study and devotional buildings, two riverside courtyards, orchards and gardens, all maintained by strictly governed servants who were forbidden to play games and obliged to attend regular prayers. Later inhabitants included Elizabeth I's ministers Lord Burleigh and the Earl of Essex, James I's Lord Treasurer Lionel Cranfield and the Duke of Beaufort who put down the Monmouth rebellion (1685) against James II. As expected, Sloane scooped up the estate to add to his own and demolished the house (1740).

But one Chelsea mansion does remain to give an idea of the 'village of palaces'. Across Beaufort Street, Cheyne Walk continues past Belle Vue House and Lodge at nos 91–2 (1771) and Mrs Gaskell's birthplace (no. 93 in 1810, she then lived at the bottom of Beaufort Street) to **Lindsey House** (1674) set behind the eagle-topped gate piers. This was the country seat of Charles II's Lord Chamberlain, the Earl of Lindsey. Divided into five (1777, to make nos 96–100) and enlarged (top floor added), it has since been home for engineer heroes Marc Isambard Brunel and his son, Isambard Kingdom Brunel (see pp. 259 and 106), and was one of Whistler's early Chelsea addresses (from 1863). Just beyond, a final clutch of Chelsea artists starts with Walter Greaves at no. 104 who admitted 'I lost my head over Whistler when I first met him and saw his painting' – Whistler did not return such enthusiasm but fondly referred to the Greaveses as 'a sort of Pegotty family' and told them 'you are the pride of one end of the Row and I am the pride the other'. Later, Hilaire Belloc also lived at no. 104 (1901–5) and Philip Wilson Steer at no. 109 (1898–1942). No. 119 was Turner's refuge from London, where he lived elderly and incognito as Mr Booth and was nicknamed Admiral Booth by locals for his keen storm-watching over the river.

This formidable band of Chelsea creativity – and this is only the cream of it – may prompt you to dash directly to find their canvases in the Tate Gallery. If not, a gentle, meandering, less mind-taxing walk through the rest of Chelsea (and past more painters' homes) and then down through Belgravia and Pimlico will bring you there eventually.

Turning right, Milmans Street leads up to King's Road, boutique windows decked out with the fore-front of British fashion in this corner. Park Walk continues northwards to St Andrew's Church, where a turn right leads through **Chelsea Park Gardens** (1916), a late bit of spacious Garden City building that began here in the 1880s to replace the closely-built, poorer dwellings. These had covered the old Sir Thomas More estate between King's Road and Fulham Road, where some 2,000 mulberry trees were planted in a disastrous eighteenth-century attempt to make silk (see p. 90). Sir Alfred Munnings, painter and President of the Royal Academy (see p. 142), lived at no. 96 (1920–56). Straight through the gardens, then left up Beaufort Street and right along Elm Park Road (catching cobbled Elm Park Lane through an arch on the left), **The Vale** runs down to the right. Here William de Morgan and his Pre-Raphaelite painter wife had another Chelsea address at no. 1. Whist-ler lived at no. 2 (1886–90), followed by illustrator Charles Ricketts and artist Charles Shanner, friends of Oscar Wilde.

Passing Mulberry Walk to go along **Mallord Street**, named after Turner's second name, AA Milne was living at no. 13 (1920–39) when *Winnie the Pooh* was published (1926), and in the 1930s Gracie Fields bought no. 28, originally built for Augustus John. Turning left into **Old Church Street** to glimpse more of Chelsea's original high street, two modern highlights are no. 64 designed by Mendelssohn and Chermayeff (1936) and no. 66 by Gropius and Maxwell Fry (1936). Opposite them, Bolton Terrace is set back from the road before the small, roadside door into the rambling, magical world of the Chelsea Arts Club (founded 1891), where the atmosphere of Whistler, Steer

and Sickert still pervades the bar, snooker table, restaurant and large garden.

The orderly King's Road squares run eastwards from here, with picturesque, small-scale and often candy-coloured terraces in between. Back down Old Church Street and left after no. 64, leafy **Carlyle Square** (1830) was built over market gardens by the Cadogan family as Oakley Square but changed its home in 1872 to honour the local Sage of Chelsea. Turning left into King's Road and glancing down Bramerton Street and wide Glebe Place (more artists' studios) on the right, the grander and more interesting houses on the road come next. No. 217 (1750) was home for James Hutton who founded the Moravian Church in England; no. 215 (1720) is where Thomas Arne possibly wrote *Rule Britannia* and actress Ellen Terry (1847–1928) certainly lived (1904–20); and past its pair, no. 213 (1720), the Venetian architect Giacomo Leoni designed no. 211 (1723) where a recent resident was British film director Carol Reed (*The Third Man, Oliver!*, etc). Across Oakley Street, local spirits of the past inspire fledgling artists at fashionable Chelsea School of Art on the left, while a batch of antique shops and markets follow on the right.

But a little detour left searches out some charming back lanes recalling Chelsea's more mixed society of later in the century. Going up Sidney Street (1845) and past Chelsea Garden Centre (stocked with good cafés and outdoor tables), James Savage's **St Luke's** church (1820–4, east window by Hugh Easton) is where Dickens married Catherine Hogarth (1836), who lived nearby. At the south-east corner of the rose-filled church garden, Britten Street runs past St Luke's Street and then right and left to the Burnsall Street Regency cottages. This surprise slice of country village dropped into central London continues on the left (past Danube Street) up Godfrey Street to Chelsea Green, a hearth-rug of grass surrounded by chic village shops. Markham Street (1830s), the second on the right, perpetuates the toytown air with the help of the Chelsea cosmeticians.

Back in King's Road and right, locals fought to save the ornate facade of the Pheasantry added to the older house by the furniture makers Joubert (1881). The house, now gone, was where Anton Dolin, Alicia Markova and Margot Fonteyn came to learn their pliées from Princess Serafine Astafieva on the first floor (1916–34), while the basement was a favourite local club for Augustus John, Pietro Annigoni and other painters and politicians.

Across and down Radnor Walk, Smith Terrace on the left runs across Smith Street to Woodfall Street, all built by Thomas Smith in 1794–1807. Now rows of immaculate cottages painted in dolly-mixture colours, they epitomise the post-war Chelsea craze for sprucing up humble homes to *bijou* grandeur.

At the top of Smith Street, **Markham Square** (1836) ahead was laid out over a field of Box Farm by Pulham Markham Evans whose family had owned the land since Tudor times. To the right, catching the splendid Victorian Markham Arms pub on the left, **Wellington Square** (1830) on the right was named after the Duke whose brother was rector of Chelsea at the time (1804–36). The first of the King's Road squares, it is the most charming: the houses are pleasantly moderate, well detailed and surround fine trees. It makes a fitting end to what many people consider to be Chelsea proper.

Further up King's Road, left through Tryon Street and across a jumble of roads, north Chelsea was one of the first extensive London developments to take up the Queen Anne style and exchange flat, white stucco facades for tall, red brick buildings with plenty of balconies and decoration. Indeed, this is London's densest district of Queen Anne, much of it speculative terraces put up by builders spurred on by the fashionable success of houses down on Chelsea Embankment. It was these houses that sealed the final link between Chelsea and London. Still mostly residential, although divided into flats, the up-market hotels are the only way to see inside one and they are often much altered.

Draycott Place (1891) runs eastwards across Draycott Avenue, the lane that bordered Chelsea Common until the 1850s. Left into **Cadogan Gardens** (1890s), this is the start of the great Cadogan Estate development, easy to follow as it is mostly named after the family. Sir Hans Sloane's younger daughter Elizabeth and her husband, Charles Cadogan, created 2nd Baron of Oakley (1718), inherited the larger slice of the Sloane estate (1753). Soon after this, Henry Holland leased part and built Hans Town (1770s) and the 3rd Baron, Charles Sloane Cadogan, was created Earl and then Viscount (1800). Later Cadogans jumped on the area's rising social tide, redeveloped much of Holland's work and built over the remaining land (1870s on); and today's descendants have held onto much of this lucrative site.

No. 25 Cadogan Gardens (1899) is on the right, now part of the Peter Jones emporium but designed by AH Mackmurdo for Whistler's disciple

Mortimer Menpes and once lined with Japanese carved wood. Back up the gardens and past Cadogan Street, **Cadogan Square** (1876–90) was built over the Hans Town centrepiece to designs of a rich amalgam of architects. The west side is the most interesting. Here Norman Shaw is at work again at nos 72 (1877), 68 (1877) and 62 (1882), interspersed with AJ Adams' nos 70, 66 and 64 (c.1878); Lord Cadogan's own architect William Young did nos 54–8 (1877–8), Ernest George and Peto designed the restrained no. 50 and the flamboyant no. 52 (1886) and Devey designed nos 28–36 (1889) where the present Lord Cadogan lives at no. 28. Moving round, the porticoed north side and the east side were all by GT Robinson except GE Street's no. 4, built for the Misses Monk (1879); and Adams' partner, JJ Stevenson, designed the south side (1877–86).

Cadogan Gate runs eastwards out of the square past **Pavilion Road**, named after the local mansion. It belonged to Henry Holland (1745–1806), son of a Fulham builder, who married Capability Brown's daughter, designed Brooks's Club in fashionable St James's (see p. 142) and enlarged Carlton House for the Prince of Wales (see p. 175). Here, he leased 89 acres from Lord Cadogan in 1771 and laid out Hans Town. Sloane Street ran down the middle, with Cadogan Place to the east, his own mansion to the west, and Hans Place north of it. Holland designed his house to double as an architectural advertisement, while his father-in-law landscaped the 21 acres of garden. Locals nicknamed it the Pavilion because Holland had designed Brighton Pavilion for the Prince of Wales. With fields either side, Hans Town was a rural delight. Although the mansion has gone (covered by Cadogan Square and Pont Street) and the houses have almost all been rebuilt, the layout of his town survives.

Just here, Pavilion Road was the service road to **Sloane Street**, which gradually moved up the social scale until today it is smart enough to be lined with Arne Jacobsen's hideous green Danish embassy (1978) to the left, followed by the most chic of boutiques (Valentino, Kenzo, Yves St-Laurent, Joseph). And, to the right, the General Trading Company sprawls over four Victorian houses, proudly displaying its three royal warrants and known to its keen Sloane Ranger customers as GTC. Worth a wander to gawp at the goodies, especially at Christmas time – you may even spot a royal doing her present shopping. Across the road stands JD Sedding's **Holy Trinity** (1888–90), a late Gothic Revival church fitted with glorious Arts and

Crafts treats: Burne-Jones and Morris's east window, Wilson and Pomeroy's chancel screen and stalls, Boucher and Onslow Ford's font, etc (tel 235 3383; open for Sun services only, 8am, 10.15am and noon).

Back up the street and right along Sloane Terrace, where the boy Byron spent holidays while he was schooled south of London in Dulwich (see p. 274), D'oyley Street leads left to Cadogan Lane, the now chic (Judy Garland lived and died here) service road for **Cadogan Place** found round to the left. Here, back to stucco land once more, the polished white terrace overlooking blossoming gardens makes a peaceful walk. At **Pont Street** (the Frenchified bridge street crossed the Westbourne River), a left turn leads across Sloane Street where Oscar Wilde was arrested at the corner Cadogan Hotel (1888) in 1895 and sent to Reading Gaol for charges of homosexuality. Beyond, Osbert Lancaster coined the term Pont Street Dutch for the large-gabled 1870s and '80s Cadogan Square cousins with plenty of terracotta detailing. Turning right into oval **Hans Place** and past another statue of Sloane, Holland's answer to Paris's Place Vendôme was where Jane Austen was living (no. 23, 1814–15) when she was entertained by the Prince Regent at Carlton House and given royal assent to dedicate her novel *Emma* to him.

Leaving by Hans Street on the east side, then left past the Sloane Street boutiques Harriet Street on the right leads into **Lowndes Square** (1833–49). This is the centrepiece of the little Lowndes Estate nestling between big brothers Cadogan and Grosvenor. William Lowndes, Secretary to the Treasury, bought his two fields and a strip of land joining them in 1723. A century later his grandson, also William, espied the fervent Belgravia building activity to the east and followed suit, laying out Lowndes Square and the Harriets (honouring William's daughter) on his north field, Lowndes Street along the strip and Lyall Street and Chesham Place on the south field. With Thomas Cubitt building three sides of the smart square (1833–49) and his brother Lewis the remaining south side, it is a fitting aperitif for the Belgravia banquet to follow.

Turning right through the square and down Lowndes Street, Motcomb Street on the left marks the beginning of **Belgravia** soil. It was here that the Westbourne River meandered through the marshy, treeless scrubland known as Five Fields, used for dawn duels, market gardens, sheep grazing, holiday duck-shooting and bull-baiting, and plagued by night-time robbers and highway-men. And it was here that the 2nd Earl Grosvenor (1764–1845, later to be created Marquess of Westminster) laid out spacious, gleaming stucco squares and terraces to make a huge, unashamedly up-market, 200-acre estate – twice the size of the earlier Grosvenor development, Mayfair (see p. 148). The dazzling white maze opened up a whole new area of London. It moved the centre of society and influence westwards, sealed the future of smart Knightsbridge, ensured the development of South Kensington, and linked Chelsea to the London puzzle. Today, Belgravia is London's most expensive address. The Duke and Duchess of Westminster, landlords of both Mayfair and Belgravia and one of the richest families in Britain, choose to live here in Eaton Square – and even they confine themselves to an upper-storey flat.

For the 2nd Earl, there was a double impetus to build. The Prince Regent came to the throne as George IV (1820–30) and began building work on his future home, Buckingham Palace (see p. 89), moving in in 1826; and Britain was enjoying new industrial and commercial wealth following the Napoleonic wars (1803–15). The estate's name had humbler origins, a Grosvenor-owned village near Leicester. As for the development itself, James Wyatt probably created the basic design of a traditional Georgian square (Belgrave) at the centre of a network of streets (1813). Thomas Cundy the Elder, his successor, then prepared the master plan, 'remarkable for its architectural character, completeness and generosity' (Summerson). For if the core of the design followed Georgian Mayfair, the scale was Regency at its grandest, inspired by Nash's Regent's Park terraces: wide, airy streets lined with ample, four- or five-storey houses set behind unified, palazzo facades and serviced by mews streets wider than many Chelsea lanes.

As Hermione Hobhouse observes: 'Belgravia seems a developer's dream: the founding of an elegant successful suburb whose inhabitants included some of the most powerful aristocrats and the richest commoners in England.' But only one of the three major developers who leased land made big money: Seth Smith fell into debt and Joseph Cundy (Thomas's brother) went bankrupt, but Thomas Cubitt became Belgravia's hero. With his revolutionary methods and Bloomsbury experience (see p. 168), his talent and his business acumen, he not only established the high quality Belgravia building but he made money and went on to develop Pimlico single-handed.

Work began in 1824, when Cubitt and his colleagues signed up. 30 years later, Belgravia was born and Mrs Gascoigne dashed off her ebullient poetic praise: 'Behold that desert now – a gorgeous town! On every side, before admiring eyes, New squares appear – fresh palaces arrive!' As for her gushing enthusiasm for Cubitt: 'A fairer wreath than Wren's should crown thy brow – HE raised a dome – a town unrivalled THOU!'. But even if Belgravia was smart from the start, today's taste for the more picturesque encourages sympathy for Disraeli's damnation as 'monotonous, . . . contrived' of its grandeur and perhaps explains why it is still London's most expensive address.

Seth Smith developed this northern chunk with relatively modest streets and a daring dash of commerce, much to the horror of contemporaries who reckoned this smart residential suburb should be 'free from the contamination of trade'. Among the **Motcomb Street** (1830s) art galleries, the facade of Joseph Jobling's south side Halkin shopping arcade survives, as does his north side Pantechnicon (1830) built as a fireproof saleroom for wines and carriages and storehouse for furniture when the great houses were closed up between social seasons. Turning left along **Kinnerton Street**, this downmarket service street for cow-keepers and tailors is now one of the prettiest Belgravia back streets, with half a dozen tiny courts off to the left – Capener's, Ann's, Frederic, etc.

Wilton Place (1825), the road into Belgravia from the Knightsbridge highway, was named after the Marquess of Westminster's father-in-law, the Earl of Wilton. Opposite, Thomas Cundy the Younger's **St Paul's Knightsbridge** (1840–3), richly decorated with brass, carving and tiles, was soon a battleground for the high church movement (tel 235 3460; open Mon–Fri 7.30am–7pm, Sat and Sun 7.30am–noon). Past Brian O'Rourke's swish Berkeley Hotel (1972), a right along Knightsbridge leads to Old Barrack Yard on the right, originally a Foot Guard's barracks (1758). To the left, Thomas Phillips's Grosvenor Crescent Mews (1826) still stables horses, as intended, and has horses to hire for a trot round Hyde Park (see p. 345). And on the right Wilton Row winds left and right to emerge into Wilton Crescent (1827).

Belgrave Square (1825–35) is to the left, Belgravia's centrepiece and the start of the grand vistas. Cubitt took the lease; three Swiss bankers put up the money; and Sir John Soane's star pupil George Basevi, who did much work in South Kensington (see p. 215) was the architect. For London's largest

square, Basevi designed the houses, railings, balconies and even the ironwork – and left his name on the portico of no. 31. To build it, Cubitt's clever wheeze was to dig the marshy clay and bake it into bricks, replacing it with soil from his firm's St Katharine Dock project (see p. 104) on the east side of the City. The houses were on a massive, palatial scale: just 11 or 12 on each side, the later south and west terraces even more sumptuous than the first two. The separate corner mansions had different architects: Robert Smirke in the north-west, HE Kendall in the south-west and Philip Hardwick in the south-east. Cubitt designed the north-east one, later swept away for Seth and Cubitt's sweeping Grosvenor Crescent (1860).

Even if Basevi's uncle, Disraeli, disapproved, the titled flocked there, from the Dukes of Bedford and Connaught to the Earls of Essex, Pembroke, Beauchamp and Albemarle and Queen Victoria's mother, the Duchess of Kent (at no. 36). Candles fluttered in the chandeliers, silver sparkled and the *beau monde* waltzed in gilded ballrooms. However, Trollope's Mr Longstaffe thought it *nouveau riche* and stuck to Mayfair. And more recently Margaret, Duchess of Argyll, remembers pre-war Knightsbridge and Belgravia as merely 'respectable', where a debutante was damned if 'she came out in Pont Street'. But today, Belgravia is tops, Mayfair eclipsed. And in Belgravia's central square, security cameras watch front doors and metal gates are locked across windows. Belgrave Square is embassy square, headquarters for the Portuguese, Spanish, Germans, Turks, Syrians, Saudi Arabians and many more. For an echo of the past, the Country Landowners' Association is at no. 16.

At the south-east corner, a left into **Chapel Street** and then a right through pretty **Groom Place** (1851 fire mark on the right) and another along **Chester Street** leads through the stables (complete with turret and clock) that serviced Hardwick's mansion (1842) for Lord Sefton. Terraces of Cubitt's **Upper Belgrave Street** (1840s) lead down past his **Eaton Place** (1820–50s), where Cubitt had his offices 1828–47 and where Chopin gave his first London recital (1848 at no. 99). On his earlier holiday in London (1837), he was suitably impressed: 'One can have a moderately good time in London if one doesn't stay too long. There are extraordinary things: Imposing toilets too narrow to turn round in. And the English! And the houses! And the palaces! And the pomp, and the carriages! Everything from the soap to the razors is extraordinary.'

Henry Hakewill's **St Peter's** (1824–7 fire-damaged 1987) is beyond. His cool Greek classic-ism was soon dismissed as a pagan temple with 'a perfect monster of a steeple' and given a Romanes-que disguise inside by Arthur Blomfield (1872–5) (tel 235 3192; open Mon–Fri 8am–5pm and Sun services at 10am). This first Belgravia church stands at the top of **Eaton Square** (1826–55), com-pleted the year Cubitt died. Named after the Gros-venor country seat in Cheshire, it is really two long terraces divided by the ancient King's Road high-way. Turning right, there are grand **views** down Cubitt's north terraces, designed by Lewis Cubitt and John Young. Then, turning left down Belgrave Place, there are more down Seth Smith's southern terraces across the highway.

South of here, past pretty Eaton Mews South, lies **Chester Square**. Here the idea was to build streets, a safer speculation. But Belgravia was already such a wild success by 1828 that Seth Smith, Joseph Cundy and a Mr Watkins formed a syndicate and laid out a square. Straight ahead, where the road becomes Eccleston Street, Ebury Mews is worth a look before going through im-maculate Chester Square to Thomas Cundy the Younger's St Michael's (1844–6) and into Elizabeth Street, kitted out with smart food shops, boutiques and restaurants.

Belgravia's secondary streets have less splen-dour but more informality and charm, displayed by the circle of Gerald Road ahead and then right turns up South Eaton Place and Chester Row. Left up Elizabeth Street and back across King's Road past Eaton Mews North, the street becomes Lyall Street where Cubitt moved to no. 3 from his several Eaton Place addresses. Turning left along Eaton Place, and roughly straight ahead into West Eaton Place and round left to Eaton Terrace, the charming mewses end with Grosvenor Cottages on the right and Eaton Terrace Mews on the left. King's Road becomes Cliveden Place on the right, while Eaton Terrace continues across the road and passes pretty Caroline Terrace to Chester Row. Dipping left to catch delightful Minera Mews and then turning back to join Bourne Street, a left turn runs down past Graham Terrace to open into **Pimlico Road**. Here the shops for antiques, interior design, flowers and food, and the Roux brothers' butch-er's, Lamartine, all clustered around the triangle of green, provide a somewhat contrived village atmosphere for local Belgravians.

To the left, Mozart composed his first symphony (1764) while staying at no. 180 Ebury Street, a road built by John Newson who came to London from

Suffolk in the 1830s to make his fortune and did just that. He also built the quieter, charming Blomfield Terrace across the road to the right. Down this and left, there is another Thomas Cundy church, **St Barnabas** (1847–50). Its Kentish ragstone exterior belies deliciously rich fittings by Pugin, Butterfield, Comper, Bodley added over the years until the whole interior became a glimmering Gothic casket of rich craftsmanship (tel 730 5054; to visit, apply to the Clergy House next door, or attend the Sun service, 9.30am).

Ranelagh Grove leads to Ebury Bridge and over the railway lines into **Pimlico**. Before the trains, the bridge crossed Grosvenor Canal (1725, enlarged 1820s) which ran from the Thames to where Victoria Station is. John Newsom kept his timber yard on one wharf; Cubitt had his building yard nearby.

If Belgravia owed its quality and success to Cubitt, Pimlico was indeed 'Mr Cubitt's District'. In 1835, after 15 years of negotiation with the Grosvenors, Cubitt had acquired all the available low-lying, marshy acres south of the canal. Then he launched into action. Over the next 30 years, with no one to compromise for, he built a less showy but more harmonious stuccoville of two leafy squares surrounded by a grid of cosy terraces with outsize welcoming porticos. As Hermione Hobhouse, biographer of Cubitt, notes: 'No other developer has had such absolute control over such a large area of London.'

By 1877, Pimlico homes were established – 'a servant or two in the kitchen, birds in the win-dows, with flowers in boxes, pianos, and the latest fashions of course.' And, typically, its already dis-tinct character was being analysed with Victorian precision: 'South Belgravia is genteel, sacred to professional men of various grades, not rich enough to luxuriate in Belgravia proper . . . here people are more lively than in Kensington, though not so grand, of course, as in Albertopolis, and yet a cut above Chelsea, which is only commercial, and ever so much more respectable than Westminster, dreadfully behind the age, vegetating the other side of the Vauxhall-bridge-road.' The relation of different parts of London to one another may have changed, but they are still analysed by many with the same biting tongue.

Pimlico today – sold off by the Grosvenors and cut off by the railway lines and the Thames – retains much of its gentility and liveliness. The white wonderland of Pimlico begins straight over the bridge with Sutherland Street. A left turn along

Clarendon Street runs across the grid of terraces, now inhabited by a select coterie of architectural historians. Another left at St George's Drive (remarkable cobbled maze of mews stabling ahead) arrives at Warwick Way. Beyond it, on the right, lies grand Eccleston Square (1835), named after another Westminster Cheshire estate. Through it and right down Belgrave Road, the Pimlico centrepiece lies on the right, **Warwick Square** (1843 on). Here Cubitt's daughter lived at the south corner, supplied with the only garden in the block. Painter James Swinton built and lived at no. 33, now run by the Warwick Arts Trust Society who hold art exhibitions and stylish evening soirées and recitals (33 Warwick Square, SW1, tel 834 7856; open during exhibitions, daily 10am–5pm; free).

Turning right down wide St George's Drive and off stuccoville into Claverton Street, young Powell and Moya won the competition for designing **Churchill Gardens** Estate (1946–62) in their final training year at the Architectural Association (see p. 166). Its heating was ingenious, using the surplus hot water from Battersea Power Station across the Thames. But as one of London's first post-war total redevelopments, it has little of the style and success of Gordon Jeeves' pre-war **Dolphin Square** housing (1937) round to the left in Grosvenor Road, where the still sought-after flats are London homes to about 70 MPs and have a communal garden, pool, restaurants (open to the public, newly decorated by Glynn Boyd Harte) and their own radio station. Beyond, St George's Square (1844) returns to Mr Cubitt's District past another Cundy church, St Saviour's (1864). A left turn into Lupus Street, then a right along charming Moreton Terrace and Place run up to Denbigh Street and right into **Warwick Way**. This is Pimlico's pulse, with Italian-dominated shops and restaurants crowding Warwick Way and Wilton Road, and the lively Tatchbrook Street fish, poultry and vegetable street market to the right.

Further along, a hop across Vauxhall Bridge Road leads into that 'vegetating' **Westminster**. Down Walcott Street, the welcome green expanse of **Vincent Square** opens out containing the playing fields for Westminster School (see p. 80). Pretty eighteenth- and nineteenth-century houses line the south-east and south-west sides, more handy homes for MPs. **The Royal Horticultural Society**, inner sanctum for flower fans, is on the north side, spread over two buildings: EJ Stebbs' Old Hall (1904) and, in Elverton Street behind, Murray Easton's New Hall (1923–8).

Founded in 1804 above Hatchards bookshop in Piccadilly (see p. 141) by John Wedgwood (brother of Josiah, the potter) and a group of keen gardeners and botanists, the society embarked upon an itinerant life. Its most significant garden stops were on the Duke of Devonshire's land at Chiswick (1821), where the gardener Paxton was scooped up by the Duke and later designed Crystal Palace (see p. 216); at Prince Albert's South Kensington cultural concourse (1861–82, see p. 220); and finally Wisley in Surrey, where land given by Sir Thomas Hanbury in 1903 is now a spectacular public garden. As for shows, the first fete was at Chiswick (1827), the first floral exhibition in the Society's Regent Street rooms (1831).

After the South Kensington demise, Inner Temple Gardens hosted the annual fete (1888–1913, see p. 131) until moved to the Royal Hospital gardens and called the Chelsea Flower Show. Here at Vincent Square, the 36,000 volumes in Linley Library (established 1868) include glorious watercolours of cerise Himalayan rhododendrons which seem to blossom off the paper, while the halls are a cocktail of colours and perfumes at the regular shows through the year, from exotic orchids to heavily perfumed old roses – less congested and cheaper than Chelsea (Vincent Square, SW1, tel 834 4333. One or two shows per month; Linley Library open for reference Mon–Fri 9.30am–5.30pm, no appointment required; to apply for six-monthly or annual membership of the RHS, apply to The Secretary, perks include 2 tickets for Members Day at Chelsea Flower Show, free entry to the regular shows, the fact-packed journal *The Garden*, permission to borrow library books. Publications, flowery gift catalogue. To visit Wisley, catch a Green Line Bus no. 715 from Oxford Circus; gardens open Mon–Sat 10am–7pm, Sun 2–7pm; charge).

Peeking down Maunsel Street, then returning along the south-east side of the square to Vauxhall Bridge Road in Pimlico, the irregularity, red brick, balconies and hanging gardens of Darbourne and Darke's Lillington Gardens Estate (1961–71) are a much happier post-war housing solution than Churchill Gardens. And in the middle rises the stripped tower of GE Street's **St James-the-Less** (1859–61) Gothic Revival church, whose exterior this time prepares you for one of the most sumptuous, moody London interiors (GF Watts fresco, Clayton and Bell windows, plenty of carving, ironwork and marble) built to honour the Bishop of Gloucester and Bristol by his three daughters, the Misses Monk for whom Street designed the house in Cadogan Square (see above) (tel 630 7726).

On down Vauxhall Bridge Road, cutting the corner through John Islip Street and Ponsonby Terrace, Henry Moore's bronze Locking Piece (1963–4) on the **Millbank** riverside heralds the Tate, found round to the left (with another four sculptures by Moore in its garden).

The **Tate Gallery** is two national collections in one: British art from the sixteenth century to around 1900, and international modern art from the Impressionists until now. The first complements the paintings in the National Gallery (see p. 88) and is straightforward; the second is very controversial – plain red canvases, kinetic contraptions and assorted bricks spark off column inches of ridicule accusing the Tate Trustees of wasting public money, ignoring some vital art developments and over-indulging in others. Opened in 1897, the gallery was named after the sugar millionaire Sir Henry Tate who gave his Victorian paintings and paid for Sidney Smith's building on the isolated site of Jeremy Bentham's octagonal prison (see p. 109). Subsequent additions (one paid for by the art dealer Joseph Duveen, two by his son) have culminated in James Stirling's beautifully proportioned and lit Clore Gallery for the Turner Collection (opened 1987), whose apple green doorway is set behind the trees and ornamental pond on the north side. This is the first of several new galleries to house special collections; and the Tate has a new and more distant northern annexe in Liverpool.

The Tate is not a maze. It is easy to seek out particular paintings. Moreover many canvases depict familiar London views – Samuel Scott's 'An Arch of Westminster Bridge', Thomas Girtin's 'The White House, Chelsea', Robert Bevan's 'House Sale at the Barbican', Charles Ginner's 'Embankment Gardens' and 'Piccadilly Circus', Oskar Kokoschka's 'View of the Thames', and the newly acquired paintings by RB Kitaj of 'Cecil Court, London WC2' and by Constable of 'The Opening of Waterloo Bridge' – bought with a £3 million public appeal.

The front hall has information on events and usually a free, up-to-date plan of what is on show in each gallery – there are weekly changes.

Beyond here, the shop is on the left as are the steps down to the basement café and the restaurant painted with Rex Whistler's fantasy mural recounting 'The Expedition in Pursuit of Rare Meats' (1926–7). Essentially, the British collection is on the left (south) side, where highlights include the starched Cholmondeley Sisters sitting up in bed with their babies, Hogarth's self-portrait, the newly acquired Gainsborough of 'The Revd John Chafy Playing the Violincello in a Landscape', social stunners by Reynolds and Stubbs, Constable's 'Flatford Mill', William Blake's haunting illustrations for Milton's *Paradise Lost* and a good block of Pre-Raphaelite canvases by Holman Hunt, Rossetti and Millais including the newly acquired Millais of 'Mrs James Wyatt Jr and her Daughter Sarah'.

The Modern Collection on the right (north side) launches with Monet, Pissarro and van Gogh, moves through Matisse, Picasso and a collection of 'ism' movements to Rothko, Jasper Johns and the stars of today, with plenty of British input – Ben Nicholson, Barbara Hepworth, Stanley Spencer, Paul Nash, Matthew Smith, Graham Sutherland, Victor Pasmore, David Hockney, Peter Blake, Howard Hodgkin, Barry Flanagan and many more.

Temporary exhibitions are found at the back. The magnificent Turner Collection is to the north (access also from the main building), where some of the 300 paintings, 20,000 drawings and nearly 300 sketchbooks left by JMW Turner (1775–1851) to the nation finally went on show 136 years after his death, together with paintbrushes, palettes, annotated guide books and letters (Millbank, SW1, tel 821 1313, for recorded information tel 821 7128; open Mon–Sat 10am–5.50pm, Sun 2–5.50pm; free, except for special exhibitions. Guided tours, lectures, workshops, films, concerts, special exhibitions, Friends and Young Friends societies (which has special openings on Sunday mornings and Monday evenings), excellent shop, café and bookable restaurant).

After a feast of prints, paintings and sculptures, there may well be a paintable sunset to glimpse above the Pimlico rooftops before heading home via Pimlico Underground.

The East End and Docklands: London's third city is reborn

Mapping it out from above: Tower Bridge for an eastwards gaze, Tower Bridge Museum for a higher one; Docklands Light Railway for a moving overview; the hilltop of Mudchute Farm for a static one; best of all, go under the Greenwich Foot Tunnel to see the whole East London sweep from the terrace in Greenwich Park.

Starting point: Bishopsgate, by Liverpool Street Station, access by Underground: Liverpool Street.

Good days to explore: Sunday for East End street markets. In this Jewish area, Saturday is quiet; Bethnal Green Museum of Childhood closes Friday.

Information: Tower Hamlets Environment Trust, 192 Hanbury Street, E1 (377 0481/2); open Mon–Fri 9am–5.30pm; extremely well-informed on Spitalfields and surrounding areas; stocks maps, walks trails and local information. Tower Hamlets Borough Information Office, see p. 4. The nearest LTB Information Centre is at the Tower, see p. 4. In addition, Whitechapel Art Gallery is well stocked with leaflets on events, and has a good café for browsing over them. To find out more about the Docklands schemes, contact Customer Enquiries, London Dockland Development Corporation, West India House, Millwall Docks, E1 (515 6000). To find out more about the East End

Jewish history, visit the Museum of the Jewish East End (see p. 170) and the Jewish Museum (p. 169). Refreshment suggestions: See p. 318.

Local festivals: Spitalfields Festival, first three weeks of June; a series of top quality concerts in Hawksmoor's Christ Church; information from Festival Office, Christchurch, Commercial Street, E1 (0483 575274). East End Festival, three weeks from mid-March; a lively platform for local-bred talent, from Bengali dance to Afro-Caribbean music; information from Peter Conway at the Arts Offices, Cheviot House, 227 Commercial Road, E1 (790 1818).

Local libraries: Central Library, Borough of Tower Hamlets, Bancroft Road, E1 (980 4366); open Mon, Tues, Thur and Fri 9am–8pm, Wed and Sat 9am–5pm; the reference Local History Library upstairs is strong on Cockney London, immigrants from Huguenots to Bengalis and the new regeneration of the Docklands, with maps and photographs to amplify books and reports, and a photocopier. Whitechapel Library, 77 High Street, E1 (247 5272/0265); open Mon, Tue and Thur 9am–8pm, Wed and Fri 9am–6pm, Sat 9am–12.30pm and 1.30–5pm; up-to-date, ethnic section strong on Bengali but weak on Judaica books which have mostly gone to Oxford University and other educational bodies.

Hard by the eastern boundary of the City, an old Huguenot shopfront stands near a synagogue where hatted and bearded Jews congregate on the pavement before the morning service. Round the corner, the action-packed morning air of Spitalfields fruit market is perfumed with fresh oranges, peaches and grapefruits. In the narrow streets to the east, the air is exotically spiced by *rogan gosht* bubbling up for The Famous Clifton Indian Restaurant. Eyes up, fabric flies through the machines of the Bengali sweat shops in upper floors. This furious rag trade competes with the latest Indian chartbusters wailing out from Sangeet Music and Bookshop. By Truman's brewery, where a woman hurries past with eggs collected from Spitalfields Farm, malty hops replace the spicy scents. And down in Wentworth Street, past the Jewish fashion shops and workrooms, Cockneys

deck their stalls out with jolly jewellery, bargain beachware, cartons of tacos or piles of non-stick frying pans. Then, fortified with a pint of Tubby Isaac's jellied eels or a cinnamon bun from Marks deli, they launch into cheery come-ons for lunchtime shoppers – 'Feel the quality, darling, six for a quid', 'Have a look, girls; here are your half-price Fred Perrys'. And Tony gives a mid-street theatrical turn on a soapbox: 'Forget about the £40 they charge at Harrods, forget about half-price stolen goods, this perfume is three pound for you – I've gone stark raving mad today.'

This is the East End today, a proud and thriving Cockney culture enriched with the traditions and trades of layers of immigrants. It stretches from the City walls eastwards through Bow, Stepney and Poplar to Stratford, West Ham, Canning Town and beyond.

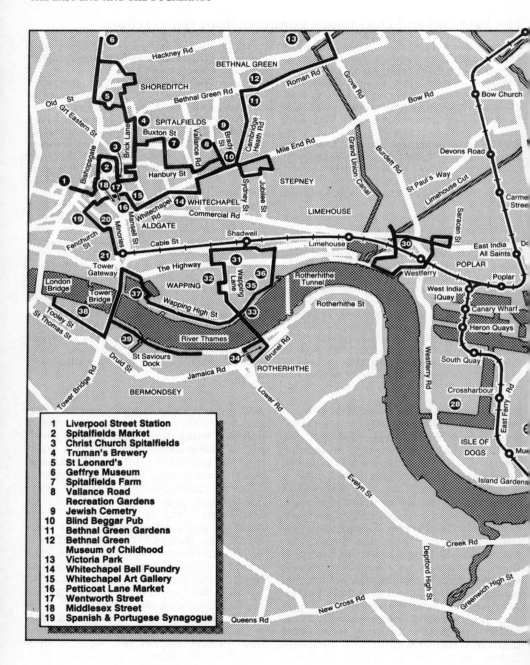

1   Liverpool Street Station
2   Spitalfields Market
3   Christ Church Spitalfields
4   Truman's Brewery
5   St Leonard's
6   Geffrye Museum
7   Spitalfields Farm
8   Vallance Road
    Recreation Gardens
9   Jewish Cemetry
10 Blind Beggar Pub
11 Bethnal Green Gardens
12 Bethnal Green
    Museum of Childhood
13 Victoria Park
14 Whitechapel Bell Foundry
15 Whitechapel Art Gallery
16 Petticoat Lane Market
17 Wentworth Street
18 Middlesex Street
19 Spanish & Portugese Synagogue

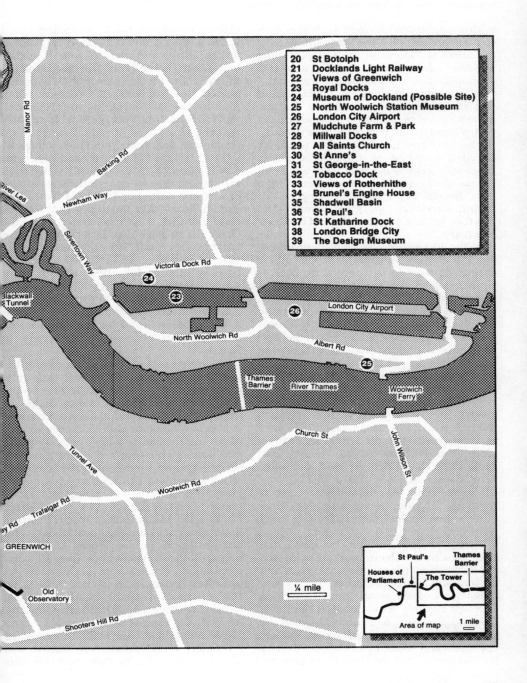

20 St Botolph
21 Docklands Light Railway
22 Views of Greenwich
23 Royal Docks
24 Museum of Dockland (Possible Site)
25 North Woolwich Station Museum
26 London City Airport
27 Mudchute Farm & Park
28 Millwall Docks
29 All Saints Church
30 St Anne's
31 St George-in-the-East
32 Tobacco Dock
33 Views of Rotherhithe
34 Brunel's Engine House
35 Shadwell Basin
36 St Paul's
37 St Katharine Dock
38 London Bridge City
39 The Design Museum

With the industrial revolution, British agricultural labourers left the fields and became the urban workforce in the fast-expanding London docks and their industrial offshoots – shipbuilding, engineering, furniture, brewing, clothing, etc. Quiet villages east of London proper exploded, became dormitory towns, and then became not just part of London but, in many people's minds, the home of true Londoners. The romantic, crowded East End of music halls, pearly kings and Cockney rhyming slang was born. For the immigrants who joined them – from Jews fleeing persecution to Bangladeshis fleeing starvation – the great London port was their landing stage and the East End their first home.

As the docks grew, the flat plain surrounding the twisting Thames was cut into a chequerboard of docks to receive the fleets of ships bringing the empire's wealth to its capital and sending out products worldwide. Such was Britain's optimism for her future that the last and biggest dock, King George V, was only completed in 1921; the Port of London Authority dredged fifty miles of the Thames deeper for the bigger ships in the 1930s; and after the Second World War's devastating bombings, a massive rebuilding programme continued until the 1950s. The Brave New World approach did not work. The docks rapidly declined and collapsed. With the arrival of container ships, the Port moved to Tilbury. East India Dock closed first, in 1967; and when King George V Dock closed in 1982, just 41 years after the technological feat of building it, the eleven-mile-long dock system from Tower Bridge to Barking Creek fell silent.

During the docks' heyday, the wealth that lined the City merchants' pockets by-passed the docks' labour force, the immigrants and the transient sailors that formed the East End population. Their high times watching Charlie Chaplin's stage debut at the Royal Cambridge music hall were matched by appalling poverty, deprivation, cholera epidemics and solace in drink, described by JH Mackay in 1891 as 'the hell of poverty.

Like an enormous, black, motionless, giant kracken, the poverty of London lies there in lurking silence and encircles with its mighty tentacles the life and wealth of the City and of the West End.' It was here that Dr Barnardo started his orphanages, William Booth founded the Salvation Army and Canon Barnett fought for healthier housing. It was here that the new breed of radical socialist and communist politicians found their followers.

This huge tract of industry and commerce was London's back yard, neatly veiled from the affluent squares and gentlemen's estates of west and north London. The City was the curtain. Now, after the docks' post-war decline, the City is its regenerator. After the Great Fire of 1666, two-thirds of the City of London was rebuilt. Since the Second World War, all but 70 of the City's 667 acres have been rebuilt. In July 1981, with a space squeeze in the City, the London Docklands Development Corporation was formed to be a catalyst to scoop up and reshape eight-and-a-half square miles of the docklands in the largest urban redevelopment project in Europe.

Their brief is to create a water city for the twenty-first century. The chosen strip runs eastwards from the Tower to Beckton on the north bank and from London Bridge to Deptford on the south bank, a spectacular land-and-waterscape with 450 square acres of docks and 55 miles of water's edge. With the government's blessing, £50 million a year for seven years and, for the enterprise zone, a set of tax incentives, LDDC drew up a master plan for four areas – Wapping and Limehouse; London Bridge City and Surrey Docks; Isle of Dogs (with a special Business Enterprise Zone) and the Royal Docks – and acted as agents for developers. LDDC then prepared the infrastructure (power, communicatior , etc), while private investors put up offices, houses and recreation facilities. By 1987, £250 million of public money and £2,200 million of private money had been poured in. By 1987, 600 companies had moved in and 12,000 homes had been built. To encourage the project, prime minister Mrs Thatcher was filmed driving a tractor there, and ministers and royals were regularly wheeled in to open completed buildings.

With astonishing speed, the stunning, water-filled setting of the docklands is reviving to become London's third city: a purpose-built, up-market, high-tech paradise of gadget-filled offices, expensive riverside apartments, sports centres, museum and entertainment complexes, and chic shopping malls with expense-account restaurants. On the still docks, ships laden with spices are replaced by floating restaurants, wind-surfers and wet-suited water-skiers. On the twisting, tidal Thames, a fast river-bus whisks high-powered businessmen to the City and Westminster, London's two older cities. Docklands even has its own airport, its own high-level railway skimming over the waters and past the gleaming buildings, and its own cable and satellite television and communications network.

Here and there a scrubbed warehouse or Georgian home recalls the past, and pockets of Victorian terraces struggle to maintain their identity sporting some strong graffiti: 'Yuppies out!', 'Mug a yuppie'. Meanwhile, the East End streets bordering the City are being spruced up. Among the Asian aromas of Spitalfields, Afro-Caribbean builders, wearing red woolly caps to protect their long tresses, restore dilapidated houses for the latest wave of immigrants, a clique of increasingly less Bohemian, middle-class professionals.

It is an exciting, fast-changing area. The East End is still full of its unquenchable spirit and romance. A glimpse round the western corner – Spitalfields, Whitechapel and Aldgate – conjures up some of its past and reveals a little of its present. Then London's new Docklands city is most easily explored by hopping on and off its own toy, the Docklands Light Railway, to see the latest progress in the two most developed areas, the businessman's dream on the Isle of Dogs and then London's latest fashionable address, Wapping and Limehouse. This massive regeneration, into which billions of pounds and dollars have been pumped, may or may not work in the long term. But it is certainly worth a look.

Starting at **Liverpool Street Station** (1874), just inside the City boundary, Edward Wilson's red-brick station, which hurtles some 60,000 pinstriped commuters into the City from the eastern counties every morning, was for poet and conservationist Sir John Betjeman 'the most picturesque and interesting of the London termini'. The Liverpool refers to Lord Liverpool, three times elected prime minister 1812–27, and not to the then thriving port on the north-west coast of England. Beside it, Charles Barry Jnr's **Great Eastern Hotel** (1884, additions 1901), the City's only large hotel, had a special underground railway track to deliver coal for heat and sea water for clients' baths and it still has two Masonic temples and a glowing glass dome in the City Gates Restaurant. This was the first site of the Royal Bethlehem Hospital (founded 1247), known as Bedlam, where the insane were chained to the wall and ducked in water or whipped to calm their tantrums. Its next home, at Moorfields (1675), was decorated with Cibber's eerie statues of Madness and Melancholy (now in the V&A) and visitors paid to stare at the caged lunatics from specially built galleries, a favourite outing finally stopped in 1770 because the tourists teased the inmates too cruelly.

Across Bishopsgate, with a glimpse at the Nat-West Tower (see p. 72) and other tubes of rooms stretching into the clouds to find more space, eighteenth-century **New Street** is in sharp contrast. Georgian houses line the left side; five acres of splendid, well-fortified warehouses built for the valuable cargo of the East Indian Company are on the right and straight ahead. Newly redeveloped to lose their insides but keep their facades, these are a taste of Docklands to come. Richard Judd designed Old Bengal warehouse on the right (1769–70); he and his successor, Henry Holland (of Hans Town fame, see p. 237), later designed the rest (1792–1820), the cobbles now prettied up with gardens, fountains and benches. Through it lies **Devonshire Square** (c.1740), built on the site of the Tudor mansion of the Cavendish family who later moved west (see p. 152), with nos 12 and 13 the earliest survivors.

Back into New Street and right, then right again down Cook Hill and Catherine Wheel Alley, a network of old Spitalfields lanes built over the site of Henry VIII's artillery ground (1537) lies across Middlesex Street. They are a microcosm of today's Spitalfields mix. **Sandys Row** runs along past old Huguenot shopfronts, with more in **Artillery Lane** on the left, and even a precision scale-maker behind one. Further along Sandys Row, the dwindling congregation for the local synagogue gossip on the street before using their keys to let themselves in for the service. Returning along the row, **Artillery Passage** is on the left, where Asian housewives in traditional, baggy, floral trousers and British woolly cardigans shop at Jarnal Food Store, near Marwah Cash and Carry and Naranjan the wholesaler. Further down, on the Crispin Street corner, Providence Row Night Refuge gives shelter to the homeless.

But before then a left into Artillery Lane then right down Gun Street opens into Brushfield Street and the heart of Spitalfields. The fruit market is ahead and a splendid **view** of Christ Church to the right, with the Jack the Ripper pub next to it.

Spitalfields has a rich history. As the City and Aldgate overspilt in the late seventeenth century, a town grew up on the fields to the east of St Mary Spital, a medieval priory and hospital. Soon known as 'the most factious hamlet of all the Tower Division', Christ Church was built to curb the nonconformity. The church also served the first tide of immigrants, the Huguenots fleeing France after the Revocation of the Edict of Nantes (1685). Many were weavers and Spitalfields, already an area for silk-weaving, became the silk centre of Georgian London. The Huguenot master weavers and dyers used their new found prosperity from damasks, velvets and brocades, usefully protected by the government ban on imported French silks, to build fine houses along Fournier, Nantes and other suitably named streets.

Weaving declined early in the last century and by the 1880s the former Georgian grandeur housed sweated labour surrounded by crowded slums. Here, the Jewish immigrants, fleeing the pogroms in Russia and Poland following the death of Tsar Alexander II (1881), changed the course of the clothing trade from exclusive silks to furs, leather and modest tailoring – trades still continued today. Meanwhile, the vegetable and fruit market (established 1682) was bought by Robert Horner (1856), a market porter made good, who lavishly rebuilt the halls. It was another market porter who, in the foggy, unlit, cobbled alleys of nearby Gunthorpe Street, found the corpse of Jack the

Ripper's first victim on August 7, 1888. Hysterical terror gripped the neighbourhood as five more prostitutes were murdered and horribly mutilated over the next eight weeks – the Ripper even teased the police by preceding his atrocities with letters explaining his next move. The murders stopped, but the Ripper was never found. It was this, London's greatest unsolved mystery, that prompted Arthur Conan Doyle to invent his super-sleuth, Sherlock Holmes (whose fictional address was 221B Baker Street, see p. 153).

Today, with slums swept away, this large patch of early Georgian houses is shared between the two latest sets of immigrants. The Indians, Pakistanis and, most of all, Bangladeshis, arrived fleeing the upheavals and resulting poverty following India's Independence (1947) and the creation of East and West Pakistan (the eastern part now called Bangladesh). They now whirl many of the tailoring machines and run local grocers, sari shops and restaurants for their compatriots. And, living among them, the rising conservation movements of the 1960s onwards bred an intrepid and brave bunch of Georgian devotees who struggled above all the odds, including ruthless developers, to save the Huguenot streets, gradually buying up available houses and restoring them to their former grandeur.

To see some of this mixed, lively society, turn left out of Gun Street, then right round the market to **Spital Square** (1720s and '30s) where silk-weavers built their homes over the site of St Mary's Priory. No. 37, a survivor on the left, now appropriately houses two champions of architectural conservation: the Society for the Protection of Ancient Buildings, founded by William Morris in 1887 and the first such society, and the Georgian Group, founded by Lord Derwent in 1937 to protect the glories of Georgian houses, squares and terraces from the maniacal developers (SPAB, 37 Spital Square, E1, tel 377 1644; Georgian Group, same address, tel 377 1722; callers can collect information on membership and activities; members may view house by appointment). But to experience a Huguenot house come to life, go through Nantes Passage on the north side of the square and into **Folgate Street** where an American anglophile, Dennis Severs, has restored no. 18 to its original condition and, for a fee, will light up the candles and give visitors a tour, conjuring up the masterweaver's life in Georgian London (to book an evening tour, write or telephone Mr Severs at 18 Folgate Street, E1, tel 247 4013; charge).

Back down Folgate Street and right into **Commercial Street**. The City Corporation pumped £2 million into Spitalfields fruit and vegetable market in 1922 to make it the biggest in Britain. Today, the market is threatened with removal eastwards to Hackney, Stratford or Leyton by 1990, and the buildings with redevelopment as yet more offices and flats. Meanwhile, on a summer morning, the porters whizz trolley-loads of French cherries around and deliver electric truck-loads of Jersey potatoes to waiting buyers. There are mangoes from India, carrots from Italy, aubergines from Holland, oranges from Israel and home-grown tomatoes and lettuces. And on chilly December mornings, the area is dotted with little fires where porters warm their hands between delivering the Christmas Brussels sprouts (Mon–Sat, 4.30am–noon). Opposite, the Jack the Ripper pub has an engraved window with a grisly list of the Ripper's victims and where they were found.

Beyond, **Christ Church** (1720) was built under the Fifty New Churches Act (1711, see St Mary-le-Strand, p. 120) and designed by Wren's pupil Nicholas Hawksmoor – the same Act and architect were used for two more great East End churches, St Anne's, Limehouse and St George-in-the-East (see below for both). The Tuscan portico leads into one of Hawksmoor's masterpieces, enriched with Flaxman's monument to Sir Robert Ladbroke and another to local house-owner Edward Peck (1737). Outside, eighteenth-century Spitalfields prosperity is continued in the gravestones, many of them French, while today's church notices hung on the railings are in both English and Bengali (tel 247 7202; if closed, apply to the Rectory at no. 2 Fournier).

Turning left and left again, the rag trade thrives in Fashion Street, where playwright Arnold Wesker once lived. At the end, sweet and spicy aromas from Asian cafes, sweetmeat shops and restaurants fill the **Brick Lane** air where Bengalis have replaced the Jewish population. Across the road, the synagogue in Heneage Street is now an Asian supermarket. Turning left, the Jami Masjid on the corner of **Fournier Street** is the epitome of Spitalfields: built as a Huguenot chapel (1743–4), it has been a Methodist chapel (1809), the Spitalfields Great Synagogue for the very orthodox Machzikei Hadath society (1897) and is now a mosque. Behind it lurks the best preserved section of Huguenot London, mostly built from 1718–28. Looking up, the houses have long windows in the weaving attics to make best use of the daylight; at street level, there are grand porticos to impress visitors.

Turning up Fournier Street, houses restored to former glory stand cheek to cheek with Bengali sweat shops, where whirling electric sewing machines have replaced the soft clicking Huguenot shuttles. More Georgian delights are along Wilkes Street on the right (with charming 1860 almshouses on Puma Court on the left); in **Princelet Street** on the right again (where a Yiddish theatre was at no. 3 and a synagogue is still at no. 19; to visit, contact the Museum of the Jewish East End, tel 346 2288/ 349 1143 or the Tower Hamlets Environment Trust, see above). And there are more in Hanbury Street, further along Wilkes Street (where the Ripper's Annie Chapman was found behind no. 29). But the Huguenots were not as grand as they made out. Spitalfields campaigner and resident Dan Cruickshank reveals the secret of no. 2 Wilkes Street, 'typical' of Spitalfields houses: 'although appearing fashionably spacious from the exterior, it is in fact cramped . . . one-room deep.'

A few yards up Brick Lane the malty hop smells, a black eagle on the bridge across the road and the tall chimney beyond announce **Truman's Brewery**, one of several East End breweries that supplied London with its famed good beer and one of the few still brewing today. Founded as the Black Eagle Brewery (1660), it was acquired by Joseph Truman (1666), who built 65–79 Brick Lane (1705–6) – Trumans had been brewing in London since 1381. His grandson Benjamin established its reputation for porter (black stout), made it one of the top three London producers and was knighted by George III. Sampson Hanbury took over, then Thomas Buxton (hence Truman, Hanbury and Buxton inscribed on many pubs) who made it the world's largest brewery (400,000 barrels a year) and was created a baronet by Queen Victoria. Today, the Truman brewery is part of Watney, Mann & Truman. The beers brewed here include Truman Best Bitter and Truman Special Mild; the grand salon of the Director's House (1740) contains the company board room; and the new glass facade was added by Arup Associates (1976).

Beyond the railway bridge, **Brick Lane Market** surges into action every Sunday at dawn – early birds carry torches in the 5am winter darkness – and is soon a classic East End market in full swing. Begun by eighteenth-century farmers as an attempt to avoid paying hefty tolls to enter the City gates, traders with smaller livestock and other goods soon joined in. In the 1920s, it was famous for its Christmas turkey auctions. Today, threatened by the inevitable developers, the stalls range from old clothes, political pamphlets, boxes of radios, armfuls of watches and hideous crockery in Brick Lane itself to the special treats of Cheshire Street on the right, Sclater Street on the left and Bacon Street further up – silver, glass, jewellery and even shellfish. Towards the top, on the left, another Spitalfields *pot pourri*: The Jolly Butchers is a Truman pub sandwiched between two Jewish bakeries (Beigel Bake's salmon and cream cheese filled beigels are irresistible) and then an Indian clothes shop and the Brick Lane Tandoor.

North of here lies **Shoreditch**, much changed since its medieval origins and its Tudor fame as the country town where James Burbage put up the first playhouse in England (1576), later moved south of the Thames and built as The Globe (see p. 73). Its entertainment tradition flourished again in the last century, when one of the most famous of the 30 or so music halls in the East End was here, The London (1856–1934), whose new facade 1893 was lit by glass braziers to welcome crowds who paid between six pence and a guinea to sit in the 1400 seats. The routine was similar in them all. The chairman pepped up the excited crowd with his patter, bashed his hammer to quell the uproar and introduced with extravagant and often rude praise up to 40 turns including dancing girls, bawdy comedians, magicians and a good sing-along before the top-of-the-bill superstars came on – perhaps Marie Lloyd, Little Titch dancing in big boots, comedian Dan Leno doing his clog dance, Charles Cockburn singing 'The Man Who Broke the Bank at Monte Carlo', Harry Champion of 'I'm 'Enery the Eighth I am' or George Robey's 'Prime Minister of Mirth'. Charlie Chaplin made his stage debut at the Royal Cambridge in Commercial Street; Gracie Fields and Stan Laurel of Laurel and Hardy played at the Queen's in Poplar. In these glittering palaces, developed from the sing-songs in pub saloon bars, the poor escaped from reality to be entertained by stars who knew what they wanted because they came from the same grimy streets. Marie Lloyd (1870–1922), who came from Hoxton, just west of Shoreditch, was the best loved of all; less successful performers got a hailstorm of bottles and rotten vegetables.

The music halls' heyday stretched from the 1850s to the 1930s, when the cinemas killed them and the songs went back to the pubs for the Friday night knees-up. Currently, the Hackney Empire was revived in 1987, with modern music and cabaret

(Mare Street, E8, tel 985 2424), the Players' Theatre thrives in the West End with Victorian music hall (see p. 293); and the Theatre Royal Stratford East continues the tradition with a blend of traditional and contemporary arts in lively monthly music-hall nights, much patronised by locals who cheer and jeer as their grandparents did (Gerry Raffles Square, E15, tel 534 0310).

Today, a quick circular spin around Shoreditch includes the best London flower market and a fascinating furniture museum. Crossing Bethnal Green Road, Brick Lane continues and then bends left to Swanfield Road where a right and left along Palissy Street reaches **Arnold Circus**. Here, Owen Fleming's Boundary Street Estate (1897–1900) was the first and one of the most enlightened of the London County Council housing schemes to replace the slums – this replaced the infamous Jago slum, a foul rookery where gang warfare was paramount, policemen entered at their peril and children were raised to 'learn cunning, spare nobody and stop at nothing', according to Arthur Morrison's novel, *Child of Jago* (1896). Out through Calvert Avenue and right, the bells of the tall, layered steeple of George Dance the Elder's **St Leonard's** church (1736–40) answered the nursery rhyme question: 'When will you pay me, said the bells of Old Bailey' with 'When I grow rich, said the bells of Shoreditch'.

About 200 yards beyond the church up Kingsland Road lies a London treat, the **Geffrye Museum**. It is a collection of English furniture and woodwork from Tudor times until 1939 displayed in 14 charming almshouses (1715) surrounding a tree-filled square. Sir Robert Geffrye (1613–1703), Lord Mayor (1685) and twice Master of the Ironmongers' Company, left a bequest to build almshouses – a popular form of charity work whose legacy is a string of small-scale buildings surrounding the City. When the Company moved the ironmongers' widows out, the council created a museum (1911) for crafts students, since the district was a furniture and cabinet-making centre. The collection is arranged chronologically, with each almshouse as a specific room. By removing parts of the dividing walls, the visitor moves through the history of English furniture: a continuous line of open-fronted rooms fully furnished with panelling, furniture, carpets, curtains, lighting, pictures and nicknacks, from the panelled Elizabethan Room and John Evelyn's Cabinet of Curiosities to the Early Georgian Room saved from Chancery Lane and two stylish 1930s rooms

(Kingsland Road, E2, tel 739 8368/9893; open Tues–Sat 10am–5pm, Sun 2–5pm; free. Workshops, special exhibitions, Friends society, shop). If it is Sunday morning, Columbia Road flower market is on. To find it, return down Kingsland Road and cross Hackney Road to go down Diss Street and Baroness Road – you will pass people leaving, triumphant, with boxes of pansies, huge bunches of lilies and giant pot plants from this oasis of green that springs up every week with a blaze of colour. It is the strong surviving spark of Baroness Burdett-Coutts's philanthropic market (1869) founded to provide the locals with cheap food.

Back down Brick Lane and under the railway bridge, Buxton Street leads left where, well down the road, a left through Allen Gardens arrives at an urban surprise: **Spitalfields Farm**. Set up in 1979, the chickens cluck about while the horses and goats quietly graze (Weaver Street, E1, tel 247 8762; open daily 9.30am–5.30pm; eggs and goat's milk for sale). On leaving, Deal Street is straight ahead; and turning right down Hanbury Street a pedestrian lane connects to Vallance Road.

Whitechapel is to the right. Lying on the main route out to Essex, it was named after its whitewashed St Mary's church and became the home for bell-founders and other metalworkers ousted from the City for their noisy craft. Intensely poor from the start, three-quarters of Whitechapel people earned less than one pound a year in 1664, the lowest wage in East London. Cheap coaching houses lined the City end of Whitechapel High Street where carts piled high with hay and vegetables, brewers' drays loaded with beer and herds of sheep and cattle pushed and shoved to squeeze into the already crowded City – scenes that continued into the 1920s and are still remembered by elderly locals.

As the docks took off, immigrant Germans were employed to refine sugar from the East India Docks, while the Irish worked as dredgers, ballast heavers and coal whippers. Crime was the norm; the slang was a language of its own. In the upper room of a back alley a manager of child thieves known as a 'kidsman' – Fagin's trade in *Oliver Twist* – would use his mistress as a prop while he trained a new 'dipper' (pickpocket) to upgrade his art from merely a 'smatter hauler' (handkerchief stealer) to the more genteel and profitable 'tooler' (picker of ladies' pockets). Then the gang would dress up as 'swells' and go to work, the tooler slipping a pretty silk handkerchief to his 'stickman'

and then strolling off after a successful 'pull' while the 'stall' impeded pursuit.

Whitechapel was where the Sephardic Jews had settled in the seventeenth century, and where over 100,000 Jews fleeing the pogroms arrived late in the last century, quickly making the district the centre of the clothing industry and Petticoat Lane the main retail market, while maintaining their language, religion, culture and dress by setting up synagogues, friendly societies, theatres and food shops. Whitechapel resembled an east European town, a Yiddish *shtetl*. At the same time, the Jews' Free School turned Yiddish-speaking immigrants into English-speaking gentlemen – the route out of the ghetto. Alfred Marks (of Marks & Spencer), Joe Loss and David Kossoff are old boys. But even with the pre-war Whitechapel Jewish population of 90,000 now reduced to 6,000 (the exodus is an anti-clockwise sweep round leafy north London) and their places taken by Asians, Saturday is quiet in Whitechapel.

For the dazzling, ostentatious Victorian West End, Whitechapel's dark mystery epitomised the East End and brought conflicting reactions. Charles Booth thought that in this 'Eldorado of the East, a gathering together of poor fortune seekers', the 'simple natural lives of the working class' were so much better than 'the artificial complicated existence of the rich'. Others were excited, one comparing Mile End Fair on Saturday night with a muddy country lane: 'The contagion of numbers, the sense of something going on, the theatres and the music halls, the brightly lighted streets and the busy crowds . . . Who could wonder that men are drawn into such a vortex?.' The scientist TH Huxley was aghast, claiming that the Polynesian savage 'in his most primitive condition [was] not half so savage, so unclean, so irreclaimable as the tenant of a tenement in an East London slum'. But for insiders, it was a different picture. The East Ender and entertainer George Lansbury wrote of 'the unexpected happiness in the middle of sordid conditions'. With such poverty and deprivation mixed with such vitality, colour and excitement, Whitechapel was a magnet for both Victorian social reformers and socialist revolutionaries.

Turning down Vallance Road, **Vallance Road Recreation Gardens** on the left has a small stone birdbath-sundial marking the spot where William Booth (1829–1912), a tall and charismatic man with flowing hair and beard, pitched a tent in an old Quaker burial ground and, with naphtha flares for light, began preaching on the night of July 2, 1865.

He continued nightly for six weeks. This was the birth of the Salvation Army which, with absolute devotion, promoted the joy of giving and the love of God. It set up soup kitchens (a penny for the poor, free for the penniless), hostels with large wooden boxes for beds and sent the Army girls, known as 'slum saviours', into the slums to tend the sick and feed the hungry. All was run with military precision, banners, bands and stirring music. Such practicality and warmth of spirit was infinitely preferable to the ways of some other Victorian saints. When Booth died, his funeral procession blocked City traffic for a day; today, the Army works in 80 countries (see also p. 171). Round the corner to the left, Durward Street leads to **Fulborne Street** on the right where, a generation after Booth, a different solution was offered to the poor: delegates for the fifth Congress of the Russian Social Democratic Labour Party in 1907 included Lenin, Stalin, Trotsky, Gorky and Litvinoff.

At the end of Durward Street, a left into Brady Street passes some eighteenth-century shops to the **Jewish Cemetery** (opened 1761, closed 1858) on the left, immaculately maintained behind closed doors – just knock to enter. Here lie Nathan Rothschild (died 1836), founder of the London line of the banking family and a patron of the 4,000-pupil Jews' Free School, and Miriam Levy, who opened the first Whitechapel soup kitchen. Back down Brady Street and left into **Whitechapel Road**, the Albion Brewery (founded 1808) on the left introduced bottled brown ale to London beer drinkers in 1899. Just beyond, the **Blind Beggar** pub is where William Booth, seeing the crowds of poor people in the taverns and gin palaces, impulsively made his first public speech in June, 1865. For modern East End anti-heroes, this is where Ronald Kray's shooting of George Cornell in the saloon bar in 1966 finally led to the arrest of the infamous Kray brothers. The ghosts of more crime tales lurk down **Sidney Street**, across the road. Here, at no. 100, Winston Churchill, then as Home Secretary in charge of the Metropolitan Police, came to witness the siege by an army of police, firemen and 20 Scots Guards of two Social Democrats from Latvia, who had tried to rob a jewellers. After six hours of shooting, the pair saw there was no hope, set fire to the house and died in the blaze.

Politics and reform crowded this corner on the borders of Whitechapel and **Stepney** – the Saxon settlement that witnessed the glory of Edward I's second parliament being held in the mansion of the Mayor of London, Henry le Waleis (1299), enjoyed Tudor prosperity and then suffered Victorian misery as a dormitory town for international dock labour and a centre for the rag trade. By 1841, Stepney's population had risen to a seething 204,000, with no drainage, over-crowding, cholera epidemics and one of the worst crime records in London. Stepney Green was the setting for Arnold Wesker's play *Chicken Soup and Barley*, and the site of the first Dr Barnardo home. Dr Thomas J Barnardo (1845–1905), an Irishman who came from Dublin to work at the London Hospital, set up his Ragged School (1865) to give local urchins warmth, food and shelter. By the time he died, 60,000 children had been given a new start in his homes whose slogan was 'no destitute child ever refused admission'.

Back up Sidney Street and right through Lindley Street to the corner of **Jubilee Street**, New Alexander Hall was where Lenin spoke at celebrations to mark the 32nd anniversary of the Paris Commune (1903), and where Rudolf Rocker, a German Libertarian and trade union leader of immigrant Jews (1895–1914), founded the Anarchist Club (1907). Left up Jubilee Street, then right along **Redman's Road** and left up Assembly Passage into **Mile End Road**, Captain Cook lived between voyages at no. 88 on the left.

Further along, on the right, the New Assembly Hall replaced the Great Assembly Hall (1883) founded by Frederick Charrington (1850–1936). After schooling at Marlborough and the gentleman's Grand Tour of the Continent, he was shocked into reality and into forsaking a vast inheritance from the family brewers when he saw the 'drunken fathers, gin-drinking mothers, ill-used children' beneath the 'high gilt letters' of his name on a family-owned pub. Throwing himself into a lifelong campaign for teetotalism, he raised money – even squeezing the family for some – to build a huge Assembly Hall with Coffee Palace, book salon selling 'pure' literature and seating for 5,000. While he fought for the closure of the jolly Lusby's music hall along the road by parading fierce billboards (ineffective) and surreptitiously noted who went in and out of the brothels and threatened to publish his lists (very effective), Charrington differed from the other East End saints. He realised there was a growing social consciousness, and he encouraged it. In 1890, he gave the Hall to William Morris, Eleanor Marx-Aveling (Karl Marx's daughter) and Prince Kropotkin to protest against Russian persecution of the

Jews; in 1895 Marx-Aveling and Kropotkin led the protest against the (Trades Union Congress) racist resolutions to exclude aliens (i.e. Russian Jews); in 1912, 8,000 Jewish tailors began their strike against the sweated labour system here; and later the same year, Charrington fed the hungry dockworkers' families during the second Dock Strike.

Just beyond the hall, a hidden treat: the Almshouses of the Trinity Brethren (1695). Built for 28 'decayed masters and commanders of ships, or the widows of such', Captain Mudd of Ratcliffe gave the land and Christopher Wren may have designed the avenue of little houses leading up to the central chapel. And to get a flavour of how the enticing glamour of Charrington's and other East End pubs contrasted with the dreary squalor of the slums, nip into Murphy's to see the mahogany fittings and cut-glass mirrors.

At Cambridge Heath Road, a 10-minute detour right leads to a giant children's playroom of old toys, board games and magnificent dolls' houses. The road runs up to **Bethnal Green**, another Saxon village whose open fields attracted the Tudor wealthy before the Spitalfields overspill of weavers and dyers and then furniture-makers, shoe-makers and the rag trade packed it to bursting point. On the right, flower-filled and well-clipped **Bethnal Green Gardens** (opened 1923) cover the original green and retain the local atmosphere. Kirby's Castle (1570) overlooked it, where Sir William Ryder, Deputy Master of Trinity House (see p. 105), lived when Pepys stored his valuables there on the second day of the Great Fire, September 3, 1666: 'About 4 o'clock in the morning, my Lady Batten sent me a cart to carry away all my money and plate and best things to Sir W Riders at Bednall Greene; which did, riding myself in my nightgown in the cart.' The diary was stored there, too. The castle later became a lunatic asylum and the gardens are still nicknamed Barmy Park.

Bethnal Green Museum of Childhood stands in more gardens across Roman Road (with a glimpse of Paradise Row on the left). This is another Victoria & Albert Museum outpost, this time for the department of dolls and toys, although the original plan was for a local museum. Set up in 1872, the collection is housed in Charles Young's train-shed building which was originally one of the temporary sheds for the V&A in South Kensington (see p. 222). It is a wonderland for adults and children. A whole dolls' house estate of mini country mansions ranges from a painted and lacquered cabinet with cheese in the pantry and chandeliers in the salon and the child Amy Miles's own dream house (1890s), with what appears to be three playrooms, to the stylish Modern Movement home, White Ladies (1935), with cocktails on the balcony and tennis and swimming pool in the garden. Then there are early Monopoly boards, Japanese puppets, German toy soldiers, Teddy Bears and dolls, electric trains and clockwork ducks, beautifully carved Noah's Arks and new toys including a witty Alice Through the Looking Glass chess set (1983) and, of course, the Royal Wedding Charger (1981) – and do not miss the childhood galleries upstairs (Cambridge Heath Road, E2, tel 980 2415/ 3204/4315; open Mon–Sat 10am–6pm; free. Workshops, special exhibitions, good child-proof shop; café being built).

East of here, along Roman Road and left down Grove Road, **Victoria Park** was the first public London park to be created for the people, not for royalty. To alleviate the appalling overcrowding, pollution and lack of sanitation (in 1839 the average life expectancy in Bethnal Green was 26 for a tradesman, 16 for an operative), 30,000 locals signed a petition to Queen Victoria. Funds were raised from selling York House (beside St James's Palace, see p. 138), 218 acres were bought and James Pennethorne (later of Battersea Park) landscaped them. Opened in 1845, Victoria Park soon had bathing and boating lakes, 40,000 trees and shrubs planted and its own song: 'The Park is called the People's Park, And all the walks are theirs, And strolling through the flowery paths, They breathe exotic airs. South Kensington, let it remain, Among the Upper Ten, Let East London, with useful things, Be left with working men.' Today, footpaths beside the Hertford Union and Regent's Canal lead east to Waltham Abbey; the boating lake has the Chinese pagoda left over from the 1847 Chinese Exhibition in Knightsbridge; the secluded Old English flower garden lies to the east; two of the alcoves from Old London Bridge are opposite the cricket pitch; and locals eat, drink, fish, swim and play bowls, tennis, hockey and netball in what is still firmly a people's park (for information tel 985 1957; cafés open in fine weather).

Back down Cambridge Heath Road and right into **Whitechapel Road**, Barnardo's London Hospital is on the left and Woods Alley opposite, just after the Underground station and as dark and dingy as when the Ripper met his second victim here, Mary Ann Nichols. Turning left down New Road, Fieldgate Street retains its red brick tenaments and is where Stalin and Litvinoff stayed at the Tower House in 1907, now a home for vagrants. **Whitechapel Bell Foundry** is at the end of the street, on Whitechapel Road, where descendants of the medieval craftsmen ousted from the City still practise their traditional trade in the Georgian buildings. Bells for Westminster Abbey were cast here; Big Ben's was recast during its disastrous saga (see p. 84); and America's Liberty Bell was made here. Across the road, locals prefer the Kosher Luncheon Club in Kasler Hall up Greatorex Street to the better-known Bloom's.

Moving west along the high road, past Aldgate East Underground station, **Whitechapel Art Gallery** is the legacy of the district's fourth great social reformer, Canon Samuel Augustus Barnett (1844–1913). He and his wife arrived as ardent missionaries to the worst parish in London: '. . . crowded and insanitary courts and alleys . . . children neglected . . . the beer shops full, the schools shut up.' The Barnetts' attitude was direct: 'The principle of our work is that we aim at decreasing not suffering but sin!'. Their assessment of the parish was harsh: the poor starve because of the alms they receive, 'never learn to work or save' and 'the want of clothes does not so loudly call for remedy as the want of interest and culture'. Fierce as they were, their three-fold initiative made a lasting impact. Barnett founded Toynbee Hall (1884, round in Commercial Street) where Lady Colin Campbell and West End choirs gave concerts and Carlyle, Milton, Wesley and later Clement Attlee gave lectures. Barnett also instigated and helped push through parliament the Artisans Dwellings Act (1875), which marked the start of slum clearance to replace rabbit warrens with healthy housing and changed the landscape of East London.

Barnett also put on painting shows, so popular that he then founded the Whitechapel Art Gallery (built 1897–9, opened 1901) to bring good visual arts to the East End on a permanent basis. CH Townsend designed the Art Nouveau building with castle towers and massively arched entrance. Today, newly restored, some of the most interesting shows of contemporary art are held here; a number of artists live in the East End so there are often local contributions; and the gallery is an informal meeting place and information centre for the area (Whitechapel High Street, E1, tel 377 0107; open Tues–Sun 11am–5pm, Wed until 8pm; free. Lectures, workshops, films, audio visuals, bookshop, good café).

Along the west wall of the gallery, narrow and eerie **Angel Alley** survives to evoke Henrietta Burnett's description of it in 1874 as ' . . . quite wrecks of houses . . . sometime a den of wild Irish'. Now, the Libertarian Freedom Press keeps the East End political spirit alive. Bloom's is beyond, the best known kosher restaurant in London, whose devoted clientele travel down from their north London prosperity for salt beef. Turning right up Commercial Street, an echo of poor Jewish days is found in Brune Street (third on the left) where the soup kitchen set up in 1902 for the Jewish poor serves the poor of the 1980s.

The tall warehouses of Commercial Street are where the rag trade hots up for the cluster of street markets that make up **Petticoat Lane**. Originally, this was the lane where a Tudor old clothes market grew up on the short cut lane linking Bishopsgate with Aldgate, where Spanish, Italian, French and Portuguese immigrants lived, just outside the City walls. With the Jewish influx, it expanded vastly to become Victorian London's largest market, totalling three miles of shops and stalls, more than half of them selling clothes. Despite driving fire engines through the crowds, pious Christians failed to prevent Sunday morning trading and it was finally authorised by a special Act of Parliament (1936). Alfred Marks, who spent his boyhood in a crowded Wentworth Street tenement and went to the Jews' Free School, remembers the Petticoat Lane beigel man making up come-on rhymes for his customers – 'Beigels for you, takes away the flu', 'When you feel hungry, don't feel blue, beigels is waiting for you.'

Today, the Jewish traders remain (although they often arrive from Golders Green, not from nearby streets); Asians have replaced the Continentals. To enjoy the market at its jolliest, pause at the stalls to hear the Cockney come-ons and see the locals bartering. Too big and well known by outsiders to have the best market prices, it does have the liveliest atmosphere and some splendid Cockney acts performed by descendants of the long gone East End musical hall stars. It is easy to find yourself buying unwanted perfume, hats and tin-openers just because of the street show. Diving westwards into **Wentworth Street**, stalls of fruit, vegetables, nuts, plants and jewellery compete with the clothes, while shops behind and streets either side sell more. Leyden Street on the right has men's clothes and then leather at the end; Goulston Street on the left mixes clothes with household linens and equipment, and Tubby Isaac's fish stall is at the bottom. Wentworth Street opens into **Middlesex**

Street, which springs to life on Sunday only to be the noisiest part of all. Turning right up it and then left through Harrow Place, **Cutler Street** has a tiny patch of hidden ground where dealers and collectors herd around 40 or so stalls sparkling with gold and jewels (prices are keen, best prices before 9am) (Wentworth Street open Mon–Fri, best at lunchtime; Middlesex Street and Cutler Street Sun mornings).

Across Houndsditch and left into **Bevis Marks Street**, an old stone carving on the new shopping arcade is the clue to finding the **Spanish and Portuguese Synagogue**, known as Bevis Marks Synagogue. One of the most sumptuous and well preserved British synagogues, it is also one of the few regularly open. Built in 1701 by Joseph Avis, a Quaker, for the newly arrived wave of Jewish refugees (see p. 170), Queen Anne contributed a beam to the galleried hall which was built like a nonconformist chapel of the time but furnished with seven splendid brass chandeliers from Amsterdam and other fine British and Dutch plate (to visit, telephone Mr Miranda on 969 3143; services on Mon and Thurs at 7.30am, Sat at 8.30am).

Aldgate lies at the bottom of the road, now reduced to a multi-roundabout but until early last century the eastern boundary of London beyond which were the separate villages and towns. Originally, it was one of the gates of Roman London, leading out to their early capital, Colchester. Later, Geoffrey Chaucer took rooms above the gateway (1374–85); and Mary Tudor entered London as Queen through it (1553). On the left, George Dance the Elder's **St Botolph** (1741–4) is a rebuilding of one of the four churches at City gates dedicated to the patron saint of travellers, worth negotiating the lorries to see JF Bentley's addition of elaborate ceiling (1881), a carving saved from St Mary's Whitechapel, and good monuments, including one to local benefactor Robert Dow (1612). Across the high street is the Hoop and Grapes, one of the City's oldest pubs in one of its oldest secular buildings.

Then to **The Docklands**. (If they seem too daunting to explore solo, see p. 40 for a guided tour.) Turning left down Minories towards the Tower, the big, blue-edged, transparent tubes on the left lead up to Tower Gateway Station of the **Docklands Light Railway**. The second Light Rail Transit system to open in Britain (September 1987, the first is in Newcastle), it is described as 'between a railway and a bus service'. Each train has two coaches, has space for 350 people and takes 14 minutes from Tower Gateway to Island Gardens. There are 15 trains an hour, each unmanned and driven by a computer; and the stations are unmanned but watched by close-circuit television (for more information, telephone 538 0311; trains run Mon–Sat 5.30am–midnight, Sun 7.30am–11.30pm; tickets from machines).

A ticket to Island Gardens – the first of three routes to be completed – provides a spectacular overview of the most advanced parts of this gigantic redevelopment (for more on their earlier history, see pp. 105–9). Speeding out eastwards, it zips through southern Whitechapel to pass on the right first the Royal Mint (where City businessmen now work) with St Katharine Dock behind and then Cable Street where 500,000 locals fought with police to prevent Sir Oswald Mosley's blackshirt Fascists marching through (1936). Then come the tower of Hawksmoor's handsome St George-in-the-East (1714–29) with Wapping surrounding London Docks behind, home of Rupert Murdoch's British newspapers: *The Times*, the *Sunday Times* and the *Sun* and the *News of the World*. After **Shadwell Station**, Stepney is on the left and Shadwell Basin behind John Walters's St Paul's (1819–20) on the right. **Limehouse Station** is beside the Rotherhithe Tunnel entrance on the right. Leaving the station, Limehouse Basin is on the right (splendid views over the river bend to Surrey Docks) and Hawksmoor's St Anne's (1714–30) on the left. After **Westferry Station** the train crosses the great wall that protected India Docks, with the Dockmaster's House surviving on the right.

Now the high-tech spectacle begins as the line turns southwards to cross three great docks with four stations: at **West India Quay**, the glittering fish weather-vane identifies Billingsgate Fish Market to the left; at **Canary Wharf**, amid the American bank buildings where three towers will soar up into the sky; at **Heron Quays** the station is on a narrow island between two long docks almost reaching the Thames at both ends, with the great Mercury Satellite disk on the left; and at **South Quay**, the upmarket, 21-storey Cascades apartments on the right look out over Surrey Docks to Tower Bridge. Heading east again, there is a splendid view back across West India Docks as the train flies across Millwall Docks and then south to **Crossharbour Station**, where a jot of old docklands survives on the left. Mudchute Farm follows on the left, a vulnerable oasis of green jealously eyed by the greedy developers, with a glimpse of Greenwich across the water. Then comes **Mudchute Park**

Station, with some more isolated Victorian terraces, before **Island Gardens Station**.

Island Gardens are right beside the station. Well-kept with lawns, flowerbeds and shady trees, and served by a small and cheerful café (open daily 9am–5.30pm) with a steaming tea-pot built into the brickwork, they provide the perfect viewing platform for one of the great London **views**, Greenwich (see p. 107). This was Wren's favourite spot for gazing at his masterpiece. And if a sailing ship glides past, even better. Keen view-seekers can go down the lift under the bubble dome to walk the cream-tiled Greenwich Foot Tunnel and then go up Greenwich Park to the Terrace where the whole of East London is mapped out. The new development stretches from London Bridge, beyond Tower Bridge, on the left, around the three bends of the river to the far end of King George V Dock on the right, some seven miles.

At this downstream end, the silver hats of the Thames Barrier are just below the giant-sized **Royal Docks**, the fourth area of the LDDC programme. Their size is equivalent to the distance from Marble Arch to the Tower; the whole of Oxford Street could drop into one dock, with room to spare.

Of the three strips of water, Royal Victoria Dock on the left will have a waterside arena, exhibition centre, hotel, cinema and possibly a **Museum of the Docklands** charting London's industrial history with huge and wondrous pieces of machinery, a steam tug and complete trade workshops to complement the bits and pieces littered about the whole docklands area – most obviously, the great cranes and, in Royal Docks, the huge 'suckers-and-blowers' which took grain out of the ships and delivered it into the warehouses. Housed in the multi-storey W Warehouse (1860s), built as a tobacco store and fully restored to be the biggest exhibit itself (or alternatively housed up at East India Dock, west of the River Lea), part one opens in 1990. But the Visitors Centre is open by appointment now (tel John Penn on 511 2612) and included in the Docklands Tour (see p. 40) (information from Museum of the Docklands, Units 39 and 41, Cannon Workshops, West India Dock, E14, tel 515 1162; an outpost of the Museum of London, who also have the latest progress information). South-east of this dock, SS Teulon's St Mark's Church (1861–2) is to be a Museum of Victorian Life (information from the Passmore Edwards Museum, Romford Road, E15, tel 519 4296/534 4545).

King George V and Albert Docks on the right are earmarked for water-sports – canoeing, water-skiing, sailing, etc. When the 10-year-long, £2,500 million project is finished, 7,000 homes will complete this water village. South of them is the Woolwich Ferry (to Deptford), the Woolwich Tunnel (lifts down to a white-tiled crossing a third-of-a-mile-long), and the little **North Woolwich Station Museum**. This tells the story of the Great Eastern Railway Company (founded 1839), which both connected London with the eastern ports and built the North Woolwich Railway encircling north London (still working, see p. 266), all set out in charming, restored station and booking office, together with the oldest surviving GER steam locomotive (1876) (Pier Road, E16, tel 474 7244; open daily Mon–Sat 10am–5pm, Sun 2–5pm; free).

In contrast, the strip between these two docks is the 2,500-foot-long runway for the latest docklands transport, **London City Airport** (opened 1987), known as Stolport. High-powered Docklands and City businessmen can nip across to the Continent, around Britain and to the tax haven Channel Islands – 'so useful for visiting a client in Jersey', remarked a stockbroker. And the newly arrived, wealthy East Enders can pop over to Paris for the weekend. The chairman of Brymon Airways, one of the two airlines operating the Dash 7 planes, went to school by Tower Bridge and claims he is 'going back to my roots', even if they are changed beyond recognition. All this will have another branch of the Docklands Light Railway speeding through it (to open 1989) and, with luck, a road bridge or tunnel across the Thames at the eastern end, the first one downstream from Tower Bridge. Already, locals come to gawp on Sundays. These are people who spent their childhood waving the big ships in and out of King George V Dock, and whose families were dockworkers for three or four generations and crossed into work on the Woolwich Ferry each morning from south bank tenements. The change from the lapping waters of a busy commercial port to still lakes of a leisure centre is a revolution.

If this seems worth exploring, it will be possible to reach it by DLR or boat when the second phase of the Docklands upheaval is complete (much will be closed to the public while building progresses). But if that was enough of a glimpse into the future, you can return to the Tower by speedy water bus. The Docklands resurgence has brought the Thames highway alive again. Thames Line run a new river bus service using catamarans to avoid a wash and thus cutting through the speed restrictions to 25 mph. It takes 30 minutes to travel from here to Chelsea in west London with the stops, about 10 minutes direct. Useful stops for Docklands exploration are West India Dock Pier (for Canary Wharf), Butler's Wharf (for the Museum of Design) and Hay's Wharf (for London Bridge City) (automatic ticket system takes coins, notes, credit cards and Capitalcards).

From Island Gardens, the easiest way to explore the **Isle of Dogs** is to get down at the DLR stations where the buildings look interesting. Eventually there will be waterside walkways around each dock.

Crossharbour is a good access point for Mudchute Farm and Park, formed by the silt dredged from the docks and set up as a 30-acre farm in 1977, the largest urban farm in Britain. The hill provides more good **views**, and you may catch the sheep being rounded up on horseback, Australian style (Pier Street, E14, tel 515 5901; park open all the time; farm found on the eastern side,open daily 8am–1pm and 2–6pm). On the other side of East Ferry Road, the buildings in Millwall Docks can be assessed from Crossharbour Bridge or the waterside paths where anglers hook fat trout, carp and bream after years of fishing restrictions. Starting on the north side of the western arm (near where the launching slip for Brunel's *Great Eastern* steamship has been discovered) and moving clockwise, they include the Island Arts Centre, the huge *Daily* and *Sunday Telegraph* printing works, the *Guardian* newspaper's hideous offices, the *Daily* and *Sunday Telegraph* editorial offices up on South Quay. Down the east side are the LDDC's showpiece headquarters, Norman Foster's West India House. London Docklands Arena, a banana shed being converted by pop impresario Harvey Goldsmith, will be Britain's largest sports centre yet built, with seating for 12,000 to watch shows ranging from pop concerts to tennis tournaments and boxing thrashes – when the even bigger Surrey Docks arena is complete, the Docklands will break one of its own records. The hotel beside it will have stunning views.

Getting down at West India Quay, the three strips of water constitute **West India Docks**. Looking south to the next quay, you can see how **Canary Wharf** is progressing and imagine the rest. This £2 billion financial centre is planned to be the new Docklands superstar, a Wall Street-on-Thames to challenge the commercial supremacy of the City since medieval times. When Dr Michael von Clemm,

then running the bank Credit Suisse First Boston, was hunting for a site for a food processing plant in early LDDC days, he went to look at the deserted West India Docks and realised how much better they would be for a financial trading centre near the overburdened City. Persuading some fellow power-brokers in the City to move there too, he imported US developer G Ware Travelstead from Kentucky, enlisted LDDC's backing, checked out the transport proposals and commissioned the biggest US architectural practice, Skidmore, Owings and Merrill, to 'develop a master plan concept that would allow a controlled growth on a large scale'.

Large it will be: a 71-acre commercial city with 12.2 million square feet of offices, two hotels, exhibition and conference centres, four full sets of shops on various levels and open long hours, 75 restaurants on the same lines, swimming pools and gyms, a telephone system that can handle 122,000 calls simultaneously, 57,000 people employed daily and parking for 8,300 cars (just in case the DLR and river buses are not enough). Essentially, the buildings along a quay the length of the Mall in St James's will include three landmark towers (they were to be 850 feet high, 50% taller than the NatWest Tower; critics shouted 'land-wrecking' and two have been reduced), and a string of internal piazzas (with waterside promenades) leading to the riverside Westferry Circus, substantially bigger than Trafalgar Square, at the west end. The DLR railway is in the middle; the airport 10 minutes away. Built in phases, the first occupants should move in in 1989, the final touches be completed at the end of the 1990s. The idea is to fulfil every human need in a twentieth-century mini-city.

For many Londoners, Canary Wharf's scale is simply too big beside the East End and Greenwich – it will undoubtedly dwarf Wren's Naval College – and its architecture has forsaken sensitivity and aesthetics for flashiness. But in Dr Von Clemm's opinion 'Canary Wharf is an unbelievable historical coincidence of an over-riding need being met by an extraordinary urban redevelopment in just the right location . . . So I'd say London has lucked out.'

In the centre dock, there are plans for a floating museum for some historic ships. Already, the *John W Mackay* (1922) is moored here, possibly the oldest steam-driven cableship in the world and complete with machinery and grandly panelled master's room and officers' saloon – and you may see proud owners of historic ships visiting London tying up beside here. Westwards, the great warehouses may give a taste of the Museum of London's docklands museum centred in the Royal Docks, together with a hotel, markets and entertainment centres. Eastwards lies Billingsgate Fish Market, moved out from the City in 1982 (to visit, see p. 325), with optimistic plans for a Chinatown project beyond, where China's main trading centre with Western Europe will include an exhibition hall, shops for everything from kites to chopsticks, a business exchange, an oriental hotel, Pagoda cinemas and a floating restaurant arranged in and around Poplar Dock and Blackwall Basin. The new site for the City's newspaper, the pink *Financial Times*, is to the north-east, while a drop of old **Poplar** is worth seeking out to the north. Up **Newby Place**, there are the Georgian terraces of Montague Terrace leading to Bazely Street on the right and, further up, a palatial rectory (c.1820) opposite Charles Hollis's **All Saints** church (1821–3), faced in Portland stone and newly restored.

The other LDDC area worth exploring is **Wapping and Limehouse**, a total contrast to the Isle of Dogs. Here, amid the new housing estates, many of the old churches and houses of two riverside hamlets that served the London port for centuries still stand, and the majestic, later riverside warehouses have been converted into up-market apartments or office space. There is less high-tech and fewer astounding water-filled vistas, but more character.

A circular stroll round **Limehouse** reveals this young and still stumbling marriage of old and new (for its earlier history, see p. 106). DLR Westferry Station is one stop from North Quay – two stops from All Saints if you went up to Poplar. Heading towards the river along Limehouse Causeway and past Dunbar Wharf on Limekiln Dock, **Narrow Street** has a rare docklands survival: a row of Georgian houses, including The Grapes pub and Booty's Wine Bar. Beyond rises the Victorian Hough's Paper Board Mill, with Limehouse Basin on the right.

Turning right up Shoulder of Mutton Lane, and then right and left into Oak Lane, **Newell Street** on the left leads up past more Georgian houses. Turning right into narrow, cobbled St Anne's Passage, Hawksmoor's magnificent **St Anne's** (1714–30) is a Docklands landmark and one of its main glories. The interior was rebuilt by Philip Hardwick after a fire (1851) and equipped with a fine organ (tel 987 1502/538 2206 to visit, or attend Sun services at 10.30 or 6pm). At the top of the street, across

Commercial Road there is a drop of the old Chinatown of Limehouse. Good Friends restaurant is in Salmon Lane straight ahead. For a handful of old streets to the east: turn right and continue into **East India Dock Road**, then cross to the north side to go up **Saracen Street**. Here, to the left and right, a few simple Chinese restaurants lurk in Nankin, Pekin and Canton streets (see p. 319).

The quickest route to **Wapping** is a two-station DLR ride from Westferry to Shadwell Station. Turning right into Cable Street, then left down Cannon Street, Hawksmoor's **St George-in-the-East** (1714–29) rises proudly, despite losing most of its guts and the lid from its main tower, as one of the great English Baroque churches. Built with Hawksmoor's two other East End churches as a result of Queen Anne's Fifty New Churches Act, plans are afoot to make it a museum of religious history. This is Wapping's landmark, although outside LDDC territory. Turning left into the Highway and right down Wapping Lane, **Tobacco Dock** on the right is the Docklands answer to Covent Garden but, in Docklands style, twice the size. DA Alexander's large, secure warehouse (1811–14) was built beside London Docks to store tobacco – for smoking, chewing and sniffing – before serving as a wool store for a century and a fur skins store after the Second World War. A forest of iron columns supported the Skin Floor, and the great brick vaults below held wine and spirits. Of many similar warehouses, this is the sole survivor. Architect Terry Farrell has restored the building; shops, restaurants and entertainments fill the galleries, floors and vaults (open daily, 7am–3am) and help serve the 2,000 Docklands households currently arriving annually to form what the LDDC officials promise will be 'an exciting new community changing tomorrow's world'. East End-born journalist Derek Jameson reacts differently: 'My East End looking like one of the snootier suburbs!', but concedes that 'for the first time in fifty years it has got a long-term future.'

Leaving by the East Quay exit at the south end and crossing one of London Docks' restored bridges, Wapping Lane runs down the river, with splendid views open westwards to the Tower. At the bottom, the views across to **Rotherhithe** may be irresistible. If so, Wapping Station on the East London Train line is just here.

Emerging from Rotherhithe Station and turning left and left again to reach Rotherhithe Street, there is a clutch of goodies. Bandram's Wharf and the Knot Garden (good views back to Wapping) are to the right; the Mayflower pub and the award-winning restoration of Thames Tunnel Mills to the left, with Hope Suffrance Wharf and East India Wharf beyond. All these surround the village church of **St Mary the Virgin** (rebuilt 1715), with rectory and schoolhouse. Further westwards, archaeologists digging just in front of the developers at Cherry Garden have made an exciting discovery: a big chunk of Edward III's stone and moated palace with two courtyards – yet another royal riverside home (possibly to be run by English Heritage and open to the public, see p. 17). Returning to the station, **Brunel's Engine House** is on the right, a mini museum of local history in the boiler house used by Marc Brunel while the Thames Tunnel (1825–43) was being built (Tunnel Road, SE16; open June–Sept on Sun, 11am–3pm, Oct–May on the first Sun of each month, 11am–3pm; free). This, the world's first under-river public thoroughfare, was opened in 1843 as a London link for dock labourers living on the south bank. Labourers building it died from fever, tunnel sickness (hookworm), explosion of sewer gas and drowning when the river broke in. But the finished result was so good it has never sprung a leak – even so, it is inspected every night. 26 years later the workers' footpath was turned into a railway line, the one used by the train back to Wapping.

To explore a little more of Wapping, turn eastwards along **Wapping High Street**, passing the great warehouses of Crane and Metropolitan Wharfs on the right and dipping into Prospect Place on the left. As the road bends left, the Prospect of Whitby pub is on the right. In **Shadwell Basin** on the left there is a particularly interesting Docklands project. The Academy of St Martin-in-the-Fields who, among more serious work, recorded the soundtrack for the film *Amadeus*, forsook Trafalgar Square to convert the ivy-clad **Wapping Hydraulic Pumping Station** (1893) into their studios, concert room and waterside café, with a tiny museum about the Pumping Station's history squeezed in too. Closed in 1977, this was the last such pumping station in the world; but in the 1930s heyday of hydraulic power the London stations pumped more than 33 million gallons of water a week under the streets of London to raise and lower everything from the organ in Leicester Square Cinema and private lifts in Mayfair mansions to Tower Bridge and the dockland locks and cranes. Spruced up, it now echoes to strains of Mozart (37 Wapping Wall, E14; tel 625 8698; concerts, Friends Society, café, bookshop).

Across the basin rises the spire of John Walter's **St Paul's** church (1812–21), one of the so-called Waterloo churches built with £1 million of government money as thanks to God for delivering Britain from Napoleon's clutches. In the earlier churches on this spot sea captains and sailors worshipped, the parents of Thomas Jefferson, 3rd President of the US, were married, and Wesley gave his last recorded sermon (1795). To reach it, go along Glamis Road and turn left over the restored and red-painted steel bascule bridge that crosses the old entrance to London Dock. To go canoeing on Shadwell Basin water, contact the Shadwell Project (Shadwell Basin, E1, tel 790 6420). On the right after the bridge, **King Edward VII Memorial Park** is eight acres of riverside grassland with good shrubs and memorials to its namesake and to explorer Sir Hugh Willoughby. Built over Shadwell Fish Market and opened in 1922, it is a quiet and green Docklands hideaway with more splendid Thames views.

Back along Wapping High Street and past the station, a thick band of warehouses is flush with the river to dock valuable mahogany and spices direct from ship to safety with no risk of quayside thieves. Now they are pricey apartments with panoramic views. A favourite Docklands 1980s game for City investors was to pioneer warehouse flat-buying, then sell on with big profits as the Docklands became fashionable with the young wealthy of the West End. Warehouses that stored valuable spices are now stocked with marble floors, whirlpool baths, indoor heated swimming pools, saunas, cable TV and high-tech video and security entry systems. With Britain's obsession for categorising society, the yuppies (young, upwardly mobile professionals) who have moved to Docklands were nicknamed 'yeppies' (young eastwardly-mobile professionals).

The first big gap is Waterside Gardens, on the southern tip of the river bend, with splendid **views** across the flat docks. Further along, there is a good **view** up Reardon Path to St George's. On and past the Victorian Gothic Oliver's Wharf (c.1870), which stored tea until 1969 and was Wapping's first warehouse conversion, and past the Town of Ramsgate pub (with surviving riverside steps beside it), the Georgian mansions of Wapping Pierhead evoke former grandeur. On the right lies Hermitage Wall and then Hermitage Basin (where a path runs up beside the canal to Tobacco Dock). On the far side, Rupert Murdoch has his bleak, prison-like News International offices, the first of the five national newspaper groups to have deserted the Fleet Street area for the Docklands.

Hugging the riverside warehouses, **St Katharine's Way** twists past Continental Wharf, Tower Bridge Wharf and President's Quay to **St Katharine Dock**, the first of the big dock expansions (1825, closed 1968) and the pioneer of dock rehabilitation. On the water, visiting cruisers and yachts and long-stay Thames barges give the three small docks the feeling of a coastal holiday village. On the land, the Dockmaster's house by the dock entrance and Ivory House in the middle of the docks are the best two survivors, seaside shops (small, expensive and not useful) line the quays, and a selection of seaside restaurants are dotted about (Dickens Inn for cheeriness and views; Tower Hotel bar and restaurants for stunning Tower Bridge views). From Monday to Friday, the occasional pinstriped businessman sits licking an ice-cream in the sunshine before returning to the World Trade Centre on the west side, a conference in Tower Hotel, or the trading floors of London Fox Futures and Options Exchange (see p. 73). Just north of here, out of the elephant-topped gateway and right along East Smithfield, Wilton's Music Hall (c.1850) is found up Ensign Street on the left, in Well Close Square by Cable Street, a surviving scrap of the great music-hall tradition (to be restored and re-opened).

For a final Docklands treat and a splendid sunset, the new river bus crosses the Thames from St Katharine Dock Pier to Butler's Wharf Pier, with Tower Bridge soaring up above the boat. (Alternatively, walk across the bridge.) Here in **Bermondsey** the mood of the old docklands is preserved the best. The air almost sniffs of warehouses impregnated with the spices they stored and the hops brewed until recently in Courage's bridge-side Horselydown Brewery (complete with river steps), once owned by Dr Johnson's friends the Thrales. Butler's Wharf, the Design Museum, St Olave's School, a nineteenth-century spice mill and a Poor Law Guardians building contribute to the corner's character, and narrow Shad Thames Street running behind the riverside warehouses has tall brick walls rising sheer either side and criss-crossed with gangway bridges on upper floors – this is where *Oliver Twist*'s Bill Sikes met his end.

Exploring downstream, St Saviour's Dock is

where pioneer dockland dweller and architect Andrew Wadsworth won an award for his conversion of New Concordia Wharf (complete with wall cranes and jetty) and took the topmost flat for himself (now sold on) – HS Goodhart-Rendel's remarkable **Most Holy Trinity** church (1960) behind it is found by following Shad Thames round to the end of the dock and turning left into Jamaica Road. Upstream, **London Bridge City** runs from Tower Bridge to London Bridge, found down the right hand lanes off Tooley Street. This is the new home for Citibank, Price Waterhouse Accountants and, for sick money-makers, there is a private hospital. And this is where US architect Philip Johnson's outsize spoof Houses of Parliament complex of offices, flats and shops topped by two 325-foot-high towers (higher than Big Ben) is possibly to go up – the Fine Arts Commission's understated opinion in their 1987 report was that it did 'not measure up to his past achievements'. Of the completed buildings, high-tech glass has been added to Goodhart-Rendel's splendid Art Deco St Olaf's House (restored) and to his Hay's Wharf where the dock has been filled in and is surrounded by shops, offices, wine-bar and pub, the whole complex known as Hay's Galleria. Back at Butler's Wharf, design knight Sir Terence Conran has founded **the Design Museum** to be an active 'broker of ideas', not just a collection of curiosities. The first of its kind in the world, it aims to stimulate design awareness and debate with a provocative design package to inspire students, businessmen, manufacturers and the public. There will be permanent and temporary shows; a display of the latest speculative designs and inventions; a study collection, slides and library open to all; restaurants and a design shop. All should open in spring 1989 (further information from Studio 4.04, 45 Curlew Street, SE1, tel 403 6933).

A riverside walkway will run uninterrupted from Tower Bridge to Cherry Garden Pier, an appropriate spot to watch the sun sink over the City and Westminster while the towers of London's third city to the east sparkle with the last warm rays. And with plans to enable cruise liners to moor near St Saviour's Dock, future visitors may have their first view of London from here, a few yards from the Bridge where London began.

London on wheels:
Under and over to far-off treats

London is not a walkable city. Even in the very centre, aching feet finally triumph over curiosity. Further afield, London is so huge that walking is impossible. Its treasures are spread from western Hampton Court to eastern William Morris treats, from the northern Royal Air Force Museum to the southern Dulwich Picture Gallery. To reach these without arriving exhausted, a combination of wheels and feet is best. Top decks of buses provide splendid views, while trains over and under the ground slice through clogged-up city traffic to connect favourite places far from each other; both systems have a variety of cheap ticket deals. Renting a bicycle is neither as mad or scary as it sounds, but London has more hills than you would think. If you get lost, locals will always help – Londoners are far more friendly than reputed. In all cases, once you take the plunge, the rewards are considerable: more access, more freedom of timing and, most of all, a closer contact with the city and its people than taking a coach tour with fellow tourists and moving around in a cocoon. So here are a few ideas to start you off exploring on wheels. To find out more about London's surrounding villages, consult Simon Jenkins's excellent *The Companion Guide to Outer London* (1981).

London by bus

Equipped with one of the bus passes or travelcards (see pp. 7–8), a day or more on the buses is an effortless way to sightsee both London and Londoners. Feet resting, you enjoy good views – best ones from the front of the top deck – and can hop off to have a closer look whenever you wish, catching a later bus to continue. If you ask, the conductor will tell you when you are near your destination. Some bus stops are only by request and in the quieter suburbs you need to press a button or tell the conductor when you want to get off. On a long journey it is worth checking when the last bus returns. If the gentle pace of a bus is enough one way, the nearest tube or train will whizz you back to Central London. Some buses suddenly terminate half way along a route, so check the place of destination displayed on the front before hopping on. Following almost any bus to its route end is fun, but here are a few tried and tested numbers, with the major stops on their routes. All except nos 27, 31, 43 and 267 include a good dose of Central London and can be picked up in Central London and pass through one or more of Hyde Park Corner, Trafalgar Square, Marble Arch and Aldwych. No. 15 is a do-it-yourself panorama of the big sights; no. 267 begins and ends in west London and stops near favourite spots otherwise tricky to reach. Page references are to more information on goodies worth hopping off to see.

Code: HPC = Hyde Park Corner (see p. 143)
    TSq = Trafalgar Square (see p. 87)
    MA   = Marble Arch (see p. 151)
    Ald = Aldwych (see p. 132)
    OC   = Oxford Circus (see p. 178)

No. 1 Greenwich (see p. 107), Ald, TSq, OC, Marylebone Station.
No. 3 Crystal Palace (good park, see p. 274), Westminster, TSq, OC, Camden Town (for Camden Lock, see p. 183).
No. 4 Archway (for Highgate, see p. 270), Islington (see p. 206), Barbican (see p. 67), St Paul's (see p. 65), Fleet Street (see p. 128), Ald, Waterloo.
No. 9 Mortlake, Barnes and Hammersmith (for riverside villages, see p. 111), Kensington (for palace and park, see p. 189), Knightsbridge (see p. 210), HPC, Piccadilly, TSq, Ald, St Paul's (see p. 65), Liverpool Street Station (for Spitalfields, see p. 247).
No. 12 Norwood Junction, Dulwich (for pictures and park, see p. 274), Westminster, TSq, Piccadilly, OC, MA, Notting Hill Gate (for north Kensington, Ladbroke Estate and Portobello Road, see pp. 196-7), Harlesden.
No. 15 East Ham, Poplar and Limehouse (in Docklands, see p. 258), Aldgate (for East End, see p. 255), Tower (see p. 101), St Paul's (see p. 65), Ald, TSq, Piccadilly Circus, OC, MA, Paddington (for Regent's Canal, see p. 186), Ladbroke Grove (for Ladbroke Estate and Portobello Road, see p. 196).
No. 19 Tooting Bec Station, King's Rd, Sloane Square (for Chelsea, see p. 229), Knightsbridge (see p. 210), HPC, Piccadilly, Bloomsbury (for museums and squares, see p. 164), Islington (see p. 206), Finsbury Park.
No. 22 Putney Common, Putney Bridge (for riverside, see p. 110), King's Road, Sloane Square (for Chelsea, see p. 229), Knightsbridge (see p. 210), HPC, Piccadilly, Holborn (for Bloomsbury museums and squares, see p. 164), Liverpool Street Station (for Spitalfields, see p. 247), Shoreditch (for East End, see p. 250).
No. 27 Archway Station (for Highgate, see p. 270), Camden Town (for Regent's Canal and Camden Lock, see p. 183), Marylebone Road (for Regent's Park, see p. 180), Paddington (for the west end of Regent's Canal, see p. 186), Notting Hill Gate (for north Kensington, Ladbroke Estate and Portobello Road, see p. 196), Kensington High Street (see p. 193), Hammersmith and Chiswick (for riverside, see p. 110), Kew (for gardens,

see p. 267), Richmond (for river and mansions, see p. 268).
No. 30 Hackney Wick, Islington (see p. 206), Marylebone Road (for Regent's Park, see p. 180), Baker St, MA, HPC, Knightsbridge (see p. 210), South Kensington (for museums, see p. 220), Putney.
No. 53 Parliament Hill Fields (for green and Hampstead, see p. 270), Camden Town (for Camden Lock, see p. 183), Great Portland Street (for Nash's London, see p. 179), OC, TSq, Westminster, Blackheath (for Greenwich, see p. 107).
No. 74 Camden Town (for Camden Lock, see p. 183), Zoo, Baker Street, MA, HPC, Knightsbridge (see p. 210), South Kensington (for museums, see p. 220), West Brompton.
No. 214 Parliament Hill Fields (for green and Hampstead, see p. 270), Camden Town (for Camden Lock, see p. 183), Islington (see p. 206), Moorgate (for the City, see p. 59).
No. 267 Hammersmith (for riverside, see p. 110), Turnham Green (for Bedford Park, see p. 267), Chiswick (for Chiswick House, etc, see p. 270), Kew Bridge (for gardens, riverside, Pumping House Station and musical museum, see pp. 267-70), Isleworth (for riverside and Syon House, see p. 269), Twickenham (for riverside, Marble Hill House, Orleans House and ferry to Ham House), Hampton Court Station (for Hampton Court House, riverside and parks).

London by bike

Bicycling in London is usually fun and friendly. Bike experts reckon some 250,000 London cycle journeys are made daily. More and more Londoners commute to work by bike. Cycling is also the most practical way of exploring. It avoids feet-exhaustion and saves time waiting for buses or detouring to delve down to the Underground. On a bike, you are free to stop and start when you wish, and if the quickest way to connect two places is by pavement, you can hop off and push for a few yards. With so many people biking in London now, from suited City dealers to mothers with babies in the front basket, car drivers are aware of cyclists; there are even special cycle lanes on some roads. But there are laws to be followed and tips to be heeded. So here are a few hints.

GETTING CLUED UP The London Cycling Campaign (LCC) is the cyclist's fount of wisdom, advice and practical help. Founded in 1978, its members work voluntarily to fight for happier London cycling. The LCC publishes the essential manual for London cycling, *On Your Bike* (£1.35), available direct from them or from bike shops. It contains all you need to know, from bike hire, traffic tips and taking a bike on a train to cycling law and how to complain about the potholes. The LCC also publishes the bi-monthly *Daily Cyclist* aimed at the regular cyclist and packed with the latest information and routes; plus a series of London Route Maps, cycle tours and inner London maps to help dodge the London lorries. To find out more, contact the London Cycling Campaign, 3 Stamford Street, SE1, tel 928 7220.

BIKE SHOPS   Here are half a dozen tried and tested ones in Central London; see the Yellow Pages telephone directory for more. Bike UK, off York Buildings, Strand, WD2 (839 2111) – found through George Court, across John Adam Street into York Buildings, then left down into a tunnel. Bike Peddlers, 50 Calthorpe Street, WC1 (278 0551). Cycle Logical, 136 New Cavendish Street, W1 (631 5060). Dial a Bike, 18 Gillingham Street, SW1 (828 4040). On Your Bike, 22 Duke Street Hill, SE1 (378 6669). Porchester Cycles, 8 Porchester Place, W2 (723 9236).

HIRING A BIKE   It is best to go to a shop near the area you want to explore, telephoning first to find out what bikes are available, together with the hire rates, the deposit rates, insurance schemes and identification required. Before taking a bike, check the seat is the right height, the bike wheels are in line, the tyres firm and the brakes good. A padlock is essential and usually provided with the bike; pumps, baskets and lights have to be bought or negotiated. Costs are around £3 per day for a three-speed bike, reduced for longer hires.

SECURITY   Bike-thieving is big business. Never leave the bike un-padlocked; it will disappear. When locking up, padlock the wheels and frame to a solid object and take all removable parts (basket, lights, pump, etc) with you.

SAFETY   It is much safer – and more pleasant – to avoid the big through roads of London (Marylebone Road, Cromwell Road, Park Lane, etc). Giant roundabouts are daunting, since car drivers play a dodgems game with each other and ignore cyclists (Hyde Park Corner, the front of Buckingham Palace, etc). Despite the number of bikes in London, people getting out of parked cars almost never look behind before opening the door, so it is best to keep well away.

THE LAW   These are the basic legal rules, although Londoners seem to be unaware of most of them. A cyclist must: obey traffic signs, have efficient brakes, have a white light in front and red light behind after lighting up time (published next to the weather forecast in the daily newspapers; otherwise, just follow the lead of the street lights); wheel a lightless bike along the left-hand side of the road at night, and have a back reflector at all times. A cyclist must not: ride on pavements or roadside footpaths, ride along bus lanes unless a road sign permits it, ride on canal towpaths, ride along motorways, or ride when under the influence of drink or drugs – the penalty is £50. To find out more, buy a copy of the *Highway Code*, available from newsagents.

BIKES AND TRAINS   An excellent combination for exploring further afield. But there are considerable restrictions. British Rail likes a bike to be labelled with the name and address of the rider; does not permit bikes on the Waterloo–City line; does not permit bikes on other lines during rush hour (Mon–Fri 7.45–9.45am into London and 4.30–6.30pm out of London); and has some reluctant guards who need to be reminded that bikes are permitted all the rest of the time. London Transport permits cyclists to take bikes on the overground parts of the Underground system and on the District, Circle and Metropolitan lines; hours are open at weekends but restricted Mon–Fri to 10am–4pm and after 7pm; and the bike is charged a child's fare. The North London Link permits bikes at all times but makes a minimal charge during rush hours.

BIKE TOURS   Like guided walks, a good way to explore new areas. London Cycling Campaign fun rides even include a summer ice-cream shop crawl. Most are at weekends; see *Time Out* or *City Limits* for lists.

ACCIDENTS   If you have an accident of any sort with a car, this is the instant six-point code in order of priority: write down the vehicle's registration number; write down witnesses' names and addresses; write down the driver's name and address; report the accident to the nearest police station; see a doctor if you are even slightly injured; contact the London Cycling Campaign.

DO-IT-YOURSELF ROUTE PLANNING Flatter areas with few main roads are easiest to begin with; the big parks and the more residential estates are perfect for first-time rides; weekends are quietest of all. Here are some ideas; see main guiding section and train trips below for more. Central spots low on traffic and high on attractiveness at all times: Hyde Park, Regent's Park, Battersea Park and Chelsea, Kensington and the Ladbroke estate. Weekend delights: the City, St James's and Mayfair, Soho and Bloomsbury. Train or Underground starts; Richmond and Twickenham, Bedford Park, Hampstead Garden Suburb, Greenwich.

London by train

In 1801, London's population was under one million; in 1901 it was 6.5 million. To serve the thousands teeming into the metropolis, public transport underwent a revolution. In 1836 the first railway opened in London, from London Bridge to Greenwich on a four-mile-long viaduct. By 1840 it had carried six million passengers. The ring of big railway termini followed, cathedrals of Victorian engineering where long snakes of carriages arrived from all over Britain bulging with passengers, commerce and supplies for the metropolis. They began with Euston (1837) and Paddington (1838), then Shoreditch (1840), Fenchurch Street (1841), Waterloo (1848) and King's Cross (1850). The next batch were Victoria (1860), Blackfriars (1864), Charing Cross (1864) Broad Street (1865) and Cannon Street (1866) in the south, bringing their loads in across the Thames; with St Pancras (1868), Marylebone (1899) and Liverpool Street (1874) in the north.

Meanwhile, crossing the seething city was a nightmare. First, the North London Railway was built (1850–1), later extended to run through the expanding satellite villages from Richmond to Woolwich and carrying 32 million passengers a year by 1880, daily workers heading for the docklands, holiday-makers off to Hampstead Heath on bank holidays. So, in 1854 the Metropolitan Railway Company was set up to build an underground railway; by 1860 it had raised the money; Marylebone and Euston roads were cut and covered again to make cheap tunnels; and on January 10, 1863 the world's first underground urban railway opened. It ran from Paddington to King's Cross, later expanded in both directions. The system mushroomed fast. The District Line came next (1868), then the Circle Line (1884) to link the main-line stations, then the Metropolitan northwards from Baker Street (1879), all run by steam trains that cleverly 'consumed their own smoke'.

In 1890, electric trains arrived, tunnels were dug deeper and the first 'Tube' opened from King William Street under the Thames to Stockwell (from Borough southwards exists today), so popular it was nicknamed the 'sardine railway' and now so extended that it runs from Morden, far south of the Thames, up to High Barnet north of the city and is the world's longest tunnel. More mushrooming followed, with first the Central Line (1900) from Shepherd's Bush to Bank, known as the 'Twopenny Tube', and then the Bakerloo (financed by an American, Charles Tyson Yerkes), and the Piccadilly, both opened 1906–7. In 1912, they stopped competing and joined forces to become the Underground.

Already in 1859, 'large numbers of the middle classes run off by rail in search of healthy villages, or farm-houses . . . where their families can be lodged, and which can be reached after business in the evening'. And the prediction was that 'the metropolis will . . . extend in an extraordinary manner: from villages which are near railways, rows of dwellings are spreading towards town, and London is branching towards the villages'. Indeed, the over and underground railways set the lines for developing suburbia, the idyllic and smoke-free estates built for the middle class. Edgware was a country village in 1921; the Tube arrived at Golders Green in 1923–4; speculators were hot on its heels, and by 1930 the population had quadrupled. The Metropolitan Line even developed the land around their north-west line themselves, coining the name 'Metro-Land' for the area.

In all, London's urban area quadrupled between the wars, much of it coated with two-storey, semi-detached villas of romantic neo-Tudor, neo-Queen Anne, neo-anything and dramatically modern styles, with gardens front and back. Although the the Metro-Land of a rural Arcadia soon became suburban sprawl, it remained the symbol of bliss, boosted by the Underground's posters ('Golders Green; a place of delightful prospects') and booklets praising country walking. After the huggermugger of London, new arrivals in the country often faced loneliness but few returned to the smokey inner city. Finally, the Victoria Line (1968–9) was opened as the world's most advanced underground railway; the Piccadilly Line was extended to Heathrow (1977), making London the first world capital to have a direct airport–city underground; and part one of the Jubilee Line opened in 1979.

The distinctive house style for the Underground emerged first with Leslie W Green's Edwardian stations, decorated with blood-red tiles and a glimmer of Art Nouveau. Then, in the 1920s and '30s the Underground became pioneers in promoting modern architecture and design, under the overall influence of Frank Pick. For Pick, no detail was left to chance, from Frank Brangwyn's posters, Edward Johnston's typeface and Charles Holden's stations to wall tiles, light fittings, and litter bins. He even took Holden on an inspirational tour of new buildings in Holland, Germany, Denmark and Sweden. The result: some of the most important contributions to British inter-war architecture and design. Pevsner thought it 'unequalled by transport design in any other metropolis'; Gavin Stamp puts the stations 'among the best British buildings of their times'. With the massive modernisaton programme started in the mid-eighties, much of this good design has been wrecked.

Today a single body, London Transport, runs the three sub-surface lines and six tube lines crisscrossing London to make up the world's biggest city railway system. Its 457 trains carry about 2.4 million passengers a day (750 million a year) along 254 miles of track (105 of them in tunnels) at an average speed of 20.5 mph, between 273 stations equipped with 69 lifts and 273 escalators. The buses and Underground together carry about six million passengers a day and cover half a million miles.

To see the early rail lines, the great 1920s and '30s stations and the latest developments, stepping off the rails to explore a few of outer London's prettier patches, old country mansions and hidden treasures, here are 13 routes: one an historical Underground tour for train fans; one the North London Link, stopping at the hearts of old villages now swallowed up into the capital; then ten very briefly outlined trips mixing train systems to seek out ancient mansions and expansive parks in what is still a reasonably idyllic suburbia; finally a trip out to Windsor Castle.

The best equipment is a travel pass (see pp. 7–8). Also, take a train map (best is the Journey Planner with all over and under ground routes) since the bowels of redecorated stations are almost mapless. To explore out from the station, a street map is useful (Nicholson's *London Streetfinder* is best). Page references are to above ground information;

the line to take to reach a station is indicated by a letter in brackets. To find out more, visit the excellent London Museum of Transport (see p. 122) and consult Douglas Rose's *The London Underground, A Diagrammatic History* (1986); Lawrence Menear's *London's Underground Stations, A Social and Architectural Study* (1983); and TC Barker and M Robbins's great two-volumed *A History of London Transport* (1975–6).

Code: M = Metropolitan
      D = District
      N = Northern
      Ce = Central
      Ci = Circle
      B = Bakerloo
      P = Piccadilly
      V = Victoria
      J = Jubilee

UNDERGROUND HISTORY ON WHEELS (good for a rainy day). To Farringdon (M), one of the first batch of stations that opened on January 10, 1863; the night before, 350 excited Victorians sat down to a sub-surface banquet here; the open section and station canopy are just as built. To Baker Street (M), also opened January 10, 1863, its honey-cream brickwork, ticket hall, gateways and soft lighting restored to glory; the history of the line on the walls, together with blow-ups of Robin Jacques's illustrations to Conan Doyle's Sherlock Holmes stories – Holmes's mythical flat was at 221B Baker Street. To Wembley Park (M), with its cottage-like wooden canopies, part of a wild plan to extend the Metropolitan line 50 miles north-west to a pleasure park with mock Eiffel Tower, connecting on to the Manchester line. Worth visiting JW Simpson's **Wembley Stadium** (1924) built for the Empire Exhibition (tours daily, 10am–4pm, every hour on the hour, no booking required) and Sir Owen Williams' Empire Pool (1934), now called Wembley Arena, site of the 14th Olympic Games (1948).

To Neasden (J), the small concrete tube contrasting with the Underground's big stock on the Metropolitan Line. Worth visiting the **Grange Museum of Local History** whose period rooms include an appropriate 1930s surburban sitting room (Neasden Lane, NW10, tel 452 8311; open Mon–Fri noon–5pm except Wed noon–8pm, Sat 10am–5pm). Through Dollis Hill (J), with its dramatically curved 1939 waiting room and canopy. To Swiss Cottage (J), where Pick's 1939 escalators make a friendly chogging noise and still have their column lighting, and where his tiles decorated with Thomas Lord's face (the cricket ground is nearby), birds, St Paul's and heraldic beasts survive. To Charing Cross (J), where on the Northern Line platforms David Gentleman added murals (1979) recounting the story of Eleanor's cross (see p. 87); and on the Bakerloo Line (named because it ran from Baker Street to Waterloo) there is a taste of the nearby National Gallery. From there, to the Museum of London Transport by foot (see p. 122).

From Covent Garden (P), the second deepest (Hampstead is the deepest), up through a string of splendid Holden stations from Manor House northwards, worth looking at each one. To Holloway (P), opened 1906, good tilework survives. To Arsenal (P), opened 1906, worth visiting Arsenal Football Club's stylish 1980s grounds. To Arnos Grove (P), opened 1932, a splendid circular station that looks like a flying saucer arrived from the moon; worth visiting the **Broomfield Museum**, a local museum housed in a seventeenth-century house amid an ornamental park, the panelled entrance hall and staircase with paintings by Verrio's pupil Gerrard Lanscroon (Broomfield Park, Palmers Green, N13, tel 882 1354 for opening times). To Cockfosters (P), opened in 1933, right by the 413-acre **Trent Park**, once part of Enfield Chase royal hunting forest, later tamed and planted (possibly by Repton), still later additions from Sir Philip Sassoon (orangery, pool, terrace, daffodils and many waterfowl), and since 1973 a delightful mixture of meadows and woodlands open to the public (especially good springtime bluebells and daffodils). To King's Cross (P), worth going up to see King's Cross and St Pancras railway stations (see p. 171).

To Angel (N), where the exposed and narrow central platform is just as it was in 1901. To Holborn (P), where a special off-shoot to Aldwych opened in 1907 to serve the merry night-life of the Strand (see p. 119). To Tottenham Court Road (Ce), where the tunnels are so straight you can almost glimpse the next station; the track was built sloping down and up to help the trains pick up speed and slow down; Eduardo Paolozzi has added glittering, colourful mosaics (1986). To Bank (Ce), where the facelift of classical coffering and caryatids echoes the nearby Bank of England (see p. 70).

To the escalator link to Monument (weekdays only; at weekends, walk down King William Street), then to Whitechapel (D) to join the East London Line and go through Marc Brunel's tunnel (see p. 259) under the Thames to Rotherhithe (see p. 258). To Whitechapel and then Tower Hill (D/Ci)

for a whizz on the new Docklands Light Railway, spinning across to the Isle of Dogs and back (see p. 255). Finally, to St James's Park (D) where Charles Holden's Broadway House (1927–9) is the London Transport Headquarters with sculptures by Epstein (Day and Night), Gill and Moore on the outside, and a mesmerising moving diagram on the main concourse which shows where all the Underground trains are on each line.

OVERGROUND: THE NORTH LONDON LINK
A splendid train ride that still feels relatively rural as it chogs from one mid-Victorian village centre to the next. A good way to do the whole trip, hopping off to explore some of the surviving village centres, is to take the Underground out to Kew Gardens (D) for a magical morning walk in the riverside Royal Botanical Gardens (open at 9.30am, see p, 267); or go on to Richmond for pretty riverside and Ham House (see p. 269), crossing by ferry (or back round by bridge) to Orleans House, Twickenham lanes and Marble Hill House (see p. 268).

Then, onto the North London Link at Richmond, its western terminus. Through Kew to Gunnersbury, where the local ex-Rothschild mansion is now **Gunnersbury Park** local museum (extravagant Rothschild horse-drawn coaches) and park (Pope's Lane, W3, tel 992 1612; open Mar–Oct Mon–Fri 1–5pm, Sat and Sun 2–6pm, Nov–Feb Mon–Fri 1–4pm, Sat and Sun 2–4pm; free). To South Acton and then Acton Central, where the agricultural land was swept away with the industrial revolution and Acton was around 1900 nicknamed 'Soapsuds Island' for its 200 laundries and by the 1930s was the biggest industrial complex south of Coventry. To Willesden Junction, a long ride cutting through what were open fields, now leafy estates.

To Kensal Rise, which became fashionable after the 54-acre **Kensal Green Cemetery** opened in 1832, the first of the huge commercial cemeteries, with trees, chapel and colonnade, gaining social acceptance as a route to paradise when George III's sixth son, the Duke of Sussex, was buried there (1843); Marc Brunel (1849), IK Brunel (1854), Charles Kemble (1854), Thackeray (1863), Leigh Hunt (1859), Anthony Trollope (1882) and Wilkie Collins (1889) followed (Harrow Road, W10, tel 969 0152; open Mon–Sat 9am–5.30pm, Sun 2–5.30pm). To Brondesbury Park, then up to High Brondesbury, where the old estate was developed with healthy, airy homes for merchants and professionals of expanding, smoky London. To two stations: West Hampstead and then Finchley Road and Frognal.

To Hampstead Heath, for Hampstead (see p. 271) and the open space of Parliament Hill (see p. 271), a good moment to stretch the legs and stroll to the next station, Gospel Oak, enjoying magnificent **views** over London on the way.

To Kentish Town, where eighteenth-century Londoners came for rural day excursions before it became a select suburb and then, in the 1840s, rows of cottage-sized villas coated the farms and meadows and it became a working class district criss-crossed with smut-and-steam-blowing railway lines, to be gentrified in the 1960s (see the pretty network focused on nearby Leverton Street). To Camden Road, well placed for Victorian workers on Regent's Canal and at the vast goods depots for St Pancras and King's Cross railway stations. To Caledonian Road and Barnsbury, and then to Highbury and Islington, all Victorian developments up on formerly playtime hills (see p. 206). To Canonbury, for a select, leafy oasis (see p. 208).

To Dalston Kingsland, Hackney Central, Homerton and Hackney Wick, packed with Victorian housing and saved by Victoria Park (see p. 253). To Stratford and West Ham in the East End, then down through the docklands stopping at Canning Town, Custom House and Silver Town to North Woolwich, where the charming restored station houses a small train museum (see p. 256), flower-filled Royal Victoria Gardens are behind, and the views across the Thames to Woolwich, where dockworkers crossed on the ferry, are little changed from when the North London Link daily brought thousands of workers down to the busy docks.

UNDERGROUND TO TWO IDYLLIC ESTATES

This is the fastest route first to London's earliest garden suburb, Bedford Park. Then to the magnificent country mansion at Osterley – if luggage is light, this is a magical last moment before leaving from Heathrow airport at the end of the line.

To Turnham Green (D), where the arrival of the train (1869) enabled Jonathan Carr, stimulated by the Aesthetic Movement of the 1870s, to make into a reality the dream of building a middle-class commuting village over 24 acres of his father-in-law's estate, **Bedford Park**. EW Godwin drew up plans (1875), Norman Shaw took over (1877) and designed many of the houses, the Tabard Pub and St Michael and All Angels church, and EJ May and

other architects contributed buildings. The whole was an Arts and Crafts enclave in the new Queen Anne style, proudly advertised as 'The Healthiest Place in the World (Annual Death Rate under 6 per Thousand), A Garden and a Bath Room with Hot and Cold water to every house' but savagely satirised by GK Chesterton: 'Thus was a village builded for all who are aesthete, Whose precious souls it fill did, with utter joy complete.' For a quick tour, see Bath Road, Priory Gardens (home of the Victorian Society, see p. 18), and the roads off Rupert and Bedford roads.

To Osterley (P), opened 1934, with its dramatic illuminated tower. A five-minute walk through Osterley village leads to **Osterley Park**, the Elizabethan house built for Sir Thomas Gresham (see p. 71) and totally transformed, decorated and furnished (from 1762) by architects William Chambers and Robert Adam for Francis and Robert Child (owners of Child's Bank). See Adam's grand portico outside and string of state rooms inside (Gobelin's tapestries in one), no detail too insignificant for the attentive Adam eye. Today with its eighteenth-century furniture arranged as in the Georgian manner, it is kept sparklingly perfect as an annexe of the V&A (with added V&A paintings), hovering in the centre of its tranquil, tree-filled park with two Georgian temples, stables, grazing cows and duck-filled lakes; sheer escapism (Isleworth, Middlesex, tel 560 3918; open Tues–Sun, Apr–Sept 2–5pm and Oct–Mar noon–4pm; grounds open daily, free; lectures, exemplary guide books, café in stables, picnics permitted).

TRAINS TO WESTERN THAMESIDE WONDERS

A remarkable concentration of goodies, accessible with some clever train-catching. Here are three routes. First the elysian fields of Kew Gardens; then post-card-pretty villages with magnificent mansions in the almost-too-perfect settings of Richmond and Twickenham, returning via Barnes; then the loop round to Syon, Kew and Chiswick.

Western wonders I By Underground to Kew Gardens (D), where the 288-acre **Royal Botanical Gardens** was first planted (1759) by George III's mother, the widowed Princess Augusta. It covered nine acres of her Kew estate, with William Aiton as head gardener, Lord Bute as botanical adviser, and Sir William Chambers as builder (Pagoda, Orangery, Ruined Arch). George III (1760–1820) inherited both his mother's Kew estate and the neighbouring Richmond Estate, where his grandfather George II and Queen Caroline had spent happy times at Ormonde Lodge (also called Richmond Lodge) and employed Capability Brown to landscape the royal garden. The estates were joined, the King moved into Kew Palace, and the gardens were enlarged and seriously planted by Sir Joseph Banks (1743–1820), who went round the world with Captain Cook and then sent gardeners off to collect specimens from all continents. Handed over to the State and further enlarged, Sir William Hooker became director (1841–65) and founded the Department of Economic Botany, the museums, the Herbarium and the Library; while WA Nesfield laid out the four great vistas (Pagoda Vista, Broad Walk, Holly Walk and Cedar Vista) and designed the lake and pond. Today despite the damage caused by the Big Storm of 1987, it is the world's foremost botanical museum and research centre – as an example, the Palm House contains every known variety of palm.

Trees, flowers, formal and informal gardens, royal buildings, glasshouses, statues and museums make a rich package to return to frequently in any weather, any month and at any time of day. It is ravishingly beautiful always. On a first visit an informal wander to drink in the atmosphere is best.

Here are just one or two favourites to guide you round (and to tempt you inside): tiny and intimate Kew Palace (1631, built by a London merchant of Dutch descent) and herbarium (with riverside gazebo), Chambers's Orangery (1761), Nash's Aroid House (1836, in fact designed as a garden pavilion for Buckingham Palace), Cambridge Cottage Garden, the rose pergola, the Ice House and the new Princess of Wales Conservatory (1987), which contains ten climatic zones, fizzes with humidity in parts, and replaces 26 old glasshouses. Then along Broad Walk to the lake, the Museum and Decimus Burton's newly restored and stunning Palm House (1844–8, with galleries for closer looks) with Queen's Beasts in front and Water Lily House (1852) to the north. Burton's newly restored and exotic Temperate House (1860–2 and 1885–9, the world's largest greenhouse when it was built; full of sticky-sweet smells and birdsong) is near Australian House packed with 20,000 antipodean plants. Chambers's Pagoda (1761) is beyond, and through great woods and Oak Avenue lies Queen Charlotte's Cottage (1770s; vaulted ceiling painted with summer flowers), where the queen went picnicking.

Finally, to the entrancing riverside view across to lion-topped Syon House before returning past the lake and among the rhododendrons and azaleas in the woods and dells along Holland and Princess walks. (Kew, Richmond, Surrey: tel 940 1171; open Mar 29–Sept 27 Mon–Sat 9.30am–6pm, Sun and bank holidays 9.30am–6pm, then closing daily at 6pm in Sept, 4pm in Oct–Jan, 5pm in Feb and 6pm in Mar; charge, annual tickets. Museums open 9.30am, glasshouses 10am, all with various closing times; Queen Charlotte's Cottage open Apr–Sept, weekends only, 11am–5.30pm, charge; Kew Palace (tel 940 3321) open daily end Mar–Sept 11am–5.30pm; charge. The Souvenir Guide includes the essential map, monthly blossoming plan and an ingenious coding system for seeking out favourite plants; guide lecturers on Tues and Thurs, bookable in writing at least a week beforehand. No dogs, picnics permitted (outside only), bad cafés – best to go round to Maids of Honour on Kew Road, catch the summer Sunday teas at St Anne's church on the green, or on to Richmond).

Western wonders II To find out more on local events, contact the information centres at Richmond Central Library, Little Green, Richmond (940 9125) and Twickenham District Library, Garfield Road, Twickenham (892 0032). For walkers, the excellent *Rural Walks Around Richmond* is sold in local shops, outlining 20 walks in the Barnes to Hampton Court area.

By Underground to Richmond (D), where a good way to see the highlights is to go down to the riverside and explore Cholmondeley Walk, Old Palace Lane, Maid of Honour Row and Richmond Palace remains.

Then, over Richmond Bridge to Twickenham to seek out the immaculately restored Palladian villa, **Marble Hill House** (1723–9), set in its spacious riverside park landscaped by royal gardener Charles Bridgeman and poet Alexander Pope; all created for Henrietta Howard, Countess of Suffolk (1688–1767) – George II's mistress – and later occupied by Mrs Fitzherbert, George IV's secret wife (see p. 139) (Richmond Road, Twickenham, Middlesex, tel 892 5115; open Sat–Thurs, Feb–Oct 10am–5pm and Nov–Jan 10am–4pm; charge; picnics permitted). At the north-west corner is Montpelier Row. Then, following the woody riverside path upstream, James Gibbs's octagonal **Orleans House Gallery** (1720) nestling in the trees is all that remains of riverside Orleans House (demolished 1926–7). Possibly built to receive George II's future wife, Caroline, the interior has rich Roman baroque plasterwork, medallions and pediment decoration, while the new adjoining gallery has regular art shows (Riverside, Twickenham, Middlesex, tel 892 0221; open Apr–Sept Tues–Sat 1–5.30pm and Sun 2–5.30pm, Oct–Mar Tues–Sat 1–4.30pm and Sun 2–4.30pm; free).

Nearby the old houses of Twickenham are in and around Bell, Water and Church lanes (with good pubs, too), where the ferry crosses from the Boat House to Ham House, quite the best way to arrive. (Beware: the ferry runs daily, 10am–6pm but not in bad weather; information on 892 9260.) From Richmond, Ham House is reached along the towpath. By car, it is found down its curving, tree-filled drive scattered with springtime daffodils.

Ham House is one of London's most extraordinary sights. Built by Sir Thomas Vavasour (1610), then the home of the Earls of Dysart (1637–1949), it appears to have been frozen in time since Elizabeth, Countess of Dysart (c.1626–98) and her second husband, the powerful Scot John Maitland, Duke of Lauderdale, employed William Samwell to add rooms on both floors and refurbished the whole palatial house in a flamboyantly baroque style. George Dysart added more fine furnishing of his own. This near-perfect, red-brick, Thameside aristocratic villa is owned by the National Trust and immaculately tended, with some period additions (notably the kitchen and a formal seventeenth-century garden) by the V&A (Richmond, Surrey, tel 940 1950; open Tues–Sun, 11am–5pm; charge, lectures, excellent teas Apr–Sept; gardens open daily and free; picnics permitted).

Extra treats in Twickenham: **York House**, a seventeenth-century mansion whose gardens down to the river were laid out by the Indian Parsee merchant Sir Ratan Tata (gardens open daily, Friday afternoon tea parties run by the Tourist Association include a house tour, for more information telephone 892 0032); and the **Rugby Football Union Headquarters** at Twickenham, where the splendid tour around hallowed 'Twickers' is a boy's delight, with a deluge of rugby facts and a peep into the changing rooms and the old bathrooms – the first game there was between Harlequins and Richmond on October 2, 1909, and Harlequins won; the first International was between England and Wales on January 15, 1910, and England won (Rugby Football Union, Twickenham, Middlesex, tel 892 8161; to join one of the two tours on Mon–Fri, at 10.30am and 2.30pm, telephone the Secretary; excellent shop for rugby fans).

By British Rail train from Twickenham or St Margaret's station to Richmond, where trains return to Waterloo, stopping at pretty Barnes for a walk down through Barnes Green to the river (see p. 111).

Western wonders III Taking the train from Waterloo, there is a loop line that makes a circle from Barnes to take in the splendours of Syon House and park, whacky Brentford Art Centre, Kew Bridge for two extraordinary museums, and Chiswick for another country mansion now engulfed in the city. The different attractions will tempt different tastebuds and the various restricted opening hours demand some planning – Syon House (not park) closed Fri, Sat and most Suns; the Kew museums open only at weekends.

To Waterloo Station to pick up the British Rail train to Kew Bridge Station; then hop on a no. 237 or 267 bus to the pedestrian entrance to Syon House, on London Road. Across the park lies the magnificent **Syon House**, sumptuous seat of the Northumberland family (see also p. 117) since the Reformation. The outside is sixteenth century, with the Northumberland lion saved from the Strand mansion (1874, see p. 117) and popped on top. The inside was totally remodelled by Robert Adam (1761) for Sir Hugh Smithson, the 1st Duke, then richly decorated, gilded and plastered, and now resplendent with ruby Spitalfields silk walls, Moorfields carpets, Matthew Boulton fireplaces, Adam tables, Wedgwood pottery and thousands of pictures. All is set in 55 acres of Capability Brown parkland (opened to the public in 1837 by the 3rd Duke), together with the pot pourri-perfumed, 6-acre formal Rose Garden in front of the river facade (entry by 10p coin); Charles Fowler's newly restored conservatory (1827) like a fairy queen's castle; a specially planted meadow; the London Butterfly House where thousands of large, intricately designed and multi-coloured wings flap lazily amid lush green leaves; and the British Motor Industry Heritage Trust Museum of historic British cars, all standing mirror-polished in vast sheds with keen curators to tell more about the Morgans, Morrises, Daimlers and Lanchesters (Brentford, Middlesex, tel 560 0881/2/3; house open Good Friday–Sept 28 Sun–Thurs noon–5pm; charge. Gardens open Mar–Oct daily 10am–6pm, Nov–Feb daily 10am–dusk; conservatory closed in winter. Butterfly House, tel 560 7272, open daily Apr–Oct 10am–5pm, Nov–Mar 10am–4pm, good shop for nature fans. Motor museum, tel 560 1378, open daily Apr–Oct 10am–5.30pm, Nov–Mar 10am–4pm. Good guidebooks for all parts; huge garden centre, health food shop, bad café; picnicking permitted). Two minutes' walk from the top of the drive is the London Apprentice riverside pub.

To Brentford Station, to find the riverside **Watermans Art Centre**, where open spaces on various levels are filled with an informal mix of art shows, music-making, café and bookshop (40 High St, Brentford, Middlesex, tel 568 1176, 24-hour information on 400 8400; open daily 11am–9pm).

To Kew Bridge Station for two eccentric but glorious weekend treats. At the **Musical Museum** (founded 1963), Frank Holland's collection (with constant additions) of pianos and reproducing piano and organ systems, from pianolas and the American violano-virtuoso to the Regal Wurlitzer are piled up in a redundant church like a curiosity shop; curator Mr Holland enthusiastically recounts their history, with plenty of demonstrations to sing along to – if you play the piano, beware (368 High Street, Brentford, Middlesex, tel 560 8108; open Apr–Oct, Sat and Sun 2–5pm; entry fee; tours last one-and-a-half hours, worth telephoning to check on times; Mr Holland insists on silence while the instruments are played, so under fives not welcome). Beside Kew Bridge, the tall tower signals **Kew Bridge Living Steam Museum** where billowing steam and grunts heave its Cornish beam engines into life every weekend, evoking the glorious steam age when Kew Pumping Station used these monster engines designed to haul water out of Cornwall's tin and copper mines to provide Londoners with drinking water, a service only stopped in 1945. Lots more to see besides, all run by mad keen enthusiasts; worth checking if one of their spectacular special events is coming up (Green Dragon Lane, Kew Bridge Road, Brentford, Middlesex, tel 568 4757; charge; special events, workshops, forge, Friends society, tea-room).

To Chiswick station, then a walk along Burlington Lane to **Chiswick House** gates. The magnificent avenue leads to a Palladian temple to the arts set in a high-walled, daringly informal but still Italian inspired paradise park. Built by the immensely refined Richard Boyle, 3rd Earl of Burlington (1695–1753, see p. 193), this country villa (1725–9) for displaying his art treasures and entertaining his cultured clique was modelled on Palladio's Villa Capra near Vicenza, with injections from William Kent on the decoration and garden, and more planting advice from royal gardener Charles Bridgeman and poet Alexander Pope, as at Marble Hill (see above). House near perfect from vaulted basements to painted top-floor ceilings (small entrance beneath the double staircase); gardens thickly and exotically planted and studded with temple and statue gems – and Inigo Jones's stone gateway taken from Beaufort House in Chelsea in 1736 (see p. 235). The exterior, black-painted window-bars are apparently as they would have been, since the Georgian architects really wanted huge plates of glass to achieve their clear, simple effects, but technology could not oblige (Burlington Lane, Chiswick, W4, tel 994 3299; house open Mar 15–Oct 15 daily 9.30am–6.30pm (closed 1–2pm), Oct 16–Mar 14 Wed–Sun 9.30am–4pm (closed 1–2pm); charge; guidebooks, nature trails; Friends society. Gardens open daily dawn to dusk; free).

Nearby, it is worth creeping round the thundering roundabout to find **Hogarth's House**, the cottage-sized Queen Anne home of painter and satirist William Hogarth (1697–1764) where he spent the summers 1749–64 surrounded by open fields, now furnished with eighteenth-century mood, memories and Hogarth London prints (Hogarth Lane, Great West Road, Chiswick, W4, tel 994 6757; open Apr–Sept Mon and Wed–Sat 11am–6pm, Sun 2–6pm, Oct–Mar Mon and Wed–Sat 11am–4pm, Sun 2–4pm; closed 1st 2 weeks of Sept and last three weeks of Dec; charge). The train then loops back via pretty Barnes (see p. 111) and Putney (see p. 110) to Waterloo.

UNDERGROUND TO NORTHERN HEIGHTS
Following two branches of the Northern Line, these are the quickest routes first to Highgate, then across the open heathland to eighteenth-century Hampstead and another cluster of fine houses, both with stunning London views. Then to the contrasting idyllic garden city of Hampstead Garden Suburb and, for militarists, the museums at Colindale.

Northern heights I To find out more about Highgate, see John Richardson's *Highgate* (1983). For a good set of Hampstead information, drop into Burgh House (see below); and see John Richardson's *Hampstead One Thousand* (1985) and Alan Farmer's *Hampstead Heath* (1984).

To Highgate (N), where the shops and magnificent houses on and around Pond Square and Hampstead High Street evoke the wealthy, elegant hilltop town famed for its 'sweet salutarie airs' and its open land and taverns for 'exercise and harmless merriment'. **Lauderdale House** (1660) sets the tone. The newly restored, first-floor salon overlooks the 29-acre hillside **Waterlow Park**, filled with magnificent trees (beeches, catalpas, yews), azaleas and birds (kestrels, parakeets) (Waterlow

Park, N6; house open daily 11am–4pm, gardens open daily dawn to dusk; café).

Highgate Cemetery, at the bottom of the park, is one of the most interesting of the London cemeteries (others include Kensal, p. 266, and Brompton, see p. 218). Opened in 1839, the 20 acres of paths twisting among the lush trees, Egyptian obelisks, stone angels and ornate catacombs were so fashionable a burial place and tourist attraction (for architecture and London views) that a 30-acre extension was opened across Swaine's Lane in 1857, the biers delivered by under-road tunnel. Prize fighter Tom Sayers (1865) and poet Christina Rossetti (1894) rest in the old, western part; George Eliot (1880), Karl Marx (1883) and Herbert Spencer (1903) in the new parts; the elaborate monuments are much restored and worth a visit (Highgate Cemetery, Swaine's Lane, N6, tel 340 1834; both sides open daily summer 10am–5pm, winter 10am–4pm (seasons change when clocks go forward and back); visits to the western side are by guided tour every hour on the hour; free access to eastern side; charge, Friends society).

The nicest way to reach Hampstead is to walk across **Hampstead Heath**, some 789 acres of rolling woodland and meadows with splendid views and a completely rural atmosphere, every drop fought for since 1829, defying both developers and 'improvers' who wanted to create another Regent's Park. From just 270 acres in 1871, to be kept 'for ever . . . open, unenclosed and unbuilt on', Parliament Hill was added (1889), then Golders Hill Park (1898) and Kenwood (1924–8), then the smaller titbits of Pitt House garden (1954), the Elms garden (1959) and the Hill garden (1960). The heath has one of the best documented flora of its kind; almost a hundred species of bird twitter in its trees. To explore a little, find Parliament Fields at the bottom of Swaine's Lane.

Moving northwards past Highgate Ponds, Kenwood House sits regally on the summit. Remodelled (1767–9) by Robert Adam for William Murray, 1st Earl of Mansfield (1705–93) and George III's Chief Justice (see p. 125), with gardens landscaped by Humphrey Repton for the 2nd Earl, it was later bought by Edward Guinness (1925), 1st Earl of Iveagh, who stashed it with goodies and then left house and contents (known as the Iveagh Bequest) to the nation – see especially the Gainsborough, Reynolds and Romney English paintings and the Dutch set (Hampstead Lane, NW3, tel 348 1286; open daily Apr–Sept 10am–7pm, Oct, Feb and March 10am–5pm, Nov, Dec and Jan 10am–4pm;

charge; lectures, concerts, good café and restaurant; picnics permitted). Cutting down west of Kenwood Lake and across to the Vale of Health, the most secret and most magical of all London gardens, Hill House, is found across Spaniards Road and into North End way, past Jack Straw's Castle pub and down a woodland path to the left to find a tiny door in the garden wall – this way is up along a pergola to find plunging lawns laced with billowing, heavy-scented azaleas; the formal entrance is in Sandy Road (open daily 9am–9pm; no dogs).

Hampstead hilltop village is just south of here, its picturesque, immaculate lanes providing hideaway homes for the rich and famous since Georgian times, with restaurants, teashops and cafés to pause in. Although folk stories say Queen Boudicca was buried in the barrow on Parliament Hill, Hampstead's golden age was as an eighteenth-century resort complete with healthy spring, race course, taverns, bowling greens and bun shops. Politicians, writers, poets and painters who have swarmed up to live in this perfect spot include William Pitt, Leigh Hunt, Byron, Keats, Constable, HG Wells, Compton Mackenzie, Sigmund Freud, RL Stevenson, Anna Pavlova, Ramsay Mac-Donald, DH Lawrence, JB Priestley, John Galsworthy, George Gilbert Scott, John Le Carré and Peter O'Toole, several of whose homes are now museums.

Good roads to seek out include Holly Bush Hill, Holly Hill, Mount Vernon, Church Row, Flask Walk, Well Walk and their surrounding lanes and focal churches. And here is a checklist for choosing a museum-house to visit on your way down the hill.

Anna Pavlova Memorial Museum, where the memory of the Russian ballerina (1881–1931) who created the part of Fokine's 'Dying Swan' (1907) is kept alive in her home, where she kept tame swans on the lake (Ivy House, North End Road, NW11; information from the Pavlova Society, 39 Lancaster Grove, NW3, tel 435 1444; open Sat 2–6pm; charge). **Fenton House** (1693), one of the best William and Mary houses surviving intact in London, is stuffed with some of George Salting's extensive ceramics collection and the impressive Benton Fletcher Collection of Musical Instruments, whose keys are often tinkled for public concerts; also a spacious garden (Hampstead Grove, NW3, tel 435 3471; open Mar on Sat and Sun 2–6pm, Apr–Oct Sat–Wed 11am–6pm; charge; lectures, concerts). **Burgh House** (1703) and garden, a tip-top Queen Anne house this time, was home of Hampstead Wells physician Dr William Gibbons (see 'WG' on the wrought iron gates), now revived by locals to have concerts in the added 1920s room, a blossoming museum of local history upstairs, and excellent tea and cakes in the basement and garden terraces (New End Square, NW3, tel 431 0144; open Wed–Sun noon–5pm; free; well equipped with information, leaflets and books on Hampstead). **Keats House**, where the Romantic poet John Keats (1795–1821) lived 1818–20 in an unpretentious Regency house which is now a re-markable mausoleum to him, saved with much American money and bulging with his letters, manuscripts, books and furniture. The garden possesses a plum tree planted on the site of the one underneath which Keats heard the songbird and wrote *Ode to a Nightingale* –˙ his fiancée, Fanny Brawne, lived next door (Wentworth Place, Keats Grove, NW3, tel 435 2062; open Mon–Sat 10am–1pm and 2–6pm; charge; good publications). Finally, a bit of a walk for pilgrims to **Freud's House** where Sigmund Freud (1856–1939), escaped from wartime Vienna in 1938 and lived here surrounded by his possessions – including his psychoanalyst's couch – until his death, after which his daughter Anna kept it as a hallowed shrine until her death (1983), when it became a museum (opened 1986) (20 Maresfield Gardens, NW3, tel 435 2002; open Wed–Sun noon–5pm; charge).

To Hampstead Station, opened 1907, retaining its blood-red and green tiles and lettering and still the deepest station of all (its liftshaft is 181-feet deep) – 300 stairs for the lift-mistrusting energetic. *Northern heights II* North from Hampstead, the next station is Golders Green (N), whose arrival in 1907 stimulated East End philanthropist Henrietta Barnett (see p. 254) to plan **Hampstead Garden Suburb**, an ideal city suburb of vernacular houses set amid trees and gardens where people 'from all walks of life' might live together in bliss and beauty. Raymond Unwin and Barry Parker made the plan (1907), with artisans' homes to the north, middle-class villas to the west, and large houses to the south near Hampstead Heath; Lutyens designed the central area terraces and St Jude's church. Today, a thoroughly middle-class enclave with not a worker's pub in sight, this leafy time-warp is best seen by taking a circular spin on the H2 minibus from the station yard, joining locals all known to the driver by name as if it were a small Italian village.

A ride on northwards to Colindale (N) is for flying, army and history enthusiasts. First, the **Royal Air Force Museum**, opened in 1972, sits on Hendon aerodrome, filling two hangars (1915) and others with 40 historic aircraft, pictures by Russell Flint, Laura Knight and David Shepherd, silver, dioramas, workshop reconstructions, cockpits and ingenious escape aids, all imaginatively used to recount the story of the RAF and its heroes and enemies, from Lord Trenchard who built up British air power to Baron Manfred von Richthofen, the German fighter-pilot nicknamed 'The Red Baron' (Aerodrome Road, NW9, tel 205 2266; open Mon–Sat 10am–6pm, Sun 2–6pm; charge; good guides, films, Friends society, restaurant, good shop for RAF fans). Next, the adjoining **Bomber Command Museum and USAF Memorial Museum**, opened in 1983, telling the story of the command (founded July 14, 1936) with the help of more aircraft including the only surviving De Havilland 9A (information as for the RAF museum). Finally, the **Battle of Britain Museum** next door, opened in 1978 to commemorate the world's first great air battle when 640 British fighters ('the Few') defeated 2,400 German Luftwaffe bombers and fighters over southern England in summer 1940, all vividly told with displays and British and German aircraft (Graham Park Way, NW9, tel 205 2266; open Mon–Sat 10am–6pm, Sun 2–6pm; charge; restaurant).

UNDERGROUND TO EASTERN CRAFTS A one-stop trip to wallow in the patterns of Arts and Crafts inspirationist William Morris, with a hidden village as *hors d'oeuvre*.

To Walthamstow Central (V) in the centre of a busy, dreary town. First, to Church End village, past rose-fronted cottages, Squire's Almshouses (1795) for 'Six Decayed Tradesmen's Widows' and St Mary's church (with large, timber-framed Ancient House beyond looking very out of place) to **Vestry House Museum of Local History**. In a building (1730) that has been a police station and workhouse, a charming and fascinating collection tells the story of Walthamstow fields to the train's arrival and the ensuing building boom, its treasures ranging from a High Victorian parlour and a Dairy milk-cart to a local copy of the Tsar's tea-set for a superior squire and the first British motor vehicle, the Bremer Car, designed by Fred Bremer, built locally and put on the road in December 1894 (Vestry Road, E17, tel 527 5544; open Mon–Fri 10am–1pm and 2–5.30pm, Sat 10am–1pm and 2–5pm; free).

To the **William Morris Gallery and Brangwyn**

ift set in a spacious municipal park. This large, anelled Georgian house, another Walthamstow ncongruity, was the childhood home for William Morris (1834–96) from 1848–58 before he went on o become a pioneering socialist (see p. 252) and the riving force behind the Arts and Crafts Movement. In addition to the substantial Morris-elated collection, artist and Morris admirer Frank Brangwyn and architect-designer AH Mackmurdo gave their own work and some Pre-Raphaelite and contemporary British paintings. All he top names are here: de Morgan tiles, Burne-Jones stained glass, Martin brothers pottery, Gimon, Barnsley and Mackmurdo furniture, Rossetti, Burne-Jones and Ford Madox Brown paintings, Brangwyn prints and drawings, and countless products of the fertile Morris imagination, from tapestries, carpets, wallpapers, fabrics, glass and metalwork to furniture, embroidery, book-design a Kelmscott Press Chaucer, 1896) and the pamphlets and photographs relating to this Socialist work (Water House, Lloyd Park, Forest Road, E17, el 527 5533 x4390; open Tues–Sat, 10am–1pm and .–5pm (or dusk if earlier), and the first Sun of the month 10am–noon and 2–5pm (or dusk); free).

OVERGROUND TO OPEN SPACE AT WIMBLE-DON, RICHMOND AND HAMPTON COURT Three good stops in Wimbledon, not all tennis elated, before a magical afternoon walk in one of the great parks nearby – Richmond, Hampton Court or Bushy.

To Southfields (D) to the **Wimbledon Lawn Tennis Museum**, to see stage-set displays of a Victorian tennis tea party, a racket maker's workshop, cocktails in a 1920s tennis club pavilion, and more, with all the elaborate and uncomfortable dresses and bonnets. They recount a century of the smart and social game for which the Wimbledon Championships began in 1877, with the added excitement of sound effects, listening posts, a film and a glimpse of Centre Court next door (The All England Club, Church Road, SW19, tel 946 6131; open Tues–Sat 11am–5pm, Sun 2–5pm; extra openings during the Championships; charge; shop or tennis fans).

To Wimbledon (D) where the two small treats only overlap in their opening hours in spring and autumn. **Southside House** (c.1665), built by Robert Pennington in the daringly new 'Dutch Barrock' baroque) style introduced by William and Mary, still quietly echoes with the chatter of Nelson, Byron and other visitors, walls lined with canvases

by Hogarth and Reynolds, quantities of quirky goodies including Tudor miniatures and Anne Boleyn's vanity case (Wimbledon Common, SW19, tel 946 7643; open Oct 1–Mar 31, Tues, Thurs and Fri, 2–5pm; charge; visits are by guided tour every hour on the hour). A 15-minute walk across the 1,000-acre **Wimbledon Common and Putney Heath**, London's largest common and a delightfully informal mix of meadows, oak woods, heather and wildflowers (and three golf courses) leads to its centrepiece, **Wimbledon Windmill**. Built around 1817 and used until 1860, it is England's only surviving hollow-post flour mill and, with the excellent windmill history museum inside, evokes the days when London was surrounded by great whirling windmills on the open fields (Windmill Road, SW19, tel 788 7655; open end Mar–end Oct, Sat and Sun 2–5pm; charge).

From here, a choice of three stunning south London parks. The no. 93 bus returns to Wimbledon Station for the British Rail train to Hampton Court Palace, formal gardens and Home Park (see p. 112). Next door to it, across Hampton Court Road, the 1100-acre Bushy Park satisfies a wilder mood in search of untamed acres (see p. 114). But right here, westwards across Roehampton Lane, is magnificent and massive **Richmond Park**, 2,358 acres of undulating grassland and bracken, dotted with copses and woods of about 200,000 trees, one of the best nature reserves in southern England.

Thoroughly royal in every way, it was Charles I who saw its pleasure potential and virtually pinched it from the local landowners by building a wall around his chosen plot whether they agreed to sell or not (1637); and today the 700 dappled fallow deer and red deer still provide venison for the royal table – beware: their Bambi faces are deceptive, especially during their Oct–Nov mating season. Make sure you see White Lodge, a Palladian mansion built (1727) as a hunting lodge for George I, now home of the Royal Ballet School (Richmond Park, Surrey, tel 748 7306; open in Aug only, daily 10am–6pm; charge); Pen Ponds in the middle, where anglers try their luck; the Isabella Plantation in the south-west corner, a 42-acre woodland with spring-scented azaleas and rhododendrons lurking beneath such unusual trees as the pocket handkerchief, strawberry, tulip and dawn redwood, most of it planted since the 1950s; and the remarkable bird life of more than 100 species, richest of all London parks (Pembroke tea house and gardens near Richmond Gate; restaurant near Roehampton Gate). Leaving by the northern Richmond Gate or

273

Kings Ride Gate, a no. 65 or 71 bus goes to Richmond for Underground and British Rail back into London.

OVERGROUND TO DULWICH, CRYSTAL PALACE AND FOREST HILL   By train or bus, or a combination, a park ramble can be sandwiched between two splendid museums, Dulwich Picture Gallery and the Horniman Museum, well·worth the effort. (Travel will be easier when the planned South London Attractions bus starts running).

By British Rail from Victoria to West Dulwich or from London Bridge to North Dulwich, to find pretty Dulwich Village which blossomed into life when Edward Alleyn, an actor who made his fortune as James I's Master of the Royal Game of Bears, Bulls and Mastiff Dogs, founded Dulwich College (1619) and Dulwich Wells spa became a fashionable eighteenth-century resort for Londoners.

First stop is **Dulwich Picture Gallery**, which opened in Sir John Soane's exquisite neo-classical building (1811–14) as the first public art gallery in England (1814). The College already owned a good collection given in 1687 by actor-manager William Cartwright, a friend of Alleyn. But the gallery's purpose was to display the sensational 400-picture bequest of Sir Francis Bourgeois (1756–1811), a gift to him from art-dealer Noel Desenfans (1744–1807) who had collected them for the King of Poland's projected National Gallery in Warsaw. When the king had to abdicate, the plan was ruined, Desenfans offered the pictures to the British government as the basis of a London National Gallery but the government failed to jump at the opportunity. So today you can wander the dozen top-lit, airy rooms and quietly enjoy what might have been the nucleus of the National Gallery of first Poland and then England – canvases by Claude, Cuyp, Rembrandt (including his four-times stolen portrait of Jacob II de Gheyn), Rubens, Van Dyck, Gainsborough, Hogarth, Canaletto and Watteau. And the mausoleum at the back contains Mr and Mrs Desenfans and Bourgeois (College Road, SE21, tel 693 5254, recorded information, 693 8000; open Tues–Sat 10am–1pm and 2–5pm, Sun 2–5pm; charge, guided tours Sat and Sun at 3pm; good guidebooks, Friends society, temporary exhibitions, education programme, concerts).

North of here, the handsome old buildings of Dulwich are found in Dulwich Village and along Village Way. To the east is **Dulwich Park**, which also belonged to the College. Its 72 acres are filled with an unusually wide variety of trees, some of them the finest British specimens of their kind - Japanese pagoda, white birch, tree of heaven, Cappadocian maple and more, with several 200-year-old oaks; plus aviary, impressive azalea and rhododendron garden (best in May), and large boating lake where paddle boaters compete with geese and ducks (café by lake).

If Dulwich Park is not a good enough inter-museum break, a no. 3 or 78 bus goes to **Crystal Palace Park** where Paxton's glass cathedral was re-erected after the Great Exhibition (see p. 216) and the 106 acres of ground spruced up and planted with terraces, gardens, walks, fountains and statues to be worthy of it. When the waterworks were at full power for a display, almost 12,000 jets were spouting. Formally opened by Queen Victoria (1854), it was a Victorian Disneyland whose fun was slowly halted by a succession of fires in the glass palace, the final and worst in 1936 when 90 fire engines failed to quench flames reportedly visible from Brighton 60 miles away. Today, the Victorian life-size prehistoric monsters survive to set the mood, the ones around the lake set out in a typically didactic Victorian way to illustrate from west to east the evolution of beasts. There is also a boating lake, a children's zoo and a café; non-stop events at the adjoining National Sports Centre (see p. 339); and open-air summer concerts (tel 778 7148/9612 for information).

From Crystal Palace Station, a British Rail train goes to Forest Hill (as does the no. 12 bus) where C Harrison Townsend's dramatic art nouveau gallery houses the **Horniman Museum** (from Dulwich Picture Gallery it is just a 15-minute walk or a ride on bus no. 185). On the outside, Robert Anning Bell's mosaic symbolises the course of human life. On the inside, the eccentric collection of Frederick J Horniman, who made his money in tea and spent the 1870s travelling and collecting, ranges over the arts, crafts and religions of the world, from Buddhism, tattooing and magic to musical instruments, board games and narcotics, with a room devoted to tea-making equipment. A fascinating, fun and quirky museum reflecting the unusual Mr Horniman (London Road, SE23, tel 699 2339/4911; open Mon–Sat 10.30am–6pm, Sun 2–6pm; workshops, lectures, concerts, shop). For broadcasting addicts, now is the moment to visit the **Vintage Wireless Museum** where Gerald Wells has assembled a remarkable collection of early televisions and wirelesses – more than a 1000 items – and shares his passion with all who visit his home (23 Rosendale Road, West District SE21, tel 670 3667 to make an appointment).

OVERGROUND EASTWARDS TO MARINE TRIUMPHS AT GREENWICH

The best way to arrive at Greenwich, one of London's top set pieces, is by boat (see pp. 93–6); second best is by Docklands Light Railway; third best is by British Rail or by road. The most stunning first view is from Island Gardens, the terminus of the DLR (see p. 255), accessible from the Greenwich side through the tunnel. As well as exploring Greenwich (see p. 107), there are museums and mansions to seek out further eastwards, best reached by train. As these tend to be special interest stops, here is a checklist for the keen.

The British Rail train route from Charing Cross passes through Waterloo and then London Bridge. From here, tracks to Greenwich follow the first London railway, which won Royal Assent in 1833 and was formerly opened on December 14, 1836 to the sound of church bells throughout south-east London and a balloon ascent by an excited Mrs Graham.

Two stops beyond Greenwich, Westcombe Park Station is for a graceful, decorated villa (1772–4) built by John Julius Angerstein, who founded Lloyd's (see p. 72) and whose painting collection kept in his Pall Mall house in town was the foundation of the National Gallery (see p. 88). George IV and Dr Johnson visited him here; today, it is a local museum, **Woodlands Local History Centre and Art Gallery** (90 Mycenae Road, SE3, tel 858 4631; open Mon, Tues, Thurs and Fri 10am–5.30pm, Sat 10am–6pm, Sun 2–6pm; free). To Charlton Station, where **Charlton House** (1607–12) was built by Sir Adam Newton, tutor to the Prince of Wales. A rare Jacobean survivor, this extravagantly decorated E-shaped mansion with towers outside and carved staircase up to plaster ceilings and marble fireplaces inside may lack stylish atmosphere now that it is a community centre but, unlike Holland House (see p. 195), it is at least open to the curious – the Summer House (c.1630) is possibly by Inigo Jones (Charlton, SE17, tel 856 3951; open Mon–Fri 9am–10.30pm, Sats by arrangement; best to telephone before going in case the rooms are in use).

To Woolwich Dockyard Station to find John Nash's tent-imitation Rotunda (1820) in the Royal Artillery barracks, housing the **Museum of Artillery** founded in 1776 and now bursting with British, French, Burmese and even Indian guns to recount the history of artillery – worth seeking out for the building alone (The Rotunda, Repository Road, SE18, tel 856 5533 × 385; open Apr–Oct Mon–Fri noon–5pm, Sat and Sun 1–5pm (Nov–Mar until 4pm; free). To Woolwich Arsenal Station where the pride of **Greenwich Borough Museum** is not so much the seventeenth-century pottery found in a Woolwich kiln but the remarkable Dawson Collection of worldwide butterflies, open by prior arrangement (232 Plumstead High Street, SE18, tel 584 1728; open Mon 2–8pm, Tues and Thurs–Sat 10am–1pm and 2–5pm; free).

OVERGROUND TO WINDSOR AND ETON

If the royal palaces littering London have whetted your appetite, the short journey to see Windsor Castle makes a perfect outing. On a steep chalk bluff rising dramatically on the south bank of the Thames, William the Conqueror built an earth and wood fortress. Henry II rebuilt much of it in stone, and most subsequent monarchs embellished and enlarged it. The Victorians created its romantic, fairytale silhouette of towers and turrets; and it is still an official residence of the Queen and her Court. Surrounding the castle are the medieval cobbled lanes of bustling Windsor town, with a Guildhall completed in 1689 by Christopher Wren (who was son of the Dean and had spent his childhood here); and the ravishingly beautiful, 4,800-acre Windsor Great Park. At the bottom of the castle hill and across the Thames lies Eton, where Henry VI founded Eton College in 1440 and today's boys dive in and out of their classrooms scattered among the bookshops, antique shops and, of course, tea-shops. If the weather is fine, you can take an afternoon cruise or stroll along the willow-shaded towpath and spot the swans and ducks. And there may be an evening show at the delightful Theatre Royal.

To help you plan your day and to steer you through the complexity of the various opening times, here are the facts and figures. Beware: the state rooms of Windsor Castle close three times during the year and St George's Chapel closes to prepare for special occasions – but there is plenty else to see.

Getting there By train: two companies raced to serve Queen Victoria with the latest transport method, so Windsor has two railway stations. From Waterloo, two trains per hour make the 50 minute journey to Sir William Tite's Windsor & Eton Riverside Station (1850); from Paddington, two trains per hour make the 35 minute journey to

Windsor & Eton Central Station (1849, rebuilt in 1897 with curving train shed, now a museum), but you need to change at Slough.

By bus: From Victoria (Eccleston Bridge), the Green Line bus route nos. 700, 702, 704 and 718 make the journey to Windsor in 60–90 minutes.

Information Windsor Tourist Information Office, Windsor Central Station, Thames Street, Windsor (0753 852010); open Apr–Oct Mon–Sat 9.30am–6.30pm and Sun 10am–6.30pm, Nov–Mar Mon–Sun 10am–4pm.

Windsor Castle (General inquiries 0753 868286) Enter through Henry VIII Gate, found up Castle Hill behind Sir Edgar Boehm's statue of Queen Victoria; precincts open daily 10am–5pm (sometimes closing earlier); good shop found to the left inside Henry VIII Gate. Here is the checklist of the castle buildings open to the public, in the order you will find them as you go up the hill from the Lower to Middle to Upper Wards:

St George's Chapel (0753 865538), open Mon–Sat 10am–4pm, Sun 2–4pm; charge; good shop; free entry to services on Mon–Sat at 7.30am, 8am and evensong at 5.15pm (sung except on Wed), and on Sun at 10.45am, 11.45am and sung Evensong at 5.15pm; closed before major events such as Garter Day (the Mon of Ascot Week, see p. 52) when 10,000 ticket-holders cram into the precincts by noon for the 3pm procession (apply by February for free tickets from The Lord Chamberlain's Office, St James's Palace, London SW1). Beyond the Chapel, through Horseshoe Cloister, good views of Eton from the terrace.

Albert Memorial Chapel (0753 862251), open Mon–Sat 10am–1pm and 2–3.45pm; free. Beyond, the massive Round Tower is on the site of William I's original fortress and was heightened 33 feet in 1829–32 for theatrical effect.

The State Apartments (0753 868286), the most difficult part to see. They are closed three times a year, when the Queen is officially in residence: mid-Mar–early May, all June and mid-Dec to the end of Dec. When open, their days and hours of opening vary so considerably that it is best to telephone *Queen Mary's Dolls' House* and the *Exhibition of the Queen's Old Master Drawings* (0753 868286) usually open Mar–Oct Mon–Sat 10.30am–5pm and Sun 1.30–5pm, Nov–Feb Mon–Sat 10.30am–3pm and Sun 1.30–5pm; charge.

Exhibition of Presents and Carriages (0753 868286), found by leaving the castle walls through St George's Gate and then turning left; usually open Mar–Oct Mon–Sat 10.30am–5pm and Sun 10.30am–3pm, Nov–Feb daily 10.30am–3pm.

Royalty and Empire Exhibition Windsor & Eton Central Railway Station (0753 57837), Madame Tussaud's outpost devoted to Queen Victoria's Diamond Jubilee of 1897, open daily Apr–Oct 9.30am–5.30pm, Nov–Mar 9.30am–4.30pm, closed for two weeks in Jan; charge.

Windsor Great Park Found by leaving the castle and returning to the statue of Queen Victoria, then turning left down High Street and left along Park Street; stunning **views** back to the south facade of the State Apartments and down the Long Walk (first laid out by Charles II) three miles to Snow Hill on top of which stands the equestrian statue (1829–31) of George III, known as the Copper Horse. Within the park, there are two special gardens: Frogmore Gardens, surrounding the royal mausoleum, open for two days in early May (the mausoleum usually is open on the Wed nearest to Queen Victoria's birthday, May 24. Tel 0753 868286 for dates); and Savill Gardens, a 35-acre woodland garden with banks of azaleas plus formal planting of roses and herbaceous borders (Wick Lane, Englefield Green, Egham, Surrey, tel 0784 35544; open daily 10am–6pm or sunset if earlier, charge; best reached by taking the 20-minute ride on a no. 441, 442 or 443 bus from Windsor). Polo: see p. 346.

River Thames To take a passenger boat, there are daily trips to Marlow and Staines from mid-May to mid-Sept (0865 243421 for times). For a good towpath walk, follow the river upstream along the Eton side for three miles to reach Dorney Court, a magnificent Tudor manor house with furniture and picture collections, a fine garden and good teas (Dorney, near Windsor, tel 06286 4638; open Easter Weekend, June–Sept on Sun, Mon and Tues 2–5.30pm, and other occasional days; charge).

Eton College Chapel (0753 869991) Found along Eton High Street, open daily 2–5pm, charge; free entry for Sun service at 10.40am.

Theatre Royal Thames Street, Windsor (0753 853888), a continuous season round the year, with especially good Christmas pantomime.

Runnymede This is the meadow where King John signed the Magna Carta (1215), a charter of liberties, to win back his rebel barons' allegiance. Take a bus (nos. 441, 442, 443 or Green Line no. 718) from just below Windsor Guildhall to the Bells of Ouseley stop in Old Windsor; then walk half a mile along the riverside to open fields and find across 200 yards of grass to the right, three memorials: Magna Carta, Kennedy Memorial and British and Commonwealth Air Forces Memorial.

Rain, rain, rain:
Staying dry and having fun

Days of drizzle, showers or bucketing sheets of rain are the London norm. For visitors from abroad, the London downpour can be a nasty shock. For Londoners, too, the unpredictable but inevitable drenchings come as a constant surprise. Few carry raincoats or brollies and those who do regularly lose them – in 1986, 22,735 were left on London buses and underground trains. The weather is a constant topic of amazed conversation. And literary references range from Shakespeare's 'For the rain it raineth every day' to the practical plea of the nursery rhyme 'Rain, rain go away, Come again another day'. So here are some tips on how to beat Londoners at their own game: first, keeping dry, then some ideas for things to do on a rain-drenched day.

The weather: The rain and sun facts

Officially, London rainfall remains resonably constant, rising noticeably in September and November. The temperature is supposed to be warmish in summer and coldish in winter, without extremes. But in June 1985, 89mm of rain tumbled down, double the month's norm and rising towards July 1981's total of 115mm on July 8 that year, a thunderstorm deluged London with 58mm of water in one hour. For summer sun, June 1987 was the dullest since records began in 1924, but June 1976 was the hottest, with an average temperature of 20.1 degrees Celsius and a water shortage. It is best to be prepared for anything.

The anti-rain kit

Over the years, the British have fought the black clouds with a barrage of special equipment – coats, boots, hats and brollies, all slotted into the social system. Until recently, most City workers carried a black brolly and briefcase. Now green Wellies and Huskies are part of the Sloane Ranger London uniform, with royal seals of approval, and the really smart look as if they are just off shooting on a Scottish estate. Meanwhile, everybody's dream is a trench coat.

The big, bulky black Wellington boots came onto the market in 1817 as the first waterproof boots. Made of rubber (hence known as gumboots sometimes), they were named after the nation's favourite hero and yet only worn by women and children. For coats, Charles Macintosh (1766–1843) patented his garments made of layers of cloth cemented together with india-rubber. In 1856 Thomas Burberry set up a draper's shop in Basingstoke and developed a cloth that did not tear and that the rain did not penetrate but that was cool and comfortable. Although he called his ingenious invention Gaberdine, Edward VII would merely call for his Burberry as the incessant rain poured down, and the name stuck.

Meanwhile, Aquascutum (Latin for water protection) launched their coats in 1851, 'soft and comforting to the touch; efficiently proofed to withstand the heaviest downpour', won a royal warrant to be 'waterproofers' to the king when he was still Prince of Wales (1897), and were the first to supply the officers of the First World War with showerproof wool trench coats. They were equipped with epaulettes to secure binocular straps, brass rings on the belt to hang hand-grenades, a gun flap on the right shoulder, a loose back yolk to push the rain off faster and cuff and collar tabs to stop water and mud getting in. And they were tested with fire hoses. This purpose-built coat is now the classic defence against the British weather.

Burberry holds warrants to keep the raindrops off the Queen and Queen Mother; Aquascutum holds one to further protect the Queen Mother. A trench coat is not cheap, but it is virtually inde-structible and can be re-reproofed to last a lifetime; and prices in the UK are up to 50% less than in the rest of the world.

One-stop shops Most large department stores stock raincoats, from Marks and Spencer on, but there are some rainproof specialists.

Aquascutum, 100 Regent Street, W1 (734 6090): Stocks the classic trench coat, with hats, brollies and much more to match. Full cleaning and valet-ing service for customers.

Burberry, 18 Haymarket, SW1 (930 3343): 'Trench 21' is the classic, now made to fit the family – men, women and children aged three upwards. All have the distinctive camel, red and black check tartan plaid lining, with Burbrollies, hats and everything else to match. Buy it at a Burberry store and you get a free monogram on the lining and 6 months' insurance.

Lillywhites, Piccadilly Circus, SW1 (930 3181): Head for the fifth floor to find a confusing top quality choice – Barbours, Partridge, Gannex, Grenfel, Britton, Puffa, Husky and much more, with all kinds of co-ordinates to match. Here too are the boots. Traditional black are so unfashion-able they are not stocked. Green is the colour. The royal favourite is Hunter; other makes include Barbours (green or blue), Lady Northampton (green or brown) and the US-made Muckers. Then to the second floor for the in-house Aquascutum shop and to the golf department for umbrellas.

Swaine Adeney Brigg and Sons, (734 4277): Found-ed in 1750, soon making whips for George III, this is an indulgent one-stop shop experience where customers glide between saddlery, gun and other departments to kit themselves out in coats and hats, exquisite gloves and monogrammed umbrellas.

James Purdy and Sons, Audley House, 57–8 South Audley Street, W1 (499 1801): Gun makers to most of the royals and the aristocracy, Purdy now also kit out country men and women with long waxed coats with back pleats, hoods, hats and more.

Specials Smith James and Sons, 53 New Oxford Street, WC1 (836 4731): Founded in 1830, this is the biggest umbrella and stick shop in town, if not in Europe. With a huge selection to ramble through, the best seller is still the black brolly with brown malacca cane handle. If you want something really special, it can be made specially for you.

James Lock & Co, 6 St James Street, SW1 (930 8874): Serious hatters since 1676 and in their latest shop since 1805, Lock's three rain hat styles – two in tweed, one in Gaberdine – can be bought off the peg or made to measure.

Hermes, 155 New Bond Street (499 8856): The Paris company, started in 1837, sells the smartest self-advertising scarves at the same prices in London as in Paris and matches them with umbrellas, hats and raincoats – the lightweight silk ones are the stuff of dreams. (They do not stock boots.)

Milletts of St Albans, 134 Chiswick High Road, W4 (994 5897): Stockists of the old fashioned black Wellington boots that are practically impossible to find today. Best to telephone first to check they have your size.

Dry delights on rain-drenched days

Of course, almost anything is possible in London at any time. But the will wilts when the grey clouds set in. So here are a few ideas to rekindle the curiosity. Some are cheap, some are not, and one or two are outside – there is a haunting magic about some corners of London under the rain. Page references are to more information.

* Shop for the anti-rain kit. Lose hours trying on trench coats, browsing for a brolly in Smith James or choosing gloves at Swaine Adeney Brigg and Son. Once you are prepared, the sun will burst out.

* Check out the directory of annual events on p. 352 to see what should be happening indoors at this time of year.

* Enjoy an indulgent breakfast in a dream set-ting; the Ritz dining room, the Dorchester Oak Room or the Meridien Piccadilly Oak Room for grandeur. Or be fashionable and sit in Patisserie

Valerie in Old Compton Street over a cosy cappuccino and the newspapers, waiting for the almond croissants to come up from the kitchens around 10am (see p. 313).

* Visit the Museum of London to seek out all the bits of London uncovered or saved from destruction when later generations have been rebuilding; Roman mosaics, Georgian shops, a model re-run of the Great Fire of London and perhaps a lecture or one of the excellent Made In London series of film shows (see p. 67).

* Go to the top floor of the National Portrait Gallery and glide over the lavender-polished wooden floors to check out who was who in London's history, from canny-looking kings and flattering bejewelled courtiers to steely-eyed statesmen and present-day stars on the ground floor (see p. 88).

* Watch British justice at work at the Royal Courts of Justice or the Old Bailey, checking out the lists with the attendants to find out which will provide the best free theatre show (see pp. 132 and 128).

* Pamper the body at a health club for the whole day. For women, the Sanctuary with big bubbling jacuzzi, trapeze-crossed swimming pool; for men and women, the Fitness Centre. Otherwise, stay at the right hotel with a club attached or take out a membership (see pp. 341–2).

* Instead of walking in a park to spot bedraggled blossoms, catch an indoors show at the Royal Horticultural Halls (see p. 241).

* Visit Westminster Abbey, bleak and gloomy in the rain with haunting history in the chapels and Chapter House and eerie wax effigies for funeral processions (see p. 77).

* Equipped with boots and raincoats, walk in the grey, soggy silence of St James's Park, where the ducks dive and dip whatever the weather. When the sun breaks through, there is an instant scene change to lush greens with background birdsong.

* Instead of clambering up to the top of St Paul's cathedral, plunge down into the crypt to wander the statues and monuments to heroes and heroines, to relax over an audio-visual display and to visit the glittering Treasury (see p. 65).

* Spend a day at one of the commercial fairs staged at the huge Olympia and Earls Court exhibition halls and their rivals. During the year, almost every fad is catered for, from Crufts and the Boat Show to camping equipment and British fashion.

* Spend a day at the V&A. Ex-director Sir Roy Strong coined the slogan; many follow his advice, exploring new rooms, catching lectures and films, eating in the vaulted basement and spending in the shop (see p. 222).

* Spend a day at the British Museum. Always plenty going on, from tours of the great domed Reading Room, lectures and films, to special exhibitions of prints and drawings, the clock room's hourly concert of chimes and two excellent shops (see p. 166).

* Spend a day at the South Bank Arts Centre. An action-packed complex, with food, art and speciality bookshops in most parts. Breakfast and art at the National Theatre might lead on to the Hayward Gallery or the Museum of the Moving Image, then art and lunchtime concert at the Royal Festival Hall, a matinee show at the NT, tea almost anywhere, a back-stage tour of the NT before cocktails and music in the foyer, and an evening choice of at least three theatres, three concerts and the National Film Theatre's screens (see pp. 117, 288).

* Spend a day at the Barbican Arts Centre. A variety pack of food, art and shops on various levels, music as the day moves on, quality concerts and plays in the afternoon and evening, a cinema in the bowels and, best of all (but only at weekends), the lush green conservatory for a country walk indoors (see pp. 67, 287).

* South Kensington culture crawl. From South Kensington Underground station there are long tunnels for the rain-weary leading directly to the Natural History, Geological, Science and V&A museums, with goodies to see, shops to spend in, and entertainment programmes (especially during school holidays) (see p. 220).

* Harrods, the best store for dreaming. Fortified with breakfast at West Side, explore acres of odd-shaped baths, taste today's food demonstrations, tinkle on a piano, choose a pet parrot, bounce on one of a thousand sofas and beds, watch a fashion show, wander amid the sparkle of Christmas decorations, play with the latest toys, have a squirt of promoted perfume, get hungry in the food halls and gorge on the unlimited tea (see p. 214).

* The theatre. The fringe clubs often do lunchtime shows; the West End and other big theatres mostly do one or two matinée performances a week, usually on Wed, Thur or Sat. Consult *Time Out* or *City Limits*, then book by telephone; this is the moment to catch a show that is sold out every evening for the next month (see p. 288).

* Opt out into dark basements to watch films. In

West End cinemas, daily shows start early afternoon – again, a good moment to avoid queues for a popular first-run movie. Among the repertory cinemas, the National Film Theatre kicks off its full daily programme around 2.30pm, with weekly membership available (see p. 296).

* Visit the Guinness World of Records to watch the world population figures spinning up by the second, buildings growing taller and reruns of sports spectaculars. Then dash into a Leicester Square cinema; brave the showers for the half-price ticket booth for a cheap matinée theatre seat; or linger over a Soho lunch.

* Watch television for the day. There are regular visitors to London from abroad who insist on a day of TV every trip. There may be only four channels, but British television is easily the best in the world (although that plainly does not always mean good) from eccentric 'Open University' subjects and children's programmes to double-bill matinée films, afternoons at the races or ringside views of the best sporting, royal and traditional events. For best preparation, pick up the current issues of the *Radio Times* and *TV Times*; the rest is free.

* Listen to the radio. Serious radio addicts can listen to John Le Carré reading his latest novel, opera from Glyndebourne or perhaps pit their own wits against the quiz show stars; again, best information from the *Radio Times*.

* Visit the National Sound Archive Library and order up some tapes and then return for a good listen, probably on another rainy day (see p. 219).

* Take the Underground out to Kew, then make a dash for the Royal Botanic Gardens where the palatial glasshouses are havens of warm, humid peace, moving from Tropical to Palm to Temperate houses (see p. 267).

* Have coffee at Liberty's on Regent Street and then wander the creaking floorboards to feast the eyes on exotic silks, satins and rugs, moving down to fine glass and porcelain, and picking up a Liberty print scarf to keep off the rain as you leave.

* Go to the Tate Gallery to enjoy the Turner pictures in Stirling's spacious, airy galleries and then have lunch in the Tate restaurant surrounded by Rex Whistler's fantasy mural (see p. 242).

* Browse in a bookshop, then hole up with your purchases until the sun reappears. Try Hatchards on Piccadilly for style, size and scope (books about London on the ground floor), followed by a relaxed lunch or tea on the top floor of Fortnum & Mason or amid the sparkling mosaics of the Criterion Brasserie at Piccadilly Circus.

* For more serious bibliophiles, there are regular book fairs in the Russell Hotel in Bloomsbury and elsewhere, excellent for picking up out-of-print favourites. Again, *Time Out* and *City Limits* carry details; (see also pp. 353–4).

* Inspect a sale at an auction house, then watch it go under the hammer the next day. Moments to peruse treasures of the Van Gogh calibre moving around the world are December, April and June. All sales are fascinating to watch – you may even pick up a carpet at Christie's or Sotheby's, a painting at less showy Bonhams or a handy fur coat and brolly at Phillips or Christie's South Kensington (see p. 328).

* If the sightseeing bug is alive and well, catch a bus and angle up to the front seat of the top deck. London traffic comes to a standstill in the rain, so there is plenty of time to identify buildings and spot sculpture on the facades and statues in the squares – you might need a handkerchief to combat the mist on the window (see p. 262 for good bus numbers).

* Watch the world at work. The City's trading floors go like a fair, rain or shine. Try Lloyd's, with building, museum, spacious gallery and people on hand to explain what's what (see p. 72), the Royal Exchange (see p. 71), Baltic Exchange (see p. 72) and London Fox, Futures and Options Exchange at St Katharine Dock (see p. 73).

* Relax in the beauty of a City church designed by Wren and listen to a lunchtime concert. To find out which concert is where, pick up the leaflet 'Events in the City of London' from the City of London Information Centre by St Paul's Cathedral (see pp. 4, 294).

* An afternoon of watching political power at work. The House of Commons and House of Lords, both open to the public, provide warmth, free theatre and interest; the Commons (rain reduces the queues) can produce better theatre, the Lords (queues usually short) has a spectacular stage set and is televised so you can watch the debate again on TV that evening (see p. 84).

* Explore Covent Garden Piazza, the covered avenues of Fowler's hall stuffed with cafés, stylish shops, daily street entertainment and weekly craft markets; for a dash of formal culture, hop across the cobbles to the London Transport or Theatre museums (see p. 120).

* Indulge in a extravagant, thoroughly English tea. Some of the best are taken on squishy sofas in the big hotels – the Hyatt Regency in Chelsea, the

Park Lane (for scones), the Hyde Park (bookable tables), the Cavendish (for chocolate cake), the Waldorf (pre-theatre or tea-dance), Le Meridien (for harp music), the Portman (post Oxford Street shopping) and Browns and Claridge's for everything – but residents take priority over non-residents.

London entertains:
Sunsets and shows to a sunrise swim

To live in London and be interested in the performing arts is to be in a perpetual tizzy, a state of elated frustration. To be a visitor, gobbling up culture by the plateful in a limited time, is even more intense. There is too much; the quantity is overwhelming.

Just to read through the *Time Out* or *City Limits* lists and criticisms for theatre, dance, concerts, opera, cinema, jazz, pop, folk, cabaret and clubs would mean missing a show. And the range is astonishing. In theatre alone the night's menu has comedies, tragedies, farces, American and British musicals, reviews, new plays, Russian plays, Reformation and Victorian plays, plays in French or German and at least one Shakespeare play. Across the arts spectrum, performers include big resident companies and orchestras, dynamic avant-garde troupes, one-man shows and international stars jetting in for three-night stands. Then there are the arts festivals scattered through the year – big ones in the City and Camden, others focusing on music, dance, jazz, opera or theatre, as if the regular London programme was not already a non-stop festival spiralling ever faster. For theatres continue to open, music groups to be founded and festivals to be launched; and space is increased by converting warehouses, sneaking into rooms above pubs, using beautiful churches

as stages and simply taking to the streets.

Having taken this cultural bull by the horns, Londoners seem to exhaust their energies. After a show, they sometimes eat out, more often eat at home. Few want to rush off for a waltz, a jig or a fling on the poker tables. And the ludicrous (but improving) licencing hours curtailing social drinking and the collapse of public transport before midnight do not help. The result is that some late-night London entertainment falls way below the standard of other capitals. Most nightclubs are pretentious and dreary, apart from those run by the whackier young people; most dinner-dance and dinner-cabaret is embarrassingly bad; the naughty Soho sex parlours are dwindling by the week; and theme evenings on the Cockney or Tudor lines are so awful they have to be experienced to be disbelieved.

Knowing the inside track and then doing some careful planning is the key to happiness. Otherwise, as with all else in London, the quantity can dazzle, leading to a disastrous evening and a loss of precious time. So here are some facts, tips and tricks, from finding free lunchtime street theatre or buying tickets for 'sold-out shows', to enjoying a glittering night at the opera, jazz in a pub, the latest comedy show and finding a taxi home afterwards. And if all the programmed partying is not enough, your

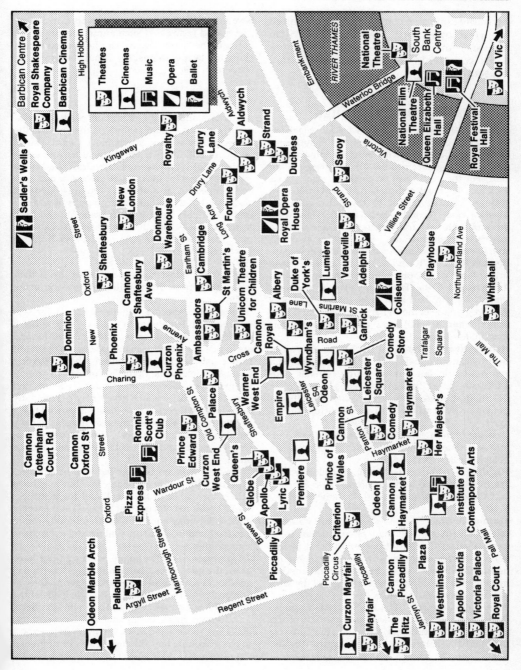

283

favourite London room can probably be hired for your own party, whether it is Syon House, Somerset House, Lord's or the dinosaur courtyard of the Natural History Museum.

Note For afternoon and evening sport, including greyhound racing and such annual events as the Horse of the Year Show, and for health and fitness clubs and beauty salons, see Fitness and fresh air chapter, p. 339.

General tips and warnings

INFORMATION   Nicholson's *London Night Life Guide* (1987 edition), (no relation to the author) is pocket-sized, packed with practical information, and is the essential manual for the tireless night bird. For the very latest on the night scene, *Time Out* has the most comprehensive entertainment listings, from ice-skating to gay clubs, with *City Limits* a close second. The LTB offices are well-stocked with lists and brochures. There are also advertisements (including latest ticket availability), features and criticisms in the quality newspapers. On Radio 4, 'Kaleidoscope' reviews the latest arts, Mon–Fri, 9.45pm, repeated the next day at 4.30pm, and 'Critics Forum' reviews the arts week on Sat, 5.45pm; best local radio tips are on LBC's AM programme in the 'What's On' spot, but Radio London and Capital give entertainment information, too.

Arts Festivals   Rhinegold Publishing brings out the invaluable annual guide *Arts Festivals In Britain and Ireland*, in late spring, listing festivals with addresses, dates, background, etc; available from 241 Shaftesbury Avenue, WC2 (240 4957), either in person or by sending £5.95 which includes postage.

Artsline   The telephone information service on arts and entertainment for disabled people, see Telephone Services, p. 6.

Kidsline   To find out what is on for children there are two telephone information services: Kidsline and Children's London, see Telephone Services, p. 6.

Finding the Stars   To know which favourite actor, musician, singer, politician or sportsman is in town, contact Celebrity Service, 10 Bond Street, W1 (499 8511) and pay high for a monthly subscription to their twice-weekly bulletin of the London movements, including hotel bookings, of the stars of stage, screen and stadium.

Free Entertainment   Plenty of it. As a springboard, daytime free shows include a variety of acts in Covent Garden Piazza, Changing the Guard at Buckingham Palace or Horse Guards' Parade, attending an art auction, watching the barristers in

law courts and, in the afternoon, visiting parliament. Day and evening shows fill the foyers of the Barbican Centre and South Bank Centre (Royal Festival Hall). There is often lunchtime and evensong music in churches and cathedrals. And evening entertainment includes outdoor summer concerts, especially at Kenwood (you only pay to sit close); and jazz and folk music in pubs. Royal and traditional pageantry is all free; major and local festivals usually include plenty of free events. For more ideas, see Mary Peplow and Debra Shipley's *London For Free* (1986).

BOOKING   Most halls and theatres open their box offices from 10am until the evening event begins.

Methods of Booking   In person: best for seat selection. By telephone to the box office using a credit card: the seats are considered paid for and are kept even after the event has begun; the credit card must usually be produced when collecting tickets. By telephone to the box office and arranging to pay on collection: there is usually a time limit for collection, after which tickets may be resold. By telephone or in person to the hall's approved ticket agency printed with its listing: a charge is usually payable, see below. By post, always give alternative seat prices and, if possible, dates and enclose an s.a.e.

Major shows are booked out well in advance, especially for Friday and Saturday, but may have tickets for earlier in the week and for matinées. While Londoners fill most of the seats in the weekdays, a Saturday audience is different, often from outside London, more dressed up and out to have a good time.

Ticket Agencies   The rogue ticket agencies have given the good ones a bad name. The dozen small good ones have formed the Ticket Agents Association and print their symbol, a triangle made of the letters TAA, on their door and on their stationery. In addition, there are several reliable big ones, including those listed below. In every case, expect to pay a booking fee, although it may be nothing if the theatre has decided to foot the agency's commission itself. Usually it is around 15–20% with First Call and Ticket Master; around 24% with Keith Prowse and the Ticket Agents Association; leaping to 60% for the rogues who rocket even higher to compete with the street touts for 'sold-out' shows. It is worth checking the fee rate and ensuring the ticket is sold at the same value as at the hall before confirming an order. As some agents only deal with higher priced tickets, it is worth asking for the full range of prices available. To book a string of shows, concerts, events and sports in one telephone call saves time and may well be worth the expense.

Keith Prowse, Banda House, Cambridge Grove, W6. Main telephone booking numbers: 741 8955 for accounts; 741 9999 for credit cards; 741 8989 for pop and sport; 741 9999 for theatre; telex 261628. In New York: 234 West 44 Street, NY10036 (212 398 1430; telex 239797). Their many London branches include: 74 Cornhill, EC3 (283 1841/9431); 171 Earls Court Road, SW5 (370 3364); 5 Grosvenor Street, W1 (629 4775); 173 Kensington High Street, W8 (938 1861); 93 Knightsbridge, SW1 (235 4892); 14 Oxford Street, W1 (631 4604/4612); 27a Shaftesbury Avenue, W1 (734 7331); 44 Shaftesbury Avenue, W1 (437 8976); 7 Southampton Row, WC1 (242 3939). Their in-hotel branches include: Browns, Claridges, Cumberland, Forum, Grosvenor House, Inn on the Park, Inter-Continental, Mayfair, Mount Royal, Park Lane, Regent Palace, Savoy, Strand Palace, Tara, Tower and Westbury. Their in-store branches include: Harrods, Selfridges and Simpson.

First Call (tel 240 7200, telex 27889); almost all booking by telephone; open 24 hours a day every day, with 60 lines and an automatic queueing system; if buying pricey tickets, the ceiling fee of around £3 per ticket is useful; have a branch in the Theatre Museum, Tavistock Street, WC2.

Ticket Master (tel 379 4444, telex 946240); almost all booking by telephone; open 24 hours a day every day, automatic queuing system; branches in WH Smith travel shops, Our Price Record shops and HMV record shops.

Ticket Touts Beware of them. They lurk near every entertainment venue where there is a popular event, assuring would-be audiences they are the only passport to obtaining a ticket. This is untrue. Furthermore, there is no guarantee whether the tout's ticket is, or is not, a forgery. Classified advertisements in the newspapers for such temptations as Centre Court tickets for Wimbledon are merely published touting. At both

levels, you pay a high price and take a high risk. There are safer and cheaper solutions.

'Sold Out' does not necessarily mean sold out. First, it is worth asking about returns, even queueing for them – miracles happen daily. Next, some halls and theatres hold back a few tickets to be sold on the day of the performance, notably the National Theatre and the RSC at the Barbican. Then, the recommended ticket agencies may be able to obtain tickets and even if they charge a fee it is lower than the touts and the tickets are genuine. Then, the Yellow Pages telephone directory lists a string of agencies who promise to solve a sold-out crisis, but fees and mark-ups should be checked carefully against the original cost of the ticket.

Sight-Lines If booking a ticket in person, it is worth checking the seat plan to make sure you can hear and/or see well enough. Ask about the rake, the angle of incline of the seats. If booking by telephone, you have to rely on the person taking the booking. They are usually very honest, often to the point of being abrupt. 'The best seats available' may not be the most expensive. And while it is sometimes worth paying more for a better position, remember the show is the same wherever you are sitting.

Seat Warnings Some concert halls (like the Albert Hall) have cheap seats behind the orchestra. Wembley is so vast it is worth paying to be near the performers. Older theatres have the biggest problems. Seat rows are close together, so long legs need aisle seats; some have blind seats behind pillars; the Queen's upper circle is too steep an incline for even those who do not normally suffer from vertigo. The view from Her Majesty's back stalls blocks out the top of the stage – audiences for Lloyd Webber's *Phantom of the Opera* missed the spectacular ending of the first act; in the Royal Opera House it is impossible to see the whole stage from the front row of the grand tier without leaning forward and blocking the view for those sitting behind; the Coliseum is vision and pitch perfect almost everywhere. In all cases, if the rake of the stalls is gradual, a small person sitting behind a tall one sees little; an upper level might be better. For dance, it is always best to be up in the first circle.

GETTING EQUIPPED For late night banking, see pp. 9–10; for chemists, see p. 326.

Dress Times have changed. In general, audiences in the pricier seats for theatre, opera, classical music and dance look tidy, men in jacket and tie, women dollied up a little; elsewhere, there is

total informality. On weekdays, most people arrive straight from the office. Saturdays are more dressy. And the real sprucing up is for the pricy seats on first nights of important West End shows and for charity galas where the patron, often a member of the Royal Family, may attend. While the old halls and theatres heat up uncomfortably, especially in the upper seats, the air-conditioning in the National Theatre and Barbican sometimes makes the air fridge-cold and a jacket or jumper is needed.
Hiring If you do not own the right outfit, it can be hired. Moss Bross, 21 Bedford Street, WC2 (240 4567) for formal men's clothes – their women's balldresses are not up to much; Contemporary Wardrobe, 66 Great Queen Street, WC2 (242 4024) for post-war high styles for both sexes; Simpsons Dress Hire, 21 Bedford Street, WC2 (836 2381) for women's clothes; Hetherington, 289 King's Road, SW3 (351 0880) for glamorous streetwise girls; Young's Dress Hire, 1–2 Berners Street, W1 (437 4422) for men's formal and informal clothes, with some modern cuts, no appointment necessary; One Night Stand, 44 Pimlico Road, SW1 (730 8708) for women's cocktail and evening dresses, with jewellery to match, appointment essential. Charles Fox, 22 Tavistock Street, WC2 (240 3111) for jewellery and more outlandish and party-time wigs and make-up. Morris Angel & Sons, 119 Shaftesbury Avenue, WC2 (836 5678), for theatrical and period costumes, perfect for a gala, grand ball or a fancy dress party.
Vital Equipment If the seat is cheap and the hall old, a cushion is a good idea. If the hall is large, a pair of binoculars helps, although some theatres have them installed in the backs of seats, unlocked by inserting a coin, usually 10p or 20p.

EATING AND DRINKING A number of West End restaurants have fixed-price pre-theatre menus and will ensure you are served a final coffee well before the orchestra strikes up or the curtain rises. Others take late bookings, although it is always worth mentioning which show you are seeing so that your table is kept should there be a 25-minute standing ovation. Inside the halls, most bars take orders for interval drinks, some do coffee and some have sandwiches and cakes, all well worth ordering before curtain-up to avoid queueing for 15 minutes and being served just as the bell goes for the second half. Beware: bar prices tend to be high, so for pre-theatre and interval drinking it may be cheaper (and less crushed) to pop round to the nearest pub. At the big concert

venues – Wembley, Hammersmith, Earls Court, etc – the food is uniformly bad and over-priced.

AT THE SHOW Concert programmes usually have helpful programme notes. The National Theatre and the RSC at the Barbican produce free cast lists as an option; a few other halls have followed. Big shows have glossy souvenir programmes.
Photography Not permitted in theatres or concert halls; sometimes permitted at large open-air shows such as at Wembley.
Tape or Video Recording Not permitted; at the opera, musicals and all types of music concerts there are usually records and tapes on sale.
Behaviour Code At a formal theatre, concert, etc, it is usual to applaud only at the end of an item and then to remain seated, not to stand. It is also unpopular to permit digital watches to bleep, to unwrap sweets noisily, to cough constantly (most halls sell mints and sucky sweets), to smoke and to arrive late – many theatres and concert halls forbid entry until a suitable moment, which may be at the interval half way through the evening. At pop concerts, sports, etc, all is much more informal.
Tipping It is traditional to tip for leaving a coat and using a well-kept washroom, but not for being shown to your seat.

LATE NIGHT TRANSPORT
By bus Most daytime services end at midnight, when the less frequent all-night service takes over.
By Underground: Each station has a notice giving the first and last departure; when the last one goes, around 11.30pm, the station is locked. If this is your last fling before leaving London, see p. 264 for night trains to Gatwick and Heathrow airports.
By taxi Possible at all hours, although there are night surcharges, see p. 8. As taxis disappear when it rains and when a crowd spills out of a hall, it is worth ordering one to collect you at the end of show (see p. 8).
By mini cab As with taxis, worth ordering for the end of a show; bookable from the Yellow Pages telephone directory; price can often be bargained down.

GETTING IN THE MOOD
Drinking For cocktails, riverside pubs and other wine bars and pubs, see Food and Drink chapter, p. 301.
Sunsets Often spectacular, their romance height-

ened by the lush parks and riverside settings. Here are a dozen favourite sunset spots: Bankside, looking across the river to the sun-sparkled tops of the City church spires and the dome of St Paul's; in front of County Hall, looking across the river and Westminster Bridge to the Houses of Parliament; Greenwich Park, from the terrace; Hampstead Heath, especially beside Kenwood House; Inn on the Park hotel, rooftop bar; Hyde Park, along Buck Hill Walk or on the Serpentine Bridge; Kew Gardens, overlooking the river opposite Syon House and staying as late as possible; Regent's Park, where the rose perfumes in Queen Mary's Garden gain sunset strength; St George's Hotel Langham Place, rooftop bar; The Mall and St James's Park, looking from the bridge towards Buckingham Palace; The National Gallery, from the portico; Waterloo Bridge, for views east and west; Tower Bridge (or cosy Tower Hotel bar), for the Thames dissolving into a golden pond.

Floodlit London Many buildings, monuments and bridges are floodlit, many looking rather better by night than by day. To catch several at once, one of the best value taxi rides is a 30-minute night drive around floodlit London, which impresses the most cynical and world-weary. To make a sort of circular trip, here are 15 illuminated set pieces: Nash's Park Crescent and Portland Place to the Wallace Collection in Manchester Square, best approached from Oxford Street (Christmas lights); Marble Arch, the remaining palatial houses at the top of Park Lane and the Dorchester and its fairy-lit tree at the bottom; the South Kensington culture complex, from the Albert Memorial and Royal Albert Hall down to the Natural History Museum and the V&A; Harrods, now lit all year round; the Embankment, from Chelsea right around to parliament, catching the illuminated bridges (especially fairy-lit Albert) and the Tate Gallery; Lambeth Palace, glowing rust-red; Parliament Square and the Houses of Parliament, good from all sides and from Lambeth Bridge; Whitehall, especially Banqueting House; Trafalgar Square, with the National Gallery and Nelson's Column (and the annual Christmas tree); Buckingham Palace, with soft gas lighting, best approached along the Mall beside partly floodlit St James's Park; Hyde Park Corner with Apsley House and then Piccadilly and Piccadilly Circus (with Regent Street for Christmas lights); The British Museum and then down Kingsway to Bush House; Inner Temple, where the lamplighter lights the gas lamps at dusk; St Paul's, best approached along Fleet Street; The Tower,

even better if you attend the Ceremony of the Keys (see p. 51); and, if you are lucky, Greenwich will be floodlit for an evening event, pure magic looking from Island Gardens to Royal Hospital. Guided evening trips: For early evening coach tours, walks and boat trips, see pp. 39–40 and 93, 96.

The big arts venues: What's what

THE BARBICAN CENTRE, Silk Street, EC2 (638 4141; 24-hour recorded information on 628 2295/9760; credit card booking every day 10am–8pm on 638 8891/628 8795; a range of cheap ticket deals). A hothouse of activity, despite its grim concrete exterior. If you are going to a play or concert, it is well worth arriving early to pick up the poster-sized, fact-ridden, folded, monthly information sheet and to explore the eight levels (see also p. 67). Briefly, this is what there is, all under one roof, so rain is no problem.

This is the London home of the Royal Shakespeare Company (RSC) who perform in two theatres, Barbican Theatre (level 3) and the smaller The Pit (level 1), sometimes new productions (especially in The Pit), sometimes productions brought from Stratford-upon-Avon, always several productions running concurrently in repertory. There are always at least 30 tickets for the Barbican Theatre and 10 for The Pit on sale at 10am on the performance day, maximum of two tickets per person; the annual Prom season has bargain prices. Backstage theatre tours are run by the RSC (to book, telephone 628 3351).

The Barbican Centre is also the London home for the London Symphony Orchestra (LSO) who perform in the Barbican Hall (level 3). There is also a cinema (level 1); a Lloyds bank (level 3); free foyer exhibitions and music (levels 3, 4 and 5); the central box office for personal booking, a lending library, music library, children's library, and bookshop (level 7); and at the top a two-tiered art gallery usually showing two exhibitions, a sculpture court and the huge, lush conservatory (level 8). In summer, there are events outside beside the lake and lunchtime and afternoon concerts in St Giles Church, across the water. In addition, there is a stream of festivals, from children's weekends to free foyer recitals.

For refreshments, there is The Waterside Café (level 5, in fact the ground level), the Cut Above restaurant (level 7, reservations on 588 3008), a wine bar with food (level 6), and bars and snack bars (levels 3, 5 and 6). If it seems too maze-like, there are guided tours (excluding backstage of the theatres) Mon–Sat 12.15pm and 5.15pm, booking essential (638 4141). The whole centre opens Mon–Sat 9am11pm, Sun noon–11pm; the vital central information desk is by the Silk Street entrance (level 5); as expected, the telephone booking system has the most sophisticated computer of its type in town.

THE SOUTH BANK CENTRE   Even bigger – the biggest in Western Europe – and so far run as several separate entities. Starting with the musical chunk, confusingly called the South Bank Centre, SE1 (928 3002; booking on 928 3191; credit card booking on 928 8800; credit card agency First Call on 240 7200; for a range of cheap ticket deals, 633 0932); composed of three concert halls, the Royal Festival Hall and the smaller Queen Elizabeth Hall and Purcell Room; the Craft Centre in Hungerford Arches (928 0643); and Feliks Topolski's 600-foot-long ongoing painting, 'A Memoir of the Century', in Hungerford Arches. Also in the three halls: Sherratt & Hughes arts bookshop, music shop, record shop, five or more foyer exhibitions, free foyer lunchtime music; and for refreshments the Riverside Café, Festival Buffet, Steak and Salt Beef Bar, Foyer Bar and Coffee Lounge. If this fascinates or confuses, there are guided tours daily at 12.45pm and 5.30pm. The whole centre opens daily 10am–10pm, or the end of the last performance; the vital central information desk is on level 1 in the Royal Festival Hall; beside it is a Computer Cab bureau, open from 6pm for booking a cab home. The centre also has information on the Hayward Gallery, built on top, which opens during exhibitions with usually two shows, café and art bookshop (928 3144; recorded information on 928 0127). See also p. 117.

The National Film Theatre comes next, South Bank, SE1 (928 3232); two cinemas showing old and new British and foreign films, usually in seasons, heavy programming squeezed into a meaty monthly booklet; big film bookshop, café, restaurant; temporary and annual membership. Beside it is the new Museum of the Moving Image (MOMI) (928 3232 for information).

Next door is the National Theatre (NT), South Bank, SE1 (information on 633 0880; 24-hour recorded booking information on 928 8126; booking on 928 2252; telex booking on 297306 Nattre G; credit card agency First Call on 240 7200; a range of cheap ticket deals). The home of the National Theatre who perform in three theatres: the Olivier

and the Lyttelton, where 40 (20 on press nights) cheap seats for each are sold on the performance day at 10am, usually only two per person, with some standing places sold if seats run out; and the Cottesloe, where some tickets are sold on the day, usually only two per person. All three have several productions running concurrently in repertory. In addition, NT Extras include intermittent Platform Performances in each theatre, usually at 6pm; a selection from the Somerset Maugham Collection of theatrical paintings hung on various levels; about four foyer art exhibitions; free foyer music before all matinées and evening performances; a large bookshop in the Lyttelton, much smaller ones in the two other theatres; and the Ovations Restaurant (reservations on 928 2033), Lyttelton Terrace Café, Box Office Buffet, Lyttelton Bar and bars and buffets for each theatre. The guided tour, including plenty behind the scenes, is one of the best, run daily, bookable at the Lyttelton Information Desk (633 0880). The whole building opens Mon–Sat 10am–end of the last performance.

Theatre, Dance and Opera

THE THEATRE YEAR   Non-stop, no closing down for summer holidays. Big Christmas shows open late autumn. The Palladium always stages a traditional Christmas pantomime; the Players Theatre does a jolly Victorian music-hall one; best of the rest are in the suburbs, such as Wimbledon and Richmond. After Christmas theatre-going quietens, except for pantomimes and family shows. Summer has the full range, plus festivals.

The London International Festival of Theatre (LIFT) in July–August (every other year) might include companies from Mexico, USSR, Nigeria and Spain, who pack fringe theatres, churches and halls with dynamic drama for three weeks, more information from 44 Earlham Street, WC2, 836 7433/7186. The City of London, the Almeida and other annual and local festivals include professional and amateur productions of theatre, dance and music, see Directory, p. 352. In late August and early September, it is worth considering a trip up to the Edinburgh Festival.

DANCE AND THE DANCE YEAR   High spots are the autumn and spring. Sadler's Wells is the London dance focus: it is the home of the Sadler's Wells Royal Ballet (the touring arm of the Royal Ballet) when they are not on tour, and has regular visits from London Contemporary Dance Theatre,

Ballet Rambert, Merce Cummingham, Michael Clarke and foreign troupes from Japan, Russia, etc. The Royal Opera House is the home of the Royal Ballet, pirouetting round the year except during August, when they sometimes dance in a huge tent in Battersea Park (cheap tickets; locals take picnics). The Place, 17 Duke's Road, WC1 (387 0161) is the home of the London Contemporary Dance Theatre, always worth a visit; also has a restaurant. The Coliseum has a summer dance season, June–Aug, with annual visits from the London Festival Ballet and a visit every other year from the Dance Theatre of Haarlem and other companies. The London Festival Ballet, a touring company, also dance at the Royal Festival Hall in the summer and at Christmas. The annual Dance Umbrella Festival (Oct–Nov) for contemporary dance is run by Riverside Studios, Crisp Road, W6 (741 4040).

OPERA AND THE OPERA YEAR   The Royal Opera is based at the Royal Opera House, where Placido Domingo, Kiri te Kanawa, Jessye Norman and others perform grand opera round the year, except August, alternating with dance. Festivals include a prom season, when seats are removed from the stalls and places sold cheaply on the day of performance. Opera relayed into the Piazza on a huge screen was initiated with astounding success in 1987 and should continue annually. The English National Opera is based at the Coliseum, where performances are always in English, usually very lively, seats are cheaper and more easily available than for the Royal Opera, and the long season is Aug–May. New Sadler's Wells Opera performs at Sadler's Wells; Welsh Opera visits the Dominion. A train ride away, Glyndebourne Festival Opera runs late May–late Aug (Glyndebourne, Lewes, Sussex, tel 0273 812321).

THE SOCIETY OF WEST END THEATRES (SWET)   The employers' association representing the owners and managers of 49 major London theatres, both the independent ones and the four state-supported national ones. SWET runs the annual Laurence Olivier Awards (announced Jan), London's answer to the Tonys, whose panel is a mixture of the theatre-going public and professionals. It publishes the fortnightly London Theatre Guide, free from theatres, libraries, LTB centres or on subscription form SWET. It runs a West End Theatre Gift Token scheme (booking on Tokenline, 379 3395), also available from any West End theatre, from the Theatre Museum and from Lon-

don post offices. And it runs various cheap ticket schemes: Sixth Form Standby Scheme; Senior Citizens Matinée Scheme; and the Leicester Square Ticket Booth (see below). To find out more, send a large s.a.e. to SWET, Bedford Chambers, the Piazza, Covent Garden, WC2.

INFORMATION AND HELP   Time Out and City Limits for the most comprehensive weekly listings of all theatre, West End and fringe; SWET's free London Theatre Guide (see above); SWET's weekly guide published in the quality newspapers; the Virgin Guide to Music, Opera and Dance in London (fortnightly, free); and the arts pages of the quality newspapers, especially the FT and the Observer, for the critics' views on the new openings. For magazines: The Stage (weekly), Dance & Dancers (monthly) and The Dancing Times (monthly). In addition, bodies to help theatre-goers include the Theatre Advice Bureau (TAB), 10a The Avenue, Hatch End, Middlesex (421 2470): founded by two actors, Ronald Barnes and Andrew Kitchen, who send enquirers a detailed questionnaire and then make up a personalised TAB Pack containing all the pertinent information – fringe and mainstream, London and provinces, with hard information on travel, food, etc.

To find out more, see The Theatres of London by Raymond Mander and Joe Mitchenson (1961, revised and expanded 1975, try for it in a second-hand bookshop) – their magnificent theatre collection is due to go on show soon at Beckenham Palace, Kent (658 7725). The British Theatre Association, Inner Circle, Regent's Park, NW1 (935 2571) has more than 250,000 theatre books (accessible to members) and runs play-readings, cheap theatre ticket schemes, etc. Westminster Central Reference Library (see p. 75) has a remarkable collection, too. The primary aim of the Theatres Trust, 10 St Martin's Court, St Martin's Lane, WC2 (836 8591) is to ensure that theatres are maintained for live entertainment.

BOOKING   See General Tips, above. For serious theatre-goers, Susie Elms's The London Theatre Scene, 3rd edition (1985) is an invaluable little book listing each main theatre with its telephone numbers, catering facilities, nearest public transport and its auditorium plan – very useful when booking by telephone. The Barbican Hall, Coliseum, NT, RSC, Royal Opera House, Sadler's Wells and many other halls have their own mailing lists (usually charging a small annual fee), priority booking systems and cheap deals. A number of theatres keep back tickets to be sold at 10am on the day of performance; worth arriving early for a popular show. For fringe theatre scattered across town, the useful Fringe Theatre Box Office, located in the Duke of York's Theatre, St Martin's Lane, WC2 (379 6002), open Mon–Sat, 10am–6pm, advises on shows, books tickets and charges 50p per booking (not per seat). For pub theatres, even more scattered, useful Pub Theatre Network, 168–70 Battersea Park Road, SW11 (622 4553) advises on what to find where.

CHEAP SEATS SWET's Leicester Square Ticket Booth, often known as the Half Price Ticket Booth, does just that. It sells tickets for most West End theatres at half price on the day of performance, adding on 80p service charge. Open at noon for matinée performances; 2.30–6.30pm for evening performances; payment by cash only; four tickets per person. Especially good for catching a matinée performance of an otherwise sold-out show. As there are always at least 20 shows on offer, listed on the booth, it is best to have a list of priorities ready in case your top choice is not available. Other cheap ticket routes: SWET's Sixth Form Standby and Senior Citizen Matinée schemes; Student Standby scheme, run by most theatres who offer unsold seats cut price to students (with student card) just before curtain up.

TIMINGS Many theatres run matinée performances, usually two a week with one of them on Saturday, usually starting between 3pm and 5pm. Evening performances tend to start between 7.30 and 8pm, with some Saturday starts at 8.30pm. Latecomers are rarely permitted to enter the auditorium until a suitable break.

The theatres

Listed below are the principal London theatres, together with telephone numbers and their advertised preferred ticket agencies; for more venues, see *Time Out* and *City Limits*. To plot the West End ones, see map, p. 283. Page references are to more information.

The code:

cc	credit card telephone number to the theatre's box office
agent cc	credit card telephone number to the theatre's approved agent/s, where bookings usually carry a fee

KP	Keith Prowse ticket agency, tel 741 9999 and see above
FC	First Call ticket agency, tel 240 7200 and see above
TM	Ticket Master ticket agency, tel 379 4444 and see above

STATE-SUPPORTED THEATRES
Coliseum, St Martin's Lane, WC2 (836 3161; cc 240 5258; agent cc 379 6433); opera in English, summer dance; friends society; best bar is the basement Dutch Bar, especially pre-show; see also p. 124.
The National Theatre, see South Bank Arts Centre, above; music before; choice of bars during intervals but higher ones have nearby terraces with good views of floodlit London; see also p. 117. Royal Opera House, Bow Street, Covent Garden, WC2 (240 1066, cc 240 1911); opera and dance; friends society for priority booking; closes Aug, when there are sometimes visiting companies. Best bar is the first-floor Crush Bar, which speaks for itself, so pre-show ordering is essential. See also p. 123.
Sadler's Wells, Rosebery Avenue, EC1 (278 8916; 24-hour information 278 5450, cc agent FC); dance and opera; friends society for priority booking; see also p. 206.
Also: The Royal Shakespeare Company, see Barbican Centre, above. Although headquartered at Stratford, the RSC London base makes it is unnecessary to make the pilgrimage, except to enjoy the town and scenery and scoop up more productions in another three theatres; but if Stratford is a must, the address is RSC, Stratford-upon-Avon, Warwickshire (0789 295623).

WEST END THEATRES About 50 independent theatres, showing on any one night a mixture of comedies, musicals, thrillers, farces and straight plays. The biggest owner is Stoll Moss, whose dozen or so theatres include the London Palladium, Drury Lane, Her Majesty's and the Coliseum, with the newly restored Playhouse latest addition. It is here that the great impresarios, helped by anonymous backers known as 'angels', mount their flashiest shows – big names include Peter Saunders who put on *The Mousetrap*, Cameron Mackintosh who produced *Cats*, *Les Miserables*, *Phantom of the Opera* and *Follies*, and now Andrew Lloyd Webber whose The Really Useful Group Plc owns the Palace Theatre and put on *Starlight Express* and *Phantom of the Opera*. Inside, the auditoria are all reasonably large and the theatre layout and jargon reflects theatre social history: the Royal Box, usually on the right side of the Dress Circle (so if you are booking seats for a Royal Gala, go for the left side) and the occasional Royal Command Performances refer to a time when the theatres were under direct control of the sovereign; patrons of the Dress Circle, the lowest circle and sometimes called Royal Circle, did indeed dress up and those seats are still usually the most expensive; the Gods, up at the top, have always been the cheapest seats; the Pit on the ground floor was second cheapest, but this whole area is now usually the Stalls, known in America as Orchestra Stalls. For more on London theatre history, the theatres and theatre societies and for a theatre history trail, see p. 289.

Adelphi, Strand, WC2 (240 7913/4, 836 7611, cc 836 7358, cc agent KP/FC/TM)

Albery, St Martin's Lane, WC2 (836 3878, cc agent KP/FC/TM)

Aldwych, The Aldwych, WC2 (836 6404/0641, cc 379 6233, cc agent FC/TM)

Ambassadors, West Street, WC2 (836 6111/2, 836 1171, cc agent FC)

Apollo, Shaftesbury Avenue, W1 (437 2663, cc 434 3598, cc agent FC)

Apollo Victoria, Wilton Road, SW1 (828 8665, cc 630 6262, cc agent FC/TM)

Cambridge, Earlham Street, WC2 (379 5299, cc agent KP/FC/TM)

Comedy, Panton Street, SW1 (930 2578, cc 838 1438, cc agent KP/FC/TM)

Criterion, Piccadilly Circus, W1 (930 3216, cc agent TM/KP)

Drury Lane, Catherine Street, WC2 (836 8108/ 240 9066/7, cc agent FC/TM)

Duke of York's, St Martin's Lane, WC2 (836 5122/3, cc 836 9837, cc agent FC/TM)

Fortune, Russell Street, WC2 (836 2238, cc 836 2239, cc agent KP/FC/TM)

Garrick, Charing Cross Road, WC2 (379 6107, cc agent KP/FC/TM)

Globe, Shaftesbury Avenue, W1 (379 6107, cc agent KP/FC/TM)

Haymarket, Haymarket, SW1 (930 9832, cc agent FC)

Her Majesty's, Haymarket, SW1 (839 2244, cc agent FC); currently the home of *The Phantom of the Opera*.

Lyric, Shaftesbury Avenue, W1 (437 3686/ 434 1050, cc 734 5156/7, cc agent FC/TM)

Mayfair, Stratton Street, W1 (629 3036, cc 629 3036, cc agent KP/FC/TM)

National Theatre, see The South Bank Centre, above.

New London, Parker Street, WC2 (405 0072, cc 404 4079, cc agent TM); currently the home of *Cats*.

Old Vic, Waterloo Road, SE1 (928 7616, cc 261 1821, cc agent FC/TM)

Palace, Shaftesbury Avenue, W1 (434 0909, cc agent FC/TM)

Palladium, Argyll Street, W1 (437 7373)

Phoenix, Charing Cross Road, WC2 (836 2294, cc agent KP/FC)

Playhouse, Northumberland Avenue, WC2 (839 4401, cc Agent KP/FC/TM)

Piccadilly, Denman Street, W1 (437 4506, cc agent FC/TM)

Prince Edward, Old Compton Street, W1 (734 8951, cc 836 3464)

Prince of Wales, Coventry Street, W1 (836 5987, cc agent FC)

Queen's, Shaftesbury Avenue, W1 (734 1166/0261/ 0120, cc 734 0120, cc agent FC)

Royal Court, Sloane Square, SW1 (730 1745/1857, cc agent FC)

Royal Shakespeare Company, see The Barbican Centre, above.

Royalty Theatre, Portugal Street, WC2 (831 0660, cc agent KP/FC/TM)

Savoy, Savoy Court, WC2 (836 8888, cc 379 6219, cc agent KP/TM)

Shaftesbury, Shaftesbury Avenue, WC2 (379 5399, cc agent KP/FC/TM)

St Martin's, West Street, WC2 (836 1443, cc agent TM); present home of *The Mousetrap*, in its 36th year in 1988.

Strand, Aldwych, WC2 (836 2660/4143/5190, cc agent KP/FC/TM)

Vaudeville, Strand, WC2 (836 9987/5645, cc agent KP/FC/TM)

Victoria Palace, Victoria Street, SW1 (834 1317/ 828 4735, cc agent FC)

Westminster, Palace Street, SW1 (834 0283/4, cc 834 0048, cc agent FC/TM)

Whitehall, Whitehall, SW1 (930 7765/839 4455, cc agent FC/TM)

Wyndham's, Charing Cross Road, WC2 (836 3028, cc agent KPO/FC/TM)

EXTRAS

Theatre in the City: Mermaid, Puddledock, Blackfriars, EC4 (638 889, cc agent KP); founded by Bernard Miles on an old theatrical site, this is the City's only theatre; visiting companies sometimes include the RSC from the Barbican.

Theatre in the park: The Open Air Theatre, Inner circle, Regent's Park, NW1 (486 2431 cc 486 1933); season June–Aug, usually three plays in repertory, of which one is usually Shakespeare; matinée and evening performances; barbeque suppers available but picnicking is best.

Theatre in the garden: Holland Park Court Theatre, Holland Park, W8 (information on 937 2542); season July–Aug.

CHILDREN'S THEATRE   Very lively in London, especially during school holidays and at weekends. At Christmas, the traditional panto-mimes have the dame played by a man and the dashing hero by a girl, with plenty of audience participation and usually a sing-along song to end; best central London one is usually at the Palla-dium. To find a puppet show, contact the Puppet Centre Trust, Battersea Arts Centre, Lavender Hill, SW11 (228 5335). Children's theatres include:

Little Angel Marionette Theatre, 14 Dagmar Passage, Cross Street, N1 (226 1787), the doyenne of giant puppet theatres.

Polka Children's Theatre, 240 The Broadway, Wimbledon, SW19 (543 4888/542 4258); a wide variety of excellent shows.

Unicorn Theatre for Children, 6–7 Great Newport Street, WC2 (836 3334); regular shows Sept–May.

Also, look out for special children's shows at the Lyric Hammersmith, the National Theatre, River-side Studios, Sadler's Wells, Tricycle Theatre and St George's Theatre in Islington. In Covent Gar-den, under St Paul's Portico, Alternative Arts runs a daily programme of theatre and entertainment, especially good at weekends; programme pinned up on the church railings; more information from 1/4 King Street, WC2 (240 5451). The Barbican Centre regularly runs days devoted to children and family entertainment.

FRINGE THEATRE   The movement of alternative theatre that mushroomed in the 1960s. Unlike the tight group of West End theatres, the fringe is scattered across London, often putting on dynamic shows with a minimum of finance in small, inti-mate rooms; a few give lunchtime as well as eve-ning performances. Ones to watch are the Almeida (with festival), ICA and Riverside, who all host companies from Britain and abroad and are often very contemporary, mix different media and are very experimental – small-scale Shakespeare to performance art; the Royal Court, Bush and Hamp-stead, where high standard, usually new plays

often transfer to the West End; and, slightly more formal, Stratford East and the Lyric Hammersmith, who often stage new plays. Here are a handful of the 60 or so fringe and pub theatres; for the useful Fringe Theatre Box Office, see Booking, p. 290.

Almeida, 1a/b Almeida Street, N1 (359 4404)

Bush, Shepherds Bush Green, W12 (743 3388)

Donmar Warehouse, 41 Earlham Street, WC2 (240 8230, cc agent TM)

Hampstead, Avenue Road, Swiss Cottage, NW3 (722 9301)

Institute of Contemporary Arts (ICA), 12 Carlton House Terrace, SW1 (930 3647, recorded infor-mation 930 6393); see also p. 176.

Lyric Hammersmith, King Street, W6 (741 2311); a splendid old theatre that was pulled down, put in store, then re-erected on top of a shopping precinct.

Riverside Studios, Crisp Road, W6 (748 3354)

Royal Court, officially part of the West End struc-ture, see above; also has a studio theatre, the Theatre Upstairs (730 2554)

Theatre Royal Stratford (Stratford East), Gerry Roffles Square, E15 (534 0310).

PUB THEATRE   About two dozen of them, all very informal, plays often watched with drink and sandwich in hand in a small back or upstairs room; often new plays, reviews or shows performed at lunchtime and evenings; most are clubs, so a small membership fee is payable. As each has its own character, it is worth contacting the Pub Theatre Network for advice, see Information above; they produce a monthly calendar of shows and a brochure about the theatres, available at the pubs or by sending an s.a.e. to PTN. Ones worth visiting include:

The Gate Theatre Club, The Prince Albert, 11 Pembridge Road, W11 (229 0706)

King's Head Theatre Club, 115 Upper Street, N1 (226 1916)

Latchmere, 503 Battersea Park Road, SW11 (228 2620)

Orange Tree, 45 New Road, Richmond, Surrey (940 3633)

Old Red Lion, St Johns Street, N1 (837 7816)

Tabard Theatre of New Writing, The Tabard, 2 Bath Road, Turnham Green, W4 (995 6035)

MUSIC HALL, CABARET, COMEDY AND REVUE   Revue grew out of the late-night cabaret and the music-hall traditions. Satirical, witty and small-scale, it was the schooling for such stars as Hermione Gingold and Gertrude Lawrence. Beyond The Fringe and the Cambridge Footlights, with Peter Cook, Dudley Moore, Jonathan Miller and Alan Bennett, took the idea to its extreme. Today, the best places are:

Comedy Store, 28a Leicester Square, WC2 (939 6665); for the wittiest, funniest and smartest comedy acts from Britain, Europe and the US; best on Saturday nights.

Donmar Warehouse, see fringe theatres; for late night revue.

Duchess Theatre, Catherine Street, WC1 (836 8243, cc 240 9648); for thriving Victorian music hall.

King's Theatre, see pub theatres; for revue over supper.

The Ritz, Piccadilly, W1 (493 8181); for seasons of smart, international stars such as Steve Ross.

Theatre Royal Stratford, see fringe theatres; for jolly monthly music-hall nights in the East End tradition; also Hackney Empire, see p. 250.

Music

THE MUSIC YEAR   Non-stop and as rich a choice as theatre. The range is huge, from contemporary classical to traditional folk. And the settings move from simple to sublime – a public concert hall, an intimate church or an echoing great cathedral, outside in a bustling piazza or lush green park, inside in a magnificent historic house or art gallery. Towards Christmas, there are carol singers in Trafalgar Square and Christmas Oratorios in the churches; at Easter Passions are sung in churches; and in summer there is a flood of music with the festivals as focal points. The major classical music festival in London is the Henry Wood Promenade Concerts (The Proms), Royal Albert Hall, SW7 (589 8212, cc 589 9465), mid-July to mid-September; eight weeks of nightly concerts, the majority classical, each broadcast live on BBC Radio 3, some on television. The Last Night ends the season with lots of audience waving and swaying to the eccentric and imperial combination of Elgar's *'Pomp and Circumstance March'*, Wood's *'Fantasia on British Sea-Songs'* and Parry and Elgar's *'Jerusalem'*. Then there is the Camden Jazz Festival, a platform for new work; the London Handel Festival; the City of London Festival, where concerts are performed in old City Livery Company halls normally closed to the public; and many more, all well advertised, see Directory on p. 352.

INFORMATION   For the full range, *Time Out* or *City Limits*. The Sunday quality newspapers carry large display advertisements for the major concert halls. For lunchtime concerts in the City churches, sometimes the only times they open, see the monthly *Events in the City of London*, available free from LTB offices and from the City of London Information Centre, St Paul's Churchyard. In addition, Radio 3 has its own full programme and broadcasts some programmes live; see daily newspapers, *Radio Times*. To attend a concert being performed expressly for a radio recording, apply to the Ticket Unit, BBC Broadcasting House, Portland Place, W1 (580 4468).

SOCIETIES   To join one of the many music societies, contact the National Federation of Music Societies, Francis House, Francis Street, SW1 (828 7320) who have a catalogue listing almost 200. To find out more about ticket concessions for young people, contact Youth and Music, 78 Neal Street, WC2 (379 6722). To find out about all aspects of new classical music, contact the Society for the Promotion of New Music, 10 Stratford Place, London W1 (491 8111), who publish a monthly 'London Events' programme. The British Music Information Centre, also at 10 Stratford Place, London W1 (499 8567) is a vast and wonderful public reference library of twentieth-century British music, scores, tapes and records (open Mon–Fri, 10am–5pm; free; twice weekly concerts).

BOOKING   See general tips, above. The principal concert halls listed in Susie Elms's *The London Theatre Scene* have useful auditoria plans. For church concerts, it is wise to book seats near the front and to dress warmly in winter; if there is no booking, arrive in good time. Apart from the classical concerts in historic houses, which book up quickly, tickets for other concerts are often available at the door; but big stars of the classics, rock and pop sell out, even at huge Wembley.

CHEAP SEATS   There are many cheap deals for early bookers, students, senior citizens, lunchtime music, matinées, etc. But the best deal is to book a series – a number of concerts connected by a theme, sometimes rather a tenuous one.

TIMINGS   Not much early morning music, except on Sunday, but plenty from lunchtime on. Lunchtime concerts tend to begin at 1pm; free foyer music in the big arts complexes around 6pm and evening concerts at 7.15–8pm. Rock, reggae, soul, folk, jazz, etc are often in pubs or clubs and tend to start between 8pm and 10pm, with late night sessions at 10–10.30pm. For children, the South Bank Centre and other halls have Saturday morning concerts.

LUNCHTIME MUSIC   Thoroughly relaxing and soothing between sightseeing or business meetings. Other benefits: usually no booking necessary, often in beautiful buildings otherwise closed, usually cheap or even free. Weekdays are best for classical concerts; Sundays for jazz in pubs and arts centres. Favourite places include: Covent Garden, for buskers, jazz trios and other informal music-making; Barbican Hall and the Royal Festival Hall for formal concerts and free foyer music; the City churches for concerts in beautiful surroundings; St Martins-in-the-Fields in Trafalgar Square; St John's Smith Square in Westminster for good food in the crypt and good music in the nave; weekday summer band performances in St James's and Regent's Parks, June–Aug, 12.30–2pm.

FOOD WITH MUSIC   A wide variety. Here is an idea of the range. Tea-dance in the Palm Court of the Waldorf Hotel, Fri–Sun; tea or cocktails with piano at Kettner's, the Savoy or Hyatt Carlton Tower; cocktails with the Hungarian Quartet at Claridge's; supper and a show at the King's Head pub theatre; hamburgers and deafening pop music at the Hard Rock Café; dinner with international cabaret at the Ritz; dinner with dancing at the Savoy; supper and jazz at Ronnie Scott's, the Pizza Express or Pizza on the Park; nightly cabaret in the ground-floor brasserie of L'Escargot and at the Pheasantry; outdoor summer concerts with picnics.

FINDING THE MUSIC
The big halls: These stage a variety of concerts, from classical to jazz and pop.
Barbican Hall, see above; home of the London Symphony Orchestra which forms the backbone of the annual programme; deemed by many musicians to have wonderful acoustics.
Royal Albert Hall, Kensington Gore, SW7 (589 8212); annual events in the enormous circular hall include huge carol concerts, a scratch Messiah sung by the whole audience and the Proms (see above); with the suspended saucers, acoustics much improved; guided tour of this huge elliptical, domed building well worth while (see p. 217).
The South Bank Centre, see above; three concert

halls. The Royal Festival Hall is the biggest and has both excellent acoustics and an 'assisted resonance system'; the smaller Queen Elizabeth Hall is used for chamber concerts, poetry readings, films, etc; the Purcell Room seats just 372 and is used for recitals, readings, etc.
Wembley Stadium and Arena, Wembley, Middlesex (902 1234); mega audiences for mega stars, from Pavarotti to Madonna.
Wigmore Hall, Wigmore Street, W1 (935 2141); built by Bechstein next to his piano showrooms, and has almost perfect acoustics for chamber music.
Churches   Used as concert halls throughout London; concerts often advertised on the church door or the information board beside the west door or on the railings. Also the best places to hear the major sacred music sung to extremely high standard (e.g. at St Paul's and Westminster Abbey) at daily evensong and on Suns – see Court page of the quality newspapers for lists and times. Here are some regular church-concert halls venues. In the City, in many beautiful Wren churches, especially St Anne and St Agnes in Gresham Street, St Mary Woolnoth in Lombard Street, St Bartholomew the Great and St Bride's. In the West End, in St James's, Piccadilly, SW1 (734 4511); St John's, Smith Square, SW1 (222 1061); St Martin-in-the-Fields, Trafalgar Square, SW1 (930 0089): and The Chapel Royal, St James's Palace. Special church events include summer Masses with full orchestra at St Paul's cathedral (information on 248 2705).
Music colleges   Students often give public concerts (and opera) during term-time, including at the Guildhall School of Music and Drama at the Barbican (628 2571); The London College of Music, 47 Great Marlborough Street, W1 (437 6120/734 8921); Queen Alexandra's House, Bremner Road, SW7 (589 4053); Royal Academy of Music, Marylebone Road, NW1 (935 5461); Royal College of Music, Prince Consort Road, SW7 (589 3643). College students also sometimes give lunchtime concerts at the RIBA, 66 Portland Place, W1 (580 5533).
Historic houses and galleries   An idea that is gaining popularity annually, this is a chance to listen to music in a very beautiful setting; worth booking in advance; sometimes a membership is necessary. Good places include: Burgh House, Ranger's House, Fenton House, Keats House, Kenwood House, Marble Hill House, Osterley House, The Royal Academy, Tate Gallery, Warwick Arts Trust.

Outside In summer, in the gardens and parks, magical on a fine evening and with a good picnic. Best of all are Saturday evenings beside the lake at Kenwood House, Hampstead Lane, NW3 (633 1707), some with fireworks; and the newer, similar tradition by the river at Marble Hill House, Richmond Road, Twickenham, Middlesex (892 5115), both run by English Heritage, see p. 17). Others include: band performances in St James's, Regent's, Hyde and Greenwich parks, June–Aug, usually afternoons and early evening; Crystal Palace Park, SE19 (633 1707) for more lakeside concerts, some with fireworks.

Finding your kind of music

CLASSICAL Found just about everywhere, see above. London has five international symphony orchestras and a multitude of other symphony and chamber orchestras who give regular concerts here. Most have friends societies for priority booking; most perform money-saving subscriptions series in the big halls.

BBC Symphony Orchestra: to attend their regular radio recording concerts at their Maida Vale studios and elsewhere, apply to the BBC, see Information above. They are the main orchestra at The Proms.

London Symphony Orchestra (LSO): plays regularly at the Barbican, its home; the only London orchestra based at a concert hall.

London Philharmonic Orchestra (LPO); offices at 35 Doughty Street, WC1 (833 2744).

Philharmonia Orchestra: offices at 76 Great Portland Street, W1 (580 9961).

Royal Philharmonic Orchestra (RPO): offices at 34 Red Lion Square, WC1 (404 0017).

Of the many other thriving London-based orchestras, ones to watch out for include: Academy of Ancient Music; Academy of St Martin-in-the-Fields (see p. 259); English Chamber Orchestra; English Consort; London Sinfonietta. In addition, London is very often part of any international orchestra's European tour – the same applies to individual musicians.

JAZZ London has a great concentration of world-class jazz musicians, many home grown, traditional and contemporary, and a special relationship with the US which encourages visiting musicians. British musicians to catch include Stan Tracy, Loose Tubes, Mike Westbrook, Kenny Wheeler (Canadian but here for 25 years) and

Humphrey Lyttleton. Early in the week is best for serious jazz lovers; later for the more social atmosphere. The several good festivals include: Bracknell (out of London), the British jazz community's annual picnic; Camden Jazz Week, part of Camden's April festival, big, adventurous, modern; Capital Jazz Festival at the Royal Festival Hall, safe if not staid. *City Limits* has the most comprehensive listing; monthly magazines include *Jazz Journal* and *The Wire*; Radio London gives the week's gigs on Saturday morning; Radio 2 has Sounds of Jazz on Sunday early evening and late Monday evening. Most places are clubs, so a small membership fee is payable; most have food. To find out more, a good read is John Fordham's *Let's Join Hands and Contact the Living* (1986), the story of Ronnie Scott, his club and his times. The main places to go are:

Ronnie Scott's Club, 47 Frith Street, W1 (439 0747); One of the longest lived and most famous jazz clubs in the world; run by a jazz musician for jazz lovers, so very sympathetic atmosphere – and you may hear the great man cracking one of his abominable but legendary jokes. Good for modern jazz, usually some well-known players, sometimes Oscar Peterson or Sarah Vaughan; George Melly at Christmas; RS plays occasionally; very different music in the new Upstairs at Ronnie Scott's. Membership brings cheaper entrance fees on some nights and a monthly magazine; best to book a table on the raised section, especially Fri–Sat; eating not compulsory at tables.

Bass Clef, 85 Coronet Street, off Hoxton Square, N1 (729 2476/2440); run by bass player Peter Ind who has the club beneath his recording studio; some of the best of young British musicians; small listening area (50–60 people), eat good food separately.

The Bull's Head pub, Lonsdale Road, Barnes, SW13 (876 5241); riverside pub run by jazz devotee Dan Fleming; back room almost a shrine to bebop, where Red Rodney, Bud Shank and others have played.

100 Club, 100 Oxford Street, W1 (636 0933); for the serious jazz fan; old-established basement with plastic tables, beer and snacks, good for modern and stomping traditional jazz; sometimes UB blues and semi-punk bands.

Pizza Express, 10 Dean Street, W1 (437 9595/439 8722); more than 20 years of pizza and mainstream jazz in a dark and smokey basement; always high quality players, (Ruby Braff, Al Cohn, etc), often dropping in for one night during a tour; good atmosphere, cheap; ordering food obligatory.

Pizza on the Park, 11 Knightsbridge, SW1 (235 5550); specialises in pianists (Roger Kellaway, Eddie Thompson, etc); eat upstairs to chat with background jazz, eat downstairs in silence with ear flapping; ordering food obligatory.
Others to check out: The Prince of Orange, Lower Road, Rotherhithe (no tel) for pub and New Orleans music; Café Italien, 19 Charlotte Street, W1 (636 4173) for food and jazz; Le Renoir, 79 Charing Cross Road, WC1 (734 2515) for brasserie and piano.

FOLK Found almost exclusively in pubs and clubs. *Time Out* gives day-by-day listings, but it is best to telephone before setting out to·ensure it is the style you fancy. Good places to check out:
Break for the Border Café, Goslett Yard, 127 Charing Cross Road, WC2 (437 8595)
Clapham Folk and Blues Club, Railway Tavern, 18 Clapham High Street, SW4 (737 0107)
Dublin Castle, 94 Parkway, NW1 (485 1773)
Half Moon, 93 Lower Richmond Road, Putney, SW15 (788 2387)
Hare & Hounds, 181 Upper Street, N1 (226 2992)
Sir George Robey, 240 Seven Sisters Road, N4 (263 4581)

ROCK, POP, SOUL AND REGGAE To find the big star concerts, see who is performing at:
Earls Court Exhibition Centre, Warwick Road, SW5 (385 1200)
Fairfield Hall, Croydon, Surrey (688 9291)
Hammersmith Odeon, Queen Caroline Street, W6 (748 4081)
Rainbow, 232 Seven Sisters Road, N4 (236 3148)
The Royal Albert Hall and Wembley Arena, see Big Halls above.
For smaller events, some clubs have a continuous character but many have theme nights or clubs-within-clubs. The best way to find what you want is to pore over the extensive day-by-day *Time Out* listings and then telephone the club to confirm what is happening that night and at what times in music, lighting, DJs, theme dress, etc – and several clubs have a Gay Night each week. Although clubs (some inside pubs) come and go with astonishing speed, here are a few that seem to stick around; many have regular nights for certain types of music, with a wide variety through the week:
Camden Palace, 1a Camden Road, NW1 (387 0248)
Dingwalls, Camden Lock, Camden High Street, NW1 (267 4967)
Gossip's, 69 Dean Street, W1 (434 4480)

King's Head, 115 Upper Street, N1 (226 1916)
Marquee, 90 Wardour Street, W1 (437 6603)
Mean Fiddler, 28a Harlesden High Street, NW10 (961 5490)
Pheasant & Firkin, 166 Goswell Road, EC1 (253 7429)
Rock Garden, The Piazza, Covent Garden, WC2 (240 3961)
Town & Country Club, 9–17 Highgate Road, NW5 (267 3334)
Wag Club, 35–7 Wardour Street, W1 (437 5534)
Wigmore Hall, see concert halls, above
Wispers, 146 Charing Cross Road, WC2 (240 2261)

Cinema

INFORMATION AND BOOKING Film in London does not compare in range with Paris, although it is far better on recent, independent American films and less popular commercial and art films. Again, *Time Out* and *City Limits* for comprehensive listings. There are two systems: West End and the independents, of which the independents have the most interesting programmes. West End programming offers a narrow range of mostly first-run films which changes on Fridays, so new films attract Friday queues, preceded by the newspaper criticisms – David Robinson in *The Times*, Philip French in the *Observer* and Nigel Andrews in the *Financial Times* are the ones to read, and they give tips for the independents, too. Booking seats is worthwhile and usually possible by telephone, but tickets may have to be collected 30 minutes before the film begins. A fee is sometimes payable at independent cinemas; membership is necessary at the National Film Theatre; prices at West End cinemas are cheaper on Monday. Many cinemas are now no smoking in parts or throughout; fast food, sweets and coffee are usually on sale, and some have bars. On television, a good range of worldwide film is screened from matinées (often old black and whites) through to late night (often 1960s or foreign language). For serious movie buffs, The British Film Institute, 21 Stephen Street, W1 (255 1444) has an unrivalled library of British and international film and television literature and documentation; publishes the monthly *Film Bulletin* and the quarterly *Sight and Sound*; and runs the National Film Archive and, on the South Bank, the National Film Theatre (festival in Nov).

TIMINGS Some have lunchtime screenings, around 1pm; most begin around 3–4pm, with two more shows at 6–6.30pm and 8–8.30pm, depending on the film's length; late night screenings (usually Fri and Sat) are around 11.30pm. Maddeningly, no advertisements specify the time of both the programme (with advertisements and trailers) and the film (after them) so another telephone call is necessary.

SCREENS   The big West End chains have chopped up many of their cinemas to make multi-screen houses, thus giving more choice, making them more money and ending with screens almost the size of television screens and no leg room for a child over 10 years old. The few cinemas with large enough screens to enjoy a film properly include: Curzon West End, Curzon Mayfair, Empire Leicester Square, Leicester Square Theatre, National Film Theatre cinema I, Odeon Marble Arch, Plaza, Warner West End.

Comfort: The most comfortable West End cinema is the sublime Curzon Mayfair, complete with two boxes; in Knightsbridge, the Minema; in the City, the Barbican.

Free films: Screened at various arts galleries including the Imperial War Museum, the National Gallery, the Tate Gallery, the V&A.

The independents and cinema clubs: This is where the interesting programming is. Often screen foreign language films; often first with foreign film festival winners. Programming may be a single film or repertory seasons related to themes. Ones to check out include the following:

Code
R screens films in repertory
L has late night films

Barbican Cinema, see Barbican Centre, above
Camden Plaza, 211 Camden High Street, MW1 (485 2443)
Chelsea Cinema, Kings Road, SW3 (351 3742)
Curzon cinemas: Curzon Mayfair, Curzon Street, W1 (499 3737); Curzon Phoenix, Phoenix Theatre, Charing Cross Road, W1 (240 9661); Curzon West End, Shaftesbury Avenue, W1 (439 4805)
Everyman Cinema, Hollybush Vale, Hampstead, NW3 (435 1525) R
Gate Cinema, Notting Hill Gate, W11 (727 4043) L
ICA Cinema, The Mall, SW1 (930 3647) R
Lumière, St Martin's Lane, WC2 (836 0691)
Metro, Rupert Street, W1 (437 0757)
Minema, 45 Knightsbridge, SW1 (235 4225)
Museum of London, London Wall, EC2 (600 3699) R

National Film Theatre, South Bank, SE1 (928 3232; membership 437 4355); see South Bank Centre.
Renoir, Brunswick Square, WC1 (837 8404)
Scala, 275–277 Pentonville Road, N1 (278 0051) R L
Screen cinemas: Screen on Baker Street, 96 Baker Street, NW1 (935 2772) L; Screen on the Green, Islington Green, Upper Street, N1 (226 3520) L; Screen on the Hill, 230 Haverstock Hill, NW3 (435 3366) L
Children's films   Many cinemas, especially the independents and clubs, have children's screenings on Saturdays. The Barbican, Institute of Contemporary Arts, National Film Theatre and the Screen cinemas all have Children's Cinema Clubs.

Other night life

There may be plenty of addresses listed in magazines but few merit a visit. Here are just a handful of good places. Again, scan *Time Out* for more.

NIGHT CLUBS AND DISCOTHEQUES   The good ones are so literally 'here today and gone tomorrow' that *Time Out*, which updates its weekly lists, suggests telephoning first to check ones on their list still exist. In general, the well established clubs, both membership and pay-on-the-door ones, have tacky interiors, dreary disco drone music and bored people hanging about. Up-market clubs make fierce membership demands and run an aggressive advertising hype, especially in the gossip columns, to make them seem attractively exclusive; experience proves otherwise. The less up-market ones, often run by young people for young people, are much more fun, often happen just one night a week, but have a much less stable lifeline; if you go to one, you may be given invitations to others, and so on. So there are very few good clubs that have long lives, good atmosphere, good music and a good crowd of people – and they are often tricky to enter.

The best:

Annabel's, 44 Berkeley Square, W1 (629 3558); smartest of the lot; the best in the world for the not-so-young – anyone under 30 or with an adventurous spirit would be bored stiff. Splendid in every detail; membership equally splendid in price and length of time to obtain: currently requires two proposers, a 6–18 month wait, £250 entry fee and then £500 a year. And in case you are wondering, there is no reciprocal membership with those riff-raff clubs overseas.

Café de Paris, 3 Coventry Street, W1 (437 2036); the best one-night wonder disco and the only one with music so good you have to dance – provided by Albert who flies in from Le Balajo in Paris every Wednesday. To get in, dress up, arrive early and hope.

The reserve set:

Town and Country Club, 9–17 Highgate Road, NW5 (267 3334); for new music, young people; pay at the door.

Empire Ballroom, Leicester Square, WC2 (437 1446); for a good bop on a large, crowded floor, friendly atmosphere; pay at the door.

The Gardens, Derry Street, off Kensington High Street, W8 (937 7994); ex-Regine's, now a good rooftop disco surrounded by lush, exotic rooftop gardens, much patronised by the over 30, wealthy Kensington international crowd.

Gossip's, 69 Dean Street, W1 (734 4111); good for young music and atmosphere, activity varies so best to telephone first; currently psychedelic Alice in Wonderland on Mondays and reggae on Saturdays; pay at the door.

Heaven, Under the Arches, Villiers Street, WC2 (839 3852); The best and most accessible of the gay clubs; most nights have a theme, often to do with dress, so it is best to telephone first; girls welcome on the weekly straight night and on others 'if they look pretty and dress right'; dress trendy; pay at the door.

Limelight, 136 Shaftesbury Avenue, W1 (434 1761); founded by Peter Gatien of New York's Limelight; claustrophobic corridors, never seems quite awake; pay at the door.

Maximus, 14 Leicester Square, WC2 (743 4111); so trendy it requires fancy dress and face paint; best after 1am; pay at the door.

The Palace, 1a Camden Palace Road, NW1 (387 0428); huge, young and fun; best to telephone to check on theme nights; dress streetwise; pay at the door.

The Palais, 242 Shepherd's Bush Road, W6 (748 2812); the revamped Hammersmith Palais with good disco, bands and huge dance floor; dress trendy or entry might be refused; pay at the door.

Piano Bar, 50 Frith Street, W1 (no tel); run by Madam Jo Jo, Queen of the Night, and her Barbettes resplendent in glamorous drag; lots of style, not much dancing; next door, Madame Jo Jo calls her second club after herself (tel 734 2473).

Stringfellows, 16–8 Upper St Martin's Lane, WC2 (240 5534); star-filled, sardine-packed, showy, spangle-glitzy; membership only.

Tramp, 40 Jermyn Street, W1 (734 0565); up-market, Sloanes, Sloanes' stars but no sparkle; membership only.

Wag Club, 35 Wardour Street, W1 (437 5534); good music, good atmosphere, good young crowd, full to bursting at weekends; currently next best after Café de Paris, goes all week; dress streetwise; pay at the door.

See also Rock suggestions, above; good for music, most have a dance floor.

DINNER DANCE AND DINNER CABARET
Usually pretty awful, apart from the informal theatrical places, see theatre section, above. But there are exceptions. Cutting across a variety of styles and moods, the good ones include:

Concordia Notte, 29–31 Craven Road, W2 (723 3725); Baroque dining room for a smart set; Latin-American cabaret; European singers; dancing.

L'Escargot, 48 Greek Street, W1 (437 2679); the ground floor brasserie has good nightly cabaret; stylish, intimate, informally sophisticated.

Gallipoli, 8 Bishopsgate Churchyard, EC2 (588 1922); good Turkish food and belly dancers in an exotic ex-Turkish bath.

Omar Khayyam, 177 Regent Street, W1 (437 3000); one night probably preferable to 1001 of Turkish and Persian food plus cabaret and belly dancers.

The Ritz, see p. 293, for chic dinner-cabaret.

Royal Roof Restaurant, Royal Garden Hotel, Kensington High Street, W8 (937 8000); essential to book a window table for gazing at London night lights between French food and fast-footing.

Savoy River Restaurant, Savoy Hotel, Strand, WC2 (836 4343); book a window table for river night lights; good food, good music, extremely elegant.

La Vie En Rose, Great Windmill Street, W1 (437 6312); food less important than the lavish cabaret and the disco's lighting tricks.

Villa dei Cesari, 135 Grosvenor Road, SW1 (828 7453); more good river views from the right tables, all very Roman except the dancing.

STRIPTEASE With the Westminster clamp-down on Soho's smut and vice (see p. 160), there is not much left. Unlicensed clubs are best left well alone: wildly overpriced and extremely unexciting – a journalist recently disguised himself to see how a foreign tourist is treated in London and ended a tedious evening £230 down. Of the licensed clubs, Raymond's Revue Bar, Walker's Court, Brewer Street, W1 (734 1593) is the best; good shows, good atmosphere; not voyeuristic or smutty; about 40% of the audience are women out with their men for an evening's entertainment; shows at 8pm and 10pm, the second show best for atmosphere. No booking necessary; pay at the door.

CASINOS   Unlike in many other cities, they abide by rigid laws, fiercely upheld, which pleases international players. The rules are designed to prevent impulse gambling. Most importantly, membership is essential and a declaration of intent to game must be signed at the club a minimum of 48 hours before playing (unless you are going as the guest of a member); non-UK residents should have identification when joining; no alcohol is served at the tables; there is no live entertainment; and no tips are given at the tables. Correct dress is a suit and tie. Most casinos have good restaurants which also serve breakfast; soft drinks, tea and snacks are usually served at the tables; and their licences for alcohol follow the general ones for bars (until 11pm) and restaurants (midnight when ordered with a meal). Timings are generally 2pm (4pm on Sun) until 4am (3am on Sat). Casinos are not permitted to advertise. To check further, contact The British Casino Association, 175 Piccadilly, W1 (493 3033).

Many casinos are rather seedy; these are anything but:

Aspinall's, 20–1 Curzon Street, W1 (629 4400); the smartest and most exclusive, in a beautiful house in the traditional Mayfair gambling area. Requires two members to propose a new member, no waiting list.

Crockford's, 30 Curzon Street, W1 (493 7771); second smartest, the second most exclusive, in an almost equally magnificent house in the same street. Normally requires a proposer, no waiting list.

London Park Tower Casino, 101 Knightsbridge, SW1 (235 6161); well run. No proposer needed, no waiting list.

The Ritz Casino, Piccadilly, W1 (491 4678); beneath the Ritz Hotel, with its style; small. A member must propose and there is then a waiting list.

Giving your own party

THE PLACE   Almost any room in London can be hired – even some royal palaces. There is no need to restrict yourself to the obvious, the hotels and restaurants. Here are a few ideas: the V&A historic house outposts – Apsley House, Ham House and Osterley; the old rooms of the V&A itself; the Soane Museum; beside Lord's Cricket Ground; the dinosaur court of the National History Museum; Marble Hill House; Leighton House, or perhaps one of the boats on Regent's canal (see pp. 183 and 186). For a smart dinner the Banqueting House in Whitehall can be yours (tel the Public Inquiries Unit, 212 3434 for information and see p. 87). On the Thames, several companies charter out boats for day and evening cruises including River Functions (Thames) Ltd, Cherry Garden Pier, SE16 (237 5134/5); Tidal Cruises Ltd, Jackson Bros (River Services) Ltd, Lambeth Pier, Albert Embankment, SE1 (928 9009); River Ride, Charing Cross Pier, Victoria Embankment, WC2 (930 0970); Catamaran Cruisers, WID Pier, Cuba Street, E14 (987 1185). For more, simply telephone the places that take your fancy as you wander around. It is surprising how many will say yes.

THE CATERING   Most historic house caretakers or owners insist on their own caterers or on one of their approved list. If not, the choice is yours. Most restaurants do outside catering, so every cuisine and price range is available. For something special, good outside caterers include Mustard Catering, 1–3 Brixton Road, SW9 (582 8496/8511) Justin de Blank Provisions Ltd, 54 Duke Street, W1 (629 3174); Searcy Tansley & Co Ltd, 136 Brompton Road, SW3 (584 3344); Leith's Good Food, 1 Sebastian Street, EC1 (251 0216); Party Ingredients Ltd, Kirtling Street, SW8 (627 3800); Graison, 17 York Road, SE1 (633 9040).

OPTING OUT   If the prospect of organising the party is exhausting, and the bank balance is healthy, put yourself in the capable hands of the best professional party-giver in London: Lady Elizabeth Anson, Party Planners, 56 Ladbroke Grove, W11 (229 9666) who provides advice, staff, food, wine, flowers and music, no detail forgotten.

CHILDREN'S PARTIES   For paper plates and tiny presents, Paperchase, 213 Tottenham Court Road, W1 (580 8496); for cakes, Art for Eating, Unit 3, Rosebery House, Rosebery Avenue, EC1 (278 2766); for entertainers, Arnold Stoker's Entertainment Agency, 32 King's Road, SW19 (540 1191); to end with a bang, Gable and Meierhans Fireworks, 97 Castlebridge, Abbey Road, NW6 (328 1968).

Late late supper and breakfast

FOR SUPPER   Canton Chinese Restaurant, 11 Newport Place, WC2 (437 6220), open 24 hours, non-stop, every day; Toddies, 241 Old Brompton Road, SW5 (373 8217), open until 7am for supper/breakfast; Up All Night, 325 Fulham Road, SW10 (352 1998), open until 6am for the dancing Sloanes; 24-hour hotel coffee shops are pretty dismal – Kensington Hilton, Londonderry, Selfridge, etc.

FOR BREAKFAST in Soho, head for Harry's, 6 Kingly Street, W1 (734 7284); open all night, every night, from 10pm round to 4.30pm, when staff clean up and rest up. Breakfast in Smithfield, with meat market entertainment: Fox and Anchor, 115 Charterhouse Street, EC1 (253 4838), Mon–Fri 6–11am; Smithfield Tavern, 105 Charterhouse Street, EC1 (253 5153), Mon–Fri 6.30–11am. Breakfast in Spitalfields, with fruit and vegetable market entertainment: The Market Café, 5 Fournier Street, E1 (247 9470), Mon–Fri 1.30am–1.30pm and Sat 1.30am–10am; Beigel Bake, 159 Brick Lane, E1 (729 0616), for salmon and cream cheese filled beigels all night, every night until 6am. See also breakfast sections of the food and drink chapter, pp. 309–19.

A new day

NEWSPAPERS   With the death of Fleet Street printing, keen news addicts must now go to the mainline railway stations for early editions, on sale around midnight on weekdays, the Sundays by 8pm on Saturday evening. In Soho enterprising newsboys are selling them by 3am; Capital Newspapers at 48 Old Compton Street and Moroni at 68 Old Compton Street open at 7.30am (Sun at 8am). Further afield, Gray's Inn News, 50 Theobalds Road, WC1 opens 4.30am.

DAWN AND BIRDSONG   Some of the dew-filled parks do not close (e.g. St James's). For dawn and sunrise: Hungerford, London and Tower bridges; and Blackfriars is good for the soft new light on the dome of St Paul's. Hampstead Heath has dawn magic – and swimming.

DAWN DIPS   Several ice-cold ponds for an early morning sobering dip.
Highgate Ponds, N6 (340 4044), men only, open around 6am in summer, later in winter.
Kenwood Pond, N6 (348 1033), women only, open around 7am in summer, later in winter.
Parliament Hill Lido, NW5 (485 3873), men and women, opens around 7am in summer only.
Serpentine Lido, Hyde Park, W1 (262 5484), men and women, open to the public around 9am in summer only. But you can join healthy members of the Serpentine Swimming Club taking their daily dips round the year, 6am–9am; just turn up, or write to Bob Kelly, Secretary, 18 Leinster Mews, W2.

Food and drink:
Eggs and bacon to champagne cocktails

It is said that a restaurant opens in London every week. If so, then less than one a week seems to close. For every big street has its multiplying batch, usually standing together in culinary competition. Somewhere in the city, every conceivable cuisine is daily sliced, chopped, steamed and simmered into life. Virtually anything that tickles your palate is to be found wherever and whenever you want in London – and with whatever surroundings you want. At one extreme, the most ostentatious eateries pander to the recent British fad of food education and food snobbery gone mad: chefs are stars, restaurants are advertisements for interior designers, fashions for outlandish ingredients change weekly, plates of food are reduced to intricate patterns of florid designs and prices are through the roof. At the other, fast food chains have invaded, put down their greasy, stodgy roots and are here to stay, smugly over-pricing their trash.

But in quieter corners, eating and drinking in London has improved beyond recognition in the last decade. Do not believe the outdated rumours. Many Londoners are now knowledgeable, critical and adventurous in their eating. To satisfy them, there are hundreds of good haunts for the hungry, romantic, formal, partying or intrepid to try. As for drink, wine lists can astound in range and even the French are impressed by the prices, the revival of real ale has made drinking in many more pubs a delight, and mushrooming wine bars have provided informal meeting-places for women as well as men.

As eating out in London is a minefield, here are some facts, warnings and tips, then some low-down on how the world's cuisines fare in London, and finally a few suggestions, a springboard of ideas to inspire experimentation or help you seek out your favourite cuisine.

Food facts

FINDING A RESTAURANT   Restaurants come and go with alarming speed, and in those that stay, the owners, chefs and interiors dance giddy changes. To learn the latest, consult the food writers in their weekly or monthly columns; one to watch especially is Fay Maschler in the *Evening Standard* (Tuesday), always up-to-the-minute, sensitive, unprejudiced and aware that going out

to a restaurant is as much to do with ambience as food. For calm contemplation and selection, these are the most useful London restaurant guides:
Fay Maschler's Guide to Eating Out In London (1986); a huge range, reliable on facts, good on food and mood, and blissfully free of cynicism.
Ledger, C: *The Virgin Guide to London's Best Restaurants*, 3rd edition (1986); also reliable and un-

snobby, helpfully arranged by bank balance and within geographical areas.

Grossman, L: *The Harpers & Queen Guide to London's 100 Best Restaurants* (1987); only 100, and many of those partly written off, so a good guide if a wider choice confuses.

Nicholson's *London Restaurant Guide* (1986), usually updated annually; mainly set out by cuisine, its great advantage is its tiny size, handy for sudden moments of peckishness.

Time Out Guide to Eating Out in London, published annually (autumn); the indefatigable *Time Out* team make this less of a selection than a bewilderingly big choice.

Of the UK guides, the classics followed to the lettuce leaf by devotees include:

Ackerman, Roy: *The Ackerman Guide to the Best Restaurants and Hotels in the British Isles* (1987).

Michelin Red Guide to England, published annually (the preceding summer).

Ronay, E: *Egon Ronay's Guide to the Hotels Restaurants & Inns of Great Britain and Ireland*, published annually (autumn of the preceding year).

Smith, D, ed.: *The Good Food Guide*, published annually (Oct–Nov of preceding year); bang up-to-date, incisive, unpretentious.

Smith, D, Mabey D and Round, J: *Budget Good Food Guide*, published annually (March); excellent for finding fair-priced food, especially ethnic, with helpful maps of non-central ethnic hotpots.

If you are flummoxed by the choice, telephone Restaurant Switchboard (888 8080), who have a wide selection of restaurants on their books. They give free advice on food and ambience; and they will make a free booking.

Food warnings and tips

THE RANGE   Best value for food and ambience is found in two seemingly contradictory places: the top and the bottom. At the top, several of the cream of London restaurants offer a fixed-price lunch menu, and some continue with a slightly pricier one for dinner; remarkable value and easily the best way to sample the milk-and-honey creations of the greatest chefs, but check carefully what is included in the price so that you are not stung by the extras. At the bottom end, the small, cheap-and-cheerful, family-run bistros do exist here, though they need seeking out, and the ethnic restaurants, most obviously Chinese Soho, and Indian Drummond Street and Brick Lane, are good value and open all hours including Sundays. The

problem is the middle range, where mediocre food and bad service are wickedly over-priced. It is certainly worth doing some research and reading menus in restaurant windows before plunging in.

BREAKFAST   A full English breakfast is one of the best value meals in town, especially in the bigger hotels and workmen's cafés. Timings tend to be 7–10am. There are two flat fee systems: either unlimited buffet or a course-by-course banquet of juice, cereal, a platter of cooked goodies, and unlimited toast and tea or coffee. No need to eat until sundown – or tea-time.

BRUNCH   A new concept to London, and so far exclusively a Sunday affair, mostly restricted to hotels. Good places include Le Caprice, the Hilton Rooftop Restaurant, Joe Allen and pricey Elephant on the River; booking essential. If you want a luxurious lie-in, Prudence McCaffrey of Bucks Fizz Breakfasts (402 9106) will deliver a champagne breakfast wrapped and tied up in ribbon.

LUNCH   Pubs are good value and atmospheric, and their food is improving; wine bars tend to have a wider range of healthier food. Restaurants are crammed with businessmen by 1pm, so book for 12.30pm or 12.45pm and order quickly to avoid long delays later except in the slickest of establishments; alternatively, eat late. To sample the creations of a top London chef, lunch is usually the moment to have the good value fixed price menu without hurting the purse. Many hotels and some department stores have flat fee lunch buffets; and hotels are the best place for a good value Sunday roast.

TEA   A meal with more myth than reality in Britain now; found in few London homes but prepared with devotion by the big hotels and a few tea-shops (many of them not British at all). Timings tend to be 3.30–5.30pm, with early arrivals gobbling the freshest scones; tea-shops have wider hours. Tea is the meal for which a table is not always bookable; in hotels, residents are given priority. Pricing tends to be flat fee for sandwiches, scones, teacakes, fancy cakes and endless tea, so it is worth acquiring an appetite; usually good value, even if it is a carbohydrate catastrophe. Of hotels, the Fri–Sun tea-dance at the Waldorf combines tea and toe-tapping in the Palm Court. Tea-shops out of the very centre that merit a detour include Tea-time, 21 The Pavement, SW4 (622 4944) and

Louis, 32 Heath Street, NW3 (435 9908). In the big stores, try Harrods buffet and the top floor of Fortnum & Mason.

ICE-CREAMS   Most English ice-cream is disgusting. The treats of American Häagen-Dazs and Frujengladje creaminess or Italian fruit sorbets are far away. To find the best, avoid the ice-cream vans and head for shops selling Loseley (British), Baskin Robbins or New England (American) or visit Gran Gelato, 7–9 in Montpelier Place, SW7 (589 4436) and Bernigra, 69 Tottenham Court Road, W1 (580 0850) for signor's home-made ice-creams using Messina recipes, or make a pilgrimage to Marine Ices, 8 Haverstock Hill, NW3 (485 8898) for fruity frozen delights.

DINNER   A good range of timings to suit the most complex evening, with the heaviest bookings 8–9pm. Many restaurants have good value, fixed price, pre-theatre menus. Many take last bookings at 11pm; Chinese, Indian and other ethnic restaurants stay open latest and, importantly, open on Sunday. Pubs tend not to serve food at night; wine bars usually do. The lounges of big hotels are excellent for a stylish snack in the evening – drink, coffee and sandwiches.

BOOKING A TABLE   Always worthwhile, whatever the meal, and two or three days ahead to eat in fashionable favourites on a Friday or Saturday evening. When booking, it is worth asking for a specific table (by the window, not by the kitchen, upstairs, downstairs, etc) and ensuring you are given it on arrival, working on the assumption that those who don't ask don't get. When the sun shines, the few restaurants with gardens or pavement get booked solid – including The Ark, Auntie's, Le Chef, Chez Gerard, Henry J Bean's, Lou Pescadou, The Ritz, Le Routier and the huge, exotic Roof Garden (lunch only). When it is chilly, those with open fires get equally booked up – including La Poule au Pot, Maggie Jones, Julie's, Camden Brasserie and Topkapi. Early eaters may find a second booking is taken for the same table and waiters will discourage lingering – at tea at The Ritz, at supper at Gavvers. Booking is also the moment to check on things that matter to you – which credit cards are accepted (some restaurants take none), air-conditioning, background music, live music, whether or not dogs are permitted. A few restaurants ask diners not to smoke at some or all of the tables. All that said, a few restaurants do not take bookings.

DRESS   In the grand hotels and in the gentlemen's clubs, a jacket and tie is expected whatever the meal or drink. If you arrive without, the porter can sometimes lend both. Elsewhere, absolute freedom in theory, but the smarter the restaurant the more it is expected that clients complement the food with dressy clothes.

BRASSERIES   A new arrival in London, and a misnomer. Most are formal restaurants; just a few have managed a relaxed, café society atmosphere where patrons can linger over a snack and the newspapers or order a full blow-out – the glittering Criterion, Soho Brasserie and La Brasserie in Fulham Road manage the mix; others should follow now that licensing laws are beginning to relax.

MENUS   Most importantly, there should be a note indicating whether or not prices include service charge (usually between 10% and 15%) and/or VAT – this makes a big difference to the final bill; if nothing is shown, ask before ordering. Fixed price menus may/may not include service, VAT and even half a bottle of wine per person. As for the food, obviously it is best to eat food in season, and a combination of waiter and guide book advice should lead to the dishes the chef prepares best.

PAYING AND TIPPING   Bills are often deceptive. Service may, or may not, be clearly itemised; VAT usually is. If in doubt, ask. As for paying up, service is not legally payable but is your choice to give if you feel it is deserved – usually 10–15%; VAT is obligatory. The whole bill including tip can be paid by credit card, provided the restaurant takes them. Beware: several do not accept any credit cards.

PICNICS   The British are mad keen on picnics, despite the unreliable weather. The best place to see the Londoners' wicker hampers out in force is at the Saturday summer concerts beside Kenwood House lake. The outstanding public parks, squares and historic houses set in formal parks rarely have good cafés – exceptions are Holland Park, Ham House (for summer tea) and Kenwood (for Sunday roast). They make ideal settings for simple sandwiches and fruit or more elaborate favourite food bought in the street markets, food shops or ordered as a carry-out from a pizzeria or an Indian or Chinese restaurant. Good food-buying stops are Soho, Neal's Yard in Covent Garden, Harrods, Fortnum & Mason (with Paxton and Whitfield for cheese in Jermyn Street behind), Selfridge's, and Marks and Spencer. Gourmet food shops and the deluxe food halls (see p. 333) will make up hampers; for the ultimate extravagance, the Champagne & Caviar Shop, 18–19 Leadenhall Market, EC3 (626 4912) will prepare a hamper tailored to the customer's choice from 100 champagnes, Russian, Iranian, Beluga or Sevruga caviar and other goodies.

Drink facts

At last, the drinking laws in England are becoming more civilised. But they are still a rabbit warren of complexity and exceptions that frustrate pub, wine bar and restaurant owners, baffle Londoners and infuriate visitors. Changes in legislation have begun; more will follow. See also Licences, below.

FINDING A PUB   The best of the five or six thousand pubs are easily missed. To find the latest favourites, buy a copy of *The London Drinker*, a monthly magazine on sale in some pubs; to select the right mood, setting and beers, invest in a guide: Aird, A, ed: *The Good Pub Guide*, published annually (the preceding early autumn); using very thin paper, a solid block of information (interior, mood, food, drink, etc) is given for each of about 4,000 British pubs, with almost 100 pages on London.

Hanson, N, ed: *The Good Beer Guide*, published annually (the preceding autumn); produced by the Campaign for Real Ale (CAMRA), it explains breweries and beers, then sends devotees off around London and Britain to sample the best; entries are short on history and mood, long on beer, appropriate for the 16-year-old campaign to stop the keg revolution of dead beer in favour of traditional British cask-conditioned beer which continues to mature in the pub cellar. Known as real ale, it is made only from pure malted barley, English hops, yeast and pure water, conditioned in the cask until the moment it is served. More information on CAMRA from 34 Alma Road, St Albans, Hertfordshire (0727 67201) who also regularly publish four in-depth area guides to London pubs (available by post) and whose members have regular meetings and receive the month magazine *What's Brewing*.

The Nicholson London Pub Guide, 3rd edition (1987);

perky entries usefully arranged by area and by theme, and even more usefully pocket sized.

McWhirter, K, ed: *The Good Wine Bar Guide 1986*; The appearance of this thick volume, almost a third of it devoted to London, shows how the wine bar has come to stay and its place in London life; long entries cover character, wines and food, with a piggy bank logo for those less greedy with their mark-up, a worldwide vintage guide up front, and much more.

LICENCES AND THE LAW   Neither logical nor straightforward. Here is the tip of the iceberg of archaic licensing nonsense – the government is about to improve this ludicrous state of affairs. If in doubt, ask the proprietor or manager of the establishment you are in.

First, pubs. With a total of 9½ hours of opening time permitted by law in English and Welsh pubs, timings tend to be 11am–3pm and 5.30–11pm. But Sunday hours tend to be shorter, noon–2pm and 7–10.30pm; some City pubs close early on weekday evenings and remain closed through weekends; and pubs in entertainment and residential areas may have extensions on Friday and Saturday evenings, with last admissions at 11pm. Wine bars have different problems, often having to abide by several drinking and eating rules depending on whether the customer is standing at the bar, sitting inside or sitting on the pavement. Cocktail bars rarely have a licence to serve alcohol without food – and some require a main course order. Restaurants have separate eating and drinking licences; larger ones have different and varying licences for each section; the most regular annoyance is when final drink orders are taken at 11pm or 11.30pm, just when post-theatre customers are arriving. However, restaurants benefited from the first breakthrough in licensing law, in 1987: they may now serve alcohol throughout the afternoon, provided 'substantial' food is served too and eaten with a 'knife and fork' – only the English could invent such a rule. Hotel bars can usually serve their residents for longer hours. Nightclub bars tend to have licences until 3am and match prices with their privilege. For very late drinking (or very early, depending on the viewpoint) pubs around the surviving food markets such as Smithfield have licences to trade in the early morning, theoretically to serve bona fide market workers only.

PUB AND BAR AGE LIMITS   Fiercely upheld, or

licences are lost. Eighteen is the youngest a person may enter a pub or bar alone and consume alcohol; children aged 14 and over may go into a pub with an adult but may not be served alcohol.

BEER   Draught beer, lager, cider and stout are sold by legal measure: a pint or half-pint.

WINE   If bought by the glass, there is no legal standard glass size, so quantity and value vary hugely. If bought by the bottle, it is up to the customer to check the label before the cork is pulled.

Drink warnings and tips

WATER   London water is safe to drink, despite the claims that every drop has passed through 10 other bodies first and is saturated with chemicals. However, it does have a distinct taste. Charitably, this may account for the Londoners' recent obsession with designer waters, both still and fizzy, foreign and home-flowing. If ordering bottled water, Perrier or Evian are usually served unless a brand is specified; British waters to try include Highland Spring, Malvern, Ashbourne, Abbey Well (with Peter Blake's portrait of David Hockney on the label).

PUBS   A pub scores points on location, historical associations, atmosphere, garden and food, but it is the British beer that counts – soft drinks tend to be expensive, wines tend to be badly kept and pricey, and foreign beers are likely to be brewed here and taste distinctly different from back home. With the breakdown of male chauvinism, few pubs freeze women out and many even have children's rooms. To play traditional pub games, there is a strict etiquette: would-be players of darts, becoming rare now, should offer to do the chalks (scoring) first and then play the winners of the previous game; for snooker or pool, put the right money on the table (unusually nominal), wait your turn and play the winner of the previous game or start afresh – it is wisest only to bet a round of drinks. As for the beer, the revival of real ale (see *Good Beer Guide*, above) in preference to the dead keg beer has led many pubs to improve their range and stock. The big seven breweries are: Allied Breweries (now Australian owned), Bass (the biggest, with 7,400 pubs and 13 breweries, Charrington IPA is their cask beer), Courage (cask John Smith's is theirs, as is Imperial Russian Stout, and

now rare bottle-conditioned beer), Greenall Whitley, Scottish & Newcastle, Watney and Whitbread (plenty of cask beers, guest beers in their pubs). Of the independent breweries whose beers are readily available in London, Iain Dobson of CAMRA recommends a taste of these: Fuller, Greene King, Pitfield, Samuel Smith, Taites and Young. To visit a hop farm, contact Whitbread Hop Farm, Beltring, Paddock Wood, Kent (0622 87068/872408).

HOTEL BARS   Depressing and dreary in all but the grand hotels where the splendidly elegant bars and lounges provide moments to sip a cocktail, watch the designer dresses being shown off by guests, gobble the cashew nuts and listen to the piano. They have the best barmen and often remain open to residents for longer hours.

WINE BARS   With their fast turnover, a reliable place to order wine by the glass, although a bottle is better value and special offers chalked up on a board the best value of all. Leaders in the wine bar revolution were Australian Don Hewitson, who now runs Cork & Bottle, Shampers and Methuselah's; and, before him, John Davy who in the 1960s pioneered the idea of selling a glass of good wine and now runs the extensive Davy's chain of wine bars. They both give priority to providing good wine and food at fair prices. The liveliest wine bars are in the City and in City workers' and Sloanes' residential areas – Chelsea, Kensington, South Kensington, etc.

COCKTAIL BARS   Rarely of American sophistication; a New Yorker is unlikely to rate a London-made dry Martini. Few have licences permitting drinking without eating, so a pre-restaurant drink is out. So head for the bars of grand hotels for a stinging cocktail mixed by the best barmen in town – the Cavendish for a Bloody Mary. Particularly English concoctions include Pimm's (gin-based), Buck's fizz (champagne and fresh orange juice); the Waldorf serves champagne in tankards.

RESTAURANTS   Spirits and cocktails tend to be pricey, so it is better value to go straight into wine. Anthony Hanson, wine merchant, claims London has a greater range of wines from all over the world than any other city, and often priced lower than in their homeland. As for English wine, some restaurants stock one or two. (To find out more, contact the English Wine Information Service, Drusilla's Corner, Alfriston, Sussex). So, in

London restaurants, wine lists can be dismayingly long. It is safest to go for the house wine, possibly more interesting to go a few notches up from it; more expensive wines have matching mark-ups. In a good restaurant the advice of the owner or wine waiter, whoever stocks the cellar, should be sound. When the waiter shows you the bottle of wine, you should check it is the one you chose before he pulls the cork. It is up to you to check the name and year carefully. With the designer-water fad, a cheeky waiter asked for water is liable to serve a bottle with a hefty mark-up, not free tap water. Many restaurants will serve decaffeinated coffee and some offer tea and infusions, if asked.

The world on your plate: The cuisine breakdown

Over the years, even centuries, the foods brought to London by the flood of immigrants – from early Italians to more recent Indians – have undergone modifications, usually either to tempt the British customer's palate, satisfy his expectations, or make the best of available ingredients. Results range from exciting through disappointing to best avoided. Cuisines range from Afghan, African, American, Austrian, Brazilian, and Burmese to Scandinavian, Spanish, Swedish, Swiss, Tex-Mex, Thai, Tunisian, Turkish, Vietnamese and Yugoslav. Here are some tips on the most commonly found ones, with one or two places to taste them. See area sections below for more.

AMERICAN Sally Clarke, who worked at Michael's Restaurant in Santa Monica and now creates Anglo-Californian cuisine at her Clarke's in Kensington (open Mon–Fri only), rates Smollensky's Balloon and Bob Payton's group – Chicago Pizza Pie Factory, Chicago Rib Shack, Henry J Bean. Paul Gambaccini, a food-keen American in London for a decade, has watched US cuisine leap across the Atlantic with beady eyes. So far, he rates Joe Allen's as a 'home away from home', Harrods West Side Express as good enough to eat in every Saturday 'to a high American standard – now there's praise', all Bob Payton's restaurants with their 'chocolate cheesecake to die for', and the brownies from Boston Back Bay Cookies stall in Harrods Food Hall, 'better than David's Cookies back home', but Hard Rock at Hyde Park Corner (629 0382) is unremarkable except for its milk shakes and its Rock 'n' Roll memorabilia; and

Baskin Robbins is poor compensation for no Häagen-Dazs or Frujengladje. For American pizza, Pizza Express is rated the bearable best of the chains, Orso is best for thin pizza but 'don't bother looking for the Greenwich Village sort'.

CHINESE Two systems, both good: cheap and cheerful, or chic, expensive and fashionable. Chinese eating used to mean going east of the City to Limehouse – a handful still stir the chop suey for new Docklands dwellers. With the Chinese arrival in southern Soho (see p. 158), cheap Chinese eating came to Central London: long menus in Chinese, fixed-price meals for the less courageous, usually Cantonese or Peking food, plenty of dim sum, informal atmosphere, lots of Chinese wielding chopsticks, open almost perpetually – all this continues. Then, as with Indian restaurants, sophistication arrived, now epitomised by Lawrence Leung's expensive but splendid Zen group. Szechuan spiciness arrived too, pioneered by the Shushan and Dragon Gate but still not as popular as it is in the US. To explore Soho Chinatown, *The Budget Good Food Guide* has a map plotting and criticising 54 restaurants.

ENGLISH Much derided due to bad restaurants; now revived to glory in several places, using both traditional recipes and a new, lighter approach. The big markets supply the English ingredients: Smithfield for meat (see p. 201), New Covent Garden and Spitalfields (see p. 249) for fruit and vegetables, Billingsgate for fish (see p. 325). Discerning chefs deal direct with producers, seeking out lamb from Wales, beef, game and salmon from Scotland, asparagus from Leicestershire, apples from Kent, etc.

Here is a day's worth of good English tasting. Yet again, the top and bottom of the market are best. For full cooked breakfast (eggs and bacon, kidneys, kippers, etc), the grand hotels are best for food and surroundings: the Inter-Continental and Waldorf rate high for buffets, the Savoy and Hyde Park for style and views, the Dorchester Oak Room for heavy splendour. Next best are the little cafés into which building-site workmen disappear after their first stint, around 9am – just watch and follow; and the pubs around the food markets, especially Smithfield, with the benefit of a breakfast pint. For traditional street snacks, stalls selling cockles, mussels, whelks and jellied eels still stand on East End corners, and braziers of roasting chestnuts, originally run by Italians, brighten the winter West

End shopping streets. For a light lunch, a Plough-man's Lunch of bread, cheese and pickle is best found at a pub that advertises its food as home-cooked – the cheese should be a freshly cut wedge, not a plastic-wrapped portion.

Lunch and dinner can be strictly traditional or more inventive. For the traditional, it is worth taking up an invitation to a London club where such male delights as Cutlets Reform and Boodles Orange Fool were created and where soups and fish-cakes are taken seriously. The nearest public versions of a club are Green's Champagne and Oyster Bar and Wilton's; the nearest to a traditional chop house is Simpson's-in-the-Strand, where huge carcases of meat are roasted daily and perfect steak and kidney pudding is made on Wednes-days. Game in season with all the trimmings is good at the Connaught, Green's, Drakes, Rules, Wilton's, the English House, Café Royal and the top hotels – venison in winter; pheasant, grouse and partridge in autumn. For fish, including oy-sters and shellfish, try cheerful Geale's, Rudland and Stubbs and Sheekey's, or go up-market to Scotts, Bentley's Restaurant and Oyster Bar and the good game restaurants (see above), or go to the City's Sweetings or Bill Bentley's Bishopgate. The season for English oysters is the months with an 'r' in them (Sept–Apr), non-British oysters are avail-able other months; British lobsters Apr–Nov; crab best Apr–Dec; mussels best Sept–Mar; Dover sole all months except Apr; salmon trout Feb–Aug; wild Atlantic salmon Feb–end Aug. Sunday lunch is still a ritual and increasingly eaten out instead of at home; each roast has its relishes – mint sauce for lamb, horseradish sauce or mustard with beef, apple sauce with pork, chutney with cold ham. The ultimate lunch is eaten on Christmas Day, when the British guzzle their way through 10 million turkeys, with roast potatoes, Brussels sprouts, stuffings and bread sauce.

English fruit puddings ladled with double cream are irresistible, especially summer pudding made with raspberries and red and black currants in July; bread-and-butter, jam roly-poly and Sussex Pond are more dangerously heavy ones. To pig out on puddings, go to the Granary, 39 Albemarle Street, W1 (493 2978), or to Simpson's-in-the-Strand.

To end, hard English cheeses such as Stilton, Leicester, Cheddar and Derby are best eaten with biscuits and crunchy celery – and a glass of port at lunchtime speeds an afternoon snooze.

For simple suppers, traditional post-theatre dishes include smoked salmon and scrambled eggs (see the restaurants above); and the best street supper is fish and chips – clues to finding the best are the number of taxis parked outside and the queues for a paper parcel of fish and chips with salt, vinegar and a gherkin. Favourite chippies include Seashell, 49–51 Lisson Grove, NW1 (723 8703) and Seafresh Fish Bar, 80–1 Wilton Road, SW1 (828 0747). All other English fast food is to be avoided.

To try the lighter creations of one of the star British chefs, try Alastair Little's food in his Soho restaurant; Shaun Thomson at Auntie's; Sally Clarke's at her Clarke's; Carla Tomasi at Frith's; Julian Jeffrey's at the Greenhouse; Richard Shepherd's at Langan's Brasserie; Philip McMullen and Winston Hansle's at Launceston Place and Simon Hopkinson's at Bibendum.

FRENCH   Again, two-tiered. Pockets of France suffused with the warmth of a family-run, provin-cial bistro or the bustle of a bubbling Parisian brasserie receive less publicity than the very formal, pricey numbers. The first league includes La Petite Auberge St Savin, The Ark, Café Rouge, St Quentin, La Bougie, Thierry's, La Fantaisie, Lou Pescadou, La Bastide, Café du Jardin, Chez Victor, Bubbs, Le Chef, Chez Gerard, La Poule au Pot, Manzi's, La Residence, Le Suquet, Le Quai St Pierre, Brasserie du Coin, Le Gamin. The second includes Le Gavroche, Le Soufflé, The Chelsea Room, La Tante Clair, and the Connaught and Capital hotels. Those in the first category are scat-tered across the city; those in the second are where the money is. Of the stars, the Roux brothers, Albert and Michel, were a driving force behind the London restaurant revolution and now run Le Gavroche, Le Poulbot, Le Gamin, Gavvers, Rouxl Britannia; Pierre Martin (ex-Cannes and ex-Fouquet) puts French sunshine and chic into his five variously priced restaurants: La Croisette, Le Suquet, Le Quai St Pierre, L'Olivier and Lou Pescadou.

GREEK   Many tavernas in Fitzrovia, spilling into Soho. The range starts at Jimmy's, a usually packed-out basement, where generations of im-poverished students try to make the waiters smile as they deliver cheap platefuls of kleftico, salad and sausage-sized chips. Progress upwards includes Beoty's on the Covent Garden fringe and the string of tavernas on Charlotte Street, several with pavement tables (essential to book even in cold weather). Tops is the nearby White Tower, only open Monday to Friday, described by Fay Maschler as mixing 'Greek Cypriot with a French influence'. To explore out of the centre, the Turkish Cypriot area is Stoke Newington and the *Budget Good Food Guide* provides a map plotting a dozen local favourites.

INDIAN   When not in India, London is the best place to eat Indian food. In Central London it has recently undergone a revolution. Flock wallpaper, cheap prices, chicken tikka and mind-blowing vindaloo menus to satisfy ex-Raj civil servants are out. The designer Indian restaurant with sophisticated menus for well-heeled fashionable eaters is in, pioneered by the Bombay Brasserie, consolidated by Amin Ali's Red Fort and Lal Qila. Now regional dishes from Goa and Bengal have their cooking methods and spices explained; cocktails precede and sorbets follow, but Kingfisher Indian beer still sneaks in between. Favourite smart places include those above and Taste of India, Malabar, Mumtaz, Sonar Gaon. The favourite central areas for the cheaper, informal but still delicious haunts are Brick Lane in Spitalfields and Drummond Street by Euston Station – here Ambala makes the best Indian sweetmeats in Britain, so good he takes orders for Indian weddings in Birmingham on his telex machine. In outer London, Southall's Indian population have made it Little India, well worth exploring with the *Budget Good Food Guide* which has a map plotting 28 Indian eateries (or take the train to Southall and head for the Broadway, the main street). There are so many Indian restaurants in London that keen spice-seekers should invest in Pat Chapman's *The Good Curry Guide 1986–7*, available from the Curry Shop, 37 The Market, Covent Garden, WC2 (240 5760).

ITALIAN   One of the mistakes on returning from a holiday in Italy is to go to a jolly Italian trattoria in London to try to perpetuate the trip. Thick, heavy sauces drown pasta, meat and fish, waiters are keener on flirting and grinding outsize peppermills than on serving, there is not a friendly mama in sight and the bill is outrageous. The most mischievous culprits seduce their prey in Soho trattorias strung with Chianti bottles. Simple, fresh Italian food prepared by the family for a reasonable charge is rare in London. A handful of finds include the Spaghetti House chain (the Holborn branch is an all-day haven for British Museum recovery), San Frediano, Ziani, Trattoria Aquilino, La Barca and the bargain Pollo at 20 Old Compton

Street (734 5917). Cicconi's is unforgivably forma and expensive but brave it to order paradise pasta then pay up and flee. Pizzarias are a separate subject: Pizza Express (in Soho) and Pizza-on-the Park provide pizza and jazz; the Pizza Pizza Pizza chain have Paolozzi's bright, primary colour decor for American deep-pan pizzas see American food above; for a favourite Londoners' treat, go to Piz zaria Castello, 20 Walworth Road, SE1 (703 2556) booking first. The best come last: the tiny Italian cafés throughout London that squeeze into corner and alleys, run by smiling, joking families who serve cappuccinos, sandwiches and doughnut from dawn to dusk.

JAPANESE   When the eastern businessmen hi London, long after their arrival in the US, carin, compatriots followed to tend to their stomachs There is now a good range, from crowded lunch time cafés that are identikit versions of Tokyo one (and with Tokyo prices) – except they lack th splendid window displays of the entire men made up in plastic – to swish showing-off centre for businessmen (Suntory, Miyama, etc), bes avoided unless someone else is signing the bill. O the first type, the City batch includes Aykoku kaku, Ginnan and Gonbei (up at King's Cross) an the West End batch around Bond Street include Masako (move off the set meals and prices soar) Ikeda, Kitchen Yakitori, Nanten Restaurant an Yakitori Bar, One Two Three, Saga and Mon (in th Cumberland Hotel).

VEGETARIAN   London is wide-eyed and awak about vegetarians. If only meat is off limits, mos restaurants serve fish, which is usually best eate simply grilled. For more total vegetarians, th Chinese, Indian, Thai, pizzaria, creperie and othe menus have quantities of good dishes. And th pioneer vegetarian restaurant Cranks at 8 Marsha Street, W1 (437 9431) now has three mor branches, all open Mon–Fri, from breakfast on and run by knowledgeable staff who cater fo vegans, too: cold dishes best, and dried frui compôte reported as 'divine'; the other branche are at 11 Central Avenue, Covent Garden Piazza WC2 (379 6508); 17–18 Great Newport Street, W (836 5226); and 9–11 Tottenham Street, W (631 3912). Sarah Brown's *Guide to Vegetarian Lon don* (1986) has 100 suggestions; the Vegetaria Society is at 53 Marloes Road, W8 (937 7739); th Vegan Society is at 33–5 George Street, Oxford.

Refreshment suggestions

While a new restaurant opens every week, upwardly mobile chefs move from kitchen to kitchen, decors are revamped, owners sell out and buy in, and menus are radically restructured. Soho and Covent Garden are especially restaurant thick, the first adding one every time a sex shop is refused its licence in the new clean-up, the second serving tourists, shoppers and theatre-goers in the streets around the restored ex-markets. In all restaurants, but especially in these two areas, it is wise to check prices carefully. Eating out in London can be memorable, fun, even sublime. It is just a question of finding the right place to satisfy your tastebuds, eyes, sensitivities and purse-strings.

The selection below is designed merely as a springboard of ideas for eating and drinking at all times of day – see the guidebooks for more and nose about the streets to see what is on offer. They are arranged in areas to coincide with the 12 day-by-day guiding chapters (see pp. 59–260); the West End has a few extras to help with pre- and post-entertainment eating. For restaurants, lunchtime suggestions tend to be for lighter food that is also lighter on the pocket, with one or two fixed-price bargains from great chefs; evening suggestions are often for a more expensive package of food, decor and ambience. So, although each is listed for its best moment, most serve other meals, too.

The code:

★ Best for a special meal; higher prices, although many claim that every meal in London is expensive unless someone else is paying.

● Particularly informal atmosphere; usually not too pricey.

🍷 Especially good wine list.

🍺 Especially good for real ales.

The cuisine is indicated after the telephone number.

THE CITY

Breakfast Le Poulbot, 45 Cheapside, EC2 (236 4379) and Rouxl Britannia, Triton Court, 14 Finsbury Square, EC2 (256 6997), both French and Roux-owned; Old Thameside Inn, St Mary Overy Dock, SE1 (403 4243/4253), breakfast Apr–Sept only, good City views.

Picnic spots The secret garden of St Dunstan-in-the-East is best; also, St Paul's Churchyard, Finsbury Circus and Square, Barbican Arts Centre.

Lunchtime restaurants Lunching is a fast-disappearing City activity. ★ Bill Bentley's Bishopsgate, Swedeland Court, 202 Bishopsgate, EC2 (283 1763), English, fish; Café Burgundy, 31 Cathedral Place, EC4 (248 2550), brasserie; ● Ginnan, 5 Cathedral Place, EC4 (236 4120), Japanese. Gow's, 81 Old Broad Street, EC2 (628 0530), English, fish; Langan's Bar & Grill, Plantation House, Mincing Lane, EC3 (220 7094), French; Le Poulbot, 45 Cheapside, EC2 (236 4379), French, best upstairs, pricey downstairs, Albert Roux nicknames it 'the pub', and ● Le Gamin, 32 Old Bailey, EC4 (236 7931), French, another Roux; ● Sweetings, 39 Queen Victoria Street, EC4 (248 3062), English, fish, crowded.

Pubs 🍺 Black Friar, 174 Queen Victoria Street, EC4 (236 5650); 🍺 Founders Arms, Bankside, SE1 (928 1899); 🍺 George, off 77 Borough High Street, SE1 (407 2056); Jamaica Wine House, St Michael's Alley, Cornhill, EC3 (626 9496); 🍺 Market Porter, 9 Stoney Street, SE1 (407 2495), brews its own beer; Old Thameside Inn, see breakfast, pub and wine with food and views; Old Wine Shades, 6 Martin Lane, EC4 (no tel) for beer and wine. 🍺 Pavilion End, 23 Watling Street, EC4 (236 6719), televisions showing cricket round the year; 🍺 Ye Olde Watling, 29 Watling Street, EC4 (248 6235);

Wine bars 🍷 Balls Bros, Great Eastern Hotel, Liverpool Street, EC2 (626 7919), jolliest of their many branches; Bow Wine Vaults, 10 Bow Churchyard, off Bow Lane, EC4 (248 1121), the City's best; 🍷 Corney & Barrow, 118 Moorgate, EC2 (628 2898); 🍷 The Pavilion, Finsbury Circus Garden, EC2 (628 8224).

Tea Not eaten in the City; head for the Waldorf or Savoy hotels.

Evening restaurants Gallipoli, 7–8 Bishopsgate Churchyard, EC2 (588 1922), Turkish in an ex-Turkish bath; or two riverside pubs: 🍺 Samuel Pepys, Brooks Wharf, 48 Upper Thames Street, EC4 (248 3048), and the 🍺 Anchor, Bankside, SE1 (407 1577), English pub, views.

WESTMINSTER Not well endowed; MPs and civil servants gossip in pubs or cross St James's Park to their Pall Mall clubs.

Breakfast 🍺 The Albert pub, Victoria Street, SW1 (222 5577); The Silver Cross pub, Whitehall, SW1 (930 8350).

Picnic spots Victoria Tower Gardens, St James's Park.

Lunchtime restaurants L'Amico, Horseferry Road, SW1 (222 4680); The Footstool, St John's, Smith Square, SW1 (222 2779) in the crypt; Kundan, Horseferry Road, SW1 (854 3434); Lockets,

Marcham Court, Marsham Street, SW1 (834 9552); National Gallery.

Pubs 🍺 Buckingham Arms, Petty France, SW1 (222 3386); The Chairmen, Queen Anne's Gate, SW1 (noted); 🍺 Clarence, Whitehall, SW1 (930 4808); Crown, Albert Embankment, SW1 (735 3723), views of parliament from upstairs room. Old Star, Broadway, SW1 (222 8755); St Stephen's Tavern, Bridge Street, SW1 (930 3230); Westminster Arms, Story's Gate, SW1 (22 8520); See also breakfast.

Wine bars 🍷 Carriages, 43 Buckingham Palace Road, SW1 (834 8871); Crowns, Crown Passage, Pall Mall (839 3960), just up from The Mall. 🍷 Methuselah's Brasserie and Wine Bar, Victoria Street, SW1 (222 3550), a Don Hewitson combination of café, bar and restaurant.

Tea National Gallery; Charing Cross Hotel, Strand, WC2 (839 7282), in the first floor lounge.

Evening restaurants thin on the ground; MPs adjourn to Methuselah's, Lockets or head for Soho (see p. 314).

THE RIVER For a day on the Thames, hopping off boats to explore the sites along the way, all these suggestions are near a boat stop. Almost all are either on, beside, overlooking or very near the water. Most are pubs, which look picturesque, produce good food and do not demand tidy clothes; good London restaurateurs still shun the spectacular riverside sites – exceptions are the expensive Elephant on the River, 129 Grosvenor Road, SW1 (834 1621) and the Savoy River Room. The order follows the twisting river, first from Westminster down to Greenwich, then from Westminster up to Hampton Court.

On the water Most boats provide hot drinks and snacks and, since the water is out of reach of the licencing laws, their bars are open most of the trip. Cruising boats offer more sustenance (see boats, pp. 93–6).

Pre-sail and post-sail stops Near Westminster pier: Silver Cross Pub, Whitehall, SW1 (930 8350), breakfast onwards. Near Charing Cross pier: Charing Cross Hotel, Strand, WC2 (839 7282); Royal Horseguards Hotel, 2 Whitehall Court, SW1 (839 3400), with summer garden; ★ Savoy Hotel River Room, Strand, WC2 (836 4343), this one is smart; and on the water: Tattershall Castle, Victoria Embankment, SW1 (839 6548), a boat-pub, and Hispaniola, Victoria Embankment, SW1 (839 3011), a boat-restaurant.

Around the Tower There is no food or drink for

sale inside the Tower. In St Katharine's Dock: The Dickens Inn (488 1226), top floor for views; Tower Hotel bar and Princes Room Restaurant (488 3580), river and bridge views. Eastwards lie The Town of Ramsgate, 62 Wapping High Street, E1 (488 2685); The Prospect of Whitby, 57 Wapping Wall, E1 (481 1095); and then The Grapes, 76 Narrow Street, E14 (987 4396). A five-minute taxi-ride over Tower Bridge and left – or a boat across the water – reaches Old Justice (237 3452), bridge views, and 🍺 The Angel (237 3608), both on Bermondsey Wall East, SE16, and 🍺 The Mayflower, 117 Rotherhithe Street, SE16 (237 4088). And just west of London Bridge, the Livery Barge Regalia is moored at Swan Lane, EC4 (623 1805). Picnics Spots: Tower Wharf; the garden in front of All Hallows by the Tower, good views of Tower and Thames; and St Dunstan-in-the-East.

Greenwich Cutty Sark, Ballast Quay, Lassell Street, SE10 (858 3146); Trafalgar Tavern, Park Row, SE10 (858 2437); The Yacht, 5 Crane Street, SE10 (858 0175). Picnic spots: Greenwich Park, the higher up the better the view.

Putney The Duke's Head, Lower Richmond Road, SW15 (788 2552).

Kew Best to cross the bridge and turn right to Strand-on-the-Green for a cluster of pretty riverside pubs: 🍺 The Bull's Head (994 0647), City Barge (994 2148) and at the end, The Bell and Crown, Thames Road (994 4164). Tea: Newmans Tea Shop, also known as The Original Maids of Honour Shop, Kew, Richmond, eat the Maids of Honour cakes where they were first baked for Henry VIII; magical summer Sunday teas at St Anne's Church, Kew Green, watching the cricket. Picnic spots: the far end of Kew Gardens, looking across the river to Syon.

Richmond Waterman's Arms, Water Lane (940 2893); White Cross, Cholmondeley Walk (940 0909); and, further off, Rose of York, Petersham Road (940 0626), and Three Pigeons, Petersham Road (940 0361). Picnic spots: Ham House and along the towpath either way.

Twickenham Riverside Inn, Riverside (892 0863), and The White Swan, Riverside (892 2166) score points for prettiness and food. Picnic spots: Marble Hill Park, the wooded towpath beyond. Two more pubs merit a detour: 🍺 Eel Pie, 9 Church Street, Twickenham (no tel); and 🍺 London Apprentice, Church Street, Isleworth (560 6136), handy for Syon Park.

Hampton Court The café and restaurant inside Hampton Court grounds leave room for improvement. Opposite the gates: The Mitre Hotel, Hampton Court Bridge (979 2264); go early for the riverside garden, depressing interior. Tea: The Palace Tea Rooms, opposite the gates; the café inside the Hampton Court Gate of Bushy Park; but best is to walk 10 minutes to the excellent Belgian Patisserie, 72 Walton Road, East Molesey (979 8123), found over the bridge and right along Creek Road.

STRAND, COVENT GARDEN, HOLBORN AND FLEET STREET

Breakfast Bar Crêperie, 21 Covent Garden, WC2 (836 2137); Boswell's Coffee House, Russell Street, WC2; Freuds, 198 Shaftesbury Av, W1 (240 9932). ★ Savoy Hotel River Room, Strand, WC2 (836 4343); ★ Waldorf Hotel, Aldwych, WC2 (836 2400).

Picnic spots The barristers monopolise most of the green spaces here and disapprove of picnicking. Lincoln's Inn Fields has greenery; Covent Garden Piazza has entertainment.

Lunchtime restaurants Covent Garden is bursting with old, new and revamped restaurants; their cafés are not as good or informal as they should be; good restaurants in the rest of the area are more rare. ● Ajimura, 51–3 Shalton Street, WC2 (240 0178), Japanese; Le Café des Amis du Vin, 11–14 Hanover Place, WC2 (379 3444), French; ● Le Café du Jardin, 28 Wellington Street, WC2 (836 8769), French; ● Le Gamin, 32 Old Bailey, EC4 (236 7931), French, owned by Roux brothers; ● Grunt's Chicago Pizza Co., 12 Maiden Lane, WC2 (379 7722), American; Joe Allen, 13 Exeter Street, WC2 (836 0651), American; Magno's, 65a Long Acre, WC2 (836 6077), French; ♥ ★ Neal Street Restaurant, 26 Neal Street, WC2 (836 8368), modern international; ● The Nosherie, 12 Greville Street, EC1 (242 1591), Jewish; Opera Terrace, 1st floor, 45 East Terrace, Covent Garden, WC2 (379 0666), English, with views; Rules, 35 Maiden Lane, WC2 (836 5314), English, best on a cold day; Simpson's-in-the-Strand, Strand, WC2 (836 9112), English, big roasts for winter warmth.

If you find yourself south of the Thames: Archduke Wine Bar, Concert Hall Approach, SE1 (928 9370) and RSJ 13a Coin Street, SE1 (928 4554), both near the South Bank Centre.

Pubs Gossip centres for local journalists, lawyers and writers for centuries, so plenty to choose from, all with strong characters. In theatrical Covent Garden: ☛ The Punch and Judy, The Market, Covent Garden, WC2 (836 1750), night in the Piazza; nearby are the Freemason's Arms, 81 Long Acre, WC2 (836 6931), ♥ Lamb and Flag, Rose Street, WC2 (836 4845), and Lemon Tree, 4 Bedfordbury, WC2 (836 1864). For a legal pint: ♥ The Cittie of Yorke, 22 High Holborn, WC1 (242 7670) Devereux, 20 Devereux Court, WC2 (583 4562); The Seven Stars, Carey Street, WC2 (242 8521); Ship Tavern, 12 Gate Street, WC2 (405 1992); For what were the journalists' pubs before they fled 'The Street': The Cartoonist, 76 Shoe Lane, EC4 (353 2828); ♥ Ye Olde Cheshire Cheese, Wine Office Court, 145 Fleet Street, EC4 (353 6170); Cock Tavern, 22 Fleet Street, EC4 (353 8570); Edgar Wallace, 40 Essex Street, WC2 (353 3120); ♥ Old Mitre, Ely Place, EC1 (405 4751); Punch Tavern, 99 Fleet Street, EC4 (353 8338).

Wine bars Bar des Amis, 11–14 Hanover Place, WC2 (379 3444), beneath the Café restaurant; ♥ Bleeding Heart, Bleeding Heart Yard, Greville Street, Hatton Garden, EC1 (242 8238); Brahms & Liszt, 19 Russell Street, WC2 (240 3661); Crusting Pipe, 27 The Market, Covent Garden, WC2 (836 1415). ♥ El Vino's, 47 Fleet Street, EC4 (353 6786), good wine and mid-day food, court battles may have won women their legal rights but they are still here on sufferance and made to feel so; Gordon's, Villiers Street, WC2 (930 1408), steep steps down to Dickensian dimness and good Madeiras. In the Upstairs Bar of the Savoy, you can peek down on the world's wealthy while sipping wine and nibbling smart snacks.

Tea The Savoy lounge or the Palm Court of the Waldorf hotel, both splendid, with the Waldorf the winner on tea-dance days, Fri–Sun (see breakfast).

Evening restaurants ♥ Beoty's 79 St Martin's Lane, WC2 (836 8768), Greek; ★ Boulestin, 1a Henrietta Street, WC2 (836 7061), French in a sumptuous setting; ♥ Melange, 59 Endell Street, WC2 (240 8077), eclectic; Oscar's Brasserie, 5–8 Temple Avenue, EC4 (353 6272); ♥ Porters, 17 Henrietta Street, WC2 (836 6466), English; ★ Savoy Hotel, see breakfast, Anton Edelmann's food in the clubby Grill or spacious River Room where there is dancing at night, the most stylish dinner-dance in town; Sheekey's, 28–32 St Martin's Court, WC2 (240 2565), English, fish; Shushan, 36 Cranbourn Street, WC2 (836 7501), Szechwan; ♥ Smith's, 33 Shelton Street, WC2 (379 0310), Anglo/French, very good atmosphere lunchtime and evenings; Taste of India, 25 Catherine Street, WC2 (836 2538), Indian; Terrazza Est, 125 Chancery Lane, WC2 (242 2601), Italian, sometimes with informal opera singing at night.

ST JAMES'S AND MAYFAIR   This is a big spending area for food. Here are the grandest hotels with stage-set public rooms. In them and near them are the most sumptuous restaurants. This is where businessmen impress their competitors and bosses, art dealers impress their clients and the world's rich have fun. To peek at the dreamworld glamour, take breakfast, tea or cocktails in one of the grand hotels. To soak it up luxuriously, linger over dinner in a top restaurant. For smaller pockets, most of the restaurants suggested for lunch remain open for dinner; and Italian cafés lurk in every passage, lane and corner.

Breakfast   Ideally, it should be in a gentleman's club. Realistically, Italian cafés are scattered thickly over the whole area. But for some style with the morning boiled egg, avoid the newly spoilt Fortnum & Mason ground floor Fountain Restaurant in favour of the mezzanine Patio, Piccadilly W1 (734 8040) or head for the grand hotels: ★ The Ritz, Piccadilly W1 (493 8181) for the most beautiful dining room in town; or try ★ Claridge's, Brook Street, W1 (629 8860); the light-drenched Terrace or ★ The Oak Room in Le Meridien, Piccadilly, W1 (734 8000); or ★ The Stafford, St James's Place, SW1 (493 0111). On Sunday, Brunch at ★ Le Caprice, see lunch.

Picnic spots   St James's Park, Green Park, Hyde Park, St George Hanover Square Gardens, and the squares open to the public – St James's, Berkeley, Hanover, Grosvenor, etc.

Lunchtime restaurants   Grand hotels are unbeatable for sumptuous, dream settings and some have star chefs – best for lunch is ★ The Ritz, its beautiful dining room overlooking Green Park; see dinner suggestions for more. For the St James's clubby atmosphere: ★ Green's Champagne & Oyster Bar, 36 Duke Street, St James's, SW1 (930 4566); ★ Wilton's, 55 Jermyn Street, SW1 (629 9955), both English, fish and game. Good value lunches include: ● Chaopraya, 22 St Christopher's Place, W1 (486 0777), Thai; ● Le Chef, 41 Connaught Street, W2 (262 5945), French bistro; ● Chicago Pizza Pie Factory, 17 Hanover Square, W1 (629 2669), American, Bob Payton's first; ● Colombina, 4–6 Duke of York Street (930 8297), Italian; ● The Crêperie, Globe Yard, 56a South Molton Street, W1 (629 4794), French; ● Criterion Brasserie, Piccadilly, W1 (839 7133), Anglo-French amid Thomas Verity's mosaics; Fortnum & Mason Patio for up-market lobster-burger; ● Ilkeda, 30 Brook Street, W1 (629 2730), Japanese; Jules Restaurant Bar, 85 Jermyn Street, SW1 (930 4700);

● Kitchen Yakitori, 12 Lancashire Court, W1 (629 9984), Japanese; Langan's Bar and Grill, 7 Down Street, W1 (491 0990) very different from (and preferred by many) nearby Langan's Brasserie, 8 Stratton Street, W1 (493 6437), French, jointly owned by Peter Langan, actor Michael Caine and chef Richard Shepherd, a theatrical and glitzy event, stars are there to be seen; One Two Three, 27 Davies Street, W1 (409 0750), Japanese; ● Smollensky's Balloon, 1 Dover Street, W1 (491 1199), Anglo-American. The Roof Restaurant, 27th floor, the Hilton, Park Lane, W1 (493 8000), international, lunch buffet, Sunday brunch or dinner, has amazing views on clear days. Lunch is also the moment to try ★ Le Caprice, Arlington House, Arlington Street, W1 (629 2239), French, fizziest at noontime. ♥ ★ Le Gavroche, 43 Upper Brook Street, W1 (408 0881), French, the Roux brothers' grandest restaurant, avoid legendary huge bills with- the fixed price menu; and ♥ ★ Le Soufflé, Hotel Inter-Continental, 1 Hamilton Place, W1 (409 3131) for Peter Kromberg's fixed price lunch.

For Oxford Street and north Mayfair shoppers, ♥ Justin de Blank, 54 Duke Street, W1 (629 3174) delicious from breakfast time on.

Pubs   For post-auction house tension and after-hours dealing, the Red Lion, 23 Crown Passage, SW1 (930 8067), near Christie's, or the Guinea, 30 Bruton Place, W1 (629 5613) near Sotheby's. In Mayfair: ● Bunch of Grapes, Shepherd Market, W1 (629 4989); ● Red Lion, Waverton Street, W1 (499 1307). In south Marylebone: Coach Makers Arms, 88 Marylebone Lane, W1 (935 9311); Dover Castle, 43 Weymouth Mews, W1 (636 9248); The Worcester Arms, 89 George Street, W1 (935 6050).

Wine bars   L'Artiste Musclé, 1 Shepherd Market, W1 (493 6150); L'Autre, 5b Shepherd Street, W1 (499 4680); ♥ Bubbles, 41 North Audley Street, W1 (499 0600); Chopper Lump, 10c Hanover Square, W1 (499 7569); Crown's, 3/4 Crown Passage, Pall Mall, SW1 (839 3960); Green's Champagne Bar, 36 Duke Street, St James's, SW1 (930 4566).

Tea   This is the serious tea-time area. Designer-dressed dames meet for multi-course teas, poised on squishy sofas in the grandest hotels. Special spoils are Browns, Albemarle Street, W1 (493 6020) for the softest sofas, given to residents first; The Cavendish, Jermyn Street, SW1 (930 2111) for top chocolate cake; Claridge's, Brook Street, W1 (629 8860), residents take priority; The Dorchester, Park Lane, W1 (629 8888) in the Promenade; Hotel Inter-Continental, 1 Hamilton Place, W1 (409 3131) for lavender sorbet amid the chinoiserie: The Park

Lane, Piccadilly, W1 (499 6321) for top scones; The Ritz, Piccadilly, W1 (493 8181), book for the second sitting; The Stafford, St James's Place, SW1 (493 0111), for intimacy. Outside the hotels: Fortnum & Mason's top floor, or the twinkle of the Criterion (see Lunch).

For Oxford Street shoppers, oases for peaceful teas are Berners Hotel, Berners Street, W1 (636 1629) and The Churchill Hotel, 30 Portman Square, W1 (486 5800).

Cocktails This is cocktail land, too; the grander the hotel, the better the experience (see tea-time count-down) – Claridge's for the Hungarian quartet, the Dorchester Promenade for showing off new outfits, the Inter-Continental (top floor) for views, the Park Lane for John Siddeley's Chinese red lacquer, and the Ritz for pink Ritz champagne. Jules Restaurant Bar (see lunch) has American style.

Evening restaurants The best time for glittering and glamorous treats, with time to linger over top food. Grandest hotel moments (details above): The ♥ ★ Connaught's back Grill and front Restaurant for elegant intimacy; The ★ Dorchester's Terrace and plush Oak Room for Anton Mosimann's cooking; Hotel Inter-Continental, 1 Hamilton Place, W1 (409 3131) for stunning views from the ★ Roof Restaurant and Bar, or Peter Kromberg's rising wonders from ♥ ★ Le Soufflé on the ground floor; ★ Four Seasons, Inn on the Park, Hamilton Place, W1 (499 0888), French, under star chef Philippe Boulot; Ninety Park Lane, Grosvenor House hotel, Park Lane (499 6363), French, the godchild of chef Louis Outhier; Le Meridien ★ Oak Room for Michel Lorain's overseeing. Restaurant treats outside hotels: ★ Cecconi's, 5 Burlington Gardens, W1 (434 6122), Italian, by-pass the meat perhaps, but not the pasta; ♥ ★ Le Gavroche, see lunch; ★ Greenhouse, 27a Hays Mews, W1 (499 3331), Anglo-French, with garden; ★ Miyama, 38 Clarges Street, W1 (499 2443), for serious Japanese food lovers; ★ Scotts, 20 Mount Street, W1 (629 5248), English, fish, with oyster pudding on Thursday in season; ★ Zen Central, 10 Queen Street, W1 (629 8089), tip top Chinese food, window seats best – if full, make the pilgrimage to Chelsea or Hampstead branches, taxi fare saved by cheaper prices.

SOHO AND BLOOMSBURY

Breakfast Continental cafés in cosmopolitan Soho. Amalfi, 31 Old Compton Street, W1 (437 7284); Bar Italia, 22 Frith Street, W1 (437 4520), complete with football match videos; Braganza, 56 Frith Street, W1 (437 5412); Harry's, 6 Kingly Street, W1 (734 8708), open all night, every night (and most of the day), from 10pm round to 4.30pm, then a quick early evening clear up; Maison Bertaux, 28 Greek Street, W1 (935 6240); Patisserie Valerie, 44 Old Compton Street, W1 (437 3466); The Swiss Centre, Leicester Square, W1 (743 1291); Le Tire Bouchon, 6 Upper James Street, W1 (437 5348).

Picnic spots A dozen garden squares including Soho, Russell and Bloomsbury, with Soho delicatessens and Berwick Street Market for picnic shopping.

Lunchtime restaurants Avoiding the mediocre, overpriced joints, Soho has a long list of good haunts. Here are a lunchtime handful: ★ Alastair Little, 49 Frith Street, W1 (734 5183), English, with AL as star chef; Arirang, 31–2 Poland Street, W1 (437 6633), Korean; ♥ ● La Bastide, 50 Greek Street, W1 (734 3300), French; Braganza, 56 Frith Street, W1 (437 5412), nouvelle French, brasserie and two restaurants; ● Cafe Loire, 12 Great Marlborough Street, W1 (434 2666), French; ● Chez Victor, 45 Wardour Street, W1 (437 6523), tiny, French; Chicago Meat Packers, 96 Charing Cross Road, WC2 (379 3277), American, Bob Payton's latest; ● Cranks, 8 Marshall Street, W1 (437 9431), the first, biggest and best of the vegetarian chain; ♥ ★ L'Escargot, 48 Greek Street, W1 (437 2879), Anglo-French; fizziest at lunchtime cabaret at night, ground-floor brasserie, dining upstairs, wine list advised by Jansis Robinson, MW; ★ Frith's, 14 Frith Street, W1 (437 3370), English; ♥ Gay Hussar, 2 Greek Street, W1 (437 0973), Hungarian; Red Fort, 77 Dean Street, W1 (437 2115), Indian; ● Soho Brasserie, 23–25 Old Compton Street, W1 (439 9301), Anglo-French; Terrazza, 19 Romilly Street, W1 (437 8991), the oldest of Mario e Franco's Italian chain; ● Le Tire Bouchon, 6 Upper James Street, W1 (437 5348), French bistro. If you are stage struck, the Palace Theatre, Shaftesbury Avenue, W1 (734 0762) for food and entertainment.

Thoughts for Fitzrovia and Bloomsbury: Charlotte Street is lined with jolly Greek restaurants, for example Animos Taverna at no. 32–34 (636 2289). ★ Auntie's, 126 Cleveland Street, W1 (387 3226), modern English; Café Bordeaux, 245 Shaftesbury Avenue, W1 (836 6328); Chez Gerard, 8 Charlotte Street, W1 (636 4975), French; Heal's Restaurant, 196 Tottenham Court Road, W1 (636 1921), modern English; ● Ikkyu, 67 Tottenham Court Road,

W1 (636 9280), Japanese; Lal Qila, 117 Tottenham Court Road, W1 (387 4570), Indian; ★ L'Etoile, 30 Charlotte Street, W1 (636 7189), French: ● Pizza Express, Coptic Street, WC1 (636 2244); ● Spaghetti House, 216 High Holborn, WC1 (831 7718), Italian, on the brasserie system of serving throughout the day; ★ White Tower, 1 Percy Street, W1 (836 8141), Parthenon of the Greeks.

Pubs Bricklayers Arms, 31 Gresse Street, W1 (636 9182); the Dog and Duck, 18 Bateman Street, W1 (437 3478); The French House, 49 Dean Street, W1 (437 2799); ☙ The Lamb, 94 Conduit Street, WC1 (242 7670); ☙ Museum Tavern, 49 Great Russell Street, WC1 (242 8987); The Plough, 27 Museum Street, WC1 (636 7964); ☙ Princess Louise, 208 High Holborn, WC1 (405 8816); Star and Garter, 21 Poland Street, W1 (no phone); White Lion, 16 Northington Street, WC1 (405 7905).

Wine bars Gazebo, 10 Argyll Street, W1 (734 2929); James Wine Bar, 46–8 James Street, W1 (487 4847); ♥ Reams, Store Street, WC1 (637 0631), handy for the BM; ♥ Shampers, 4 Kingley Street, W1 (437 1692); Tracks, 17a Soho Square, W1 (439 2318).

For a cocktail, Rumours, 33 Wellington Street, WC2 (836 0038) is in a former flower market building, now filled with the fashion-conscious cocktail-sipping young; or beautiful Kettners, 29 Romilly Street, W1 (437 6437), then a pizza in the plush dining room.

Tea Patisserie Valerie or Maison Bertaux in Soho, see Breakfast; further north, Lascelles Old English Teahouse, 2 Marlborough Court, off Carnaby Street, W1 (439 2366), delicious cakes in tiny teahouse; in Bloomsbury, the Russell Square café if the sun shines, Hotel Russell drawing room if not.

Evening restaurants Chinese Soho is best in the evening and Sunday lunchtime; Charlotte Street continues as for lunch; Bloomsbury students go home. ● Diamond, 23 Lisle Street, W1 (437 2517), Chinese, favourite of chef Nico Ladenis; L'Entre-côte Café de Paris, St Martin's Lane, W1 (836 7272), French; Au Jardin des Gourmets, 5 Greek Street, W1 (437 1816), French; ★ The Lindsay House, 21 Romilly Street, W1 (493 0450), revival designer English; ● Manzi's, 1–2 Leicester Street, WC2 (734 0224), French, ground-floor painted room best; ● Melati, 21 Great Windmill Street, W1 (437 2745), Malaysian; ● Melati, 31 Peter Street, W1 (437 2011), Malaysian, both Melatis founded by one family, now firmly separate; ● New World, 1 Gerrard Place, W1 (734 0677), Chinese, favourite of

chef Anton Mosimann and critic Fay Maschler; The Szechuan, 56 Old Compton Street, W1 (437 2069), Chinese.

THE NASH SWEEP: REGENT STREET, REGENT'S PARK AND REGENT'S CANAL All these are on or very near the Nash beat. The order assumes breakfasting on the street, then progressing into the park and along the canal.

Breakfast Café Marengo, 5 Regent Street, W1 (839 6251); Liberty's, 210–20 Regent Street, W1 (734 1234); St George's Hotel, Langham Place, W1 (580 0111) for rooftop views at all times of day. Also Maison Sagne, 105 Marylebone High Street, W1 (935 6264) for pre-Tussauds fortification.

Picnic spots Regent's Park for green horizons and Queen Mary's Garden roses; Primrose Hill for breathtaking views.

Lunchtime restaurants ● Ceylon Tea Centre, 22 Regent Street, W1 (930 8632); ● The Criterion, Piccadilly Circus, W1 (839 7133), French; Café Royal, 68 Regent Street, W1 (437 9090), plush Café Wilde (cocktail bar and brasserie) opens onto the street; the sumptuous ★ restaurant is behind, probably the prettiest high Edwardian dining room in London; Veeraswamy's, 99–101 Regent Street, W1 (734 1401), Indian, window table bookable; The Magic Moment, basement of Lindys, 233 Regent Street, W1 (499 6176), for food and magicians. Inside Regent's Park: ● Rose Garden Restaurant, Queen Mary's Gardens, Inner Circle, NW1 (935 4010); ♥ Tea Pavilion, south of Queen Mary's Gardens and by the tennis courts; ● Broad Walk Pavilion, halfway up Broad Walk; the Zoo, good for clandestine lunches amid the roars and screeches.

Canal eating At Camden: ♥ HQ, Camden Lock, NW1 (485 9987); ♥ Le Routier, Camden Lock, NW1 (485 0360), French; Le Bistroquet, 273–5 Camden High Street, NW1 (485 9607) and Camden Brasserie, 216 Camden High Street, NW1 (482 2114), both French, both just out of water sight; and the Raj Bhel Poori House, 19 Camden High Street, NW1 (388 6663), South Indian. On the water: The Gallery Boat, moored opposite 15 Prince Albert Road, NW1 (485 8137); the Sunday lunch or Tues-Sat evening cruise on *My Fair Lady*, Camden Lock-Little Venice and back, bookable at Jenny Wren, 250 Camden High Street, NW1 (485 4433/6210). At Little Venice: Didier, 5 Warwick Place, W9 (286 7484), just out of water sight; or hie up to L'Aventure, 3 Blenheim Terrace, NW8 (624 6232), both French.

Pubs The Clifton, 96 Clifton Hill, NW8 (624 5233); Ordnance Arms, 29 Ordnance Hill, MW8 (722 6143), with fish and chips on Fri and Sat; Warwick Castle, Warwick Place, W9 (286 6868), with weekend barbeques.

Wine bars ❢Bill Bentley's, 239 Baker Street, NW1 (935 3130); Hamish's, 85–7 Parkway, NW1 (267 3591); ❢ Odettes, 130 Regent's Park Road, NW1 (586 5486); Shampers, 4 Kingly Street, W1 (437 1692).

Tea The Criterion, Liberty's and St George's Hotel, see above. For splendid neighbourhood tea-rooms: Jaquet, 75 St John's Wood Road, NW8 (722 3438); Maison Sagne, 105 Marylebone High Street, W1 (935 6240), for post Tussauds recovery.

Evening restaurants If still in Regent Street, head eastwards into Soho or westwards into Mayfair, see above. From Regent's Park, dive down into north Marylebone for Asuka, 209 Baker Street, W1 (486 5026), Japanese; ❢ Langan's Bistro, 26 Devonshire Street, W1 (935 4531), French, this was originally Odin's (q.v.) with Peter Langan of Langan's Brasserie in Mayfair doing the cooking; ★ Odin's, 27 Devonshire Street, W1 (935 7296), the grander version of Langan's Bistro; and ❢ Topkapi, 25 Marylebone High Street, W1 (486 1872), Turkish; or go west to Mumtaz, 4–10 Park Road, N1 (723 0549), Indian. See also canal eating, above.

KENSINGTON AND NOTTING HILL

Breakfast If you are off to Kensington Palace, the little Tea Kiosk in the north-west corner of Kensington Gardens opens around 9am, depending upon staff. Otherwise: Maison Bouquillon, 41 Moscow Road, W2 (727 4897) for a Spanish–French mixture of croissants and pepitos with coffee or hot chocolate; Royal Garden Hotel, Kensington High Street, W8 (937 8000), a window seat on the tenth floor. In Holland Park: Julie's Bar, 137 Portland Road, W11 (727 7985); Tootsies, 120 Holland Park Avenue, W11 (229 8567).

Picnic spots Kensington Gardens, Holland Park or the more intimate garden of Leighton House.

Lunchtime restaurants Best position is The Roof Garden, 6th floor, 99 Kensington High Street (entrance in Derry Street), W8 (937 7994), Anglo-French, lush planting and splendid views, lunch Mon–Fri, brunch on Sun. Clarke's, 124 Kensington Church Street, W8 (221 9225), Californian-influenced English, for Sally Clarke's creations noon or night; ● Costas, 14 Hillgate Street, W8 (229 3794), Greek, with garden; La Residence, 148 Holland Park Avenue, W11 (221 6090), lunchtime fixed price menu.

Pubs Plenty of good locals in this leafy residential area, especially for thirsty antique hunters. In inner Kensington: Catherine Wheel, 23 Kensington Church Street, W8 (937 3259); Churchill Arms, 119 Kensington Church Street, W8 (727 4242); Elephant & Castle, 40 Holland Street, W8 (937 0316). In West Kensington: The Scarsdale, 23 Edwardes Square, W8 (937 4513); The Greyhound, 1 Kensington Square, W8 (937 7140). On Campden Hill: ⬛ Windsor Castle, 114 Campden Hill Road, W8 (727 8491). In Holland Park: Prince of Wales, Princedale Road, W11 (727 9000); Duke of Clarence, 203 Holland Park Avenue, W11 (603 5431). Around Portobello Road: The Colony, 175 Westbourne Grove, W11 (229 1774); Duke of Norfolk, 202 Westbourne Grove, W11 (229 3551); Finche's (Duke of Wellington), 179 Portobello Road, W11 (727 6762); Portobello Star, 171 Portobello Road W11 (229 8016); Sun in Splendour, 7 Portobello Road, W11 (727 5444); Uxbridge Arms, 13 Uxbridge Street, W8 (727 7326).

Wine bars A good set for up-market locals. Drinks, 21 Abingdon Road, W8 (937 6504); Hollands, 6 Portland Road, W11 (229 3130); Jimmie's, Kensington Palace Barracks, Kensington Church Street, W8 (937 9988); Julie's Bar, see breakfast; Mildreds, 135 Kensington Church Street, W8 (727 5452); Scandie's, 4 Kynance Place, SW7 (589 3659).

Tea A good choice. Julie's and Maison Bouquillon, see breakfast; Mario's café in Holland Park; The London Toy and Model Museum, 21–3 Craven Hill, W2 (262 7905); Maison Pechon, 127 Queensway, W2 (229 0746); Patisserie Parisienne, 24 Phillimore Gardens, W8 (938 1890).

Evening restaurants ❢ The Ark, 122 Palace Gardens Terrace, W8 (229 4024), with a younger sister Ark at 35 Kensington High Street, W8 (937 4294), totally different character; L'Artiste Assoiffé, 306 Westbourne Grove, W1 (727 4714); The Belvedere, Holland House, Holland Park, W8 (602 1238), French, the only proper restaurant in a London park; Boyd's Glass Garden, 135 Kensington Church Street, W8 (727 5452) ❢ Chez Moi, 1 Addison Avenue, W11 (603 8267), French; ❢ Geales, 2 Farmer Street, W8 (727 7969), for formal fish 'n' chips; ❢ Hiroko, Kensington Hilton, 179 Holland Park Avenue, W11 (603 3355/5003), Japanese; ❢ Julie's, see breakfast; Launceston Place, 1a Launceston Place, W8 (937 6912); English; Kingfisher, Halcyon Hotel, 81 Holland Park, W11 (727

315

7288); ♥ Maggie Jones, 6 Old Court Place, Kensington Church Street, W8 (937 6462), English; Malabar, 27 Uxbridge Street, W8 (727 8800), Indian; Monsieur Thompson's, 29 Kensington Park Road, W11 (727 9957), French; La Pomme d'Amour, 128 Holland Park Avenue, W11 (229 8532), French.

SMITHFIELD AND CLERKENWELL TO ISLINGTON AND CANONBURY

Breakfast To enter the meaty Smithfield spirit, a hearty pub breakfast of bacon, eggs, sausage and even chops or steak, washed down with a pint of bitter: Fox and Anchor, 115 Charterhouse Street, EC1 (253 4838), breakfast Mon–Fri 6–11am; Smithfield Tavern, 105 Charterhouse Street, EC1 (253 5153), breakfast Mon–Fri 6.30–11am. For a gentler start: Café St Pierre, 9 Clerkenwell Green, EC1 (251 6606); Quality Chop House, 94 Farringdon Road, EC1 (837 5093), founded as 'The Progressive Working Class Caterers', now serving serious breakfast to middle-class clients who sit reading the *Guardian* in the old mahogany pews. In Islington: The Garbanzo Coffee House, 411 City Road, EC1 (833 2888), trendy, like much of Islington wakes late, open 10am; and for Camden Passage shoppers The Dome, Upper Street, N1 (226 3414).

Picnic spots No large parks here but Myddelton Square has rosebeds and Canonbury has the pretty New River Walk – Islington's stretch of Regent's Canal needs tidying up.

Lunchtime restaurants In Smithfield and Clerkenwell: Bubbs, 329 Central Markets, Smithfield, EC1 (236 2435), French, closes early (9.30pm) just as the meat lorries are already arriving; Café St Pierre, see breakfast, French; Rudland and Stubbs, 35–7 Greenhill Rents, EC1 (253 0148), English. In Islington: ★ Frederick's, Camden Passage, N1 (359 2888); ♥ Moussaka-on-the-Green, Islington Green, N1 (354 1952); ♥ Solopasta, 26 Liverpool Road, N1 (359 7648), Italian, crushed, excellent; Young's, 154–5 Upper Street, N1 (226 8463), Chinese, this one for Cantonese and Peking, the chef of the sister restaurant at 19 Canonbury Lane, N1 (226 9791); cooks Szechuan.

Pubs The Smithfield, see Breakfast; also ☞ Hand and Shears, 1 Middle Street, Smithfield, EC1 (600 0257). In Islington, pubs are antique market stallholders' meeting place: Camden Head, 2 Camden Walk, N1 (359 0851); Eagle, 2 Shepherdess Walk, N1 (253 3561); The Fallen Angel, 65 Graham Street, N1 (253 3996), crazily painted, run as a young people's brasserie; ☞ George IV,

Copenhagen Street, N1 (833 1114); ☞ Island Queen, 87 Noel Road, N1 (226 5507), more whacky interiors; King's Head, 115 Upper Street, N1 (226 1916), drink and eat before, during and after the theatre show; Slug and Lettuce, 1 Islington Green, N1 (226 3864). In Canonbury: ☞ Compton Arms, 4 Compton Avenue, Canonbury Lane, N1 (359 2645).

Wine bars Almeida, 1 Almeida Street, N1 (226 0931), home-made food in a theatre-café, avant-garde theatre next door; ♥ Café St Pierre, see Breakfast; Serendipity, The Mall, Camden Passage, N1 (359 1932).

Tea No tea-rooms here; The Fallen Angel pub does the job; see also Breakfast spots in Islington.

Evening restaurants In Clerkenwell: Le Café du Marché, 22 Charterhouse Square, EC1 (608 1609), French in an old warehouse. In Islington: Due Franco, 207 Liverpool Road, N1 (607 4112), jolly Italian; ● M'sieur Frog, 31a Essex Road, N1 (226 3495), French; Sona Gaon, 46 Upper Street, N1 (226 6499), Indian; ● Trattoria Aquilino, 31 Camden Passage, N1 (226 5454), tiny family-run Italian.

KNIGHTSBRIDGE AND SOUTH KENSINGTON

Breakfast Important for a heavy museum day. For fortification, windowside breakfast at the Hyde Park Hotel, 66 Hyde Park, SW1 (235 2000), to glimpse the Hyde Park Barracks horses exercising in Hyde Park around 7.30am or trotting off to the Horse Guards around 10.30am. Snappier starts: Italian cafés behind Knightsbridge Green and in Hans Crescent; Le Métro, 28 Basil Street, SW3 (589 6283). Inside Harrods: West Side Express café (entrance in the south-west side) and The Georgian Restaurant (4th floor) (730 1234). Also, La Brasserie, 272 Brompton Road, SW3 (584 1668), a real brasserie; Joe's Cafe, 126 Draycott Avenue, SW3 (225 2217), sleek and stylish, dawn to dusk.

Picnic spots This is smart private square area; public lawns include tree-filled Princes Gardens, the Natural History Museum, Hyde Park and Kensington Gardens.

Lunchtime restaurants Harrods has restaurants on every floor for every taste; others nearby include ♥ ★ Capital Hotel, 22–4 Basil Street, SW3 (589 5171), tip top French; ● Chicago Rib Shack, 1 Raphael Street, Knightsbridge, SW3 (581 5595), American; Fantaisie Brasserie, 13 Knightsbridge Green, SW1 (589 0509), French and beautiful; ♥ Stockpot, 6 Basil Street, SW3 (589 8627), cheap 'n' cheerful amid the big spenders. The V&A basement restaurant is exemplary; other South Ken museums leave visitors to starve, so food nearby includes: Au Bon Acceuil, 27 Elystan Street, SW3 (589 3718), French; ● Bangkok, 9 Bute Street, SW7 (584 8529), Thai; ● Daquise, 20 Thurloe Street, SW7 (584 4944), Polish; ★ Hilaire, 68 Old Brompton Road (584 8993), French; ♥ Lou Pescadou, 241 Old Brompton Road, SW5 (370 1057), French, merits the walk for Pierre Martin's cheaper restaurant; Ognisko Polski (known as The Hearth), 55 Exhibition Road, SW7 (589 4670), Polish, a club but welcomes non-members for vodka and flaki; ● Paper Tiger, 10 Exhibition Road, SW7 (584 3737), Chinese Szechuan; Tui, 19 Exhibition Road, SW7 (584 8359), Thai. See also Breakfast.

Pubs A good way to relax from the South Ken culture. Admiral Codrington, 17 Mossop Street (589 4603); Australian, 29 Milner Street, SW3 (589 3114); Bunch of Grapes, 207 Brompton Road, SW3 (589 4944); Ennismore Arms, 2 Ennismore Mews, SW7 (584 0440); Enterprise, 35 Walton Street, SW3 (584 8858), borrow cards, cribbage and dominoes for a quiet game; Hoop & Toy, Thurloe Place, SW7 (589 8360); King George IV, Montpelier Square, SW1 (589 1016), one of several in the old Knightsbridge lanes; The Loose Box, 136 Brompton Road, SW3 (584 9280); Paxton's Head, 153 Knightsbridge, SW1 (584 8054); Tattershall's Tavern, Knightsbridge Green, SW1 (584 7122); ♥ Zetland Arms, 2 Bute Street, SW7 (589 3813).

Wine bars ♥ Basil's, Basil Street Hotel, 8 Basil Street, SW3 (581 3311); ♥ Bill Bentley's, 31 Beauchamp Place, SW3 (589 5080); Draycott's, 114 Draycott Avenue, SW3 (584 5359); ♥ Le Metro, 28 Basil Street, SW3 (589 6286), top rosette from *The Good Wine Bar Guide 1986*; The Loose Box, 136 Brompton Road, SW3 (584 9280); Punch's, 30 Old Brompton Road, SW7 (581 0099); The Wine Gallery, 232 Brompton Road, SW1 (584 3493).

Tea Culture and shopping stimulate the appetite. The V&A basement restaurant is good. Best value is Harrods' Georgian Restaurant (fourth floor) buffet tea, 3.30–5.30pm, for a flat fee the sweet-toothed serve themselves and gobble until they feel sick. Others: Daquise, 20 Thurloe Street, SW7 (584 4944); Gloriette, 128 Brompton Road, SW3 (589 4750); Hyde Park Hotel, see Breakfast, bookable; Les Specialités St Quentin, 256 Brompton Road, SW3 (225 1664). For sumptuous post-museum tea and cocktails, Blakes Hotel, see evening restaurants.

Evening restaurants ★ Blakes, 33 Roland Gardens, SW7 (370 6701), international; Bombay Brasserie, 140 Courtfield Close, Courtfield Road, SW7 (370 4040), Indian, pioneer of interior designed up-market spice-eating, book a table in the airiest conservatory in town; The Phoenicia, 11 Abingdon Road, W8 (937 0120), Lebanese; St Quentin, 243 Brompton Road, SW3 (589 8005), not a brasserie at all, a smart fast evening restaurant; Turner's, 87–9 Walton Street, SW3 (584 6711) for ex-Capitol Graham Turner's creations.

CHELSEA, BELGRAVIA AND PIMLICO As a smart residential area full of Sloanes with money to spend on having a good time, the many restaurants fill with local atmosphere during the week. The newest gourmet area is Sloane Avenue, where the powerful alliance of Sir Terence Conran and Simon Hopkinson has added another restaurant to the chic enclave now that the magnificently tiled Bibendun (ex-Michelin) building has been refurbished (81 Fulham Road, SW3, tel 581 5817).

Breakfast For the Chelsea mood, munch Chelsea buns overlooking Cadogan Place in the smart Chelsea Room of the Hyatt Carlton Tower hotel, Cadogan Place, SW3 (235 5411). Or join Sloanes for informal coffee and croissants at the Oriel Brasserie, Sloane Square (730 4275). For Sunday brunch, join cosmopolitan London at ★ The Elephant on the River, 129 Grosvenor Road, SW1 (834 1621); or try Bendicks, 195 Sloane Street, SW3 (235 4749), and L'Express, 16 Sloane Street, W1 (235 9869), in the basement of Joseph Pour La Maison.

Picnic spots Best is Battersea Park. The Chelsea Pensioners prefer visitors not to picnic in the Royal Hospital grounds.

Lunchtime Restaurants ♥★ La Tante Claire, 68–9 Royal Hospital Road, SW3 (352 6045), for Pierre Koffman's French creations and his fixed price lunch menu. More realistically: ♥ Asterix, 329 King's Road, SW3 (352 3891), crêperie; ♥ La Bersagliera, 372 King's Road, SW3 (352 5993), tiny Italian; ♥ Le Casino, 77 Lower Sloane Street, SW1 (730 3313), Peter Ilic's cheap 'n' cheerful joint; ♥ Chelsea Kitchen, 98 King's Road, SW3 (589 1330), International; ♥ Como Lario, 22 Holbein Place, SW1 (730 2954), Italian; ♥ The Dolphin Brasserie, Dolphin Square, Chichester Street, SW1 (828 3207), Art Deco delight overlooking the swimming pool; Drakes, see evening, for Sunday lunch; Gavvers, 61–3 Lower Sloane Street, SW1

(730 5983), French, owned by the Roux brothers, noontime good, or second sitting for dinner; ♥ General Trading Company, 144 Sloane Street, SW1 (730 6400) for Justin de Blank's basement bistro; Hoizin, 72 Wilton Road, SW1 (630 5108), Chinese fish; ♥ Motcombs, 26 Motcomb Street, SW1 (235 6382); ♥ The Tent, 15 Eccleston Street, SW1 (730 6922), Anglo-French. See also Sloane breakfast haunts. In the isolated Tate, there is a ♥ ★ restaurant (best to book) and a designer café.

Pubs Plenty of good ones, to save the pocket from pricey restaurants.

In Chelsea: Cadogan Arms, 298 Kings Road, SW3 (no tel); Chelsea Potter, 119 King's Road, SW3 (352 9479); ♥ Cross Keys, 2 Lawrence Street, SW3 (352 1893); King's Head and Eight Bells, 50 Cheyne Walk, SW3 (352 1820); Man in the Moon, 392 King's Road, SW3 (352 5075), sometimes theatre upstairs; Phene Arms, 9 Phene Street, SW3 (8391); Surprise, 6 Christchurch Street, SW3 (352 0455).

In Belgravia: ♥ Antelope, 22 Eaton Terrace, SW1 (730 7781); Duke of Wellington, 63 Eaton Terrace, SW1 (730 3103); ♥ Grenadier, 18 Wilton Row, SW1 235 3074) ex-officers' mess; ♥ Nag's Head, 53 Kinnerton Street, SW1 (235 1135); Star Tavern, 6 Belgrave Mews West, SW1 (235 3019); Turks Head, 10 Motcomb Street, SW1 (235 2514).

In Pimlico: Morpeth Arms, Millbank, SW1 (834 6442); ♥ Orange Brewery, 37 Pimlico Road, SW1 (730 5378), brews its own beers in the cellar, 'SW1' and the stronger 'SW2'; St George's Tavern, 14 Belgrave Road, SW1 (730 5378). For pre- and post-Tate Gallery: Paviours, Page Street, SW1 (834 2150).

Wine bars Blushes, 52 King's Road, SW3 (589 6640); Charcos, 1 Bray Place, SW3 (584 0765); Chimes, Churton Street, SW1 (821 7456); ♥ Ebury Wine Bar, 139 Ebury Street, SW1 (730 5447), one of the best. Henry J Beans, 195 King's Road, SW3 (352 9255), mixes American memorabilia and jollity with American beers and cocktails.

Tea Hyatt Carlton Tower hotel foyer, see Breakfast, the best package for tea, setting, piano music and flowers.

Evening restaurants ♥ ★ Chelsea Room, Hyatt Carlton Tower, see Breakfast, for Bernard Gaume's delicacies; Drakes, 2a Pond Place, SW3 (584 4555), good traditional country-in-town English; ♥ The Hungry Horse, 196 Fulham Road, SW10 (352 7757/ 8081), a pioneer for traditional English food; ♥ Mijanou, 143 Ebury Street, SW1 (352 3546), French, for Sonia Blech's inventive dishes; ♥ Nineteen, 19 Mossop Street, SW1 (589 4971), interna-

tional, full of youngish locals; La Poule au Pot, 231 Ebury Street, SW1 (730 7763); Pomegranates, 94 Grosvenor Road, SW1 (828 6560), international; Red Pepper, 7 Park Walk, SW10 (352 3546), Chinese Szechuan; San Frediano, 63 Fulham Road, SW3 (584 8375), Italian, very jolly; Le Suquet, 104 Draycott Avenue, SW3 (581 1785), fish; ♥ ★ La Tante Claire, see Lunch, advanced booking essential; Thierry's, 342 King's Road, SW3 (352 3365), friendly French; Ziani, 45 Radnor Walk, SW3 (352 2698), designer Italian, with a second, larger edition at 112 Cheyne Walk, SW10 (352 7534). Culinary devotion may merit the pilgrimage over the river to ★ L'Arlequin, 123 Queenstown Road, SW8 (622 0555).

DOCKLANDS With the upheavals of this whole area, the pubs, such an integral part of its history, seem to be the only unchanging elements. All else is in flux. See also River eating section.

Breakfast In Spitalfields: The Market Café, 5 Fournier Street, E1 (247 9470), fruit market workers down robust meals Mon–Fri 1.30am– 1.30pm and Sat 1.30am–10am; Meraz Cafe, 56 Hanbury Street, E1 (247 2538) or the Sweet and Spicy, 40 Brick Lane, E1 (247 1081), for Asian breakfast. Beigel Bake, 159 Brick Lane, E1 (729 0616) makes Jewish salmon and cream cheese filled beigels, served daily 1pm–6am. For English buffet breakfast: City Gates Restaurant, Great Eastern Hotel, Liverpool Street, EC2 (283 4363); Tower hotel, see River eating p. 310.

Picnic spots Bethnal Green Gardens for flowers; Victoria Park for trees and space; top of Mudchute Farm hillock for high-tech views; Island Gardens for idyllic Greenwich views.

Lunchtime restaurants Bloom's, 90 Whitechapel High Street, E1 (247 6001), Jewish; The Cherry Orchard, 241–5 Bethnal Green Road, E2 (980 6678), vegetarian; Kosher Luncheon Club, Morris Kasler Memorial Hall, 13 Greatorex Street, E1 (247 0039); Whitechapel Art Gallery café, 80–2 Whitechapel High Street, E1 (377 0107).

Pubs For the riverside pubs, see River eating p. 310. Many inland pubs are still an integral part of East End life; many were supplied by local breweries active until recently; several have ungentrified interiors; some have evening entertainment. Ignore any hastily pinned up signs saying 'no travellers' – they are aimed at gypsies, not guide-book-clutching visitors. Ferry House, 26 Ferry Street, E14 (987 5141); Five Blades and

Bladebone, 27 Three Colts Street, E14 (987 2329); ☛ Hollands, 9 Exmouth Street, Stepney, E1 (790 3057), merits a detour; ☛ Hoop and Grapes, 47 Aldgate High Street, EC3 (no tel), one of the oldest, good food; Royal Cricketers, 211 Old Ford Road, E2 (980 3259); Still and Star, 1 Little Somerset Street, E1 (488 3761).

Wine bars As the City moves eastwards to gentrify the East End and docklands, the first cork of a new wine bar is pulled almost monthly. Older arrivals include: Bootys, 92 Narrow Street, E14 (987 8343); City Limits, 16–8 Brushfield Street, E1 (377 9877); Grapeshots, 2/3 Artillery Passage, E1 (247 8215).

Tea Island Gardens café (open daily 9am–5.30pm), overlooking Greenwich – magic moments as the light softens.

Evening restaurants In Spitalfields: the glorious bazaar of Indian bistros, many to rival homeland versions, is seriously threatened by developers, so go fast; the system is to wander Brick Lane and the streets off it, select one you like, get a table and order and then, if it does not hold a licence for drink, go and collect a pint of lager from the nearest pub. In Limehouse: Pockets of Chinatown that served the Chinese ship-workers and sailors last century are, so far, unthreatened by developers. All very local, very informal haunts, so it is vital to make a reservation in advance, or entry may be refused. Good Friends, 139 Salmon Lane, E14 (987 5541); New Friends, 53 West India Dock Road, E14 (987 1139); Young Friends, 11 Pennyfields, E14 (987 4276); Chinatown, 795 Commercial Road, E14 (987 2330).

Spend, spend, spend

A London shopping addict can buy and browse all day every day for an infinite length of time and never visit the same shop twice. But there is so much else to do in London, too. So, by trial and error, Londoners and visitors establish their favourite shopping grounds both for daily life and for delicious flights of fancy, learning what is stacked where in their chosen stores. Having mastered their inside spending track, strong and often contradictory truths emerge: Oxford Street to be avoided at all times, 'except for Marks and Spencer's who have their new lines first'; sales to be avoided, 'but I got a Liberty dress for just £30 last January'; Christmas shopping to be avoided, but 'weren't the Regent Street lights good this year'; and Harrods to be avoided, except 'the cheeses are the best', 'I have an account card simply for the florist' and 'the toy department keeps the boys happy for hours'.

But shopping in London can be miserable and frustrating. A long shopping list can easily send the buyer criss-crossing the city, wasting time and money on transport and ending the day with no purchases, sore feet and often tears. So here are some hints and tips for happy shopping, from day-to-day essentials to big art buys, from street market bargains to putting your feet up with mail order catalogues, from tiny boutiques to huge department stores.

Tips, facts and warnings

INFORMATION   The key to happy spending. These are the books, magazines and newspapers to consult:

Newspapers   The *Financial Times*, the pink paper for money-makers, softens for the Saturday 'Weekend' section where Lucia van der Post gives discerning, up-to-the-minute shopping news. In *The Independent*, Suzie Menkes reveals the latest fashion news on Wednesdays.

Magazines   *Time Out* has a weekly streetwise Sell Out section and regular features focusing on a small area of London with exhaustive detail. *Harpers & Queen*, the glossiest of monthlies, has a Bazaar shopping section and so many advertise-ments that there is a directory for shopping addres-ses; and *Vogue*, the other monthly glossy, has a Shophound section and ditto for advertisements; both for up-market designer spending. *Cosmo-politan*, *Elle* and *Company* are for mainstream fashion and accessories; *Blitz*, *I.D.* and *The Face* for the most streetwise styles and ideas.

Books   These are the most useful:
Time Out Guide to Shopping in London, published annually (early summer): Shopping in London for the uninitiated before this was first published in 1986 was hit and miss, and often miss. Now the *TO* team have done all the leg-work; packed with facts and tips, all in 200 pages. Essential.

Forshaw, A and T Bergstrom: *The Markets of London* (1986); reliable for both history, travel and tips.

Grunfeld, N: *The Royal Shopping Guide* (1984): A perky, annotated list of the shops that hold royal warrants, from floor polish makers to jewellers; most proudly print their royal patron's crest on their product's wrapping and on their shopping bags, so you can shop where the royals shop and let everyone else know.

Perlmutter, K: *London Street Markets* (1984); the facts, history and tips, with a subject index for speedy searching.

MONEY Paying by cash often enables the buyer to strike a bargain. Some stores accept cheques over £50 if the buyer has proof of identity. For travellers' cheques, many stores accept sterling ones for a small handling charge but accept other currencies with a higher exchange rate than banks, so it is best to cash them there. For credit cards, there is usually an upper limit beyond which the trader will make a surreptitious telephone call to head office to check the buyer's credibility.

In-store credit cards To speed up shopping and delay payment, some stores have their own credit cards. The two most useful are the Fraser Card, for The Army & Navy, Barkers, DH Evans and Dickins & Jones; and the Debenhams card, which also covers Harvey Nichols, Hamley's, Rayne and Burtons. Others include Austin Reed, Burberrys, Debenhams, Fenwick, Habitat, Harrods, John Lewis (also covers Peter Jones), Laura Ashley, Liberty, Marks and Spencer, Mothercare, Next, Ryman, Selfridges (also covers all Sears shops including Lilly & Skinner and Wallis), Warehouse and more.

VAT Value Added Tax is currently rated at 15% in Britain and payable on almost everything (current exceptions include food, books, children's clothes). All non-UK passport holders are exempt from VAT if they are taking the goods out of the UK within three months. But they must first pay it, then reclaim it. As it can be a fair sum, it is worth the effort. The system works as follows for non-UK passport holders living outside the EEC (for EEC passport holders, see below).

First, ensure the shop operates a Retail Export Scheme and how much must be spent in that shop to use it (the minimum is usually £75–100). Then, taking your passport to go shopping, tell the assistant before you pay that you want to use the 'Export scheme'. You must then produce your passport (and some shops need to see your return air ticket),

the shop completes the VAT407 form and you take part of it away, having agreed how the refund is to be paid; in department stores it is often necessary to get an export sales bill from each department you shop in, then take them to a central export desk. It is wise to keep a separate note of the name and address of each shop.

On leaving Britain, all goods bought on the 'export scheme' should be in hand luggage. At customs (Heathrow has a special VAT area), goods bought must be displayed and matched up with their VAT407 forms; customs officers stamp the forms and send them back to each shop; the shops send the customer their refund, usually a sterling cheque unless otherwise agreed. If the goods are being mailed or have been packed in the suitcase, they must be shown to local customs officials on arrival at your home airport, the forms stamped and sent back to the shop.

The system for EEC passport holders is the same for buying the goods, except that it is worth remembering that there is a minimum figure on each object below which VAT cannot be reclaimed: £45 for Ireland, £165 for Greece and Denmark, and £207 elsewhere. It is also worth noting before you leave home what the local purchase tax rate will be on each item you buy here when you return home with it. Then, instead of showing goods and forms to customs officers on leaving Britain, they are shown to customs on arrival at home, when the forms for claiming UK VAT are stamped and sent back and the local purchase tax (which may be higher or lower for each article) is payable. This law fully lives up to legends of British bureaucracy.

SHOPPING AND THE LAW The law is very protective towards the shopper. Useful things to know include: goods in sales should be perfect unless labelled otherwise ('second', etc); a trader's claims for a product must be upheld or he must refund the money (e.g. a raincoat advertised as waterproof that soaks through in a light shower); all toys on sale must pass safety requirements (no lead, sharp edges, etc).

Payment and the law More useful notes. Paying deposits leads to a tricky legal position if the goods turn out not to be what you want. They are best avoided. A trader does not have to accept cheques or credit cards unless there is a sign displayed, then he does. Always ask for an itemised receipt so that any faulty goods can be returned.

Faults and the law More useful notes. Every product comes with an unwritten guarantee that it should perform its duty, so if a fault caused before you owned it develops, return it; written guarantees (eg for electrical goods) usually have a card to be completed and returned to the makers. If there is a fault, take the product back to the shop together with the receipt and the trader should offer a replacement, refund or credit note; you may refuse to accept a credit note; in the event of any problems about refunds for faulty goods ask for the manager or deal direct with the shop's head office.

Mail order and the law Yet more useful notes. Usually, if goods arrive faulty or not as described, you have two weeks to return them and then your money is reimbursed, together with the postage if they were faulty.

Street merchants Otherwise known as rip-off merchants. Worth watching their soap-box shows; not worth buying their Italian designer-labelled shirts run up in Dalston or their French perfume brewed in Bethnal Green.

PREPARATION   If you know exactly what you want, it is always worth telephoning to check it is in stock before traipsing across London or braving a downpour, or both.

Timings The majority of shops open Monday to Saturday, from around 9am to around 5.30pm. Being London, there are then a string of exceptions. Small, specialist shops may keep short hours, art galleries often close on Saturdays, etc, so it is worth telephoning to check the hours. Conversely, many shops now stay open late (see below), notably the wonderful Waterstone's chain of bookshops; most Oxford Street shops close between 7 and 8pm on Thursday; most Knightsbridge shops close at around 7pm on Wednesday; many Covent Garden shops regularly close around 7pm. On Sunday, the law ensures most shops remain closed, but street markets blossom throughout the city.

Seasonal shopping and sales The London shopping year. From mid-November, the Christmas lights in Oxford and Regent streets and the extended shopping hours lure Londoners into a frenzy of spending. Immediately pre-Christmas, Oxford Street, Mayfair, Knightsbridge and Chelsea are one big shopping crush. The atmosphere can be cheerful and exhilarating, with hot chestnuts roasting in the streets and splendid window displays – Selfridges usually has the best. Harrods (for splendour) and Woolworth's (for value) have the best decorations. The January sales begin the first weekday after Boxing Day with

equal crushes; advertised everywhere, useful sales lists are published in the newspapers – the cleverest people buy next year's Christmas presents; Harrods' bargains can be bought by mail order with credit cards, avoiding the scrum; the most expensive shops (department stores and boutiques) generally make the biggest reductions. Valentine's Day (February 14) has been commercialised, exchanging romance for heart-shaped cards, chocolates, panties and even pizzas. Mother's Day (March) receives the same treatment, when flowers double in price. Easter comes next, with chocolate Easter eggs and bunnies. Summer clothes often arrive while snow is on the ground; then the summer sales start in July, just when the sun comes out, with more advertising and more helpful lists in newspapers. August is dull, waiting for September winter stock.

In the shops – regular services Depending on its size and prestige, a shop may offer a string of useful services: an in-store card (see above), credit (at an Annual Percentage Rate of interest – APR), mail order service (for all or some goods), glossy catalogue (see below), alteration and repair services (see below), beauty parlours, cafés and restaurants, delivery service (see below), postal and shipping service and the Retail Export Scheme for VAT (see above). Some stores give their cardholders priority shopping at saletimes – Harvey Nichols normally give cardholders a pre-sale viewing day and an extra 10% off sale prices.

In the shops – extra services Wrapping is almost never up to Paris standards; a few stores such as Harrods and Selfridges have wrapping departments, but charge. Clothes bought from good designer shops can usually be altered by in-house steamstresses for a minimal charge; belts can have extra holes punched on the spot; watchstraps can be altered. Buying art and antiques, every gallery has its regular craftsman who will polish, clean, frame, etc. For nursing mothers, Selfridges, Debenhams, DH Evans, John Lewis, Liberty, Hamleys, Harrods and others have special rooms; for dogs, Harrods has a kennel.

Deliveries Some shops take telephone orders for credit card or account customers and then deliver, so no need to budge from the sofa. Having visited a shop, some deliver free within a certain radius; some charge; some are reluctant to deliver at all.

Catalogues and mail order – armchair shopping Saves hours travelling, searching and queueing. The more glamorous catalogues may have a price tag; others are free. Some stores only mail order the items in their catalogues; others devote a department to their clients' postal and shipping wishes. Catalogues to dream over include Aspreys, Harrods, Fortnum & Mason; ones to use include Early Learning Centre, General Trading Company, Habitat, Halcyon Days, Hatchards, Harvey Nichols, Heal's, Goodes, Laura Ashley, Liberty, Next, Penhaligon's, Reject China Shop.

For mail order shopping outside London, try: The Gift Catalogue, Lionkeen Ltd, Pudding Cake Lane, Rolvenden, Near Cranbrook, Kent (0580 240211); Tridias, 124 Walcot Street, Bath (0225 69455).

Museum, galleries and societies shopping One of the best ways of buying clever and unusual presents; often very high quality at fair prices, with part of the profit going to the cause. Either visit the gallery or send for its catalogue for armchair mail ordering; good ones include the Royal Horticultural Society, British Museum, London Transport Museum, National Gallery, Royal Academy, the Tate, the V&A. Some give reductions to members of Friends Societies for all or some of the goods -- the V&A lops off 10%. Especially good buys include the annual diaries and address books illustrated with items from the museum, gallery or society. For a cross-section of museum buys, the Design Centre, 28 Haymarket, SW1 (839 8000) usually stocks a good range; and the Museums and Galleries of Great Britain, 24–5 Catherine Hill, Frome, Somerset (London inquiries: 960 1650) has a mail order catalogue with a good selection.

Shopping by area

One good shop attracts another. So Central London has pockets which are shoppers' delights. With some pre-planning, a whole shopping list can be ticked off within a few hundred yards, with no trudging across town. Alternatively, some are heaven for daydreaming. Here are a few areas thick with good quality shops, each good for a blitz buy-out; the street markets (see below) have encouraged other areas. If you plunge into one and want to come up for air and sustenance a few hours later – or need a bracing, pre-spree breakfast – see suggestions for that area in the Food and Drink chapter, pp. 309–19.

COVENT GARDEN   Revitalised fruit and flower market, now one of the thickest concentrations of shops in town; especially good for crafts, specialist shops, presents, avant-garde young, fashion ac-

cessories. The Market in the piazza has two (sometimes three) layers of shops (The Doll's House, Pollocks' Toy Theatres, Biography Bookshop, Strangeways, Trivia, S Fisher, The Candle Shop) plus craftsmen's stalls. Surrounding streets that deserve a detour include Wellington Street (Penhaligon's), Russell Street (Knutz), The Strand (postage stamps galore), New Row (Naturally British), James Street (Patricia Roberts, Scribbler) and Floral Street (Jones, Sanctuary for opting out). North of here is the good concentration of Long Acre (Dillons Arts Bookshop, Stanford, Covent Garden General Store), Neal Street (Kite Store, The Hat Shop, Neal Street East), Shelton Street, Earlham Street (Contemporary Applied Arts, The Badge Shop), Shorts Gardens, Endell Street (Detail) and Neal's Yard (healthy bakery, farmshop, dairy, wholefoods, etc). North again, across New Oxford Street (James Smith's umbrellas), lies Bloomsbury with Museum Street, Coptic Street and Great Russell Street (bookshops galore; Westaway & Westaway for woollens; the British Museum shops). And eastwards is Chancery Lane (London Silver Vaults).

ST JAMES'S AND PICCADILLY   Quietly sophisticated, thoroughly English, royal warrants by the dozen, old shops as beautiful as the products they sell; St James's with small specialist shops patronised by generations of Londoners, Piccadilly and Regent Street with larger shops still full of sophisticated calm. Streets to explore include St James's (Berry Bros, Lock), King Street (Christie's, Spink), Duke Street (more art), Bury Street (Paul Longmire and art), Jermyn (Floris, Paxton and Whitfield, Ivan's, shirtmakers), Piccadilly (Swaine Adeney Brigg, Simpson, Hatchards, Fortnum's, The Royal Academy, Gered) and the arcades (Princes, Piccadilly and Burlington). See also Regent Street and Piccadilly Circus.

MAYFAIR   So chic and high-flying international that most people are reduced to window-shopping in Valentino and Asprey, The Fine Art Society and Sotheby's. This is where the world's rich kit out themselves and their houses with clothes, jewels and serious art. The backbone is Old (southern half) and New (northern half) Bond Street (Arthur Ackermann, Agnew, Charbonnel et Walker in Old Bond Street; Asprey, Cartier, Boucheron, Hermes, Gucci, Ferragamo, Versace, Armani, The Fine Art Society, The White House, Sotheby's, Fenwick's, Smythson's, etc in New Bond Street). Good streets off it and nearby include Grafton Street (Zandra Rhodes); Albemarle and Dover streets (art); Burlington Arcade (Richard Ogden, woollens); Cork, Old Burlington and Maddox streets (art), Savile Row (tailors and a General Trading Store outpost); Brook Street, South Molton Street and their neighbours (designer fashion, Browns, Katherine Hamnett, Prestat, Colefax & Fowler, Grays Antique Market, Phillips auctioneers), with St Christopher's Place (avant-garde fashion) across Oxford Street. Further west is South Audley Street (Goode's).

SOHO, CHARING CROSS ROAD AND TOTTENHAM COURT ROAD   Soho for fun and high fashion shopping, as in Covent Garden, but often cheaper and on the sharper side of trendy; southern part for Chinatown (see p. 155); north of Shaftesbury Avenue for old-established food shops and newly arrived clothes shops, music shops, fabric shops and services for the streetwise – competing with restaurants to take over closed-down sex parlours. They are scattered through these tight-knit streets: Good Soho streets include Old Compton (Patisserie Valerie), Frith, Dean (music), Wardour, Poland, Berwick (daily street market, Fratelli Camisa, Borovick Fabrics), Broadwick (Just Facts), Brewer (Lina Stores, Vintage Magazine Centre, Japan Centre), Upper St John, Beak (Anything Left Handed), Great Marlborough (books and music) – Carnaby Street staggers on in jaded shoddiness. The long south-to-north eastern Soho boundary road is Charing Cross Road for new and old books (Waterstone's, Ian Shipley, Zwemmer, Zwemmer OUP) changing its name after it crosses Oxford Street to become Tottenham Court Road (electrical shops, Heal's, Habitat, Paperchase).

REGENT STREET AND PICCADILLY CIRCUS
This long street is mostly brushed with the elegance of its up-market west side; big shops and often big spending, with Piccadilly Circus in the middle. Below the circus, Regent Street (often known as Lower Regent Street) is parallel to Haymarket (Design Centre, Burberry). Across Piccadilly Circus (Lillywhites, Tower Records, Boots) lies the string of good Regent Street shops (Austin Reed, Acquascutum, Waterstone, Garrard, Mappin & Webb, Hamleys, Reject China Shop, Rosenthal, Villeroy & Boch, Henry's, Jaeger, Liberty, Dickins & Jones, Laura Ashley, Secret Garden, Scottish Woollens).

KNIGHTSBRIDGE   Local shops for London's best-addressed residents. Many Mayfair boutiques have an outpost here to serve local ladies of leisure. The glitzy shopping drag stretches from the top part of Sloane Street round past Harrods and down Brompton Road and the bazaar bustle of Beauchamp Place to the newly christened Brompton Cross area (Walton Street/top of Sloane Avenue) – and then pushes even further west along Fulham Road, hotspot for interior designers. Good streets include Sloane Street (the Joseph cluster, Truslove & Hanson, Friends, Kenzo, Laura Ashley, Pulbrook & Gould), with Motcomb and West Halkin (art and interiors) off to the east; Knightsbridge (Harvey Nichols, Harrods, Lucienne Phillips), Brompton Arcade (Italian Paper Shop), Brompton Road (Scotch House, Yves St-Laurent) and Montpelier Street (Gran Gelato); Beauchamp Place (Reject China Shop, Bruce Oldfield, Janet Reger, Stanley Lesie, Caroline Charles, Maison Panache, The Beauchamp Place Shop), Walton Street (smart interiors, Nina Campbell, Danielle, the Monogrammed Linen Shop, Dragons, Walton Street Stationery Company, Saville Edells) and Fulham Road (Conran, Paperchase, Divertimenti, Parrots, Butler & Wilson, Occasions, Tatters, Piero de Monzi, The Watch Gallery, Mary Fox Linton). And up at the V&A, one of the best in-house museum shops and the Crafts Council Shop.

CHELSEA   Traditional Sloane Ranger shopping around Sloane Square; becomes more avant garde and fun past the crop of antique markets further down King's Road. Streets to check out are the bottom part of Sloane Street (General Trading Company, Presents, Partridges), Sloane Square (Peter Jones, David Mellor), Blacklands Terrace (John Sandoe), Bourne Street (Elizabeth David); Pimlico Road (interiors and antiques, Upstairs Shop, Mr Fish, After Dark, Woods Wilson, Lane Fine Art) and King's Road (Designer's Guild, Osborne & Little, Reject Shop, Chelsea Gardener, Chelsea Antique Market, Antiquarius Antique Market, Chenil Galleries, Tiger Tiger, The Last Detail, Rococo, Glamour City).

HAMPSTEAD   One of the nicest places to shop. The beautiful hilltop village's discerning, cultured residents are the magnet for a cluster of excellent shops in the pretty lanes serviced with brasseries and restaurants for breathers. Shops to seek out include: Comme Ci Comme Ça, Caroline Brunn, Chic of Hampstead, The New Shop, Collections (for discount designer clothes), Christin Baybars toyshop and new and old bookshops for the bookish Hampstead set – if the sun shines, browse through your book on Hampstead Heath.

OXFORD STREET   It might be the place to avoid at all costs – some Londoners claim not to have clapped eyes on it for five-year stretches – but it does have some redeeming shops and the biggest branches of several chains, all best attacked early in the morning, early in the week. From west to east they include: Marks and Spencer Marble Arch (their flagship, new lines arrive here first), Tie Shop, Selfridges, St Christopher's Place (off to the north); then past Bond Street Underground station are the HMV music shop, South Molton Street, New Bond Street and Oxford Circus (biggest Sock Shop, biggest Benetton); beyond is The Pantheon (the other huge Marks and Spencer), The Body Shop (biggest) and Virgin Megastore. And branches of Body Shop, more Sock Shop, more Tie Rack, more Benetton, Dixon's, Stefanel, Next, Claude Gill and Athena bookshops are dotted all along. Beware: the whole street crawls with rogue street traders.

Shopping where, when and how you wish

STREET MARKETS   London's traditional street markets for food, antiques and clothes still thrive, and some grow bigger. Some are weekly, some daily; stallholders' banter is a delight after stuffy shop assistants; and bargains are to be found. In all cases, early arrivals find the best bargains; close inspection saves later disappointments (you cannot return goods); all prices can be bartered down; fancy designer labels/picture signatures should be viewed with a certain scepticism: pickpockets abound. At antique markets, it is worth taking a magnifying glass, tape measure and other equipment to ensure the buy is the right one. Here is a cross-section of the most interesting and lively in Central London, with page references to more information on character, days and timings. To find out more, see books in Information, above.

Bermondsey Market (also known as New Caledonian Market), SE1, Fri, antiques, take a torch and get there at dawn to compete with serious collectors and dealers – starts 6am.

Berwick Street, W1, Mon–Sat, fruit and veg, see p. 162.

Brick Lane, E1, Sun morning, complete mixture, see p. 249.

Camden Lock, NW1, Sat–Sun, mixture with plenty of crafts, see p. 183.

Camden Passage, N1, Wed and Sat, antiques, see p. 207.

Charing Cross Collectors' Market, WC2, for regular and eccentric collectors.

Columbia Road, E2, Sun morning, flowers and plants, see p. 251.

Covent Garden Market, The Piazza, WC2, Tues–Sat, crafts, see pp. 121–2.

Jubilee Market, Covent Garden, WC2, Mon for antiques, Tues–Sat general.

Leadenhall, Bishopsgate, EC3, Mon–Fri, splendid covered market for food, see p. 73.

Leather Lane, EC1, Mon–Sat (best Mon–Fri lunchtimes), mixture with plenty of rag trade, see p. 127.

Petticoat Lane and surrounding streets, E1, Mon–Fri and Sun morning (best), complete mixture with emphasis on rag trade, see p. 254.

Portobello Road, W11, Mon–Sat for fruit and veg, Fri–Sat for antiques, see p. 197, backed up with shops including a good set of craft shops around Portobello Green and bookshops in Blenheim Crescent.

To see (or buy at) the wholesale markets which supply the surging London population with their food, visit one of these as early as bearable or at the end of a night on the tiles:

Billingsgate, 87 West India Dock Road, E14, Tue–Sat 5.15–8.30am, Sun 6–8.30am (shellfish only), fish, traders are mostly joined by public shoppers on Sat.

New Covent Garden Market, Nine Elms Lane, SW8, Mon–Fri 3am–11am, fruit, vegetables and flowers that used to be sold in Covent Garden; pay to enter. Beware: if you are going by taxi, arrange for it to wait or to collect you; otherwise you are stranded.

Smithfield, EC1, Mon–Fri 5–10am, meat; see p. 201.

Spitalfields, Commercial Street, E1, Mon–Fri 4.30–11am, Sat 4.30–9am, fruit, vegetables and flowers; free, see p. 249.

LATE NIGHT AND SUNDAY SUPPLY SHOPS Shops remain open until at least 7pm on Thursday in the Oxford Street area and Wednesday in the Knightsbridge area; many Covent Garden shops keep regular late hours; daily hours extend in the run up to Christmas in all areas. In addition, here are some life-savers.

Chemists Boots, Piccadilly Circus, W1 (734 6126), open Mon–Fri 8.30am–8pm, Sat 9am–8pm, with optician department; this is the biggest of the Boots chain.

Garden Pharmacy Perfumery, 118 Long Acre, WC2 (240 3111), open Mon–Fri 8.30am–8pm, Sat 9.30am–8pm, Sun 1–7pm.

Underwoods: This chain of chemists has good stock and keeps the most extensive hours. Branches include: 254 Earls Court Road, W8 (370 2232), Mon–Sat 9am–10pm, Sun 10am–10pm; 8 Queensway, W2 (229 9006), Mon–Sat 9am–11pm, Sun 10am–11pm; 114 Queensway, W2 (229 1183), open Mon–Sat 9am–10pm, Sun 10am–10pm; 267 Tottenham Court Road, W1 (580 1686), Mon–Fri 8.30am–9pm, Sat 9am–8pm, Sun 11am–8pm.

Also: Bliss Chemist, 5 Marble Arch, W1 (723 6116), daily 9am–midnight; Bliss Chemist, 50 Willesden Lane, NW6 (624 8000), out of the centre but open daily 9am–2am.

Food For late night and Sunday food shopping, from pâté to pudding with wines to match and flowers and chocolates for presents: Partridges, 132 Sloane Street, SW1 (730 0651), open daily 8.30am–9pm, the best for gourmet foods. Others: Apollo Food and Wines, 93 Shaftesbury Avenue, W1 (437 1570), open daily, 24-hours, good for post-theatre and post-Soho guzzling.

Europa Supermarkets all open daily, 8/9am–11pm, their delicatessen counters usually closing at 10pm. Central London ones include: 174 Fulham Road, SW10 (370 2394); 134 Gloucester Road, SW7 (370 4894); 26 Kendal Street, W2 (723 1879); 279b King's Road, SW3 (351 0722); 75/77 Old Brompton Road, SW7 (584 3387); 65–71 Sloane Avenue, SW3 (589 6171); 160–1 Sloane Street, SW1 (730 9108); 125 Strand, WC2 (836 0483).

Lalami: Conduit Street, W1 (491 4149), open Mon–Fri 8am–11pm, Sun 9am–9pm.

WH Cullen has some shops which open long hours every day including: 25 Eccleston Street, SW1 (730 8946), open Mon–Sat 8am–8pm (Sat until 7pm), Sun 9am–6pm; 182 Fulham Road, SW10 (352 7056), open Mon–Sat 7.30am–midnight, Sun 8am–11pm; 112 Holland Park Avenue, W11 (221 7139), open daily 7.30am–11pm.

Presents The food shops supply wine, flowers and chocolates. For something more, The Covent Garden General Store, 111 Long Acre, WC2 (240 0331) opens Mon–Sat 10am–midnight, Sun

11am–8pm; Knutz, 1 Russell Street, WC2 (836 3117), open Mon–Sat 11am–8pm, the best for whacky and witty presents; Reject China Shops at 33–5 Beauchamp Place, SW3 (581 0737, open Sun) and 134 Regent Street, W1 (434 2502).

Books Waterstone bookshops have at last brought US evening book-buying habits to London and have good stock and knowledgeable staff. Their London branches are: 121–5 Charing Cross Road, WC2 (434 4291), open Mon–Fri 9.30am–7.30pm, Sat 10.30am–7pm; 193 Kensington High Street, W8 (937 8432), open Mon–Fri 9.30am–10.30pm, Sat 9.30am–7pm, Sun noon–7pm; 99 Old Brompton Road, SW7 (581 8522), open Mon–Fri 9.30am–10.30pm, Sat 9.30am–7pm, Sun noon–7pm; 88 Regent Street, W1 (734 0713), open Mon–Fri 9.30am–9.30pm, Sat 9.30am–7pm, Sun noon–7pm; 62 Southampton Row, WC1 (831 9019), open Mon–Fri 9.30am–6pm (Thurs until 7pm), Sat 1–5pm.

ONE-STOP SHOPS For speedy shopping, this is the easiest way to tick off a long shopping list in one shop. Most have: extensive in-store services (see above); an in-store credit card (see above); a system of collecting parcels all together at the end of the spree; and operate the retail export scheme (see VAT, p. 321 above). Sale prices are often the best bargains in town. The bigger buildings may seem like rabbit warrens, but essential day-to-day items (stationery, stockings, haberdashery, perfumes, make-up, food) are usually on the ground floor, household hardware in the basement, and clothes, china, linens and toys on the upper floors, topped by beauty salons (see pp. 348–50) and restaurants. Traditional department stores are on the wane; newer, multi-product stores such as General Trading Company, Laura Ashley and Next are multiplying. The following selection have a good range, quality goods and efficient service:

Aquascutum, 100 Regent Street, W1 (734 6090): The Raincoat (see Rain, chapter, p. 278) plus everything to wear under, over and around it.

Army & Navy Stores, 105 Victoria Street, SW1 (834 1234): off the big spending beat, so less crowded.

Austin Reed, 103 Regent Street, W1 (734 6789); a man's spree should start with a shave in the glorious 1920s basement barber's.

Burberry, 161 Regent Street, W1 (930 3343); The Alternative Raincoat (see Aquascutum), plus everything to wear under, over and around it.

Debenhams, 334–8 Oxford Street, W1 (580 3000):

fashion for body and home, good glass and china; information desk on ground floor.

Dickins & Jones, 224 Regent Street, W1 (734 7070): Plenty of instore designer shops for one-stop designer shopping.

Fenwicks, 63 New Bond Street (629 9161): well-stocked, up-market emporium for Mayfair ladies (and a few men) and Bond Street workers; ground floor jewellery, stockings, belts and petticoats put instant chic into smart evenings.

Fortnum & Mason, 181 Piccadilly, W1 (734 8040): probably the most exclusive; ground floor hall, stationery and Christmas decorations are all stuff of dreams, see also p. 142.

General Trading Company, 144 Sloane Street, SW1 (730 0411): much more than a Sloane heaven; the Chelsea answer to Liberty's, with quality (if pricey) buys in all departments, especially china and glass; even the royals trot in to shop here.

Harrods, Knightsbridge, SW1 (730 1234): Londoners have a love–hate relationship with it; all visitors explore it; most people who enter its different world leave it clutching something in a moss-green bag; for much more information, see p. 214.

Harvey Nichols, Knightsbridge, SW1 (235 5000): far more elegance and style than its Harrods neighbour, proved in the stationery and designer departments and the rooftop restaurant.

Jaeger, 200–6 Regent Street, W1 (734 8211): chic fashion for men and women, with newly expanded accessories and leisure departments.

John Lewis, Oxford Street, W1 (629 7711): mostly sells good for the house; this and Peter Jones (see below) are part of the group which claims their prices 'are never knowingly undersold' and refunds the difference if proved otherwise.

Laura Ashley, 256–8 Regent Street, W1 (437 9760/ 734 5824): this is the flagship store; good for filling a wardrobe or decking out a house with tiny floral prints or stripes; no longer cheap.

Liberty & Co, 210–20 Regent Street (734 1234): top design and craftsmanship in every department; the best one-stop store for fashion essentials, accessories, quality presents, oriental goods and British and imported fabrics; excellent follow-up service.

Marks and Spencer: Marble Arch, 458 Oxford Street, W1 (935 7954) or The Pantheon Store, 173 Oxford Street, W1 (437 7722); these are the two biggest of the chain and stock the latest lines, basketfuls of the old lines, the full food range and the new perfumery, household and high fashion lines. Often known as 'Marks & Sparks' or plain 'M

& S', even Mrs Thatcher admits to buying her undies here.

Peter Jones, Sloane Square, SW1 (730 3434): this is where Sloanes kit out their Fulham homes, so it is well stocked with safe, modernish designs – and 'never knowingly undersold' (see John Lewis).

Selfridges, 400 Oxford Street (629 1234): built by an American on American lines (see p. 152); ground floor perfumery, the biggest in Europe, food hall a wonderland; upper floors not of the same standard.

Simpson, 203 Piccadilly, W1 (734 2002): up-market, mostly male shopping for much more than just their DAKS macks.

THE CHAINS   The quality chains usually have a flagship store or two or three stores that have the fullest range of goods. Below are the principal addresses of a few good chains whose branches are scattered throughout the city.

Benetton: the largest shop stocking the fullest range of the primary-coloured Italian clothes is at 255 Regent Street, W1 (493 8600).

The Body Shop: the biggest selection of natural, vegetable-based smells, potions, and creams, with brushes, sponges and all else to go with them is at 64–6 Oxford Street, W1 (631 0027). Other big ones include: Unit 13, The Market, Covent Garden, WC2 (836 2183), 32 Great Marlborough Street, W1 (437 5137), 59 King's Road, SW3 (584 0163) and 113 Victoria Street, SW1 (630 5588).

Boots: see chemists under Late Night shopping, above.

Europa: see food under Late Night shopping, above.

Marks and Spencer: see One-stop shops, above.

Next: really a department store spread over various sites, each branch with its own lines and characters. The shortest route to visit them all is: Next Collection (classic), Next Man and Next Interiors, 160 Regent Street, W1 (343 2515); Next Accessories, Next Two (young), Next Essentials, Next Man and Next Florist at 327–9 Oxford Street, W1 (409 2746), Next-to-Nothing (cheap) at 129–31 Oxford Street, W1 (734 4754).

Ryman: a large chain of stationers stocking good design at competitive prices, the biggest store at 6 Great Portland Street, W1 (636 3468/637 2668), just north of Oxford Circus.

Sock Shop: the foot panderer's paradise, with the most socks, stockings and tights in nylon, cotton and even silk, for men and women, is at 257–9 Oxford Circus, W1 (493 4039).

Tie Rack: the largest selection of ties, bow-ties and tie hangers, go to 487a Oxford Street, W1 (493 4344), at the Marble Arch end.

Underwoods: see chemists under Late Night shopping, above.

WH Smith: the store that has the biggest range of newspapers, stationery and books as well as computer equipment, toys and games and the travel section (for Ticketmaster entertainment booking, see p. 285), is at Holborn Circus, 124 Holborn, EC1 (242 0535); second biggest is at Sloane Square, 36 Sloane Square, SW1 (730 0351), but no toys or travel.

Waterstone: see bookshops under Late Night shopping, above.

Finding What You Want

It may be wine, art, clothes, shoes or simply a blitz buy at Marks and Spencer that you seek. Whatever the object of your desires, the choice of shops for every subject is bewildering. Here is a tiny selection as a guide to making a few good London buys.

ART AND ANTIQUES A helpful, hefty manual for hunting down what you want is *The British Art & Antiques Directory*, published annually (usually October). For more instant information, Sotheby's magazine stall and good newsagents sell the weekly *Antique Trade Gazette*, the monthly *The Antique Collector* and specialised collecting magazines.

At auction Easy once you conquer fear – and good places to take a close peek at the world's finest creations as they move from one private collection to another. Each auction house has a list of sales and advertises in the newspapers; alternatively, telephone. Each sale has a catalogue and has free viewing times when experts are on hand to explain and advise. It is important to check items carefully for condition and, if for the home, size (tape measure, magnifying glass and small torch are handy). It is best to decide upon an upper price limit before the auction and then keep to it and check out beforehand the various charges (premiums, VAT, shipping, etc). Currently, an export licence is necessary for pricier items. Then off you go. Bonham's, Montpelier Street, Knightsbridge, SW7 (584 9161); Bonham's Chelsea, 65–9 Lots Road, SW10 (351 7111); Christie, Manson and Woods, 8 King Street, SW1 (839 9060); Christie's South Kensington, 85 Old Brompton Road, SW7 (581 7611); Lots Road Chelsea Galleries, 71 Lots Road, SW10 (351 5784); Phillips, Son & Neale, 7 Blenheim Street, W1 (629 6602); Sotheby's, 34–5 New Bond Street, W1 (493 8080).

At markets Indoors: Antiquarius, 135–41 King's Road, SW3 (351 5353); Chelsea Antique Market, 245a & 253 King's Road, SW3 (352 5689); Gray's Antique Market, 58 Davies Street, W1 (629 7034); Grays Mews Antique Market, 1 Davies Mews, W1 (629 7034).

Outdoors: Bermondsey, Camden Lock, Camden Passage, Portobello and others, see Street Markets above.

At art fairs A non-stop string of them, some general, some specialist, from the Contemporary Art Fair (end May) to the Burlington House Fair (every two years). June is mega-fair month: Grosvenor House Fair, The Dorchester Fair (porcelain and glass) and Olympia. Find advertisements and lists in *The Antique Trade Gazette* and *The Antique Collector*.

At art colleges The degree shows (June–July) are selling exhibitions, a good moment to give much-needed patronage to blossoming talent. Ones worth seeking out include: Camberwell School of Arts and Crafts, Central School of Art and Design, Chelsea School of Art, London College of Fashion, London College of Printing, Royal Academy Schools, Royal College of Art and St Martin's School of Art.

In the galleries and shops The biggest concentrations are in the St James's to Mayfair sweep and from the top half of Kensington Church Street down into Portobello Road – Kensington Church Street alone has more than 50, some of which stock a useful map of which is where. Other good clusters include: Camden Passage, Pimlico Road, Motcomb Street, Fulham Road, King's Road. For lists and maps, pick up a copy of *Galleries*, a thick booklet published monthly and distributed free at most galleries. Whatever you are searching for, it is well worth visiting the auction houses as well to see the range and quality on offer.

Art Nouveau, Art Deco Chenil Galleries, 181 King's Road, SW3 (351 5353, shared with Antiquarius) for Pruskin and other good stalls; Richard Dennis, 144 Kensington Church Street, W8 (727 2061); David Gill, 60 Fulham Road, SW3 (589 5946); L'Odeon, 173 Fulham Road, SW3 (581 3640); Maria Merola, 108 Kensington Church Street, W8 (221 8490).

Books, maps, prints Good areas are the lanes south of the British Museum and Cecil Court, off St Martin's Lane. Shops to seek out include: Maggs Bros, 50 Berkeley Square, W1 (493 7160); Bernard

Quaritch, 5 Lower John Street, W1 (734 2983), very splendid, the biggest and makes the biggest deals; Quinto Bookshops, 83 Marylebone High Street, W1 (935 9303) and 48a Charing Cross Road, WC2 (379 7669), the Marylebone shop is nicest; Ben Weinreb, 93 Great Russell Street, WC1 (636 4895). Bloomsbury Book Auctions, 3 Hardwick Street, EC1 (636 1945) hold good auctions twice a month. In Knightsbridge, Charles Woodruff, 26 Yeoman's Row, SW3 (584 0370, by appointment only). All of these have good stock on London.

Carpets and textiles Mysterious but alluring subjects for most people. Best to go and see a few at the V&A, buy a copy of *Hali* magazine at the V&A shop (or subscribe to it at Kingsgate House, Kingsgate Place, NW6, tel 328 9341), watch a few go under the hammer at the auction houses and then visit some of these shops, all well-established and reliable. Bernadout & Bernadout, 7 Thurloe Place, SW7 (584 7658), big stock with a large turnover; The Contemporary Textile Gallery, 10 Golden Square, W1 (439 9071), for new modern carpets; David Black Oriental Carpets, 96 Portland Road, W11 (727 2566), established the market for kilims and now has oldest to newest pieces; Heskia, 19 Mount Street, W1 (629 1483), up-market decorative; C John, 70 South Audley Street, W1 (493 5288), up-market decorative, supplies the royals; Alexander Juran, 74 New Bond Street, W1 (629 2550), for decorative and collectors' market; Clive Loveless, 29 Kelfield Gardens, W10 (969 5831, by appointment only), for tribal and nomadic textile collectors; Clive Rogers, 1st floor, 50 South Molton Street, W1 (629 4478), wide-ranging stock; The Rug Shop, 1 Elystan Street, SW3 (584 8724), decorative rugs and kilims; The Textile Gallery, 4 Castellain Road, NW9 (286 1747, by appointment only), Michael Franses's treasures for collectors; Vigo Carpet Gallery, 6a Vigo Street, W1 (439 6971), large decorative and collectors' stock; Zadah Persian Carpets, 1st floor, 20 Dering Street, W1 (493 2622).

Clocks Bobinet, 102 Mount Street, W1 (408 0333); J Carlton-Smith, 17 Ryder Street, SW1 (930 6622); Ronald Lee, 1–9 Bruton Place, W1 (499 6266), and several in and around Camden Passage.

Coins Worth visiting Cutler Street market on Saturday morning (see p. 255); then to AH Baldwin & Co, 7 Blenheim Street, W1 (493 2445) for auctions; Seaby's, 8 Cavendish Square, W1 (631 3707); Spink & Son Ltd, 5 King Street, SW1 (930 7888).

Furniture For English: Mallett & Son Ltd, 40 New Bond Street, W1 (499 7411); Norman Adams, 8 Hans Road, SW3 (589 5266); Stair & Co, 120 Mount Street, W1 (499 1784) – and for English enamel boxes, etc to go with it, Halcyon Days, 105 New Bond Street, W1 (629 8811). For continental: Partridge, 144–6 New Bond Street, W1 (629 0834); William Redford, 9 Mount Street, W1 (629 1165); OF Wilson, Queens Elm Parade, SW3 (352 9554). For early furniture: Barling of Mount Street, 112 Mount Street, W1 (499 2858). There are equally interesting batches on Pimlico and Fulham roads.

Glass WGT Burne, 11 Elystan Street, SW3 (589 6074); Delomosne & Son Ltd, 4 Campden Hill Road, W8 (937 1804).

Militaria Under Two Flags, 4 St Christopher's Place, W1 (935 6934).

Oriental Odile Cavendish, 14 Lowndes Street, SW1 (235 2491, by appointment), especially lacquer; Ciancimino, 99 Pimlico Road, SW1 (730 9950); Shirley Day, 91b Jermyn Street, SW1 (839 2804); Eskenazi Ltd, Foxglove House, Piccadilly, W1 (493 5464); John Sparks Ltd, 128 Mount Street, W1 (499 2265); Spink & Son Ltd, 5–7 King Street, SW1 (930 7888); Woods Wilson, 103 Pimlico Road, SW1 (730 2558). For India in particular: Joss Graham, 10 Eccleston Street, SW1 (730 4370); Indar Pasricha, 3 Shepherd Street, W1 (493 0771); Spink & Son (see above); Tooth Paintings, 29 New Bond Street (491 0864).

Paintings, drawings, engravings, prints A vast array of galleries, many of whom mount exhibitions to rival the museums; see *Galleries* magazine, above; see also pp. 140–48 for a selection of galleries stocking antique and contemporary pictures. A cluster of mixed treats to start with might include: Arthur Ackermann & Sons (sporting), 3 Old Bond Street, W1 (493 3288); Thomas Agnew & Son, 43 Old Bond Street, W1 (629 6176); The Leger Galleries (English), 13 Old Bond Street, W1 (629 3538); Connaught Brown (turn-of-the-century), 2 Albemarle Street, W1 (408 0362); and for contemporary art Marlborough Fine Art (modern), 6 Albemarle Street, W1 (629 5161); Marlborough Graphics, 39 Old Bond Street, W1 (629 5161); and CCA Galleries (prints), 8 Dover Street, W1 (499 6701).

Porcelain, pottery The Antique Porcelain Company, 149 New Bond Street, W1 (629 1254); Heirloom & Howard, 1 Hay Hill, W1 (493 5868), for armorial antiques; Jonathan Horne, 66b&c Kensington Church Street, W8 (221 5658); Rogers De Rin, 76 Royal Hospital Road, SW3 (352 9007); also, Richard Dennis, see Art Nouveau.

Silver, jewellery Most of these stock both new

and old pieces. Asprey, 165 New Bond Street, W1 (493 6767); N Bloom, 40 Conduit Street, W1 (629 5060); JH Bourdon-Smith, 24 Mason's Yard, SW1 (839 4714); Garrard, 112 Regent Street, W1 (734 7020), worth a visit for the shop alone; Hennell, 12 New Bond Street, W1 (629 6888); DS Lavender, 16b Grafton Street, W1 (629 1782); The London Silver Vaults, Chancery House, 53–65 Chancery Lane, WC2 (242 3844) for a warren of overflowing shops; SJ Phillips Ltd, 139 New Bond Street, W1 (629 6261); SJ Shrubsole, 43 Museum Street, WC1 (405 2712); Wartski, 14 Grafton Street, W1 (493 1141). For more jewellers who have old and new sparkles: Boucheron, 180 New Bond Street, W1 (493 0983); Cartier, 175 New Bond Street, W1 (493 6962); Chaumet, 178 New Bond Street, W1 (629 0136); Collingwood of Conduit Street, 46 Conduit Street, W1 (734 2656), adorn British royal necks, wrists and ears; Stuart Devlin, 90/92 St John Street, EC1 (235 547), creates miracles for the Queen and others; Charles De Temple, 52 Jermyn Street, SW1 (499 3639); Tiffany, 25 Old Bond Street, W1 (409 2790). It is also worth exploring the little shops all along Hatton Garden; good prices.

Russian Tzigany, 28–9 Dover Street, W1 (491 1007); The Winter Palace, 69 Kensington Church Street, W8 937 2410).

Scientific instruments Harriet Wynter, 50 Redcliffe Road, SW10 (352 6494).

Stamps Monthly exhibitions at the Strand Palace Hotel, WC2 (836 8080) and the National Postal Museum (see p. 67), the big centres focus on the Strand around Stanley Gibbons International, 399 Strand, WC2 (836 8444), with nearby London International Stamp Centre, 27 King Street, WC2, where 40 or so merchants deal in their speciality. To find out more, contact the British Philatelic Trust, Alder House, 1 Aldersgate Street, EC1 (726 6721); the British Philatelic Federation, 314 Vauxhall Bridge Road, SW1 (828 4416).

BEAUTY PRODUCTS AND PERFUMES The Body Shop, see Chains, above; Boots, see Late Night Shopping, above; Cosmetics à la Carte, 16 Motcomb Street, SW1 (235 0596), for made-to-measure cosmetics; Crabtree and Evelyn, 6 Kensington Church Street, W8 (937 5029); Czech and Speake, 39c Jermyn Street, SW1 (439 0216); Floris, 89 Jermyn Street, SW1 (930 2885); Mary Chess, 7 Shepherd Market, W1 (629 5152) for almost too English perfumes; Neal's Yard Apothecary, 2 Neal's Yard, WC2 (379 7222); Penhaligon's, 41

Wellington Street, WC2 (836 2150); The Secret Garden, 153 Regent Street, W1 (439 3101), aromatherapist using natural fragrant oils, beautifully packaged for daily use. For men: Ivan's, 20 Jermyn Street, SW1 (930 8753); George Trumper, 9 Curzon Street, W1 (499 1850). See also Health and fitness centres and Opting Out sections of Fitness, Fresh air and Peace chapter, pp. 341, 349–50.

BOOKS More than 500 shops to choose from, including specialists for dance, motorcars, India and foreign languages. The best of the generalists, all with good staff, will know where to send a specialist: Dillons Arts Books, 8 Long Acre, WC2 (836 1359); Dillons University Bookshop, 82 Gower Street, WC1 (636 1577); Hatchards, 187 Piccadilly, W1 (439 9921), much better than its two branches; John Sandoe, 10 Blacklands Terrace, SW3 (589 9473); Ian Shipley, 70 Charing Cross Road, WC2 (836 4872) for arts; Truslove & Hanson, 205 Sloane Street, SW1 (235 2128); Waterstone, see Late Night shopping above; Zwemmer, 80 Charing Cross Road, WC2 (836 4710). All these stock numerous volumes on London; in addition, there are dazzling concentrations of London books at the LTB Information Office at Victoria Station (see p. 3), and at the Architectural Association bookshop (see p. 166).

CHEMIST See Late Night shopping, above.

CLOTHES Men's and women's clothes: the best way to find what you want is to flick through the fashion magazines (see Information, above). On the street, good areas are on and around Bond Street and Knightsbridge for designer clothes; Regent Street and Knightsbridge corner for traditional British; King's Road, Covent Garden, St Christopher's Place, Soho and the eastern end of Kensington High Street (Kensington Market, Hyper Hyper) for pace-setting young fashion. See Areas, One-stop shops and Chain stores, above.

Here are a few suggestions for specific items:

Accessories For Sock Shop and Tie Rack, see Chains, above. Accessorize, Unit 22, The Market, Covent Garden, WC2 (240 2107); Cobra, 5 Portobello Green, 281 Portobello Road, W10 (960 4874); Timney Fowler, 388 King's Road, SW3 (351 6562); Hermes, 155 New Bond Street, W1 (499 8856) for The Scarf; Hyper Hyper, 26–40 Kensington High Street, W8 (937 6964); Kensington Market, 49–53 Kensington High Street, W8 (937 1572); TM Lewin & Sons, 106 Jermyn Street,

SW1 (930 4291) for special ties; Paul Longmire, 12 Bury Street, SW1 (930 8720), for the smartest cufflinks, tie-pins and key rings which are also supplied to the Queen; Reputation, 186 Kensington Park Road, W11 (221 7641) for scarves, brollies, etc; Paul Smith, 43–4 Floral Street, WC2 (379 7133); The Watch Gallery, 129 Fulham Road, SW3 (581 3239), with a glass of wine while you select your timekeeper; XYZ, 74 Heath Street, NW3 (794 3242).

Children's clothes   The two big stores are Mothercare, 461 Oxford Street, W1 (629 6621) with clothes, equipment and good books, and Marks and Spencer, see Chains above. More specialised shops include: Additions, 52 Chiltern Street, W1 (486 3065) for the fashionable; Children's Bazaar, 162c Sloane Street, SW1 (730 8901) for second-hand bargains; InStep, 45 St John's Wood High Street, W8 (722 7634) for shoes of all kinds, carefully fitted, with cartoon videos to keep kids happy; Kid's Plus, 9 Church Street, NW8 (723 5517) for British and worldwide fashion favourites from Osh Kosh on; Kid's Stuff, 482 Roman Road, E3 (981 1652), good value and worth a visit if you are checking out the adult Roman Road bargains nearby, see Sale Shops, below; Laura Ashley, 9 Harriet Street, SW1 (235 9796) for prettiness; Little Perishers, 139 Upper Street, N1 (226 3344) for up-market clothes; Meeny's USA, 163 Draycott Avenue, SW3 (581 2163), now for US and more; Please Mum, 22 Sloane Street, SW1 (235 5303), over-the-top extravaganzas, worth a window-shop; Youngsters, 230 Portobello Road, W10 (221 2910) for traditional and modern; Zero Four Plus, 53 South Molton Street, W1 (493 4920) for designer clothes and nursery extras.

Costume and fashion jewellery   Annabel Jones, 52 Beauchamp Place, SW3 (589 3215) for old, new and glittering fun; André Bogaert, 5 South Molton Street, W1 (493 4869); Butler & Wilson, 189 Fulham Road, SW3 (352 3045) for Sloane sparkles; Chapel Market (indoor arcade), N1 for stalls piled high with jolly gems; Comme Ci Comme Ça, 63 Heath Street, NW3 (431 3361); Lesley Craze, 5 Essex Road, N1 (226 3200) for a wide choice of rising contemporary jewellers; Detail, 49 Endell Street, WC2 (379 6940); Fior, 22 New Bond Street, W1 (589 0053); Isis, 3 Portobello Green, 281 Portobello Road, W10 968 5055); David Joseph, 33 Clerkenwell Road, EC1 (250 1462) for contemporary designers; Ken Lane, 66 South Molton Street, W1 (584 5299); Liberty, see One-stop shops above, ground floor dripping with delights; Sheer Deca-

dence, 44 Monmouth Street, WC2 (379 4161). To see what other young jewellers are creating, catch one of the occasional selling exhibitions at the Goldsmith's Hall, Foster Lane, EC2 (606 8971). For pricier rocks, see Silver, jewellery, under Antiques above.

Dressmakers, ballgowns   Antiquarius, 135 King's Road, especially Biddulph & Banham; Belville-Sassoon, 73 Pavilion Road, SW1 (235 3087) for Ascot elegance; Chelsea Design Company, 65 Sidney Street, SW3 (352 4636); Droopy and Browns, 16 St Christopher's Place, W1 (935 3198); David Fielden, 137 King's Road, SW3 (351 1745); Hetherington, 289 King's Road, SW3 (351 0880); Fred's, Smith Street, SW3 (730 2754) for the young; Bruce Oldfield, 27 Beauchamp Place, SW3 (584 1363); Zandra Rhodes, 14a Grafton Street, W1 (499 6695); Rich Bitch, 83 Marylebone High Street, W1 (486 4688); Tatters, 74 Fulham Road, SW3 (584 1532).

Hats   Traditional men's: Bates, 21a Jermyn Street, SW1 (734 2722); Herbert Johnson, 13 Old Burlington Street, W1 (439 7397); Lock & Co, 6 St James's Street, SW1 (930 5849). High fashion women's: David Shilling, 44 Chiltern Street, W1 (935 8473); Stephen Jones, 34 Lexington Street, W1 (734 9666). Young and fun: The Hat Shop, 58 Neal Street, WC2 (836 6718); Marina Killery, 44 Addison Road, W14 (602 5421); Kirsten Woodward, 26 Portobello Green Arcade, W10 (960 0090).

Hiring clothes   see Entertainment chapter, pp. 285–6.

Leather   Etienne Aigner, 6–7 New Bond Street, W1 (491 7764) for all things, especially gloves; Henry's, 185 Brompton Road, SW3 (589 2011) and 201 Regent Street, W1 (437 6542) for sumptuous bags and baggage; Loewe, 25a New Bond Street, W1 (629 2961) for top Spanish leather; Mulberry, 12 Gees Court, St Christopher's Place, W1 (493 2546) for bags, belts and brollies.

Lingerie   As visitors are usually spotted filling two, even three wire baskets with knickers and bras, half the world must buy their undies from Marks and Spencer, see Chains above. For something more exciting: Bradley's, 83–5 Knightsbridge, SW1 (235 2902); Courtenay, 22–4 Brook Street, W1 (629 0542); Keturah Brown, 85 Regent's Park Road, NW1 (586 0512), for designer natural fabrics; Rose Lewis, 40 Knightsbridge, SW1 (235 6885), the tops for well-made, well-fitted, serious style; Madeleine Salons de Lingerie, 12 Henrietta Place, W1 (580 8575) for designer undies and expert fitting; Rigby & Peller, 2 Hans Road, SW1

(589 9293) for hand-made and high style corsetry; Ann Summers, 18 Edgware Road, W2 (262 4357), for unashamedly sexy undies, with branches in Soho; The White House, 51–2 New Bond Street, W1 (629 3521).

Rain For the anti-rain kit, see pp. 277–8.

Sale shops The best way to buy several designer outfits for the cost of one. Collections, 4 England's Lane, NW3 (586 1015); The Constant Sales Shop, 56 Fulham Road, SW3 (589 1458). It is also worth heading for the East End for designer bargains: Petticoat Lane Designer Fashion Market, between Middlesex and Goulstons streets, Sunday morning; 424, 424 Roman Road, E3 (980 4500); Dash, 511 Roman Road, E3 (980 9545); Ice, 504 Roman Road, E3 (980 2892); Zee E3, 434–6 Roman Road, E3 (981 3333). Camden Lock market has two or three stalls of high British fashion at low prices.

Second-hand shops A growing market and the best way to buy either cheap newish post-war fashions or more expensive proper antiques. American Classics, 20 Endell Street, WC2 (831 1210) for the James Dean look; Annie's, 10 Camden Passage, N1 (359 0796), also at 400–5 King's Road, SW10 (351 5229); Antiquarius, see Antiques above especially Biddulph & Benham at Stand Y5; Blax Period & Original Clothing, 8 & 11 Sicilian Avenue, WC1 (404 0125) for both sexes; Cobwebs, 60 Islington Park Road, N1 (359 8090); Cornucopia, 12 Tatchbrook Street, SW1 (828 5752); Cuba, 56 New Oxford Street, WC1 (580 7740); Designs, 60 Rosslyn Hill, NW3 (435 0100); Hackett Gentlemans Clothiers, 65c New King's Road, SW6 (731 2790/7129), merits a detour for the young fogey look; High Society, 46 Cross Street, N1 (226 6863); Pamela, 93 Walton Street, SW3 (589 6852), quiet quality; Phlip, 191 King's Road, SW3 (352 4332); Plug, 291 Portobello Road, W10 (969 7150); Redress, 51 Endell Street, WC2 (240 5006); Spatz, 48 Monmouth Street, WC2 (379 0703); Sam Walker, 41 Neal Street, WC2 (240 7800), for men, especially cufflinks and buttons.

Shoes Someone once counted the shoeshops in Oxford Street and was then too exhausted to do anything else all day. For something more special than the chains: Manolo Blahnik, 40 Old Church Street, SW3 (352 8622); Church's Shoes, 163 New Bond Street, W1 (499 9449); George Deliss, 41 Beauchamp Place, SW1 (584 3321), for hand-made shoes; Ferragamo, 24 Old Bond Street, W1 (629 5007); Maud Frizon, 30 Old Bond Street, W1 (493 5989); Charles Jourdan, 39–43 Brompton Road, SW3 (581 3333); Hobbs, 47 South Molton Street, W1 (629 0750); John Lobb, 9 St James's Street, SW1 (930 3664), who shoe royal feet; The London Espadrille Centre, 79 King's Road, SW3 (351 4634); Johnny Moke, 396 King's Road, SW10 (351 2232); Pied à Terre, 19 South Molton Street, W1 (629 1362) and elsewhere; Rayne, 15–6 New Bond Street, W1 (493 9077); Russell & Bromley, 24 New Bond Street, W1 (629 6903), their largest London store, huge selection of own make and others.

Tailoring and bespoke men's clothes For tailors: Blades, 8 Burlington Gardens, W1 (734 8911); Douglas Hayward, 95 Mount Street, W1 (499 5574); Huntsman, 11 Savile Row, W1 (734 7441); Kilgour, French & Stanbury, 8 Savile Row, W1 (734 6905); Henry Poole, 15 Savile Row, W1 (734 5985); and for a more fashion-conscious cut Tommy Nutter, 19 Savile Row, W1 (734 0831). For shirts: Ashley & Blake, 42 Beauchamp Place, SW3 (584 2682); Beale & Inman, 131 New Bond Street, W1 (629 4723); Mr Fish, 52 Pimlico Road, SW1 (730 3193), Lady Miranda Nuttall buys the amazing cloth, Michael F has it tailored; Harvie & Hudson, 77 & 79 Jermyn Street, SW1 (839 3578); Hilditch & Key, 73 Jermyn Street, SW1 (930 5336); New & Lingwood, 53 Jermyn Street, SW1 (493 9621); Sulka, 19 Old Bond Street, W1 (493 4468), especially for silk shirts, pyjamas and dressing-gowns; Turnbull & Asser, 71–2 Jermyn Street, SW1 (930 0502). For both men and women: Hawes & Curtis, 2 Burlington Gardens, W1 (493 2200); Thresher & Glenny, Lancaster Place, The Strand, WC2 (836 4608).

Woollens Benetton, see Chains above; Berk, 45–50 Burlington Arcade, W1 (493 0028), for classics; Bill, 93 New Bond Street, W1 (629 2837) for classics; Canterbury of NZ, 101 Marylebone High Street, W1 (486 0702); The China Market and Reject Wool Shop, Unit 26, The Market, Covent Garden, WC2 (836 6010) for seconds and end-of-line knits from top Scottish houses; Edna Ronay, 141 King's Road, SW3 (352 1085), her woollens also sold in Liberty's; Ehrmen, 21/22 Vicarage Gate, W8 (937 4568), for Kaffe Fasset designs; No. 1 Copenhagen Street, 1 Copenhagen Street, N1 (833 3929) for one-off young British designs; Peal & Co, 37 Burlington Arcade, W1 (493 9220) for exciting cashmere. Patricia Roberts, 31 James Street, WC1 (379 6660), 60 Kinnerton Street, SW1 (235 4742) and 236 Brompton Road, SW3 (589 9741) for dazzling colour; The Scotch House, 2 Brompton Road, SW1 (581 2151) for classics; Scottish Merchant, 16 New Row, WC2 (836 2207), for fashionable tradition; Westaway &

Westaway, 62–5 Great Russell Street, WC1 (405 4479) and 92 Great Russell Street, WC1 (636 1718), the second for hand-knitted Shetland and Aquascutum, both for bargain prices.

CRAFTS   Very lively in London. First stops are the Contemporary Applied Arts, 43 Earlham Street, WC2 (836 6993) and the Crafts Council Gallery and Information Section, 12 Waterloo Place, SW1 (930 4811); both are showcases for British craftsmen, with exhibitions and a service to find craftsmen to commission and information on the London crafts scene – the Crafts Council has a useful London map plotting the crafts shops it recommends (its shop is in the V&A). Camden Lock Market, see above, has a cluster of good shops open Tues–Sun; The Apple Market, Covent Garden, has more, see above. The Craftsmen Potters Shop, 7 Marshall Street, W1 (437 7605), will arrange a studio visit to see more of a potter's work. Other shops include: Anatole Orient, 318 Portobello Road, W10 (969 4119), for rising and risen British ceramicists (several other crafts shops near by); Casson Gallery, 73 Marylebone Lane, W1 (487 5080); Coleridge, 192 Piccadilly, W1 (437 0106) for studio glass; Contemporary Textiles Gallery, 10 Golden Square, W1 (439 9071); The Glasshouse, 65 Long Acre, WC2 (836 9785); Harlequin House, 3 Kensington Mall, W8 (221 8629) for puppets; JK Hill, 151 Fulham Road, SW3 (584 7529); A & T Hinks, Unit 18, 21 Wren Street, WC1 (278 3815) for jack-in-the-boxes; Kikapu, 38 King Street, WC2 (240 6098); Naturally British, 113 New Row, WC2 (240 0551). Two Clerkenwell complexes are well worth contacting: Pennybank Chambers, Clerkenwell Road, EC1 (251 0276) for about 80 craftsmen, see p. 203; 31 Clerkenwell Close, EC1 (251 4821, by appointment only) for 160 units of specialist craftsmen, see p. 204. Design agent Sharon Plant has her crafts and design showcase house in Highbury (354 3073, by appointment only) so customers can see pieces in situ before commissioning one for themselves.

FLORISTS   The flower stalls on street corners and by Underground stations have quality blossoms and keep late hours. They often stand on sites handed down through the family; good ones for both flowers and local gossip from the flower men are outside Green Park Underground station and in Belgrave Square. The most perfect London guest asks his hostess for the colours of her dining-room decoration and then orders from a florist an arrangement complementing it to be delivered in the early evening. Florists usually take telephone orders with credit cards; some are members of Interflora for sending flowers, plants and grand bouquets Londonwide, nationwide and worldwide – the risk is that the shop used the other end might be inferior to the one where you order this end. Good florists include: Caroline Dickenson, 35 Park Street, W1 (499 6363), whose flowers are flown in from the South of France (including very long stemmed roses) twice a week, which accounts for the exceptional quality; Felton & Sons, 220–224 Brompton Road, SW3 (589 4433); The Flowersmith, 34 Shelton Street, WC2 (240 6688); Janda, for telephone orders (732 3641/2/3, 24-hour booking on 0892 834263); Edward Goodyear, 45 Brook Street, W1 (629 1508) and at 45 Knightsbridge, SW1 (235 8344) and in The Savoy Hotel, The Strand, WC2 (836 4343), whose Brook Street branch arranges the blossoms for Claridge's next door; Kenneth Turner, 8 Avery Row, W1 (499 4952/3) for arrangements only; Moyses Stevens, 6 Bruton Street, W1 (493 8171) for everything; Joan Palmer, 31 Palmer Street, SW1 (222 4364) where the flowers to be sent are selected from her shop and then packaged up; Pulbrook and Gould, 181 Sloane Street, SW1 (235 3920/3186) where the flowers are extra fresh and long-lasting as many come up from the country gardens of Lady P and her friends.

FOOD – GENERAL

Food halls   Best deluxe food halls are Fortnum & Mason, Harrods and Selfridges; best mainstay food hall is Marks and Spencer. See also Late Night shopping for One-stop shops.

General gourmets   Good for buying instant delicious meals, especially picnics; see also Late Night shopping above. Les Amis Gourmands, 30 James Street, WC2 (836 4665), French; Athenian Grocery, 16a Moscow Road, W2 (229 6280), Greek, Lebanese and more; Bartholdi & Son, 4 Charlotte Street, W1 (636 3762), Swiss; Beetons, 3 Abingdon Road, W8 (937 3442); Boucherie Lamartine, 229 Ebury Street, SW1 (730 4175), owned by the Roux brothers, and much more like *a patisserie-traiteur* – lemon pie a dream; I Camisa, 61 Old Compton Street, W1 (437 4686) Italian; The Delicatessen Shop, 23 South End Road, NW3 (435 7315); Fouqet of Knightsbridge, 58 Beauchamp Place, SW3 (581 5540), direct from Paris; The German Food Centre, 44 Knightsbridge, SW1 (235 5760); Gourmets des Gascognes, 3 Hillgate Street, W8 (221 4131), *patisserie-traiteur extraordinaire*; The

Greek Food Centre, 12 Inverness Street, NW1 (485 6544); Hobbs & Co, 29 South Audley Street, W1 (409 1058); JA Centre, 348–356 Regent's Park Road, N3 (346 1042), Japanese, even sushi; Justin de Blank Provisions, 42 Elizabeth Street, SW1 (730 0605); Lina Stores, 18 Brewer Street, W1 (438 6482), Italian; Lisboa, 54 and 57 Golborne Road, W10 (969 1052 for delicatessen, 968 5242 for patisserie), Portuguese; Loon Fung Supermarket, 42–4 Gerrard Street, W1 (437 7332), even stock frozen dim sum; Neal's Yard complex, WC2, with Bakery (836 5199), Farm Shop (836 1066) and the Wholefood Warehouse round at 31 Shorts Gardens, WC2 (836 5151); Rosslyn Delicatessen, 56 Rosslyn Hill, NW3 (431 2309), for French and Jewish foods; The Spanish Delicatessen, 125 Ledbury Road, W11 (229 2127); Les Specialités St Quentin, 256 Brompton Road, SW3 (225 1664); The Swedish Table, 7 Paddington Street, W1 (486 7077), a drop of Sweden.

FOOD – SPECIALIST SHOPS   These are a few treats, but the gourmet shops (see above) are often excellent for patisserie and cheeses.

Bakes and cakes   Ambala Sweet Centre, 112 Drummond Street, NW1 (387 3521), for the best Indian sweetmeats this side of Delhi; Justin de Blank Hygienic Bakery, 46a Walton Street, SW3 (589 4743), their croissants have a royal warrant; Louis, 32 Heath Street, NW3 (435 9908); Patisserie Samedi, 880d Brompton Road, SW7 (584 1885); Petticoat Lane Bakeries, 41–3 Wentworth Street, E1 (247 2953), Jewish; See also the Gourmet food shops above, and breakfast and teatime suggestions in the Food and Drink chapter, pp. 309–19, many of which sell their bread and cakes over the counter, too.

Cheese   Jeroboams, 24 Bute Street, SW7 (225 2232); The London Cheese Company, 21 Goodge Street, W1 (631 4191); Neal's Yard, whose huge range of English cheeses includes many unusual and unpasteurised ones, see General Gourmet shops above; Paxton and Whitfield, 93 Jermyn Street, SW1 (930 9892), who run a mail order service, a cheese club and give advice on which cheeses will travel best. See also Harrods, who stock about 500.

Chocolate   Harrods and Selfridges food halls have international dreamworlds for chocaholics. In addition: Bendicks, 55 Wigmore Street, W1 (935 7272); Charbonnel et Walker, 24 Old Bond Street, W1 (629 4396), their chocolates are no longer coded by number, but they can still be packed in huge circular boxes with the receiver's name in gold-foiled chockies; Prestat, 14 Princes Arcade, W1 (629 4838), especially good for truffles and seasonal chocolates; Mirandy et Filles, 3 Park Road, Baker Street, NW1 (262 1906), formerly Clare's Chocolates, whose name they still use; Rococo, 321 King's Road, SW3 (352 5857), newer arrival, with added lusciousness.

Health food   Neal's Yard complex, see gourmet shops above, outdoes all the others and merits a detour.

Ice-Cream   See p. 303.

Tea, coffee   For tea: The Tea House, 15a Neal Street, WC2 (240 7539); Whittards of Chelsea, 111 Fulham Road, SW3 (589 4261), merits a detour for teas and tisanes imported direct from all over the world. For coffee: Algerian Coffee Stores, 52 Old Compton Street, W1 (437 2480); L Fern & Co, 27 Rathbone Place, W1 (636 2237); HR Higgins, 42 South Molton Street, W1 (499 5912); Monmouth Coffee House, 27 Monmouth Street, WC2 (836 5272). For both: The Drury Tea and Coffee Company, 37 Drury Lane, WC2 (836 2607), 3 New Row, WC2 (836 1960) and 3 Mepham Street, SE1 (928 0144).

INTERIORS, THE HOME   Best areas for general shops are Tottenham Court Road and Chelsea; best for current design and specialists shops is Covent Garden; best for safe modernish design and specialists is Chelsea. To evaluate the state of British design, visit its showcase, The Design Centre, 28 Haymarket, SW1 (839 8000) with a shop on ground and first floors and reference information and services in the basement.

General stores   Colefax & Fowler, 39 Brook Street, W1 (493 2231); Conran Shop, 77 Fulham Road, SW3 (589 7401) for Sir Terence Conran's sharp-eyed design team's selection, especially glass and tableware; Designer's Guild, 271 & 277 King's road, SW3 (351 5775) for Patricia Guild's designs and now Howard Hodgkin's fabrics; Joseph Pour La Maison, 16 Sloane Street, SW1 (235 9868); Habitat, 196 Tottenham Court Road, W1 (631 3880) and Heal's, 196 Tottenham Court Road, W1 (636 1666), designer knight Sir Terence Conran's flagships; The Irish Shop, 11 Duke Street, W1 (935 1366) and 80 Buckingham Gate, SW1 (222 7132); Practical Styling, 16–18 St Giles High Street, WC2 (240 3711); Reject Shop, 245 Brompton Road, SW3 (584 7611), 234 King's Road, SW3 (352 2750) and 209 Tottenham Court Road, W1 (580 2895); Sanderson, 53 Berners Street, W1 (636 7800).

Specialists Authentics, 42 Shelton Street, WC2 (240 9845); Cole & Son, 18 Mortimer Street, W1 (580 5369) for English chintzes and hand-painted wallpapers; The Copper Shop, 48 Neal Street, WC2 (836 2984); Crucial, 204 Kensington Park Road, W11 (229 1940) for the whackiest new designs; David Mellor, 26 James Street, WC2 (379 6947) for kitchen supplies; Divertimenti, 68–72 Marylebone Lane, W1 (935 0689) and 139–41 Fulham Road, SW3 (581 8065) for designer kitchen supplies; Givens Irish Linen Store, 207 King's Road, SW3 (352 6352); Mary Fox Linton, 249 Fulham Road, SW3 (351 0273); The Monogrammed Linen Shop, 168 Walton Street, SW3 (589 4033); One Off, 56 Neal Street, WC2 (379 7796); Osborne & Little, 304 King's Road, SW3 (352 1456); Zoffany, 27a Motcomb Street, SW1 (235 5295) for fabrics and wallpapers.

For china, glass and cutlery Garrard, see Silver in antiques, above; General Trading Company, see One-stop shops, above; Gered Wedgwood & Spode, 173 Piccadilly, W1 (629 2614), contrary to popular belief this is where the largest selection of Wedgwood and Spode is to be found outside the factories; Thomas Goode, 19 South Audley Street, W1 (499 2823), probably the widest selection, certainly the most beautiful china shop; Liberty, see One-stop shops, above; Reject China Shop, 33–5 Beauchamp Place, SW3 (581 0737), open Sunday, with another branch at 134 Regent Street, W1 (437 3576). For Royal Doulton fans, the London headquarters of the International Collectors Club is Royal Doulton Gallery, 167 Piccadilly, W1 (749 9191). See also Crafts, above.

MUSIC Music maniacs like Paul Gambaccini and John Savage agree that London is the world centre for buying back music, re-issues of both UK and US records – indeed, all post-war popular music.

The record mega-stores Good for discounts, so worth comparing prices. Virgin Megastore, 14–16 Oxford Street, W1 (631 1234), owner Richard Branson's aim is to stock everything released, good back rock list; HMV, 363 Oxford Street, W1 (629 1240), especially classical Our Price Records, 33 King's Road, SW3 (730 1061), the biggest branch of a big chain; Tower Records, Swan & Edgar Building, Piccadilly Circus, W1 (439 2500), open until midnight, especially strong on classical and musicals.

Specialists Soho is the centre. Boosey & Hawkes, 295 Regent Street, W1 (580 2060) for sheet music and instruments; Chappell, 50 New Bond Street, W1 (491 2777) for sheet music and instruments;

Colletts, 129–31 Charing Cross Road, WC2 (734 0782) for all Eastern European; Daddy Kool, 94 Dean Street, W1 (437 3535) for reggae; Dobells, 21 Tower Street, WC2 (240 1354) for new and old jazz and blues; Early Music Shop, 47 Chiltern Street, W1 (935 1242); 58 Dean Street, W1 (437 4500) for musical and film sound tracks; Groove Records, 52 Greek Street, W1 (437 4711) for soul and up-to-the-minute US imports (cash buys only); Novello, 8 Lower James Street, W1 (734 8080) for sheet music and books; Ray's Jazz, 180 Shaftesbury Avenue, WC2 (229 8541) for new and old jazz including 78s; Rough Trade, 130 Talbot Road, W11 (229 8541) for the best stock of independent and underground music in the UK; Stern's, 116 Whitfield Street, W1 (387 5550) for African and Latin.

Stores devoted to second-hand records include: Honest Jon's Records, 278 Portobello Road, W10 (969 9822) for all popular music; Plastic Passion, 2 Blenheim Crescent, W11 (229 5424) for 60s psychodelia; Rock On, 3 Kentish Town Road, NW1 (no tel) for rock 'n' roll, R & B.

NEWSPAPERS AND MAGAZINES For early newspaper buying see Entertainment chapter, p. 300. WH Smith is the biggest chain, see Chains above. Newsagents with a wide stock that includes plenty of foreign publications include Capital Newsagents, 48 Old Compton Street, W1 (437 2479), good for Greek, Israeli, Turkish, Portuguese and Indian; Capital Newsagents, 33 Queensway, W2 (229 8007), as good as its Soho brother, with added Arabic stock; A Morone & Son, 68 Old Compton Street, W1 (437 2847), for worldwide stock; Newspoint, 104–6 Long Acre, WC2 (240 7645), good for European, American and Australian.

Specialists Birthday issues of *The Times* 1880–94, Capital House, Market Place, W3 (993 5092); Comic Showcase, 17 Monmouth Street, WC2 (240 3664) for UK and US, new and old; David Godfry's Old Newspaper Shop, 37 Kinnerton Street, SW1 (235 7788); Gray's Inn Road street stalls for old copies of The Times and others; Japan Centre Musashi, 66–8 Brewer Street, W1 (439 8035) for the latest Japanese newspapers, mags and books; The London Comic Shop, 39 Great Russell Street, WC1 (636 1011) for all kinds, worldwide, new and old; Sotheby's bookstall, see above, for art and antique trade magazines; The V&A museum for art magazines; The Vintage Magazine Shop, 39–41 Brewer Street, W1 (439 8525).

PHOTOGRAPHY   To have films developed fast and well, two groups offer a 60-minute service and a same-day enlargement service: Photo Inn has branches at 12 Oxford Street, W1 (580 5858), the top of South Molton Street (629 7911) and elsewhere; City Photo branches include 237 Regent Street, W1 (493 7579) and The Trocadero, Piccadilly Circus, W1 (437 4580) which opens Mon–Sat 10am–10pm and Sun noon–10pm. In addition, the chemists Boots and Underwoods develop films.

Photographic shops   These are good for supplies, repairs and sometimes hiring (book well in advance in summer). Advance Technical AI Cameras, 9/12 St Anne's Court, off Wardour Street, W1 (734 0895), on-site craftsmen; Fox Talbot Cameras, 443 Strand, WC2 (379 6522); Jessop Photo Centre, 67 New Oxford Street, W1 (240 6077); Keith Johnson, 11 Great Marlborough Street, W1 (439 8811), EC Kingley & Co, 93 Tottenham Court Road, W1 (387 6500); Pelling and Cross, 104 Baker Street, W1 (380 1144).

To see or buy photographs   Hamiltons Gallery, 13 Carlos Place, W1 (499 9493); The Photographers' Gallery, 5–8 Great Newport Street, WC2 (240 5511); The Special Photographers Gallery, 21 Kensington Park Road, W11 (221 3489).

PRESENTS   Of course, any shop might produce the perfect present you seek, but here are some shops devoted to presents. See also Museum Shopping, Art and Antiques, Beauty and perfumes, Crafts, Florists suggestions above, and Stationery and Toys below. Of the one-stop shops, Liberty's is the best, followed by the General Trading Company for Chelsea shoppers, see above, and the more lighthearted Covent Garden General Store, see Late Night shopping, above.

Specialists   The Badge Shop, 18 Earlham Street, WC2 (836 9327); Break of Day, 10 Beauchamp Place, SW3 (581 3293), for delicate quality; Halcyon Days, 14 Brook Street, W1 (269 8811) for mini-antiques; Knutz, 1 Russell Street, WC2 (836 3117) for a good joke; Mysteries, 11 Monmouth Street, WC2 (240 3688) for psychic everything; Neal Street East, 5 Neal Street, WC2 (240 0136) for eastern delights; Nina Campbell, 9 Walton Street, SW3 (225 1011), pretty and pricey; Parrots, 56 Fulham Road, SW3 (584 5699), a Sloane favourite; Presents, 129 Sloane Street, SW1 (730 5457), another lighthearted Sloane seducer; Saville Edells, 25 Walton Street, SW3 (584 4398), pricey, useful and useless prezzies; Strangeways, 19 The Market, Covent Garden, WC2 (379 7675) for joke teapots and clocks. Two that merit the detour as you go to Camden Passage in Islington: Preposterous Presents, 262 Upper Street, N1 (226 4166) for wit, magic and jokes; and Gill Wing, 194 Upper Street, N1 (359 7697) opposite, for more stylish but still witty presents.

STATIONERY   Paperchase, 167 Fulham Road, SW3 (589 7839), with its bigger offspring at 213 Tottenham Court Road, W1 (580 8496) for paper everything and plenty of colour; Ryman's, see Chains above. For more specialists shops: Italian Paper Shop, 11 Brompton Arcade, SW3 (589 1668) for the most beautiful papers; Lefax, 28 Shelton Street, W1 (836 1977); Oggetti, 100 Jermyn Street, SW1 (930 4694) for high style; Penfriend, Bush House Arcade, Bush House, Aldwych, WC2 (836 9809) for pens and repairs of every kind; Phillip Poole, 182 Drury Lane, WC2 (405 7097) for traditional ink pens; Scribblers, 29 James Street, WC2 (240 7640); Smythson, 54 New Bond Street, W1 (629 8558), the smartest of all; The Walton Street Stationery Company, 97 Walton Street, SW3 (589 0777). Harrods is reputed to have the best Filofax department.

SPORT   Best general store is huge Lillywhites, Piccadilly Circus, SW1 (930 3181); poor seconds are Astral Sports and Leisure, basement of DH Evans, 318 Oxford Street, W1 (629 8800) for sports in general; and Olympus Sportswear, 301 Oxford Street, W1 (409 2619).

Specialists   Alpine Sports, 215 Kensington High Street, W8 (938 1911) for skiing, another branch at 956–8 Strand, WC2 (839 5161); Anello and Davide, 94 Charing Cross Road, WC2 (836 5019) for dancing; Cobra 2,000, 111 Oxford Street, W1 (439 1082) for stylish ballgame equipment; Freed's, 94 St Martin's Lane, WC2 (240 0432) for dancing; WH Gidden, 11d Clifford Street, W1 (734 2788) for good value country sporting clothes; Holland & Holland, 33 Bruton Street, W1 (499 4411) for guns, etc; House of Hardy, 61 Pall Mall, SW1 (839 5515), for anglers – some known to practise casting off with a new rod in the street; James Purdey & Sons, 57 South Audley Street, W1 (499 1801) for guns; Swaine, Adeney, Brigg & Sons, 185 Piccadilly, W1 (734 4277) for riding; Captain OM Watts, 45 Albemarle Street, W1 (493 4633) for sailing. For country sports, see Rain chapter, pp. 277–8; for workout clothes, see Health and fitness centres, p. 341.

TOYS, GAMES Hamleys, 188–96 Regent Street, W1 (734 3161) may be the biggest toy emporium in the world but it stocks a lot of junk among a few good items. To find out more about British hand-made toys, and how to commission them, contact The British Toymakers Guild, 240 The Broadway, SW19.

Quality toys and games Children's World, 29 Kensington High Street, W8 (937 6314) for books; Kristin Baybars, 3 Mansfield Road, Gospel Oak Village, NW3 (267 0934), merits a detour for British handmade toys; The Dolls House, 29 The Market, Covent Garden, WC2 (379 7243), all handmade and beautiful; Early Learning Centre, 225 Kensington High Street W8 (937 0419) and King's Road, SW3 (581 5764) for the current favourite education-al toys, famed throughout English speaking coun-tries; Frog Hollow, 15 Victoria Grove, W8 (581 5493) for tiny to big toys, open Sun; Galt, 30 Great Marlborough Street, W1 (734 0829) for edu-cational wooden toys; Harrods toy department, see One-stop shops above; Harvey Johns, 16–20 Parkway, NW1 (485 1718) for tiny to big toys and plenty of traditional games; Humla Children's Shop, 235 Camden High Street, NW1 (267 7151) for wooden German toys among the clothes; The Kite Shop, 69 Neal Street, WC2 (836 1666) in kits or ready to fly; The Party Place, 67 Gloucester Ave-nue, NW1 (586 0169) for everything for a good party, even the clown; Pollock's Toy Theatres, 44 The Market, Covent Garden, WC2 (379 7866) one of the best for old fashioned and modern toys and excellent jigsaw puzzles, with another shop attached to Pollock's Toy Museum, see p. 163; The Singing Tree, 69 New King's Road, SW6 (736 4527) for dolls' houses and their furnishings; Eric Snook, Unit 32, The Market, Covent Garden, WC2 (379 7681) for handmade specials; Steam Age, 19 Abingdon Road, W8 (938 1982) for model trains, even the answerphone message begins with a steam train whistle; Tiger Tiger, 219 King's Road, SW3 (352 8080) for a huge range of traditional and modern, many handmade, plus party fun; The Tree House, 235 Kensington High Street, W8 (937 7497) for tiny to big toys.

For older children and adults Beatties of Lon-don, 202 High Holborn, WC2 (405 6285) for model cars, railways, board games and more; Cabaret Mechanical Theatre, Units 33 and 34, The Market, Covent Garden, WC2 (379 7961) for contemporary automata; Games People Play, 5 Wellington Ter-race, Bayswater Road, W2 (727 9275) for war games, US games and multi-lingual Scrabble;

Just Games, 62 Brewer Street, W1 (734 6124) for beautifully made games; Virgin Games Centre, 100 Oxford Street, W1 (637 791) for regular and fashionable favourites.

TRANSPORT For hiring bicycles, see p. 263; to buy one, go to Condor Cycles, 144–8 Gray's Inn Road, WC1 (837 7641). To buy a classic vintage car: Paradise Garage, Downers Cottages, Old Town, Clapham SW4 (720 0054, best to telephone before-hand) for magnificent vehicles to buy or hire.

WINE London has the best range of wines at the best prices. To prime yourself on the wine scene, consult Jancis Robinson's *The Wine Book*, and for more in-depth reading her *Vines, Grapes and Wines*. The magazines with the latest tips are *Decanter* and *Wine*, both published monthly. To learn a little more, there are two good courses: Christie's Wine Course, Christie's South Kensington (Fine Art Course), 63b Old Brompton Road, SW7 (581 3933) and Leith's School of Food and Wine, 12 St Albans Grove, W8 (229 0177).

Buying at auction Great fun and there are bar-gains to be found but it is worth doing some homework on prices before raising your hand by mistake – a 1784 bottle of Château d'Yquem bot-tled for Thomas Jefferson went for £39,600 in 1986. As the quantities in each lot are large, it is often easier to buy with a few friends and then split the booty. Both everyday and special wines are offered but beware of wine merchants off-loading stock that their discerning clients would consider too old – for example, a simple white Muscadet over three years old. Before the auction there is a tast-ing, usually in the evening. The auction price does not include VAT, and it is important to check the catalogue carefully for each lot to see what taxes are payable – lots offered 'In Bond' will require hefty import duty to be paid. Regular wine auctions are held at Christie's, Christie's South Kensington and Sotheby's, see Art and Antiques, above.

Wine merchants Give reliable advice and attend to their clients' needs very well, but prices may be slightly higher. The best include: Berry Brothers & Rudd, 3 St James's Street, SW1 (930 1888/839 9033); Corney & Barrow, 118 Moorgate, EC2 (638 3124); Haynes Hanson & Clark, 36 Kensington Church Street, W8 (937 4650). Of the less grand, two cur-rent recommendations are Ostlers, 63a Clerken-well Road, EC1 (250 1522) and La Vigneronne, 105 Old Brompton Road, SW7 (589 6113), both good for their unblinkered approach, their range and for their regular wine tasting evenings (small fee).

High street shopping Best of the chains: Oddbins, who have central branches at 23 Earlham Street, WC2 (836 6331), 142 Fulham Road, SW10 (373 5715), 7 George Street, W1 (935 6727), 141 Notting Hill Gate, W11 (229 4082) and elsewhere. For supermarket wines, Sainsbury's, Tesco and Waitrose all have excellent selections, from everyday wines to own-label champagnes.

Warehouse shopping Current best are Majestic Wine Warehouses, where wine is sold by the case only, slightly further out but worth the journey; nearest branches are Unit B2 Albion Wharf, Hester Road, SW11 (223 2983), Arch 84, Goding Street, SE11 (587 1830).

Fitness and fresh air; beauty and peace

When the thought of one more museum, monument, show or shop is too much to bear, relax. For spectators, there is almost every kind of sport to watch in or near the city, and the best of British and world sport is broadcast on TV. For participants, many sports are readily accessible. For relaxing the body and mind more gently, there is a good range of health, fitness and dance centres. And for a stroll or a reviving jog amid trees and blossoms, the London parks are unsurpassed in quantity, quality and beauty.

Here is a selection, with information on how to find out more. If you are staying in a top hotel, the hall porter can often arrange golf, tennis, etc. If you have friends in London who are members of sports clubs, it is worth accepting any invitations to play or visit; facilities and settings are usually excellent. For a weekly checklist of events to watch and join, see *Time Out* and *City Limits*. Large newsagents stock a host of specialist magazines, from *Running* to *Bodytalk*, all packed with information on the latest events, equipment and gossip. Lillywhites, Piccadilly, W1 (930 3181) is a good general sports store; see p. 336 for more. To keep dry while watching sport in the rain, see p. 278.

Sport

SPORT ON TELEVISION AND RADIO   Events covered on television depend to an extent on British participation and taste. Big events such as Wimbledon tennis and cricket test matches are covered so well it is almost better than attending in person. Other British favourites given hours of air time include horse racing and snooker. Big blocks of sports broadcasting are on Saturday and Sunday afternoons and evenings and on Wednesday evening; Channel 4 caters for minority sports, including American football. For radio, test matches are broadcast live on Radio 3, sometimes through the night when played abroad; Wimbledon, soccer and other British obsessions are broadcast on Radio 2, which also gives an hourly sports bulletin every afternoon with a 15-minute sports round-up at 6.45pm. As schedules change, see daily newspapers for the most accurate programmes.

MAIN MULTI-SPORT SPECTATOR VENUES
Alexandra Palace, Wood Green, N22 (883 6477)
Crystal Palace National Sports Centre, Ledrington Road, SE19 (778 0131)
Royal Albert Hall, Kensington Gore, SW7 (589 8212)
Wembley Stadium and Arena, Wembley, Middlesex (902 1234)

PRIVATE SPORTS CLUBS   Some of these have reciprocal membership with clubs around the world; some, not all, have waiting lists for membership.
Cannons Sports Club, Cousin Lane, EC4

(283 0101); currently the largest commercial sports club in town; its riverside facilities include aerobics floor, badminton, basketball, beauty treatments, 3,000-square-foot gym, martial arts, sauna, snooker (6), solarium, squash (10), swimming pool (20m), table tennis (5), tennis (singles only) and more, plus bars, cafés, laundry, clothes and equipment for hire; extensive reciprocal memberships worldwide; a number of members' privileges in London.

Hurlingham Club, Fulham, SW6 (736 8411); long waiting list for this beautiful club and grounds equipped with croquet, golf, squash, swimming pool and tennis courts; but some reciprocal memberships, and members may take guests.

Paddington Sports Centre, Castellain Road, W9 (286 8448); bowls greens (2), squash (2), tennis courts (10, 4 of them floodlit); playing-in test for the tennis.

Queens Club, Palliser Road, W14 (381 4213); long waiting list to play rackets, real tennis, squash and tennis; the public can watch real tennis matches and can buy tickets for the Queens Tennis Tournament (June) from Keith Prowse booking agency (see p. 285).

Roehampton Club, Roehampton Lane, SW15 (876 5505); golf, gym, squash (6), swimming pool, tennis (3 indoor, 16 outdoor).

YMCA, 112 Great Russell Street, WC1 (637 8131); aerobics (classes), badminton (4), gym (multi-gym and free-weights), handball, sauna, solarium, squash (2), swimming pool (25m); everything the indoor sports fanatic or keep fit expert wants.

HOTELS WITH SPORTS AND HEALTH FACILITIES

Facilities are open to residents, with the overwhelming advantages of being right on hand, high quality, relatively cheap and rarely overcrowded – they might even compensate for the high cost of the room. Non-resident membership is usually limited, expensive and has a waiting list, but it is worth asking; temporary non-resident membership is unusual.

Berkeley, Wilton Place, SW1 (235 6000); rooftop indoor pool for sunset swims surrounded by café/bar, with nearby exercise bikes, massage, sauna, solarium.

Grosvenor Health Club, Grosvenor House Hotel, Park Lane, W1 (499 6363 x4592); aerobics (classes), gym (classes), massage, sauna, solarium, swimming pool (20m), whirlpools (2), plus health food bar.

Holiday Inn Marble Arch, George Street, W1 (723 1277); beauty treatments, gym, sauna, solarium, swimming pool (22m).

Holiday Inn Swiss Cottage, King Henry's Road, NW3 (722 7711); beauty parlour, gym, sauna, solarium, swimming pool (small), table tennis.

Hyatt Carlton Tower, 2 Cadogan Place, SW1 (235 5411); aerobics, beauty parlour, gym, steam, sauna, solarium. Sparkling new, rooftop and second only to Champneys at Le Meridien.

Kensington Close, Wrights Lane, W8 (937 8170); gym, sauna, solarium, squash (2), swimming pool (20m).

Le Meridien, Piccadilly, W1 (734 8000); Champneys Health Club fills the basement; beauty and massage parlour, billiard room, gym, solarium, squash (2), swimming pool (12m square), Turkish bath (unisex), whirlpool, plus library and brasserie. The swishest and most luxurious in town; the best free perk to come with any London hotel room; costs a pricey penny for non-residents.

Rembrandt: Aquilla, 11 Thurloe Place, SW7 (225 0225); aerobics, beauty therapy and massage, gym (with power jog), solarium, steam, swimming pool (16m), whirlpool and sauna in each dressing room, yoga.

PUBLIC PARTICIPATION SPORTS CENTRES

As fitness is now fashionable, facilities mushroom by the week. Here are a few of the best. The London boroughs run a variety of good sports centres, sports in parks, and swimming pools and tend to list them in the telephone directory under their boroughs (if at all) rather than the centre's name (see p. 11 for a list of boroughs). The royal parks also organise sports. For the more serious, it is worth contacting the organisation for a specific sport for advice on where to find the current best conditions and equipment. To find the nearest sports centre, telephone Sportsline (222 8000).

Chelsea Sports Centre, Chelsea Manor Street, SW3 (352 6985); badminton (1), squash (1), swimming pool (25m).

Colombo Street Sports Centre, 22 Colombo Street, SE1 (261 1658); badminton (3), boxing, karate, table tennis (2), tennis (2), yoga.

Crystal Palace National Sports Centre, Crystal Palace, SE19 (778 0131); comprehensive facilities include an arena (for basketball, volleyball and karate), badminton (4), gym, netball (6), ski-slope, squash (10), swimming pools (one 50m, one for diving, one for training), tennis (6).

Dolphin Square, Grosvenor Road, SW1 (798 8686);

sauna, solarium, squash (8), swimming pool (18m).

Elephant and Castle Recreation Centre, 22 Elephant and Castle, SE1 (582 5505); badminton (6), gym, squash (4), shallow swimming pool (with wave machine and slide), table tennis.

Kensington Sports Centre, Walmer Road, W11 (727 9923); badminton (3), sauna, solarium, squash (3), steam, swimming pool (33m), tennis (6).

Lee Valley Regional Park, headquarters at PO Box 88, Enfield, Middlesex (9002 717711); a huge park with various newly built, all-weather sports facilities including Picketts Lock Sports Centre (see below); Banbury Sailing Centre, Walthamstow Avenue, E4 (531 119); Eastway Cycle Circuit Pavilion, Temple Mill Lane, E15 (534 6085); Lea Bridge Riding School, Lea Bridge, E10 (556 2629); and Lee Valley Ice Centre, Lea Bridge Road, E10 (533 3151).

Michael Sobell Sports Centre, Hornsey Road, Islington, N7 (607 1632); extensive facilities exclude a pool but include badminton/tennis (7), basketball, climbing, cricket, gym, sauna, solarium, squash (6), trampoline.

The Oasis, 32 Endell Street, WC2 (831 1804); aerobics, badminton (2), karate, gym, sauna, solarium, squash (3), swimming pools (indoor 25m and outdoor 26m), table tennis (2).

Paddington Recreation Ground, Randolf Avenue, W9 (625 4303); bowling greens (6), cricket nets (6), tennis (17).

Picketts Lock Sports Centre, Picketts Lock Lane, N9 (803 4756); part of Lee Valley Park; extensive facilities include badminton (17), football, 9-hole golf, netball (4), putting, sauna suite, snooker, squash (8), swimming pool, table tennis, tennis (4).

Queen Mother Sports Centre, 228 Vauxhall Bridge Road, SW1 (798 2125/834 4725); archery, badminton, fencing, gym, swimming pools (3: general 35m, teaching and diving), table tennis, tennis, trampoline, volley ball and more.

Seymour Leisure Centre, Bryanston Place, W1 (798 1421); gym (with hi-tech and weight training, requires induction course), sauna, solarium, squash (2), steam, swimming pools (2, 30m and 30m), whirlpool. Membership required for squash.

Thorpe Park, Staines Lane, Chertsey, Surrey (09328 62633); 500-acre theme park near London devoted to the history and achievements of maritime Britain; water-based attractions include a Thunder River Ride down 470 metres of churning foamy water, watersports and roller-skating.

HEALTH AND FITNESS CENTRES   Although many of these run graded membership systems, the instant day membership rate makes them immediately accessible. See also hotel health clubs, where membership comes free with a room booking. London is now awash with Nautilus gym equipment; aerobics, dancing and yoga are still rising in popularity. Each club has its own balance of self-indulgent pampering to energetic exercise so it is worth a little telephone research to find the perfect mix for you.

Body Workshop, Lambton Place, Westbourne Grove, W11 (221 7989); Barbara Dale helps you make the body work at beginner, intermediate and advanced levels; yoga, too.

Club on the Park, 140 Battersea Road, SW11 (627 3158); aerobics, gym (Schnell, classes), sauna, solarium, whirlpool (ladies only), plus bar and restaurant.

Dance Works, 16 Balderton Street, W1 (629 6183); 10 studios for top training in every kind of dance, with stretching and sweating sessions, too; annual and monthly membership.

The Fitness Centre, 11 Floral Street, WC2 (836 6544); for a serious working out session, this currently has the most space and most equipment in town; Alexander technique, aromotherapy, beauty treatments and nutrition advice, chiropody, dance (classes in ballet, jazz and tap), outstanding gym (including computerised equipment), martial arts classes, sauna, solarium, steam and much more.

Holmes Place Health Club, Holmes Place, 188a Fulham Road, SW10 (352 9452); dance studios (2), gym, hair salon, swimming pool.

Pineapple Covent Garden, 7 Langley Street, WC2 (836 4004); the first of Debbie Moore's health-giving Pineapples, with 13 studios for every kind of exercise, dance and keep fit facility plus sauna and large shop. All Pineapples do Hydra-Fitness training.

Pineapple, 38 Harrington Road, SW7 (581 0466); the most beautiful of the Pineapples, amid Victorian splendour, marble and stained glass, with all Pineapple facilities.

Pineapple West, 60 Paddington Street, W1 (487 3444); still the Pineapple facilities, with the largest dancing space (Makarova and Baryshnikov have pranced on it) and Lyn Marshall to give yoga classes.

St James's Sauna and Health Club, Byron House, 7–9 St James's Street, SW1 (930 5870); a men-only club in clubland; beauty treatments, gym, massage, sauna, solarium, plunge pool, reflexology, restaurant and more.

Sanctuary, 11 Floral Street, WC2 (240 9635); a pampering paradise for women only: beauty treatments, exercise classes, sauna, steam, swimming pool (51ft, swing above), huge whirlpool, plus brasserie and piles of glossy magazines.

Westside Health Club, 201–7 Kensington High Street, W8 (937 5386); aerobics, beauty treatments, gym, osteopath, sauna, solarium, steam, yoga. See also YMCA, above.

THE COUNT-DOWN: SPORTS TO WATCH AND PLAY There is so much sport in London that this is merely a springboard, with spectator highlights to seek out, participation tips and information on how to find out more. BEWARE: for major spectator sports the touts, ticket agencies, tour operators and classified advertisements of the newspapers lure you to buy tickets for sold-out finals at exorbitant prices. Usually, there is a cheaper way of going, such as queueing to stand or waiting for a second-hand ticket at Wimbledon. Also, to be there might not be as good as watching on television, even if you lose some of the atmosphere. And all big events are televised.

American football Best of the British teams are the London Ravens (play at Richmond on Sundays) and the Olympians (play at Streatham); big events are at Wembley (May) and Crystal Palace. But for class, Channel 4 brings British viewers American football from the US on Sundays and two major league US teams come over for a pre-season game at Wembley (Aug).

Angling The people sitting with line and hook along the London canals and in the big parks all have the essential fishing permit for that place, obtainable from the London Anglers' Association, 183 Hoe Street, London E17 (520 7477), or Roest Road Hall, Hervy Park Road, E17. More serious anglers should go up to Scotland for some salmon fishing amid stunning scenery, found by scanning the classified advertisements in quality newspapers.

Athletics Watch Britain's top middle-distance runners at Crystal Palace. For information on other events and for suitable clubs to play in, contact the Amateur Athletics Association, Francis House, Francis Street, SW1 (828 9326).

Badminton A growing sport with the fashionable and young who watch the All England Championships at Wembley (Mar), other games at the Royal Albert Hall (including the British Airways Masters, Oct) and play in sports centres and clubs. For information on watching and playing, contact the Badminton Association, National Badminton Centre, Bradwell Road, Loughton Lodge, Milton Keynes (0908 568822)

Ballooning Richard Branson's hop across the Atlantic in 1987 was part of the balloon boom in Britain. Spectacular multi-balloon meets take place annually at Leeds Castle in Kent, Bristol and other picturesque spots; see *Time Out* and *City Limits* for details. To have a magical first ride, the ballooning clubs run weekends for around £200, with a credit note if bad weather prevents an ascent. For lists of events and of ballooning clubs, send a 50p postal order or cheque to Mr Green, the British Ballooning and Airship Club, PO Box 1006, Birmingham (021 643 3224); the Capital Ballooning Club meets on the last Wed of each month at Biggles Wine Bar, Mason's Yard, Duke Street, SW1 and flies from Potters Bar and elsewhere.

Baseball and softball London Warriors play at Richmond Athletic Club and are in the British National league. To play, join US exiles in Regent's Park on Sunday afternoons; visitors are encouraged to join in. On TV, Channel 4 sometimes broadcasts the world series (Sept–Oct).

Basketball See Crystal Palace, Kingston and other top clubs at the national finals at Wembley (Apr) where the Harlem Globetrotters make an annual visit; the National Cup finishes at the Royal Albert Hall (Dec). For information on more London events and on London clubs, contact Mr Horn, London secretary for the English Basketball Association, 26 Ickenham Close, Ruislip, Middlesex (0895 673955); the EBA is based at Calomaz House, Lupton Avenue, Leeds (0532 496044).

Billiards and snooker The big London games are at Wembley (Jan), with others around Britain during the year given hours of TV time. To play, many pubs have tables and some snooker clubs have temporary membership. Centre Point 24-hour Snooker and Gymnasium Club, New Oxford Street, WC1 (240 6886/6880) has 13 tables, gym, whirlpool and is indeed open round the clock. Beware: in clubs, do not bet more than a round of drinks.

Bowls Best enjoyed informally, watching gentlemen rolling the balls over immaculate lawns in London parks; the most central spots are in Hyde Park, near the Royal Albert Hall, and in Finsbury Square, an oasis on the northern borders of the City. On TV, Superbowl is in the autumn (usually

Oct). To play, apply to the clubs, but they are likely to be reluctant to let you play right away.

Boxing   See the big fights at Wembley and the Royal Albert Hall (and soon at the Docklands); see the London Amateur Boxing Association championships at the Royal Albert Hall (Mar) and the ABA National championships at Wembley (first Friday in May), interspersed with other big fights at 'small house venues' advertised in the press. Big fights are broadcast. For a list of events, send an s.a.e. to the ABA London branch, 68–9 Central Buildings, Southwark Street, SE1 (407 2194).

Bridge   To find out about major events, contact the English Bridge Union, 15b High Street, Thame, Oxfordshire. To watch, learn and play, contact the London School of Bridge, 38 King's Road, SW3 (589 7201).

Climbing   None to see; but if this is your game, go to the Michael Sobel Sports Centre (see above).

Cricket   The addicts value Lord's for beauty and the Oval for cosmopolitan crowds and jollity. Lord's Cricket Ground, St Johns Wood, NW8 (289 1615 for ticket enquiries, 286 8011 during May–Sept for prospects of play), see also p. 185; the Middlesex home ground and scene of Test matches and finals of major competitions. Oval Cricket Ground, The Oval, Kennington, SE11 (735 4911 for score and prospects of play); the Surrey home ground. Sunday league games at either are well worth catching; regulars to Lord's take their sandwiches with them. Elsewhere, little clubs throughout London play on summer evenings and at week-ends (Kew Green is particularly pretty, with home-made tea at the church, as is Vincent Square on the Westminster–Pimlico borders); and one of the best cricket day trips out of London is to Canterbury, with the cathedral as backdrop – it also has a tree on the pitch. On TV and Radio 3, the Test matches are usually broadcast live. To play, men and women should put on their trainers and go and ask the people playing if they may join – there are usually several simultaneous games played on summer evenings in Regent's Park. Out of season, compensation is a tour of Lord's and its museum (see p. 185).

Croquet   Well worth the small admission charge to watch play in the beautiful and immaculate grounds of the Hurlingham Club. To play, go to pretty Fulham Palace grounds where kings and bishops have putted balls through hoops on the old croquet lawn; alternatively, dream of exclusive membership of Hurlingham or make friends with a member.

Cycling   The big moments in London are the last stage of the Round Britain Milk Race (May) and the last city of the Kellogg's City Centre Cycling (Aug) which is broadcast on Channel 4. The Tour de France is also on TV. To bike for sport, there is a purpose built track at Lee Valley Park. For information on sporty cycling to watch and do, contact the British Cycling Federation, 16 Upper Woburn Place, WC1 (387 9320). To bike for pleasure or transport, contact the London Cycling Campaign, see p. 262; and for out of town tours the Cyclists Touring Club, 69 Headrow Road, Godalming, Surrey (04868 7217).

Flying   To see the planes, go to the observation deck at Heathrow, best morning and evening (see p. 23). To fly, contact the London School of Flying, Elstree Aerodrome, Hertfordshire (953 4343) or the three clubs at Biggin Hill Civil Airport, Kent: King Air Flying Club (0959 75088); The Surrey and Kent Flying Club (0959 72255); and Air Touring (0959 73133).

Football   (Association Football): To see the FA Cup final (May) or the Littlewoods Challenge Cup (Apr) at Wembley, the touts will charge heavily for tickets; but both are televised. However, it is easy to buy tickets for the schoolboy internationals at Wembley (spring) to see the stars of the future. It is also easy to visit during the season (Aug–May) one of the 12 London clubs listed below (their dates of founding and becoming professional are in brackets), whose games are on Saturday afternoons and some weekday evenings. Beware: it is best not to sport the colours of either team; it is wise to buy a seat before the match day or to avoid standing behind the goals if you want to stand; violence tends to occur in the streets before and after a game, so be streetwise.

Arsenal (1886, 1891), Highbury Stadium, Avenell Road, Highbury, N5 (359 0131/226 0304); colours: red and white.

Brentford (1889, 1899), Griffin Park, Braemar Road, Brentford, Middlesex (847 2511/560 2021); colours: red, white and black.

Charlton Athletic (1905, 1920), Selhurst Park, SE25 (771 6321/635 4462); colours: red and white.

Chelsea (1905, 1905), Stamford Bridge Ground, Fulham Road, SW6 (385 5545/381 6221); colours: blue and white.

Crystal Palace (1905, 1905), Selhurst Park, SE25 (653 4462/771 5311); colours: blue and red.

Fulham (1879, 1898), Craven Cottage, Stevenage Road, SW6 (736 6561/7035); colours: white and black.

Leyton Orient (1881, 1903), Leyton Stadium, Brisbane Road, E10 (539 2223/4483); colours: red and white.

Millwall (1885, 1893), The Den, Cold Blow Lane, SE14 (639 3143); colours: blue and white.

Queen's Park Rangers (1885, 1893), Rangers Stadium (Loftus Road), South Africa Road, W12 (743 0262); colours: blue and white.

Tottenham Hotspur (Spurs) (1882, 1895), White Hart Lane, 748 High Road, Tottenham, N17 (808 3030 for dial-a-seat service, 808 1020 for match and ticket information, 801 3323 for ticket office); colours: blue and white.

West Ham United (1900, 1900), Upton Park, Green Street, E13 (472 3322 for dial-a-ticket service, 470 1325 for match and ticket information); colours: claret, blue and white.

Wimbledon (1889, 1964), Plough Lane Ground, 45 Durnsford Road, Wimbledon, SW19 (946 6311); colours: blue and yellow.

To play, it is easiest to go to Hyde Park or Regent's Park and just ask to join any game where the players are not dressed in uniform shirts – men and women are welcome.

Golf See the stars at Wentworth, Sunningdale and elsewhere outside London, possibly flying up to the beautiful seaside course at St Andrew's in Scotland. To play on a private course is pricey and needs a member's introduction or reciprocal arrangement with your home club; but there are several attractive public courses around London where charges are low and there is usually equipment for hire; best to go weekdays to avoid crowds and to telephone beforehand to check there is no special event on. Public courses include: Addington Palace, Gravel Hill, Croydon, Surrey (654 3061), no equipment for hire, open to non-members Mon–Fri only; Beckenham Place Park, Beckenham, Kent (650 2292), equipment for hire, booking unnecessary except for Sat and Sun mornings; Bromley Golf Course, Magpie Hall Lane, Bromley (462 7014), equipment for hire, no booking; Richmond Park, Roehampton Gate, SE15 (876 3205), equipment for hire, essential to book for weekends. To find out more, contact the English Golf Union, 1–3 Upper King's Street, Leicester (0533 553042).

Gliding To find out about events and to glide, contact the British Gliding Association, Kimberley House, Vaughan Way, Leicester, (0533 531051).

Greyhound racing Laying a few bets as you watch the hounds hurtle round the track from your dinner table makes an evening with a difference.

Racing goes on throughout the year on weekday evenings; with betting starting at 20p, it can be a cheap evening's entertainment. See the low life at Harringay and Catford; ask the waitresses to take your bets at Wembley; best all-round facilities at Walthamstow and Wembley. For good views and a base for the evening, book a table in the restaurant. These are the five London tracks, all easily accessible: Catford Stadium, Catford Bridge, SE6 (690 2261); Hackney Stadium, Waterden Road, E15 (986 3511); Harringay Stadium, Green Lanes, N4 (800 3474/6); Walthamstow Stadium, Chingford Road, E4 (527 2252); Wembley Stadium, Empire Way, Wembley (902 8833).

Gymnastics Watch the skilful twisting and leaping at the Royal Albert Hall and Wembley; big competitions are usually televised; more information from the British Amateur Gymnastics Association, 2 Buckingham Avenue East, Slough, Berkshire (0753 34171). For amateur play, The Fitness Centre is the best in town.

Hang gliding To watch the finals of the British League (Aug) and the Bleriot Cup (Aug) and learn of other events, contact Joan Lane, 35 Springfield, Bradford-on-Avon, Wiltshire (02216 6427). To find a gliding club, contact the British Hang Gliding Association-Cranfield Airfield, Cranfield, Bedfordshire (0234 751688) and go for tuition above the rolling hills of the South Downs; or go to British Skyrides Hang-gliding School, Biggin Hill, Kent (0959 73996).

Horse-racing To satisfy the British obsession, plenty to see near London during the Mar–Nov flat season and winter steeplechasing (Aug–May), with endless hours relayed on TV. Off-course betting is legal, well governed and straightforward in Britain: just walk into a high street betting office, ask the person behind the counter how the system works, and in some of the smarter places you can watch races on the betting shop TVs while sitting down with a cup of tea. Big races begin with the 1,000 Guineas and 2,000 Guineas at Newmarket (Apr–May); then royals, society and busloads of day-trippers flocking to Epsom for The Derby (first Wed in June); then even more royals, higher society and bigger hats at Ascot (mid-June); then glorious Goodwood (July) where the Swettenham Stud Sussex Stake is the richest mile race in Europe. There are public stands for all; and while applications for a ticket to the Royal Enclosure at Ascot have to be with Her Majesty's Representative at St James's Palace by March (see p. 53), 40,000 tickets for the Grandstand (with access to

the paddocks) are sold daily during Ascot Week; for the Richmond Enclosure at Goodwood, take out annual membership. For a more informal flutter on the horses, hop on a train for a day out to a stunning country setting, taking a picnic if the weather is good and laying a few bets with the Tote or the bookmakers; some courses have weekday evening meetings; details of the day's races are in the newspapers, in-depth details *in Sporting Life* and the *Racing Post*, with more help from the Racing Information Bureau, Winkfield Road, Ascot, Berkshire (0990 25912). The royal family, in particular the Queen Mother and Princess Margaret, can often be seen in the stand at Sandown Park (for the Royal racing colours, see pp. 45–6). These courses are easy to reach from London:
Ascot, Grandstand Office, Ascot Racecourse, Ascot, Berkshire (0990 22211); train Waterloo–Ascot
Epsom, Epsom Grandstand Association, Race Course Paddock, Esher, Surrey (03727 26311); train Waterloo–Tattenham Corner
Goodwood, Chichester, Sussex (0243 774107); train Victoria–Chichester, then bus
Kempton, Sunbury-on-Thames, Middlesex (0932 782292); train Waterloo–Sunbury
Lingfield Park, Lingfield, Surrey (0342 834966); train Victoria–Lingfield Park
Newmarket, Jockey Club Office, High Street, Newmarket, Suffolk (0638 664151); train Liverpool Street–Cambridge, then coach
Royal Windsor Races, Windsor, Berkshire (0753 864726); train Waterloo–Windsor & Eton Riverside or Victoria–Windsor, then bus or 20-minute walk
Sandown Park, Esher, Surrey (0372 63072); train Waterloo–Esher

Horse-riding Show jumping fans can see the Horse of the Year Show (Oct) at Wembley and the Olympia International Show Jumping Championships (Dec) at Olympia, Kensington, W14 (inquiries to Earls Court, tel 385 1200). Or they can take a train out to the Royal Windsor Horse Show (May) at Windsor and spot a spattering of royals, information from the Royal Mews, Windsor Castle, Windsor, Berkshire (0753 860633); take a train up to the Royal International Horse Show (June) at the National Exhibition Centre, Birmingham (021 780 4141); or go out to Hickstead for the Nations Cup Week (June), the Derby Meeting (Aug) and other events, information from the All England Jumping Course, Hickstead, Sussex (0273 834315). More information from the British

Show Jumping Association, British Equestrian Centre, Stoneleigh, Warwickshire (0203 552511). To ride in central London, book up early at the remaining London mewses being used for their original stabling purposes: Bathurst Riding Stables, 63 Bathurst Mews, W2 (723 2813), minimum age six; Ross Nye's Riding Establishment, 8 Bathurst Mews, W2 (262 3791), minimum age 8; Lilo Blum's Riding School and Stables, 32 Grosvenor Crescent Mews, SW1 (235 6846), no minimum age. To ride in a more rural setting in beautiful Richmond Park, go to Roehampton Gate Stables, Richmond Park, Surrey (876 7089); there is also riding in Lee Valley Park; stables tend to close Mondays.

Ice-hockey See the Lea Valley Lions, Streatham Redskins and other top London teams during the Sept–Apr season, with the championship play-offs at Wembley (Apr–May) and televised.

Ice-skating See the St Ivel Gala and Championships (Oct) at Richmond, both televised. To skate, there are five good rinks open daily with morning, afternoon and evening sessions and boots for hire: Lee Valley Park and Michael Sobell Sports Centre (see above); Queens Ice Skating Club, Queensway, W2 (299 0172); Richmond Ice Rink, Clevedon Road, by Richmond Bridge (892 3646); Streatham Ice Rink, 386 Streatham High Road, SW16 (769 7861).

Lacrosse If the English meet the Americans or Australians at The Oval (see cricket for details), that is the match to catch.

Motor sports The best place to go and watch near London is Brands Hatch, Fawkham, Kent (0474 872331); racing most weekends round the year, usually motorbikes on Sat, cars on Sun, but big meets for either take over for two or three days; as big annual races vary in venue and date, it is best to send for a year diary, then go by train, bus, car or helicopter; if driving, the pretty lanes are more pleasant than the motorway. See the Grand Prix on TV, wherever it takes place. To race, book in for a Day Out at Brands Hatch, where amateur drivers roar round the course with an instructor, receive some lessons and then, if they are up to scratch, go out in a single seater Formula First, bookable at Brands Hatch (0474 872367).

Mountaineering and rock scrambling To climb, contact the British Mountaineering Council, Crawford House, Precinct Centre, Booth Street East, Manchester (061 273 5835) who offer advice on safety and supply route maps.

Netball See England play Australia, Jamaica and

other big stars in the international at Wembley (Nov); more information from the All England Netball Association, Francis House, Francis Street, SW1 (828 2176). To play, contact the Secretary of the AENA Middlesex branch, telephone 360 8036.

Orienteering For a list of national events to watch and fixed courses in London to maintain your skills, contact the British Orienteering Federation, Riversdale, Dale Road North, Darley Dale, Matlock, Derbyshire (0629 734042) and ask for their south-east information pack.

Parachuting To jump, contact the British Parachuting Association, Kimberley, 47 Vaughan Way, Leicester (0533 519635/519778) for a list of suitable clubs. Some clubs run weekend (or two weekday) courses when, after instruction, you can do a free fall from on high, possibly as a tandem free fall with the instructor just behind you to open your rip-cord at the right moment.

Petanque This, and not bowls, is apparently what Sir Francis Drake was playing at Portsmouth in 1588 when he learnt of the Spanish Armada's approach. A growing sport in the south-east, especially Kent where pubs often have their own 'terrain' laid out. To play in London, pick up a set at a games shop and head for a park. More information from the British Petanque Association, 126 Rosebank Road, Countesthorpe, Leicester.

Polo The nearest place to see this ultimate rich man's sport played with consummate skill by worldwide teams is at Guards' Polo Club, Smiths Lawn, Windsor Great Park, Englefield Green, Egham, Surrey (0784 34212); Apr–Sept, weekends and weekdays. But the most important high-goal tournament in England is the Gold Cup (July) played in a stunning setting by Cowdray Castle at Cowdray Park Polo Club, Midhurst, West Sussex (073081 3257); end Mar–end Aug, weekends and July weekdays.

Real tennis See Henry VIII's favourite game played at Hampton Court, round on the garden side (see p. 114); at Queen's, members and their guests may watch; at Lord's, only invited VIPs see the skilful show. To play, contact Queen's Club (see above).

Rambling For a stride out over nearby countryside, conducted country walks are cheap and one of the nicest and most relaxed ways to glimpse the English scenery. Contact the Ramblers Association, 1/5 Wandsworth Road, SW8 (582 6826/6878) for a programme of events; wear stout shoes and take waterproofs; lunch is usually at a pub.

Roller-skating To watch or join in the fun,

boogying and acrobatics, it is best to telephone to check timings before joining a roller disco session. Inside: Colombo Sports Centre, Picketts Lock Sports Centre (for all, see above). Outside: Battersea Park and the South Bank Arts complex, both best on weekend afternoons.

Rowing Out of town, high society don blazers, frocks and hats for Henley Royal Regatta (June–July see p. 52), whose finals clash with Wimbledon tennis finals. Although Henley has now sold out to commerce, who use it to entertain customers and prized workers, it can still be very pretty; for more information contact Henley Royal Regatta, Regatta Headquarters, Henley-upon-Thames, Oxon (04912 2153). In London, see the Oxford v Cambridge race (April), which starts its upriver course to Mortlake at Putney Bridge; the Head of the River race (Mar) which is processional so there is plenty to see over a length of time; the Doggett Coat and Badge race (July) from London Bridge to Chelsea (see p. 63); the Devizes to Westminster Canoe Marathon (Easter); more information from the British Canoe Union, 45 High Street, Addlestone, Surrey (0932 841341). To row with one of the Thames clubs or to learn, contact the Amateur Rowing Association, 6 Lower Mall, London W6 (748 3632) who produce a comprehensive British Rowing Almanac. For something more informal, hire a boat in a park – Battersea, Hyde, Regent's, Victoria, etc (see pp. 232, 150, 180, 253).

Rugby league See the Challenge Cup finals at Wembley (May) when northern fans descend on London, or watch on TV. Fulham are the only London professional club. Plenty of matches on TV throughout the season (Aug/Sept–May).

Rugby union No chance of getting tickets to see an international at Twickenham (unless you pay the touts outrageous prices), but it is televised live; easy to attend the Varsity Match (Oxford v Cambridge, Dec); fairly easy to see the John Player Cup Final (Apr–May). Well worth booking to join a tour of Twickenham's hallowed rooms and stand (Rugby Football Union, Twickenham, Middlesex, tel 892 8161, see also p. 269). However, there is a good chance of seeing a club match during the season (Sept–May) in the trouble-free, friendly atmosphere of one of the 10 London clubs listed below:

Blackheath FC (est. 1853), Rectory Field, Blackheath, SE3 (858 8541/852 7622); the oldest organised club, playing their first game against Richmond in 1863.

Harlequins (est. 1866), Stoop Memorial Ground,

Twickenham, Middlesex (892 3080); a founder member of the Rugby Football Union which Edwin Ash formed in 1871; hero WW Wakefield won 31 caps for England (1920–7).

London Irish RFC (est. 1898), The Avenue, Sunbury-On-Thames (892 0051/948 0850); KW Kennedy won 45 caps (1965–75).

London Scottish RFC (est. 1878), Richmond Athletic Ground, Richmond, Surrey (289 1611); AF McHarg won 44 caps (1968–79).

London Welsh RFC (est. 1885), Old Deer Park, Kew Road, Richmond, Surrey (661 1328); JPR Williams won 55 caps (1969–81).

Metropolitan Police RFC (est. 1923), Police Sports Club, Imber Court, Embercourt Road, East Molesey, Surrey (230 3999).

Richmond FC (est. 1861), Athletic Ground, Richmond, Surrey (549 8540); another old club, founded by Edwin Ash (see Harlequins, above); played its first match against Blackheath in 1863; hero CW Ralston played for England 22 times (1971–5).

Rosslyn Park RFC (est. 1879), Priory Lane, Upper Richmond Road, Roehampton, SW15 (672 1255 x4160); hero AG Ripley played for England 24 times (1972–6).

Saracens RFC (est. 1876), Bramley Sports Ground, Gren Road, Southgate, N14 (486 1122).

Wasps RFC (est. 1867), Repton Avenue, Sunbury, Middlesex (034282 2980).

Running Recreational running is on the increase in London. More than 20,000 compete in the annual London Marathon (early May); very popular, so book early to enter, or sit back and watch on TV. For this and other fun runs, see *Running Magazine*. To run with company, contact the big sports centres and see *Time Out* or *City Limits*. The friendly London Hash House Harriers (c/o Mick McAlinden, 12 Park House Road, N11, tel 361 0887) meet at least once a week to run a route with cut-out points for the less energetic and a final meeting-up pub at the end; mid-week runs in Central London, weekends at Osterley and other places further out. To run alone, the London parks are ideal; up-market hotels produce jogging maps. A good green stretch is to take the Underground to Queensway and then jog through Kensington Gardens, Hyde Park, Green Park and St James's Park; another is to explore the Bloomsbury squares (see p. 168); another is to go around Regent's Park and along the Regent's Canal towpath; another is to dart between the sculptures along Victoria Embankment Gardens (see p. 118).

Skateboarding Decreasingly fashionable, but the best places to watch and spin around yourself are the South Bank Arts complex and the half-pipe at Crystal Palace.

Skiing See it on TV throughout the season. Keep up your skills on the man-made dry slopes of Alexandra Park, Woolwich, Crystal Palace, and Lee Valley Park sports centres.

Snooker See Billiards

Soccer See Football

Softball See Baseball

Speedway See this and banger and stockcar racing in the cheap, cheerful and unglamorous settings of Hackney and Wimbledon stadiums (see Greyhound racing, above), a good outing.

Squash See the British Open Championships at Wembley (Apr). To play: this boom game for the young and fashionable is now levelling off, so the clubs are less overburdened. However, most courts are in private clubs, top central clubs are expensive, public courts are booked well in advance. If desperate, pay heavily to join a club, go to one of the sports centres listed above, or go out to Wembley Squash Centre, Wembley (902 9230), booking a court in advance and taking your food as the catering is bad. For private, well-run squash clubs, Mike Corby runs five in the City: Cotton's Sports Club, London Bridge City, Tooley Street, EC1 (403 1171) – squash (6) and swimming pool (25m); Cutlers Square and Racquets Club and Gymnasium, 9 Devonshire Square, EC2 (626 3161); Lambs Squash Club, 1 Lambs Passage, Chiswell Street, London EC1 (638 3811/2/3/4); London Bridge Sports Centre, off Swan Lane, London Bridge, EC4 (623 6895/6); and Spitalfields Sports Centre, London Fruit Exchange Building, Brushfield Street, E1 (247 9786/9). For a tournament directory and a list of London clubs, send £1 and an s.a.e. to the Squash Rackets Association, Francis House, Francis Street, SW1 (828 3064).

Street hockey An immensely skilled and acrobatic game of ice-hockey on roller skates following ice-hockey rules, mostly played by black people and a growing London favourite. Watch for the *City Limits* Street Warriors team; see the agility at the Elephant and Castle Recreation Centre (Mar–Sept).

Swimming See the big competitions at Crystal Palace, some televised. To swim, London is well equipped with public pools built as amenities for locals and therefore heavily subsidised, well maintained, cheap and free from membership restrictions; to find your nearest, telephone the recreation department of the local borough or ask at the town hall or library. Beware: do not swim in the Thames; it is strongly tidal and can kill – one person drowned in 1986. If a daily swim is crucial, stay at the right hotel or go to your nearest public pool.

To swim outdoors, pools include Oasis, two ponds (one for men, one for women) on the Highgate side of Hampstead Heath with space to sunbathe if the weather goes mad, and the Serpentine in Hyde Park, W2 (724 3104, see p. 300).

To swim indoors, see the sports centres, clubs and health clubs, above. Crystal Palace and Brixton have Olympic-sized pools; Porchester Baths, Queensway, W2 (229 9950) has pool (30m), squash (2) and splendid Turkish baths (with their own telephone number, 798 3688).

To swim for fun with slides, wave machines, waterslides and other machines, try the Elephant and Castle Recreation Centre or go out to the top favourite, The Tubes and Wild Water Ride at Richmond.

For an early morning dip, see p. 300.

Tennis The top tournament is the All England Lawn Tennis Championships at Wimbledon (end June), first held in 1877. To gobble strawberries and sip champagne (18 tons and 12,000 bottles went down in 1986) for a fortnight and watch the balls bounce on the Centre Court, apply to the All England Lawn Tennis and Croquet Club, Church Road, SW19 (946 2244) to enter the ballot by the preceding December 31. Or arrive on the day and queue patiently for tickets to all courts; leaving ticket-holders are encouraged to drop their tickets into a box, so late afternoon arrivals can often pay a nominal fee for a good seat and a few hours' play. TV, radio, newspapers and conversation focus on the courts throughout. For the other 50 weeks, the Wimbledon Lawn Tennis Museum is compensation (see p. 273). Before Wimbledon, Queen's Club run the Stella Artois tournament (June); during the colder months, tournaments continue inside at Wembley and the Royal Albert Hall; for more information, contact the Lawn Tennis Association, or the Lawn Tennis Foundation, both at Queen's Club, Barons Court, W14 (385 4233/2366), who also have details on where to play throughout London. There are almost 2,000 courts in Central London (10,000 in Greater London) but competition for them is fierce and booking essential. Many parks have courts run by the local borough; a few have privately run courts; sports centres have well kept courts; daytime bookings are often more available.

In addition, try Regent's Park public courts, between Outer Circle and Queen Mary's Garden, NW1, no telephone, 8 courts, booking office; Thom Golf and Tennis School, Outer Circle, near the zoo, Regents Park, NW1 (723 4588), 3 courts, block bookings taken for a regular slot; Hyde Park, near Alexandra Gate, The Carriage Road, SW1 (262 5484), 3 courts, personal booking only. Visitors can play at the London Indoor Tennis Club, Alfred Road, Westbourne Green, W2 (286 1985), 3 indoor courts, coaches, partners, gym and the Vanderbilt Racquet Club, 31 Sterne Street, W12 (743 9816), overseas membership. More information from The Tennis Bureau, 160 Tower Bridge Road, SE1 (403 2467).

Ten Pin Bowling See the snazziest computerised scoreboards and the hottest players rolling and posing – and compete with them – at Lewisham Bowl, 11–29 Belmont Hill, SE13 (318 9691), open daily 10am–midnight.

Water-skiing See the British championships at Thorpe Park; to see less spectacular water acrobatics, go to King George V dock and other parts of the Docklands at weekends. To ski boatless, Thorpe Park has a two-cable circuit: just plug in and go around, always plenty of room, and cheap; to ski in town, contact The Royal Dock Waterski Club, Gate 16, King George V Dock, Woolwich Manor Way, E16 (511 2000).

Windsurfing Like water-skiing, a growing sport to be seen at weekends in the Royal Docks of the reviving Docklands.

Opting out: Sit back and be beautified

Hairdressers and beauticians: sit back and daydream as sensitive hands massage your scalp; and have your hands and toes preened while the scissors clip and dryer blows. The big department stores have top floor beauty salons: Essanelle salons in Dickins & Jones, DH Evans and Fenwicks; and the Glemby salons using Orlane products in Harvey Nichols (terrific electrolysist) and Selfridges. *Harpers & Queen* glossy magazine has the latest London beauty information. Here is a tiny selection of some of the current best and most pampering:

BARBERS
Austin Reed, 103 Regent Street, W1 (734 6789); splendid 1920s basement for male pampering.

Cuts Barber Shop, 23a Frith Street, W1 (734 2171); for streetwise men; hair chopped daily but telephone to check when George the shaver is in.

Trufitt & Hill, 23 Old Bond Street, W1 (493 2961); for a shave, a manicure, a beard trim and more.

George F Trumper, 9 Curzon Street, W1 (499 1850/ 2932); a gentleman's oasis, found through the front shop lined with shelves of smelly potions.

BEAUTICIANS

The Beauty Clinic, 413a Fulham Palace Road, SW6 (736 7676); perfect for pavement-weary feet.

Katherine Corbett, 21 South Molton Street, W1 (493 5905); wonderful for disposing of all unwanted things to make the skin more pearly.

Face Facts, 75 George Street, W1 (486 8287); give lessons, especially good for cosmetic camouflage.

Arsho Grimwood, Steiner Salon, Royal Garden Hotel, Kensington, W8 (937 8000); book way ahead to be tended by a medically-trained beautician.

Eve Lom, 3 Upper Wimpole Street, W1 (935 9988); Perfect cleansing of the London filth, recommended by Leslie Kenton of *Harpers & Queen*.

Marguerite Maury Aromotherapie, Suite 101, Park Lane Hotel, W1 (493 6630); magical facials and body massage to revive and renew.

Clare Maxwell-Hudson, 87 Dartmouth Road, NW2 (450 6494); she comes to you, to add to the pampering.

Nailomania, 1 Hinde Street, W1 (486 8079); with the aid of plastic, acrylic and much care, the direct route to beautiful hands and feet.

HAIRDRESSERS   Most also give beauty treatments:

Allan Soh, 11a Brompton Arcade, SW1 (581 5941); individual creations by one of the trendiest of the trendy take several hours and cost a pretty penny but look wizzard.

The Cadogan Club, 182 Sloane Street, SW1 (235 3814); eavesdrop on the latest Sloane obsessions while the herbal shampoos take effect; full beauty treatments from facials to massage, too.

Cifford Austin Hunt, 55 Kensington Church Street, W8 (937 2150); Pampering for men and women can be extended into series of visits before a big occasion.

Cuts Company, 114 Kensington Church Street, W8 (727 2171); for streetwise hair for both sexes; see also barbers, above.

D Map, 7 Upper James Street, W1 (734 1050); ceiling painting to amuse during shampooing, dentists' chairs for streetwise clipping in comfort.

Neville Daniel, 175 Sloane Street, SW1 (245 6151) and 107–8 Marylebone High Street, W1 (487 4048); clients include the Queen and beauty expert Leslie Kenton, two good heads of hair to recommend themselves.

Edmonds, 40 Beauchamp Place, SW1 (589 5958); relaxed and laid back for men and women, many of whose mops are in the public eye.

John Frieda, 75 New Cavendish Street, W1 (636 1401); tend royals, stars and nobodies with equal care.

Hari & Friends, 30 Sydney Street, SW3 (352 2295); top cutters for top heads in need of a trim or shape up, male and female.

Harrods Hair and Beauty Salon, Knightsbridge, SW1 (730 1234); the grandest and longest hair-dos whipped into shining healthiness; globe-trotters find their dream chiropodist here.

Harvey Nichols, Knightsbridge, SW1 (235 5000); loyal followers travel miles for weekly cosseting from top to toe.

Hugh At 161, 161 Ebury Street, W1 (730 2196); loving care for the local Belgravia ladies's locks, but no beauty treatments.

Leonard, 6 Upper Grosvenor Street, W1 (629 5757); luxury and styles to suit the traditional Mayfair ladies; the Day At Leonard's pampers every corner with massage, facial, make-up and more.

Michael John, 23a Albemarle Street, W1 (629 6969 for women, 499 7529 for men); Michael Rasser is still here, John Isaacs runs the Beverley Hills branch. Top of the tree for sensitivity to all locks – long or short, straight or curly, blue rinse or bang up-to-date; especially good at colour for men and women; manicure, pedicure and own-make beauty products too. If you cannot get to them, they will come to you.

Molton Brown, 58 South Molton Street, W1 (629 1872); Men and women emerge looking like themselves and not a chocolate box confection; hair accessories and glorious own-make beauty products (also available at Liberty's and Harrods); 20-minute mini make-up advice sessions.

Trevor Sorbie, 10 Russell Street, WC2 (240 3816); good for a short, up-to-the-minute snip, and recommended for colour.

Sweeney's, 48 Beauchamp Place, SW3 (589 3066); men from Lord Montague to Rod Stewart are shaped here; women follow in flocks.

Vidal Sassoon: for women, 60 South Molton Street, W1 (491 8848); for men, 56 Brook Street, W1 (493 5428); hair, nails and own-make beauty products all up to standard.

BEAUTY PRODUCTS   In addition to the own-makes from the hairdressers listed above, these should fulfil every need:

The Body Shop, 64–6 Oxford Street, W1 (631 0027); of the dozen or so branches, this is the biggest, stuffed with multi-coloured potions, soaps and scrubbers oozing conceivable and inconceivable perfumes.

Harrods, Knightsbridge, SW1 (730 1234); acres of pink space on the ground floor to wander and sniff around.

Selfridges, 400 Oxford Street, W1 (629 1234); probably the best stocked beauty and perfume department; often the only place in London for unusual imported brands such as Lancaster from Monaco.

The Secret Garden, 153 Regent Street, W1 (439 3101); London's first aromatherapist, using natural fragrant oils in therapy, delicious-smelling and beautifully packaged for everyday use; in-house herbalist.

The parks: Space and green peace

The parks are a London glory. Almost 11% of Greater London is parkland, some 67 square miles (174 square kilometres) scattered across the capital as tiny triangles that were once village greens, formal manicured lawns planted with dazzling annuals, leafy squares surrounded by terraces, walled secret gardens, great tracts of deceptively informal landscaped airiness or acres of heath and woodland. These are the Londoners' playgrounds. They are their own back gardens, each loved almost possessively for its cumulative layers of childhood memories, summer parties, romantic trysts and centuries of history.

For locals and visitors, the parks relieve the seemingly endless grey streets, squares and skyscrapers. Despite the developers' greed, the monarchs and later the people of London have fought for and protected these precious places. They evolved for different reasons.

The royal parks were once personal possessions of the sovereign, much-prized hunting grounds for royal relaxation. Though open to the public today, they still belong to and are run by the Crown – Jennifer Adams and her 180 staff keep the central ones clipped, mowed and planted. Then there is common land that once surrounded the walled City of London and its satellite villages. Here the people grazed their sheep and cattle, beat their carpets clean and collected firewood – the origin of

Hampstead Heath and Wimbledon Common – until the eighteenth- and nineteenth-century London expansion and the rise in land values. The lords of the manor then enclosed thousands of common acres and started selling them off to make fast cash, all halted by public outcry and the Metropolitan Commons Act of 1866. There are also parks created specifically for the public by Victorian campaigners, to improve the conditions and health of the crowded poor areas. Victoria Park came first (1842), then Battersea (1846), a movement that gained momentum with the creation of the London County Council, later the Greater London Council.

Meanwhile, the independent City of London Corporation was authorised by parliament (1878) to buy land within 25 miles of its walls, keeping it in its natural condition for the benefit of City dwellers – Epping was their first purchase (1878), Highgate Wood and others followed. Finally, the squares, the key to London's building character, received their official protection in 1931. Even if some remain firmly locked to all but local residents, they still work as dark green, lush oases amid the city hubbub.

Today London has a staggering 1,700 parks, ranging from the four-acre walled Chelsea Physic Garden to the 6,000 acre Epping Forest. The wildlife in them is extraordinary, well-established in woodland, marsh, meadow and heath or newly-arrived on bomb sites and derelict yards. Some 2,000 varieties of plants grow wild. Despite the loss of thousands of London trees in the Big Storm of 1987, some of the finest specimens of common and unusual trees growing in Britain are still in London. And a hundred different kinds of birds nest here and a hundred more pass through as they migrate, from kingfishers in Hackney to parakeets in Chiswick. In addition, the bigger parks have lakes, rivers and canals for watching wildlife and going boating, statues and historic houses for a dash of culture, sports from cricket to horse-riding, bandstands for music and cafés for sustenance.

Exploring them and returning to favourites to find peace and to enjoy particular corners is as much part of discovering London as dipping into the different museums or finding a favourite pub. Heaven in London might become sunset in July wandering through Queen Mary's Rose Garden, the spring daffodils and bluebells of Holland Park, a misty winter view of Greenwich from Island Gardens, sunshine boating on the Serpentine, watching the ducks in St James's Park or a summer evening concert beside the lake at Kenwood.

TO FIND OUT MORE

Books

Crowe, A: *The Parks and Woodlands of London* (1987)
Forshaw, A and Bergstrom, T: *The Open Spaces of London* (1986)
Goode, D: *Wild in London* (1986)
Jennett, S: *The Official Guide to the Royal Parks of London* (1979)
Meller, H: *London Cemeteries* (1983)
Simms, E: *Wild Life in the Royal Parks* (1974).

Societies

Ecological Parks Trust, The Old Looms House, Back Church Lane, E1 (481 0893); sets up ecological parks in London.

Friends of the Earth 377 City Road, EC1 (837 0731); local London groups have set up nature reserves within existing parks.

Green Heritage Service, 3 Mayfield Road, Thornton Heath, Croydon Surrey (689 4197); devoted to studying and preserving London's open spaces.

London Wildlife Trust, London Ecology Centre, 80 York Way, N1 (278 6612/3); members are very active in setting up nature reserves, protecting threatened areas, and publicising its work with a newsletter, Wild London.

National Gardens Scheme, 57 Lower Belgrave Street, SW1 (730 0359); their annual booklet, *Gardens of England and Wales*, known as 'The Yellow Book', lists over 2,000 private gardens that are opened to the public, together with descriptions, dates open and entry costs.

Royal Horticultural Society; see p. 241.

Royal Society for the Protection of Birds (RSPB), The Lodge, Sandy, Bedfordshire (0767 80551); the 14 local London groups concentrate on the city's feathered life and habitat and run RSPB events; newly improved catalogue of bird-decorated presents.

The Tradescant Trust, 74 Coleherne Court, London SW5 (373 4030); runs the Museum of Garden History, see p. 81.

THE PARKS   Here are a handful of favourites, with page references to more information. Andrew Crowe's exhaustive, practical and compact book is the best springboard to park exploration.

The royal parks: Bushy Park (see p. 114), Green Park (see p. 143), Greenwich Park (see p. 107), Hampton Court (see p. 112), Hyde Park (see p. 151), Kensington Gardens (see p. 190), Primrose Hill (see p. 184), Regent's Park (see p. 182), Richmond Park (see p. 273) and St James's Park (see pp. 89–90).

Other airy delights, from small to spacious: The Barbican Conservatory (only open Sat and Sun, see p. 287), Battersea Park (see p. 232), Bishop's Park (see p. 110), Bunhill Fields (see p. 68), Chelsea Physic Garden (see p. 234), Chiswick House Gardens (see p. 270), Crystal Palace Park (see p. 274), Dulwich Park (see p. 274), Gray's Inn Gardens (see p. 127), Hampstead Heath (all parts, see p. 271), Highgate Cemetery (see p. 271), The Hill Garden, Hampstead (see p. 271), Holland Park (see p. 195), Island Gardens (see p. 256), Kensal Green Cemetery (see p. 266), Leighton House Garden (see p. 195), Lincoln's Inn Fields (see p. 125), London Butterfly House, Syon Park (see p. 269), Museum of Garden History (see p. 81), Osterley Park (see p. 267), Pirelli Garden in the V&A Museum (see p. 225), Ranelagh Gardens (see p. 231), Regent's Canal towpath (see p. 183), Royal Botanical Gardens, Kew (see p. 267), St Dunstan-in-the-East churchyard (see p. 73), Syon Park (see p. 269), Trent Park (see p. 266), Victoria Tower Gardens (see p. 85) and Waterlow Park (see p. 270).

EXTRAS   The most exciting new garden to look forward to is the 9-acre Lambeth Palace haven, currently being restored by the energetic Rosalind Runcie, wife of the Archbishop of Canterbury, and due to open in 1988 (see p. 81).

To wallow in the best gardens out of town, wander the Royal Horticultural Society's immaculate acres at Wisley (see p. 241).

To peek behind the London facades at those legendary, lovingly tended English gardens, check out the National Garden Schemes 'Yellow Book' (see above) to find out which of 60 or so London gardens are open (mostly Apr–Sept).

The London Year:
A month-by-month directory of events

The London year runs non-stop. Whenever you arrive, there is plenty going on. Here are some of the annual events to look out for, from music festivals and London traditions to sports finals and shopping sales. Page references lead to more information about the event or its venue; see pp. 339–48 for more on all sports events.

A long-lasting event is mentioned in each of the months it covers, e.g. Henry Wood Promenade Concerts, July–September. Sports, traditional and other events whose dates vary from year to year are in both their possible months, e.g. Henley Royal Regatta always ends on the 27th Sunday of the year and therefore begins at the end of June or early July. Bank holidays are included because there are often good shows and events in the parks and big stadia, but museums tend to close. Events outside London are of national interest and easy to reach. To find out exactly what's on this week, consult the current *Time Out* or *City Limits*, or visit one of the London Tourist Board Information Centres or the City of London Information Centre (see pp. 3–4).

JANUARY

Arts festivals London International Mime Festival; Park Lane Group Young Artists & 20th Century Music Series.

Sport Snooker; football; gymnastics (Gold Top Champions Cup); rugby union (Internationals); tennis (World Double championships).

Traditions Baddeley Cake (6th; Theatre Royal, Drury Lane, see p. 120); Charles I Commemoration Procession and wreath-laying by Royal Stuart Society (last Sun, St James's Palace to Trafalgar Square, see p. 87); Chinese New Year Parade (Gerrard Street, Soho); Epiphany Gifts (6th; Chapel Royal, St James's Palace, see p. 138); The Queen spends the month at Sandringham.

Other Bank holiday on New Year's Day (1st), with parade along Piccadilly and Regent Street. Antiques and Collectors' Fair; Christmas street illuminations (until 6th, see Nov) and pantomimes in theatres and on ice (see Dec) continue; The Holiday Show; International Boat Show; International Silver & Jewellery Fair & Seminar; January shopping sales (see p. 322); Model Engineer Exhibition; Racing Car Show.

FEBRUARY

Arts festivals English Folk Dance and Song Festival (Royal Albert Hall).

Sport Football; rugby union (Internationals).

Traditions Blessing the Throats Service (St Etheldreda's Church, see p. 128); Chinese New Year Parade (Gerrard Street, Soho); Clowns Service (Holy Trinity, Dalston, E8); royal gun salutes on Accession Day (6th, Accession Day, see p. 52); Shrove Tuesday (the day before Ash Wednesday and the beginning of Lent, pancake races at Covent Garden, events at Lincoln's Inn, Westminster School and elsewhere); Sir John Cass memorial service (St Botolph's, Aldgate); Stationers' Service (Ash Wed, St Faith's Chapel in St Paul's Cathe-

dral); Trial of the Pyx (Goldsmiths' Hall, see p. 67).
Other Crufts Dog Show; International Silver & Jewellery Fair & Seminar.

MARCH

Arts festivals Camden Festival (see p. 173, including Jazz Week); Country Music Festival; East End Festival.
Sport Badminton (All England championships); boxing (London Amateur championships); football; gymnastics (*Daily Mirror* USSR Gymnastics display); rowing (Head of the River race); rugby union (Internationals; John Player Cup Final).
Traditions Bridewell Service (2nd Tues, St Bride's, see p. 129); Druid Ceremony (20th, the Spring Equinox, on Tower Hill); Oranges and Lemons Service, St Clement Danes, see p. 130); St David's Day (1st, Windsor Castle); St Patrick's Day 17th, Queen Mother inspects the Irish Guards).
Other British Summer Time begins (see p. 11); Daily Mail Ideal Home Exhibition; London International Book Fair.

EASTER WEEKEND

Arts festivals International Festival of Country Music.
Sport Rowing (Devises to Westminster Canoe Marathon); horse-racing.
Traditions Butterworth Charity (Good Friday; St Bartholomew the Great, (see p. 201); Easter Passions sung in churches and concert halls (see p. 294); The Royal Maundy (Thurs before Good Friday, see p. 53); Easter Parade (Easter Sunday; Battersea Park); Harness Horse Parade of working horses (Easter Monday; Regent's Park); Hot Cross Bun Ceremony (Good Friday; Widow's Son Inn, 75 Devons Road, E3).
Other Bank holiday on Good Friday and Easter Monday. International Model Railway Exhibition.

APRIL

Arts festivals Camden Festival (see p. 173, including Jazz Week); London Handel Festival; Silk Cut Festival (country music).
Sport Basketball; football (Littlewoods Challenge Cup); horse-racing (Grand National, Liverpool; Newmarket races); ice-hockey; polo; rowing (Oxford v Cambridge race); squash (British Open championships).
Traditions John Stow's Commemorative Service (St Andrew Undershaft); Primroses laid by Disraeli's statue (19th, Parliament Square, see p. 35); Royal gun salutes on the Queen's birthday

(21st, see p. 52), the Queen spends mid-March and all April at Windsor (so State Apartments close, see pp. 275–6); St George's Day, patron saint of England (23rd, red cross flag of St George flies above English parish churches); Shakespeare's birthday (23rd, Southwark Cathedral); Spital Sermon (Thurs after Easter, St Lawrence Jewry); Tyburn Walk (last Sun, Old Bailey to Tyburn Convent, see p. 151).
Other Chelsea Spring Antiques Fair; Covent Garden opera proms (see p. 289); London International Book Fair; Royal Horticultural Society Spring Flower Show (see p. 241).

MAY

Arts festivals Covent Garden May Fayre (St Paul's Churchyard, see p. 115); Glyndebourne Festival Opera (see p. 289); London International Opera Festival; Piccadilly Festival.
Sport American Football; boxing (ABA National championships); cricket; cycling (Round Britain Milk Race); football (FA Cup Final); horse-racing (Newmarket); horse-riding (Badminton Horse Trials, see also p. 51; Royal Windsor Horse Show); ice-hockey; polo; flying (Biggin Hill Air Fair); rugby league (Challenge Cup finals); running (London Marathon).
Traditions Beating the Bounds (Ascension Day, St Peter ad Vincula in the Tower of London, see p. 102, All Hallows by the Tower, see p. 104, and St Clement Danes); Beating Retreat (Horse Guards Parade, see p. 51); Dunkirk Veterans Service and Parade (St Lawrence Jewry, see p. 68); Florence Nightingale Memorial (12th, Westminster Abbey, see p. 109); Lilies and Roses Ceremony (21st, Tower of London); Oak Apple Day (Royal Hospital, Chelsea, see p. 231); Pepys Commemorative Service (St Olave's, see p. 105); Private Fire Brigades Competition (Guildhall Yard, see p. 68).
Other Bank holidays for May Holiday (1st Mon) and Spring Holiday (last Mon). Chelsea Flower Show (see p. 227) and related picture exhibitions; Contemporary Art Fair (see p. 328); Covent Garden opera proms (see p. 289); London–Brighton Historical Commercial Vehicle Run (Battersea Park, three-day fair); open-air art exhibition, Victoria Embankment Gardens (see p. 118); Morris dancing (Wed evenings, by Westminster Abbey); Royal Academy Summer Exhibition (see p. 142).

JUNE

Arts festivals Almeida International Festival of Contemporary Music and Performance (see

p. 292); Alternative Arts Festival of Street Theatre (see p. 115); Capital Radio Music Festival; Covent Garden Dance Festival; Glyndebourne Festival Opera (see p. 289); Greenwich Festival (see p. 93); Kensington and Chelsea Festival (see p. 187); Open Air Shakespeare Season (see p. 181); Piccadilly Festival; Spitalfields Festival (see p. 243).

Sport Cricket; horse-racing (The Derby, Epsom; Ascot Week, see also p. 53); horse-riding (Royal International Horse Show, Birmingham; Nations Cup Week, Hickstead); polo; rowing (Henley Royal Regatta); tennis (Stella Artois tournament, Queen's; All England Lawn Tennis championships, Wimbledon).

Traditions Beating Retreat (Horse Guards Parade, see p. 51); The Bubble Sermon and Procession (1st Tues, St Martin's-within-Ludgate, EC4); Election of the Lord Mayor's Sheriffs (24th, see p. 68); Garter Ceremony (Windsor, see p. 52) conducted by the Queen who spends most of June at Windsor (so State Apartments close, see p. 276); royal gun salutes on Coronation Day (2nd) and Prince Philip's birthday (10th, see p. 52); Skinners' Installation Procession (2nd Thurs after Whitsun, to St Mary Aldermary); Sounding Retreat (see p. 51; Beating Retreat); Strawberry Fayre (see p. 115); Trooping the Colour (Horse Guards Parade, see p. 54)

Other Antiquarian (Park Lane Hotel) and PBSA (Hotel Russell) book fairs; Coliseum summer dance season (see p. 289); Dorchester Ceramics Fair, Fine Art and Antiques Fair (Olympia) and Grosvenor House Antiques Fair (see p. 328); Calthorpe Summer Celebrations (see p. 155); Midsummer at St Mary's Primrose Hill (see p. 173); Morris dancing (Wed evenings, by Westminster Abbey); open-air concerts at Kenwood House and Marble Hill House (see p. 295); Royal Academy Summer Exhibition (see p. 142).

JULY

Arts festivals Almeida International Festival of Contemporary Music and Performance (see p. 292); Alternative Arts Festival of Street Theatre (see p. 115); Bracknell Jazz Festival (see p. 295, information on 0344 427272); Capital Radio Music Festival (including Jazz Festival, see p. 295); City of London Festival (see p. 59); Clerkenwell Festival (see p. 199); Cyprus Week; Glyndebourne Festival Opera (see p. 289); Hackney Festival; Henry Wood Promenade Concerts (see p. 293); London International Festival of Theatre (LIFT) (see p. 288); National Festival of Music for Youth; Open Air

Shakespeare Season (see p. 181); Richmond Festival (see p. 93); Sanskritik Festival of the Arts of India. The annual Festival of London is launched in 1988.

Sport Cricket; horse-racing (Goodwood); polo (Gold Cup); rowing (Henley Royal Regatta); tennis (All England Lawn Tennis championships, Wimbledon).

Traditions Doggett's Coat and Badge rowing race (see p. 63); the Queen's State Visit to Scotland (see p. 54); Grocers' Procession (near 10th, to St Stephen Walbrook, see p. 64); Procession of Our Lady of Mount Carmel (see p. 199); Road Sweeping by the Vintners' Company (2nd Thurs, Vintners' Hall, Kennet Wharf Lane, EC4, to St James Garlickhythe); Swan Upping (Sunbury-on-Thames to Whitchurch, see p. 100).

Other Albert Street Carnival (see p. 173); Bloomsbury Fair (see p. 155); Coliseum summer dance season (see p. 289); Fitzrovia Fair (see p. 155); July summer shopping sales (see p. 322); Morris dancing (Wed evenings, by Westminster Abbey); National Gallery evening openings (see p. 88); open-air concerts at Kenwood House and Marble Hill House (see p. 295); Queen Square Fair (see p. 155); Royal Academy Summer Exhibition (see p. 142); Royal Garden Parties (see p. 53); Royal Tournament (see p. 53).

AUGUST

Arts festivals Alternative Arts Festival of Street Theatre (see p. 115); Edinburgh Festival (Scotland); Glyndebourne Festival Opera (see p. 289); Greenwich Clipper Week (see p. 93); Henry Wood Promenade Concerts (see p. 293); London International Festival of Theatre (LIFT) (see p. 288); Not The RSC (theatre, see p. 290); Notting Hill Carnival (see p. 187); Open Air Shakespeare Season (see p. 181); South Bank Summer Music (see p. 288); Summer in the City (see p. 59). The annual Festival of London is launched in 1988.

Sports American football; cricket; cycling (Kellogg's City Centre race); football; horse-riding (Derby Meeting, Hickstead); sailing (Cowes Week, see also p. 52); Greater London Horse Show, Clapham Common; London Riding (Horse Parade); polo.

Traditions Cart marking (Guildhall Yard); royal gun salutes on the Queen Mother's birthday (4th, see p. 52); the Queen spends the month at Balmoral, Scotland.

Other Bank holiday for Late Summer Holiday (last Mon), with local fairs on Hampstead Heath and elsewhere. Coliseum summer dance season (see p. 289); Morris dancing (Wed evenings, by Westminster Abbey); National Gallery evening openings (see p. 88); open-air concerts at Kenwood House and Marble Hill House (see p. 295); the Royal Ballet dance in the Tent, Battersea Park (see p. 289); RHS Summer Flower Show (see p. 291).

SEPTEMBER
Arts festivals Covent Garden Music Festival; Edinburgh Festival (Scotland); Henry Wood Promenade Concerts (see p. 293); Jermyn Street Festival (see p. 134); Thamesday (between Waterloo and Westminster bridges); Punch and Judy puppet festival (last Sun, Covent Garden Piazza, see p. 122).
Sports Cricket; football; polo.
Traditions Autumn Equinox (22nd or 23rd, Primrose Hill, see p. 184); Battle of Britain Memorial Service (Westminster Abbey, see p. 77); Christ's Hospital Boys Service and March (St Matthew's Day, from Church of the Holy Sepulchre, Holborn Viaduct, to Mansion House); Clog and Apron Race (Broad Walk, Kew Gardens, see p. 267); Cromwell's Commemoration Speech (3rd, Oliver Cromwell's statue, in front of the Houses of Parliament, see p. 85, with procession by The Roundhead Association on nearest Sun); Horseman's Sunday (2nd last Sun, Church of St John and St Michael, W2), with procession, then Horse Show in Kensington Gardens; Admission of Sheriffs (Guildhall), with the Lord Mayor's Election the following day (see p. 68); Private Fire Brigades Competition (Guildhall Yard, see p. 68); the Queen spends the month at Balmoral, Scotland.
Other Annual conferences of political parties (Conservative and Labour alternate between Blackpool and Brighton); British Craft Show (Syon House, see p. 269); Burlington House Antiques Fair, Chelsea Autumn Antiques Fair (see p. 328); City of London Flower Show (Guildhall, see p. 68; Royal Horticultural Society Great Autumn Flower Show (see p. 241), preceded there by the Royal National Rose and National Chrysanthemum societies annual shows.

OCTOBER
Arts festivals Dance Umbrella (see p. 289); Early Music Centre Festival (Wigmore Hall and South Bank Centre, see p. 288); National Brass Band Festival; Nettleford Festival (music); Royal Court Young Writers' Festival (see p. 229).
Sports Badminton; football; horse-riding (Horse

of the Year Show); ice-skating (St Ivel Gala championships).
Traditions Basketmakers' Procession (last Wed, to St Margaret Pattens, see p. 73); Harvest Festival (services in many churches including St Mary-at-Hill, Eastcheap, see p. 73, for fishermen, and St Martin-in-the-Fields, see p. 88, for the London costermongers, who are dressed up and known as the Pearly Kings and Queens); Law Courts open with Judges' Service and Parade (Westminster Abbey to Houses of Parliament); The Lion Sermon (16th, St Katharine Cree, Leadenhall Street); National Service for Seafarers (Wed nearest to the 21st, St Paul's Cathedral); Quit Rents Ceremony (Royal Courts of Justice); Trafalgar Day (Sat evening reunion at the Royal Albert Hall, then parade and service at the Cenotaph the next morning); State Opening of Parliament (see p. 53); Vintage Festival (1st Tues, St Olave's Church, see p. 105).
Other British Philatelic Exhibition; British Summer Time ends (see p. 11); The Motorfair; Park Lane Antiques Fair (see p. 328); RHS Early October Fruit and Vegetable Show (see p. 241).

NOVEMBER
Arts festivals Dance Umbrella (see p. 289); London Film Festival (see p. 296); Royal Court Young Writers' Festival (see p. 229).
Sports Football; gymnastics (New Zealand Lamb International Rhythmic Gymnastics); netball; tennis (Benson & Hedges championship).
Traditions American Thanksgiving Day (4th Thurs, US Ambassador attends an interdenominational service at St Paul's Cathedral); Guy Fawkes Day (5th, public fireworks displays); London–Brighton Veteran Car Run (1st Sun, from Hyde Park Corner); Lord Mayor's Show (2nd Sat), with Lord Mayor's Admission (preceding Fri) and Lord Mayor's Banquet (following Mon, see p. 69); Remembrance Sunday (Sun nearest the 11th, see p. 53); St Cecelia's Day Service (22nd, Church of the Holy Sepulchre Without Newgate, Holborn Viaduct, see p. 128); St Katharine's Day Service and distribution of new coins (St Katharine Dock, see p. 104); State Opening of Parliament (see p. 53).
Other Christmas street illuminations (Oxford, Regent, Jermyn and Bond streets); World Travel Market.

DECEMBER
Arts festivals London Student Drama Festival.
Sports Basketball; football; gymnastics (Craft In-

ternational); horse-riding (Olympia International Show Jumping championships); rugby union (Varsity Match).

Traditions Boar's Head Presentation and Procession (Butchers' Hall to Mansion House); Carol-singing around the Christmas Tree (Trafalgar Square) and throughout London; Festival of Nine Lessons and Carols and other Christmas music performed in churches and concert halls (see p. 294); pantomimes in the theatres (see p. 288) and on ice (Wembley, see p. 339); the Queen attends Christmas morning service at St George's Chapel, Windsor Castle (see p. 275, so State Apartments close for the last fortnight of Dec); The Dickens Drive (from Dickens House, see p. 172, to Eaton Square); Dr Johnson's Memorial Service (18th, Westminster Abbey); Watch Night (31st, St Paul's Cathedral); New Year's Eve gathering (midnight, Trafalgar Square).

Other Bank holiday for Christmas Day (25th) and Boxing Day (26th). Christmas exhibition at Bethnal Green Museum of Childhood (see p. 253); Christmas street illuminations (see Nov); Father Christmas visits toy departments of big stores (see p. 326); National Cat Club Show; Royal Smithfield Show (livestock); World Travel Market.

Key dates in London's history

Note: ruling houses are included below, but see pp. 47–9 for a full list of monarchs and their dates

43 Roman Emperor Claudius invades Britain; builds London Bridge a few years later and establishes a port and garrison called Londinium.

60 Boudicca, queen of the Iceni tribe, burns down London; the Romans rebuild.

70 Roman military supply base at Southwark, London's first suburb.

200 Romans encase London in a wall pierced by seven gates; population about 50,000.

410 Emperor Honorius renounces responsibility for London's defence; London wanes and disappears from historical record.

604 According to the chronicler Bede, the first St Paul's cathedral built for Mellitus, first bishop of London.

7th & 8th centuries Anglo-Saxons of Kent, then Mercia, control London, called Ludenwic.

829 Egbert of Wessex, a Saxon, unites England as one kingdom.

842 Vikings ravage London. 350 Viking ships later storm London (851); Viking Danes control London (871–2).

886 King Alfred, the Saxon and Christian, defeats the Viking Danes and establishes London as an international market-town.

994 Renewed Viking attacks on London begin; after the Saxon king Aethelred dies (1016), Canute, the Viking Dane, accepted as king of England; succeeded by his son, Harthacnut.

1042 Edward, surviving son of Aethelred, becomes king; known as 'The Confessor' for his piety.

1052 Edward makes London his capital; sets up his court at Thorney Island, south-west of the city walls, and endows St Peter's church with land and a new abbey church; Westminster is thus established as the royal centre, separate from the commercial City of London.

1066 William I, the Conqueror, defeats Harold II at the Battle of Hastings, then defeats London and is crowned at Westminster Abbey; Normans rule until 1154.

1070s William I begins building the White Tower in the Tower of London, the royal defence against the City of London mob.

1097–9 William II builds Westminster Hall (rebuilt 1394–9), part of the Palace of Westminster which remains the principal royal residence until 1529.

1100–32 City merchants win right from Henry I to collect taxes and elect sheriffs; he wins their support as king.

1123 St Bartholomew's Hospital and Priory founded, followed by St John of Jerusalem Priory and Clerkenwell Nunnery (both c.1140); medieval London has 13 monastic houses and more than 120 churches; population about 18,000.

1154 Henry II initiates Plantagenet rule which lasts until 1399.

1176 Peter de Colechurch's stone London Bridge built, the only bridge in London until 1739.

1191 Richard I formally recognises City of London as a self-governing community.

1192 Henry FitzAilwin becomes the first mayor of London.

1197 City merchants win lucrative management of the Thames from Richard I; reverts to the monarchy in 1857.

1215 City supports King John financially and wins royal recognition of independent status from Westminster; City then supports rebelling barons who draft the Magna Carta.

1245–69 Henry III begins rebuilding Westminster Abbey; consecrated 1269.

1280 Old St Paul's Cathedral completed.

1282 Llywelyn The Last of Wales dies; from now on, England and Wales share the same monarch.

1290 Jews expelled; invited to return 1656.

1348–50 A population of about 50,000 ravaged by Black Death (bubonic plague).

1381 Mayor William Walworth stabs and kills Wat Tyler, leader of the Peasants' Revolt, quelling the army of labourers who had occupied London for two days.

1399 Henry IV initiates Lancastrian rule until 1461.

1411–40 Guildhall built, administrative centre of the City.

1461 Edward IV initiates Yorkist rule which lasts until 1485 and in gratitude for City support during the Wars of the Roses (1455–85), knights many merchants.

1477 William Caxton publishes the first book printed in England, on his press at Westminster.

1485 Henry VII initiates Tudor rule which lasts until 1603; London flourishes; population leaps from about 75,000 in 1500 to 200,000 (186,000 within the City walls) in 1600.

1529 Cardinal Wolsey's fall: Henry VIII makes Whitehall Palace his principal town royal residence and Hampton Court Palace a favourite country one.

1533 Henry VIII breaks with Rome, becomes head of the Church of England; dissolution of the monasteries begins (1536), 800 closed by 1540, their lands acquired by merchants who become the new gentry.

1566 Royal Exchange founded, to enable London to compete with Amsterdam in trading.

1574 Theatres banned from the City; Bankside in Southwark becomes entertainment centre; the Burbages build the Globe in 1599 (burnt down 1613).

1603 James VI of Scotland becomes James I of England, initiating Stuart rule; from now on, England, Scotland and Wales share the same monarchy.

1605 Gunpowder plot to blow up Parliament and the royal family fails.

1613 New River Head opens at Finsbury, bringing clean water to the City.

1620 The *Mayflower* sets sail, carrying the Pilgrim Fathers to the New World.

1631 Inigo Jones designs Covent Garden piazza, the first planned square; Jones also designs Queen's House, Greenwich (1616–35), Banqueting Hall, Whitehall (1619–22) and Queen's Chapel (1623–7).

1637 Hyde Park opened by Charles I, the first public royal park.

1643 Civil War begins. The City finances Parliament; Charles I beheaded 1649; Oliver Cromwell presides over The Commonwealth 1649–53 and the Protectorate 1653–9; a period of fierce Puritanism.

1660 Restoration of the monarchy; Charles II on the throne and Roman Catholic Stuart rule continues until 1714. Royal Society formally constituted.

1665 Great Plague kills almost 100,000 and drives the wealthy out to suburbs; St James's Square laid out, launching the development of aristocratic St James's, Mayfair and Marylebone; Theatre Royal Drury Lane built, one of only two legitimate theatres with royal patents.

1666 Sept 2–5, Great Fire begins in Pudding Lane and destroys four-fifths of the City.

1670 Christopher Wren begins designing his 51 City churches; Wren also designs St Paul's Cathedral (1675–1711), Royal Hospital, Chelsea (1681–91), Hampton Court Palace East east and south wings (1689–94), Kensington Palace (1689–96) and Greenwich Hospital (1696–1702).

1675 Foundation stone laid for Wren's new St Paul's Cathedral; Royal Observatory built at Greenwich to mark the meridian and British naval supremacy.

1680s Lloyd's marine insurance market founded in Edward Lloyd's coffee house, but not formalised until 1871.

1685 After the revocation of the Edict of Nantes, French Protestants seek religious refuge in England, many settling in Soho and Spitalfields.

1689 William and Mary move into Kensington Palace which becomes a royal London residence until 1762; development of Kensington follows.

1694 Bank of England founded to finance war with France.

1698 Whitehall Palace burnt down, except for Banqueting Hall; St James's Palace becomes official royal residence, which it still is, and remains a principal royal home until 1762.

1700s Population about 575,000 (208,000 within the City walls), the largest city in Western Europe, 20 times the next biggest English city and containing one tenth of the nation's inhabitants.

1714 George I initiates Hanovarian rule.

1715 Lord Burlington and Colen Campbell design Burlington House; Burlington also designs his Chiswick House (1725–9). 1725–31 Grosvenor Square laid out, centrepiece of the Grosvenor family's Mayfair development.

1733 William Kent designs the Treasury Building, followed by Berkeley Square (1744–5) and Horse Guards (1745–55).

1737 Satires staged at the Theatre Royal Haymarket lead to the Lord Chamberlain acquiring powers of censorship on all public theatre performances (finally lifted in 1968).

1739 Westminster Bridge opens, central London's second bridge.

1754 Royal Society of Arts founded, followed by the Royal Academy (1768), Royal Institution (1799) and Royal Horticultural Society (1804).

1759 British Museum opens; new building 1823–8.

1761–8 Robert Adam remodels Syon House, followed by Osterley (1762–7), Kenwood (1767–9) and, with brothers James and John, designs The Adelphi (1768–74) and many fashionable homes.

1762 George III and Queen Charlotte move into Buckingham House; St James's Palace now merely the official residence.

1773 Merchant venturers focus their dealings at New Jonathan's coffee house, formalised as the Stock Exchange in 1802.

1801 First population census: 959,000 (128,000 in the City).

1802 London the largest port in the world. West India Dock, the first enclosed dock, opens; earth dug from later docks stabilises the marshy Battersea Park and Belgravia.

1811 Lord's Cricket Ground for the MCC (founded 1787) moved to its present site.

1816–28 John Nash lays out Regent Street, Carlton House Terrace, Piccadilly and Oxford circuses, Regent's Park and Regent's Canal – the canal joins Grand Union Canal to link London with growing Midlands industry; Nash also transforms Buckingham House (1820 on), remodels St James's Park (1827–9) and designs the Theatre Royal, Haymarket (1820–1) and All Souls, Langham Place (1822–4).

1811–17 Waterloo Bridge is the first of a series of new or rebuilt bridges, marking the nineteenth century growth of London and its south bank suburbs. Bridges that follow: Southwark (1814–19), Vauxhall (1816), Hammersmith (1824–7, rebuilt 1883–7), London (rebuilt 1831), Chelsea (1851–8), Westminster (rebuilt 1852–62), Blackfriars (rebuilt 1860–9), Lambeth (1861), Wandsworth (1870–3), Albert (1871–3), Putney (rebuilt 1882–6), Battersea (rebuilt 1886–90), Tower (1886–94).

1824 National Gallery founded; gallery built 1832–8, after Trafalgar Square cleared of royal stables and laid out (1830).

1825–35 Belgrave Square laid out, centrepiece of the Grosvenor family's development of fashionable Belgravia behind Buckingham Palace; Thomas Cubitt's Pimlico development follows.

1826 University College established, earliest part of the University of London, founded 1836 and reorganised 1900. George IV moves into Buckingham Palace; Carlton House demolished.

1829 Horse-drawn bus service begins along Marylebone Road; Sir Robert Peel establishes Metropolitan Police force to patrol all London outside the City boundaries.

1830 London Zoo opens.

1833–52 Parliament sanctions railway to be built London Bridge–Greenwich, 1833; first railway opens, London Bridge–Greenwich, 1836. The first batch of termini follow: Euston (1837), Paddington (1838), Fenchurch Street (1841), Waterloo (1848), King's Cross (1850).

1834 Palace of Westminster (Houses of Parliament) burns down; rebuilt mostly 1835–60, designed by Charles Barry and Augustus Welby Pugin.

1837 Queen Victoria, aged 18, crowned; rules 63 years until death in 1901.

1841   Royal Botanical Gardens at Kew open to the public.

1843   The world's first underwater pedestrian tunnel opens, Rotherhithe–Wapping.

1845   Victoria Park in the East End opens, the first park created for Londoners; Battersea Park, the second, opens 1853.

1847–8   Following the Great Potato Famine in Ireland, over 100,000 Irish arrive and form 20% of London's population.

1849   Cholera epidemic kills 14,000; lack of hygiene peaks in 1858 when the stench of the drains emptying into the Thames is known as the Great Stink. By 1865, £4 million spent on Bazalgette's 83-mile-long sewerage system, plus a string of health acts passed.

1851   Population: 2,363,000 (128,000 in the City). The Great Exhibition, held in Hyde Park, has six million visitors. Inspires plan for South Kensington museums, halls and colleges, including the first permanent buildings for the Victoria & Albert Museum (1855–6), Royal Albert Hall (1867–71), Science Museum (1864), Natural History Museum (1873–80) and Imperial College (1907).

1860   Victoria Station opens, marking the railway expansion; Blackfriars (1864), Charing Cross (1864), Broad Street (1865), Cannon Street (1866), St Pancras (1868), Liverpool Street (1874) and Marylebone (1899) complete the ring of London termini.

1863   Metropolitan Railway opens, the world's first urban underground train service, Paddington–King's Cross; District (1868) and Circle (1884) lines follow.

1864–76   George Gilbert Scott designs the Albert Memorial, followed by St Pancras Station (1868–74) and the Foreign Office (1868–73).

1864–70   Joseph Bazalgette's Victoria Embankment built, claiming 37 acres from the Thames.

1870   First tramcar service runs Brixton–Kennington and Whitechapel–Bow.

1872   Richard Norman Shaw designs the Royal Geographical Society; Shaw also designs Bedford Park (with E. W. Godwin) and houses on Chelsea Embankment (1875–80).

1874–82   Royal Courts of Justice (Law Courts) built, centralising the courts of Westminster and the Inns.

1875   First plans for Bedford Park, an idyllic garden city suburb; Hampstead Garden City follows in 1907.

1877–86   Shaftesbury Avenue slices through Soho, soon lined with theatres.

1880s   Many Jews arrive, fleeing anti-semitic pogroms in Russia and Poland, and settle in the East End.

1884–9   The Savoy hotel built, the first deluxe hotel; the Connaught (1894–6); Claridge's (remodelled 1895), the Ritz (1906) and the Dorchester (1928–31) follow.

1888   London County Council established to govern the 117 square miles of London, except the City; first London Dock strike protests at low wages.

1890   First Tube runs, King William Street–Stockwell (Northern Line), with electric trains in deep level tunnels; extensions follow, plus Central (1900), Bakerloo (1906–7) and Piccadilly (1906–7) lines.

1895–1903   Westminster Cathedral built.

1897   Queen Victoria on the throne for 60 years, Diamond Jubilee celebrations throughout the year; Tate Gallery opens.

1901–5   Harrods builds new store at Knightsbridge; Selfridges grand store follows (1907–28).

1901   Population: Greater London 6,506,000 (27,000 in the City).

1901–13   The Mall laid out; Aston Webb designs the Admiralty Arch, Queen Victoria Memorial and Buckingham Palace east front; Webb also designs the new wing and facade for the V&A (1899–1901).

1909   Port of London Authority take over administration of the docks to tackle rivalry of railways and Liverpool port.

1910   London Palladium built, one of 60 big halls for variety and music-hall entertainment.

1912   Second London Dock Strike; King George V Dock the last great dock, is begun (opens 1921); 8,000 East End Jewish tailors strike against the sweated labour system.

1914–18   First World War.

1922   First daily wireless programmes broadcast from Savoy Hill; BBC established in 1927 and begins television broadcasting from Alexandra Palace in 1936.

1927–9   Charles Holden designs Broadway House; Holden also designs many Underground stations (1930s) and University of London's Senate House (1932 onwards).

1930s   Many Jews arrive, fleeing fascist persecution in Europe, and settle in the East End.

1936   Battle of Cable Street; Edward VIII abdicates 325 days after his coronation to marry Mrs Simpson.

1930s & '40s Population of Greater London at its peak, about 10 million; immigrants include many Greeks from Cyprus; Green Belt encircling London established to control suburban expansion.

1939–45 Second World War. Blitz bombings destroy a third of the City of London and much of the docks (1940); following German invasion of Poland, 33,000 Poles arrive and set up a Government-in-exile (1940).

1947 Following post-war developers' destruction, Town and Country Planning acts are passed to protect buildings of historic and architectural importance. By 1986, more than 30,000 London buildings listed.

1950s & '60s Many Asians arrive, after the upheavals following India's Independence (1947) and the creation of East and West Pakistan; many Chinese arrive from the New Territories and settle in Soho; many Afro-Caribbeans arrive and settle in Brixton, some in Notting Hill.

1951 Population: Greater London 8,193,000 (5,000 in the City); Festival of Britain held on South Bank to relieve post-war austerity includes building of Royal Festival Hall.

1952 Elizabeth II succeeds; coronation June 2, 1953.

1956 Clean Air Act puts an end to London smog.

1959–82 Bomb-devastated Barbican area developed as high-rise housing and arts complex.

1960s The Beatles, Mary Quant, Carnaby Street and King's Road help create "swinging London"; tall buildings significantly change skyline: Hilton Hotel (1961–3), Centre Point (1963–7), London Telecom Tower (1963–6), Hyde Park Barracks (1967–70).

1965 Greater London Council established to run London, replacing LCC.

1967 Civil Amenities Act passed so that conservation areas can be identified and protected. By 1986, more than 300 London areas protected.

1973 Britain joins the European Economic Community (EEC).

1974 Covent Garden market moves to Nine Elms; locals save, restore and revive market buildings.

1976 National Theatre complex opens; Museum of London opens.

1977 Underground to Heathrow airport opens, the world's first such capital city-airport link.

1979 General Election: Conservative Party win and Mrs Thatcher becomes Britain's first woman prime minister; re-elected 1983 and 1987.

1981 London Docklands Development Corporation (LDDC) established to revitalise the 450 square acres of redundant dock area.

1981 Richard Seifert's NatWest Tower, 600 feet tall, is completed as the tallest building in Britain.

1982 London International Financial Futures Exchange (LIFFE) moves into Royal Exchange and becomes the largest such exchange outside the US; Billingsgate Market moved to West India Dock; Barbican Centre opens; Thames Barrier completed to protect London from flooding; King George V Dock is the last dock to close.

1985 Redevelopment of 10-acre Broadgate site in the City begins.

1986 Population of Greater London: 6,775,200, swelled by 7,570,000 visitors. Parliament abolishes the Greater London Council.

1987 Theatre Museum opens, as do the Docklands Light Railway, the Clore Gallery adjoining the Tate, London City Airport and the Princess of Wales Conservatory in the Royal Botanical Gardens.

1988 Museum of the Moving Image opens.

Select bibliography

A volume on one aspect or other of London life – from parks and pubs to churches and children – is published every week. To browse over the latest, visit the LTB bookshop at Victoria Station (see p. 3), devoted exclusively to London, or one of the general bookshops suggested on p. 330. To seek out more unusual books, or books now out of print, visit a second-hand bookshop (see p. 328) or one of the libraries listed in Chapter 5 (see p. 55).

As a springboard for London learning, here are a few general books – for specialist volumes, see the appropriate pages above (e.g. restaurant guides on p. 301, park guides on p. 351 and guides for children's London on p. 19). An asterisk indicates an especially well illustrated book.

HISTORY AND ARCHITECTURE
* Barker, F & Jackson, P: *London: 2000 years of a city and its people* (Macmillan, 1974, paperback 1983)
* Barker, F & Hyde, R: *London: As it might have been* (John Murray, 1982)
  Bebbington, G: *London Street Names* (Batsford, 1987)
  Beier, A L & Finlay, R: *The Making of the Metropolis: London 1500–1700* (Longman, 1986)
  Briggs, A: *Victorian Cities* (Penguin, 1968)
* Byrne, A: *London's Georgian Houses* (The Georgian Press, 1986)
* Cameron, R & Cooke, A I, ed: *Above London: Collection of Aerial Photographs in Colour* (The Bodley Head, 1980)
* Carr, R J M, ed: *Dockland: An illustrated historical survey of life and work in east London* (North East London Polytechnic, 1986)
  Clark, J: *Saxon and Norman London* (Museum of London, 1980)
* Coen, T & Forshaw, A: *The Square Mile: The City of London in colour* (Batsford, 1987)
  Cruickshank, D & Wyld, P: *London: The Art of Georgian Building* (Architectural Press, 1975)
* Davies, A: *The Map of London: From 1746 to the Present Day* (Batsford, 1987)
* Fishman, W J & Breach, N: *The Streets of East London* (Duckworth, 1979)
  George, M D: *London Life in the Eighteenth Century* (1925, Penguin edition 1966)
  Gray, R: *A History of London* (Hutchinson, 1978)
  Hall, J & Merrifield, R: *Roman London* (HMSO & Museum of London, 1986)
* Hessenberg, I, ed: *London in Detail* (John Murray, 1986); 2,000 photographs of London building and street details
* Hibbert, C: *London: The Biography of a City* (1969, Penguin edition 1980)
* Hobhouse, H: *Lost London: A Century of Demolition and Decay* (Macmillan 1979)
* Jones, C: *The Great Palace: The Story of Parliament* (BBC, 1983)

Kennedy, C: *Mayfair: A Social History* (Hutchinson, 1986)

Kent, W: *An Encyclopaedia of London* (Dent, revised edition 1951)

Longford, E: *Victoria R I* (Weidenfeld & Nicolson, 1964)

Lyders, C & Harrison, A, eds: *Docklands Heritage: Conservation and Regeneration in London Docklands* (LDDC, 1987)

Merrifield, R: *London City of the Romans* (Batsford, 1983)

Milne, G: *The Great Fire of London* (Historical Publications, 1987)

* Olsen, D J: *The City as a Work of Art: London, Paris and Vienna* (Yale, 1986)

* Olsen, D J: *The Growth of Victorian London* (Batsford, 1976)

Pritchett, V S: *London Perceived* (Hogarth, 1986)

* Procter, A & Taylor, R, eds: *The A–Z of Elizabethan London* (Guildhall Library with Harry Margary, 1979); the first in a series of historical atlases which now includes Georgian, Regency and Victorian London

Rasmussen, S E: *London: The Unique City* (Jonathan Cape, 1937)

Richardson, J: *Covent Garden* (Historical Publications, 1979)

* Schofield, J: *The Building of London: from the Conquest to the Great Fire* (Colonnade, 1984)

* Service, A: *The Architects of London: and their buildings from 1066 to the present day* (Architectural Press, 1979)

* Shakespeare, N: *Londoners* (Sidgwick, 1986)

Stamp, G: *The Changing Metropolis* (Penguin, 1987)

Summerson, J: *Georgian London* (1945, Penguin edition 1978)

* *Survey of London*, vols I–XCII (1900 ad seq) plus monographs (1896 ad seq); this formidable project to survey all London is currently published by Athlone Press, with H Hobhouse as editor; the latest volume is *Southern Kensington: Kensington Square to Earls Court*

* Sykes, C S: *Private Palaces: Life in the Great London Houses* (Chatto & Windus, 1985)

Thornbury, W & Walford, E: *London Recollected: Its History, Lore and Legend*, vols I–V (first published as Old and New London in 1872–8, republished by The Alderman Press, 1985–7)

* Trench, R & Hillman, E: *London under London: A subterranean guide* (John Murray, 1984)

Walford, E: *Village London: The Story of Greater London*, vols I & II (first published as Great London in 1883–4, republished by The Alderman Press, 1883–4)

* Weightman, G & Humphries, S: *The Making of Modern London* (Sidgwick & Jackson); vol I, 1815–1914 (1983); vol II, *1914–39* (1984). Vol III, *1939–45 London at War*, is by J Mack and S Humphries vol IV, *1945–85*, is by S Humphries and J Taylor.

* Weinreb, B & Hibbert, C: *The London Encyclopaedia* (Macmillan 1983, paperback edition 1987); a massive reference book of 5000 entries

Wilson, D G: *The Thames: Record of a Working Waterway* (Batsford, 1987)

GUIDES FOR SPECIAL INTERESTS

* Barker, F & Silvester-Carr, D: *The Black Plaque Guide to London* (Constable, 1987); a light-hearted complement to the blue plaques for the famous, black plaques are for the infamous

* Blatch, M: *A guide to London's churches* (Constable, 1978)

* Byron, A: *London statues: A guide to London's outdoor statues and sculpture* (Constable, 1981)

* Ebel, S & Impey, D: *A guide to London's riverside* (Constable, 1985)

* Fido, M: *Murder Guide to London* (Weidenfeld, 1986)

Gibson, P: *The Capital Companion: A street-by-street guide to London and its inhabitants* (Webb & Bower, 1985)

* Jones, E & Woodward, C: *A Guide to the Architecture of London* (Weidenfeld & Nicolson, 1983)

McAuley, I: *Guide to Ethnic London* (Michael Haag, 1987)

Pevsner, N: *London I: The Cities of London and Westminster*, Penguin, 1971, (third edition revised by B Cherry 1973)

Phillips, T: *A London Docklands Guide: a gazetteer to points of historical and architectural interest* (Peter Marcan Publications, 1986)

Piper, D: *The Companion Guide to London* (Collins, sixth edition 1977); Piper is your companion for 28 walks

* Saunders, A: *The Art and Architecture of London: An illustrated guide* (Phaidon, 1984)

* Stamp, G & Amery, C: *Victorian Buildings of London 1837–1887: An Illustrated Guide* (Architectural Press, 1980)
  Waddell, H: *London Art and Artists Guide* (Art Guide Publications, fourth edition, 1986)
  Williams, G E: *Guide to Literary London* (Batsford, 1987)

PERSONAL VIEWS AND JOURNALS

Ash, R: *The Londoner's Almanac: Containing Lists of London's Best & Worst* (Century, 1985)
Benedictus, D: *The Absolutely Essential Guide to London* (Sphere, 1986)
Bowle, J, ed: *The Diary of John Evelyn* (Oxford University Press, 1985); Evelyn lived 1620–1706
Brazil, D: *Naked City: 150 Faces of Hidden London* (Macdonald, 1987)
* Canning, J. ed: *The Illustrated Mayhew's London* (Weidenfeld & Nicolson 1986)
* Casson. H: *Hugh Casson's London* (Dent, 1983); a painter's view
Jackson, P, ed: *George Scharf's London: Sketches and watercolours of a changing City, 1820–50* (John Murray, 1987)
* Latham, R, ed: *The Illustrated Pepys* (Bell & Hyman, 1978); short extracts from the diary (1660–69) of Samuel Pepys, who lived 1633–1703
Latham, R, ed: *The Shorter Pepys* (Bell & Hyman, 1985); longer extracts from the eleven-volumed diary, but no pictures
Nairn, I: *Nairn's London* (Penguin, 1966)
Pottle, F A, ed: *Boswell's London Journal 1762–1763* (Heinemann, 1951); James Boswell lived 1740–95
Wheatley, H B, ed: *John Stow: The Survey of London* (Everyman, revised edition 1987); John Stow lived 1525–1605

Index

Note: Numbers in **bold** indicate main reference.